CRETNEY'S FAMILY LAW

AUSTRALIA
Law Book Co.
Sydney

CANADA and USA
Carswell
Toronto

HONG KONG
Sweet & Maxwell Asia

NEW ZEALAND
Brookers
Auckland

SINGAPORE and MALAYSIA
Sweet & Maxwell Asia
Singapore and Kuala Lumpur

CRETNEY'S FAMILY LAW

Other Titles in the Textbook Series

Employment Law

Equity & Trust

Environmental Law

Criminal Law

Land Law

Public Law

Tort

Contract

CRETNEY'S FAMILY LAW

Textbook Series

By Rebecca Probert BA, LLM
School of Law, University of Warwick

Sixth Edition

First Edition ⎫ as *Elements of Family Law* 1987
Second Edition ⎬ 1992
Third Edition 1997
Fourth Edition 2000
Fifth Edition 2003
Sixth Edition 2006

Published in 2006 by
Sweet & Maxwell Limited of
100 Avenue Road, London NW3 3PF
(http://www.sweetandmaxwell.co.uk)

Typeset by Interactive Sciences Ltd, Gloucester
Printed in Great Britain by
William Clowes Ltd, Beccles, Suffolk

No natural forests were destroyed to make this product;
only farmed timber was used and replanted

A C.I.P. catalogue record for this book is available from the British Library

ISBN–10 0–421–93100–0
ISBN–13 978–0421–93100–8

DEDICATION

For Liam

PREFACE

It has been a daunting task to follow in the footsteps of so eminent a family lawyer as Stephen Cretney, but I hope that this new edition has maintained the high standards that he set. The aim remains the same: to serve the needs of readers—whether lawyers or not—who need a concise guide to the basic principles of English family law. The focus is on legislative provisions and reported cases, together with the issues of policy that they raise. The reader who is interested in the way in which the law works in practice—whether from the perspective of the practitioner or those who experience the law—will have to supplement this book with more specific texts.

Family law is a fast-moving area, and some chapters have been extensively revised. The Civil Partnership Act 2004 has had a profound impact on most areas of family law, since it replicates the majority of the statutory provisions applicable to spouses for the benefit of civil partners. The Domestic Violence, Crimes and Victims Act 2004 has made a number of amendments to the circumstances in which domestic violence remedies may be obtained and enforced, while the Gender Recognition Act 2004 provides for the legal recognition of gender reassignment. Other areas of family law are changing more slowly: the law relating to marriage, outlined in Part One, still retains the imprint of earlier centuries. The law is stated as at April 28, 2005—although Ch.8 was later revised to take account of the House of Lords' decision in *Miller v Miller; McFarlane v McFarlane*—and the reader should be alert to any subsequent changes in the law.

References to reported cases are normally to the specialist *Family Law Reports*, or else to the *Family Court Reports*. More recent cases are reported with a neutral citation, but alternatives are listed in the Table of Cases.

I would like to thank Dr Stephen Cretney once again for entrusting me with his textbook, and for his exceedingly helpful, witty and erudite comments on the draft chapters with which I have bombarded him. Professor Judith Masson has also been extremely generous in giving me the benefit of her expertise in the field of child law. I would also like to thank Kevin Symons at Sweet and Maxwell for his support and patience, and my students at the University of Warwick for making lecturing in family law a positive pleasure. I owe a huge debt of gratitude to my husband Liam D'Arcy Brown, who once again read and commented on draft chapters, provided practical support throughout the writing process in the form of delicious dinners, and demonstrated considerable patience in the weeks leading up to our wedding—which took place the day after the deadline for this edition. This edition is dedicated to him, in the full and certain hope that he will never need to consult it in anger.

Rebecca Probert

TABLE OF CONTENTS

		page
Preface		ix
Abbreviations		xix
Table of Cases		xxi
Statutes		xli
Statutory Instruments		xlix

1   INTRODUCTION: THE FAMILY AND THE LAW

A: Defining "The Family" and Family Law	1–001
The concept of the family	1–001
Family life	1–002
The scope of "family law"	1–003
The administration of family law	1–004
The nature of family law	1–005
B: Demographic and Social Change	1–006
The decline of marriage?	1–007
The rise of cohabitation	1–008
The increase in the number of births outside marriage	1–009
Step-families	1–010
The rise of single-person households	1–011
Multi-culturalism	1–012
The role of the extended family	1–013
Family roles	1–014
C: Family Law and Human Rights	1–015
Giving effect to Convention rights	1–016
The scope of the Convention	1–017
Convention rights	
The impact of the Convention	1–025
D: The Structure and Approach of this Book	1–026

Part 1: FORMAL RELATIONSHIPS

Introduction	I–001

2   FORMING A MARRIAGE OR CIVIL PARNERSHIP

A: Introduction	2–001

B: Marriage Formalities   2–002
  Preliminaries to marriage   2–003
  The marriage ceremony   2–008
  Registration of marriages   2–013
C: Failure to Comply with the Required
  Formalities   2–014
D: The Presumptions in Favour of Marriage   2–018
E: Reform   2–019
F: Civil Partnerships   2–020
G: Conclusion   2–021

3 NULLITY
A: Introduction: Void and Voidable Marriages   3–001
  The modern law of nullity   3–002
  The approach of the chapter   3–003
B: Void Marriages   3–005
  Prohibited degrees: blood relationships and legal relationships 3–005
  Minimum age   3–012
  Defective formalities   3–013
  Bigamy   3–014
  Parties of same sex   3–015
  Polygamous marriages   3–016
C: Voidable Marriages   3–017
  Incapacity to consummate   3–018
  Wilful refusal to consummate   3–022
  Lack of consent   3–025
  Mental Disorder   3–032
  Gender reassignment   3–033
  Venereal disease   3–034
  Pregnancy by another   3–035
  Bars to a decree   3–036
D: Effects of a Decree   3–040
E: Void and Voidable Civil Partnerships   3–044
  Void civil partnerships   3–045
  Voidable civil partnerships   3–046
  Effects of an order   3–047
F: Conclusion: Do We Need the Law of Nullity   3–048

4 EXITS: DIVORCE AND DISSOLUTION
A: Introduction   4–001
B: Evolution of the Law   4–002
  The "matrimonial offence" 1857–1969   4–003
  Pressures for reform   4–004
  "The Field of Choice"   4–005
C: The Modern Law   4–006
  Petitioning for divorce   4–007
  The five facts   4–008
  Appraisal of the 1969 Reforms   4–023

D: **Reform?**   4–027
    The scheme of the Family Law Act 1996   4–028
    The parts of the Family Law Act that are in force   4–029
    The reasons for the non-implementation of Pt II of the Family
        Law Act   4–033
    Where next?   4–034
E: **Divorce and Religion**   4–035
F: **Dissolution of Civil Partnerships**   4–036
G: **Conclusion**   4–037

Part 2: FAMILIES—FORMAL AND INFORMAL

Introduction
    Family law and family crises   II–001
    Formal and informal families   II–002
    The consequences of marriage   II–003
    The consequences of formal relationships   II–004
    The rights of cohabitants   II–005
    The significance of parenthood   II–006
    The structure of Part II   II–007

5 OWNERSHIP OF FAMILY ASSETS
  A: **Introduction**   5–001
    When is ownership relevant?   5–002
  B: **Formal Requirements**   5–003
  C: **Informal Methods of Acquiring an Interest**   5–007
    Resulting trust   5–009
    Common intention constructive trusts   5–010
    Proprietary estoppel   5–016
    Choosing between estoppel and trusts   5–019
    Improvements to the property   5–020
  D: **Consequences of Ownership**   5–021
  E: **Rights against Third Parties**   5–022
    Ordering sale   5–023
    Are third parties bound by informally created rights?   5–026
    Protection against undue influence and misrepresentation 5–029
  F: **Ownership of Personal Property**   5–030
  G: **Conclusion**   5–035

6 PROTECTION FROM VIOLENCE AND HARASSMENT
  A: **Introduction**   6–001
  B: **Orders Under Pt IV of the Family Law Act 1996**   6–002
    Non-molestation orders   6–003
    Occupation orders   6–006
    Emergency protection   6–015
    Enforcement of orders   6–016
  C: **Other Civil Remedies**   6–017
    Injunctions under the Supreme Court Act   6–018
    The Protection from Harassment Act 1997   6–019
  D: **Conclusion**   6–025

7 FAMILY MAINTENANCE
A: **Introduction** 7–001
B: **Family Maintenance—The Role of the State** 7–002
C: **Enforcing Adults' Obligations to Support
Children** 7–008
The Child Support Act 1991 7–009
Assessment by the Courts of the Obligation to Support Children 7–020
D: **Court Orders for Maintenance** 7–025
E: **Conclusion** 7–029

8 DEALING WITH ASSETS UPON RELATIONSHIP BREAKDOWN
A: **Introduction** 8–001
B: **Private Ordering and its Limits** 8–002
Cohabitation contracts 8–003
Prenuptial agreements 8–004
Separation agreements 8–005
Consent orders 8–006
Financial Dispute Resolution appointments 8–007
C: **Orders the Court can Make** 8–008
D: **The Exercise of the Court's Discretion** 8–013
First consideration to the welfare of children 8–014
The duty to consider "all the circumstances" 8–018
Seeking a "clean break" 8–035
E: **Reconsidering Financial Arrangements** 8–040
F: **Conclusion** 8–045

9 RIGHTS ON DEATH
A: **Introduction** 9–001
B: **Division of the Estate Upon Intestacy** 9–002
C: **The Inheritance (Provision for Family and
Dependants) Act 1975** 9–005
D: **The Family Home** 9–019
E: **Conclusion** 9–024

Part 3: CHILDREN, THE FAMILY AND THE LAW

Introduction III–001
The family as a private unit III–001
Family and the state III–002
*The legal structure for determining issues about children's
upbringing: the Children Act 1989* III–003
The scope of the Children Act 1989 III–008
Organisation of the text III–009

10 LEGAL PARENTAGE
A: **Introduction: What is a Parent?** 10–001
B: **Establishing Parentage** 10–002
The common law presumptions 10–003
Are the presumptions still relevant? 10–004

The availability of samples 10–005
Safeguards 10–006
C: **Human Assisted Reproduction** 10–007
D: **Surrogate Parenting** 10–015
Surrogacy and parentage 10–016
Are surrogacy agreements enforceable? 10–023
E: **The Child's Right to Know About His or Her Origins** 10–024
F: **Conclusion** 10–025

11 PARENTAL RESPONSIBILITY AND CHILDREN'S RIGHTS
A: **Introduction** 11–001
B: **The Concept and Content of Parental Responsibility** 11–002
Responsibilities rather than rights 11–002
The content of parental responsibility 11–003
Overruling parental wishes 11–004
General constraints on parental responsibility 11–005
Responsibility and accountability 11–006
Parental rights and the Human Rights Act 1998 11–007
C: **Who is Entitled to Exercise Parental Responsibility?** 11–008
The relevance of marriage 11–008
Deserving and undeserving fathers 11–010
Automatic parental responsibility 11–011
Ways of acquiring parental responsibility 11–014
Ways of losing parental responsibility 11–027
Shared parental responsibility 11–028
Responsibility not transferable 11–029
Action by a person without parental responsibility 11–030
Authority without obligation? 11–031
D: **"Parental Responsibility" and Children's Rights** 11–032
The Gillick decision 11–033
The Gillick rationale: mature children entitled to take their own decisions? 11–034
Limitations on Gillick doctrine 11–035
E: **Conclusion** 11–039

12 THE COURTS' POWERS TO MAKE ORDERS DEALING WITH CHILDREN'S UPBRINGING: THE PRIVATE LAW
A: **Introduction** 12–001
B: **Does the Court have Jurisdiction?** 12–002
The "spin-off" jurisdiction 12–003
"Free-standing" applications 12–004
C: **Private Law Orders Under The Children Act 1989** 12–016
The menu of orders 12–017
Conditions and directions 12–021
Restrictions on the court's power to make orders 12–022
Key controversies 12–025

D: Ancillary Orders   12–034
E: Family Proceedings under the Inherent
   Jurisdiction   12–039
F: International Child Abduction   12–047
   The 1983 Hague Convention on the Civil Aspects of International
   Child Abduction   12–048
   Non-Convention Countries   12–055
G: Conclusion   12–056

13 COURT ORDERS DEALING WITH CHILDREN'S UPBRINGING:
   THE STATE'S ROLE
   A: Introduction—State Intervention: The Historical
      Background   13–001
      The Children Act 1989   13–002
      The approach of this chapter   13–003
   B: Local Authorities' Powers and Duties to Provide
      Services for Children   13–004
   C: Protective Measures   13–007
      The range of protective orders   13–008
      Emergency powers   13–009
      Should an application for a care or supervision order be made? 13–012
      The nature of care proceedings   13–013
      The threshold criteria   13–019
      Should the court make an order   13–026
   D: Children Looked After by a Local Authority   13–030
      Accommodation   13–031
      Implementing the care plan   13–036
      Contact with parents   13–037
      Ending the care order?   13–038
      Leaving care   13–039
   F: Remedies Available Where the Local Authority has Failed   13–044
   G: Conclusion   13–049

14 SHOULD THE COURT MAKE AN ORDER? THE WELFARE PRINCIPLE
   A: Introduction   14–001
   B: The Fundamental Principle: Child's Welfare
      Paramount   14–002
   C: The Welfare Principle   14–006
      No delay   14–007
      Is the order necessary?   14–008
      The welfare checklist   14–009
   D: The Welfare Principle and Human Rights   14–017

15 ADOPTION
   A: Introduction   15–001
   B: The Concept of Adoption   15–002
   C: Eligibility to Adopt and to be Adopted: The Law   15–014
   D: The Role of the Adoption Agency   15–017
   E: The Role of the Birth Parents   15–024

F: The Role of the Court   15–029

The powers of the court   15–030

Dispensing with consent   15–033

Should the court make an order?   15–036

Should an order for contact be made?   15–043

G: Inter-Country Adoptions   15–044

H: Conclusion   15–045

Index   *page* 367

TABLE OF ABBREVIATIONS

ACA	Adoption and Children Act 2002
CA	Children Act 1989
CPA	Civil Partnership Act 2004
CSA	Child Support Act 1991
DVCVA	Domestic Violence, Crimes and Victims Act 2004
ECHR	European Convention on Human Rights
FLA	Family Law Act 1996
GRA	Gender Recognition Act 2004
HFEA	Human Fertilisation and Embryology Act 1990
HRA	Human Rights Act 1998
I(PFD)A	Inheritance (Provision for Family and Dependants) Act 1975
LPA	Law of Property Act 1925
MA	Marriage Act 1949
MCA	Matrimonial Causes Act 1973
TLATA	Trusts of Land and Appointment of Trustees Act 1996

TABLE OF CASES

A (A Child) (Adoption of a Russian Child), Re [2000] 1 F.L.R. 539; [2000] 1 F.C.R. 673 15–034

A (A Child) (Permission to Remove Child from Jurisdiction: Human Rights); Sub Nom: G-A (A Child), Re [2000] 2 F.L.R. 225; [2001] 1 F.C.R. 43 12–028

A (A Child) (Temporary Removal from Jurisdiction), Re; Sub Nom: W v A [2004] EWCA Civ 1587; [2005] 1 F.L.R. 639 .... 12–027, 12–028

A (A Minor) (Child of the Family), Re [1998] 1 F.L.R. 347; [1998] 1 F.C.R. 458 7–021

A (A Minor) (Paternity: Refusal of Blood Test), Re [1994] 2 F.L.R. 463; [1994] Fam. Law 622, CA (Civ Div) 10–004, 10–005

A (Children) (Conjoined Twins: Medical Treatment) (No.1), Re; Sub Nom: A (Children) (Conjoined Twins: Surgical Separation), Re [2001] Fam. 147; [2001] 2 W.L.R. 480; [2001] 1 F.L.R. 1 .... 11–003, 11–004, 12–042

A (Children) (Interim Care Order), Re [2001] 3 F.C.R. 402; (2001) 165 J.P.N. 968, Fam Div 13–020

A (Children) (Shared Residence), Re [2001] EWCA Civ 1795; [2002] 1 F.C.R. 177, CA (Civ Div) 12–027

A (Placement of Child in Contravention of Adoption Act 1976 s.11), Re [2005] 2 F.L.R. 727, Fam Div 15–012, 15–018

A and W (Minors) (Residence Order: Leave to Apply), Re; Sub Nom: A (Minors) (Residence Order), Re [1992] Fam. 182; [1992] 3 W.L.R. 422 .... 12–011, 14–003

A v A (A Minor) (Financial Provision) [1994] 1 F.L.R. 657; [1995] 1 F.C.R. 309 7–024

A v A (Elderly Applicant: Lump Sum); Sub Nom: A v A (Duxbury Calculations) [1999] 2 F.L.R. 969; [1999] 3 F.C.R. 433 .... 8 030

A v A (Family: Unborn Child); Sub Nom: A v A (Child of the Family) [1974] Fam. 6; [1974] 2 W.L.R. 106 7–021

A v A (Shared Residence and Contact); Sub Nom: A v A (Children: Shared Residence Order) [2004] EWHC 142; [2004] 1 F.L.R. 1195 12–027

A v B (Financial Relief: Agreements); Sub Nom: A v B (Ancillary Relief: Separation Agreement) [2005] EWHC 314; [2005] 2 F.L.R. 730 8–005

A v Essex CC [2003] EWCA Civ 1848; [2004] 1 W.L.R. 1881 .... 13–047, 15–022, 15–045

A v Liverpool CC (1981) 2 F.L.R. 222, HL 12–046

A v United Kingdom [1998] 2 F.L.R. 959; [1998] 3 F.C.R. 597, ECHR 11–003

AB (A Minor) (Adoption: Unmarried Couple), Re Sub Nom: AB (Adoption: Joint Residence), Re; AB (A Minor) (Adoption: Parental Consent), Re [1996] 1 F.L.R. 27; [1996] 1 F.C.R. 633 15–016

AK v Australia (148/1999) (2004) 11 I.H.R.R. 967, UN CAT 3–026

A County Council v DP see Oxfordshire CC v DP

A Local Authority v B (Emergency Protection Orders); Sub Nom: X Council v B (Emergency Protection Orders) [2004] EWHC 2015; [2005] 1 F.L.R. 341 ... 13–011, 13–012

A Local Authority v K; Sub Nom: A County Council v K [2005] EWHC 144; [2005] 1 F.L.R. 851 13–017

A Local Authority v PD [2005] EWHC 1832; [2005] E.M.L.R. 35, Fam Div 12–044

A Local Authority v S [2004] EWHC 1270; [2004] 2 F.L.R. 129 13–018

A Local Authority v W, L, W, T and R *see* W (Children) (Identification: Restrictions on Publication), Re

Abbey National Building Society v Cann [1991] 1 A.C. 56; [1990] 2 W.L.R. 833 5–028

Adams v Adams [1984] 5 F.L.R. 768, CA 14–010

Adoption Application (Payment for Adoption), Re; Sub Nom: Adoption Application (Surrogacy) (AA 212/86), Re [1987] Fam. 81; [1987] 3 W.L.R. 31; [1987] 2 F.L.R. 291 10–015

Akintola v Akintola (Transfer of Tenancy) [2001] EWCA Civ 1989; [2002] 1 F.L.R. 701 8–015

Al Habtoor v Fotheringham *see* Al-H v F

Al-H v F [2001] EWCA Civ 186; [2001] 1 F.L.R. 951 12–049

Ali v Khan [2002] EWCA Civ 974; (2002–03) 5 I.T.E.L.R. 232 5–009

Al-Khatib v Masry [2004] EWCA Civ 1353; [2005] 1 F.L.R. 381 8–002

Alliance & Leicester Plc v Slayford [2001] 1 All E.R. (Comm) 1; [2001] C.P. Rep. 52; [2000] E.G.C.S. 113, CA 5–029

Ampthill Peerage, The [1977] A.C. 547; [1976] 2 W.L.R. 777 10–002

An NHS Trust v MB [2006] EWHC 507, Fam Div 11–004

Anufrijeva v Southwark LBC; Sub Nom: R. (on the application of Anufrijeva) v Southwark LBC; R. (on the application of N) v Secretary of State for the Home Department; R. (on the application of M) v Secretary of State for the Home Department [2003] EWCA Civ 1406; [2004] Q.B. 1124 1–019

Archer v Archer [1999] 1 F.L.R. 327; [1999] 2 F.C.R. 158 4–020

Ash v Ash [1972] Fam. 135; [1972] 2 W.L.R. 347 4–013

Atkinson v Atkinson [1988] Fam. 93; [1988] 2 W.L.R. 204 8–009

Attar v Attar (No.2) [1985] F.L.R. 653 8–029

B (A Child) (Adoption Order), Re [2001] EWCA Civ 347; [2001] 2 F.L.R. 26 .. 15–012, 15–043

B (A Child) (Interim Care Orders: Renewal), Re [2001] 2 F.L.R. 1217; [2001] Fam. Law 802 13–014

B (A Child) (Section 91(14) Order: Duration), Re [2003] EWCA Civ 1966; [2004] 1 F.L.R. 871 12–005

B (A Minor) (Adoption Application), Re [1995] 1 F.L.R. 895; [1995] 2 F.C.R. 749 15–040

B (A Minor) (Adoption Order: Nationality), Re [1999] 2 A.C. 136; [1999] 2 W.L.R. 714; [1999] 1 F.L.R. 907, HL 15–015, 15–039

B (A Minor) (Child Abuse: Custody), Re [1990] 2 F.L.R. 317; [1991] F.C.R. 757 14–014

B (A Minor) (Residence Order: Status Quo), Re [1998] 1 F.L.R. 368; [1998] 1 F.C.R. 549 14–012

B (Adoption Order: Jurisdiction to Set Aside), Re; Sub Nom: B (Adoption: Setting Aside), Re [1995] Fam. 239; [1995] 3 W.L.R. 40, CA 15–003

B (Children) (Care: Interference with Family Life), Re; Sub Nom: B (Children) (Children: Patient Confidentiality), Re; B (Children) (Interim Care Order), Re [2003] EWCA Civ 786; [2003] 2 F.L.R. 813 13–026

B (Children) (Non-Accidental Injury: Compelling Medical Evidence), Re [2002] EWCA Civ 902; [2002] 2 F.L.R. 599 13–017

B (Children) (Removal from Jurisdiction), Re [2001] 1 F.C.R. 108, CA (Civ Div) 12–028

B (Children) (Removal from Jurisdiction), Re; S (A Child) (Removal from Jurisdiction), Re [2003] EWCA Civ 1149; [2003] 2 F.L.R. 1043 12–028

B (Children), Re [2005] EWCA Civ 643, CA (Civ Div) 12–028, 14–012

B (Consent to Treatment: Capacity), Re; Sub Nom: B v NHS Hospital Trust; B (Adult: Refusal of Medical Treatment), Re [2002] EWHC 429; [2002] 2 All E.R. 449 11–038

B (Deceased), Re; Sub Nom: Bouette v Rose [2000] Ch. 662; [2000] 2 W.L.R. 929; [2000] 1 All E.R. 665 9–013

B (Minors) (Parentage), Re [1996] 2 F.L.R. 15; [1996] 3 F.C.R. 697 ..... 10–001, 10–007, 10–012

B v A, C and D (Acting by Her Guardian) [2006] EWHC 2 .... 10–012, 11–017, 11–027

B v B (A Minor) (Residence Order) [1992] 2 F.L.R. 327; [1993] 1 F.C.R. 211 ... 11–030, 14–008

B v B (Adult Student: Liability to Support); Sub Nom: B v B (Financial Provision for
 Child) [1998] 1 F.L.R. 373; [1998] 1 F.C.R. 49   7–020

B v B (Financial Provision: Welfare of Child and Conduct) [2002] 1 F.L.R. 555; [2002]
 Fam. Law 173, Fam Div 8–014, 8–026

B v B (Mesher Order) [2002] EWHC 3106; [2003] 2 F.L.R. 285   8–010

B v B (Minors) (Custody, Care and Control); Sub Nom: B v B (Custody of Children)
 [1991] 1 F.L.R. 402; [1991] F.C.R. 1   14–015

B v B (Occupation Order) [1999] 1 F.L.R. 715; [1999] 2 F.C.R. 251   6–012

B v B (Residence Order: Reasons for Decision); Sub Nom: B (A Minor) (Residence
 Order: Reasons), Re [1997] 2 F.L.R. 602; [1998] 1 F.C.R. 409   14–009

B v B (Residence: Condition Limiting Geographic Area) [2004] 2 F.L.R. 979; [2004] Fam.
 Law 651, Fam Div   12–028

B v P (Adoption by Unmarried Father); Sub Nom: B (A Child) v RP; B (A Child)
 (Adoption by One Natural Parent to the Exclusion of Other), Re; B (A Child)
 (Adoption: Natural Parent), Re; B (A Child) (Sole Adoption by Unmarried Parent),
 Re; B (Adoption by Unmarried Father), Re [2001] UKHL 70; [2002] 1 W.L.R. 258;
 [2002] 1 F.L.R. 196 .... 14–017, 15–016

B v P (Adoption by Unmarried Father); Sub Nom: B (A Child) v RP; B (A Child)
 (Adoption by One Natural Parent to the Exclusion of Other), Re; B (A Child)
 (Adoption: Natural Parent), Re; B (A Child) (Sole Adoption by Unmarried Parent),
 Re; B (Adoption by Unmarried Father), Re [2001] UKHL 70; [2002] 1 W.L.R.
 258   15–039

B v United Kingdom (36337/97); P v United Kingdom (35974/97) [2001] 2 F.L.R. 261;
 [2001] 2 F.C.R. 221   1–020

B v United Kingdom (36536/02) [2006] 1 F.L.R. 35; [2005] 3 F.C.R. 353 .... I–001, 3–009

B v United Kingdom [2000] 1 F.L.R. 1; [2000] 1 F.C.R. 289   11–010

Banik v Banik (No.1) [1973] 1 W.L.R. 860; [1973] 3 All E.R. 45   4–021

Banik v Banik (No.2) (1973) 117 S.J. 874   4–021

Bank of Baroda v Dhillon [1998] 1 F.L.R. 524; [1998] 1 F.C.R. 489   5–026

Bank of Ireland Home Mortgages Ltd v Bell [2001] 2 All E.R. (Comm) 920; [2001] 2
 F.L.R. 809   5–025

Banks v Banks see B v B (Occupation Order)

Barca v Mears [2004] EWHC 2170; [2005] 2 F.L.R. 1   5–024

Barclays Bank Plc v Khaira [1993] 1 F.L.R. 343; [1993] Fam. Law 124, CA (Civ Div)   5–012

Barclays Bank Plc v O'Brien [1994] 1 A.C. 180; [1993] 3 W.L.R. 786   5–029

Barder v Caluori; Sub Nom: Barder v Barder [1988] A.C. 20; [1987] 2 W.L.R. 1350 ...   8–044

Barony of Moynihan, Re [2000] 1 F.L.R. 113; [2000] Fam. Law 21 .... 10–006, 11–009

Barrass v Harding [2001] 1 F.L.R. 138; [2001] 1 F.C.R. 297   9–014

Barrett v Barrett [1988] 2 F.L.R. 516; [1988] F.C.R. 707   8–025

Barrett v Enfield LBC [2001] 2 A.C. 550; [1999] 3 W.L.R. 79; [1999] 2 F.L.R. 426, HL   13–047

Bellenden (formerly Satterthwaite) v Satterthwaite [1948] 1 All E.R. 343, CA   8–042

Bellinger v Bellinger [2003] UKHL 21; [2003] 2 A.C. 467   3–015

Berkshire CC v B [1997] 1 F.L.R. 171; [1997] 3 F.C.R. 88   13–037

Berrehab v Netherlands (A/138); Sub Nom: Berrehab v Netherlands (10730/84) (1989)
 11 E.H.R.R. 322; The Times, June 30, 1988, ECHR   1–002

Best v Samuel Fox & Co Ltd [1952] A.C. 716; [1952] 2 All E.R. 394 ....   II–003

Bhaiji v Chauhan [2003] 2 F.L.R. 485; [2003] Fam. Law 558, Fam Div   4–007

Birch v Birch [1992] 1 F.L.R. 564; [1992] 2 F.C.R. 545   4–013

Birmingham City Council v H (Care Order) [1992] 2 F.L.R. 323; [1993] 1 F.C.R. 247   12–021

Birmingham Midshires Mortgage Services Ltd v Sabherwal (Equitable Interest) (2000)
 80 P. & C.R. 256, CA (Civ Div)   5–028

Bishop v Plumley [1991] 1 W.L.R. 582; [1991] 1 All E.R. 236   9–013

Blunkett v Quinn [2004] EWHC 2816; [2005] 1 F.L.R. 648   10–005

Bradley v Bradley [1973] 1 W.L.R. 1291; [1973] 3 All E.R. 750   4–013

Bristol and West Building Society v Henning [1985] 1 W.L.R. 778; [1985] 2 All E.R.
 606   5–028

Brixey v Lynas (No.1); Sub Nom: B v L (No.1) 1997 S.C. (H.L.) 1; 1996 S.L.T. 908;
 [1996] 2 F.L.R. 499 .... 14–011, 14–013
Buffery v Buffery [1988] 2 F.L.R. 365; [1988] F.C.R. 465 4–006
Burns v Burns [1984] F.L.R. 216, CA 5–013, 5–015
Burris v Azadani [1995] 1 W.L.R. 1372; [1995] 4 All E.R. 802; [1996] 1 F.L.R. 266 6–018

C (A Child) (Care Orders), Re [2001] EWCA Civ 810; [2001] 3 F.C.R. 381, CA (Civ
 Div) 14–007
C (A Child) (Foreign Adoption: Natural Mother's Consent: Service), Re [2006] 1 F.L.R.
 318; [2006] Fam. Law 8, Fam Div 15–016
C (A Child) (Immunisation: Parental Rights), Re; Sub Nom: B (A Child) (Immunisation:
 Parental Rights), Re; C (Welfare of Child: Immunisation), Re; F (A Child) (Immu-
 nisation: Parental Rights), Re [2003] EWCA Civ 1148; [2003] 2 F.L.R. 1095; [2003]
 EWHC 1376 12–020
C (A Child) (Residence Order), Re [2003] EWCA Civ 407, CA (Civ Div) 14–015
C (A Child) (Secure Accommodation Order: Representation), Re; Sub Nom: M (A
 Child) (Secure Accommodation Order), Re [2001] EWCA Civ 458; [2001] 2 F.L.R.
 169 13–041
C (A Child), Re [2006] EWCA Civ 235, CA (Civ Div) 12–027
C (A Minor) (Adoption Order: Conditions), Re; Sub Nom: C (A Minor) (Adoption:
 Contract with Sibling), Re [1989] A.C. 1; [1988] 2 W.L.R. 474 15–043
C (A Minor) (Adoption: Parental Agreement: Contact), Re [1993] 2 F.L.R. 260; [1994]
 2 F.C.R. 485 15–039
C (A Minor) (Family Assistance Order), Re [1996] 1 F.L.R. 424; [1996] 3 F.C.R. 514 12–035
C (A Minor) (Interim Care Order: Residential Assessment), Re; Sub Nom: C (A Minor)
 (Local Authority: Assessment), Re [1997] A.C. 489; [1996] 3 W.L.R. 1098; [1997] 1
 F.L.R. 1, HL 13–014, 13–036
C (A Minor) (Leave to Seek Section 8 Orders), Re [1994] 1 F.L.R. 26; [1994] 1 F.C.R.
 837 .... 11–035, 12–012
C (A Minor) (Medical Treatment: Court's Jurisdiction), Re; Sub Nom: C (A Minor)
 (Detention for Medical Treatment), Re [1997] 2 F.L.R. 180; [1997] 3 F.C.R. 49 11–038
C (A Minor) (Wardship: Medical Treatment) (No.2), Re [1990] Fam. 39; [1989] 3 W.L.R.
 252 12–040
C (Abduction: Interim Directions: Accommodation by Local Authority), Re [2003]
 EWHC 3065; [2004] 1 F.L.R. 653 .... 12–001, 12–048
C (Abduction: Settlement) (No.2), Re [2005] 1 F.L.R. 938; [2005] Fam. Law 440, Fam
 Div 12–053
C (Adoption: Religious Observance), Re; Sub Nom: C (A Child) (Care Proceedings:
 Care Plan), Re; R. (on the application of C) v Waltham Forest LBC [2002] 1 F.L.R.
 1119; [2002] Fam. Law 497 .... 15–040, 15–043
C (Child Abduction) (Unmarried Father: Rights of Custody), Re; Sub Nom: C (Child
 Abduction) (Custody Rights: Unmarried Father), Re; G (A Child) (Custody Rights:
 Unmarried Father), Re; G v M [2002] EWHC 2219; [2003] 1 W.L.R. 493 12–049
C (Children) (Prohibition on Further Applications), Re; Sub Nom: C (Children: Con-
 tact), Re [2002] EWCA Civ 292; [2002] 1 F.L.R. 1136 .... 12–005, 12–032
C (Contact: No Order for Contact), Re [2000] 2 F.L.R. 723; [2000] Fam. Law 699, Fam
 Div 12–031
C (Residence: Child's Application for Leave), Re [1995] 1 F.L.R. 927; [1995] Fam. Law
 472 12–012
C v C (A Minor) (Custody Appeal); Sub Nom: C (A Minor), Re [1991] 1 F.L.R. 223;
 [1991] F.C.R. 254 14–015
C v C (Application for Non Molestation Order: Jurisdiction) [1998] Fam. 70; [1998] 2
 W.L.R. 599; [1998] 1 F.L.R. 554 6–003
C v C (Financial Relief: Short Marriage); Sub Nom: C v C (Financial Provision: Short
 Marriage) [1997] 2 F.L.R. 26, CA 8–014
C v Flintshire CC (formerly Clwyd CC); Sub Nom: C v A Local Authority [2001] EWCA
 Civ 302; [2001] 2 F.L.R. 33 13–047
C v Solihull MBC [1993] 1 F.L.R. 290; [1993] Fam. Law 189 14–007

CH (Contact: Parentage), Re [1996] 1 F.L.R. 569; [1996] Fam. Law 274, Fam Div   10–010
CL v East Riding Yorkshire Council *see* L (A Child) (Care Proceedings: Responsibility
   for Child's Injury), Re
CO v CO (Ancillary Relief: Pre Marriage Cohabitation) [2004] EWHC 287; [2004] 1
   F.L.R. 1095   8–030
Campbell v Griffin [2001] EWCA Civ 990; [2001] W.T.L.R. 981   5–017
Campbell v Mirror Group Newspapers Ltd; Sub Nom: Campbell v MGN Ltd [2004]
   UKHL 22; [2004] 2 A.C. 457   1–024
Cannon v Cannon; Sub Nom: C (Abduction: Settlement) (No.1), Re [2004] EWCA Civ
   1330; [2005] 1 W.L.R. 32   12–054
Carabott v Huxley (2005) 102(34) L.S.G. 30, CA (Civ Div)   6–016
Carlton v Goodman; Sub Nom: Goodman v Carlton [2002] EWCA Civ 545; [2002] 2
   F.L.R. 259   5–005
Carr-Glynn v Frearsons [1999] Ch. 326; [1999] 2 W.L.R. 1046; [1999] 1 F.L.R. 8, CA   9–023
Chalmers v Johns [1999] 1 F.L.R. 392; [1999] 2 F.C.R. 110   6–013
Chief Adjudication Officer v Bath [2000] 1 F.L.R. 8; [2000] 1 F.C.R. 419   2–020
Churchill v Roach [2002] EWHC 3230; [2004] 2 F.L.R. 989 .... 9–011, 9–013, 9–017
Citro (A Bankrupt), Re; Citro (A Bankrupt), Re [1991] Ch. 142; [1990] 3 W.L.R. 880;
   [1991] 1 F.L.R. 71, CA   5–024
City of London Building Society v Flegg [1988] A.C. 54; [1987] 2 W.L.R. 1266   5–028
Clark v Chandler; Sub Nom: Chandler v Clark [2002] EWCA Civ 1249; [2003] 1 P. &
   C.R. 15   9–023
Clark v Clark [1999] 2 F.L.R. 498; [1999] 3 F.C.R. 49   8–033
Claughton v Charalambous [1999] 1 F.L.R. 740; [1998] B.P.I.R. 558   5–024
Cleary v Cleary [1974] 1 W.L.R. 73; [1974] 1 All E.R. 498   4–011
Clough v Killey [1996] N.P.C. 38; (1996) 72 P. & C.R. D22, CA (Civ Div)   5–015
Clutton v Clutton [1991] 1 W.L.R. 359; [1991] 1 All E.R. 340; [1991] 1 F.L.R. 242 .... 8–010, 8–035
Cole (A Bankrupt), Re; Sub Nom: Ex p. Trustee v Cole [1964] Ch. 175; [1963] 3 W.L.R.
   621   5–030
Conran v Conran [1997] 2 F.L.R. 615; [1998] 1 F.C.R. 144   8–027
Corbett v Corbett (otherwise Ashley) (No.1) [1971] P. 83; [1970] 2 W.L.R. 1306 ... 3–015, 3–019
Cordle v Cordle [2001] EWCA Civ 1791; [2002] 1 W.L.R. 1441   8–026
Cornick v Cornick (No.1) [1994] 2 F.L.R. 530; [1994] 2 F.C.R. 1189   8–044
Cotterell v Cotterell [1998] 3 F.C.R. 199, CA (Civ Div)   4–006
Coventry (Deceased), Re; Sub Nom: Coventry v Coventry [1980] Ch. 461; [1979] 3
   W.L.R. 802   9–014
Cowan v Cowan [2001] EWCA Civ 679; [2002] Fam. 97   8–032
Cox v Jones [2004] EWHC 1486; [2004] 2 F.L.R. 1010 .... 5–014, 5–032
Croydon LBC v A (No.1) [1992] Fam. 169; [1992] 3 W.L.R. 267 .... 12–019, 12–034
Cunliffe v Fielden; Sub Nom: Fielden v Cunliffe [2005] EWCA Civ 1508; [2006] 2 W.L.R.
   481   9–016
Curley v Parkes [2004] EWCA Civ 1515; [2005] 1 P. & C.R. DG15, CA (Civ Div)   5–009

D (A Child) (Intractable Contact Dispute: Publicity), Re; Sub Nom: F v M (Contact
   Orders) [2004] EWHC 727; [2004] 1 F.L.R. 1226   12–033
D (A Child) (Residence: Ability to Parent), Re [2001] EWCA Civ 742; [2001] 2 F.C.R.
   751, CA (Civ Div)   14–011
D (A Child) (Threshold Criteria: Issue Estoppel), Re [2001] 1 F.L.R. 274; [2001] 1 F.C.R.
   124   13–015
D (A Child), Re [2005] EWCA Civ 743   14–015
D (A Minor) (Adoption Order: Validity), Re [1991] Fam. 137; [1991] 2 W.L.R. 1215;
   [1991] 2 F.L.R. 66, CA   15–015
D (Children) (Care: Change of Forename), Re [2003] 1 F.L.R. 339; [2003] Fam. Law 77,
   Fam Div   14–013
D (Children) (Shared Residence Orders), Re; Sub Nom: D v D (Children) (Shared
   Residence Orders) [2001] 1 F.L.R. 495; [2001] 1 F.C.R. 147   12–027
D (Minors) (Adoption by Step-Parents), Re (1981) 2 F.L.R. 102   15–037

D (Minors) (Residence: Imposition of Conditions), Re [1996] 2 F.L.R. 281; [1996] 2 F.C.R. 820 12–021

D (Prohibited Steps Order), Re; Sub Nom: D v D (Ouster Order) [1996] 2 F.L.R. 273; [1996] 2 F.C.R. 496 12–034

D v D (County Court Jurisdiction: Injunctions) [1993] 2 F.L.R. 802; [1994] Fam. Law 8 12–021

D v D (Financial Provision: Periodical Payments) [2004] EWHC 445; [2004] 1 F.L.R. 988 8–038

D v D (Nullity: Statutory Bar) [1979] Fam. 70; [1979] 3 W.L.R. 185 3–039

D v East Berkshire Community NHS Trust *see* JD v East Berkshire Community Health NHS Trust

DP v United Kingdom (38719/97) [2003] 1 F.L.R. 50; [2002] 3 F.C.R. 385 13–048

Dawson v Wearmouth [1999] 2 A.C. 308; [1999] 2 W.L.R. 960; [1997] 2 F.L.R. 629, CA ... 14–009

De Lasala v De Lasala [1980] A.C. 546; [1979] 3 W.L.R. 390 8–006

Drake v Whipp [1996] 1 F.L.R. 826; [1996] 2 F.C.R. 296 5–008

Durham v Durham; Hunter v Edney (otherwise Hunter); Cannon v Smalley (otherwise Cannon) (1885) L.R. 10 P.D. 80, PDAD 3–026

Duxbury v Duxbury [1987] 1 F.L.R. 7; [1987] Fam. Law 13, CA (Civ Div) 8–030

Dyer v Dyer (1788) 2 Cox Eq. Cas. 92 5–009

Dyson Holdings Ltd v Fox [1976] Q.B. 503; [1975] 3 W.L.R. 744 1–001

E (A Minor) (Care Order: Contact), Re [1994] 1 F.L.R. 146; [1994] 1 F.C.R. 584 13–037

E (A Minor) (Wardship: Medical Treatment), Re [1993] 1 F.L.R. 386; [1994] 5 Med. L.R. 73, Fam Div 11–038

E (Children) (Residence Order), Re [2001] EWCA Civ 567; [2001] 2 F.C.R. 662, CA (Civ Div) 14–014

E (Family Assistance Order), Re [1999] 2 F.L.R. 512; [1999] 3 F.C.R. 700 .... 12–035, 13–048

E (Minors) (Residence: Imposition of Conditions), Re; Sub Nom: E (Minors) (Residence Orders), Re [1997] 2 F.L.R. 638; [1997] 3 F.C.R. 245 12–028

ET (Serious Injuries: Standard of Proof), Re [2003] 2 F.L.R. 1205; [2003] Fam. Law 871, Fam Div 13–018

Edgar v Edgar [1980] 1 W.L.R. 1410; [1980] 3 All E.R. 887 8–005

Edwards v Lloyds TSB Bank Plc [2004] EWHC 1745; [2005] 1 F.C.R. 139 5–025

Elsholz v Germany [2000] 2 F.L.R. 486; [2000] 3 F.C.R. 385 1–021

Espinosa v Bourke; Espinosa v Isaacs; Espinosa v Wilson [1999] 1 F.L.R. 747; [1999] 3 F.C.R. 76 9–014

Evans v Evans (1989) 153 J.P. 78; [1989] 1 F.L.R. 351 8–033

Evers Trust, Re; Sub Nom: Papps v Evers [1980] 1 W.L.R. 1327; [1980] 3 All E.R. 399 5–021

Eves v Eves [1975] 1 W.L.R. 1338; [1975] 3 All E.R. 768 5–014

F (Abduction: Unmarried Father: Sole Carer), Re [2002] EWHC 2896; [2003] 1 F.L.R. 839 12–049

F (Adoption: Welfare of Child: Financial Considerations), Re [2003] EWHC 3448; [2004] 2 F.L.R. 440 15–011

F (Children) (Contact Orders: Domestic Violence), Re; Sub Nom: F (Children) (Restrictions on Applications), Re [2005] EWCA Civ 499; [2005] 2 F.L.R. 950 12–031

F (Children) (Shared Residence Order), Re [2003] All E.R. (D) 258 12–027

F (In Utero), Re [1988] Fam. 122; [1988] 2 W.L.R. 1288; [1988] 2 F.L.R. 307, CA 12–046

F (Minors) (Specific Issue: Child Interview), Re; Sub Nom: F (Minors) (Solicitors Interviews), Re [1995] 1 F.L.R. 819; [1995] 2 F.C.R. 200 12–020

F v Child Support Agency [1999] 2 F.L.R. 244; [1999] 2 F.C.R. 385 10–005

F v F (Ancillary Relief: Substantial Assets) [1995] 2 F.L.R. 45; [1996] 2 F.C.R. 397 8–004

F v G (Child: Financial Provision) [2004] EWHC 1848; [2005] 1 F.L.R. 261, Fam Div 7–024

F v Lambeth LBC; Sub Nom: F (Children: Care Planning), Re [2002] 1 F.L.R. 217; [2001] 3 F.C.R. 738 13–031

FM (A Child) v Singer [2004] EWHC 793, QBD III–004

Fisher v Fisher [1989] 1 F.L.R. 423, CA 8–028

Fitzpatrick v Sterling Housing Association Ltd [2001] 1 A.C. 27; [1999] 3 W.L.R. 1113;
    [1998] 1 F.L.R. 6, CA 1–001, 1–002, 1–008
Flavell v Flavell [1997] 1 F.L.R. 353; [1997] 1 F.C.R. 332 .... 8–037, 8–041
Fleming v Fleming [2003] EWCA Civ 1841; [2004] 1 F.L.R. 667 .... 8–009, 8–037, 8–041
Flintshire CC v K [2001] 2 F.L.R. 476; [2001] 2 F.C.R. 724 15–044
Ford v Ford [1987] Fam. Law 232, CC (Croydon) 3–024
Foster v Foster [2003] EWCA Civ 565; [2003] 2 F.L.R. 299 8–030
Francis v Manning [1997] EWCA 1231, CA 7–024

G (A Child) (Domestic Violence: Direct Contact), Re [2000] 2 F.L.R. 865; [2001] 2
    F.C.R. 134 14–010
G (A Child) (Interim Care Order: Residential Assessment), Re; Sub Nom: G (A Child)
    (Interim Care Orders: Inpatient Assessment), Re; Kent CC v G [2005] UKHL 68;
    [2005] 3 W.L.R. 1166 13–014
G (A Minor) (Adoption: Illegal Placement), Re [1995] 1 F.L.R. 403; [1995] 3 F.C.R. 26 ... 15–018
G (A Minor) (Parental Responsibility: Education), Re [1994] 2 F.L.R. 964; [1995] 2
    F.C.R. 53 11–028
G (Care: Challenge to Local Authority's Decision), Re [2003] EWHC 551; [2003] 2
    F.L.R. 42 .... 1–021, 11–028
G (Children) (Permission to Terminate Paternal Contact), Re; Sub Nom: G (Children)
    (Adoption: Contact), Re [2002] EWCA Civ 761; [2003] 1 F.L.R. 270 15–043
G (Children) (Residence: Making of Order), Re [2005] EWCA Civ 1237; [2006] Fam.
    Law 93 14–008
G (Children) (Residence: Same Sex Partner), Re [2005] EWCA Civ 462; [2005] 2 F.L.R.
    957 .... 11–024, 12–018
G (Children) (Residence: Same Sex Partner), Re; Sub Nom: CG v CW [2006] EWCA Civ
    372; [2006] 1 F.C.R. 681 .... 1–005, 11–024, 12–026, 14–015
G (Financial Provision: Liberty to Restore Application for Lump Sum), Re [2004]
    EWHC 88; [2004] 1 F.L.R. 997 .... 8–021, 8–030
G and R (Child Sexual Abuse: Standard of Proof), Re [1995] 2 F.L.R. 867, CA (Civ
    Div) 13–021
G v F (Non Molestation Order: Jurisdiction); Sub Nom: G v G (Non Molestation Order:
    Jurisdiction) [2000] Fam. 186; [2000] 3 W.L.R. 1202; [2000] 2 F.L.R. 533 6–004
G v G (Financial Provision: Equal Division) [2002] EWHC 1339; [2002] 2 F.L.R. 1143 ... 8–032
G v G (Financial Provision: Separation Agreement); Sub Nom: Wyatt-Jones v Gold-
    smith [2004] 1 F.L.R. 1011, CA (Civ Div); affirming [2000] 2 F.L.R. 18 8–005
G v G (Matrimonial Property: Rights of Extended Family) [2005] EWHC 1560; [2006]
    1 F.L.R. 62 .... 5–014, 8–032
G v G (Minors: Custody Appeal) [1985] 1 W.L.R. 647; [1985] 2 All E.R. 225 1–005
G v G (Occupation Order: Conduct) [2000] 2 F.L.R. 36; [2000] 3 F.C.R. 53 6–013
G v G (Periodical Payments: Jurisdiction to Vary) [1998] Fam. 1; [1997] 2 W.L.R. 614;
    [1997] 1 F.L.R. 368, CA 8–037
G-A (A Child) (Permission to Remove Child from Jurisdiction: Human Rights) see A (A
    Child) (Permission to Remove Child from Jurisdiction: Human Rights)
Gandhi v Patel; Sub Nom: Ghandi v Patel [2002] 1 F.L.R. 603; [2002] Fam. Law 262 2–017
Garcia v Garcia [1992] Fam. 83; [1992] 2 W.L.R. 347; [1992] 1 F.L.R. 256, CA 4–017
Gereis v Yagoub [1997] 1 F.L.R. 854; [1997] 3 F.C.R. 755 2–016
Ghaidan v Godin-Mendoza; Sub Nom Ghaidan v Mendoza; Godin-Mendoza v Ghai-
    dan; Mendoza v Ghaidan [2004] UKHL 30; [2004] 2 A.C. 557 ... 1–001, 1–002, 1–007, 1–016,
    1–023
Gillett v Holt [2001] Ch. 210; [2000] 3 W.L.R. 815; [2000] 2 F.L.R. 266, CA 5–017
Gillick v West Norfolk and Wisbech AHA [1986] A.C. 112; [1985] 3 W.L.R. 830 11–033,
    11–034, 11–035, 11–036, 14–010
Gissing v Gissing [1971] A.C. 886; [1970] 3 W.L.R. 255 .... 5–005, 5–013, 5–015
Glass v United Kingdom (61827/00) [2004] 1 F.L.R. 1019; [2004] 1 F.C.R. 553 11–004
Gloucestershire CC v P; Sub Nom: P (A Minor) (Residence Orders), Re [2000] Fam. 1;
    [1999] 3 W.L.R. 685; [1999] 2 F.L.R. 61 12–015
Goodman v Gallant [1986] Fam. 106; [1986] 2 W.L.R. 236; [1986] 1 F.L.R. 513, CA 5–005

Goodwin v United Kingdom (28957/95) [2002] I.R.L.R. 664; [2002] 2 F.L.R. 487; [2002] 2 F.C.R. 577 .... I–001, 3–015

Gordon v Gordon [1903] P. 141, PDAD 10–003

Gorman (A Bankrupt), Re [1990] 1 W.L.R. 616; [1990] 1 All E.R. 717; [1990] 2 F.L.R. 284 5–013

Grant v Edwards [1986] Ch. 638; [1986] 3 W.L.R. 114 5–019

Gully v Dix; Sub Nom: Dix (Deceased), Re [2004] EWCA Civ 139; [2004] 1 W.L.R. 1399 ... 9–011, 9–012

H (A Child) (Adoption: Consultation of Unmarried Fathers), Re; Sub Nom: H (A Child) (Adoption: Disclosure), Re; G (A Child) (Adoption: Disclosure), Re [2001] 1 F.L.R. 646; [2001] 1 F.C.R. 726 .... 11–010, 15–028

H (A Child) (Contact: Domestic Violence), Re [2005] EWCA Civ 1404; [2006] 1 F.C.R. 102, CA (Civ Div) 12–031

H (A Child) (Residence), Re [2001] EWCA Civ 742 12–026

H (A Child) (Residence), Re [2002] 3 F.C.R. 277, CA (Civ Div) 14–015

H (A Minor) (Abduction: Rights of Custody), Re; Sub Nom: H (A Child) (Removal from Jurisdiction), Re [2000] 2 A.C. 291; [2000] 2 W.L.R. 337; [2000] 1 F.L.R. 374, HL 12–049

H (A Minor) (Care Proceedings: Child's Wishes), Re [1993] 1 F.L.R. 440; [1993] Fam. Law 200 14–010

H (A Minor) (Contact), Re [1994] 2 F.L.R. 776; [1994] 2 F.C.R. 419 10–010

H (Agreed Joint Residence: Mediation), Re; Sub Nom: B v O (Residence Orders: Parental Contact) [2004] EWHC 2064; [2005] 1 F.L.R. 8 12–026

H (Child Abduction) (Unmarried Father: Rights of Custody), Re [2003] EWHC 492; [2003] 2 F.L.R. 153 12–049

H (Child Orders: Restricting Applications), Re [1991] F.C.R. 896, CA (Civ Div) 12–005

H (Children) (Child Abduction: Grave Risk), Re; Sub Nom: H (Children) (Abduction), Re [2003] EWCA Civ 355; [2003] 2 F.L.R. 141 12–052

H (Children) (Contact Order) (No.2), Re [2002] 1 F.L.R. 22; [2001] 3 F.C.R. 385 14–017

H (Children) (Termination of Contact), Re; Sub Nom: H (Children) (Terminating Contact Orders: Local Authorities Powers), Re [2005] EWCA Civ 318; [2005] 2 F.L.R. 408 13–037

H (Minors) (Local Authority: Parental Rights) (No.3), Re; Sub Nom: H (Minors) (Adoption: Putative Father's Rights) (No.3), Re [1991] Fam. 151; [1991] 2 W.L.R. 763; [1991] 2 All E.R. 185 11–017

H (Minors) (Sexual Abuse: Standard of Proof), Re; Sub Nom: H (Minors) (Child Abuse: Threshold Conditions), Re; H and R (Child Sexual Abuse: Standard of Proof), Re [1996] A.C. 563; [1996] 2 W.L.R. 8; [1996] 1 F.L.R. 80, HL 13–018, 13–021

H (Minors) (Wardship: Sexual Abuse), Re; Sub Nom: H (Minors) (Wardship: Interim Custody), Re; H (Suspected Child Abuse: Interim Decisions), Re [1992] 1 W.L.R. 243; [1991] 2 F.L.R. 416 14–014

H (Minors) (Welfare Reports), Re [1990] 2 F.L.R. 172; [1991] F.C.R. 866 12–037

H (Minors: Prohibited Steps Order), Re [1995] 1 W.L.R. 667; [1995] 4 All E.R. 110; [1995] 1 F.L.R. 638 .... 12–019, 12–034

H and A (Children) (Paternity: Blood Tests), Re [2002] EWCA Civ 383; [2002] 1 F.L.R. 1145 .... 2–019, 10–003, 10–004, 10–005, 10–024

H v H (Financial Provision: Special Contribution) [2002] 2 F.L.R. 1021, Fam Div 8–032

H v H (Residence Order: Leave to Remove from Jurisdiction) (Note) [1995] 1 F.L.R. 529; [1995] 2 F.C.R. 469 14–009

H v M (Property: Beneficial Interest) [1992] 1 F.L.R. 229; [1991] F.C.R. 938 .... 5–012, 5–014

H-J v H-J (Financial Provision: Equality); Sub Nom: HJ v HJ (Financial Provision: Equality) [2002] 1 F.L.R. 415; [2002] Fam. Law 176, Fam Div 8–028

Haas v Netherlands (36983/97) [2004] 1 F.L.R. 673; [2004] 1 F.C.R. 147 1–002

Hadjimilitis v Tsavliris (Divorce: Irretrievable Breakdown) [2003] 1 F.L.R. 81; [2002] Fam. Law 883, Fam Div 4–006

Hale v Tanner [2000] 1 W.L.R. 2377; [2000] 2 F.L.R. 879 6–016

Hall & Co v Simons; Sub Nom: Harris v Scholfield Roberts & Hall; Barratt v Ansell (t/a
  Woolf Seddon); Barratt v Woolf Seddon; Cockbone v Atkinson Dacre & Slack;
  Harris v Scholfield Roberts & Hill [2002] 1 A.C. 615; [2000] 3 W.L.R. 543; [1999] 1
  F.L.R. 536, CA   8–006
Hanlon v Law Society [1981] A.C. 124; [1980] 2 W.L.R. 756   8–019
Haringey LBC v C (A Child) [2004] EWHC 2580; [2005] 2 F.L.R. 47   13–020
Harris (formerly Manahan) v Manahan [1996] 4 All E.R. 454; [1997] 1 F.L.R. 205   8–006
Harris v Harris [2001] 1 F.C.R. 68; *Independent*, January 15, 2001 (C.S); *Daily Telegraph*,
  December 19, 2000, CA (Civ Div)   8–041
Harrogate BC v Simpson [1986] 2 F.L.R. 91; (1985) 17 H.L.R. 205   1–001
Hawes v Evenden [1953] 1 W.L.R. 1169; [1953] 2 All E.R. 737, CA   1–001
Hepburn v Hepburn [1989] 1 F.L.R. 373; [1989] F.C.R. 618   8–036
Heseltine v Heseltine [1971] 1 W.L.R. 342; [1971] 1 All E.R. 952   5–008
Hipgrave v Jones; Sub Nom: Jones v Hipgrave [2004] EWHC 2901; [2005] 2 F.L.R. 174   6–020,
                                                                                                                                        6–024
Hirani v Hirani (1983) 4 F.L.R. 232, CA (Civ Div)   3–028
Hockenjos v Secretary of State for Social Security [2004] EWCA Civ 1749; [2005] Eu.
  L.R. 385 .... 7–006, 12–027
Hokkanen v Finland (A/299–A); Sub Nom: K v Finland (19823/92) [1996] 1 F.L.R. 289;
  [1995] 2 F.C.R. 320; (1995) 19 E.H.R.R. 139   12–029
Holman v Howes [2005] All E.R. (D) 169   5–021
Hoppe v Germany (28422/95) [2003] 1 F.L.R. 384; [2003] 1 F.C.R. 176, ECHR   14–017
Horner v Horner [1982] Fam. 90; [1982] 2 W.L.R. 914   6–003
Hosking v Michaelides [2004] All E.R. (D) 147 .... 5–020, 5–024
Hunter v Canary Wharf Ltd; Sub Nom: Hunter v London Docklands Development
  Corp [1997] A.C. 655; [1998] 1 W.L.R. 434; [1997] 2 F.L.R. 342   6–018
Hunter v Murrow; Sub Nom: H v M (Abduction: Rights of Custody) [2005] EWCA Civ
  976; [2005] 2 F.L.R. 1119   12–049
Huntingford v Hobbs [1993] 1 F.L.R. 736; (1992) 24 H.L.R. 652   5–005
Hurst v Supperstone; Sub Nom: Supperstone v Hurst [2005] EWHC 1309; [2006] 1
  F.C.R. 352   5–015
Hussey v Palmer [1972] 1 W.L.R. 1286; [1972] 3 All E.R. 744   5–008
Hyde v Hyde; Sub Nom: Hyde v Hyde and Woodmansee (1865–69) L.R. 1 P. & D. 130;
  [1861–73] All E.R. Rep. 175, Divorce Ct   2–001
Hyett v Stanley [2003] EWCA Civ 942; [2004] 1 F.L.R. 394   5–019
Hyman v Hyman; Hughes v Hughes [1929] A.C. 601, HL; affirming [1929] P. 1, CA   8–002

I v N [2003] EWHC 327   14–010
Ignaccolo-Zenide v Romania (31679/96) (2001) 31 E.H.R.R. 7, ECHR   12–029

J (A Child) (Custody Rights: Jurisdiction), Re; Sub Nom: Jomah v Attar; J (Child
  Returned Abroad: Human Rights), Re; J (A Child) (Return to Foreign Jurisdiction:
  Convention Rights), Re; J (A Child) (Child Returned Abroad: Convention Rights)
  [2005] UKHL 40; [2006] 1 A.C. 80 .... 1–005, 12–055
J (A Child) (Leave to Issue Application for Residence Order), Re [2002] EWCA Civ 1346;
  [2003] 1 F.L.R. 114 .... 12–011, 12–012
J (A Minor) (Prohibited Steps Order: Circumcision), Re; Sub Nom: J (A Minor)
  (Specific Issue Orders: Muslim Upbringing and Circumcision), Re; J (Specific Issue
  Orders: Child's Religious Upbringing and Circumcision), Re [2000] 1 F.L.R. 571;
  [2000] 1 F.C.R. 307   11–028
J (Abduction: Acquiring Custody Rights by Caring for Child), Re [2005] 2 F.L.R. 791;
  [2005] Fam. Law 605, Fam Div   12–049
J (Children) (Abduction: Child's Objections to Return), Re; Sub Nom: J (Children)
  (Child Abduction: Child Appellant), Re [2004] EWCA Civ 428; [2004] 2 F.L.R.
  64   12–053
J (Children) (Residence: Expert Evidence), Re [2001] 2 F.C.R. 44, CA (Civ Div)   14–015
J v C (Child: Financial Provision) [1999] 1 F.L.R. 152; [1998] 3 F.C.R. 79 .... 7–023, 7–024
J v C [2005] EWHC 1016, Fam Div   11–003

J v C; Sub Nom: C (An Infant), Re [1970] A.C. 668; [1969] 2 W.L.R. 540 .... 14–015, 15–003

J v J; Sub Nom: SRJ v DWJ [1999] 2 F.L.R. 176; [1999] 3 F.C.R. 153 8–036

J v ST (formerly J) (Transsexual: Ancillary Relief); Sub Nom: ST v J (Transsexual: Void
    Marriage) [1998] Fam. 103; [1997] 3 W.L.R. 1287 3–043

J v V (Disclosure: Offshore Corporations) [2003] EWHC 3110; [2004] 1 F.L.R. 1042 8–004,
    8–020, 8–021, 8–027

JD v East Berkshire Community Health NHS Trust; Sub Nom: MAK v Dewsbury
    Healthcare NHS Trust; D v East Berkshire Community NHS Trust; K v Dewsbury
    Healthcare NHS Trust; RK v Oldham NHS Trust [2005] UKHL 23; [2005] 2 A.C.
    373 13–047

Jenkins v Livesey (formerly Jenkins) [1985] A.C. 424; [1985] 2 W.L.R. 47 8–043

Jennings (Deceased), Re; Sub Nom: Harlow v National Westminster Bank Plc [1994] Ch.
    286; [1994] 3 W.L.R. 67 9–014

Jennings v Rice [2002] EWCA Civ 159; [2003] 1 F.C.R. 501 5–018

Jones v Maynard [1951] Ch. 572; [1951] 1 All E.R. 802 5–030

Judd v Brown; Sub Nom: Bankrupts (Nos.9587 and 9588 of 1994), Re [1999] 1 F.L.R.
    1191; [1999] B.P.I.R. 517; [1998] 2 F.L.R. 360 5–024

Julian v Julian (1972) 116 S.J. 763 4–022

K (A Child) (Secure Accommodation Order: Right to Liberty), Re; Sub Nom: W BC v
    DK; W BC v AK [2001] Fam. 377; [2001] 2 W.L.R. 1141; [2001] 1 F.L.R. 526, CA 13–041

K (A Minor) (Adoption: Foreign Child), Re; Sub Nom: K (Adoption and Wardship), Re
    [1997] 2 F.L.R. 221; [1997] 2 F.C.R. 389 .... 12–043, 15–003, 15–044

K (Children) (Non Accidental Injuries: Perpetrator: New Evidence), Re; Sub Nom: K
    (Children) (Adoption Orders: Fresh Evidence), Re; K (Children) (Adoption: Free-
    ing Order), Re [2004] EWCA Civ 1181; [2005] 1 F.L.R. 285 14–007

K (Children), Re [2005] EWCA Civ 1226, CA (Civ Div) 13–021

K (Minors) (Wardship: Criminal Proceedings), Re [1988] Fam. 1; [1987] 3 W.L.R. 1233;
    [1988] 1 F.L.R. 435 12–044

K v Finland (25702/94) (No.2); Sub Nom: T v Finland (25702/94) (No.2) [2001] 2 F.L.R.
    707; [2001] 2 F.C.R. 673 .... 13–029, 13–037

K v K (Ancillary Relief: Prenuptial Agreement) [2003] 1 F.L.R. 120; [2002] Fam. Law
    877, Fam Div 8–004, 8–014, 8–025

KD (A Minor) (Ward: Termination of Access), Re [1988] A.C. 806; [1988] 2 W.L.R. 398;
    [1988] 1 All E.R. 577 .... 14–015, 14–017

KR v Bryn Alyn Community (Holdings) Ltd (In Liquidation); Sub Nom: Various
    Claimants v BACHL; Various Claimants v Bryn Alyn Community (Holdings) Ltd
    (In Liquidation) [2003] EWCA Civ 85; [2003] 3 W.L.R. 107; [2003] 1 F.L.R. 1203 13–047

Karner v Austria (40016/98) [2003] 2 F.L.R. 623; [2004] 2 F.C.R. 563 .... 1–023, II–005

Kaur v Singh [1972] 1 W.L.R. 105; [1972] 1 All E.R. 292 3–024

Keegan v Ireland (A/290) [1994] 3 F.C.R. 165; (1994) 18 E.H.R.R. 342, ECHR 1–002

Kelly v BBC [2000] 3 F.C.R. 509, Fam Div 14–003

Kelly v DPP [2002] EWHC 1428; (2002) 166 J.P. 621 6–020

Kinch v Bullard [1999] 1 W.L.R. 423; [1998] 4 All E.R. 650; [1999] 1 F.L.R. 66 9–023

King v DPP [2001] A.C.D. 7; Independent, July 31, 2000 (C.S), DC 6–020

Kingsnorth Finance Co Ltd v Tizard; Sub Nom: Kingsnorth Trust Ltd v Tizard [1986]
    1 W.L.R. 783; [1986] 2 All E.R. 54 5–027

Kirklees MBC v S (Contact to Newborn Babies); Sub Nom: S (A Child) (Care Proceed-
    ings: Contact), Re [2006] 1 F.L.R. 333; [2005] Fam. Law 768 13–037

Kosmopoulou v Greece (60457/00) [2004] 1 F.L.R. 800; [2004] 1 F.C.R. 427 12–029

Kotke v Saffarini [2005] EWCA Civ 221; [2005] 2 F.L.R. 517 9–011

L (A Child) (Care Proceedings: Responsibility for Child's Injury), Re; Sub Nom: CL v
    East Riding Yorkshire Council [2006] EWCA Civ 49; [2006] 1 F.C.R. 285 13–024

L (A Child) (Care: Assessment: Fair Trial), Re; Sub Nom: C (A Child) (Care Proceed-
    ings: Disclosure of Local Authority's Decision Making Process), Re [2002] EWHC
    1379; [2002] 2 F.L.R. 730 1–021

L (A Child) (Contact: Domestic Violence), Re; V (A Child) (Contact: Domestic Vio-
    lence), Re; M (A Child) (Contact: Domestic Violence), Re; H (Children) (Contact:
    Domestic Violence), Re [2001] Fam. 260; [2001] 2 W.L.R. 339; [2000] 2 F.L.R. 334,
    CA 12–029, 12–030, 12–031, 14–010
L (Care Proceedings: Human Rights Claims), Re [2003] EWHC 665; [2003] 2 F.L.R.
    160 13–048
L (Contact: Genuine Fear), Re [2002] 1 F.L.R. 621; [2002] Fam. Law 341, Fam Div ...   12–031
L Teaching Hospitals NHS Trust v A; Sub Nom: L Teaching Hospital NHS Trust v A
    [2003] EWHC 259; [2003] 1 F.L.R. 1091 .... 10–001, 10–010, 10–011, 10–012, 12–005
L v Finland [2000] 2 F.L.R. 118; [2000] 3 F.C.R. 219   1–002
Lambert v Lambert; Sub Nom: L v L (Financial Provision: Contributions) [2002]
    EWCA Civ 1685; [2003] Fam. 103 .... 8–030, 8–032
Lancashire CC v B (A Child) (Care Orders: Significant Harm); Sub Nom: Lancashire
    CC v W (A Child) (Care Orders: Significant Harm); Lancashire CC v A (A Child);
    BW (Care Orders), Re; B and W (Children) (Threshold Criteria), Re [2000] 2 A.C.
    147; [2000] 2 W.L.R. 590 .... 13–007, 13–012, 13–024
Langley v Liverpool City Council [2005] EWCA Civ 1173; [2006] 1 W.L.R. 375   13–010
Lau v DPP [2000] 1 F.L.R. 799; [2000] Crim. L.R. 580   6–020
Le Brocq v Le Brocq [1964] 1 W.L.R. 1085; [1964] 3 All E.R. 464   4–014
Le Foe v Le Foe; Woolwich Plc v Le Foe [2001] EWCA Civ 1870, CA (Civ Div);
    affirming [2001] 2 F.L.R. 970 .... 5–013, 8–033
Le Marchant v Le Marchant [1977] 1 W.L.R. 559; [1977] 3 All E.R. 610 .... 4–006, 4–019
Lebbink v Netherlands (45582/99) [2004] 2 F.L.R. 463; [2004] 3 F.C.R. 59   1–002
Lightfoot v Lightfoot-Brown [2005] EWCA Civ 201; [2005] 2 P. & C.R. 22   5–013
Lissimore v Downing [2003] 2 F.L.R. 308; [2003] Fam. Law 566, Ch D   5–017
Livingstone-Stallard v Livingstone-Stallard [1974] Fam. 47; [1974] 3 W.L.R. 302   4–013
Lloyds Bank Plc v Rosset [1991] 1 A.C. 107; [1990] 2 W.L.R. 867 .... 5–008, 5–012, 5–013, 5–014,
                                                                                            5–015, 5–016
Lomas v Parle [2003] EWCA Civ 1804; [2004] 1 W.L.R. 1642   6–025
Lowson v Coombes [1999] Ch. 373; [1999] 2 W.L.R. 720; [1999] 1 F.L.R. 799   5–009

M (A Child) (Contact: Parental Responsibility), Re [2001] 2 F.L.R. 342; [2001] 3 F.C.R.
    454 11–018
M (A Child) (Refusal of Medical Treatment), Re; Sub Nom: M (A Child) (Medical
    Treatment: Consent) [1999] 2 F.L.R. 1097; [1999] 2 F.C.R. 577 ..... 11–036, 12–041, 12–043
M (A Minor) (Care Order: Threshold Conditions), Re; Sub Nom: M (A Minor) (Care
    Order: Significant Harm), Re [1994] 2 A.C. 424; [1994] 3 W.L.R. 558   13–021
M (A Minor) (Child's Upbringing), Re [1996] 2 F.L.R. 441; [1996] 2 F.C.R. 473, CA (Civ
    Div) 14–012, 14–013, 14–015
M (Children) (Contact: Long Term Best Interests), Re; Sub Nom: M (Children) (Intrac-
    table Contact Dispute: Court's Positive Duty), Re [2005] EWCA Civ 1090; [2006] 1
    F.L.R. 627 .... 12–031, 14–010
M (Contact: Family Assistance: McKenzie Friend), Re; Sub Nom: M (Contact: Parental
    Responsiblity: McKenzie Friend), Re [1999] 1 F.L.R. 75; [1999] 1 F.C.R. 703   11–018
M (Intractable Contact Dispute: Interim Care Order), Re; Sub Nom: CDM v CM [2003]
    EWHC 1024; [2003] 2 F.L.R. 636   12–038
M (Residence), Re see N-B (Children) (Residence: Expert Evidence), Re
M (Sperm Donor Father), Re [2003] Fam. Law 94, Fam Div   12–018
M (Threshold Criteria: Parental Concessions), Re [1999] 2 F.L.R. 728; [1999] Fam. Law
    524, CA (Civ Div)   13–015
M and B (Children) (Contact: Domestic Violence), Re [2001] 1 F.C.R. 116, CA (Civ
    Div) 12–031, 14–010
M and N (Minors), Re [1990] Fam. 211; [1989] 3 W.L.R. 1136; [1990] 1 F.L.R. 149 ....   III–001
M and R (Minors) (Child Abuse: Expert Evidence), Re; Sub Nom: M and R (Minors)
    (Expert Opinion: Evidence), Re [1996] 4 All E.R. 239; [1996] 2 F.L.R. 195 ..... 13–027, 14–014
M v B [2005] EWHC 1681; [2006] 1 F.L.R. 117 .... 3–026, 12–040
M v Birmingham City Council [1994] 2 F.L.R. 141; [1995] 1 F.C.R. 50   13–025

M v M (Divorce: Jurisdiction: Validity of Marriage); Sub Nom: A-M v A-M (Divorce: Jurisdiction: Validity of Marriage) [2001] 2 F.L.R. 6; [2001] Fam. Law 495, Fam Div 2–017

M v M (Financial Relief: Substantial Earning Capacity) [2004] EWHC 688; [2004] 2 F.L.R. 236 8–022

M v M (Maintenance Pending Suit) [2002] EWHC 317; [2002] 2 F.L.R. 123 8–021

M v M (Parental Responsibility); Sub Nom: J (A Minor) (Parental Responsibility), Re [1999] 2 F.L.R. 737; [1999] Fam. Law 538 11–018

M v M (Prenuptial Agreement) [2002] 1 F.L.R. 654; [2002] Fam. Law 177, Fam Div 8–004

M v Secretary of State for Work and Pensions; Sub Nom: Secretary of State for Work and Pensions v M; Langley v Bradford MDC [2006] UKHL 11; [2006] 2 W.L.R. 637 .. 1–002, 1–023

M, T, P, K and B (Children) (Care: Change of Name), Re [2000] 2 F.L.R. 645; [2000] Fam. Law 601, Fam Div 14–010, 15–043

Mabon v Mabon [2005] EWCA Civ 634; [2005] Fam. 366 .... 11–038, 12–012

McFarlane v McFarlane; Parlour v Parlour [2004] EWCA Civ 872; [2005] Fam. 171 ..... 8–036, 8–037

Marckx v Belgium (A/31) (1979–80) 2 E.H.R.R. 330, ECHR 1–002

Martin v Martin [1978] Fam. 12; [1977] 3 W.L.R. 101 8–010

Martin v Myers [2004] EWHC 1947, Ch D 2–019

Maskell v Maskell [2001] EWCA Civ 858; [2003] 1 F.L.R. 1138 8–044

May v May [1986] 1 F.L.R. 325; [1986] Fam. Law 106, CA (Civ Div) 14–011

Mehta (otherwise Kohn) v Mehta [1945] 2 All E.R. 690; 174 L.T. 63, PDAD 3–031

Mesher v Mesher [1980] 1 All E.R. 126 (Note); The Times, February 13, 1973, CA (Civ Div) 8–010

Messina (formerly Smith otherwise Vervaeke) v Smith (Messina Intervening); Messina (formerly Smith otherwise Vervaeke) v Smith (Member of Public Showing Cause); Messina (formerly Smith otherwise Vervaeke) v Smith (Queen's Proctor Showing Cause) [1971] P. 322; [1971] 3 W.L.R. 118 3–031

Midland Bank Plc v Cooke [1995] 4 All E.R. 562; [1997] 6 Bank. L.R. 147; [1995] 2 F.L.R. 915 .... II–005, 5–015

Miller v Miller; McFarlane v McFarlane [2006] UKHL 24 ..... 8–001, 8–009, 8–013, 8–014, 8–018, 8–019, 8–022, 8–023, 8–024, 8–025, 8–027, 8–029, 8–030, 8–031, 8–032, 8–033, 8–036, 8–037, 8–041, 8–045

Miller v Miller; Sub Nom: M v M (Short Marriage: Clean Break) [2005] EWCA Civ 984; [2006] 1 F.L.R. 151; [2005] EWHC 528 .... 8–030, 8–033, 8–045

Minton v Minton [1979] A.C. 593; [1979] 2 W.L.R. 31, HL 8–013, 8–035

Minwalla v Minwalla [2004] EWHC 2823; [2005] 1 F.L.R. 771 .... 8–020, 8–027

Mollo v Mollo; Sub Nom: Mollo v Diez [2000] W.T.L.R. 227; [1999] E.G.C.S. 117, Ch D 5–012

Mortgage Corp v Shaire; Mortgage Corp v Lewis Silkin (A Firm) [2001] Ch. 743; [2001] 3 W.L.R. 639 5–025

Mossop v Mossop [1989] Fam. 77; [1988] 2 W.L.R. 1255; [1988] 2 F.L.R. 173, CA 5–020

Mouncer v Mouncer [1972] 1 W.L.R. 321; [1972] 1 All E.R. 289 4–016

N (A Child) (Residence Order: Procedural Mismanagement), Re; Sub Nom: N (A Child) (Residence: Appointment of Solicitor: Placement with Extended Family), Re [2001] 1 F.L.R. 1028; [2001] Fam. Law 423, CA (Civ Div) 14–015

N (A Child), Re [2006] EWCA Civ 357, CA (Civ Div) 11–037

N (A Minor) (Adoption), Re [1990] 1 F.L.R. 58; [1990] F.C.R. 241 15–040

N (Section 91(14) Order), Re; Sub Nom: N (A Minor) (Residence Order: Appeal), Re; N (A Minor) (Section 91(14) of the Children Act 1989), Re [1996] 1 F.L.R. 356; [1996] 2 F.C.R. 377 12–005

N v N (Financial Provision: Sale of Company) [2001] 2 F.L.R. 69, Fam Div 8–023

N-B (Children) (Residence: Expert Evidence), Re; Sub Nom: M (Children) (Residence: Expert Evidence), Re [2002] EWCA Civ 1052; [2002] 2 F.L.R. 1059 14–015

National Provincial Bank Ltd v Ainsworth; Sub Nom: National Provincial Bank Ltd v Hastings Car Mart Ltd [1965] A.C. 1175; [1965] 3 W.L.R. 1 6–014

Norris v Norris; Haskins v Haskins [2003] EWCA Civ 1084; [2003] 1 W.L.R. 2960; [2002]
   EWHC 2996   8–032
North Yorkshire CC v SA; Sub Nom: A (A Child) (Care Proceedings: Non-Accidental
   Injury), Re [2003] EWCA Civ 839; [2003] 2 F.L.R. 849   13–024
Nottinghamshire CC v P; Sub Nom: P v Nottinghamshire CC [1994] Fam. 18; [1993] 3
   W.L.R. 637; [1993] 2 F.L.R. 134, CA 12–024, 12–038, 13–008
Nutting v Southern Housing Group Ltd [2004] EWHC 2982; [2005] 1 F.L.R. 1066   1–007

O (A Child) (Contact: Withdrawal of Application), Re; Sub Nom: O (A Child) (Termina-
   tion of Contact), Re [2003] EWHC 3031; [2004] 1 F.L.R. 1258   12–032
O (A Child) (Supervision Order: Future Harm), Re [2001] EWCA Civ 16; [2001] 1 F.L.R.
   923   13–029
O (A Minor) (Contact: Imposition of Conditions), Re [1995] 2 F.L.R. 124; [1995] Fam.
   Law 541   12–031
O (Children) (Hearing in Private: Assistance), Re; Sub Nom: O (Children) (Representa-
   tion: McKenzie Friend), Re; WR (A Child) (Representation: McKenzie Friend), Re;
   W (Children) (Representation: McKenzie Friend), Re [2005] EWCA Civ 759; [2006]
   Fam. 1   1–020
O (Transracial Adoption: Contact), Re; Sub Nom: O (A Minor) (Adoption), Re [1995]
   2 F.L.R. 597; [1996] 1 F.C.R. 540   15–043
O and N (Children) (Non-Accidental Injury: Burden of Proof), Re; Sub Nom: O and N
   (Children) (Care: Preliminary Hearing), Re; B (Children), Re; B (A Child) (Non-
   Accidental Injury: Compelling Medical Evidence), Re [2003] UKHL 18; [2004] 1
   A.C. 523   13–028
O-S (Children: Care Order), Re [2001] EWCA Civ 2039; [2002] 1 F.C.R. 689, CA (Civ
   Div)   14–014
O'Neill v O'Neill [1975] 1 W.L.R. 1118; [1975] 3 All E.R. 289   4–013
Osman v United Kingdom (23452/94) [1999] 1 F.L.R. 193; (2000) 29 E.H.R.R. 245   13–047
Oxfordshire CC v DP; Sub Nom: A County Council v DP [2005] EWHC 1593; [2005] 2
   F.L.R. 1031   13–015
Oxfordshire CC v L (Care or Supervision Order); Sub Nom: Oxfordshire CC v B (Care
   or Supervision Order) [1998] 1 F.L.R. 70; [1998] 3 F.C.R. 521   13–005
Oxley v Hiscock; Sub Nom: Hiscock v Oxley [2004] EWCA Civ 546; [2005] Fam. 211   5–015

P (A Child) (Abduction: Custody Rights), Re; Sub Nom: P (A Child) (Abduction:
   Consent), Re; P (A Child) (Abduction: Acquiescence), Re [2004] EWCA Civ 971;
   [2005] Fam. 293   12–051
P (A Child) (Financial Provision), Re; Sub Nom: P v T [2003] EWCA Civ 837; [2003] 2
   F.L.R. 865 .... 7–020, 7–024, 14–003
P (A Child) (Parental Dispute: Judicial Determination), Re [2002] EWCA Civ 1627;
   [2003] 1 F.L.R. 286   14–008
P (A Minor) (Parental Responsibility), Re [1998] 2 F.L.R. 96; [1998] 3 F.C.R. 98   11–018
P (A Minor) (Residence Order: Child's Welfare), Re; Sub Nom: P (Section 91(14)
   Guidelines: Residence and Religious Heritage), Re [2000] Fam. 15; [1999] 3 W.L.R.
   1164; [1999] 2 F.L.R. 573, CA 12–005, 14–013
P (Medical Treatment: Best Interests), Re [2003] EWHC 2327; [2004] 2 F.L.R. 1117 ...   11–038
P (Terminating Parental Responsibility), Re [1995] 1 F.L.R. 1048; [1995] 3 F.C.R. 753   11–027
P v G (Family Provision: Relevance of Divorce Provision) [2004] EWHC 2944; [2006] 1
   F.L.R. 431   9–016
P v P (Consent Order: Appeal Out of Time) [2002] 1 F.L.R. 743, Fam Div   8–043
P v P (Inherited Property) [2004] EWHC 1364; [2005] 1 F.L.R. 576, Fam Div 8–022, 8–027,
                                                                                            8–030, 8–032
P v R (Forced Marriage: Annulment: Procedure) [2003] 1 F.L.R. 661; [2003] Fam. Law
   162, Fam Div 3–001, 3–028
P v United Kingdom (56547/00) [2002] 2 F.L.R. 631; [2002] 3 F.C.R. 1 .... 1–003, 1–020, 13–029,
                                                                                            13–037, 13–048
Palau-Martinez v France (64927/01) [2004] 2 F.L.R. 810; (2005) 41 E.H.R.R. 9   14–013
Pascoe v Turner [1979] 1 W.L.R. 431; [1979] 2 All E.R. 945   5–018

Paul v Constance [1977] 1 W.L.R. 527; [1977] 1 All E.R. 195 5–030
Payne v Payne; Sub Nom: P v P (Removal of Child to New Zealand) [2001] EWCA Civ
    166; [2001] Fam. 473 12–028
Pearson v Franklin (Parental Home: Ouster) [1994] 1 F.L.R. 246 12–034
Pettitt v Pettitt; Sub Nom: P v P [1970] A.C. 777; [1969] 2 W.L.R. 966 5–001
Phillips v Peace [1996] 2 F.L.R. 230; [1996] 2 F.C.R. 237 .... 7–020, 7–023
Piglowska v Piglowski [1999] 1 W.L.R. 1360; [1999] 3 All E.R. 632 8–042
Pini v Romania (78028/01) [2005] 2 F.L.R. 596; (2005) 40 E.H.R.R. 13 1–002
Poel v Poel [1970] 1 W.L.R. 1469; 114 S.J. 720, CA (Civ Div) 12–028
Portsmouth NHS Trust v Wyatt (No.1); Sub Nom: Wyatt (A Child) (Medical Treatment:
    Parents Consent), Re [2004] EWHC 2247; [2005] 1 F.L.R. 21 12–040
Portsmouth NHS Trust v Wyatt (No.2); Sub Nom: Wyatt (A Child) (Medical Treatment:
    Continuation of Order), Re [2005] EWCA Civ 1181; [2005] 1 W.L.R. 3995 12–040
Potter v Potter (1975) 5 Fam. Law 161, CA (Civ Div) 3–023
Pounds v Pounds [1994] 1 W.L.R. 1535; [1994] 4 All E.R. 777; [1994] 1 F.L.R. 775 8–006
Practice Note (Official Solicitor: Sterilisation) [1996] 2 F.L.R. 111; [1996] 3 F.C.R. 94 12–043
Pratt v DPP [2001] EWHC Admin 483; (2001) 165 J.P. 800 6–020
Preston v Preston [1982] Fam. 17; [1981] 3 W.L.R. 619 8–029
Prince v Massachusetts (1944) 321 U.S. 158 .... III–001
Pritchard Englefield (A Firm) v Steinberg [2004] EWHC 1908; [2005] 1 P. & C.R. DG2,
    Ch D 5–025

Q (A Minor) (Parental Order), Re [1996] 1 F.L.R. 369; [1996] 2 F.C.R. 345 .... 10–011, 10–018,
                                                                                                    10–019, 10–023
Q v Q [2005] EWHC 402; [2005] 2 F.L.R. 640 8–025

R (A Minor) (Residence: Contact: Restricting Applications), Re; Sub Nom: R (A Minor)
    (Leave to Make Applications), Re; [1998] 1 F.L.R. 749; [1998] 2 F.C.R. 129 .... III–005
R (A Minor) (Wardship: Consent to Treatment), Re [1992] Fam. 11; [1991] 3 W.L.R.
    592 11–038
R. (A Child) (Adoption: Contact Orders), Re [2005] EWCA Civ 1128; [2006] 1 F.L.R.
    373 .... 12–011, 15–043
R. (A Child) (Care: Plan for Adoption: Best Interests), Re [2006] 1 F.L.R. 483; [2006]
    Fam. Law 10, Fam Div 15–019
R. (A Child) (IVF: Paternity of Child), Re; Sub Nom: R (A Child) (Contact: Human
    Fertilisation and Embryology Act 1990) (No.2), Re; D (A Child) (IVF: Paternity of
    Child), Re; R (A Child) (Parental Responsibility: IVF Baby), Re; B v R [2005]
    UKHL 33; [2005] 2 A.C. 621; [2003] EWCA Civ 182 1–002
R. (A Child) (Surname: Using Both Parents), Re [2001] EWCA Civ 1344; [2001] 2 F.L.R.
    1358 .... 11–009, 14–013
R. (A Minor) (Adoption: Access), Re [1991] 2 F.L.R. 78; [1991] F.C.R. 1006, CA 15–003
R. (A Minor) (Residence: Religion), Re; Sub Nom: R (A Minor) (Religious Sect), Re
    [1993] 2 F.L.R. 163; [1993] 2 F.C.R. 525, CA 14–013
R. (Adoption), Re [1967] 1 W.L.R. 34; [1966] 3 All E.R. 613 .... 15–015, 15–034
R. (Children) (Residence: Shared Care: Children's Views), Re [2005] EWCA Civ 542;
    [2006] 1 F.L.R. 491 12–027
R. v C [2001] EWCA Crim 1251; [2001] 2 F.L.R. 757 6–020
R. v Colohan see R. v C
R. v Evans [2004] EWCA Crim 3102; [2005] 1 W.L.R. 1435 6–005
R. v H [2001] 1 F.L.R. 580; [2001] 1 F.C.R. 569 6–020
R. v Hampshire CC Ex p. H [1999] 2 F.L.R. 359; [1999] 3 F.C.R. 129, CA 13–045
R. v Hills see R. v H
R. v Human Fertilisation and Embryology Authority Ex p. Blood; Sub Nom: R. v
    Human Fertilisation and Embryology Authority Ex p. DB [1999] Fam. 151; [1997]
    2 W.L.R. 807; [1997] 2 F.L.R. 742, CA 10–011, 10–013
R. v McNaughten; Sub Nom: R. v M; R. v McNaghten [2003] EWCA Crim 3479; The
    Times, January 15, 2004, CA (Crim Div) 6–001
R. v Pearce [2001] EWCA Crim 2834; [2002] 1 W.L.R. 1553 .... II–005

R. v R (Leave to Remove); Sub Nom: R v R [2004] EWHC 2572; [2005] 1 F.L.R. 687,
Fam Div 12–028

R. v R (Lump Sum Repayments) [2003] EWHC 3197; [2004] 1 F.L.R. 928 8–009

R. v R (Rape: Marital Exemption); Sub Nom: R. v R (A Husband) [1992] 1 A.C. 599;
[1991] 3 W.L.R. 767 .... II–003

R. v Registrar General Ex p. Smith [1991] 2 Q.B. 393; [1991] 2 W.L.R. 782; [1991] 1
F.L.R. 255, CA 15–006

R. v Tameside MBC Ex p. J (A Child) [2000] 1 F.L.R. 942; [2000] 1 F.C.R. 173 13–006

R. (on the application of A) v Lambeth LBC; Sub Nom: A v Lambeth LBC; R. v
Lambeth LBC Ex p. A [2001] EWCA Civ 1624; [2002] 1 F.L.R. 353, CA 13–046

R. (on the application of Anton) v Secretary of State for the Home Department [2004]
EWHC 2730; [2005] 2 F.L.R. 818 12–046

R. (on the application of Axon) v Secretary of State for Health [2006] EWHC 37; [2006]
1 F.C.R. 175 11–033

R. (on the application of Baiai) v Secretary of State for the Home Department; R. (on
the application of Bigoku) v Secretary of State for the Home Department; R. (on
the application of Tilki) v Secretary of State for the Home Department; R. (on the
application of Trzcinska) v Secretary of State for the Home Department [2006]
EWHC 823; The Times, April 14, 2006, QBD (Admin) I–001, 2–007

R. (on the application of Bibi) v Camden LBC [2004] EWHC 2527; [2005] 1 F.L.R.
413 12–027

R. (on the application of Carson) v Secretary of State for Work and Pensions; Sub Nom:
Carson v Secretary of State for Work and Pensions; R. (on the application of
Reynolds) v Secretary of State for Work and Pensions [2005] UKHL 37; [2006] 1
A.C. 173; [2005] 2 W.L.R. 1369 1–023

R. (on the application of CD) v Isle of Anglesey CC; Sub Nom: CD (A Child) v Isle of
Anglesey CC [2004] EWHC 1635; [2005] 1 F.L.R. 59 14–010

R. (on the application of Ford) v Revenue and Customs Commissioners; Sub Nom: R.
(on the application of Ford) v Board of Inland Revenue [2005] EWHC 1109, QBD
(Admin) 7–006

R. (on the application of G) v Barnet LBC; R. (on the application of W) v Lambeth
LBC; R. (on the application of A) v Lambeth LBC [2003] UKHL 57; [2004] 2 A.C.
208 13–005

R. (on the application of Kehoe) v Secretary of State for Work and Pensions; Sub Nom:
Secretary of State for Work and Pensions v Kehoe; Kehoe v Secretary of State for
Work and Pensions [2005] UKHL 48; [2006] 1 A.C. 42 7–018

R. (on the application of L (A Child)) v Manchester City Council; R. (on the application
of R (A Child)) v Manchester City Council [2001] EWHC Admin 707; [2002] 1
F.L.R. 43 13–033

R. (on the application of Mellor) v Secretary of State for the Home Department; Sub
Nom: R. v Secretary of State for the Home Department Ex p. Mellor [2001] EWCA
Civ 472; [2002] Q.B. 13 1–022

R. (on the application of Plymouth City Council) v HM Coroner for Devon; Sub Nom:
Plymouth City Council v County of Devon Coroner [2005] EWHC 1014; [2005] 2
F.L.R. 1279 1–018

R. (on the application of Rose) v Secretary of State for Health; Sub Nom: Rose v
Secretary of State for Health [2002] EWHC 1593; [2002] 2 F.L.R. 962 10–024

R. (on the application of the Crown Prosecution Service) v Registrar General of Births,
Deaths and Marriages; Sub Nom: J and B, Re [2002] EWCA Civ 1661; [2003] Q.B.
1222 .... I–001

R. (on the application of the Howard League for Penal Reform) v Secretary of State for
the Home Department (No.2) [2002] EWHC 2497; [2003] 1 F.L.R. 484 13–042

R. (on the application of Ullah) v Special Adjudicator; Sub Nom: Ullah v Special
Adjudicator; Do v Secretary of State for the Home Department; R. (on the
application of Ullah v Secretary of State for the Home Department; Do v Immigration Appeal Tribunal [2004] UKHL 26; [2004] 2 A.C. 323 1–016

R. (on the application of Williamson) v Secretary of State for Education and Employment; Sub Nom: Williamson v Secretary of State for Education and Employment [2005] UKHL 15; [2005] 2 A.C. 246 .... 11–001, 11–003

R. (on the application of X) v Gloucestershire CC [2003] EWHC 850 13–046

Rampal v Rampal (Ancillary Relief); Sub Nom: Rampal v Rampal (No.2) [2001] EWCA Civ 989; [2002] Fam. 85 3–043

Rees v Newbery; Sub Nom: Lankesheer (Deceased), Re [1998] 1 F.L.R. 1041; [1998] Fam. Law 320, Ch D 9–013

Rees v United Kingdom (A/106); Sub Nom: Rees v United Kingdom (9532/81) [1987] 2 F.L.R. 111; (1987) 9 E.H.R.R. 56 3–015

Reiterbund v Reiterbund [1975] Fam. 99; [1975] 2 W.L.R. 375; [1974] 1 W.L.R. 788 .... 4–020, 4–022, 7–002

Richards v Green (1984) 11 H.L.R. 1; (1983) 268 E.G. 443, CA (Civ Div) 4–013

Richards v Richards [1984] A.C. 174; [1983] 3 W.L.R. 173 .... 6–012, 6–025

Richardson v Richardson (No.2) [1996] 2 F.L.R. 617; [1997] 2 F.C.R. 453; [1994] 2 F.L.R. 1051, Fam. Div. 8–017

Robinson v Bird; Sub Nom: Robinson v Fernsby; Scott-Kilvert's Estate, Re [2003] EWCA Civ 1820; [2004] W.T.L.R. 257 9–014

Robinson v Murray; Sub Nom: Murray v Robinson [2005] EWCA Civ 935; [2006] 1 F.L.R. 365 6–016

Roddy (A Child) (Identification: Restriction on Publication), Re; Sub Nom: Torbay BC v News Group Newspapers [2003] EWHC 2927; [2004] E.M.L.R. 8 11–038

Roper v Roper and Porter [1972] 1 W.L.R. 1314; [1972] 3 All E.R. 668 4–011

Rose v Rose (Divorce: Consent Orders) (No.1) [2002] EWCA Civ 208; [2002] 1 F.L.R. 978 .... 8–006, 8–007

Rowe v Prance [1999] 2 F.L.R. 787; [2000] W.T.L.R. 249 5–030

Royal Bank of Scotland Plc v Etridge (No.2); Barclays Bank Plc v Coleman; Barclays Bank Plc v Harris; Midland Bank Plc v Wallace; National Westminster Bank Plc v Gill; UCB Home Loans Corp Ltd v Moore; Bank of Scotland v Bennett; Kenyon-Brown v Desmond Banks & Co (Undue Influence) (No.2) [2001] UKHL 44; [2002] 2 A.C. 773; [2001] 3 W.L.R. 1021 5–029

S (A Child) (Abduction: Custody Rights), Re; Sub Nom: S (A Child) (Abduction: Grave Risk of Harm), Re; S (A Child) (Return to Jurisdiction: Israel), Re [2002] EWCA Civ 908; [2002] 1 W.L.R. 3355 12–052

S (A Child) (Change of Names: Cultural Factors), Re [2001] 2 F.L.R. 1005; [2001] 3 F.C.R. 648 14–013

S (A Child) (Contact Dispute: Committal), Re [2004] EWCA Civ 1790; [2005] 1 F.L.R. 812 12–031

S (A Child) (Contact: Promoting Relationship with Absent Parent), Re [2004] EWCA Civ 18; [2004] 1 F.L.R. 1279 .... 12–029, 12–032

S (A Child) (Identification: Restrictions on Publication), Re; Sub Nom: S (A Child) (Identification: Restriction on Publication), Re [2004] UKHL 47; [2005] 1 A.C. 593 .... 1–024, 12–044

S (A Child) (Residence Order: Condition) (No.2), Re [2002] EWCA Civ 1795; [2003] 1 F.C.R. 138, CA (Civ Div) 12–028, 14–012

S (A Child) v Knowsley BC; S (A Child) v Walters; S (A Child) v Cusick; S (A Child) v Shaw [2004] EWHC 491; [2004] 2 F.L.R. 716 13–041

S (A Minor) (Independent Representation), Re [1993] Fam. 263; [1993] 2 W.L.R. 801 12–012

S (A Minor) (Parental Responsibility), Re [1995] 2 F.L.R. 648; [1995] 3 F.C.R. 225 11–002

S (Children) (Care Order: Implementation of Care Plan), Re; Sub Nom: W and B (Children) (Care Plan), Re; W (Children) (Care Plan), Re; W (Children) (Care Order: Adequacy of Care Plan), Re [2002] UKHL 10; [2002] 2 A.C. 291; [2001] EWCA Civ 757 .... 1–016, 13–036

S (Children) (Specific Issue Order: Religion: Circumcision), Re [2004] EWHC 1282; [2005] 1 F.L.R. 236 12–020

S (Contact: Children's Views), Re [2002] EWHC 540; [2002] 1 F.L.R. 1156 14–010

S v B (Abduction: Human Rights) [2005] EWHC 733; [2005] 2 F.L.R. 878 12–052

S v B (Ancillary Relief: Costs) [2004] EWHC 2089; [2005] 1 F.L.R. 474, Fam Div 8–027
S v N [2003] All E.R. 14–012
S v S (Ancillary Relief: Consent Order); Sub Nom: S v S (Divorce: Setting Aside Consent
    Order) [2002] EWHC 223; [2003] Fam. 1 8–044
S v S (Financial Provision: Departing from Equality) [2001] 2 F.L.R. 246; [2001] 3 F.C.R.
    316 8–028
SA, Re [2005] EWHC 2942; [2006] Fam. Law 268, Fam Div 12–040
SK (An Adult) (Forced Marriage: Appropriate Relief), Re; Sub Nom: SK (Proposed
    Plaintiff), Re [2004] EWHC 3202; [2006] 1 W.L.R. 81 12–040
SRJ v DWJ *see* J (SR) v J (DW)
Sahin v Germany (30943/96) [2003] 2 F.L.R. 671; 15 B.H.R.C. 84 1–021
Salgueiro da Silva Mouta v Portugal (33290/96) [2001] 1 F.C.R. 653; (2001) 31 E.H.R.R.
    47 1–023
Santos v Santos [1972] Fam. 247; [1972] 2 W.L.R. 889 4–016
Savage v Dunningham [1974] Ch. 181; [1973] 3 W.L.R. 471 5–013
Scott v Scott (1986) 150 J.P. 333; [1986] 2 F.L.R. 320 12–037
Secretary of State for Work and Pensions v Jones [2003] EWHC 2163; [2004] 1 F.L.R.
    282 10–005
Sekhon v Alissa [1989] 2 F.L.R. 94; [1989] Fam. Law 355, Ch D 5–009
Shaw v Shaw [2002] EWCA Civ 1298; [2002] 2 F.L.R. 1204 8–043
Sheffield City Council v E; Sub Nom: E (Alleged Patient), Re [2004] EWHC 2808; [2005]
    Fam. 326 3–026
Singh v Entry Clearance Officer, New Delhi [2004] EWCA Civ 1075; [2005] Q.B. 608 1–001,
    1–003, 15–044
Singh v Singh [1971] P. 226; [1971] 2 W.L.R. 963 .... 3–020, 3–028
Sledmore v Dalby (1996) 72 P. & C.R. 196; [1996] N.P.C. 16, CA (Civ Div) 5–018
Smith v Clerical Medical and General Life Assurance Society [1993] 1 F.L.R. 47; [1992]
    F.C.R. 262, CA (Civ Div) 3–008
Smith v Smith; Sub Nom: Smith (Deceased), Re [1992] Fam. 69; [1991] 3 W.L.R. 646;
    [1991] 2 F.L.R. 432, CA 8–044
Sorrell v Sorrell [2005] EWHC 1717; [2006] 1 F.L.R. 497 8–032
South Glamorgan CC v B; Sub Nom: South Glamorgan CC v W and B [1993] 1 F.C.R.
    626; [1993] Fam. Law 398 13–014
Southwark LBC v B [1998] 2 F.L.R. 1095; [1999] 1 F.C.R. 550 13–021
Spence (Deceased), Re; Sub Nom: Spence v Dennis [1990] Ch. 652; [1990] 2 W.L.R. 1430;
    [1990] 2 F.L.R. 278, CA 3–042
Stack v Dowden; Sub Nom: Dowden v Stack [2005] EWCA Civ 857; [2006] 1 F.L.R. 254 ... 5–005,
    5–015, 5–019, 5–035
Stephenson v Stephenson [1985] F.L.R. 1140; [1985] Fam. Law 447, CA (Civ Div) 14–011
Sullivan v Sullivan (1818) 2 Hag. Con. 238 3–031
Suss v Germany (40324/98) [2006] 1 F.L.R. 522; [2005] 3 F.C.R. 666 12–029
Suter v Suter [1987] Fam. 111, [1987] 3 W.L.R. 9; [1987] 2 F.L.R. 232, CA 8–015, 8–021
Sutton v Mishcon de Reya [2003] EWHC 3166; [2004] 1 F.L.R. 837 .... 5–006, 8–003
Sylvester v Austria (36812/97); Sylvester v Austria (40104/98) [2003] 2 F.L.R. 210; [2003]
    2 F.C.R. 128 12–029
Szechter v Szechter [1971] P. 286; [1971] 2 W.L.R. 170 .... 3–028, 3–029

T (A Child) (Contact: Alienation: Permission to Appeal), Re [2002] EWCA Civ 1736;
    [2003] 1 F.L.R. 531 12–032
T (A Child) (Order for Costs), Re [2005] EWCA Civ 311; [2005] 2 F.L.R. 681 12–032
T (A Minor) (Adoption: Contact Order), Re [1995] 2 F.L.R. 251; [1995] 2 F.C.R. 537 15–043
T (A Minor) (Care Order: Conditions), Re [1994] 2 F.L.R. 423; [1994] Fam. Law 558 13–037
T (A Minor) (Wardship: Representation), Re; Sub Nom: CT (A Minor) (Wardship:
    Representation), Re [1994] Fam. 49; [1993] 3 W.L.R. 602 12–041
T (Accommodation by Local Authority), Re [1995] 1 F.L.R. 159; [1995] 1 F.C.R. 517 13–045
T (Children) (Abduction: Child's Objections to Return), Re; Sub Nom: T (Children)
    (Abduction: Custody Rights), Re [2000] 2 F.L.R. 192; [2000] 2 F.C.R. 159 12–053

T (Children) (Abuse: Standard of Proof), Re; Sub Nom: T (Children) (Sexual Abuse: Standard of Proof), Re [2004] EWCA Civ 558; [2004] 2 F.L.R. 838 .... 13–017, 13–018
T (Children) (Interim Care Order), Re [2001] EWCA Civ 1345; [2001] 3 F.C.R. 175, CA (Civ Div) 13–021
T (Judicial Review: Local Authority Decisions Concerning Child in Need), Re [2004] 1 F.L.R. 601; [2004] Fam. Law 176 13–046
T v T (Consent Order: Procedure to Set Aside) [1996] 2 F.L.R. 640; [1997] 1 F.C.R. 282 ... 8–043
T v T (Financial Relief: Pensions) [1998] 1 F.L.R. 1072; [1998] 2 F.C.R. 364 .... 8–025, 8–034
Tameside and Glossop Acute Services NHS Trust v CH (A Patient) [1996] 1 F.L.R. 762; [1996] 1 F.C.R. 753 11–038
Tanner v Tanner (No.1) [1975] 1 W.L.R. 1346; [1975] 3 All E.R. 776 5–008
Thain (An Infant), Re; Sub Nom: Thain v Taylor [1926] Ch. 676, CA III–006
Thomas v Fuller-Brown [1988] 1 F.L.R. 237; [1988] Fam. Law 53, CA (Civ Div) 5–013, 5–020
Thomas v News Group Newspapers Ltd; Sub Nom: Thomas v Hughes; Thomas v News Group International Ltd [2001] EWCA Civ 1233; [2002] E.M.L.R. 4 6–021
Thomas v Thomas [1995] 2 F.L.R. 668; [1996] 2 F.C.R. 544, CA 8–021
Thompson v Thompson (Financial Provision) [1991] 2 F.L.R. 530; [1992] 1 F.C.R. 368, CA 8–044
Thurlow v Thurlow [1976] Fam. 32; [1975] 3 W.L.R. 161 4–013
Tribe v Tribe [1996] Ch. 107; [1995] 3 W.L.R. 913 5–009
Trippas v Trippas [1973] Fam. 134; [1973] 2 W.L.R. 585 8–018

U (A Child) (Serious Injury: Standard of Proof), Re; Sub Nom: LU (A Child), Re; LB (A Child), Re; B (A Child) (Serious Injury: Standard of Proof), Re [2004] EWCA Civ 567; [2005] Fam. 134 13–018
U (A Child), Re [2003] EWCA Civ 27 14–010
Upton v National Westminster Bank Plc [2004] EWHC 1962; [2004] W.T.L.R. 1339, Ch D 11–009

V (A Child) (Care Proceedings: Human Rights Claims), Re [2004] EWCA Civ 54; [2004] 1 W.L.R. 1433 13–048
V (A Minor) (Adoption: Consent), Re [1987] Fam. 57; [1986] 3 W.L.R. 927 15–043
V v V (Ancillary Relief: Power to Order Child Maintenance) [2001] 2 F.L.R. 799; [2001] Fam. Law 649 .... 7–017, 7–029
V v V (Children) (Contact: Implacable Hostility) [2004] EWHC 1215; [2004] 2 F.L.R. 851 .... 12–032, 12–033
V v V (Financial Relief) [2005] 2 F.L.R. 697; [2005] Fam. Law 684, Fam Div 8–036
Vaughan v Vaughan [1973] 1 W.L.R. 1159; [1973] 3 All E.R. 449 6–003
Venema v Netherlands (35731/97) [2003] 1 F.L.R. 552; [2003] 1 F.C.R. 153, ECHR 13–048

W (A Child) (Abduction: Conditions for Return), Re; Sub Nom: W (Abduction: Domestic Violence), Re [2004] EWCA Civ 1366; [2005] 1 F.L.R. 727 12–047
W (A Child) (Parental Contact: Prohibition), Re; Sub Nom: W (A Child) (Section 34(2) Orders), Re [2000] Fam. 130; [2000] 2 W.L.R. 1276; [2000] 1 F.L.R. 502 13–037
W (A Minor) (Medical Treatment: Court's Jurisdiction), Re; Sub Nom: J (A Minor) (Consent to Medical Treatment), Re [1993] Fam. 64; [1992] 3 W.L.R. 758 11–038
W (Children) (Identification: Restrictions on Publication), Re; Sub Nom: A Local Authority v W [2005] EWHC 1564; [2006] 1 F.L.R. 1 12–044
W (Wardship: Relatives Rejected as Foster Carers), Re [2003] EWHC 2206; [2004] 1 F.L.R. 415 .... 12–044, 13–033
W v H (Child Abduction: Surrogacy) (No.1) [2002] 1 F.L.R. 1008; [2002] Fam. Law 345, Fam Div 10–001
W v J (A Child) (Variation of Financial Provision) [2003] EWHC 2657; [2004] 2 F.L.R. 300 12–045
W v Oldham MBC; Sub Nom: W (A Child) (Non-accidental Injury: Expert Evidence), Re; GW v Oldham MBC [2005] EWCA Civ 1247; [2006] 1 F.L.R. 543 13–017
W v United Kingdom (A/121); Sub Nom: W v United Kingdom (9749/82) (1988) 10 E.H.R.R. 29, ECHR; (1984) 6 E.H.R.R. CD565, Eur Comm HR 1–021

W v W (Nullity: Gender); Sub Nom: W v W (Physical Inter-sex) [2001] Fam. 111; [2001]
    2 W.L.R. 674; [2001] 1 F.L.R. 324 3–015
WM (Adoption: Non-Patrial), Re [1997] 1 F.L.R. 132; [1997] 2 F.C.R. 494 15–016
Wachtel v Wachtel (No.2) [1973] Fam. 72; [1973] 2 W.L.R. 366 .... 8–022, 8–033
Wagstaff v Wagstaff [1992] 1 W.L.R. 320; [1992] 1 All E.R. 275 8–031
Watson (Deceased), Re [1999] 1 F.L.R. 878; [1999] 3 F.C.R. 595, Ch D 9–010
Wells v Pickering; Sub Nom: Pickering v Wells [2002] 2 F.L.R. 798; [2002] Fam. Law
    812 5–025
Wells v Wells; Sub Nom: W v W (Financial Provision: Company Shares) [2002] EWCA
    Civ 476; [2002] 2 F.L.R. 97 .... 8–023, 8–029
Whiston v Whiston [1995] Fam. 198; [1995] 3 W.L.R. 405; [1995] 2 F.L.R. 268, CA 3–043
White v White [2001] 1 A.C. 596; [2000] 3 W.L.R. 1571; [2000] 2 F.L.R. 981, HL 8–001, 8–008,
            8–013, 8–014, 8–019, 8–023, 8–027, 8–029, 8–030, 8–032, 8–037, 8–044,
            8–045
White v White; Sub Nom: W v W (Joinder of Trusts of Land Act and Children Act
    Applications) [2003] EWCA Civ 924; [2004] 2 F.L.R. 321 5–021
Whiting v Whiting [1988] 1 W.L.R. 565; [1988] 2 All E.R. 275; [1988] 2 F.L.R. 189, CA 8–036,
            8–038
Williams & Glyn's Bank Ltd v Boland; Williams & Glyn's Bank Ltd v Brown [1981] A.C.
    487; [1980] 3 W.L.R. 138 5–027
Williams v Lindley [2005] EWCA Civ 103; [2005] 2 F.L.R. 710 8–044
Woolford v DPP 2000 W.L. 664496 6–020

X (Children) (Care Proceedings: Parental Responsibility), Re; Sub Nom: X (A Child)
    (Parental Responsibility Agreement: Child in Care), Re [2000] Fam. 156; [2000] 2
    W.L.R. 1031; [2000] 1 F.L.R. 517 11–017
X (Minors) v Bedfordshire CC; M (A Minor) v Newham LBC; E (A Minor) v Dorset CC
    (Appeal); Christmas v Hampshire CC (Duty of Care); Keating v Bromley LBC
    (No.2) [1995] 2 A.C. 633; [1995] 3 W.L.R. 152, HL 13–047, 13–048
X Council v B see A Local Authority v B (Emergency Protection Orders)
X v X [2002] 1 F.L.R. 508; [2002] Fam. Law 98, Fam Div 8–005
X, Y and Z v United Kingdom (21830/93) [1997] 2 F.L.R. 892; [1997] 3 F.C.R. 341 ... 1–002

Y (Leave to Remove from Jurisdiction), Re [2004] 2 F.L.R. 330; [2004] Fam. Law 650,
    Fam Div 12–028
Yousef v Netherlands (33711/96) [2003] 1 F.L.R. 210; [2002] 3 F.C.R. 577 14–017

Z (A Minor) (Freedom of Publication), Re; Sub Nom: Z (A Minor) (Identification:
    Restrictions on Publication), Re [1997] Fam. 1; [1996] 2 W.L.R. 88; [1996] 1 F.L.R.
    191, CA 12–019
Z v United Kingdom (29392/95) [2001] 2 F.L.R. 612; [2001] 2 F.C.R. 246 .... 1–019, 3–015, 13–048
Z v Z (Abduction: Children's Views) [2005] EWCA Civ 1012; [2006] 1 F.L.R. 410 12–053
Zaffino v Zaffino see Z v Z (Abduction: Children's Views)
Zawadka v Poland (48542/99); Sub Nom: Zawadkaw v Poland (48542/99) [2005] 2 F.L.R.
    897; [2006] 1 F.C.R. 371 .... 1–017, 12–029, 14–017

Table of Statutes

1753 Clandestine Marriages Act 2–001
1837 Wills Act (7 Will 4 & 1 Vict.
    c.26) 9–001
    s.7 11–036
1857 Divorce and Matrimonial
    Causes Act 1–001, 4–003
1870 Married Women's Property
    Act II–004
1882 Married Women's Property
    Act (45 & 46 Vict. c.75) ... II–004
1925 Law of Property Act (15 & 16
    Geo.5 c.20) 5–021
    s.36 9–023
    s.52 5–004
    s.53(1) 5–007
    s.53(1)(b) 5–005
    s.53(1)(c) 5–005
    s.53(2) 5–007
    s.196(3) 9–023
    s.199 5–027
1925 Administration of Estates Act
    (15 & 16 Geo.5 c.23)
    s.46 .... 9–002, 9–003
1926 Adoption of Children Act (16
    & 17 Geo.5 c.29) 15–001
1933 Children and Young Persons
    Act (23 & 24 Geo.5 c.12)
    s.1(7) 11–003
1948 Children Act (11 & 12 Geo.6
    c.43) 1–003, 13–001
1949 Marriage Act (12, 13 & 14
    Geo.6 c.76) .. 2–002, 2–009, 2–016
    s.3 2–004
    s.3(1)(b) 2–004
1949 Adoption of Children Act (12,
    13 & 14 Geo.6 c.98) 15–006
1956 Sexual Offences Act (4 & 5
    Eliz.2 c.69)
    s.1 .... II–003

1964 Married Women's Property
    Act (c.19) 5–031
1967 Matrimonial Homes Act
    (c.75) 6–008, 6–014
1968 Civil Evidence Act (c.64) 10–003
1969 Family Law Reform Act
    (c.46) 11–032
    s.20 10–005
    s.20(1A) 10–006
    s.21(1) 10–005
    s.21(2) 10–005
    s.21(3) 10–005
    s.26 10–004
1969 Children and Young Persons
    Act (c.54) 13–043
1969 Divorce Reform Act (c.55) 3–048,
    4–005, 4–007, 4–015, 4–027,
    8–008
1970 Law Reform (Miscellaneous
    Provisions) Act (c.33) 5–020,
    5–032
    s.3(1) 5–032
    s.3(2) 5–032
1970 Marriage (Registrar General's
    Licence) Act (c.34) 2–009
1970 Matrimonial Proceedings and
    Property Act (c.45) 8–008
    s.37 .... 5–020, 5–034
1971 Nullity of Marriage Act (c.44) ... 3–002,
    3–025
1972 Civil Evidence Act (c.30)
    s.3 13–017
1973 Matrimonial Causes Act
    (c.18) 3–002, 3–022, 4–005,
    4–014, 5–020, 7–027,
    7–028, 7–029, 8–008, 8–013,
    8–035, 12–003
    Pt.II 8–001
    s.1(1) 4–006
    s.1(2) 4–008

1973	Matrimonial Causes Act —*cont.*	
	s.1(2)(a)	4–009
	s.1(2)(b)–(e)	4–036
	s.1(2)(b)	4–010, 4–013
	s.1(2)(d)	4–015
	s.1(2)(e)	4–015
	s.2(1)	4–012
	s.2(3)	4–013
	s.2(6)	4–016
	s.5	4–018
	s.9	4–007
	s.10(2)	4–015, 4–017
	s.10A	4–035
	s.11	3–004
	s.11(c)	3–015
	s.11(d)	3–016
	s.12	3–017, 3–033
	s.12(1)	3–018
	s.12(b)	3–022
	s.12(c)	3–025
	s.12(g)	3–015
	s.12(h)	3–015, 3–033
	s.13	3–036
	s.13(1)	3–039
	s.13(4)	3–037
	s.17	4–006
	s.17(1)	7–028
	s.18(1)	7–028
	s.18(2)	7–028
	s.19	3–014
	s.24A	8–012
	s.25	8–006, 8–018, 8–027, 8–036
	s.25(1)	8–014
	s.25(2)	8–018
	s.25(2)(a)	8–018
	s.25(2)(b)	8–026
	s.25(2)(c)	8–028
	s.25(2)(d)	8–029, 8–030
	s.25(2)(e)	8–030
	s.25(2)(f)	8–031, 8–032
	s.25(2)(g)	8–032, 8–033
	s.25(2)(h)	8–033
	s.25A	8–036
	s.25A(1)	8–036
	s.25A(2)	8–036, 8–037
	s.25A(3)	8–039
	s.27	7–026
	s.28(1A)	8–037
	s.31	8–041
	s.31(7A)	8–041
	s.33A	8–006
	s.34(1)	8–002
	s.35	8–005
	s.41	12–003

1975	Inheritance (Provision for Family and Dependants) Act (c.63)	7–005, 8–039, 9–005, 9–006, 9–009, 9–013, 9–016, 9–018
	s.1(3)	9–009
	s.1(1A)	9–009
	s.1(1B)(b)	9–009
	s.3(2)	9–016
	s.3(4)	9–013
1975	Children Act (c.72)	15–006, 15–008, 15–013, 15–017, 15–031
1976	Legitimacy Act (c.31)	
	s.1(3)	3–042
1976	Adoption Act (c.36)	15–008, 15–016, 15–018, 15–037, 15–039
	s.16	15–035
1976	Domestic Violence and Matrimonial Proceedings Act (c.50)	6–002
1977	Rent Act (c.42)	1–002
1978	Domestic Proceedings and Magistrates Courts Act (c.22)	7–027, 7–029, 12–003
1978	Adoption (Scotland) Act (c.28)	15–037
1981	Supreme Court Act (c.54)	
	s.37	6–018
	s.41(2)	12–041
1981	British Nationality Act (c.61)	
	s.1(5)	15–004
	s.50	11–009
1983	Marriage Act (c.32)	2–009
1984	Child Abduction Act (c.37)	
	s.1	12–028
1984	Matrimonial and Family Proceedings Act (c.42)	8–033
	Pt.III	12–003
1984	Police and Criminal Evidence Act (c.60)	
	s.24(2)(n)	6–022
	s.24(6)	6–023
1985	Surrogacy Arrangements Act (c.49)	10–023
	s.2(3)	10–023
1985	Social Security Act (c.53)	8–011
1985	Child Abduction and Custody Act (c.60)	12–048, 14–005
1985	Housing Act (c.68)	9–020
1986	Marriage (Prohibited Degrees of Relationship) Act (c.16)	3–007, 3–008
	s.10(2)	3–009
1986	Insolvency Act (c.45)	5–024
	s.335A(2)	5–024
	s.336(4)	5–024
	s.336(5)	5–024
	s.337(5)	5–024

1986	Family Law Act (c.55)	12–047
	s.1	12–047
1987	Crossbows Act (c.32)	11–036
1987	Family Law Reform Act (c.42) 11–009,	11–010
	s.28	3–042
1987	Minors Contracts Act	11–036
1988	Housing Act (c.50)	9–020
1989	Law of Property (Miscellaneous Provisions) Act (c.34)	
	s.2 .... 5–004, 5–006,	8–003
1989	Children Act (c.41) 5–021, 7–011, 7–020, 7–022, 7–024, 7–029, III–003, III–008, 11–002, 11–003, 11–008, 11–010, 11–015, 11–025, 11–027, 11–031, 12–001, 12–002, 12–003, 12–014, 12–015, 12–018, 12–022, 12–031, 12–041, 12–042, 12–046, 12–047, 12–056, 13–001, 13–002, 13–004, 13–007, 13–008, 13–014, 13–016, 13–019, 13–023, 13–043, 13–048, 14–006, 15–006, 15–008, 15–011, 15–036,	15–041
	Pt.1	12–003
	Pt.II 12–003,	12–041
	Pt.III	13–004
	Pt.IV	12–003
	s.1 .... 14–002, 14–017,	15–036
	s.1(1)	11–004
	s.1(2)	14–006
	s.1(3) 13–008, 13–026, 14–006, 14–015,	14–017
	s.1(3)(g)	13–029
	s.1(4)	14–009
	s.1(5) 12–002, 13–008, 13–026, 14–006,	14–008
	s.2(1)	11–012
	s.2(2)	11–013
	s.2(6)	11–027
	s.2(7)	11–028
	s.2(8)	11–028
	s.2(9)	11–029
	s.2(11)	11–029
	s.3	12–019
	s.3(5)	11–030
	s.4	11–016
	s.4(1)(a)	11–018
	s.4(1)(b)	11–017
	s.4(2A)	11–027
	s.4A 11–019,	15–008
	s.5	11–023
	s.5(6)	11–023
	s.5(7)	11–023

1989	Children Act—cont.	
	s.5(7)(b)	11–023
	s.5(8)	11–023
	s.7 .... III–008, 10–003, 10–024,	11–002
	s.7(1)	12–036
	s.8 .... III–008, 11–037, 12–001, 12–003, 12–004, 12–005, 12–006, 12–010, 12–013, 12–016, 12–021, 12–023, 12–034, 12–044, 12–056, 13–026, 14–003, 14–009, 14–010, 14–014, 14–016, 15–013,	15–043
	s.8(1)	12–017
	s.8(3) 12–003,	12–039
	s.9(3)	12–015
	s.9(5)	12–024
	s.9(6)	12–023
	s.9(7)	12–023
	s.10(1)(a)(ii)	12–010
	s.10(1)(b)	14–016
	s.10(3)	12–015
	s.10(4)(a)	12–005
	s.10(5) 12–006,	12–009
	s.10(5A)	12–009
	s.10(8)	12–012
	s.10(9)	12–011
	s.10(10)	12–008
	s.11(4)	12–027
	s.11(7)	12–021
	s.12(1)	11–023
	s.12(2) 11–023,	12–018
	s.12(3)	11–024
	s.12(5)	12–023
	s.13 12–028,	14–009
	s.13(1)(a)	12–018
	s.14(4)	15–013
	s.14(6)(b)	15–013
	s.14(7)	15–013
	s.14(8)	15–013
	s.14A(2)(b)	15–013
	s.14A(5)	15–013
	s.14C(1)	11–021
	s.14C(1)(a)	15–013
	s.14C(1)(b)	15–013
	s.14D	15–013
	s.14F	15–013
	s.15 .... 5–002, 7–020, 8–045,	III–008
	s.16	12–036
	s.17 .... 13–005, 13–006,	13–042
	s.17(1)	13–005
	s.17(1)(b) 13–005,	13–030
	s.17(3)	13–005
	s.17(6)	13–005
	s.17(10)	13–005
	s.17A	13–005
	s.17B	13–005
	s.20 13–006,	13–030
	s.20(1)	13–006

1989   Children Act—*cont.*
    s.20(3) 13–006
    s.20(4) 13–006
    s.22(3) 13–030
    s.22(5) 12–009, 13–030
    s.23(1) 13–030
    s.23(4) 13–033
    s.25 13–041
    s.26 13–045
    s.26(1) 15–043
    s.26(2A) 13–036
    s.26A 13–045
    s.31 .... 12–040, 13–019
    s.31(1) 13–008, 13–029
    s.31(2) 13–014, 13–019, 13–024,
                                    15–031
    s.31(2)(b)(i) 13–024
    s.31(3A) 13–029
    s.31(9) 13–019, 14–014
    s.31(10) 13–020
    s.31(11) 13–014
    s.31A 13–029
    s.33(1) 13–030
    s.33(3)(a) 11–025
    s.33(3)(b) 11–028
    s.33(4) 11–028
    s.33(6) 11–025
    s.34(1) 13–037
    s.34(3) 13–037
    s.34(6) 13–037
    s.34(11) 13–037
    s.37 .... III–008, 13–008, 13–014
    s.37(3) 12–037
    s.38 .... III–008, 13–014
    s.38(3) 13–026
    s.38(6) 13–014
    s.38(7) 13–014
    s.38A 13–011
    s.38B 13–011
    s.39(1) 13–038
    s.41(1) 13–016, 14–010
    s.41(5) 13–016
    s.41(6) 14–010
    s.43 13–012
    s.44 13–010
    s.44(1)(b) 13–011
    s.44(1)(c) 13–011
    s.44(4)(c) 11–024, 11–025, 13–011
    s.44(5) 13–011
    s.44(5)(b) 11–026
    s.44(6) 13–011
    s.44(7) 11–036
    s.44A 13–011
    s.44A(2)(b)(i) 13–011
    s.44B 13–011
    s.45(5) 13–011
    s.45(10) 13–011
    s.46(1) 13–010

1989   Children Act—*cont.*
    s.46(2)(b) 15–043
    s.47 .... 13–012, 13–042, 13–048
    s.47(5A) 13–012
    s.66(1) 15–011
    s.67(1) 15–011
    s.91(14) 12–005, 12–006, 13–038
    s.91(15) 13–038
    s.100(2) 12–041
    s.105 7–021
    s.105(1) 14–014
    Sch.1 .... 7–020, 7–021, III–008
    Sch.1, para.4(1) 7–024
    Sch.1, para.4(2) 7–024
    Sch.2, para.7 13–005
    Sch.3 13–029
    Sch.3, para.6(1) 13–029
    Sch.8, para.7A 15–011
    Sch.13, para.45(2) 12–042
1990   Human Fertilisation and Em-
    bryology Act (c.37) 7–011,
             10–007, 10–009, 10–012,
              10–013, 10–014, 10–016,
                     10–017, 10–024
    s.27(1) 10–008
    s.27(2) 10–022
    s.28 .... 10–011, 15–016
    s.28(2) 10–010, 10–011, 10–013,
                               10–016
    s.28(3) 10–011, 10–013
    s.28(5)(c) 10–022
    s.28(5A)–(5I) 10–013
    s.28(6)(a) 10–012
    s.30 11–021
    s.30(1) 10–021
    s.30(1)(a) 10–018
    s.30(1)(b) 10–018
    s.30(5) 10–019
    s.30(6) 10–019
    s.36 10–023
    Sch.3 10–012
1990   Courts and Legal Services Act
    (c.41) 10–010
    Sch.16, para.2 10–003
1991   Child Support Act (c.48) 7–002,
            7–008, 7–009, 7–010, 7–011,
            7–012, 7–014, 8–026, 8–045,
                   10–005, 14–005
    s.6 .... 7–013, 7–017, 7–018, 7–020
    s.26 10–004
1992   Social Security Contributions
    and Benefits Act (c.4)
    s.144(3) 7–006
    Sch.10, para.5 7–006
1992   Social Security Administra-
    tion Act (c.5)
    Pt.V 7–006

1994 Criminal Justice and Public
Order Act (c.33) II–003
1994 Marriage Act (c.34) 2–009, 2–015,
2–017
1995 Pensions Act (c.26) 8–008, 8–011
1995 Child Support Act (c.34) 7–015
1995 Law Reform (Succession) Act
(c.41) 9–004, 9–009, 9–013
1996 Family Law Act (c.27) .. 4–027, 4–028,
4–029, 4–030, 4–034, 5–002,
6–002, 6–003, 6–010, 6–017,
6–025, 12–003, 12–034
Pt.I 4–034
Pt.II 4–030, 4–033
Pt.III 4–030
Pt.IV ... 5–021, 6–001, 6–002, 6–014,
6–016
s.1 4–033
s.15 5–021
s.22 4–031
s.22(1) 4–031
s.29 .... 4–032, 4–033
s.33 6–006
s.33(1) 6–008
s.33(1)(b) 6–007
s.40 6–006
s.41 6–013
s.42(5) 6–005
s.42A 6–016
s.45(1) 6–015
s.45(2) 6–015
s.45(3) 6–015
s.46(3A) 6–016
s.46(4) 6–016
s.47 6–016
s.47(2) 6–016
s.62 .... 6–004, 8–045
s.62(1)(a) 6–004
s.62(3)(ea) 6–004
Sch.6 13–011
Sch.7 8–045
1996 Marriage Ceremony (Pre-
scribed Words) Act
(c.34) 2–009
1996 Trusts of Land and Appointment of Trustees Act
(c.47) 5–021, 6–006
s.12 5–021
s.14 .... 5–021, 5–025
s.15 .... 5–021, 5–025
1996 Education Act (c.56)
s.7 11–005
s.444 11–005

1997 Protection from Harassment
Act (c.40) ... 6–001, 6–004, 6–005,
6–016, 6–018, 6–019, 6–021,
6–022, 6–025
s.1 .... 6–020, 6–022
s.1(2) 6–020
s.1(3) 6–021
s.2 6–023
s.2(3) 6–022
s.3 6–024
s.3(2) 6–024
s.3(3) 6–024
s.3(6) 6–024
s.5 6–023
s.5A 6–023
s.7(1)(a) 6–020
s.7(4) 6–020
s.12 6–021
1998 Crime and Disorder Act
(c.37) 11–006, 13–043
s.11 .... 12–003, 13–043
s.12 12–003
s.14 13–043
1998 Human Rights Act (c.42) 1–002,
1–014, 1–015, 1–016, 5–024,
7–018, III–001, 11–007,
12–044, 13–014, 13–048,
14–017
s.1 1–016
s.1(1) 1–016
s.3 1–016
s.4 1–016
s.6 .... 1–016, 1–017
s.10 1–016
1999 Adoption (Intercountry As-
pects) Act (c.18) 15–044
1999 Access to Justice Act (c.22) 4–032,
8–042
s.55 8–042
1999 Welfare Reform and Pensions
Act (c.30) 8–008, 8–011, 8–033
1999 Immigration and Asylum Act
(c.33) 3–007
2000 Care Standards Act (c.14) 15–017
2000 Child Support, Pensions and
Social Security Act (c.19) ... 7–009,
7–012, 7–014, 7–018, 10–004,
10–006
2001 Regulatory Reform Act
(c.6) 2–018
2002 Land Registration Act (c.9)
s.116 5–018
Sch.3, para.2 5–027
2002 Divorce (Religious Marriages)
Act (c.27) 4–035

2002   Adoption and Children Act
         (c.38) 6–001, III–009, 10–021,
                  11–008, 11–015, 11–017,
                  11–019, 11–022, 12–003,
                  12–005, 12–023, 12–031,
                  13–005, 13–036, 13–045,
                  15–006, 15–007, 15–008,
                  15–013, 15–015, 15–016,
                  15–028, 15–031, 15–035,
                  15–036, 15–039, 15–042,
                       15–044, 15–045
         s.1(2) 15–019, 15–036
         s.1(3) 15–036
         s.1(4) 15–019
         s.1(4)(a) 15–037
         s.1(4)(c) 15–036, 15–039
         s.1(4)(f) 15–036, 15–042
         s.1(6) 15–036
         s.1(7)(a) 15–036
         s.3 15–017
         s.4 15–008
         s.9(3) 12–015
         s.12 15–021
         s.19 15–023
         s.20 15–026
         s.21 .... 13–038, 15–023, 15–031
         s.23A 13–039
         s.23B 13–039
         s.23C 13–039
         s.23D 13–039
         s.23E 13–039
         s.25 .... 11–020, 11–025, 15–023
         s.26 .... 15–031, 15–036
         s.26(3) 15–031
         s.27(4) 15–031
         s.32 15–027
         s.42 15–032
         s.44(1) 15–018
         s.44(4)(b) 15–020
         s.46 15–004
         s.46(6) 15–032
         s.47(4) 15–032
         s.47(5) 15–032
         s.47(7) 15–032
         s.47(8) 15–015
         s.47(9) 15–015
         s.49(4) 15–015
         s.49(5) 15–015
         ss 50–51 15–016
         s.51(2) 15–008
         s.51(3) 15–016
         s.51(4) 15–016
         s.52 15–033
         s.52(3) 15–026
         s.52(4) 15–032
         s.52(5) 15–026
         s.52(10) 15–028
         s.57 15–006

2002   Adoption and Children Act
         —cont.
         s.58(4) 15–006
         s.60(3) 15–006
         s.61(3) 15–006
         s.61(4) 15–006
         s.62 15–006
         s.67 .... 10–022, 15–004
         s.67(2) 15–004
         s.67(3)(a) 15–008
         s.77 15–006
         s.78 15–006
         s.79(6) 15–006
         s.79(7) 15–006
         s.80 15–006
         s.81 15–006
         s.83 15–044
         s.92(4) 15–018
         s.93 15–018
         s.94 15–018
         s.95 15–018
         s.96 15–018
         s.97 10–022
         s.111 11–016
         s.112 .... 11–018, 15–008
         s.115 11–022
         s.118 13–036
         s.122 14–010
         Sch.2 15–006
2002   Nationality, Immigration and
         Asylum Act (c.41)
         s.9 11–009
2003   Human Fertilisation and Em-
         bryology (Deceased Fa-
         thers) Act (c.24) 10–013
2003   Anti-social   Behaviour   Act
         (c.38) 11–006
2003   Sexual Offences Act (c.42) 3–011
         s.25 3–011
         s.27 3–011
         s.28 3–011
         s.64 3–011
         s.65 3–011
2004   Gender Recognition Act (c.7) .. 3–005,
                       3–015, 3–033
         s.2 3–015
         s.3 3–015
         s.9 3–015
2004   Asylum   and   Immigration
         (Treatment of Claimants,
         etc.) Act (c.19) 2–007
2004   Domestic Violence, Crime and
         Victims Act (c.28) ... 6–004, 6–013,
                       6–016, 6–023
         s.5 13–024
2004   Children Act (c.31) 11–003, 12–017,
                  13–001, 13–012, 15–011
         s.58 11–003

2004 Children Act—*cont.*
s.60 13–043
2004 Civil Partnership Act (c.33) 1–001,
1–007, 1–013, 2–001, 2–019,
3–045, 3–046, 4–036,
II–002, II–005, 5–021,
6–002, 6–004, 6–008, 6–014,
7–005, 7–025, 8–013, 9–001,
9–009, 10–011, 10–018,
15–016
s.1 2–001
s.2(1) 2–019
s.6 2–001
s.41 4–036
s.44(5) 4–036
s.49 3–045
s.50 3–046
s.56 .... 4–036, 7–028

2004 Civil Partnership Act—*cont.*
s.65 .... 5–020, 5–034
s.72 8–001
s.74 5–020
s.74(5) 5–032
Sch.1 3–005
Sch.5 .... 8–001, 8–008, 8–035
Sch.5, Pt.9 7–026
Sch.5, para.7(1)(c) 8–010
Sch.5, para.10 8–012
Sch.5, para.20 8–014
Sch.5, para.21 8–018
Sch.6 7–027
Sch.6, para.48 7–021
Sch.8 9–020
Sch.24, para.5 7–005
2005 Education Act (c.18)
s.116 11–005
2006 Family Law (Scotland) Act ... 5–035

TABLE OF STATUTORY INSTRUMENTS

1983 Adoption Agencies Regulations (SI 1983/1964)
reg.15(2) 15–006

1991 Placement of Children with Parents etc. Regulations (SI 1991/893) 13–032

1991 Family Proceedings Rules (SI 1991/1247) 4–016, 4–036
r.4.3 12–010
r.9(5) 14–010

1994 Parental Responsibility Agreement (Amendment) Regulations (SI 1994/3157) ... 11–017

1997 Fireworks (Safety) Regulations (SI 1997/2294) 11–036

1997 Land Registration Rules (SI 1997/3037) 5–005

1999 Family Proceedings (Amendment No.2) Rules (SI 1999/3491) 8–002

2000 Reporting of Suspicious Marriages and Registration of Marriages (Miscellaneous Amendments) Regulations (SI 2000/3164) 2–007

2001 Child Support (Maintenance Calculations and Special Cases) Regulations (SI 2001/155)
reg.3 7–014

2001 Child Support (Variations) Regulations (SI 2001/156) 7–015

2002 Fostering Services Regulations (SI 2002/57) 13–033

2004 Review of Children's Cases (Amendment) Regulations (SI 2004/1419) 13–036

2004 Human Fertilisation and Embryology Authority (Disclosure of Donor Information) Regulations (SI 2004/1511) 10–024

2005 Adoption Agencies Regulations (SI 2005/389) 15–017, 15–020
reg.17 15–022
reg.17(1)(f) 15–022
reg.31 15–022
reg.35(4) 15–026
reg.36(3)(a) 15–023
reg.36(4)(a) 15–023

2005 Disclosure of Adoption (Post-Commencement Adoptions) Regulations (SI 2005/888) 15–006
reg.4 15–006

2005 Adoption Information and Intermediary Services (Pre-Commencement Adoptions) Regulations (SI 2005/890) 15–006

2005 Adopted Children and Adoption Contact Registers Regulations (SI 2005/924)
r.6(1) 15–006
r.7(1)(b) 15–006

2005 Special Guardianship Regulations (SI 2005/1109) 15–013

2005 Children (Private Arrangements for Fostering) Regulations (SI 2005/1533) ... 15–011

2005 Restriction on the Preparation of Adoption Reports Regulations (SI 2005/1711) 15–018

2005 Suitability of Adopters Regu-
     lations (SI 2005/1712) 15–020
2005 Civil Partnership (Amend-
     ments to Registration
     Provisions) Order (SI
     2005/2000)   2–019
2005 Family Procedure (Adoption)
     Rules (SI 2005/2795) 15–028
     r.23 15–028
     r.72(1)(a) 15–026
     r.108 15–028

2005 Tax and Civil Partnership
     Regulations   (SI2005/
     3229)   9–021
2005 Independent Review of Deter-
     minations   (Adoption)
     Regulations   (SI
     2005/3332) 15–021
2006 Child Benefit (General) Reg-
     ulations (SI 2006/223)
     reg.3   7–004

Chapter 1

Introduction: The Family and The Law

A: Defining "The Family" and "Family Law"

The concept of the family

The "family" is at once both very easy and very difficult to define. It is easy in the **1–001** sense that most people would be able to give a list of those whom they personally regard as "family". But this is also what makes it so difficult to find a comprehensive definition. One person's definition is not necessarily the same as another's, and both may be different from the concept of family encapsulated by the law. Should "family" status be determined by marriage, by blood ties, by self-definition, or by function? An example of the latter approach is provided by the judgment of Waite L.J. in *Fitzpatrick v Sterling Housing Association Ltd* [1998] 1 F.L.R. 6, CA:

> "The question is more what a family does than what a family is. A family unit is a social organisation which functions through its linking its members closely together. The functions may be procreative, sexual, sociable, economic, emotional The list is not exhaustive."

Some indication of the modern diversity of family life against which such questions are asked is provided by the judgment of Munby J. in *Singh v Entry Clearance Officer, New Delhi* [2004] EWCA Civ 1075:

> "in our multi-cultural and pluralistic society the family takes many forms . . . Many marry according to the rites of non-Christian faiths. There may be one, two, three or even more generations living together under the same roof . . . Children live in households where their parents may be married or unmarried. They may be the children of polygamous marriages. They may be brought up by a single parent. Their parents may or may not be their natural parents . . . Some children are brought up by two parents of the same sex . . . The fact is that many adults and children, whether through choice or circumstance, live in families more or less removed from what until comparatively recently would have been regarded as the typical nuclear family." (para.63)

How far the "traditional" family consisting of married parents and their dependent children is typical is considered further below (paras 1–006 *et seq.*). How the law treats these different family relationships will take the rest of the book to describe. For present purposes, what is of interest is how the law's concept of "family" has changed in recent years. For many years, family law was largely concerned with the status of marriage and the consequences of marital breakdown. (In *A Century of Family Law*, published in 1957—the centenary of the Divorce and Matrimonial Causes Act 1857—14 of the 16 chapters focused on the rights of married couples, and only two on the legal position of children.) This focus on marriage has changed significantly in the intervening decades. Parenthood, rather than marriage, is now arguably the key relationship in family law through which rights and responsibilities are channelled. At the same time, a wider range of adult relationships has been accepted as familial. Cohabiting couples with children were accepted as being members of one another's family—for some limited purposes—as early as the 1950s (see *e.g. Hawes v Evenden* [1953] 1 W.L.R. 1169), although unmarried childless couples had to wait until 1976 for such recognition (*Dyson Holdings Ltd v Fox* [1976] QB 503). And there has been an even more dramatic change in the law's attitude to same-sex couples. As Munby J noted in *Singh v ECO, New Delhi* [2004] EWCA Civ 1075:

> "Within my professional lifetime we have moved from treating such relationships as perversions to be stamped out by the more or less enthusiastic enforcement of repressive criminal law to a ready acknowledgment that they are entitled not merely to respect but also, in principle, to equal protection under the law."
> (para.62)

Even as little as ten years ago family law essentially adopted a three-tiered approach, privileging marriage, conferring limited rights on heterosexual cohabitants, and offering occasional recognition of the wider family. Same-sex couples did not even feature in this hierarchy, and it was initially held in *Harrogate v Simpson* [1986] 2 F.L.R. 91 that they did not constitute a "family" in the eyes of the law. As a result of the decision of the House of Lords in *Fitzpatrick v Sterling HA* [1999] 3 W.L.R. 1113, HL, however, a same-sex partner was recognised as a member of his cohabitant's family, thus scraping on to the bottom tier of the hierarchy. Not long after, in *Ghaidan v Goden-Mendoza* [2004] UKHL 30, the House of Lords further held that it was discriminatory to distinguish between opposite-sex couples and same-sex couples in the context of succession to tenancies, and held that a same-sex partner was entitled to the same rights as a heterosexual partner. As Baroness Hale noted:

> "homosexual relationships can have exactly the same qualities of intimacy, stability and inter-dependence that heterosexual relationships do . . . [M]arried and unmarried couples, both homosexual and heterosexual, may bring up children together . . . Homosexual couples can have exactly the same sort of inter-dependent couple relationship as heterosexuals can . . . Some people, whether heterosexual or homosexual, may be satisfied with casual or transient relationships. But most human beings eventually want more than that. They want love. And with love they often want not only the warmth but also the sense of belonging to one another which is the essence of being a couple. And many couples also come to want the stability and permanence which go with sharing a home and a life together, with or without the children who for many people go to

make a family. In this, people of homosexual orientation are no different from people of heterosexual orientation." (para.142)

Same-sex couples thus attained the second tier. Finally, in 2004, Parliament passed the Civil Partnership Act, which created the new status of civil partnership, modelled on marriage but open only to same-sex couples. The Act came into force on December 5, 2005 and by January 31, 2006 3,648 same-sex couples had entered into civil partnerships, of which 2,510 were between two men and 1,138 between two women. By registering a civil partnership, such individuals are thereby opting into virtually the same rights and responsibilities that are accorded to married couples. Furthermore, the Civil Partnership Act equates the position of same-sex cohabitants with that of heterosexual counterparts. As a result, family law still adopts a three-tiered approach, but the content of the tiers differs considerably.

Despite these extensive reforms, the current law remains unsatisfactory in a number of respects. On the one hand, there is the question of whether equality has really been achieved by allowing same-sex couples to enter into a civil partnership: while this new institution may be the *legal* equivalent of marriage, is it the same in terms of social recognition? The plethora of references to "same-sex marriages" in the media when the first civil partnerships were formalised in December 2005 suggests that there is an emerging public perception to this effect (although the term "gay marriage" is also used in a pejorative sense by opponents). In a growing number of countries, same-sex couples are entitled to marry: the Netherlands was the first to allow same-sex marriage in 2001, followed by Belgium in 2003, and then Spain and Canada in 2005. Other jurisdictions are considering whether to follow suit. Various attempts have been made by a number of US States to make provision for same-sex marriage, but at present the only state to allow such marriages is Massachusetts. In the light of these initiatives the Civil Partnership Act appears to be a less radical option.

Similarly, while the 2004 Act conferred the same rights on unregistered same-sex cohabitants as were already enjoyed by opposite-sex cohabitants (for examples see paras 6–009 and 9–009), the reality is that the legal treatment of cohabitants is fragmented and inconsistent. The present position can perhaps best be summarised by saying that cohabitants are treated in the same way as married or partnered couples for certain purposes, given different rights in other contexts, and ignored the rest of the time. Given the resulting patchwork of legal rights, it is unsurprising that a (mistaken) belief in "common law marriage" is strong among cohabitants. A person who is treated as a spouse in the context of welfare benefits (see para.7–005) might reasonably expect that the same rules apply to pensions or indeed to provision at the end of a relationship, but would be sadly disappointed (see Ch.8). One option for reform that was suggested when the Civil Partnership Bill was being debated was that heterosexual cohabiting couples should also have the opportunity to register a partnership. This option is unattractive for a number of reasons. First, the law would be asymmetrical: heterosexual couples would have the option of marriage or civil partnership, while same-sex couples would only have the option of entering into a civil partnership. Secondly, such a reform would not protect those cohabitants—probably the majority—who failed to register their relationship. Why would the 59 per cent of cohabitants who believe that they have a "common law marriage" register a partnership in order to obtain rights that they think they already enjoy?

Successive Early Day Motions have been tabled—with the support of 119 MPs—calling upon the government "to introduce a new law to provide a safety net for couples of whatever sexual orientation who live together as its next priority." (see *e.g.* Hansard April 19, 2006). At present the Law Commission is examining the rights of cohabitants when a relationship ends, and is expected to issue a consultation paper in 2006 with a final report in 2007. It is to be hoped that this will address the current deficiencies of the law.

Family life

1–002   The changing attitudes to different family forms outlined above have been influenced at least in part by the incorporation of the European Convention on Human Rights into English law by means of the Human Rights Act 1998 (see further para.1–015). This has required the courts to give more careful consideration to what is meant by the term "family life". Article 8 of the Convention provides that everyone has the right to respect for his private and family life, his home, and his correspondence". Interference with this right may be justified on a number of grounds, which are examined further below (para.1–021): for present purposes the key issue is how "family life" is defined.

The European Court of Human Rights has adopted an explicitly functional approach in deciding whether or not "family life" exists in any given case. As it explained in *Lebbink v The Netherlands* [2004] 2 F.L.R. 463:

> "The existence or non-existence of 'family life' for the purposes of Art 8 is essentially a question of fact depending upon the real existence in practice of close personal ties." (para.36)

Despite this functional approach, attention is also paid to the form of the relationship. Thus family life automatically exists between married couples, and between them and any child born of the marriage from the moment of birth, even if the parents have separated (*Berrehab v The Netherlands* (1989) 11 E.H.R.R. 322, para.21). Family life also exists automatically between cohabiting parents and their child (see *e.g. Keegan v Ireland* (1994) 18 E.H.R.R. 342). However, the blood tie alone is neither necessary nor sufficient (see *e.g. Haas v The Netherlands* [2004] 1 F.L.R. 673) to create family life. In *X, Y and Z v UK* [1997] 2 F.L.R. 892, for example, family life was held to exist between the female-to-male transsexual partner of the mother and the child she had borne as the result of artficial insemination. Relationships created by adoption are entitled to equal respect, and in *Pini v Romania* [2005] 2 F.L.R. 596, ECHR, the court even held that in the circumstances of that case the potential relationship between adopters and child fell within the scope of Art.8. *Lebbink* itself shows that family life may be established without a significant investment of time and effort. In this case the parents of the child never cohabited during their three-year relationship, but the father was present at the birth, visited regularly, and babysat once or twice. The court held that family life had been established in this case. Nor is "family life" confined to the nuclear family: it was noted in *Marckx v Belgium* (1979) 2 E.H.R.R. 330 that "family life within the meaning of Art.8 includes at least the ties between near relatives, for instance those between grandparents and grandchildren, since such relatives may play a considerable part in family life" (at para.45), although the tie between grandparent and grandchild may not be seen as equivalent to the tie between parent and child (see *e.g. L v Finland* [2000] 2 F.L.R. 118).

Before the passage of the Human Rights Act there were few occasions when the English courts were required to consider whether particular combinations of individuals constituted a "family." Family law, somewhat surprisingly, rarely defines eligibility to rights in terms of "family" status: depending on the context, rights are conferred on spouses, civil partners, children, and a variety of relatives. One exception is the Rent Act 1977—now of limited application—which provides that members of a tenant's family can succeed to a tenancy upon the tenant's death. This explains why the major breakthroughs in the legal definition of "family"—such as *Fitzpatrick v Sterling HA* [1999] 3 W.L.R. 1113, HL, and *Ghaidan v Godin-Mendoza* [2004] UKHL 30—have all occurred in the context of housing law. In recognising that same-sex partners constitute a family, the law of this jurisdiction was actually in advance of the European Court of Human Rights, which has yet to recognise the relationship between same-sex cohabitants—or indeed that between heterosexual cohabitants—as constituting "family life" (see the authorities discussed in *Secretary of State for Work and Pensions v M* [2006] UKHL 11).

Since the implementation of the Human Rights Act, the courts have had to consider whether "family life" exists when considering claims that rights under Art.8 have been infringed. A similarly functional approach to that adopted by the Strasbourg court can be seen in decisions such as *Re R (a child)* [2003] EWCA Civ 182, in which it was noted that "[f]amily life does not inevitably flow from genetic fatherhood, although it often will. It may flow from looking after a child to whom one is not related by blood, but the length and intensity of that relationship will be particularly relevant."

It will be clear from the above discussion that there is no single legal concept of the family, but rather a set of shifting ideas about family relationships and about the rights that they entail.

The scope of "family law"

This section considers three fundamental questions: first, what does "family law" **1–003** actually include; secondly, what form does regulation of the family take; and, thirdly, what are the limitations of the law in this context?

The answer to the first question is in part dictated by convenience and the need to identify a coherent body of law that fits into the confines of the standard university course. Even so, the perceived scope of "family law" may alter over time. In 1957 the then Master of the Rolls, Lord Evershed, perceived no definitional problem, simply proclaiming that "family law" was not a term of art, but merely "a convenient means of reference to so much of our law . . . as directly affects that essential unit of the English social structure, the family" (*A Century of Family Law*, pp.vii–iii). But many laws affect the family—for example: employment laws, in allowing for "family-friendly" policies; housing laws, in providing accommodation for families; the benefit system, in providing support for families—and legal rules of this kind may be of more day-to-day significance to many families than the rules relating to divorce or child protection. While such topics are important, they tend to fall outside the scope of most family law courses. A more precise definition of family law might be that it defines family statuses—*e.g.* through marriage or parenthood or adoption—and stipulates when the law may intervene to protect family members.

The second question raises the point that regulation may take many different forms. It is clear that there has been a move away from the idea that it is the role of the state and the law to prescribe moral standards for the populace. Today it is difficult to believe that as late as the start of the twentieth century Parliament was debating whether it should be legal for a widower to marry the sister of his deceased wife, with opponents of such a reform drawing on Biblical sources to justify their opposition.

By contrast, at the end of the twentieth century the Home Office paper *Supporting Families* (1998) suggested that it was not for the Government to tell people how to run their lives (although the rest of the paper did not quite support this stance). A similar shift can be seen in the courts: to quote Munby J once more, "[t]he days are past when the business of the judges was the enforcement of morals or religious belief." (*Singh v ECO, New Delhi* [2004] EWCA Civ 1075, para.64). Yet the move away from moral prescriptions is not the same as a decline in state regulation of the family. There has at the same time been an increased willingness to intervene in family life. The view that the privacy of family life is to be respected has given way to the recognition that support for individual family members may require that privacy to be breached. There is a greater recognition that the home is not always a haven to be protected against state intervention, but may in fact be an effective prison in which the economically or physically powerful (usually men) dominate and abuse the weak and vulnerable (usually women and children), and that a failure to intervene effectively endorses such abuse.

The law has attempted to address the imbalance of power within the family in a number of ways. Legislation has been passed to ensure formal equality between spouses: the rules that in the past gave husbands power over their wives' bodies and property have been consigned to history. The law has also recognised the need for remedies to address the continuing inequality of many family relationships: the courts may now interfere with property rights by excluding a violent partner from the family home (see Ch.6) and by reallocating property on divorce or dissolution (Ch.8). The vulnerability of children within the home has also been recognised. Towards the end of the nineteenth century, child neglect was widely publicised, and the state responded with measures of regulation, inspection, and (increasingly) assistance. The Education Act 1870 introduced the principle of compulsory education, and thus has some claim to be the most radical legislative interference with the right for the family to transmit its own values to succeeding generations. In other contexts too, legislation grappled with the problem of how far the state should be empowered to take compulsory measures to override the once sacrosanct parental right to control children's upbringing. Eventually, the Children Act 1948 (one of the keystones of the post-World War II welfare state) cast on the state extensive responsibilities to care for children in need. Since then there has been what one judge has described as a "cascade of legislation" dealing with these matters. The powers and duties of the state in relation to children and their families are now so extensive that certain aspects of the family law syllabus could fairly be described as a branch of public law rather than private law (see Ch.13). Yet constraints on undue intervention in family life remain, bolstered by Art.8 of the ECHR and its guarantee of respect for private and family life. The fact that the state has to maintain a delicate balance between interfering in family life unnecessarily and failing to protect vulnerable members of the family is illustrated by the cases of *P, C and S v UK* [2002] 3 F.C.R. 1, ECHR and *Z v UK* [2001] 2 F.L.R. 612, ECHR, the former finding a breach of human rights on account of the local authority's action and the latter finding a breach on the basis of the authority's *inaction* (see para.13–048).

Despite this level of intervention, family law rarely *directly* prescribes how family members should behave towards one another. The law's view of the obligations that family members owe to one another generally manifests itself through the way in which breaches of those obligations are dealt with. For example, the fact that adultery is a basis for divorce suggests that spouses owe obligations of fidelity towards each other, but the law contains no specific statement to this effect. (By contrast, Art.212 of the French Civil Code states that spouses owe one another fidelity, support and assistance.) The remedies now available in cases of domestic violence indicate that certain forms of behaviour are not to be tolerated, and the fact that the state can intervene if the family poses a threat to minor children shows that a certain standard of parenting is expected. In recent years there has, however, been a shift towards more explicit guidance, perhaps motivated by the fact that family behaviour does not suggest that the general public has fully assimilated the messages "radiated" by the law about the importance of civilised separation and co-operative post-separation parenting. Although the "information meetings" piloted in the context of divorce reform were ultimately abandoned (see para.4–033), guidance and counselling for parents is deployed both where their children are involved in criminal activities (see para.11–006), and where the parents themselves are in conflict over contact (see para.12–032).

One final point on the scope of family law relates to its limitations—some perhaps inherent, some attributable to the fact that the state's ability to intervene is limited by the resources made available for the task. The fact that the law endorses equality in relationships does not ensure that relationships will be equal. Similarly, the fact that there are legal mechanisms for protecting vulnerable family members does not mean that the vulnerable are thereby safe. The criminal statistics demonstrate the reality that home and family are still often associated with violence: women are more likely to be assaulted by someone that they know than by a stranger. Stories of children abducted and killed by strangers attract considerable media attention, but children are far more likely to die at the hands of their parents, and there are families in which children are repeatedly abused by the very adults who are supposed to protect them.

The administration of family law

Even if there is a legal solution to a particular family problem, there remains the **1–004** separate question about the nature of the legal procedures that should be invoked. Three key issues arise in this context: first, the question of the appropriate court to deal with different issues; secondly, the promotion of alternatives to litigation; and, thirdly, the nature of court proceedings in family law cases.

One persistent theme in the administration of family law is the need for the system to adapt to parental separation on a mass scale. When judicial divorce was first made available in 1857 (see para.4–003), it could only be granted by a panel of three judges in the High Court in London, the aim being to impress on litigants the seriousness of their actions. By contrast, government policy is now that cases "should start at the lowest appropriate level" (DCA, *Focusing judicial resources appropriately: The Right Judge for the Right Case* (CP25/05), p.26). At present family matters may be dealt with in three different tiers of courts: the High Court, the county courts, and family proceedings courts (the latter being magistrates' courts having a family jurisdiction). While all three tiers have concurrent jurisdiction in disputes involving children—with the result that cases may be begun in any tier—this is not necessarily the case for other matters, such as the granting of divorces. The government has indicated that its long-term objective is to create a single Family Court (DCA, *A Single Civil Court? The Scope for unifying the civil and family jurisdictions of the High Court, the county courts and the Family Proceedings Courts* (CP(R) 06/05), p.42), which would involve more work, across a broader range of family matters, being handled by the family proceedings courts. While the creation of such a court would require primary legislation, a number of initiatives—such as the new unified court administration in operation from April 2005—have already been put in place to ensure that cases are heard at the most appropriate level. What is "appropriate" is indicated by the statement in *Focusing judicial resources appropriately* that:

> "The assumption should be that, with limited exceptions, cases should not be dealt with by High Court judges unless they have exceptional features which justify their being dealt with at this senior level." (p.6)

A second theme evident in the succeeding chapters is that litigation—particularly in its more adversarial form—is in any case an inappropriate means of dealing with many family disputes. Quite apart from the fact that the law is perceived to be a blunt instrument for dealing with family life, there is the risk that litigation may cause damage to family relationships. Thus obtaining a divorce hardly ever involves the parties disputing in court whether or not the marriage has, for legal purposes, irretrievably broken down (see para.4–007). Moreover, the parties are strongly encouraged to settle the consequences of separation—in relation to both the division of property and the issue of post-separation parenting—between themselves or with the assistance of a mediator (see paras 8–002 and 12–033). Issues of child support are generally allocated to an administrative body—the Child Support Agency—rather than the courts (see Ch.7). In addition, individuals are encouraged to regulate their financial affairs to preclude later disputes (see *e.g.* para.5–005). The current policy is to promote alternatives to litigation—or at least adjudication—as far as possible.

It should be noted that the somewhat negative view of lawyers that lies behind attempts to promote alternatives such as mediation is somewhat unfair in the light of the way in which practitioners engage with family law. The Family Law Protocol aims to "encourage a constructive and conciliatory approach to the resolution of family law disputes", and family lawyers certainly perceive themselves as adopting such an approach (see J. Eekelaar, M. Maclean and S. Beinart, *Family Lawyers* (Oxford, Hart Publishing, 2000), and see para.4–034). Procedural developments have increasingly come to involve not only the parties' legal representatives but even the judges. This is vividly demonstrated in a revealing research project conduced by Davis and Pearce (see "The Hybrid Practitioner" [1999] Fam. Law 547). They record a typical case in which the parties' lawyers negotiated "at the door of the court" for one and a half hours, and agreed everything except for the precise time at which weekend contact between father and daughter would finish. Davis and Pearce record:

> The judge "listened sympathetically. She suggested 6.30 p.m. in term time and 7.30 p.m. in holidays. However, Mrs Jones remained firm, arguing that Karen herself did not want the later time. The . . . judge effectively chaired some further discussion as to the return time. She made it clear that the final decision must be based on what Karen was saying. She gave time for everyone to express their point of view, 'Are you quite sure? I haven't written anything down yet'."

A third theme relates to the nature of proceedings that do make it to court. As the above extract shows, family cases are markedly dissimilar from the system of "adversarial" justice traditional in the common law courts—in which each party puts his or her viewpoint to a judge who is confined to choosing between the solutions they put forward. In dealing with disputes over children the courts are not confined to the options presented by the parties, and the "inquisitorial" role of the court has been highlighted, particularly in proceedings where the issue is whether a child should continue to live with parents who are suspected of harming him or her (see para.13–015).

This leads on the next point, the question of whether family law is distinctively different from other legal subjects in its approach to disputes.

The nature of family law

Lord Evershed's statement that family law is "not a term of art" would seem to suggest **1–005** that there is nothing to distinguish family law from other legal subjects, apart from its content. Almost half a century later, the prevailing view is that family law is different from other subjects in a number of crucial respects. O'Donovan has argued that:

> "subjects such as contract or trusts are based on a legal construct, a concept that springs from the mind of the lawyer but that has no correspondent in the material world ... It is otherwise with family law. The subject is organised around a notion—the family—which is taken for granted and is not legally defined." (*Family Law Matters* (1993), p.10).

Of course, as O'Donovan acknowledges, the law also plays a significant role in constructing a particular view of the family. Judges and legislators are influenced by ideas about the form that families *should* take, as well as evidence of the form that families do take. The extent to which other legal subjects are not rooted in "real life" is also open to debate. But it can be claimed with some justification that non-legal matters have a greater role to play in family law than in other subject areas.

First, family law is highly discretionary, in order to accommodate the diversity of family life ("All happy families are alike, but an unhappy family is unhappy after its own fashion", as Tolstoy suggested in *Anna Karenin*). This means that there is also greater scope for different judges to reach different decisions (or even for the same judges to reach different decisions if the facts of the cases are slightly different). Any attempt to apply reported cases to the facts of a new situation must take into account the variety of facts that may have influenced the earlier cases. The discretionary nature of family law also affects the role of the appeal court. An appellate court is only entitled to interfere if the trial judge's decision is so plainly wrong that he or she must have given far too much weight to a particular factor: *G v G* [1985] 1 W.L.R. 647, HL. As Baroness Hale emphasised in *Re J (Child Returned Abroad: Convention Rights)* [2005] UKHL 40, findings of credibility and primary fact, and the evaluation and balancing of various factors, are matters for the trial judge.

Secondly, there is a heavy reliance on expert evidence in cases involving children. For example, the legal rule that decisions about a child's upbringing should be determined by what would be in the best interests of the child concerned is influenced by contemporary views about what is best for children, often informed by experts in child development. As Wilson J. has argued, child law is both different from and in certain respects more difficult than other areas of law, since "it centres upon the future of children, and, indeed, not just upon their practical and economic but also upon their psychosocial future." ("The Misnomer of Family Law" [2003] Fam Law 29). In addition, medical evidence may be necessary to determine whether the injuries of a child have been inflicted deliberately or can be attributable to natural causes (although the limitations of medical evidence in such cases have attracted much attention in recent years, see para.13–017).

Thirdly, views about family life may change in the light of new research or policies, with the result that the speed of change is perhaps faster in family law than in other areas of law. Thorpe L.J. acknowledged the pace of change in *CG v CW and G (Children)* [2006] EWCA Civ 372: "we have moved into a world where norms that seemed safe twenty or more years ago no longer run." (para.43) The reader should therefore be alert to the changes that have occurred between the text being written and being read. Yet in some areas of family law the pace of change is somewhat slower: as Chs 2 and 3 indicate, the law relating to marriage is still heavily influenced by its history and in many respects differs little from the rules that operated in the nineteenth century.

As the former Lord Chancellor, Lord Irvine, once commented, "when it comes to family law we all think that our views are as good as those of anyone else" (*Hansard* (HL) December 11, 1996, col.1095). We all come to the subject with our own preconceptions. This may make family law seem like an easy subject, on which every one can have a valid opinion. But one of the challenges for those interested in family law is to try to stand aside from their own experience of family life, and look at the evidence objectively.

This is perhaps a convenient point at which to introduce some of the social and demographic changes that have occurred in family life in recent decades.

B: DEMOGRAPHIC AND SOCIAL CHANGE

1–006   The twentieth century was a period of great change for the family. This section examines the changes that have occurred in the structure of the family, and in the roles of different members of the family. There is a long-standing debate about the relation-ship between the law and the demographic position: do changes in the law cause changes in family life, or does the law simply respond to demographic change? The issue is by no means clear-cut (see, *e.g.* para.4–001 below in the context of divorce reform), and the reader should reflect on the demographic changes described below when reading the chapters dealing with the substantive law.

The decline of marriage?

1–007   The twentieth century witnessed a rise and fall in the popularity of marriage. By the late 1960s, marriage had become an almost universal experience: less than five per cent of 16-year-olds were expected to die unmarried. Even in the late 1970s, the Home Office felt able to conclude that "[i]t is no longer fashionable to predict that marriage, in any recognisable form, is about to give way to radically new forms of sexual partnership. Marriage has never been more popular, even if it has never been more risky" (*Marriage Matters*, 1979). In fact, the downward trend had begun in 1973, and continued virtually unabated until 2001. Since then there has been a slight rise, although the optimism engendered by the fact that 2004 saw the third successive annual rise in marriages should be tempered by the fact that it also witnessed the fourth successive rise in divorces in the UK as a whole. The Home Office at least got it right in saying that marriage has become more "risky", in the sense that there is now a greater risk of a marriage ending in divorce (see para.4–001, below).

Despite these changes, marriage remains an important institution, both in demographic terms, and in terms of its legal significance. There are still many more married than unmarried couples, and, despite the increase in the number of births outside marriage, married couples are more likely to have children than are cohabitants. In 2004, the majority of dependent children—66 per cent—were living in a family in which the parents were married. The rise in divorce does not necessarily indicate a wholesale rejection of the institution of marriage, since many divorcing couples remarry. Moreover, modern marriages will often last longer than the marriages of Victorian couples, largely due to changes in life expectancy. They may also be qualitatively different from those of our forebears—those who believe the Victorian age to be the golden age of family values should read Phyllis Rose's *Parallel Lives* (Random House, 1984).

Marriage also remains important for the purposes of family law, since the law controls who can and cannot marry and confers certain rights on married couples (see further, para.II–002). It is also important in defining the rights that are available to *unmarried* couples. Marriage is taken as the standard against which other heterosexual relationships must be measured: legislation tends to use the formulation "living together as if they were husband and wife." (Following *Ghaidan v Godin-Mendoza* [2004] UKHL 30 the same standard applied briefly to same-sex cohabitants—see *e.g. Nutting v Southern Housing Group* [2004] EWHC 2982 (Ch)—but in the wake of the Civil Partnership Act 2004 the appropriate question to ask is whether such a couple are living together as if they were civil partners—although the answer yielded is likely to be the same, see in particular para.7–005.)

The rise of cohabitation

Both the greater delay before marriage, and the overall fall in the numbers marrying, **1–008** can be attributed to the increase in the number of couples who choose to cohabit either as a prelude, or alternative, to marriage.

It is clear that the majority of marriages are now preceded by a period of cohabitation. In 2002, 87 per cent of couples who were marrying in a civil ceremony had identical addresses, although amongst those marrying in a religious ceremony the proportion was only 59 per cent. (This figure conceals some interesting variations—85 per cent of those marrying in a Unitarian ceremony gave identical addresses, as compared to only 7 per cent of Jehovah's Witnesses and 6.5 per cent of Sikhs.) Pre-marital cohabitation was slightly more popular amongst those who had already been married and divorced than amongst those embarking upon matrimony for the first time (and, it should also be noted, divorce is more prevalent among those who have lived together before marriage, although the precise correlation between these two facts is not clear-cut.

It is less clear whether cohabitation can be seen as a long-term alternative to marriage. The median duration of cohabiting relationships (other than those that lead to marriage) is significantly shorter than the median duration of marriages, and cohabiting couples are also less likely to have children. Such factors will obviously have an influence on the needs of such couples if their relationship breaks down.

The approach of the law to cohabiting couples is gradually changing. As Waite L.J. noted in *Fitzpatrick v Sterling Housing Association Ltd* [1998] Ch. 304, CA:

> "As [cohabitation] became more open, so attitudes towards it became less judg-mental. That included the attitude of the courts, where notwithstanding that the encouragement of marriage as an institution remains a well-established head of public policy, the respect due to the sincerity of commitment involved in many such relationships is reflected in judicial terminology—terms like 'partner' now being more generally used than the once preferred references to 'common-law spouse', 'mistress' or even ... 'living in sin.' "

Yet cohabiting couples do not by any means enjoy all the rights that are conferred upon married couples, nor, indeed, is there any consensus about the regulation of cohabiting relationships.

The increase in the number of births outside marriage

1–009   The relationship between the adults may be of lesser importance than whether or not they have children. In 2004, 42 per cent of births occurred outside marriage—a total of 269,724. Of these, 83 per cent were jointly registered, mostly by couples who gave the same address (and for the legal implications of joint registration, see para.11–016, below). Many of these couples will go on to marry at a later date. Others will split up, leaving one partner as a lone parent (and of course many marriages will end, leaving one parent with care of the children). In 2005, 24 per cent of children were living in a lone-parent household, usually with their mother. Again, however, it is important to recognise that the majority of children—65 per cent in 2004—live with both natural parents.

Step-families

1–010   The prevalence of divorce and remarriage means that there are a large number of step-families. *De facto* step-families may also be created where a lone-parent cohabits. Overall, around 10 per cent of families with dependent children include children from previous relationships. Since it is still more common for children to live with their mother after their parents divorce or separate, over 80 per cent of such families consist of the children, their mother and her new husband or partner. What should be the status of the new partner in such cases? And should the new partner have any obligation to support his or her step-children? The legal options are explored in Chs 11 and 15, and the financial obligations in Ch.7. It is unfortunate that there is no simple term to distinguish between formalised and cohabiting partners in this context, since the law makes a number of distinctions between the two. The term "step-parent" generally denotes a person who has entered into a formal relationship with the parent—whether marriage or a civil partnership—and will be used in this way in this book.

The rise of single-person households

Another dramatic trend is the increase in single-person households, particularly **1–011**
among younger people: in 2005, 29 per cent of households contained only one person.
Such persons are not necessarily bereft of "family": they will usually have relatives,
and perhaps ex-partners and children living in a different household. They may even
have a current partner who maintains a separate household: the concept of "living
apart together" is increasingly recognised and it has been estimated that around two
million men and women—excluding students and adult children living at home—have
partners in another household. In addition, friends may play an important role,
providing the same support as a family:

> "I know we're all psychotic, single and completely dysfunctional and it's all done
> over the phone . . . but it's a bit like a family, isn't it?" (Helen Fielding, *Bridget
> Jones's Diary* (Picador, 1997)

Multi-culturalism

England and Wales is an increasingly multi-cultural society: by 2001 the ethnic **1–012**
minority population accounted for 8 per cent of the UK population. This change
poses new challenges for the law. What should be the status, for example, of a marriage
that is valid according to the parties' own religious law but which does not comply
with the statutory requirements? How is the law to deal with informal home-sharing
practices in which the parties' conception of their rights does not fit within any
mechanism of English law? How far should cultural expectations shape the division of
assets on divorce, or the courts' assessment of the best interests of a child? Such issues
will be considered throughout the book.

The role of the extended family

Family law tends to focus on the relationships between couples, or between parents **1–013**
and their minor children. Relatively little attention is paid to wider kin, or relationships between adult children and their parents. One reason for this may be that it is
rare for relatives, other than the nuclear family, to share a home together. Elderly
parents are increasingly less likely to move in with their adult children: either they
remain at home, perhaps with informal care being provided by an external source as
they become frailer, or they move into residential care. It is even rarer for a household
to contain more than one family: only one per cent of households contain two or more
families (although for South Asian households the figure is 10 per cent). There is,
however, a tendency for adult children to remain at home for longer periods, refusing
to fly the nest: in 2005, 57 per cent of young men aged between 20 and 24 and 38 per
cent of women in the same age range were still living with their parents. Such
arrangements are generally transitory: among those aged between 30 and 34 only 8 per
cent of men and 3 per cent of women were still living at home.

However, the fact that relatives do not often share living accommodation does not
necessarily mean that they will not play an important role in family life. In particular,
grandparents may have an important role to play in providing child-care, or in looking
after children who have been taken into care by the local authority (see Ch.13). In

Supporting Families (1998) it was noted that 92 per cent of grandparents were in touch with their grandchildren, and 47 per cent helped out by providing care for them. The way in which the law perceives the role of grandparents will be relevant in determining disputes between parents and grandparents over who should care for the children (see paras 12–011 and 14–015, below).

Similarly, informal care is more likely to be provided by someone who does not live in the same household as the person being cared for. Relatives constitute a high proportion of informal carers, with the burden primarily falling upon adult daughters. As the population ages—the 2001 census found that 21 per cent of the population was over the age of 60, one per cent more than the proportion under the age of 16—the position of carers is likely to attract more attention.

When Parliament was debating the Civil Partnership Act 2004, the House of Lords passed an amendment that would have enabled relatives who had been sharing a home for at least 12 years, and who had attained the age of 30, to enter into a civil partnership. The ostensible purpose of this was to provide protection—such as exemption from inheritance tax—for relatives who had shared a home for a significant period of time, although commentators suspected that the true reason was the desire to create a distinction between marriage and civil partnerships, and reduce the latter to a desexualized institution equally applicable to family members. While there may be a need to provide greater legal protection for relatives who share homes and lives, civil partnerships do not seem an apt mechanism to achieve this.

Family roles

1–014   The "traditional" breadwinner-housewife model is no longer the norm: in 2004, 90 per cent of fathers and 67 per cent of mothers with dependent children were in paid employment. Fewer women are having children, and those who do tend to have smaller families: the average number of children per family was only 1.8 in 2004. The care of pre-school children may, however, require a temporary absence from the labour market: in 2004, only 59 per cent of married or cohabiting mothers with children under the age of five were in employment, compared to the 77 per cent whose children were aged between five and ten. Employment rates are lower for lone mothers (34 per cent and 57 per cent respectively), and indeed for lone fathers, 67 per cent of whom are in paid employment. This reflects the difficulties in one person combining the roles of breadwinner and carer (as opposed to both roles being shared between two persons).

It should however be noted that much of the increase in female employment has been in part-time work. Almost 50 per cent of women with one child work part-time, and this figure rises to over 60 per cent for those who have two or more children. Moreover, absences from the labour market for the purpose of child-rearing may have a significant effect on life-time earnings. This will affect the resources available to the household, and, equally importantly, to the individuals within the household, and has implications for the ability of women to acquire an interest in the family home (see Ch.5), as well as for the effect of relationship breakdown (see Ch.8). Another important point to note is the decline in the proportion of *men* who are in paid employment: while in 1971 92 per cent of men of working age were in employment, by 2004 this figure had fallen to 80 per cent. Accordingly, there is now a higher proportion of households where *neither* partner is in paid employment than in the past, as well as a higher proportion of households where *both* partners are employed.

The question as to who performs such unpaid but essential tasks such as housework, child-care, and caring for the elderly also has important ramifications for many areas of family law. The evidence suggests that the burden of unpaid work falls largely, although by no means solely, upon women. The importance of such work has been recognised in some areas of the law (see para.8–032, below), but not in others (see para.5–013, below). The question as to who takes responsibility for childcare will also be relevant if the courts are required to determine with which parent a child should live (see Chs 11 and 13).

The role of children within the family has undergone a profound shift. In the nineteenth century children would often work from an early age to supplement the family income. (Karl Marx claimed that children needed more protection against economic exploitation by their own parents than against exploitation by their employers). Modern children consume, rather than provide, the family income, and more attention is focused on the duty of parents to support their minor children than whether adult children should support their elderly parents.

In brief, therefore, it is clear that the form of the family, and roles within the family, have both undergone significant change. One important factor in bringing about *legal* change has been the advent of the Human Rights Act, which will now be considered.

C: FAMILY LAW AND HUMAN RIGHTS

The UK is a signatory to a number of international conventions designed to protect **1–015** human rights generally (*e.g.* the United Nations Declaration of Human Rights) or the rights of particularly vulnerable members of society (see *e.g.* the United Nations Convention on the Rights of the Child). For present purposes the most important of these conventions is the European Convention for the Protection of Human Rights and Fundamental Freedoms. This differs from the other conventions mentioned in two respects. First, any individual who believes that his or her rights have been infringed may petition the European Court of Human Rights in Strasbourg. A finding by the court that the UK has breached its obligations under the Convention obliges the government to amend the relevant law to bring it into line with the Convention, to compensate the applicant if ordered to do so, and to take such other steps as were required of it. Successful applications are thus important both for the individual concerned and in prompting legislation that the Government might otherwise not have introduced (see for example para.3–015).

Secondly, and even more importantly, the European Convention on Human Rights was incorporated into English law by the Human Rights Act 1998 and thus, unlike many other international conventions, is directly enforceable in the domestic courts. This possibility does not render the right of individual petition to the European Court unnecessary, as an individual may have no domestic remedy. But it is clear that the fact that human rights arguments can now be raised in the domestic courts has greatly increased the likelihood of a litigant seeking to invoke the Convention. Since the 1998 Act came into force on October 2, 2000 it has had a profound impact on family law, and for that reason a brief explanation of the approach of the Act and the provisions most often invoked in this context is appropriate.

Giving effect to Convention rights

1–016 The Human Rights Act 1998 sought to reconcile the objective of "bringing rights home" with the traditional understanding of the sovereignty of the Westminster Parliament. For this reason, the Act does not provide in a straightforward way that the Convention shall have effect as part of English law, but instead seeks to give effect to what it defines (at s.1) as the "Convention rights" in a number of different ways. First, it establishes a "rule of interpretation". Legislation is to be "read and given effect" in a way that is compatible with "Convention rights" if it is possible to do so (s.3), and, in determining questions relating to such rights, the courts must take into account the jurisprudence established by the European Court, even if the application of an English precedent would lead to a different result. As Lord Steyn noted in *R (Ullah) v Special Adjudicator* [2004] 2 A.C. 323:

> "The duty of national courts is to keep pace with the Strasbourg jurisprudence as it evolves over time: no more, but certainly no less." (para.20)

Secondly, s.6 provides that it is unlawful for a "public authority"—a term which includes the court itself—to act in a way that is incompatible with a Convention right, and s.7 gives "victims" of any such unlawful act the right either to rely on the Convention right in any legal proceedings, or to institute legal proceedings against the relevant authority. Thirdly, s.4 provides a procedure whereby a court may make a declaration that a statutory provision is incompatible with a Convention right. If it does so, a Minister may make an order effecting the necessary changes, if such action is considered to be necessary and there are "compelling reasons" for adopting the special procedure laid down by the Act rather than bringing a bill before Parliament in the usual way (s.10, and for an example see para.3–009).

Finally, it should be noted that the 1998 Act did not incorporate Art.13 of the Convention (which states that "[e]veryone whose rights and freedoms as set forth in this Convention are violated shall have an effective remedy before a national authority notwithstanding that the violation has been committed by persons acting in an official capacity."). The effect of this was explained in *Re S (Minors) (Care Order: Implementation of Care Plan); Re W (Minors) (Care Plan: Adequacy of Care Plan)* [2002] UKHL 10:

> "In Convention terms, failure to provide an effective remedy for infringement of a right set out in the Convention is an infringement of Art.13. But Art.13 is not a Convention right as defined in s.1(1) of the Human Rights Act. So legislation which fails to provide an effective remedy for infringement of Art.8 is not, for that reason, incompatible with a Convention right within the meaning of the Human Rights Act" (*per* Lord Nicholls, para.60).

Perhaps the key provision in this scheme is s.3, since this enables the court to interpret legislation in a way that is compatible with the Convention, even if this was not the original intention of Parliament (see *Ghaidan v Godin-Mendoza* [2004] UKHL 30, *per* Lord Nicholls at para.29). The scope of the Human Rights Act is thus dependent on the meaning that is given to "interpretation". It is clear that the courts may be required to adopt an "unnatural" interpretation of legislation in order to ensure its compatibility with the Convention. It is also accepted that "interpretation" extends to the inclusion of extra words, or the deletion of offending terms. But the courts cannot adopt an interpretation that is diametrically opposed to the intentions of Parliament. Thus in *Re S (Minors) (Care Order: Implementation of Care Plan); Re W (Minors) (Care Plan: Adequacy of Care Plan)* [2002] UKHL 10, Lord Nicholls stressed that the distinction between interpreting legislation, which was the role of the courts, and amending it, which was the role of Parliament, had to be maintained.

"For present purposes it is sufficient to say that a meaning which departs substantially from a fundamental feature of an Act of Parliament is likely to have crossed the boundary between interpretation and amendment. This is especially so where the departure has important practical repercussions which the court is not equipped to evaluate." (para.40)

Similarly, in *Ghaidan v Godin-Mendoza*, he acknowledged that

"[t]he meaning imported by the application of section 3 must be compatible with the underlying thrust of the legislation being construed." (para.33)

This suggests that the more important or radical the change might be, the less likely the courts are to take action. In addition, the consequences of adopting a particular interpretation must also be taken into account. If a particular interpretation raises major policy questions it is likely to be a matter for Parliament rather than the courts.

The scope of the Convention

The Convention was drawn up in the wake of World War II and sought to protect the **1–017** individual against the state. If this were its only function, its application to disputes between family members would be somewhat limited. But the Convention is a "living" document, and the Court has held that signatory States have positive obligations to take steps to promote the rights guaranteed in the Convention. Furthermore, while the Act does not *directly* affect disputes between private individuals—thus a father, for example, could not simply bring an action against the mother for breach of his Convention rights if he was denied contact with his child—it can have an *indirect* effect. Courts are within the statutory definition of "public authority" in s.6 and are thus obliged to act in a way that is compatible with Convention rights. The combination of these factors means that Convention rights must be taken into account even in intra-family disputes. As the Court explained in *Zawadka v Poland* [2005] 2 F.L.R. 897:

"The court recalls that the essential object of Art.8 is to protect the individual against arbitrary interference by public authorities. There may, however, be positive obligations inherent in an effective "respect" for family life. These obligations may involve the adoption of measures designed to secure respect for family life even in the sphere of relations between individuals, including both the provision of a regulatory framework of adjudicatory and enforcement machinery protecting individuals' rights and the implementation, where appropriate, of specific steps." (para.53)

Convention rights

1–018 With these points in mind, consideration should be given to the articles of the Convention that are of most relevance to family law.

(1) *Right to life*

Article 2 of the Convention protects the right to life, subject to certain very narrowly defined exceptions. The state is not only under a duty not to take a person's life, but is also under a positive duty to protect a person's right to life. A failure to protect a child or other family member known to be at risk within the family might therefore fall within its scope (see *e.g. R (Plymouth C.C.) v HM Coroner* [2005] EWHC 1014 (Admin)).

(2) *Prohibition of torture*

1–019 Similarly, Art.3, which provides that "no one shall be subjected to torture or to inhuman or degrading treatment or punishment", may not seem to be immediately relevant to family law, but has been invoked in the context of parental punishment (see para.11–003) and where a local authority failed to protect children from abuse (see *e.g. Z v UK* [2001] 2 F.L.R. 612, ECHR, also para.13–048, below). It has also been suggested that it has a role to play in the protection of victims of domestic violence (see *e.g.* S. Choudhry and J. Herring, "Righting Domestic Violence" (2006) I.J.L.P.F. 95). Article 3 may also require the state to take positive action to provide welfare support, on the basis that, as Lord Woolf C.J. explained in *Anufrijeva v Southwark LBC* [2003] EWCA Civ 1406:

> "There is a stage at which the dictates of humanity require the State to intervene to prevent any person within its territory suffering dire consequences as a result of deprivation of sustenance." (para.35)

—although, as he pointed out, the European Court has not as yet found any state to be in violation of Art.3 on this ground.

(3) *Procedural rights*

1–020 Article 6 of the Convention, which specifies the procedural rights that are to be observed in determining legal rights, has been invoked in a number of cases. It provides that:

> "in the determination of his civil rights and obligations . . . everyone is entitled to a fair and public hearing . . . by an independent and impartial tribunal established by law. Judgment shall be pronounced publicly but the press and public may be excluded from all or part of the trial in the interest of morals, public order or national security in a democratic society, where the interests of juveniles or the protection of the private life of the parties so require, or to the extent strictly necessary in the opinion of the court in special circumstances where publicity would prejudice the interests of justice."

The reference to "public" does not prevent cases being heard in private—as many family law cases are—where this is necessary to protect the interests of the parties involved (see *e.g. B v UK* [2001] 2 F.L.R. 261, ECHR). The importance of the proceedings being "fair" has on occasion required the provision of legal representation to the parties (see *e.g. P, C and S v UK* [2002] 3 F.C.R. 1, ECHR), or at least the assistance of a *McKenzie* friend (*In The Matter of the Children of Mr O'Connell, Mr Whelan and Mr Watson* [2005] EWCA Civ 759) and is relevant in determining the extent to which family members should be able to play a role in legal proceedings.

(4) *Rights to respect for private and family life*

Article 8 provides that:

1–021

(1) Everyone has the right to respect for his private and family life, his home and his correspondence.

(2) There shall be no interference by a public authority with the exercise of this right except such as is in accordance with the law and is necessary in a democratic society in the interests of national security, public safety or the economic well-being of the country, for the prevention of disorder or crime, for the protection of health or morals, or for the protection of the rights and freedoms of others.

The way in which the courts have interpreted "family life" for these purposes was considered above (para.1–002). It should be noted that the qualifications set out in Art.8(2) are more extensive than those found in other articles. Of particular significance for present purposes is the fact that the Art.8 rights of one person may have to yield to the rights of another person. How the courts should balance the Art.8 rights of different family members is a hotly-contested issue, particularly in the context of the law relating to children. Is the welfare principle—which dictates that the welfare of the child is to be the court's paramount consideration in deciding certain questions—compatible with the balancing of rights required by Art.8? On this point opinion is divided, with the courts generally asserting that it is compatible, and academic commentators arguing that it is not. The debate is considered in more detail in Ch.14: at this stage it should simply be emphasised that the issue is not simply a conflict between adult rights and children's welfare, since children themselves have rights under Art.8.

The European Court has also held that Art.8 connotes certain procedural safeguards in addition to the substantive right to family life. The question to be posed, according to *W v UK* (1988) 10 E.H.R.R. 29, is:

"whether, having regard to the particular circumstances of the case and notably the serious nature of the decisions to be taken, the parents have been involved in the decision-making process, seen as a whole, to a degree sufficient to provide them with the requisite protection of their interests." (at para.64)

This idea of "sufficient involvement" and what it entails has been developed in a number of subsequent cases (see *e.g. Elsholz v Germany* [2000] 2 F.L.R. 486, and *Sahin v Germany; Sommerfeld v Germany* [2003] 2 F.L.R. 671), and the domestic courts have also begun to emphasise the importance of this dimension to Art.8 (see *e.g. Re L (Assessment: Fair Trial)* [2002] EWHC 1379 (Fam) and *Re G (Care: Challenge to Local Authority's Decision)* [2003] EWHC 551 (Fam)).

(5) *The right to marry and found a family*

1–022 Article 12 of the Convention provides that "men and women of marriageable age have the right to marry and to found a family, according to national laws governing the exercise of this right." In recent years this has been invoked (with varying degrees of success) by transsexuals seeking recognition of their reassigned sex for the purposes of marriage (see para.3–015), by a couple unable to marry because of the family relationship between them (see para.3–009) and by couples or individuals seeking access to assisted reproduction (see *e.g. R v SSHD Ex p. Mellor* [2001] EWCA Civ 472; *Evans v UK* [2006] All E.R. (D) 87).

(6) *Non-discrimination*

1–023 Article 14 of the Convention provides that "[t]he enjoyment of the rights and freedoms set forth in this Convention shall be secured without discrimination on any ground such as sex, race, colour, language, religion, political or other opinion, national or social origin, association with a national minority, property, birth or other status". The final words mean that other forms of discrimination may be outlawed by the court to reflect changing social norms. For example, it has been accepted that discrimination on the basis of sexual orientation is prohibited by Art.14 (see *e.g. Salgueiro da Silva Mouta v Portugal* [2001] 1 F.C.R. 653, ECHR), and, further, that "very weighty reasons" have to be advanced before such discrimination can be regarded as compatible with the Convention (*Karner v Austria* [2004] 2 F.C.R. 563, ECHR). While the protection of the "traditional family" in principle constitutes such a reason, it is difficult to invoke this argument in practice, on account of the requirement of proportionality. As the court explained in *Karner v Austria*:

> "The aim of protecting the family in the traditional sense is rather abstract and a broad variety of concrete measures may be used to implement it. In cases in which the margin of appreciation afforded to member states is narrow, as is the position where there is a difference in treatment based on sex or sexual orientation, the principle of proportionality does not merely require that the measure chosen is in principle suited for realising the aim sought. It must also be shown that it was necessary to exclude persons living in a homosexual relationship from the scope of [the legislation] in order to achieve that aim." (para.41)

The court unsurprisingly held that this had not been shown (and see also *Ghaidan v Godin-Mendoza*). After all, as Baroness Hale noted in *Secretary of State for Work and Pensions v M* [2006] UKHL 11:

> "No one has yet explained how failing to recognize the relationships of people whose sexual orientation means that they are unable or strongly unwilling to marry is necessary for the purpose of protecting or encouraging the marriage of people who are quite capable of marrying if they wish to do so." (para.113)

It should also be noted that Art.14 does not prohibit discrimination *per se*, but only discrimination in the enjoyment of rights guaranteed by the Convention. In other words, it is necessary to show some link between the discrimination and one of the rights set out in the Convention. The appropriate approach to this question was set out by Lord Nicholls in *R (Carson) v Secretary of State for Work and Pensions* [2005] 2 W.L.R. 1369, but it should be noted that the House of Lords has dismissed earlier suggestions that even a tenuous link with one of the Convention rights would suffice (see *Secretary of State for Work and Pensions v M* [2006] UKHL 11).

(7) Freedom of expression

The applicability to family law of the guarantee of freedom of expression set out in **1–024** Art.10 may not be immediately obvious, but what if the media seek to publish information about a child, or the child's family, that would damage the well-being of the child? Art.10 is not an absolute right, and the exceptions set out in Art.10(2) include "the protection of the reputation or rights of others." It is also clear that the Art.10 rights of the media may conflict with the Art.8 rights of the individual. How is such a clash to be resolved? In *Re S (Identification: Restrictions on Publication)* [2004] UKHL 47, Lord Steyn set out four propositions relating to the interplay between Art.8 and Art.10, distilled from the earlier decision of the House of Lords in *Campbell v MGN Ltd* [2004] UKHL 22:

> "First, neither Article has *as such* precedence over the other. Secondly, where the values under the two Articles are in conflict, an intense focus on the comparative importance of the specific rights being claimed in the individual case is necessary. Thirdly, the justifications for interfering with or restricting each right must be taken into account. Finally, the proportionality test must be applied to each." (para.17)

The application of this process of parallel analysis is considered further below (para. 12–044). It has also been argued that this process should be applied if other Convention rights are in conflict—for example, in balancing the Art.8 rights of father, mother and child in a dispute over contact—although to date the courts have shrunk from such an approach (see S. Choudhry and H. Fenwick, "Taking the Rights of Parents and Children Seriously: Confronting the Welfare Principle under the Human Rights Act" (2005) 25 O.J.L.S. 453, and para.14–017).

The impact of the Convention

This brief outline of the Convention will have given the reader some idea of the **1–025** different contexts in which the rights it guarantees may be relevant, and should be borne in mind in reading the succeeding chapters. Its impact must be judged on the extent to which it has changed the substantive law.

D: THE STRUCTURE AND APPROACH OF THIS BOOK

In an introductory textbook of this kind it is not possible to do any more than present **1–026** the key topics and issues within family law, and an element of selection is inevitably required. Since it is not aimed at practitioners, details of procedure and practice are not included. Moreover, despite the increasingly international nature of family law, there is not sufficient space to do justice to the fascinating questions that arise if a case involves an international element. (For example, in what circumstances will a marriage celebrated abroad—perhaps polygamously, perhaps between parties of the same-sex—be recognised in this country? Will an order granted by the courts of one country be enforced in another? When do the courts of this country have jurisdiction to hear a case involving nationals of another country?) The reader who is interested in pursuing such questions should refer to the growing literature on the nature of international family law (see *e.g.* J. Murphy, *International dimensions in family law* (Manchester University Press, 2005): the subject-matter of this book is the law of England and Wales, and cases with an international dimension will not be considered. The two exceptions to this are the important topics of child abduction and international adoption, which are considered in Chs 12 and 15 respectively.

The book is divided into three parts. Part I deals with formal relationships, focusing on the way that the law regulates entry into and exit from marriage and civil partnership. Part II is largely about money and property: how individuals may acquire interests in the family home (Ch.5), the sources of maintenance for intact and broken families (Ch.7), and how property is divided when a relationship comes to an end either during the lifetime of the parties (Ch.8), or when one party dies (Ch.9). Chapter 6 also deals with such themes, but its main focus is domestic violence. In Part III the focus shifts to the position of children (although the presence of children will of course be relevant to many of the themes discussed in earlier chapters). It examines the rules by which parentage is determined (Ch.10), the extent of parental responsibility and children's rights (Ch.11), the way in which the courts determine intra-family disputes and disputes between families and the state (Chs 12 and 13), the welfare principle that applies to both sets of disputes (Ch.14), and, finally, the law relating to adoption (Ch.15). Each part is preceded by a short introduction that highlights the key issues.

PART ONE

FORMAL RELATIONSHIPS

INTRODUCTION

The designation of a relationship as "formal" as opposed to "informal" is no reflec- **I–001** tion on the quality of the relationship, but merely distinguishes relationships that have been formalised by church or state from those that have not. Since December 5, 2005 two types of formal relationship—marriage and civil partnership—have co-existed side by side. As only opposite-sex couples may marry, and only same-sex couples may enter into a civil partnership, it cannot be said that a couple has a choice between the two, unlike in the Netherlands, where both registered partnerships and marriage are available to same-sex and opposite sex couples alike. But there is, in any case, no real difference between a marriage and a civil partnership in terms of the rights to which each gives rise: apart from a few minor differences, the regulation of, and package of rights consequent upon, a civil partnership is the same as for marriage. By contrast, while the law has begun to confer rights on cohabitants, they do not enjoy the same rights as either spouses or civil partners. The consequences of these different relation- ships are considered later in the book: Part I focuses instead on how individuals may enter into, and exit from, marriages and civil partnerships.

In order to enter into a valid marriage or civil partnership, the parties must have the capacity to do so and comply with the necessary formalities. This may sound simple enough, but there are a number of difficult social and moral issues that the law has had to resolve: how far should the law regulate when, how, and whom one can marry? It is clear that Art.12 of the European Convention (see para.1–022) does not prevent a state from enacting laws that place restrictions on the form that a valid marriage must take, or on the ability of certain couples to marry, for example because they are too young or because they are closely related to one another. The restrictions should not, however, impair the very essence of the right to marry: and in recent years UK law has been found to be in breach of Art.12 both by the European Court (see *e.g. B and L v UK* [2006] 1 F.L.R. 35 and *Goodwin v UK* [2002] 2 F.C.R. 576, discussed at paras 3–009 and 3–015 below), and by the domestic courts (*R (ota Baiai) v Secretary of State for the Home Department* [2006] EWHC 823 (Admin), considered at para.2–007 below).

It is also clear that those couples who meet the criteria specified in the legislation should be allowed to marry without any further restrictions being imposed:

> In *R. ota CPS v Registrar-General of Births, Deaths and Marriages* [2002] EWCA Civ 1661, the Crown Prosecution Service wished to prevent a couple from marrying. The man was accused of murder, and the major evidence against him was contained in a statement by his cohabitant. She subsequently wished to retract her statement and the couple declared their intention to marry. If she became his spouse, she could not be compelled to give evidence against him. The

Registrar-General refused to prevent the marriage from going ahead, and the Court of Appeal endorsed his approach.

With these points in mind, the law governing the formal creation and termination of marriages and civil partnerships can now be considered.

Chapter 2

FORMING A MARRIAGE OR CIVIL PARTNERSHIP

A: INTRODUCTION

According to the definition of marriage proffered in *Hyde v Hyde* (1866) L.R. 1. & D. **2–001**
130 (and still recited at the start of civil ceremonies), marriage is "the voluntary union
for life of one man and one woman to the exclusion of all others." At a time when it
is predicted that one in three marriages will end in divorce, this has the quality of an
aspiration rather than an accurate description. Furthermore, as a *definition* of marriage, it is deficient in that it fails to identify the central legal difference between
married and cohabiting couples, namely that the former have gone through a valid
ceremony of marriage and the latter have not. By contrast, s.1 of the Civil Partnership
Act 2004 provides, with more precision than passion, that "a civil partnership is a
relationship between two people of the same sex . . . which is formed when they
register as civil partners of each other."

Increasingly, the procedure chosen for entering into a formal legal relationship is
secular rather than religious: in 2004, 68 per cent of marriages were celebrated
according to civil rather than religious rites. For civil partners no such choice exists, as
the 2004 Act specifies that a civil partnership may not be registered in religious
premises (s.6). The popularity of civil marriage is very much a recent phenomenon:
only in 1996 did the number of civil marriages exceed the number celebrated according
to religious rites. Historically, though, marriage law is closely linked with religious
practice: for centuries marriage was governed by the church, which stipulated that
certain formalities should be observed, although the failure to observe the required
formalities did not necessarily render the marriage void. Mutually expressed consent
to marriage was sufficient to bind the parties, although the presence of a minister of
the Church of England was necessary for the ceremony to confer full *legal* rights. By
the mid-eighteenth century the problem of clandestine marriages—marriages which
were celebrated before a priest of the Church of England but which did not conform
to the church's requirements—was thought to have become so acute that Parliament
intervened, and the Clandestine Marriages Act 1753 gave statutory force to the
church's requirements. Henceforth, a marriage that did not comply with the necessary
formalities was void. Only Jews and Quakers—along with members of the Royal
Family—were exempted from the requirement that marriages be conducted according

to the rites of the Church of England. Catholics and Dissenters had to wait until 1836, when the Marriage Act introduced civil ceremonies and the possibility of marriage according to the rites of other religions. Even today these distinctions persist, and the legal regulation of a marriage celebrated according to religious rites differs according to whether the rites in question are Anglican, Jewish or Quaker, or of other denominations or religions. The importance of a sound understanding of the history of marriage laws was also demonstrated in 2005 when the Prince of Wales announced his intention to marry Mrs Parker-Bowles in a civil ceremony (see R. Probert, "The wedding of the Prince of Wales: Royal Privileges and Human Rights" (2005) *Child and Family Law Quarterly* 363 on the special rules that apply to member of the Royal Family in this context).

For the sake of clarity, this chapter will deal with the formalisation of marriages and civil partnerships separately, since the procedure for registering a civil partnership is not only exclusively secular but also different in a number of respects from civil marriage. There are also certain rules developed by the courts in relation to marriage that have no counterpart in the Civil Partnership Act. Part B sets out the formalities for a valid marriage, while Part C explains the consequences of failing to comply with those formalities (which vary according to the extent to which the ceremony departs from the form prescribed by statute). The state's preference for marriage over unregulated cohabitation can be seen in the presumptions in favour of marriage, which place the onus of disproving the marriage on the person seeking to challenge it. These presumptions have been invoked in a number of cases in order to uphold marriages where the formalities had not been observed, and are considered in Part D. Recent proposals for reform are highlighted in Part E, and the procedure for formalising a civil partnership is dealt with in Part F.

B. MARRIAGE FORMALITIES

2–002   The modern law, largely contained in the Marriage Act 1949, is complex—indeed, the Law Commission has commented that it is "not understood by members of the public or even by all those who have to administer it" (see Law Com. No.53, Annex. para.6). All that can be done in an introductory textbook such as this is to highlight some of the main characteristics of the law. There are three elements: the preliminaries, the ceremony itself, and the registration of the marriage.

Preliminaries to marriage

2–003   Two aspects need to be considered under this heading: first, the requirement that parental consent be obtained if either party is of marriageable age but under 18; secondly, the requirement for advance publicity to be given to the parties' intention to marry. There is also the broader question as to why such preliminaries are necessary.

(1) Parental consent (sometimes) required

2–004   Parental consent is normally required for the marriage of those who have passed their sixteenth birthday but have not attained the age of 18 (s.3 of the Marriage Act 1949), although its absence does not in fact render the marriage void. A parent with parental responsibility (see Ch.11) or the child's guardian may give consent. The legislation also stipulates whose consent is required if the child is in local authority care, or placed for adoption, or the subject of a residence order or special guardianship order: the rules are rather detailed, but basically the consent of those persons (or institutions) who have parental responsibility for the child will be required.

Changes in the law in this area reflect the shifting balance of power between parent and child. In the eighteenth century, a marriage under the age of 21 without parental consent would, in certain circumstances, be void. Today parental consent is only required for those under 18, and, as mentioned, its absence does not render the marriage void, although the parties may be liable to prosecution for making a false statement. The court can also override a refusal to give the necessary consent (s.3(1)(b)). In addition, the rules are of much less importance than was once the case because of the trend towards marriage later in life: the latest figures indicate that the average age at first marriage is now over 31 for men and 29 for women.

(2) *Publicising the intention to marry*

The law requires the parties' intention to marry to be publicised before a marriage can be solemnised. The objective is to give an opportunity for people to point to what the Book of Common Prayer describes as a "just cause or impediment" to the intended marriage, for example that either the bride or groom is already married, or under age. More recently, the system has been used to ascertain the *bona fides* of those entering into marriage, in an attempt to ensure that they are not flouting the immigration rules. **2–005**

At present, there are two procedures for publishing the intention to marry: Anglican and civil. An Anglican ceremony can be preceded by certain civil preliminaries, but Anglican preliminaries may not be used before a civil ceremony.

(a) Anglican preliminaries

Over 90 per cent of Church of England ceremonies are preceded by banns (the announcing of the parties' intention to marry in the church on three consecutive Sundays), due to a mixture of tradition (banns were first introduced in the twelfth century), and cost (they are the cheapest preliminary). Alternatively, the parties may obtain a common licence from the Church authorities or a special licence issued on behalf of the Archbishop of Canterbury. A special licence may authorise a marriage at any time and in any place. **2–006**

(b) Civil preliminaries

The Immigration and Asylum Act 1999 has standardised the procedure to be followed for all other marriages. If there is to be a civil ceremony, or a non-Anglican religious ceremony, the parties must obtain a superintendent registrar's certificate. Both must give notice in person (although not necessarily together) of their intention to marry to the superintendent registrar of the district where they have had their usual place of residence for at least seven days. If the parties live in different districts, each must give notice in the relevant district. Each must give details of his or her name, marital status, occupation, place of residence and nationality. Evidence of any of these details may be required. All this information is entered in the marriage notice book, which is open for inspection by the public. After giving notice, there is a waiting period of 15 days before the marriage can be solemnised, although the Registrar General has power to shorten this period if the applicant can show "compelling reason" for doing so. This waiting period applies to each notice of marriage, so if one of the parties gives notice later than **2–007** the other, they must wait for 15 days after the second notice before the marriage can be solemnised.

It may seem odd that provisions about marriage formalities are contained in a piece of legislation dealing with immigration and asylum, but the avowed aim of the reforms was to tackle the problem of "sham" marriages by giving the superintendent registrar the chance to meet both parties. Indeed, control over the marriages of those subject to immigration control has been tightened still further. Suspected cases of sham marriages are to be reported to immigration authorities: Reporting of Suspicious Marriages and Registration of Births, Deaths and Marriages (Miscellaneous Amendments) Regulations 2000, SI 2000/3164. The Asylum and Immigration (Treatment of Claimants, etc) Act 2004 requires those subject to immigration control to give notice at specified registration centres, and the notice will not be accepted unless the person subject to immigration control either has entry clearance for the purpose of marriage, or the written consent of the Secretary of State. The scheme has, however, been declared to be incompatible with both Art.12 and Art.14 of the European Convention:

> In *R (Baiai and others) v Secretary of State for the Home Department* [2006] EWHC 823 (Admin), Silber J. held that although it was possible to impose restrictions on the right to marry in the interests of an effective immigration policy, the restrictions under the 2004 Act were not a proportionate means of achieving this aim, due to the lack of a rational connection between the restrictions and the aim. This decision was influenced by the fact that the restrictions did not apply to marriages celebrated according to the rites of the Church of England, and in particular by the failure of the Secretary of State to provide any justification for applying the scheme to non-Anglican religious marriages.

There are special preliminaries to facilitate the marriage of the terminally ill, the housebound, prisoners, and people in psychiatric hospitals.

The marriage ceremony

2–008 The legislation permits four types of ceremony: civil marriage; marriage according to the rites of the Church of England; Jewish and Quaker marriages; and marriages according to the rites of a recognised religion in a registered and licensed place of worship.

(1) Civil ceremonies

2–009 The legal requirements are simple in the extreme. Under rules laid down in the Marriage Act 1949, as amended by the Marriage Ceremony (Prescribed Words) Act 1996, the parties must declare that they are free lawfully to marry (or that they know of no legal reason, or lawful impediment, to the marriage). They then either "call upon these persons here present to witness that I, A.B., do take thee, C.D., to be my lawful wedded wife (or husband)" or say "I, A.B., take you (or thee), C.D., to be my wedded wife (or husband)". These bare formalities are usually supplemented by readings or music. In the past, there was a requirement that the proceedings be totally secular. This was sometimes interpreted restrictively, with Shakespearean sonnets and Robbie Williams' *Angels* being banned on the basis that they contained religious references. While the use of any religious *service* at a civil ceremony is prohibited by statute, the guidance issued to registrars now allows readings or songs that include "incidental" religious references, although readings from sacred texts such as the Bible or Koran remain prohibited, as does the singing of hymns. Such prohibitions are intended to maintain the distinction between religious and secular ceremonies: religious groups in particular are concerned to ensure that the "special" nature of a religious service is retained.

Local authorities must provide register offices for the celebration of civil marriages. A register office ceremony takes place in the office, "with open doors", and two or more witnesses must be present. It is a fundamental principle of English law that a marriage ceremony be a public event, although celebrities and public figures have ensured privacy by careful timing or other means. As a result of changes made by the Marriage Act 1994, the parties may choose a register office outside their own registration district. It was hoped that the change in the law would encourage local authorities to provide more attractive amenities and would introduce an element of competition between different authorities; and it seems that many local authorities have taken steps (with some success) to make register office ceremonies more attractive.

The Marriage Act 1994 also increased the choice of venues by allowing civil marriages to be solemnised on "approved premises". The local authority has the task of establishing that (amongst other matters) the premises provide "a seemly and dignified venue" with no recent or continuing connection with any religion; that the marriage room is identifiable and separated from any other activity on the premises at the time of the ceremony; that the premises are to be regularly available to the public for weddings, and that the public will be allowed free access to the premises. There are also restrictions on the sale and consumption of food and alcoholic beverages in the hour preceding the ceremony. In spite of these restrictions, it appears that the "approved premises" wedding has met a substantial demand. A wide range of venues has been approved, including castles, football grounds, zoos, and the department store Selfridges. Most, however, are hotels, able to offer a package including the wedding, reception, and honeymoon suite. There has been a steady increase in the numbers of such weddings: in 2004, 31 per cent of marriages were celebrated in approved premises.

Again, special provision is made for civil marriages of the terminally ill, some psychiatric patients and those in prisons, hospitals or other such places (see the Marriage (Registrar-General's Licence) Act 1970 and the Marriage Act 1983).

(2) *The Church of England*

The marriage must be celebrated by "a clerk in Holy Orders in the Church of **2–010** England". The celebrant will use one of the forms of service authorised by the Church. Just under two-thirds of all marriages with a religious ceremony take place in Anglican churches. The clergy are obliged by law to celebrate the marriages of those who satisfy the statutory residence requirements whatever the intending parties' religion (or lack of it). There are, however, certain statutory exceptions to this. For example, while there is no absolute rule against the remarriage of a divorcé(e) in church, individual parish priests may still refuse to conduct a ceremony involving a divorcé(e). Similarly, a parish priest may refuse to marry a person who has undergone gender reassignment (see s.5B of the Marriage Act 1949 and para.3–015 below).

(3) *Jewish and Quaker weddings*

The celebration of Jewish and Quaker marriages has, ever since 1753, been entirely a **2–011** matter for the religions concerned. There is no legal regulation of the content or location of the ceremony, nor of who may celebrate such a marriage. The state's role is limited to requiring that the parties comply with the civil preliminaries outlined above, and that any such marriage be registered.

(4) Marriages in a registered place of religious worship

2–012 By contrast, the regulation of marriages according to other religious rites is more extensive: both the place and the celebrant are regulated, and, as with civil weddings, certain prescribed words must be included in the service.

It is possible for any building which is a place of meeting for "religious worship" to be registered for the purposes of marriage. There are two hurdles here. First, the interpretation of the expression "religious worship" for this purpose has occasioned difficulty. Mosques and Sikh or Hindu temples undoubtedly fall within the definition; but the courts have held, for example, that the expression does not extend to the practices of Scientologists: *Ex p. Segerdal* [1970] 2 Q.B. 697. Furthermore, not all places of worship are registered for marriages: for example, out of 621 mosques that are certified as places of worship, only 127 are registered as places where marriages can be celebrated. In *Chief Adjudication Officer v Bath* [2000] 1 F.L.R. 8, CA, problems arose where the parties, recent immigrants, married in an unlicensed Sikh temple (see para.2–018 below). If a couple wish to marry in an unregistered place of worship, then they must go through an additional civil ceremony of marriage in order to have a legally binding marriage. The form of the ceremony to be used (usually conducted by a minister of the religion concerned) is a matter for the parties and the body controlling the building, subject to one vital qualification. This is that at some stage in the proceedings the parties must make the statements required by the Marriage Act 1949, as amended by the Marriage Ceremony (Prescribed Words) Act 1996 (set out above) in either English or Welsh. Rather surprisingly, there is no requirement that the parties understand the language used.

Registration of marriages

2–013 All marriages celebrated in this country must be registered in accordance with the prescribed statutory procedures (see s.53 of the 1949 Act). Registration provides proof that the ceremony took place, and also facilitates the collection of demographic information. A failure to register a marriage, however, has never been a basis for holding the marriage void. This leads on to the next topic: what are the consequences of failing to comply with the required formalities?

C: FAILURE TO COMPLY WITH THE REQUIRED FORMALITIES

2–014 Again, the current law is complex. In brief, failure to comply with the required formalities may have one of three consequences. First, the omission may be a relatively minor one, and the validity of the marriage will not be affected. Secondly, the marriage may be void if the parties have "knowingly and wilfully" failed to comply with certain formalities. Thirdly, there may be no marriage at all—what is termed a non-marriage—if the ceremony bears no resemblance to that required by the law.

(1) Valid despite non-compliance

2–015 The Act expressly states that certain irregularities, such as marrying without parental consent, do not affect the validity of the marriage. It is silent as to the consequences of some minor irregularities, for example, the requirement that the marriage be celebrated "with open doors", and that certain prescribed words be used. It seems probable that such irregularities would not affect the validity of the marriage: they are directory rather than mandatory.

(2) *Void for failure to comply*

The Marriage Act 1949 provides that a marriage is void if the parties "knowingly and **2–016** wilfully" disregard any of a number of specified requirements (for example, the requirement to give notice to the Registrar). For example:

> In *Gereis v Yagoub* [1997] 1 F.L.R. 854, FD, a marriage took place in a Greek Orthodox church that had not been licensed for the celebration of marriage. The parties were aware of this fact. However, they did not go through the additional civil ceremony that they were advised was necessary. In the circumstances, the judge held that they had knowingly and wilfully failed to comply with the law and the marriage was accordingly void.

(3) *Non-marriage*

But what is the position if the parties fail to comply with the necessary formalities but **2–017** genuinely believe that their marriage is valid? It has recently been stated in *A-M v A-M* [2001] 2 F.L.R. 6, FD, that if a couple marry outside the forms specified by the Marriage Act 1949, the marriage is to be classified as non-existent rather than void, a classification that has severe consequences for the rights of the parties (see para.3–001):

> In this case, the parties, who were both domiciled abroad, went through a Muslim ceremony of marriage in their London flat. They intended it to create a valid marriage and the ceremony was conducted by an Islamic mufti. The marriage was polygamous as the husband was already married, but, under Islamic law, he was entitled to marry more than one wife. The husband was subsequently advised that the ceremony would not create a valid marriage, and various unsuccessful attempts were made to remedy this. Some years later, the husband decided to divorce his wife. The question for the court was whether there was a marriage to dissolve. It was held that the ceremony in the flat could not create a valid marriage, as it was outside the forms stipulated by the Marriage Act. To complicate matters, the court in fact decided that the parties *were* married, but on different grounds (see below, para.2–018).

This interpretation of the Marriage Act was followed in *Gandhi v Patel* [2001] 1 F.L.R. 603, FD (which involved a polygamous Hindu marriage in a restaurant). Whether or not a marriage is outside the forms specified by the Marriage Act is a question of degree. In *Gereis v Yagoub* [1997] 1 F.L.R. 854, FD, the judge considered whether the marriage should be classified as a non-marriage but decided that it was sufficiently close to the forms prescribed by the Marriage Act as it "bore the hallmarks of an ordinary Christian wedding and . . . both parties treated it as such." (at 858). While it is sensible for non-compliance to be a matter of degree, it would be indefensible for a Sikh or Muslim marriage to be struck down in circumstances in which a Christian marriage would be upheld.

D: THE PRESUMPTIONS IN FAVOUR OF MARRIAGE

2–018 The decision in *A-M v A-M* that the ceremony in the flat did not create a valid marriage was not the end of the story. The judge held that, as the parties had lived together for nearly twenty years, acknowledging each other and recognised by others as husband and wife, it should be presumed that they had gone through a valid ceremony of marriage, based on the legal presumption that couples who live together and are reputed to be married have in fact gone through a valid ceremony of marriage.

As the marriage in *A-M v A-M* would have been polygamous, it had to be presumed that the ceremony had taken place abroad, in a country that allowed polygamy, while both were domiciled in countries that allowed polygamy, since one's capacity to marry (as opposed to the form of the ceremony) is governed by one's domicile. The lack of evidence that the wife had travelled to such a country with the husband during the relevant period was not seen as a problem. Under Islamic law a marriage could be celebrated in the wife's absence "providing that she had at some stage signed a power of attorney, whether knowing exactly what it was, or what or was for, or not" (at 16).

The court was following the decision of the Court of Appeal in *Chief Adjudication Officer v Bath* [2000] 1 F.L.R. 8, in which the presumption was invoked to uphold a marriage that had taken place between recent immigrants in the early 1950s:

> The couple had lived together until the husband's death 37 years later and no question was cast upon the validity of their marriage until Mrs Bath was refused a widow's pension. The reasoning of the court is very unclear. As the parties never doubted the validity of their marriage, they had had no incentive to take steps to go through a second ceremony. The court did not presume that they had done so, but it is also unclear whether they were willing to presume that the original ceremony was valid. Robert Walker L.J. noted that "if in this case the husband and wife had been compelled by adverse circumstances to separate soon after the ceremony, so that no presumption arose from cohabitation, I feel real doubt whether they could have been regarded as lawfully married under English law." (at 22). It seems that the court was motivated by (understandable) sympathy for Mrs Bath, but the idea that a marriage can slowly mature into validity by the mere passage of time is not one that has hitherto been part of English law.

Quite apart from the tortuous reasoning involved in these cases, it is increasingly questionable whether a presumption that presupposes a sharp social differentiation between unmarried and married couples should have a role to play in the twenty-first century (for a more realistic approach see *Martin v Myers* [2004] EWHC 1947). It is interesting to note that in other contexts the courts have been keen to downplay the role of presumptions that are based on the assumptions of earlier generations (see, *e.g. Re H and A (Children)* [2002] EWCA Civ 383, below at para.10–004). The law of marriage is, to a degree, still carrying the legacy of the eighteenth-century's social mores.

There is a second presumption in favour of marriage, namely that if a man and woman go through a ceremony of marriage, and afterwards live together and are reputed to be married, then it is presumed that the necessary formalities have been observed. This presumption still has an important role to play, placing the burden of proof on the person who seeks to challenge the validity of the marriage.

E: Reform

The Government has proposed to change the way in which marriages are publicised, **2–019** celebrated and registered (*Civil Registration: Vital Change—Birth, Marriage and Death Registration in the Twenty-First Century* (2002) Cm 5355). Under these proposals, Church of England ceremonies would be preceded by the same formalities as all other ceremonies. Couples would be required to give notice of their intention to marry to their "local registration service provider" and obtain a schedule confirming that their marriage could proceed. They would then be offered a free choice as to where and when the marriage could take place—subject to the agreement of the celebrant. This would mean that the validity of a marriage would no longer be affected by whether or not the place where it was celebrated was registered or not. The distinction between religious and civil ceremonies would be retained: the local registration service provider would appoint civil celebrants, while religious celebrants would have to be approved by the Registrar General. Registration would also be updated, with a new central database becoming the legal record of marriage. It was initially intended that such reform could and would be achieved under the Regulatory Reform Act 2001, but the Government has since accepted that changes of this nature require primary legislation (see *Registration Modernization: A Position and consultation paper on the delivery of the local registration service in England and Wales*, published in November 2005).

F: Civil Partnerships

The proposed procedure for civil marriage was also intended to apply to civil partner- **2–020** ships, but the relevant regulations have amended the 2004 Act (see the Civil Partnership (Amendments to Registration Provisions) Order 2005 SI 2005/2000), with the result that the applicable procedure is broadly similar to the existing rules for civil marriage. Registration of a civil partnership cannot take place in religious premises, and no religious service is permitted. One difference in the registration of a civil partnership, as compared to the celebration of a civil marriage, is that no prescribed words are required for the former. Instead, s.2(1) of the 2004 Act merely states that "two people are to be regarded as having registered as civil partners of each other once each of them has signed the civil partnership document": consent, ceremony and proof all rolled into one. The partnership is then registered.

As in the case of civil marriage, there are separate procedures for the house-bound, the detained, and the terminally ill to register a civil partnership.

G: Conclusion

For the majority of couples who marry or enter into a civil partnership, much of the **2–021** law discussed in the remainder of this book will not be relevant. After all, the majority of marriages are ended by death rather than by divorce, and there is no reason to believe that the position will be any different for civil partners. Others, however, will wish to "uncouple", and the next two chapters examine the various ways of doing so.

Chapter 3

NULLITY

A: INTRODUCTION

What are the essential attributes of a marriage or civil partnership in the eyes of **3–001** English law? One would search in vain for any explicit list in the statute books. Instead, what the law regards as essential to these formal relationships must be inferred from the grounds on which each can be annulled. It should be noted at the outset that nullity—of either a marriage or civil partnership—is conceptually distinct from the termination of such relationships by the respective mechanisms of divorce or dissolution (on which see Ch.4). In the case of divorce or dissolution, a marriage or civil partnership is brought to an end because of the behaviour of one or both of the parties; by contrast, annulment effectively wipes out the marriage or civil partnership because of some fundamental obstacle to its very existence. The obstacle may relate to the individual—for example if he or she is under the age of 16, or has already entered into a formal relationship—or it may relate to the couple—for example if they are closely related to each other.

Before divorce was widely available, individuals might have recourse to the law of nullity as a functional substitute: the most famous example is of course Henry VIII, whose marriages to Catharine of Aragon, Anne Boleyn and Anne of Cleves were all ended by what would today be called decrees of nullity rather than "divorces" in the modern sense. Now that divorce is widely available, this function of the law of nullity is only of relevance to those couples who have religious scruples about divorce— annulments, being rooted in ecclesiastical law, are more acceptable to some elements of the Christian church than is divorce (and see also *P v R (Forced Marriage: Annulment: Procedure)* [2003] 1 F.L.R. 661 on their significance for certain ethnic minority communities).

When contrasting the 251 decrees of nullity granted in 2005 with the 142,393 divorces the same year it is easy to imagine that the law of nullity has little social significance today. But it is important to bear in mind that, in addition to the factors that may invalidate a marriage or civil partnership after it has been celebrated, the law of nullity has an inhibitory effect, in that a particular obstacle may mean that the parties are prevented from going through a ceremony in the first place. In addition, parts of the law of nullity once thought to be of little practical significance are acquiring new relevance: for example, the possibility of annulling a marriage on the basis that one of the parties entered into it under duress is of considerable significance in tackling the problem of forced marriages today.

This distinction between those factors that are likely to prevent a ceremony from taking place, and those that may invalidate the effect of an otherwise valid ceremony, broadly corresponds to that between the grounds that render a marriage or civil partnership void, and those that render it merely voidable. This distinction between void and voidable is—as is the case with much of the English law of marriage—a product of the historical development of the law. It can today be said to distinguish between the grounds that the state sees as fundamental to the creation of a formal relationship, and those grounds that are a matter for the parties themselves, since any "interested person" may take proceedings if the marriage or civil partnership is void, whereas only the parties themselves are entitled to seek an annulment if the defect is one that merely renders it voidable. The other main differences between the two categories are as follows:

Void marriage or civil partnership	Voidable marriage or civil partnership
Never existed	Valid until annulled by the court
Unnecessary (but possible) to obtain a decree or (in the case of a civil partnership) an order declaring that it is void	Necessary to obtain a decree or (in the case of a civil partnership) an order in order to annul the marriage
Can be pronounced void even after the parties have died	Can only be annulled during the lifetime of the parties
No bars	Decree/order may be barred in certain specified circumstances (see further paras 3–036 et seq. and 3–046

This basic distinction between a marriage or civil partnership that is voidable and one that is void is comprehensible enough. The legal *consequences* of each are, however, difficult to reconcile with this distinction: logic has been tempered by sympathy in that even a void marriage or civil partnership—which, in the eyes of the law, never existed—may attract certain legal consequences. The reason is that, to avoid hardship, many of the legal consequences of a valid marriage have been attached even to void marriages, provided that a decree of nullity is obtained, and the same principle now applies to civil partnerships. Hence, although it is never strictly necessary to obtain either a decree annulling a marriage that is void, or an order annulling a void civil partnership, it may be very much in the interests of one of the parties to do so. This can be illustrated by considering the case of a woman who has entered into a bigamous marriage. That "marriage" is void. But if either party petitions for a decree to annul the marriage, the court would, on granting that decree, have the same powers to make orders for financial relief for her as if it were dissolving a valid marriage by divorce. Bringing proceedings to establish that there is no marriage or civil partnership thus, paradoxically, seems to create legal consequences similar to those that would flow from the termination of a valid marriage or civil partnership. Whether the court is willing to exercise those powers in any particular case—for example where the petitioner knew of the legal obstacle—is another matter, which is considered further below (at para.3–043).

It should also be noted that the court has no such jurisdiction where the ceremony is so deficient that it results in merely a *non-marriage* (or non-partnership), which explains why the courts resorted to such tortuous reasoning in cases such as *CAO v Bath* to avoid this unpalatable result (see para.2–018).

The modern law of nullity

As noted above, the law of nullity is rooted in ecclesiastical law, and until 1857 the **3–002** ecclesiastical courts had exclusive power to annul marriages. The newly created Divorce Court that then took over this jurisdiction was directed to proceed as far as possible on the same principles that the ecclesiastical courts had applied. New grounds were added by statute in 1937, requiring the courts to formulate new principles, and the law was comprehensively reformed by the Nullity of Marriage Act 1971 (and subsequently consolidated in the Matrimonial Causes Act 1973, which is still the governing legislation in this area). While the doctrines of the ecclesiastical courts may—as applied in the case law between 1858 and 1971—still be relevant in interpreting the statutory provisions, recourse to these old doctrines is discouraged now that the law has been codified (save in so far as case law provides a guide to the legislative intent). The doctrines formulated by canon lawyers of past centuries can have even less relevance to civil partnerships.

The approach of the chapter

Given the importance of the historical development of the law, the differences in **3–003** terminology, and the (admittedly few) substantive differences between marriage and civil partnerships, it is convenient to consider marriage and civil partnerships separately. Some cross-referencing will be required, since the existence of a civil partnership will in itself create certain obstacles to a marriage (see paras 3–005 and 3–014). The categories of "void" and "voidable" marriages are examined in Parts B and C respectively. The effects of granting a decree are set out in Part D, and Part E considers all three issues in relation to civil partnerships. The concluding section discusses whether the law of nullity is necessary in the twenty-first century.

B: VOID MARRIAGES

In brief, under s.11 of the Matrimonial Causes Act 1973, the grounds on which a **3–004** marriage is void are:

(i) that the parties are within the prohibited degrees;

(ii) that either party is under the age of 16;

(iii) that the parties have knowingly and wilfully failed to comply with the requisite formalities;

(iv) that either party is already in an existing formal relationship (marriage or civil partnership);

(v) that the parties are of the same sex;

(vi) that the marriage was polygamous and contracted overseas while either party is domiciled in England and Wales.

These grounds will now be considered in turn:

Prohibited degrees: blood relationships and legal relationships

3–005 It is understandable that the law might wish to prohibit sexual relationships with close blood relatives—for example in order to protect children from being sexually exploited by their relatives or from concern about the increased likelihood of the development of inherited genetic disorders. The "prohibited degrees" in English law, however, extend beyond relationships of consanguinity (the blood relationship), to relationships created by marriage (relationships by affinity). Relatives by affinity are called "affines" and consist of the spouse (or former spouse) of one's own relatives, and relatives of one's spouse (or former spouse)—in other words, in-laws and step-relations. The prohibitions on marriages between affines originated in the canon law doctrine whereby marriage makes man and woman one flesh: if husband and wife were one flesh, the wife's sister was effectively the man's sister.

In recent years, justification for prohibiting marriages between affines has been based on broader considerations of social policy, linked to exploitation and to the confusion of roles that may result from sexual relationships that transgress the rules—*e.g.* a man having sex with his wife's daughter from a previous relationship (although it should be noted that there is not an exact overlap between relationships that cannot be formalised and relationships that are criminalised, see para.3–011 below). These broader considerations of social policy also explain why the same prohibitions have been extended to civil partners, and why the registration of a civil partnership will itself create a new set of "prohibited degrees" for the purposes of marriage as well as for future civil partnerships (CPA 2004 Sch.1). A further twist is added by the Gender Recognition Act 2004, which allows for the legal recognition of a transsexual in his or her acquired gender (see further below, para.3–015).

Another "legal relationship" that is relevant for these purposes is that of adoption, although the prohibitions are different again from those that apply to those related by blood.

More specifically, the following restrictions apply:

(1) Blood relatives

3–006 English law prohibits an individual from marrying a parent, child, grandparent, brother or sister, uncle or aunt, nephew or niece. The same restrictions apply to siblings of the half-blood—*i.e.* those who have only one parent in common. Unlike some other western systems of law, cousins are free to marry.

(2) Affines

3–007 The law on affines is less simple, with different rules applying to different categories of relationship. The law has sought to strike a balance between the need to avoid sexual exploitation within the family and the desire to ensure that individuals can marry the person of their choice. Take the example of a step-daughter: it is easy to understand why the law might wish to prevent a marriage between her and the man who helped bring her up, but it is less easy to justify any prohibition if she was an adult living away from home at the time when the man in question married her mother, and if the parties only met and fell in love after the mother's death. Is there any justification for not allowing the couple to marry in the latter case—especially when there would be no such restriction if the man in question had merely cohabited with the girl's mother?

Over the years, the law has been progressively relaxed. The increase in divorce and remarriage since the end of World War II greatly increased the risk that a couple who had never in fact been members of the same family unit would be debarred from marriage by reason of a legal relationship created by a relative's marriage, and this was one of the factors which led to the liberalisation of the law by the Marriage (Prohibited Degrees of Relationship) Act 1986. The basic principle of the 1986 legislation is that marriage with relatives by affinity is now permitted, but in two cases certain conditions have to be fulfilled:

(a) Step-child/step-parent

A marriage with a step-child is only permitted if (a) both parties are 21 or over; and **3–008** (b) the younger has not been a "child of the family" in relation to the elder at any time before the child attained the age of 18. (For present purposes it is sufficient to say that a child of the family is somebody who has been "treated" as a child of a particular marriage.) In effect, the law does not allow a marriage where one of the parties has effectively acted as the other's father or mother during the step-child's childhood:

> In *Smith v Clerical Medical and General Life Assurance Society and Others* [1993] 1 F.L.R. 47, CA, a man married the mother of a 13-year-old girl and they all lived together in the same household. Six years later the man left with the girl, and they set up house together, apparently intending to marry. Such a marriage would have been void before the enactment of the 1986 Act, and it remained prohibited after that Act since the girl had (before attaining 18) lived with her intended husband in the same household and he had treated her as a child of the family.

(b) Parents in law/son or daughter-in-law

The prohibitions relating to the former spouse of one's son or daughter are, somewhat **3–009** arbitrarily, more restrictive than those relating to the child of one's former spouse. A man may not marry his son's former wife unless both of the parties intending to marry have attained the age of 21, and—more significantly—unless both his son and his son's mother are dead. Thus:

> In *B and L v UK* [2006] 1 F.L.R. 35, A and B's son C married L. After both of the marriages had ended in divorce, a relationship developed between B and L, his daughter-in-law. B and L wanted to marry, but were informed that they would be unable to do until both C and his other parent, A, were dead.

When the law was challenged by the parties before the European Court of Human Rights, the Government argued that the restriction was not absolute, not only because the parties might be able to marry at some point in the future if A and C both died, but also because of the possibility of seeking exemption from the rules by means of a private Act of Parliament. However, this possibility was one of the factors that led the Court to hold that there had in fact been a violation of Art.12:

"The inconsistency between the stated aims of the incapacity and the waiver applied in some cases undermines the rationality and logic of the measure . . . there is no indication of any detailed investigation into family circumstances in the Parliamentary procedure and . . . in any event, a cumbersome and expensive vetting procedure of this kind would not appear to offer a practically accessible or effective mechanism for individuals to vindicate their rights." (*B and L v UK* [2006] 1 F.L.R. 35, at para.40).

The court also pointed out that the bar on marriage was not backed up by prohibitions on the relationship itself—the law did not criminalise relationships between a father-in-law and daughter-in-law—thereby undermining any argument that the ban on marriage protected family relationships.

Shortly after the decision of the European Court in *B and L v UK*, the government indicated its intention to change the law. Under s.10(1)(b) of the Human Rights Act 1998, legislative amendments may be made by Ministerial order if the European Court has held a provision of the legislation to be incompatible with the European Convention. Further restrictions are imposed by s.10(2), which states that there must be "compelling reasons" for adopting this procedure. In February 2006 a proposal for a draft Marriage Act 1949 (Remedial) Order 2006 was laid before Parliament. The Joint Committee on Human Rights subsequently recommended that a draft order in the same terms should be laid before Parliament and approved the procedure adopted (*Sixteenth Report*). This obviates the need for primary legislation, and once the relevant order takes effect, it will be possible for a man to marry his daughter-in-law (or a woman her son-in-law). However, the law relating to marriages between step-relations remains unchanged.

(3) Adoption

3–010   There are two rules that have a special bearing in cases where a child has been adopted. Under the "legal transplant theory" (see para.15–003) the adopted child ceases to be the child of the original birth parents and becomes legally the child of the adoptive parents. Despite this, the child remains within the same prohibited degrees in relation to the natural parents and other relatives as if there had been no adoption. Hence, a marriage between a couple who are brother and sister by blood will be void even if neither of them knows about the relationship. (There are now special provisions in the legislation entitling a person to have access to the recorded facts about the birth, so that the slight risk that a couple will marry in ignorance of the biological relationship has been reduced, see further para.15–006 below.)

The second rule is that an adoptive parent and the adopted child are deemed to be within the prohibited degrees, and they continue to be so notwithstanding that the child is subsequently adopted by someone else. This clearly reflects the policy that the law should discourage sexual relationships within the home circle. However, there are no other express prohibitions arising by reason of adoption, and it is thus possible, for example, for an adopted child validly to marry his adoptive sister, assuming that they are not otherwise within the prohibited degrees. This is somewhat at odds with the policy in other areas of deterring relationships within the home circle.

(4) Prohibited relationships

3–011   By contrast, the policy of deterring relationships within the home circle is a key theme within the Sexual Offences Act 2003. Since 1908 it has been a criminal offence for a person knowingly to have sexual intercourse with certain relations. The 2003 Act replaced the old offence of incest with a number of new offences. They key point here is the way in which those offences overlap with the prohibited degrees of marriage. Sections 64 and 65, for example, deal with sex between adult family members and criminalise penetrative sex between a person and his or her parent, grandparent, child, grandchild, sibling (whether full or half), aunt, uncle, nephew or niece. This expanded list is still narrower than the prohibited degrees of marriage, since it does not include in-law and step-relationships. By contrast, the new offence of "sexual activity with a child family member" (s.25) is much wider, including, for example, foster parents and cousins who have lived in the same household, who are entitled to marry (for a full list see s.27). It would of course be absurd if 17-year-old cousins who had validly married or entered into a civil partnership were to be subject to criminal sanctions for consummating their relationship, and s.28 of the 2003 Act does provide that conduct that would otherwise constitute an offence under s.25 will not be an offence between married couples or civil partners. No such defence applies to those who are intending to marry: the courtship of such couples must therefore be either chaste or criminal.

Minimum age

A marriage is void if either party is under 16 years of age. This rule (which applies **3–012** whether or not either knew the facts) should be distinguished from the rule that requires parental consent where a person intending to marry is under 18 years of age. Failure to comply with the parental consent rule has no effect on the validity of the marriage. Thus if a 17-year-old girl gets married without her parents' consent the validity of the marriage will not be affected. In contrast, a marriage between a boy of 17 and a girl whom everyone believes to be 16 is void if it is subsequently (perhaps many years later) established that she was in fact one day short of her sixteenth birthday, even if both sets of parents consented to the marriage.

This rule seems capable of creating hardship. It is true that the "teenage" marriage is now something of the past for most people in this country but this is not necessarily true for some ethnic minorities. If a couple marry, genuinely but mistakenly believing that they have both attained the appropriate legal age to do so, it seems harsh to hold the union void. Moreover, if a couple have lived together for many years believing their marriage to be valid, it would seem to be quite wrong to let a third party challenge it—perhaps to gain financial benefit under the succession laws. These criticisms have particular force in cases where one party was born in a country with no reliable system of birth registration and no one realised that he or she was in fact under 16 at the time of the marriage.

Defective formalities

The effect of failing to comply with the formalities required for a valid marriage **3–013** partnership is discussed in Ch.2.

Bigamy

An individual may only have one formal relationship at a time: a purported marriage **3–014** is void if, at the time of the ceremony, either party was already validly married or in a subsisting civil partnership. It remains void even if the pre-existing spouse or civil partner dies, or if the pre-existing formal relationship is legally terminated, although in such cases there is no obstacle to the second union being validly formalised thereafter. The belief of the parties to the second union that the first had already come to an end is irrelevant for these purposes if such belief, although genuine, is unfounded.

Problems may arise if there is no evidence as to whether the former spouse or civil partner was still alive at the date of the later ceremony. Such cases can often be resolved by applying a presumption that a person is dead if there is no evidence that he was alive throughout a continuous period of seven years: see s.19 of the MCA.

Parties of same sex

3–015   Section 11(c) of the Matrimonial Causes Act 1973 provides that a marriage is void if the parties are not respectively male and female. This may appear simple enough, but what about transsexuals? The medical term for transsexualism is "gender identity dysphoria" and as the European Court of Human Rights explained (in *The Rees Case* [1987] 2 F.L.R. 111) transsexuals are generally people who: "whilst belonging physically to one sex, feel convinced that they belong to the other; they often seek to achieve a more integrated, unambiguous identity by undergoing medical treatment and surgical operations to adapt their physical characteristics to their psychological nature." Is a male-to-female transsexual male or female for the purposes of marriage?

At common law the answer was that a male-to-female transsexual remained male within the context of marriage: *Corbett v Corbett* [1971] P. 83. A person's sex was fixed for all time at birth, and was tested by reference to gonadal, genital and chromosomal factors. If these factors were congruent, they were decisive, and psychological factors were excluded from consideration. In this view a person born with male genitalia and male chromosomes remained "male" for the purpose of marriage, notwithstanding the fact that such a person might have undergone extensive surgery, possessed the external attributes of a woman, lived and been accepted as a woman, and in most ways have become philosophically, psychologically and socially a woman.

This remained the law for over 30 years, although judges increasingly expressed unease at such an approach. The scope of the decision in *Corbett* was restricted in *W v W (Nullity: Gender)* [2001] 1 F.L.R. 324, Charles J, which was a case of inter-sex rather than transsexualism (*i.e.* the sex of the child had not been clear at birth and remained ambiguous). The judge held that where the biological criteria were not congruent, other factors could be taken into account.

A more significant challenge came from the European Court of Human Rights, which, after upholding UK law in earlier cases, finally decided in *Goodwin v UK* [2002] 2 F.C.R. 576, ECHR, that the UK's policy on the legal status of transsexuals breached Art.12, which protects the right to marry, and Art.8, which protects the right to respect for private and family life:

> A post-operative male-to-female transsexual claimed that her rights under Art.12 were breached as she could not marry her partner under English law, which continued to treat her as a man for the purposes of marriage. The European Court of Human Rights held that while the right to marry was subject to the

national laws of the contracting states, "the limitations thereby introduced must not restrict or reduce the right in such a way or to such an extent that the very essence of the right is impaired" (at 604). In the case before it, the applicant "lives as a woman, is in a relationship with a man and would only wish to marry a man. She has no possibility of doing so. In the court's view, she may therefore claim that the very essence of her right to marry has been infringed." (at 604). See also *I v UK* [2002] 2 F.C.R. 612.

Even following the decision in *Goodwin*, the English courts did not feel able to interpret the law so as to ensure consistency with Arts 8 and 12. Instead, the House of Lords declared it to be incompatible with the European Convention on Human Rights (*Bellinger v Bellinger* [2003] UKHL 21). The harshness of the decision in *Bellinger* was, however, mitigated by the fact that the government had already announced that it planned to introduce legislation to reform the law, and the Gender Recognition Act 2004 was passed.

As a result, under the Gender Recognition Act 2004, an adult may make an application for a gender recognition certificate from a Gender Recognition Panel, which consists of both legal and medical members. The Panel must grant the application if the applicant has or has had gender dysphoria, "has lived in the acquired gender throughout the period of two years ending with the date on which the application is made" and "intends to continue to live in the acquired gender until death" (GRA s.2).

A number of points should be made about this process. First, the issue has become a medical rather than a legal one: under s.3 the applicant is required to produce reports from two medical practitioners or one medical practitioner and a chartered psychologist diagnosing gender dysphoria. Secondly, there is no requirement that the applicant should have undergone surgery. This ties into the third point, namely the difficulty of disproving the applicant's intention to live in the acquired gender until death. There is no prohibition on seeking a subsequent gender recognition certificate to revert to one's original sex.

If the applicant is married, the panel can only grant an interim gender recognition certificate, and the union must be annulled before a full certificate can be granted. The grant of an interim certificate is itself a ground on which a marriage is voidable (MCA s.12(g), and see para.3–033 below). When the decree of nullity has been made absolute, a full gender recognition certificate will be issued and "the person's gender becomes for all purposes the acquired gender" (GRA s.9).

As a result, a transsexual will be able to enter into a formal relationship in his or her reassigned sex. Thus a male-to-female transsexual may either enter into a marriage with a man (or, if she so wishes, a civil partnership with a woman). A male-to-female transsexual who was previously married to a woman may choose to enter into a civil partnership with the same women after the marriage has been annulled and the full certificate issued, but it is not possible simply to convert a marriage into a civil partnership (or vice versa). It should also be noted that there is no *obligation* upon a person who has undergone gender reassignment surgery to seek legal recognition of the reassigned sex: accordingly, a male-to-female transsexual who has not sought legal recognition of this reassignment may marry, or remain married to, a woman.

Despite the changes made by the Gender Recognition Act, certain differences in legal treatment remain. First, no clergyman is obliged against his conscience to solemnise the marriage of a person who has acquired a new gender under the Act.

Secondly, those who marry a person unaware that he or she has undergone gender reassignment may seek to annul the marriage (MCA s.12(h), and see further below at para.3–033). This means that the marriage of, for example, a male-to-female transsexual who has satisfied the Gender Recognition Panel that she fulfils the legislation's criteria, and has obtained a gender recognition certificate, can still be challenged by her spouse simply on the basis that she is a transsexual. This seems to go against the explicit declaration that the newly recognised gender is to be valid for all purposes. It could be argued that fairness to the other spouse requires the option of annulling the marriage. But again, this assumes that a marriage to a transsexual is so fundamentally different to any other marriage that such an option should be preserved. Thirdly, there remains a risk that the marriage could be challenged on the basis of non-consummation—a possibility that is considered further below (para.3–019).

One final point should be noted. Given the emphasis that the European Court placed on the fact that Ms Goodwin was in a relationship with a man and would only wish to marry a man, it may also be questioned whether a challenge under Art.12 of the Convention by a same-sex couple wishing to *marry* might prove successful in the future.

Polygamous marriages

3–016 Section 11(d) of the Matrimonial Causes Act 1973 (as amended) provides that an actually polygamous marriage entered into after July 31, 1971 is void if either party to the marriage was at the time domiciled in England and Wales. The question of how far English law will recognise polygamous marriages contracted by those domiciled abroad is beyond the scope of this book (see J. Murphy, *International dimensions in family law* (Manchester University Press, 2005), for a discussion of the law).

C: VOIDABLE MARRIAGES

3–017 The grounds on which a marriage is voidable are listed in s.12 of the Matrimonial Causes Act 1973 as follows: non-consummation (due either to incapacity or to wilful refusal); lack of consent; the fact that one spouse had undergone gender reassignment before the marriage or during it; venereal disease, pregnancy by a third party, and mental illness.

Even if the petitioner is able to establish one of the above grounds, a decree may still be denied if one of the statutory bars is applicable. Certain bars—those imposing time limits on petitions and those stipulating that the petitioner must have been ignorant of the facts relied upon—apply to only some of the grounds, and are discussed below where appropriate. One bar, however, is applicable to all of the grounds on which a marriage may be voidable—namely that the petitioner had acted in such a way as to lead the respondent to believe that no petition would be brought—and it is discussed in more detail at the end of this section.

Incapacity to consummate

3–018 Section 12(1) provides that a marriage shall be voidable if it has not been consummated owing to the incapacity of either party to consummate it. This is a statutory codification of a basic principle of the canon law: although marriage was formed simply by consent, it was an implied term of the contract that the parties had the capacity to consummate it. Physical capacity was thus as much a basic requirement of marriage as the intellectual capacity to consent. The law is in this respect still influenced by its origins in the canon law.

It is possible for a spouse to petition on the basis of his or her *own* incapacity. Whichever party petitions, it is for the petitioner to prove that the incapacity exists. The court has power to order a medical examination, and may draw adverse inferences against a party who refuses to be examined.

The key principles of the law can be summarised as follows:

(1) *Meaning of consummation*

Consummation means sexual intercourse that is "ordinary and complete": there must **3–019** be both erection and penetration for a reasonable length of time. It is not necessary for either party to have an orgasm, nor is infertility relevant. Despite this apparently expansive definition (which would seem to rob the requirement of consummation of any purpose, whether sex is regarded as either a matter of procreation or of recreation) there are limits as to what the law regards as "ordinary and complete" intercourse. Only heterosexual intercourse counts for this purpose, and only where the vagina is penetrated by the penis.

It is possible that the marriage of a person who has undergone gender reassignment may be vulnerable to challenge on this ground. The problem is most obvious where such a person has not undergone gender reassignment surgery, but even where such surgery has been carried out, the courts have been unwilling to recognise the parties as capable of "ordinary and complete" intercourse (see *e.g. Corbett v Corbett* [1971] P.83). Whether any of the bars listed in s.13 would provide a defence is considered further below (see para.3–039).

(2) *The nature of the incapacity*

Incapacity will be deemed to be incurable if any remedial operation is dangerous, or **3–020** if the respondent refuses to undergo an operation. Some cases of incapacity have psychological origins, but questions of causation are irrelevant in deciding the issue of capacity. It follows that it is immaterial that the impotence is only in relation to the spouse (that is to say that the respondent is capable of having intercourse with other partners). It also follows that a spouse who suffers from what is traditionally called "invincible repugnance" to the act of intercourse with the other will, for this purpose, be regarded as incapable of consummating the marriage. But it would seem that some element of psychiatric or physical aversion is necessary, and that a rational decision not to have intercourse is insufficient:

> In *Singh v Singh* [1971] P. 226, the petitioner was a 17-year-old Sikh girl who reluctantly went through a marriage ceremony arranged by her parents with a man she had never previously met. Karminski L.J. said that she "never submitted to the physical embraces of the husband, because . . . it does not appear that she saw him again". Since she did not want to be married to this man it was "understandable that she did not want to have sexual intercourse with him" but (the judge said) this was "a very long way from an invincible repugnance", and her petition was dismissed.

(3) Must the incapacity have existed at the time of the marriage?

3–021 It was a basic requirement of the canon law that the incapacity must have existed at the date of the marriage. It remains the case that the fact that the parties have had intercourse with each other *prior* to the marriage ceremony is irrelevant to the issue of whether the marriage has been consummated. More difficult questions arise in relation to supervening capacity: what if the spouse is incapacitated as a result of an accident on the way from the wedding to the honeymoon? The canon law would have refused a decree of nullity in such a case, reflecting the great theoretical difference between recognising that incapacity could be said to have prevented a marriage coming into existence at all (which the church was prepared to accept) and dissolving a valid marriage because of some supervening cause (which would have been incompatible with the church's teaching about marriage and divorce). The position under the current law is less clear, because the Act does not specifically require that the incapacity should have existed "at the time of the celebration of the marriage". Since it seems clear that the statutory codification of the law in 1971 was not intended to effect any change, the courts might well interpret the provision in the light of the classical distinction between nullity and divorce and refuse a decree in such a case.

Wilful refusal to consummate

3–022 Section 12(b) of the Matrimonial Causes Act 1973 provides that a marriage is voidable if it has not been consummated owing to the wilful refusal of the respondent to consummate it. (It should be noted that it is not possible petition on the basis of one's *own* refusal, in contrast to the situation where non-consummation is due to incapacity.) This ground is something of an anomaly, since the law of nullity generally deals with conditions existing at the time of the marriage, and wilful refusal is by definition something which occurs after marriage. It does not derive from the canon law, being instead the creation of statute (the Matrimonial Causes Act 1937). Thus in interpreting this ground the canon law is of no direct relevance.

The key features of the law are as follows:

(1) Refusal

3–023 A decree will only be granted if an examination of the whole history of the marriage reveals "a settled and definite decision" on the part of the respondent, "come to without just excuse". A husband (it has been held) must use appropriate tact, persuasion and encouragement and his wife will not be guilty of wilful refusal if he has failed to do so. Moreover:

> In *Potter v Potter* (1975) 5 Fam. Law 161, CA, a wife was refused a decree because the husband's failure to consummate resulted from natural "loss of ardour" after a prolonged history of sexual difficulties.

(2) Without excuse

3–024 If the respondent can show a "just excuse" for the refusal to consummate there is no wilful refusal:

> In *Ford v Ford* [1987] Fam. Law 232, the marriage had taken place whilst the husband was serving a sentence of five years' imprisonment. During visits he was

left alone with his wife for periods of up to two hours. She had heard from other visitors that it was not unusual in such circumstances for intercourse to take place, but the husband refused. The judge held that this did not justify a finding that the husband had wilfully refused to consummate the marriage: as having sex would have been in breach of the Prison Rules, this provided him with a just excuse for his refusal. However, the fact that the husband has asked to be taken to his ex-girlfriend's house upon his release from prison and had refused to have anything to do with his wife did justify a decree of nullity being granted under this heading.

The question of whether there is a just excuse for refusal to consummate a marriage has also arisen in a rather different context. Among some religions it is the practice for the parties to go through a civil marriage ceremony and a separate religious ceremony. The first will be necessary for the legal recognition of the marriage if the place where the marriage is to be celebrated is not licensed (see para.2–012 above), while the latter is equally essential to the religious recognition of the marriage. In these circumstances, it has been held that a husband's failure to organise the religious ceremony is not merely a just excuse for the wife's refusing to consummate the marriage but itself amounts to a wilful refusal on his part to consummate. Thus:

In *Kaur v Singh* [1972] 1 W.L.R. 105, a marriage was arranged between two Sikhs. A civil ceremony took place, but the husband (notwithstanding the fact that he knew it to be his duty) refused to make arrangements for the religious ceremony. It was held that the wife was entitled to a decree on the grounds of his wilful refusal to consummate the marriage.

Such cases also illustrate that a refusal to consummate the marriage may be encompassed within a more general refusal to have anything to do with the other spouse.

Lack of consent

For the canon law, marriage was created by the consent of the parties, and without **3–025** true consent there could be no marriage. As a result of a somewhat controversial amendment made by the Nullity of Marriage Act 1971, a marriage celebrated after July 31, 1971 to which either party did not validly consent (whether in consequence of duress, mistake, unsoundness of mind or otherwise) is no longer void, but only voidable: see now s.12(c) of the MCA 1973.

Cases of lack of consent usually involve situations in which there has in fact been an *expression* of consent but where this apparent consent is subsequently claimed not to be real. The problem for the law is how to balance the principle that marriage must be based on the free and genuine consent of the parties with the need to ensure that apparently valid legal unions are not avoided by subsequent claims relating to the existence of a state of mind or belief that was not evident at the time of the ceremony.

English law seeks to resolve this juristic dilemma by, on the one hand, refusing to allow private reservations or motives to vitiate an ostensibly valid marriage, whilst on the other hand accepting that there may be cases in which there has been no consent at all.

The law is complex, and the cases can best be considered under the three heads specifically referred to in the legislation: (a) insanity; (b) duress and fear; and (c) mistake and fraud. Whatever the basis of the claim, the petition must be brought within three years of the date of the marriage.

(1) Insanity

3–026   Marriage (according to a nineteenth-century judge) is a very simple contract, which does not require a high degree of intelligence to understand (Sir James Hannen P. in *Durham v Durham* (1885) 10 P.D. 80 at 81). Mental illness or incapacity will only affect the validity of consent if either party was, at the time of the ceremony, incapable of understanding the nature of marriage and the duties and responsibilities it creates. This test of capacity was recently endorsed in *Sheffield CC v E* [2004] EWHC 2808 (Fam), in which Munby J. summarised the modern duties and responsibilities as follows:

> "Marriage, whether civil or religious, is a contract, formally entered into. It confers on the parties the status of husband and wife, the essence of the contract being an agreement between a man and a woman to live together, and to love one another as husband and wife, to the exclusion of all others. It creates a relationship of mutual and reciprocal obligations, typically involving the sharing of a common home and a common domestic life and the right to enjoy each other's society, comfort and assistance." (para.132)

From this it is clear that an individual does not need a particularly precise understanding of the legal rights and responsibilities of marriage in order to have capacity to enter into such a union. As Chisholm J. declared in the Australian case of *AK and NC* (2004) F.L.C. 93–178 "if there were such a requirement, few if any marriages would be valid." Indeed, Munby J.'s summary is more accurate as a statement of social practice than as an account of legal obligations: one assumes that most spouses do love each other, but it cannot be claimed that there is a legal "duty of love" save in the very narrow sense that a marriage is voidable if it has not been consummated.

As this discussion shows, incapacity is hard to establish. There is an alternative mental illness ground which was introduced by legislation in 1937 precisely because it was so difficult to establish lack of consent: (see para.3–032, below). If the incapacity of an individual is established in *advance* of the marriage, the inherent jurisdiction of the court may be invoked to prevent a marriage taking place (see *e.g. M v B, A and S (By the Official Solicitor)* [2005] EWHC 1681 (Fam), and para.12–040 below).

(2) Duress and fear

3–027   Of rather more significance is the law dealing with marriages entered into as a result of duress or fear. Such forced marriages should be distinguished from the arranged marriages that form part of the culture of many ethnic minority communities. In an arranged marriage, the parties give their free consent to marry one another. In a forced marriage, by contrast, the apparent consent of at least of one the parties is achieved by force or threats. The Forced Marriage Unit, a joint initiative of the Home Office and the Foreign and Commonwealth Office, deals with around 250 cases per year. It is likely that forced marriages are more widespread than even this might suggest: for obvious reasons there is no reliable source of statistics. The issue is sometimes seen as a clash between different cultural and religious traditions, but while many faiths endorse *arranged* marriages, the Home Office has stressed that "no major world faith condones forced marriages" and that describing it as a religious issue may simply feed prejudices (Home Office, *A choice by right: The report of the working group on forced marriage* (HMSO, 2002)).

(a) The "overborne will" test

The question for the court is whether there has been a real consent. Hence (it has been **3–028** said) "where a formal consent is brought about by force, menace or duress"—a yielding of the lips, not of the mind—it is of no legal effect (*Szechter v Szechter* [1971] P.286). At one time, case law supported the view that only a threat of immediate danger to life, limb or liberty could suffice to justify the granting of a decree of nullity on this ground. But the reality is that a weak-minded person's will may be overcome by threats that would have had no impact on a stronger character, and in *Hirani v Hirani* (1982) 4 F.L.R. 232, the Court of Appeal held that the test is simply whether the threats or pressure are such as to destroy the reality of the consent and to overbear the will of the individual. Hence a decree could be granted to a 19-year-old Hindu girl told by her parents to break off a relationship with a Muslim boyfriend and to "marry someone we want you to, otherwise pack up your bags and go". Had the old "threat to life or liberty" test applied, it seems doubtful whether she (or many other victims of forced marriage) would be able to succeed. It would appear that the test in *Hirani* is now widely viewed as the appropriate one to apply (see *e.g.* Home Office, *A choice by right: The report of the working group on forced marriage* (HMSO, 2002), and *P v R (Forced Marriage: Annulment: Procedure)* [2003] 1 F.L.R. 661).

Even so, if the marriage is deliberately contracted (albeit only out of a sense of obligation to family or religious tradition) it cannot be annulled on this ground:

> In *Singh v Singh* [1971] P.226, the bride had never seen her husband before the marriage, and only went through the ceremony out of a "proper respect" for her parents and Sikh traditions. The court refused to annul the marriage because there was no evidence of fear.

(b) The nature of the threats

It should also be noted that the threats need not emanate from the other party, or from **3–029** family members: in *Szechter v Szechter* [1971] P. 286, threats to life and liberty arising from the policies of a totalitarian regime were held to suffice. In that case the parties had married so that they would be allowed to leave the country and thus avoid imprisonment. Whether such cases should be seen as a matter of duress is perhaps open to question: although the parties were no doubt frightened, their decision to marry was a conscious and a rational one: they wanted to be married so that they could enjoy the legal consequences of matrimony.

(c) Access to the law

It should be borne in mind that the real problem for the victim of a forced marriage **3–030** may not be the law's definition of duress but rather access to the law (see, *e.g.* Home Office, *A choice by right: The report of the working group on forced marriage* (HMSO, 2002)). Recent initiatives have focused on raising awareness and improvements in practice—for example, among immigration authorities—rather than changes to the substantive law of marriage. The Government is also consulting on whether to make forcing a person into a marriage a specific criminal offence: see the consultation paper published jointly by the Foreign and Commonwealth Office and the Home Office, *Forced Marriages: A Wrong Not a Right* (2005).

(3) Mistake and fraud

3–031 Generally neither mistake nor fraud renders a marriage void. The maxim *caveat emptor*—let the buyer beware—applies, it has been said, just as much to marriage as it does to other contracts. Even fraud is not a vitiating factor if it induces consent, but only if it procures the appearance without the reality of consent. Hence, mistake can only be relevant if it destroys an apparent consent. Thus a mistake as to the identity of the other party (more plausible when brides wore heavy veils until the knot was tied) will invalidate the marriage but a mistaken belief that the other party has certain attributes will not. So if I marry A under the belief that he is B, then this is sufficient to invalidate the marriage; but if I marry A erroneously believing him to be rich then the marriage will be unimpeachable. Similarly, and rather more plausibly, a mistake as to the nature of the ceremony will invalidate the marriage. The mistaken belief that the petitioner was appearing in a police court, or that the ceremony was a betrothal or religious conversion ceremony (*Mehta v Mehta* [1945] 2 All E.R. 690) have been held sufficient to invalidate the marriage. The fact that one of the parties was so drunk (or under the influence of drugs) as not to know what was happening will also be sufficient (*Sullivan v Sullivan* (1812) 2 Hag. Con. 238 at 246). By contrast, a mistake about the legal consequences of marriage is insufficient: *Messina v Smith* [1971] P. 322.

Mental disorder

3–032 In 1937 a new ground was introduced, namely that at the time of the marriage either party, though capable of giving a valid consent, was suffering (whether continuously or intermittently) from mental disorder of such a kind, or to such an extent, as to be unfit for marriage. "Mental disorder" now has the meaning defined in the Mental Health Act 1983. A petitioner may rely on his or her own mental disorder for the purpose of a petition on this ground, which is primarily intended to cover the case where, although the afflicted party is capable of giving a valid consent, the mental disorder makes him or her incapable of carrying on a normal married life. The petition must be brought within three years of the marriage.

Gender reassignment

3–033 Two new grounds have been added to s.12 of the Matrimonial Causes Act 1973 as a result of the passage of the Gender Recognition Act 2004. First, if an individual has obtained a gender recognition certificate before entering into a marriage, and the other party to the union is unaware of this fact, the latter is entitled to petition for nullity within the first three years of the marriage (MCA s.12(h)). Secondly, if an individual seeks legal recognition of gender reassignment while married, then the Gender Recognition Panel can only issue an interim gender recognition certificate. The grant of such a certificate is a ground on which either party may base a nullity petition, which must be brought within six months of the issue of the certificate.

Venereal disease

A marriage is voidable on the basis that at the time of the marriage the respondent was **3–034** suffering from venereal disease in a communicable form. The petitioner must have been unaware of this fact at the time of the marriage and must bring the petition within three years.

Pregnancy by another

A marriage is voidable on the basis that at the time of the ceremony the respondent **3–035** was pregnant by some person other than the petitioner. (It should however be noted that a wife cannot petition on the basis that her husband has impregnated another woman.) The petition must be brought within three years, although a decree may be barred if the petitioner was aware of the facts (not just that the woman was pregnant but also that she was pregnant by someone else).

Bars to a decree

If one of the grounds set out above is established, the petitioner will usually be entitled **3–036** to a decree. However, the petition may still fail if one of three bars contained in s.13 of the Matrimonial Causes Act 1973 can be established.

(1) *Time*

In the case of proceedings founded on lack of consent, venereal disease, pregnancy by **3–037** a third party, or gender reassignment, it is an absolute bar that proceedings were not instituted within three years of the marriage. (There is a restricted power to extend this period in cases of mental illness: see s.13(4).) Where the petition is based on the issue of a gender recognition certificate to a married person, the time limit is shorter—only six months—and there is no provision for it to be extended.

(2) *Knowledge of defect*

A petition founded on the respondent's venereal disease, pregnancy by a third party or **3–038** gender reassignment pre-dating the marriage will fail unless the petitioner can satisfy the court that, at the time of the ceremony, the petitioner was ignorant of the facts alleged.

(3) *"Approbation"*

The court shall not grant a decree of nullity if the respondent satisfies the court that **3–039** the petitioner, with knowledge that it was open to him to have the marriage avoided, so conducted himself in relation to the respondent as to lead the respondent reasonably to believe that he would not seek to do so; and, in addition, that it would be unjust to the respondent to grant the decree (MCA s.13(1)).

This replaces the complex and uncertain bar of approbation inherited from the ecclesiastical courts. Three separate matters must be proved:

    (i) *conduct* by the petitioner in relation to the respondent which resulted in the respondent reasonably believing that the petitioner would not seek a decree of nullity;

(ii) *knowledge* on the petitioner's part at the time of the conduct relied on that the marriage could be annulled; and

(iii) *injustice* to the respondent if a decree were granted.

These bars have been relevant in one not uncommon situation: the case of companion-ship marriages. Suppose, for example, that an elderly couple marry on the under-standing that they are not to have sexual relations and that their marriage is to be "for companionship only". After living together for some years, the husband changes his mind and seeks to have sexual relations. The wife (who had at the husband's request given up a job carrying pension rights) refuses. Will she be able successfully to defend a nullity petition alleging wilful refusal? It would seem that if the wife could prove that the husband knew that nullity was available in cases of non-consummation, she might do so, since in this case the loss of pension rights could perhaps constitute injustice to her.

A new twist on this example relates to the situation of a spouse who, prior to the marriage, underwent gender reassignment but who is in the eyes of the law unable to consummate the marriage. If the marriage has lasted for some time a court might decide that the criteria set out above are met. If, on the other hand, the couple part within a fairly short period then it is unlikely that this bar would be established.

But it is important to note that there is no general public interest bar to the grant of nullity decrees. The law is now only concerned with the conduct of the parties towards each other and with injustice to the respondent. It is not concerned with representations that have been made to third parties, or with considerations of public policy. For example:

> In *D v D (Nullity: Statutory Bar)* [1979] Fam. 70, the fact that a couple adopted a child (and thus represented to the court considering the adoption application that they were husband and wife) did not debar one of them from subsequently petitioning for nullity on the ground of wilful refusal. The fact that it might be thought contrary to public policy to allow either party subsequently to assert that the marriage was a nullity was not relevant.

D: EFFECTS OF A DECREE

3–040 At one time a void marriage had no legal consequences: in the eyes of the law the parties were not, and never had been, any more than cohabitants. Even if the marriage were only voidable, the result was the same, since the decree of nullity operated retrospectively. However, over the years the law has been reformed in attempts to meet the hardship that was sometimes caused by the common law rules:

(1) *Voidable marriages: decrees not retroactive*

3–041 Under the law as it stood before 1971, the parties to a voidable marriage were validly married until annulment, but once a decree absolute had been pronounced they were deemed never to have been married. In 1971, the rule was abolished as being anom-alous, inconvenient and uncertain. A voidable marriage that is annulled is now treated as if it had existed up to the date of the decree.

(2) *The status of children*

Children of voidable marriages are legitimate because the marriage is treated as valid **3–042** unless and until it is annulled. At common law, the child of a void "marriage" was illegitimate. However, in 1959 statute provided that the child of a void marriage is to be "treated as" legitimate provided that at the time of conception (or at the time of the celebration of the marriage if later) both or either of the parties reasonably believed that the marriage was valid. It is immaterial that the belief in the validity of the marriage was based on a mistake of law: (see s.1(3) of the Legitimacy Act 1976 as amended by s.28 of the Family Law Reform Act 1987). But a child will only be treated as legitimate under these provisions if the birth occurred *after* the void marriage (see, *Re Spence dec'd* [1990] 2 F.L.R. 278, CA) and the legislation only applies where the father was domiciled in this country at the time. The significance of this is, however, much reduced by the fact that the marital status of a child's parents is now irrelevant for most purposes (see para.11–009 below).

(3) *Financial provision for the parties*

If the court grants a decree of nullity in respect of a marriage, it has the same power **3–043** to make financial orders against either party in much the same way as it would have on granting a decree of divorce in respect of a valid marriage. Thus although there is no legal need to obtain a decree of nullity in respect of a void marriage, there are practical advantages to so doing. Similarly, a "spouse" who has obtained a nullity decree is eligible to apply to the court for reasonable provision out of the other's estate after the death.

But the fact that the court has power to make financial orders does not mean that it will in fact do so. There has been some difference of judicial opinion as to the principles to be applied. In *Whiston v Whiston* [1995] 2 F.L.R. 268, CA, the Court of Appeal held that a bigamist was not entitled to financial provision. Had she remained a cohabitant she would have received nothing. Accordingly, any rights to financial relief flowed from the fact that she had committed the crime of bigamy and her claim was defeated by the principle of public policy debarring a criminal from profiting from the criminal act. In subsequent cases, judges have preferred to rely on the discretion afforded by the legislation rather than lay down any absolute rule. In *S-T (formerly J) v J* [1998] Fam. 103, CA, where the claimant, a female-to-male transsexual, had committed perjury by declaring himself free to marry a wealthy young woman, the court refused to extend *Whiston* beyond the crime of bigamy. In that particular case, it decided not to award the claimant anything, but justified this by reference to its wide discretion. More recently, the Court of Appeal in *Rampal v Rampal* [2001] EWCA Civ 989 held that *Whiston* did not establish a rule that *no* bigamist was entitled to apply for financial relief. Thorpe L.J. commented that "absolute rules in the field of family law are inevitably, and usually swiftly, challenged by the exceptional case."

E: Void and Voidable Civil Partnerships

The grounds on which an order may be sought to annul a civil partnership are **3–044** virtually identical to those examined above, but there are a number of significant differences.

Void civil partnerships

3–045 The grounds on which a civil partnership is void are listed in s.49 of the Civil Partnership Act 2004:

> (i) that the parties are within the prohibited degrees;
>
> (ii) that either party is under the age of 16;
>
> (iii) that the parties have knowingly and wilfully failed to comply with the requisite formalities;
>
> (iv) that either party is already in an existing formal relationship (civil partnership or marriage);
>
> (v) that the parties are not of the same sex;

The omission from this list requires little explanation. It was unnecessary for the 2004 Act to make provision for the recognition of "polygamous" civil partnerships contracted overseas, since no jurisdiction in the world recognises multiple civil partnerships. It should also be noted that a person who enters into concurrent civil partnerships in this country does not commit the offence of bigamy—which remains applicable only to individuals who contract concurrent marriages—but would be guilty of perjury, since he or she would have made a formal and untruthful declaration that there were no impediments to the civil partnership. The second civil partnership would of course be void.

It should also be noted that the remedial order intended to allow marriages between in-laws (see above para.3–009) does not extend to civil partnerships, since Art.12 protects only the right to marry, not the right to enter into a civil partnership. However, the relevant provisions of the Civil Partnership Act 2004 prohibiting a civil partnership between—for example—a man and his former son-in-law, have not been brought into force, and the government has indicated that they will be repealed to ensure parity between spouses and civil partners.

Voidable civil partnerships

3–046 The grounds on which a civil partnership is voidable are (CPA 2004, s.50):

> (i) lack of consent;
>
> (ii) mental disorder;
>
> (iii) respondent was pregnant by a third party;
>
> (iv) the issue of an interim gender reassignment certificate to either party;
>
> (v) respondent had undergone gender reassignment prior to the civil partnership.

There are three omissions from this list (and one inclusion) that require some explanation. It is not possible to annul a civil partnership on the basis of either non-consummation or the fact that one party suffers from a communicable venereal

disease. As noted above, the legal definition of "consummation" is explicitly heterosexual and the government took the view that it should not be extended to same-sex
couples. The Women and Equality Unit responsible for the reform further stated that
it was not "appropriate in present day circumstances to include [transmission of a
venereal disease] as a ground to nullify a civil partnership." (*Response to Civil
Partnership: A framework for the legal regulation of same-sex couples* (November
2003).) It did not explain why it remains appropriate in the context of marriage.
Together, this three omissions mean that there is nothing within the 2004 Act—apart
from the restrictions on partnerships with close kin—that acknowledges the sexual
dimension to civil partnerships. To some, this is an advantage: the Church of England,
for example, has stated that it is willing to accept its ministers entering into civil
partnerships as long as they abstain from sex (see *Civil partnerships—A pastoral
statement from the House of Bishops of the Church of England*, issued on July 25, 2005).
To others, it may seem that the goal of equal treatment has not yet been achieved (see
further para.1–001).

It might be thought that the possibilty of a civil partnership being annulled on the
basis that one of the parties was pregnant by a third party at the time of the
partnership was a little remote, but the availability of assisted reproduction (see
further Ch.10) means that the inclusion of this ground in the 2004 Act is justified.

An order annulling a civil partnership may be barred in the circumstances set out
above in relation to marriages.

Effects of an order

The effects of an order annulling a civil partnership mirror those of a decree annulling   **3–047**
a marriage.

F: CONCLUSION: DO WE NEED THE LAW OF NULLITY?

As suggested at the start of this chapter, the law of nullity is important for an   **3–048**
understanding of the nature of marriage and civil partnership, since it defines who can
legally enter into such relationships. Indeed, the law of nullity is an inevitable concomi-
tant of the fact that the law defines who can legally formalise a relationship: if, for
example, a marriage or civil partnership between close relations or two 15-year-olds
were *not* void, then the prohibition would be an empty one.

This is not to say that *all* of the grounds on which a marriage or civil partnership
can be annulled serve a useful function. In view of the unpleasantness of nullity
proceedings (which may involve medical examinations and will normally involve a full
court hearing), it is sometimes suggested that the concept of the voidable marriage
might be abolished, and that instead the parties should be left to obtain a divorce
based on the breakdown of their marriage. This has been done in Australia, but the
Law Commission rejected such a solution for this country. It has been suggested that
for some—particularly perhaps members of some ethnic minorities—divorce still
carries a stigma, and that a decree of nullity is a more acceptable alternative in such
cases.

Yet, for the vast majority of the population the law of nullity has lost much of its
practical importance. Even a void marriage or civil partnership now carries legal
consequences. More fundamentally, divorce or dissolution is more readily available to

terminate an unsatisfactory relationship, which means that there is much less need to turn to the law of nullity to find an alternative legal way of escape. The law has been totally transformed since the Divorce Reform Act 1969 introduced a new ground for divorce—which forms the subject matter of the next chapter.

Chapter 4

Exits: Divorce and Dissolution

A: Introduction

For the lawyer, a marriage or civil partnership creates a legal status from which legally **4–001** enforceable rights and duties arise; and from the same legalistic perspective, divorce or dissolution simply terminates that legal status. The termination of the legal relationship is not necessarily coterminous with the termination of the personal relationship: a couple may have cohabited for only a few days after formalising their relationship and thereafter lived apart for many years, consumed with mutual hatred and bitterness. But so far as the law is concerned they remain united in the eyes of the law and entitled to the rights flowing from their legal relationship. Conversely, divorce or dissolution does not necessarily bring the parties' personal relationships to an end, not least because there will often be children for whom arrangements will have to be made over the years.

It is important to bear in mind the distinction between legal status and personal relationship when assessing the rise in divorce over the past century. As the grounds for divorce have been progressively relaxed, the number of divorces has risen. But while it is clear that reform of the divorce law leads to an increase in the number of divorces, this does not necessarily indicate that it leads to increased marital breakdown. Of course, if divorce was not available—as in Ireland until relatively recently— there would be no divorces, but it would be naïve to believe that the parties to an unsatisfactory marriage would necessarily stay together. The increased prevalence of divorce does, however, mean that divorce has become an increasingly acceptable way of ending a marriage, with the result that the social constraints on divorce have weakened considerably. Divorce no longer poses an insuperable barrier to a political career, although so far the only person to have achieved the position of Prime Minister while married to a divorced person is Margaret Thatcher. The example set by the Royal Family has changed dramatically: a revival of the ban on divorced persons at court would thin the family circle somewhat. Changing attitudes towards "personal fulfilment" give greater weight to individual happiness than to the maintenance of the marriage tie. Giddens, for example, has commented on the rise of the "pure relationship" that is "continued only in so far as it is thought by both parties to deliver enough satisfaction for each individual to stay within it" (*The Transformation of Intimacy* (1992) Polity Press, p.58). In addition, higher expectations of marriage have arguably led to greater disillusionment.

While the last few years has seen a levelling off in both the number of divorces (which could by itself be attributed to the decline in the number of marriages) and, more significantly, in the rate of divorce, the UK still has one of the highest divorce rates in Western Europe. In 2005 there were 151,654 petitions for divorce and 142,393 decrees were made absolute. The median duration of a marriage that is ended by divorce is 11.5 years, and two in every five marriages are expected to end in divorce. Even if such figures represent a fall in the number of divorces since the numbers peaked in 1993, they still provoke considerable concern, especially as over half of the marriages that end in divorce involve children under the age of 16. It remains to be seen whether civil partnerships—which can be terminated by dissolution on virtually the same grounds as are available to terminate a marriage—prove equally vulnerable to breakdown.

The implications of relationship breakdown (including the division of assets and the arrangements to be made for the children, which are considered in Chs 8 and 12 respectively) are a major component of any family law course. This chapter focuses on the circumstances in which the law allows marriages and civil partnerships to be terminated. There are a few differences in terminology: a marriage is ended by *divorce*, a civil partnership by *dissolution*; a spouse will *petition* for divorce, while a civil partner makes an *application*; and the terms *petitioner* and *applicant* are used accordingly. For this reason, it is more convenient to discuss divorce and dissolution separately. Part B describes the evolution of the law, in order to establish the basis of the modern law and to set the low divorce rate of earlier generations in context. Part C considers the modern law, and Part D the proposals that have been advanced for reform. Part E looks briefly at the relationship between civil and religious divorces, such as the Jewish *get*. Finally, Part F considers the grounds on which a civil partnership may be terminated.

B: EVOLUTION OF THE LAW

4–002   The modern law of divorce cannot be understood without some knowledge of its historical development. Until the Reformation, English law followed the canon law of the Catholic Church in not permitting divorce in the sense in which that word is used today. The ecclesiastical courts were able to grant annulments (as explained in Ch.3), as well as divorces *a mensa et thoro*. The latter freed the spouses from the obligation to cohabit but did not allow them to remarry. By the eighteenth century a procedure for divorce by private Act of Parliament—which did allow the parties to remarry—had been developed. This, however was expensive—it was popularly estimated to cost at least a thousand pounds—and time-consuming, and it became clear that reform was necessary.

The "matrimonial offence" 1857–1969

4–003   The Matrimonial Causes Act 1857 accordingly created the Court for Divorce and Matrimonial Causes, which had the power to dissolve marriages (as well as to grant annulments and judicial separations, the latter corresponding to the old divorce *a mensa et thoro*). This power was initially somewhat limited. The petitioner had to prove that the respondent had committed adultery, that the petitioner was himself free of any matrimonial guilt, and that there had been no connivance or collusion between the parties. A wife had in addition to prove that her husband had "aggravated" his adultery by cruelty or two years' desertion or had committed incest, bestiality, rape or sodomy. Divorce by judicial process was thus made available, but only to an injured and legally guiltless spouse.

Modifications were made to the law over the years. In 1923, Parliament allowed a wife to petition for divorce on the ground of adultery alone, and in 1937 the grounds for divorce were widened to include cruelty, desertion and incurable insanity. With the exception of this last ground, it was still not possible to obtain a divorce against an "innocent" spouse. Where the marriage had broken down through the fault of neither party, or where the "innocent" spouse was unwilling to initiate the divorce, there was no legal redress. Some men and women simply left their legal spouses and set up new families, either (bigamously) remarrying or simply cohabiting.

Pressures for reform

Not surprisingly, there was strong pressure for change, not only from those who **4–004** wished to be able to remarry but also from those within the legal profession who disliked the intrusive questioning rendered necessary by the legal requirements. In the years following World War II, there were a number of Bills designed to allow divorce based simply on the fact that the parties had separated. These attracted considerable support, but the crucial breakthrough came with the publication in 1966 of a report by a group established by the Archbishop of Canterbury, *Putting Asunder.* It may seem odd that the Church of England, which remains opposed to divorce, should have been involved in putting forward proposals for reform, but the Church drew a distinction between what it was bound to require of its own members and what it ought to say about secular laws. The report of the Archbishop's Group favoured, as the lesser of two evils, the substitution of the doctrine of breakdown for that of the matrimonial offence. It was considered that, in order to answer the question of whether the marriage had indeed broken down, the court should carry out a detailed inquest into "the alleged fact and causes of the 'death' of a marriage relationship". The group also proposed that the court should be obliged to refuse a decree (notwithstanding proof of breakdown) if to grant it would be contrary to the public interest in justice and in protecting the institution of marriage.

"The Field of Choice"

The Lord Chancellor referred *Putting Asunder* to the newly established Law Commis- **4–005** sion. The Commission was influenced by research that revealed the prevalence of "stable illicit unions", and the assumption that liberalising divorce law would enable such unions to be regularised. It took as its starting point that a good divorce law should seek "(i) to buttress, rather than to undermine, the stability of marriage; and (ii) when, regrettably, a marriage has irretrievably broken down, to enable the empty legal shell to be destroyed with the maximum fairness, and the minimum bitterness, distress and humiliation" (*Reform of the Grounds of Divorce—The Field of Choice* (1966)). The Commission rejected the Archbishop's Group's proposal that an inquiry be held in every case into the breakdown. It was thought that such an inquiry would be humiliating and distressing to the parties, and would necessitate a vast increase in expenditure of money and human resources. Eventually, the Commission and the

Archbishop's Group reached agreement on the principle ultimately embodied in the Divorce Reform Act 1969. This principle—which remains the law—is that breakdown should be the sole ground for divorce. However, breakdown itself is not a justiciable issue but is to be inferred from certain facts. The legislation listed five "facts": three that were similar to the old matrimonial offences of adultery, cruelty and desertion, and two new grounds based on separation for specified periods of time. These reforms were consolidated in the Matrimonial Causes Act 1973, which forms the current law of divorce.

C: THE MODERN LAW

4–006   The clear statutory message of the Matrimonial Causes Act 1973 is that the sole ground for divorce is the irretrievable breakdown of the marriage (s.1(1)). While in legal theory this statement is true, in practice it is misleading. First, relationship breakdown, without proof of one of the five facts, will not be sufficient to terminate the legal relationship.

> For example, in *Buffery v Buffery* [1988] 2 F.L.R. 365, CA, the parties to a 20-year marriage had grown apart, no longer had anything in common, and could not communicate. The Court of Appeal accepted that the marriage had broken down, but, since the wife had failed to establish any of the five facts, a decree could not be granted.

Secondly, once one of the statutory facts *has* been proved, the breakdown of the marriage will almost automatically be inferred. Although in theory the specified facts are merely the necessary evidence from which the court may infer breakdown, in practice they give rise to such a strong presumption that it is almost impossible for the respondent to rebut the presumption:

> In *Le Marchant v Le Marchant* [1977] 1 W.L.R. 559, the husband petitioned for divorce on the basis of five years' separation (see further para.4–015) and a decree was granted notwithstanding the wife's denial that the marriage had broken down irretrievably and her protestations that she still loved her husband. It takes two to make a marriage. (By contrast, in *Cotterell v Cotterell* (1998) 3 F.C.R. 199, CA, the Court of Appeal held that the court should first consider whether the marriage has irretrievably broken down and only then go on to consider what it regarded as the subsidiary question of whether one of the "facts" had been made out. However, this decision stands on its own and seems to have been decided *per incuriam*—in plain English, the decision is clearly wrong.) In any event, the almost universal use of the "special procedure" explained below (at para.4–007) deprives the court of any real opportunity to investigate the question of break-down. Of course, a respondent may (and occasionally does) defend a divorce case simply on the issue of whether the marriage has in truth irretrievably broken down. But legal aid will not be available for this purpose and few solicitors would advise a client to spend money on a defence that is almost certain to fail. Indeed, in *Hadjimilitis v Tsavliris* [2003] 1 F.L.R. 81, Fam Div, the husband's insistence that the marriage had not broken down reinforced his wife's allegations that he sought to control her actions, and the accusations that he levelled against his wife

only served to convince the judge that a divorce should be granted. In truth, the five facts have become the grounds for divorce notwithstanding the theory—which must be remembered in the examination room—that irretrievable breakdown is the only ground for divorce.

It should also be noted that the legislation retained the option of judicial separation, which may be granted upon proof of any of the five facts (MCA s.17).

Petitioning for divorce

Before examining the five facts upon which a divorce may be based, the practicalities **4–007** of petitioning for divorce should be considered. First, there are restrictions as to *when* a petition may be brought. Between 1937 and 1984 a petition could not be brought within the first three years of the marriage, unless it was shown that the case was one of exceptional hardship suffered by the petitioner or one of exceptional depravity on the part of the respondent. In 1984 Parliament accepted that this provision was unsatisfactory, not least because it involved the making of distressing and humiliating allegations in more than a thousand cases each year. But it was thought desirable to retain some restriction on the availability of divorce early in marriage so as—symbolically at least—to assert the state's interest in upholding the stability and dignity of marriage, and to prevent divorce being apparently available within days of the marriage ceremony. The current law is that that no petition for divorce shall be presented to the court before the expiration of the period of one year from the date of the marriage (s.3). While this period cannot be shortened, regardless of the circumstances, other legal remedies can be used to provide legal redress—short of terminating the marriage—during the first year. In addition, the conduct of the respondent during that year is not irrelevant, as the petitioner may rely on matters that occurred during that period as grounds for a divorce.

Secondly, although the Divorce Reform Act 1969 revolutionised the conceptual basis of the divorce law, far and away the most significant change in the reality of the divorce process was the introduction in 1973 of a so-called "special procedure". It is true that this procedure is only applicable to undefended divorce cases, but almost all divorce petitions are today undefended. The "special" procedure is thus no longer special. As Wilson J. noted in *Bhaiji v Chauhan* [2003] 2 F.L.R. 48:

"The continued use of the label . . . well illuminates the time-warp in which the law and practice governing the dissolution of marriage have become caught." (para.5).

The "special procedure" carefully preserved the theory that divorce was a judicial act, since a marriage can only be dissolved by a judicial decree pronounced in open court. But the parties do not have to attend court, and the decision as to whether the grounds for divorce are satisfied is made on the basis of written evidence. As Mr John Diamond, writing in *The Times*, put it: the court sends the forms, "you post them back: that's it". Although practice may to some extent differ from court to court, it seems that the courts do not usually seek to investigate statements made in a petition that is undefended, although the recent case of *Bhaiji v Chauhan* [2003] 2 F.L.R. 48—in which the suspicions of court staff were aroused by a number of identically-worded petitions—shows that this stage of the proceedings is not a mere formality. The forms are scrutinised by a district judge in private, and it is his duty to satisfy himself that the petition and other documents are in order. Once this is done, the pronouncement of the decree *nisi* follows as a matter of course. Six weeks and one day after the decree nisi has been granted, the petitioner may apply for the decree to be made absolute. If the petitioner for some reason fails to apply for the decree absolute, then the respondent may do so after a further three months have passed (MCA s.9). It should be noted that it is not until the decree absolute has been granted that the marriage is legally terminated and the parties free to marry again.

The five facts

4–008 In view of the way in which petitions for divorce are dispatched, the grounds for divorce may seem almost irrelevant. But it is still essential to frame the petition in terms of one of the five facts and lawyers need to have an understanding of the statutory provisions—and the way in which they have been interpreted by the courts—in order to be able to complete the relevant documents correctly. The reader will note that much of the case-law in this area dates from the 1970s, reflecting both the fact that this is when the courts first had occasion to interpret the reforms introduced in the 1969 legislation, and the dearth of defended divorces in the past three decades. While the cases described in the following account are important in that they established how the statutory provisions should be interpreted, judicial pronouncements from this era on the expectations of married couples should be treated with caution, given the profound changes that have occurred in the past few decades.

The five facts from which irretrievable breakdown of a marriage can be inferred are set out in s.1(2) of the Matrimonial Causes Act 1973, and are as follows:

(1) *Adultery*

4–009 To establish the "adultery" fact it is necessary to show "[t]hat the respondent has committed adultery and the petitioner finds it intolerable to live with the respondent" (s.1(2)(a)). This requires two distinct matters to be proved:

(a) The fact of the respondent's adultery

4–010 Adultery involves voluntary or consensual sexual intercourse between a married person and a person (whether married or unmarried) of the opposite sex who is not the other's spouse. (Sexual intercourse with a person of the *same* sex does not constitute adultery in the eyes of the law, although it would almost certain come within the scope of s.1(2)(b), considered below.) It is no longer necessary for the petitioner to identify the adulterer, and a petitioner seeking to rely on this ground may thus simply state in the petition that the respondent has committed adultery.

(b) The petitioner finds it intolerable to live with the respondent

4–011 The policy of the 1969 reforms was that adultery should be relevant only in so far as it was a symptom of marital breakdown. As a result, the legislation added the requirement that the petitioner should find it intolerable to live with the respondent. However, it is not necessary that the petitioner should find the respondent's *adultery* intolerable.

In *Cleary v Cleary and Hutton* [1974] 1 W.L.R. 73, the Court of Appeal held that the "fact" is established if the petitioner genuinely finds it intolerable to live with the respondent, even if the adultery has not played any significant part in the breakdown of the marriage. The legislation does not require the petitioner to allege "that the respondent has committed adultery by reason of which the petitioner finds it intolerable to live with the respondent."

The fact that there need be no link of this kind could lead to apparently bizarre results. In *Roper v Roper* [1972] 1 W.L.R. 1314 at 1317, Faulks J. suggested that a wife might even divorce a husband who had committed a single act of adultery because he blew his nose more than she liked. But this interpretation gives effect to the plain words of the section, and it is consistent with the aim of the legislation that breakdown of marriage should be the sole ground for divorce.

(c) Six months living together a bar

If one spouse knows that the other has committed adultery, but has continued to live **4–012** with him or her thereafter for six months or more, a divorce petition cannot be based on that act of adultery (s.2(1)). Conversely, if they have lived together for less than six months after the adultery, the fact that they have done so is to be disregarded "in determining . . . whether the petitioner finds it intolerable to live with the respondent." The object of this rule was to make it clear that a couple could seek a reconciliation without running the risk that by living together the innocent party would be held to have forgiven the adultery.

(2) *Respondent's behaviour*

Section 1(2)(b) of the Matrimonial Causes Act allows the court to infer breakdown on **4–013** proof of the "fact" that "the respondent has behaved in such a way that the petitioner cannot reasonably be expected to live with him"; and it appears that this is the "fact" most often alleged, particularly in wives' petitions. In many cases the behaviour complained of may be extremely serious—for example domestic violence. (The fact that wives are more likely to petition for divorce than husbands is not necessarily an indication that women are responsible for the breakdown of the marriage.) In other cases the allegations may appear more trivial: for example, in *Livingstone-Stallard v Livingstone-Stallard* [1974] Fam. 47, CA, the court had to consider the parties' methods of washing their underwear, whilst in *Richards v Richards* [1984] F.L.R. 11, HL, it was alleged that the husband never remembered the wife's birthday or wedding anniversary, did not buy her Christmas presents, failed to give her flowers on the birth of their child and failed to notify her parents of the event, refused to take her to the cinema, and refused to dispose of a dog which had caused considerable damage to the matrimonial home.

It should be noted that the question for the judge is not whether such behaviour is unreasonable *per se*, but whether it is unreasonable to expect the petitioner to continue to live with the respondent in the circumstances. The test is objective insofar as the question to be answered is: can the petitioner "reasonably be expected" to live with the respondent? But the court must consider the particular parties to the suit before it: for example, are the parties as bad as each other (see *e.g. Ash v Ash* [1972] Fam. 135), or, alternatively, is one party particularly sensitive to the other's behaviour (see *e.g. Birch v Birch* [1992] 1 F.L.R 564)? The Court of Appeal (*O'Neill v O'Neill* [1975] 1 W.L.R. 1118) has favoured an approach which puts the issue in terms of a direction to a jury:

"Would any right-thinking person come to the conclusion that this husband has behaved in such a way that his wife cannot reasonably be expected to live with him, taking into account the whole of the circumstances and the characters and personalities of the parties?" The test is, therefore, what could reasonably be expected of these parties; but the determination of what is "reasonable" in this context obviously requires the making of value judgements about the nature of marriage and about the obligations and standards of behaviour implicit in the marriage contract. Acceptable standards of behaviour vary over time: it is hard to imagine a modern court endorsing the suggestion in *Ash v Ash* [1972] Fam. 135 that a violent spouse could be expected to live with one equally violent, especially given the evidence that female violence is generally not equivalent to male violence (see further para.6–001).

The fact that the test focuses on what is to be expected of the petitioner, rather than the culpability of the respondent, means that this ground may be satisfied even where the behaviour in question is attributable to mental or physical illness. But the cases provide no clear answer to the question of principle: what is it reasonable to expect one spouse to tolerate? In *Thurlow v Thurlow* [1976] Fam. 32, where a husband was granted a decree against his epileptic and bed-ridden wife, it was said that the court would take full account of the obligations of married life, including "the normal duty to accept and share the burdens imposed upon the family as a result of the mental or physical ill-health of one member". But in practice the fact that the health of the petitioner or that of the family as a whole is likely to suffer from continued cohabitation is a powerful factor influencing the court in favour of granting a decree.

Can the respondent say that the fact that the petitioner has gone on living in the same household proves that the petitioner can reasonably be expected to live with him? The Act contains a provision (s.2(3)) which is intended to facilitate reconciliation by enabling the parties to live together for a short period without losing the right to seek divorce if the attempt is unsuccessful. In deciding whether the petitioner can reasonably be expected to live with the respondent, the court must disregard cohabitation for periods of up to six months after the final incident alleged. Longer periods do not constitute an absolute bar, but the longer the period the more likely it is that the court will draw the inference that the petitioner could reasonably be expected to put up with the respondent's behaviour. But the petitioner is entitled to attempt to refute any such inference that they can reasonably be expected to live together, and in *Bradley v Bradley* [1973] 1 W.L.R. 1291 (where the wife was still living in a four-bedroom council house with the husband and seven children), the Court of Appeal held that she should be allowed to prove that it would be unreasonable to expect her to go on living there.

(3) Desertion

4–014 Desertion is one of the traditional matrimonial offences, and, unlike the other matrimonial offences of adultery and cruelty, survived the 1969 reforms unaltered. It is, however, unnecessary to consider the earlier case-law on this topic in any detail, encrusted as it is with the preoccupations of previous generations of judges. Today, the availability of other options means that very few petitions are based on desertion. In brief, the main elements of desertion are: (1) the fact of separation; and (2) the intention to desert. The necessary factual separation can be established even if the couple remains under the same roof, although if there is still any sharing (however minimal) of a common life—for example, sharing a common living room, or taking meals together—the parties are not deemed to have separated:

In *Le Brocq v Le Brocq* [1964] 1 W.L.R. 1085, the wife excluded her husband from the matrimonial bedroom by putting a bolt on the inside of the door. There was no avoidable communication between them, but the wife continued to cook the husband's meals, and he paid her a weekly sum for housekeeping. Because of this, he failed to establish desertion: there was, as Harman L.J. put it, "separation of bedrooms, separation of hearts, separation of speaking: but one household was carried on . . . "

To establish the intention to desert what is required is an intention (usually of course inferred from the words and conduct of the spouse alleged to be in desertion) to bring the matrimonial union permanently to an end. A separation will not amount to desertion if the petitioner has consented to it, or if there is good cause for the separation—for example where the party who left was ill-treated by the other—or if the respondent lacks the mental capacity necessary to form the intention to desert.

The desertion must have lasted for a continuous period of two years immediately preceding the presentation of the petition. Thus if the spouse returns before the filing of the petition, no decree can be granted even if he or she has been absent for more than two years. However, brief reunions do not affect the ability of a spouse to petition on this ground: periods up to an aggregate of six months will be disregarded in determining whether the period was continuous, although the time spent together will not count towards the two year period.

(4) *Living apart*

The fourth and fifth facts from which breakdown may be inferred both involve the **4–015** parties living apart for a specified period of time. Section 1(2)(d) requires proof that the parties have lived apart for a continuous period of at least two years immediately preceding the presentation of the petition and that the respondent consents to a decree being granted. Section 1(2)(e) merely requires proof that the parties have lived apart for a continuous period of at least five years immediately preceding the presentation of the petition. These provisions were conceptually revolutionary. They effectively permitted what the divorce law had for more than a century refused, in the first case, divorce by consent and in the second the divorce of a spouse who is innocent of any matrimonial offence. It was claimed during the debates on the 1969 Divorce Reform Act that the latter would amount to a "Casanova's charter". When the Act came into force, five years' separation was the second most popular ground for divorce—which in itself suggested that the Act was being used to terminate marriages that had long ceased to exist in fact rather than generating a new sense of irresponsibility. In fact, neither of the separation grounds has been as popular as the architects of the 1969 reform predicted, although the past few years has seen a slight increase in the number of petitions based on the fact of two years' separation (34 per cent in 2004, in contrast to 24 per cent in 1991), or on five years' separation (although still less than 10 per cent in 2004). Most petitioners continue to allege adultery or "behaviour", perhaps because this offers a quicker route to divorce.

It is important to be aware of the similarities and differences between s.1(2)(d) and (e). The same definition of living apart applies to each, and in each case some additional protection is afforded to the respondent by virtue of s.10(2). In the case of a petition based on five years' separation, however, there is an extra defence that may in certain limited situations lead to a divorce being refused. These will be considered in turn:

(a) The meaning of "living apart"

4–016 The statute provides that a couple shall be treated as living apart "unless they are living with each other in the same household." (s.2(6)). The courts have held that "living apart" involves both physical and mental elements. So far as physical separation is concerned, the courts adapted the old law of desertion and held that what is in issue is separation from a state of affairs rather than from a place. The question to be asked is whether there is any community of life between the parties. If, therefore, the husband and wife share the same living room, eat at the same table, or perhaps watch television together, they are still to be regarded as living in the same household. The fact that the couple do so "from the wholly admirable motive of caring properly for their children" is immaterial (*Mouncer v Mouncer* [1972] 1 W.L.R. 321). As David Lodge put it in his 1996 novel *Therapy*: "Apparently the British divorce courts are very strict on laundry . . . If she knowingly washed his socks it could screw up his petition, he says." (Penguin, 1996, at 166).

So far as the mental element is concerned, the Court of Appeal in *Santos v Santos* [1972] Fam. 247 held that living apart could only start for the purposes of this "fact" when one party recognises that the marriage is at an end—that is to say, when the spouses are, in common parlance, "separated", rather than simply living apart by force of circumstances. But (rather bizarrely) the court also held that it was not necessary for the one spouse to communicate the belief that the marriage was at an end to the other. The *Santos* decision was based on the assumption that consensual divorces based on separation require close judicial scrutiny, but this reasoning has been completely undermined by the adoption of the so-called special procedure: (see para.4–007 above). It is true that the procedural rules require a petitioner to state on oath "the date when and the circumstances in which you came to the conclusion that the marriage was in fact at an end" (Form M7(e) of the FPR 1991); and the district judge will need to be satisfied that the documentation has been correctly completed. But it is only in exceptional cases that there will be an opportunity for any probing of that evidence to take place; and accordingly in practice the only result of the *Santos* decision seems to be to complicate the law. No doubt petitioners who do not have access to legal advice may not realise the importance of stating that they had come to the conclusion that the marriage was over more than two or five years ago, and occasionally a petitioner will have to pay the penalty for innocently telling the truth.

(b) Protection for the respondent

4–017 Under s.10(2) the respondent may apply to the court after the granting of a decree *nisi* for consideration of his or her financial position after the divorce. In such a case the court must not make the decree absolute unless it is satisfied that the financial arrangements are "reasonable and fair" or "the best that can be made in the circumstances". This provision was originally enacted when the court had less extensive financial powers than it now enjoys, and for that reason is today rarely invoked. But it may still be applied in certain circumstances (see *e.g. Garcia v Garcia* [1992] 1 F.L.R. 256, CA). In essence this provision enables the court to make sure that everything has been properly dealt with before the marriage is finally terminated.

(c) The "grave hardship" defence

4–018 Section 5 provides that the court may dismiss a petition founded solely on five years' separation if two distinct conditions are satisfied: first, that dissolution will result in "grave financial or other hardship to the respondent" and, secondly "that it would in all the circumstances be wrong to dissolve the marriage". This defence (although far narrower than some supporters of the 1969 reforms led people to believe) is of some importance, since it occasionally prevents the dissolution of a marriage which has irretrievably broken down. In addition, the threat of invoking the defence may be a powerful weapon in negotiating the terms of the financial settlement to be made following divorce. It may be difficult to establish the necessary elements of the defence:

(i) The hardship must result from the divorce, not from the breakdown: The respondent **4–019** must prove that his or her position as a divorced spouse is worse than it would be as a separated spouse. This is difficult to do. It is, for example, true that many divorced people suffer serious financial problems; but the court has wide powers to make financial orders on divorce, and any problems usually stem from the fact that there is insufficient money to keep two households, rather than from the legal termination of the marriage. Most cases under this section concern the loss of pensions that would be payable to a spouse or widow (see *e.g. Le Marchant v Le Marchant* [1977] 1 W.L.R. 559), but the court now has greater powers to reallocate pensions on divorce (see para.8–011).

(ii) "Grave financial hardship": The word "grave" has its ordinary meaning of "impor- **4–020** tant or very serious". It is not sufficient to show that a spouse will lose something, and a spouse is not entitled to be compensated pound for pound for everything that he or she will lose in consequence of the divorce.

In *Reiterbund v Reiterbund* [1975] Fam. 99, CA, a 52-year-old divorceé would lose her entitlement to the state widows' pension if her 54-year-old ex-husband died before she reached the age of 60. But the risk of him dying in the next eight years was not great, and even if he did she would receive exactly the same income under the supplementary benefit system as under the state widow's pension scheme. The court refused to withhold a divorce.

At the other end of the financial scale:

In *Archer v Archer* [1999] 1 F.L.R. 327, CA, a 55-year-old consultant orthopaedic surgeon had a large income but few substantial capital assets. His 54-year-old wife claimed that she would suffer grave hardship because if (as was statistically probable) he pre-deceased her, the £18,000 maintenance order against him would come to an end, since periodical payments only endure for the life of the payer (see para.8–009, below). But the wife had her own investments amounting to nearly £300,000 and she owned a house worth more than £200,000. The Court of Appeal agreed that the loss of the maintenance payments could not, in the circumstances, be regarded as "grave" hardship.

(iii) Hardship other than financial hardship: Although it is, in theory, open to a **4–021** respondent to establish non-financial hardship, there has been no reported case in which such a defence has succeeded. In particular, the courts have taken a robust approach to pleas based on religious belief. It is not enough for the respondent to show that divorce is contrary to his or her religion and that divorce will cause unhappiness and a sense of shame; there must be evidence of some specific hardship flowing from the divorce:

> In *Banik v Banik* [1973] 1 W.L.R. 860 a Hindu wife's pleadings that she would be ostracised if divorced were held to establish a *prima facie* case of grave hardship. However, the evidence was eventually held not to substantiate her claim and a decree was granted: *Banik v Banik (No.2)* (1973) 117 S.J. 874.

4–022   (iv) 'Wrong in all the circumstances'': If, but only if, the court is satisfied that grave financial or other hardship would be caused by a divorce, will it proceed to the next stage, and consider whether it would "in all the circumstances" be wrong to dissolve the marriage. This involves the court in balancing the hardship against the policy embodied in the modern divorce law, which, as Finer J. put it in *Reiterbund v Reiterbund* [1974] 1 W.L.R. 788 at 798, "aims, in all other than exceptional circumstances, to crush the empty shells of dead marriages". There seem to have been few cases in which a decree has been refused; but *Julian v Julian* (1972) 116 S.J. 763, is one such:

> The husband was 61 and the wife 58. Neither was in good health. The wife was receiving periodical payments from the husband. If the husband predeceased her these payments would cease and she would in addition lose her right to a police widow's pension, leaving her with only a very small total income. The decision that it would be wrong to grant a divorce and thus (as the law then stood) deprive her of the pension was largely based on the belief that it was not particularly hard on the husband to deprive him of the chance to remarry.

Appraisal of the 1969 reforms

4–023   The 1969 reform certainly achieved its objective of allowing the "empty legal shells" of many marriages that had irretrievably broken down to be crushed. In its first year of operation (1971) nearly 30,000 petitions were based on the ground that the parties had lived apart for five years, and it is reasonable to suppose that many of these were cases in which the respondent had refused to divorce the other. Marriage had ceased to be legally indissoluble. But the Act has been much less successful in its other declared objectives.

(1) *Failing to buttress marriages*

4–024   There is now a concern that saveable marriages are being terminated by divorce. The last Conservative government, when advancing proposals for reform, expressed the opinion that some divorce petitions "represent a "cry for help" which may not reflect a seriously thought out decision to end the marriage."

(2) *Failing to minimise bitterness, distress and humiliation*

4–025   Proponents of the 1969 reforms assumed that couples would choose to petition on the "civilised" ground of separation for two years where both were agreed on divorce. This belief was soon proved false. In fact, around two-thirds of all divorce petitions are still based on adultery or "behaviour". In 1988 the Law Commission concluded that the necessity of making allegations in a divorce petition "drew the battle-lines" at the outset and that the hostility engendered in this way made the divorce process painful not only for the parties but also for the children. The incidents relied on in the petition may be (as the Law Commission put it in 1990) exaggerated, one-sided or even untrue, and those who believed themselves denied any realistic possibility of putting the record straight might well suffer what has been described as a burning sense of injustice.

(3) *The gap between theory and practice*

There are a number of ways in which the theory of the divorce law differs from **4–026** practice. First, as noted above, while the "irretrievable breakdown" of the marriage is the sole ground for divorce, the circumstances capable of establishing breakdown are limited. The fact alleged may have no connection with the reason for the breakdown of the marriage. Secondly, the introduction of the special procedure has meant that most allegations are not investigated. Thirdly, while fault is relevant to the process of obtaining a divorce, it has very little significance in the resolution of questions concerning care of the children and allocation of property. The Law Commission's allegation that couples found the law confusing was, however, somewhat undermined by its suggestion that couples were colluding to obtain divorces more quickly on one of the "fault" grounds—an indication that some couples understood the system all too well.

D: REFORM?

Such concerns led the Law Commission to consider the current law and put forward **4–027** proposals for reform *(The Ground for Divorce* (1990) Law Com. No.192). It suggested that irretrievable breakdown should remain the sole ground for divorce, but that such breakdown should be ascertained by more objective criteria. This was to be achieved by removing the current "facts" from which breakdown is inferred but making divorce a longer process, during which the parties would reflect on whether the marriage had indeed broken down.

The Conservative Government, after an extensive further consultation process, accepted the main thrust of the Law Commission's proposals for "divorce after a period for the consideration of future arrangements and for reflection". The Family Law Bill containing these reforms did not have an easy passage through Parliament. The idea of "no-fault" divorce was controversial, and many concessions had to be made to groups whose ideology was very different from that which had influenced the drafting of the Bill. The Bill eventually passed into law as the Family Law Act 1996 but implementation of the main provisions was delayed in order that pilot schemes might be carried out to test the effectiveness of the new procedures. The results of these schemes did not satisfy the Labour government—which had, when in opposition, supported the Bill—and on January 16, 2001 it was announced that the main provisions of the Act would not be implemented after all.

Thus the scheme established by the 1969 Act, for all its deficiencies, remains the law. While it is unnecessary to have a detailed knowledge of the Family Law Act 1996, the reasons for the rejection of the scheme shed light on the current government's policy towards divorce. It is also necessary to consider those parts of the Family Law Act that *have* been implemented. The following paragraphs accordingly sketch out the framework of the 1996 Act (for a more detailed discussion see the fourth edition of this work), the parts of it that are in force, and the reasons why the key provisions were not brought into force.

The scheme of the Family Law Act 1996

4–028 The scheme of the 1996 Act was far more complex than the original scheme proposed by the Law Commission. In brief, it would have required a person contemplating divorce to attend an information meeting, either alone, or with his or her spouse. Three months later, he or she would be able to file a statement that the marriage had broken down. There then would follow a period for reflection and consideration. The standard period would be nine months but this would be extended automatically if the couple had children under the age of 16 and in addition either party would be able to apply for an extension. However, the period would not be extended if there was an occupation order or non-molestation order in force in favour of the child (on which see Ch.6), or if delay would be detrimental to the welfare of any child. After this period either party would be able to apply for a divorce, although the divorce would not be granted if the parties had not made arrangements for the future.

The parts of the Family Law Act that are in force

4–029 Certain parts of the 1996 Act—the provisions asserting the general principles to be kept in mind by those carrying out functions under the new divorce law (Pt I), and making provision for marriage support and governing public funding for mediation (Pt III)—were brought into force on March 21, 1997.

(1) *The general principles*

4–030 In a departure from the normal form of legislation, s.1 set out the principles that were to inform the application of the Act, which indicate the conflicting ideals to which the Act gave expression:

> "The court and any person, in exercising functions under or in consequence of Pts II and III of the Act . . . shall have regard to the following general principles:
>
> (a) that the institution of marriage is to be supported;
> (b) that the parties to a marriage which may have broken down are to be encouraged to take all practicable steps, whether by marriage counselling or otherwise, to save the marriage;
> (c) that a marriage which has irretrievably broken down and is being brought to an end should be brought to an end:
>
>> (i) with minimum distress to the parties and to the children affected;
>> (ii) with questions dealt with in a manner designed to promote as good a continuing relationship between the parties and any children affected as is possible in the circumstances; and
>> (iii) without costs being unreasonably incurred in connection with the procedures to be followed in bringing it to an end; and
>
> (d) that any risk to one of the parties to a marriage, and to any children, of violence from the other party should, so far as reasonably practicable, be removed or diminished."

It would be difficult to argue with the hope that marriages will not break down or with the desire that any divorces can be managed amicably (and cheaply). One might, however, question how far the law is able to facilitate such aims. Moreover, this section now stands somewhat isolated, since it has no application to the way in which the courts interpret the current law. It does apply to Pt III of the Act, to which we shall now turn.

(2) *Marriage support*

Marriage support has been defined as "activity aimed at helping people to establish **4–031** and maintain successful relationships with their partners" and mainly takes the form of counselling for couples or individuals whose marriage is in difficulty (*The Funding of Marriage Support*, Report by Sir Graham Hart, 1999, para.10). Traditionally these services have been provided by voluntary agencies—notably Relate, formerly the National Marriage Guidance Council. Public funding was first provided as long ago as 1947 but the level of support was always uncertain and unpredictable and seemed generally to be given on a severely restricted basis. Sir Graham Hart's 1999 Report recommended that the Lord Chancellor's Department should play a more active role in these matters, and that government should substantially increase the level of funding and also provide leadership on policy matters.

Section 22(1) sought to put funding for marriage support on a more secure basis. It conferred an express statutory power to make grants in connection with: (a) the provision of marriage support services; (b) research into the causes of marital breakdown; and (c) research into ways of preventing marital breakdown. However, Government departments appear to be playing pass-the-parcel with the issue of marriage support: responsibility passed from the Home Office to the Lord Chancellor's Department and then to the Department for Education and Skills. The nature of the support being offered has also changed: the remit of the Advisory Group on Marriage and Relationship Support, established in 2002, included support for non-marital relationships, and in 2004, under the auspices of the DfES, the Marriage and Relationship Support Grant was subsumed within the "Strengthening Families Grant Programme". Section 22 does not appear to have had a long-lasting effect.

(3) *Mediation*

Marriage support is intended to save marriages: it is hoped that the parties will not go **4–032** through with the divorce they had contemplated. Mediation has a different objective: it is concerned to help divorcing couples negotiate their own arrangements for the consequences of breakdown—particularly in relation to the arrangements to be made about children's upbringing and about financial matters. It was hoped that mediation would play a major part in the reformed process under the Family Law Act and that couples would use the period for "reflection and consideration" to make arrangements for the future once they had decided that their marriage could not be saved. To this end provisions were included for the court to draw the parties' attention to the possibility of mediation. More significantly, under s.29 of the Act, a person seeking legal aid in matrimonial proceedings would have to attend a meeting with a mediator to determine whether mediation is suitable to deal with the issues arising.

While mediation may have been central to the Family Law Act, it was not dependent on the Act's implementation and is promoted by the Legal Services Commission as an alternative to litigation. Section 29 itself was repealed by the Access to Justice Act 1999 but remains part of the Legal Services Commission's funding code.

The reasons for the non-implementation of Pt II of the Family Law Act

4–033 While the Lord Chancellor did not provide detailed reasons for his decision not to implement the main provisions of the Family Law Act, some clues are provided by the results of the schemes that were set up to pilot the key procedures of Act. Two components of the proposed scheme were tested: information meetings and mediation.

The information meetings were intended to provide general information about the divorce process, and about issues such as marriage support, mediation and legal aid. Six different types of information meetings were tested, with information being provided through individual face-to-face meetings, group presentations or CD-Roms. The 7,863 men and women who attended the meetings found them "generally helpful", but there were few signs that the meetings helped them save their marriages or encouraged them to resolve issues through mediation. Fifty-five per cent of those attending the meetings were already separated (and a subsequent follow-up study found that 65 per cent of the sample had either divorced or were in the process of doing so, while only 19 per cent remained living with their spouse: see *Picking up the Pieces: Marriage and Divorce Two Years After Information Provision* (DCA, 2004)). A number did try counselling or mediation after the meeting (23 per cent and 10 per cent respectively over the subsequent two years), but more consulted a solicitor (73 per cent). Since attendance at these meetings was voluntary those attending were not necessarily typical of the divorcing population, and the results may over-estimate the numbers willing to contemplate mediation or counselling.

Research was also carried out into publicly-funded mediation. Those referred under s.29 of the Act were described as "compliant, but not obviously enthusiastic", and only 30 per cent of such cases were deemed suitable for mediation. In many cases, the other party was not willing to attend. It was also found that even where the parties did reach agreement through mediation, the legal costs were not significantly reduced.

The pilot schemes indicated that the procedures laid down by the Family Law Act would do little to save marriages or money and as such did not fulfil the principles set out in s.1 of the Act.

Where next?

4–034 It is doubtful whether any divorce law could achieve the aims set out in Pt I of the Family Law Act. It is unrealistic to expect divorce to be a civilised process if it takes place against a backdrop of betrayal, domestic violence or child abuse. However civilised the process is in theory, the extent to which it can reduce the acrimony between the parties is questionable.

In contrast to the assumptions about what the *law* could achieve, the debates surrounding the 1996 Act revealed a negative view of *lawyers*. By contrast new developments reveal a more positive view of the role that lawyers play in the divorce process. In March 2001, the Lord Chancellor announced plans to pilot new Family Advice and Information Networks (FAINs). This time, solicitors were to be at the forefront of developments as the persons responsible not only for giving legal advice but also referring clients to mediation, counselling and other services. At the time of writing, pilot schemes had been running for a number of years. The aims of the Family Advice and Information Networks do sound remarkably familiar; they are to:

"facilitate the dissolution of broken relationships in ways which minimise distress to parents and children and which promote ongoing family relationships and co-operative parenting [and] provide tailored information and access to services that may assist in resolving disputes and/or assist those who may wish to consider saving or reconciling their relationship." (Legal Services Commission, *Developing Family Advice and Information Services* (2002), para.2.1)

It is clear from this that some lessons have been learnt from the failure of the Family Law Act—for example that people tend to want specific rather than general information and that as most will consult a lawyer this may as well be built into the scheme. Yet the similarity between the aims of FAINs and the objectives of the "good divorce law" outlined by the Law Commission in the 1960s suggests that for the past forty years or so the question has not been what the law should be trying to achieve, but how it can best achieve it. In this respect FAINs might seem to reflect the triumph of hope over experience.

E: DIVORCE AND RELIGION

As noted above, the fact that the respondent has religious objections to divorce will **4–035** not be sufficient to prevent the legal termination of the marriage. If both parties have religious objections to divorce they may prefer the option of a judicial separation, which, as noted above, is available upon proof of any of the five facts without the need to establish that the marriage has broken down. In common with the divorce *a mensa et thoro* granted by the ecclesiastical courts before 1857 a judicial separation does not end the marriage, but merely allows the parties to live separately (although since cohabitation cannot now be compelled even if the parties have separated without an order, this is of limited significance). More importantly, the court has the same powers to reallocate resources as upon divorce (see Ch.8).

One further issue to be considered is the difference between civil divorce—the subject of this chapter—and religious divorce. A civil divorce is not regarded as effective to dissolve a marriage by certain religious groups. If, for example, a Jewish husband refuses to grant a *get*—a Jewish divorce—the parties remain married under Jewish law even if they are no longer regarded as husband and wife under English law. Section 10A of the Matrimonial Causes Act 1973 (as inserted by the Divorce (Religious Marriages) Act 2002) now allows either party to apply for the divorce not to be made absolute until a declaration is made by both parties that they have taken the necessary steps to dissolve the marriage in accordance with their own religious usages. The result is that a wife can prevent her husband from divorcing her in the eyes of English law but leaving her bound to him according to their own religious law. She cannot, however, force him to grant a religious divorce. The provision is thus of limited scope, and at present applies only to Jewish divorces.

F: DISSOLUTION OF CIVIL PARTNERSHIPS

For same-sex couples, the debate has to date focused on the right to enter into a legally **4–036** recognized relationship. Yet it is inevitable that some civil partnerships will break down, and the question thus arises: in what circumstances can a civil partner seek dissolution of the partnership? The Civil Partnership Act provides that an application for a dissolution order may be made on the basis that the partnership has irretrievably broken down; there are, however, only four facts from which such breakdown may be inferred (s.44(5) of the CPA 2004). Adultery was omitted on the basis that it "has a specific meaning within the context of heterosexual relationships and it would not be possible nor desirable to read this across to same-sex civil partnerships." (Women and Equality Unit, *Response to Civil Partnership: A framework for the legal regulation of same-sex couples* (November 2003), p.35). This does not mean that a civil partner will be unable to apply for dissolution where his or her partner is unfaithful: such infidelity might well be considered to be behaviour of such a kind that the applicant could not reasonably be expected to live with the respondent. In all other respects the law regulating the dissolution of a civil partnersip is identical to that described above: thus there is a bar on any application before one year has elapsed from the formation of the civil partnership (s.41), the facts from which breakdown may be inferred are identical to those listed in s.1(2)(b)–(e) of the MCA 1973 (s.44(5) of the CPA), and dissolution may be refused on the basis of grave financial or other hardship where the application is based on five years' separation. There is even the possibility of a separation order (s.56), which parallels the grant of a judicial separation to spouses, and civil partners will be able to take advantage of the "special procedure" (see the amended Family Proceedings Rules 1991)

G: CONCLUSION

4–037   As this chapter has shown, it has become increasingly easy (at least in legal terms) to obtain a divorce. The grounds are such that virtually any spouse will be able to obtain a divorce sooner or later. However, while divorce brings closure to the status of marriage, to what extent does it end the obligations between the parties? The support functions of marriage may continue after the divorce, as Chs 7 and 8 demonstrate, and a divorced spouse may even claim provision from the estate of the other (see Ch.9). It is these practical consequences of marriage that Part II examines.

PART TWO

FAMILIES—FORMAL AND INFORMAL

INTRODUCTION

Family law and family crises

Part I considered how the formal status of marriage or civil partnership might be acquired and terminated. By contrast, the topics covered in Part II focus on the various crisis points that may arise in such relationships: for example if one party inflicts violence on the other (Ch.6) or refuses to support the other (Ch.7). It also deals with the reallocation of property when the relationship is terminated by divorce or dissolution (Ch.8) or death (Ch.9). The dominance of such crises in family law texts reflects the idea that the law has little role to play in intact families—although it would perhaps be more accurate to say that the law that affects ongoing families (such as housing, social security, and employment law) is not defined as "family law". While there is insufficient space in an introductory text of this kind to do justice to all the laws that affect the family, it is important to recognise that there is this wider framework of laws that regulate, support, and sometimes undermine the family. A brief sketch of some of the laws affecting intact families is provided in Ch.5 (which considers the situation where the family home is threatened by a claim from a third party such as a mortgagee or creditor) and Ch.7 (which highlights the significance of employment and state support in family maintenance). **II–001**

Formal and informal families

A second important aspect of the topics covered in Part II is that many are of relevance to couples who have not formalised their relationship as well as to spouses and civil partners. Over the years there has been a degree of convergence between the legal rights of spouses and of cohabiting couples. Marriage has become more like cohabitation, in that married couples are now increasingly treated as two individuals, rather than as a unit, while cohabiting couples now enjoy certain legal rights that were formerly reserved to married couples. However, in certain situations married couples are still treated as a unit, while cohabitants by no means enjoy all of the rights of married couples. As a result of the Civil Partnership Act 2004, most of the statutory provisions that apply to married couples have been extended to same-sex couples who have entered into a civil partnership, and the statutory provisions that previously applied only to heterosexual cohabitants "living together as husband and wife" have been extended to same-sex couples who are "living together as if they were civil partners." Despite this assimilation, a number of points need to be borne in mind. First, the Civil Partnership Act eschewed the straightforward option of simply stating that all rules applicable to married couples would henceforth be applicable to married couples. While the 2004 Act meticulously applies to civil partners most of the statutory provisions relevant to spouses, it does not deal with the common law. The question **II–002** thus arises as to whether there are any common law rules that will apply only to married couples and not to civil partners. Secondly, there remains a crucial distinction between those couples that have formalised their relationship and those who have not. Thirdly, however, this distinction is sometimes undermined by a further important shift within family law, namely the shift away from formal legal ties and towards parenthood as the key relationship for channelling rights and responsibilities. These points will be considered in turn.

The consequences of marriage

II–003 At common law, husband and wife were deemed to be one person. This meant that they could not, for example, give evidence against one another, sue one another, or be convicted of stealing from one another. This position has now been modified by statute, although some remnants of the doctrine of unity still remain. The law of evidence now makes statutory provision about the competence and compellability of spouses, while citizenship and immigration are dealt with by statute and delegated legislation. Some of the changes to the law are surprisingly recent: it was only in *R v R* [1992] 1 A.C. 599, HL, that it was finally established that a husband could be guilty of raping his wife (see now s.1 of the Sexual Offences Act 1956, as amended by the Criminal Justice and Public Order Act 1994). Earlier authorities had held that, upon marriage, a woman consented to her husband exercising his "marital rights" and could not withdraw that consent.

A second common law doctrine was that by marriage a husband and wife became entitled to each other's "consortium"—in essence, to each other's society, assistance, comfort and protection. Any further definition is difficult: as Lord Reid suggested in *Best v Samuel Fox & Co Ltd* [1952] A.C. 716, "it seems to me rather to be a name for what the husband enjoys by virtue of a bundle of rights, some hardly capable of precise definition." (at 736).

It seems unlikely that these doctrines, rooted as they are in the history of marriage, will be held applicable to civil partnerships. As this discussion shows, the special position of spouses has been largely modified by statute. The question of whether the nebulous rights encompassed by the doctrine of unity and the doctrine of consortium apply to civil partners is unlikely to be of practical importance.

The consequences of formal relationships

II–004 One long-vanished aspect of the doctrine of unity was that, upon marriage, a woman's property vested in her husband. Nineteenth-century feminists and lawyers campaigned against the injustice of this rule, and legislation was eventually passed to ensure that, as a general principle, the wife would retain her separate property upon marriage (Married Women's Property Acts 1870 and 1882). As a result, it became a cardinal principle of English law that marriage had no impact on the property rights of the spouses. This remains true today, with one or two minor exceptions, and is equally true of civil partnerships. Thus, if it becomes necessary to ascertain the ownership of the home during the marriage or civil partnership, the parties will have to rely on the rules of property law, which apply to all persons regardless of their status (at least in theory, see para.5–019, below). Spouses and civil partners have statutory rights to *occupy* the shared home (see para.6–014, below) but no automatic rights to a property interest in it.

The corollary of the rule that the wife's property passed to the husband upon marriage was that a husband had an obligation to support his wife. Statute has now imposed mutual obligations of support upon spouses, as well as upon civil partners, and the ways in which this duty to maintain may be enforced are considered in Ch.7.

In contrast to the separation of property during a marriage or civil partnership, the courts have the power to reallocate property upon divorce or dissolution (Ch.8). Where the relationship ends in death the survivor will in most cases (and subject to the terms of the deceased's will) be entitled to the bulk of the assets (Ch.9). The status of the parties thus has a significant effect on their legal rights and responsibilities.

The rights of cohabitants

As noted above, cohabitants now enjoy at least some of the rights formerly reserved to **II–005** their married counterparts. Yet the law still draws a firm distinction between those who have formalised their relationship and those who have not. The widespread belief that living together for a certain period of times creates a "common law marriage" and confers upon the parties the same rights as if they were married has no truth in it. The myth may in fact have an adverse effect on cohabiting couples if, as a result of a belief that they are protected by the law, they fail to make the necessary arrangements that would secure them protection (for example making contracts, wills, or declarations of trust). It is likely that the mistaken belief in protection is stronger among heterosexual couples than among same-sex cohabitants, since until recently the latter had little reason to believe that the law offered them any protection. Whether this alters as a result of the passage of the 2004 Act remains to be seen.

Even where rights are conferred upon cohabiting couples, such rights tend to be inferior to those granted to married couples in the same situation. A bereaved cohabitant has no automatic right to receive anything from the estate of the deceased, and the terms upon which provision may be claimed are less favourable than those that apply to married couples (see Ch.9). A cohabitant who is a victim of domestic violence may apply to the court for an order excluding the other partner from the home, but the relevant rules make a number of distinctions between married and cohabiting couples (Ch.6). Even the law of property, supposedly blind to the status of the parties, may make distinctions between married and cohabiting couples (as illustrated by the importance attached to the fact that the parties were married in *Midland Bank v Cooke* [1995] 2 F.L.R. 915, CA, para.5–015 below). The only context in which cohabitants are assured parity is in the context of means-tested welfare benefits—in that the assets of cohabiting couples are aggregated in the same way as those of married couples, to ensure that the former do not obtain any advantage over the latter.

While the European Convention on Human Rights has provided a justification for the elimination of discrimination against same-sex couples, it has not been seen as justifying the elimination of differences between those who have formalized their relationship and those who have not. Thus:

In *R. v Pearce* [2001] EWCA Crim 2834, a man convicted of murdering his brother appealed on the basis that his cohabitant of 19 years had been compelled to give evidence, which would not have been possible had they been married. He submitted that a marriage certificate should not be the touchstone of compellability in 2001, and that his rights under Art.8 had been infringed. The Court of Appeal dismissed his appeal on the basis that the interference with his Art.8 rights had been necessary for the prevention of crime. Any exceptions relating to the compellability of witnesses should be as narrow as possible.

More broadly, the European Court of Human Rights has accepted that the protection of the "traditional family" is in principle a legitimate aim: see *e.g. Karner v Austria* [2003] 2 F.L.R. 623. It seems unlikely, therefore, that a cohabitant would be able to claim the same rights as a spouse or civil partner on the basis of discrimination.

The significance of parenthood

II–006   The importance of parenthood, as opposed to the legal relationship between the parents, will become more obvious in Part III, but the presence of children will have an important impact on the rights and responsibilities of the adults within the family as well. The presence of children may be relevant in determining the occupation of the family home (see Chs 5 and 6), and the obligation to support one's children arises regardless of the relationship between the parents (see Ch.7). Children are the "first consideration" for the courts in deciding how the assets of the spouses should be divided upon divorce (Ch.8). They figure less heavily in Ch.9, which is concerned with the division of assets upon death—largely because of the assumption that the children of the deceased will be adults and no longer in need of support.

The structure of Part II

II–007   Chapter 5 looks at the ways in which individuals may acquire interests in the family home or other family assets. Ownership of property is also relevant to Chapter 6, which looks at domestic violence, since the right to exclude a violent person from the family home may depend on the property rights of the victim. Ownership of assets may also affect the ability of the victim to leave the relationship. Chapter 7 considers the different sources of maintenance for intact and broken families: the state, in the form of benefits, one's own earnings, and maintenance from a parent or former partner. The final two chapters examine how property is divided when a relationship comes to an end either by divorce or dissolution (Ch.8), or by death (Ch.9).

Chapter 5

OWNERSHIP OF FAMILY ASSETS

A: INTRODUCTION

The title of this chapter may be somewhat misleading, in that the ownership of "family **5–001** assets" is, in principle, governed by strict principles of property law, which take little account of the fact that such assets may have been purchased for the common use of the parties. In *Pettitt v Pettitt* [1970] A.C. 777, HL, Lord Upjohn opined that "the expression "family assets" is devoid of legal meaning and its use can define no legal rights or obligations."

Nor is this merely a terminological issue. One frequent criticism of the law in this area is the fact that it does not reflect the reality of modern family life. The way in which a couple organise their financial affairs—perhaps one partner paying the mortgage, one paying bills and other household outgoings—may determine who owns what, even if neither of the parties were aware of the significance of their actions.

The majority of this chapter will focus on the family home, since this is usually the most significant single asset of the parties, as well as providing shelter for the family. In addition, more complicated questions arise in relation to the family home than in relation to other assets. Most owner-occupiers purchase their home with the assistance of money lent by a bank or building society, the home being acquired providing the security for the debt. The asset-value of the home—or "equity"—is the difference between the amount borrowed and the current market value of the property. A house purchased for £200,000 with a 90 per cent mortgage begins with a loan of £180,000 and £20,000 equity. If the market value of the house increases by 50 per cent in three years the equity is increased by the rise in value (to £120,000) and by the amount of the mortgage that has been repaid. Of course, interest normally has to be paid on the money borrowed and many owner-occupiers spend a third or more of their income on mortgage payments. The high cost of mortgage repayments raises a number of issues, not least whether two incomes are required to pay them and the responsibility for making such payments if the relationship breaks down (see further paras 6–006 and 8–009 below). For present purposes, it should be noted that the existence of a mortgage may affect how interests in the home are calculated, and raises the possibility of a claim by the lender to repossession of the property if the family are unable to meet the mortgage repayments. The steep rises in house prices raises further issues: it should, for example, be borne in mind that even a relatively short period may have a significant impact on the financial position of the parties, to the detriment of the party who does not have an interest in the property.

This chapter looks first at how interests in property may be formally created (Part B), and then the ways in which informal equitable interests may arise through statute, the law of trusts or estoppel (Part C). Part D considers the consequences of ownership for the parties themselves in terms of their rights of occupation, and Part E examines how far property interests are protected against third parties such as mortgagees, creditors or trustees in bankruptcy and the likelihood of the family being able to remain in occupation of the home against the wishes of a third party. Other family assets should not be forgotten, and Part F looks at the rules relating to ownership of personal property, such as chattels and bank accounts. First, however, a brief explanation of the relevance of the rules outlined in this chapter:

When is ownership relevant?

5–002 Knowledge of the rules relating to ownership and occupation of the family home is of importance to family lawyers for a number of reasons. First, few special rules apply to the property of married couples or civil partners during the currency of their relationship. Their rights over the family home are determined almost solely by the application of general principles of property law. While the couple are living in harmony it may not seem to matter who owns what, but the issue will become one of crucial importance if there is a dispute with a third party such as a mortgagee, creditor or trustee in bankruptcy. In such a case it will be important to ascertain what proportion of the home is owned by the bankrupt, for example, in order to determine what property will be available to meet his or her debts (and what will be left to the family). In addition, in such cases the value of the home as an asset is in conflict with its role of providing shelter: the court may need to decide whether the home should be sold, in order to realise its value, or whether the family should be allowed to remain in occupation. Ownership of the family home will also need to be established when one of the parties dies, to determine the value of the estate.

Furthermore, if the relationship between the adult members breaks down, the question arises as to who should remain in residence and who should leave. The court has an extensive statutory discretion to reallocate the resources of spouses or civil partners upon divorce or dissolution, irrespective of the strict property rights of the parties (see Ch.8). By contrast, there is no equivalent statutory regime to reallocate the assets of unmarried couples when they separate. Thus for cohabitants, and indeed for relatives who share or contribute to the purchase of a home, it is the rules of property law that govern the division of property at the end of the relationship, as well as if there is a dispute with a third party. There are two exceptions to this: first, the courts have a discretionary power to order the transfer of certain tenancies between cohabitants under the Family Law Act 1996 (considered in Ch.8); secondly, there is the possibility of an order in favour of a child of the parties under s.15 of the Children Act 1989 (considered in Ch.7).

Many of the cases involving the determination of entitlement to the house and other property are therefore concerned with unmarried couples. But since every relationship must end in either separation or death, property law will, at some point or another, be relevant to every family.

B: FORMAL REQUIREMENTS

The formalities required depend on the nature of the transaction: **5–003**

(1) Transfer of legal title

The purchase of a property normally occurs in two stages. First, the parties enter into **5–004**
a contract for the purchase. Section 2 of the Law of Property (Miscellaneous Provisions) Act 1989 requires such a contract to be made in writing and signed by the parties. Once such a contract has been made the parties are bound to go ahead with the transaction, which is completed when the legal title is conveyed to the purchaser and registered with the Land Registry. Section 52 of the Law of Property Act 1925 provides that a deed is necessary to convey or create any legal estate in land. The significance of this for present purposes is that if the conveyance of the family home was taken in the name of one partner it follows (in the absence of any subsequent conveyance) that the other can make no claim to be entitled to the legal estate.

Ownership of the legal estate is important in a number of respects. The legal owner is entitled to deal with the legal estate and can, for example, sell it or create a legal charge over the property without needing to seek the permission of any other person, even if the property is the family home. But it is in many ways the beneficial owner of the property who is the *real* owner, since it is the beneficial owner who is entitled to the proceeds of sale if the property is sold (or, if there is more than one beneficial owner, to share in the proceeds proportionate to their interests in the property). The legal owner may also be the beneficial owner of the property, but it is also possible that he or she is holding the property on trust for one or more beneficiaries.

(2) Declaration of trust

If two persons buy a house together, it is often the case that the house will be registered **5–005**
in their joint names. However, the mere fact that the *legal* title to a property is in the joint names of the parties does not necessarily mean that the *beneficial* title will be jointly owned. In *Goodman v Carlton* [2002] EWCA Civ 545 Ward L.J. made an impassioned plea for conveyancers to take steps to ascertain how their clients wish to share the beneficial interest and ensure that this is formally recorded:

> "I ask in despair how often this court has to remind conveyancers that they would save their clients a great deal of later difficulty if only they would sit the purchasers down, explain the difference between a joint tenancy and a tenancy in common, ascertain what they want and then expressly declare in the conveyance or transfer how the beneficial interest is to be held because that will be conclusive and save all argument. When are conveyancers going to do this as a matter of invariable standard practice? This court has urged that time after time. Perhaps conveyancers do not read the law reports. I will try one more time. ALWAYS TRY TO AGREE ON AND THEN RECORD HOW THE BENEFICIAL INTEREST IS TO BE HELD. It is not very difficult." (para.44)

The difference between a joint tenancy and a tenancy in common is that, in the former, a joint tenant does not own a distinct share in the property, while tenants in common *do* own distinct shares in the property. If the property is sold, each joint tenant is entitled to the proceeds of sale in equal shares, while tenants in common are entitled to shares reflecting their respective interests in the property, which may be either equal or unequal. Since 1997, if two or more persons are registered as joint owners, they must complete a declaration as to their beneficial interests in the property (Land Registration Rules 1997). The standard transfer form requires them to state whether they are joint tenants, tenants in common in equal shares or whether they hold the property on other trusts (for example, for themselves in unequal shares or for other persons who have contributed to the purchase). This is sufficient evidence of a trust and is conclusive as to the shares of the parties in the absence of fraud or mistake (*Goodman v Gallant* [1986] 1 F.L.R. 513, CA). This reform is likely to have an important impact on disputes over ownership in the future. Yet the courts still deal with many cases where the property was acquired before 1997, as indeed was the case in *Goodman v Carlton*. And other less explicit declarations in the transfer may not have the same effect:

> In *Huntingford v Hobbs* [1993] 1 F.L.R. 736 the transfer contained a declaration by the purchasers that the survivor of them would be entitled to give a valid receipt for capital money. For present purposes the precise meaning of that phrase is unimportant: the key point is that such a declaration was consistent with the right of survivorship inherent in a joint tenancy. However, the Court of Appeal held that it was also consistent with other arrangements and so did not constitute an express declaration of trust.

The same decision was reached in *Stack v Dowden* [2005] EWCA Civ 857, a result that made sense in the light of the (hardly surprising) fact that the couple had not understood the effect of the declaration.

Moreover, the practice instigated in 1997 has no application where the property was acquired in the name of only one person. In such a situation the legal owner may still choose to declare a trust in favour of another person or persons. The trust need not be in a set form, but must, if it relates to land, be evidenced in writing: s.53(1)(b) of the Law of Property Act 1925. Thus:

> In *Gissing v Gissing* [1971] A.C. 886, HL, the matrimonial home had been conveyed into the husband's sole name. When the marriage broke up he told his wife: "Don't worry about the house—it's yours. I will pay the mortgage payments and all other outgoings." That statement by itself gave the wife no enforceable rights: there was no deed that could displace the legal estate, and no written document to satisfy the requirements of s.53(1)(b).

In addition, it is not possible to dispose of an equitable interest except by a written disposition (s.53(1)(c) of the LPA).

(3) *Contract*

5–006 The parties may choose to set out their respective rights in the family assets in a contract. A contract that involves the transfer or other disposition of an interest in land must be made in writing according to s.2 of the Law of Property (Miscellaneous Provisions) Act 1989.

While contracts purporting to regulate the division of assets on divorce or dissolution are not binding on the courts (as to which see further para.8–004), there is no objection to a formal contract regulating the ownership of the home during the relationship. Rather different considerations arise in relation to contracts between cohabiting couples. In the past it has been suggested that a contract between cohabitants—even if drawn up in accordance with the requirements of contract law—might be struck down as contrary to public policy on the basis that to uphold such a contract would be to undermine marriage. In *Sutton v Mishcon de Reya* [2003] EWHC 3166 (Ch), however, Hart J. drew a distinction between a contract for sexual relations outside marriage and a contract entered into by a cohabiting couple to deal with financial matters. The former would be void, while the latter—assuming that the general requirements of the law of contract had been met—would be valid (see further para.8–003). Indeed, the government's current *Living Together* campaign is actively encouraging cohabiting couples to enter into contracts, which suggests confidence that such contracts would be upheld by the courts in case of dispute.

(4) *Exempted transactions*

The fact that couples are entitled to declare trusts or enter into contracts does not **5–007** mean that they will, and many do not. What happens if there is no formal declaration regarding the beneficial ownership of the property? Under s.53(2) of the Law of Property Act 1925, the formal requirements imposed by s.53(1) do not affect the "creation or operation of resulting, implied or constructive trusts". In addition, the legal owner may be estopped from denying the other's beneficial interest in the property. These transactions are exempted from the formal requirements outlined above. Since couples often do not make formal arrangements regarding their property—especially where one partner moves into a house owned by the other—these doctrines have provided an important means of acquiring an interest in the property, and will now be considered.

C: INFORMAL METHODS OF ACQUIRING AN INTEREST

There has, over the years, been considerable difference of judicial opinion about the **5–008** circumstances in which the court will find that a person has acquired an interest in property despite the lack of any formal arrangements. Various different methods have been used in the attempt to do justice between the parties: trusts, estoppel, and even contractual licences (see *e.g. Tanner v Tanner* [1975] 1 W.L.R. 1341, CA). This section will focus on the ways in which it is possible to acquire a proprietary interest, but this hardly reduces the scope for disagreement, since the division of opinion—among both judges and academics—as to the circumstances that will give rise to a trust or estoppel has been considerable. At one time it was thought by some that the court could impose a trust whenever it would be "inequitable" for the legal estate owner to keep the property for himself alone (*Heseltine v Heseltine* [1971] 1 W.L.R. 342 at 346, CA), and that the court could impose a trust whenever justice and good conscience required (*Hussey v Palmer* [1972] 1 W.L.R. 1286, CA). But as a result of a series of decisions, culminating in the decision of the House of Lords in *Lloyds Bank v Rosset* [1991] 1 A.C. 107, HL, it is clear that the jurisdiction is in fact much more restricted. Unfortunately, notwithstanding the apparent clarification made by the House of Lords in *Rosset* there remains considerable uncertainty in the law. Peter Gibson L.J. commented in *Drake v Whipp* [1996] 1 F.L.R. 826, CA "as is notorious, it is not easy to reconcile every judicial utterance in this well-travelled area of law." This should be borne in mind when reading the following summary of the law.

Resulting trust

5–009 If one partner provides all or part of the purchase price for a family home that has been conveyed into the name of the other, there is a presumption that the former will be entitled to a share in the property proportionate to the amount of his or her contribution. If, therefore, one partner pays £100,000, and the other pays £300,000 of a total purchase price of £400,000, the first will in principle be entitled in equity to a one-quarter interest in the property under a resulting trust. However, since making a contribution to the purchase price only raises a *presumption* of resulting trust, it is possible to rebut it with appropriate evidence. Thus if there is evidence that the contribution was intended as a gift or a loan, the presumption of resulting trust will be rebutted (see *e.g. Sekhon v Alissa* [1989] 2 F.L.R. 94).

Traditionally, a contribution from a husband to his wife, a fiancé to his fiancée or a father to his child was presumed to be a gift—the so-called presumption of advancement. The presumption of a resulting trust was supplanted in such cases. Just as the presumption of resulting trust could be rebutted by evidence of intention to make a gift, the presumption of advancement could be rebutted by evidence that there was no intention to make a gift. Today this presumption is rarely applied, as there is often evidence that a gift was not intended (see *e.g. Ali v Khan* [2002] EWCA Civ 974, CA). It is also recognised that the strength of the presumption is weakened because it reflects the assumptions of a by-gone era—there is no presumption of advancement in the case of a contribution from a wife to her husband, a fiancée to her fiancé, or even a mother to her child. However, one situation in which the presumptions may be relevant is where property has been transferred into the name of one person for some improper reason, for example, to keep it out of the divorce proceedings in which one of the parties is involved, or so that one party may continue to be eligible for means-tested state benefits. If the relationship between the parties subsequently breaks down, and the person whose name does not appear on the legal title wishes to claim an interest in the property, the starting presumption assumes new importance. If the presumption of resulting trust applies, the claimant can establish his or her entitlement to an interest in the property without needing to explain why the property was transferred into the name of the other party alone (see *e.g. Lowson v Coombes* [1999] 1 F.L.R. 799). By contrast, if the presumption of advancement applies, the husband, father or fiancé must provide evidence that there was no intention to make a gift—which will inevitably expose the illegal purpose underlying the transaction. Understandably, the court will not uphold a claim to an interest in property based on an illegality of this kind. As a result, the success of a claim depends not on the nature of the illegal purpose but on the identity of the claimant. The distinction seems bizarre and the courts have sought to escape from such arbitrary results by refining the doctrine so that, for example, evidence of the illegal purpose can be adduced as long as it was not carried into effect (see *Tribe v Tribe* [1996] Ch. 107, CA). In 1999 the Law Commission published a consultation paper (*Effect of Illegality on Contracts and Trusts*, Law Com No.154), proposing that courts should have a "structured discretion" whether to enforce arrangements that had an illegal element. A further report is expected in 2006.

Now that spouses have mutual obligations to support one another and parents have equal obligations to support their children, the sex-specific nature of the presumption—which has no application to civil partners—looks decidedly dated. In

2005 the Family Law (Property and Maintenance) Bill, sought to abolish the presumption in relation to married or engaged couples, but failed to secure a second reading, as is all too often the fate of private members' bills.

The idea of the resulting trust was developed long before the practice of purchasing a property with the assistance of mortgage finance emerged (see *e.g. Dyer v Dyer* (1788) 2 Cox Eq. Cas. 92; 30 E.R. 42), and the extent to which payments subsequent to the purchase can give rise to a resulting trust is a moot point. In *Curley v Parkes* [2004] EWCA Civ 1515 the Court of Appeal reiterated the orthodox rule that "a resulting trust crystallises on the date that the property is acquired" (*per* Peter Gibson LJ at para.18). This meant that mortgage repayments would not give rise to a resulting trust (although assuming liability for the mortgage would, since the mortgagor is deemed to have contributed the amount of the sum borrowed to the purchase price). On the same basis the judge dismissed the argument that the payment of the removal costs or the solicitors' fees and expenses could give rise to a resulting trust.

Such contributions could potentially give rise to a constructive trust, which will now be considered.

Common intention constructive trusts

The constructive trust has many manifestations, and this chapter is concerned only **5–010** with the "common intention" constructive trust. It is important to emphasise this, as this type of constructive trust is based on the actual or imputed intentions of the parties regarding their beneficial interests, rather than being imposed irrespective of the intentions of the parties (although in some of the cases that follow the distinction may seem to be more apparent than real). In order to establish a constructive trust it must first be established that the parties have a common intention to share the beneficial interest in the property, and, secondly, that the claimant has relied upon that common intention to his or her detriment.

(1) *Establishing a common intention to share the beneficial interest*

There are two situations in which the court may find a common intention: in the first **5–011** situation such intention is expressed, while in the second it is inferred from the parties' conduct.

(a) Discussions leading to agreement or understanding

In *Lloyds Bank v Rosset* [1991] A.C. 107 Lord Bridge of Harwich said that the first and **5–012** fundamental question which must always be resolved is whether there have "at any time prior to the acquisition of the disputed property, or exceptionally at some later date, been discussions between the parties leading to any agreement, arrangement or understanding reached between them that the property is to be shared beneficially".

In some (exceptional) cases, there may be clear evidence that the parties had made an agreement about beneficial entitlement:

> For example, in *Barclays Bank v Khaira* [1993] 1 F.L.R. 343, a husband and wife signed a Land Registry form, in the presence of a witness, which purported to transfer their house to the wife. Although the document was stamped, it was never presented to the Land Registry for registration and was thus ineffective to transfer the legal estate to the wife. However, the trial judge held that the transfer form was "the best evidence a court could reasonably expect of an express

domestic arrangement as to the sharing of a beneficial interest", which was capable of being effective to give the wife an equitable interest in the property.

But in most of the cases that have come before the courts the matter has been much less clear-cut. The courts have sometimes found on rather slight evidence that there was an understanding between the parties. For example, excuses as to why the claimant was not on the legal title to the property have been construed as acknowledgements that the claimant was to have an equitable interest in the property.

> In *H v M (Property: Beneficial Interest)* [1992] 2 F.L.R. 229, Ch D, a second-hand car dealer told his cohabitant, a former Bunny Girl, that the house would have to be in his name for "tax reasons" and that when they were married she would have half. The judge was satisfied that the discussions established the existence of mutual expectations that the beneficial interest was to be shared equally.

The discussions must also make it clear that the other person is to have an interest in the property, not just a right to live there.

> In *Mollo v Mollo* (1999) EGCS 117, Ch D, a mother purchased a house for her adult sons to occupy, informing them that title was to remain in her name since they were not sufficiently responsible. The court held that the common intention that the property was to provide accommodation for the sons was a long way from a common intention that they were to own it beneficially.

One final point should be noted. Although the claimant is required to show evidence of a common intention to share the beneficial interest, the fact that the legal owner subsequently denies any such intention does not prevent the court from finding that there was in fact such a shared intention at an earlier stage. If the issue is disputed it is a matter for the judge to decide whose evidence is more convincing. Thus in *Cox v Jones* [2004] EWHC 1486 (Ch) Mann J. preferred the claimant's evidence that there had been discussions about the ownership of the property in dispute, suggesting that it would be natural for there to be conversations about joint ownership in the context of the relationship, which was one with "with long-term commitments potentially close at hand" (para.67). It may be "natural", but there are many couples who never get round to discussing the issue of ownership. How can a common intention be established in a case of this kind?

(b) Drawing inferences from conduct

5–013   In the absence of evidence of such an understanding or arrangement, the court will consider whether an intention to share the beneficial interest can be inferred from the conduct of the parties. In *Lloyds Bank v Rosset* [1991] A.C. 107, HL, Lord Bridge (with whom the other Law Lords agreed) stated that it was "at least extremely doubtful" whether anything short of a direct contribution to the purchase price by the partner who was not the legal owner (whether initially or by payment of mortgage instalments) could justify the drawing of the inference of a common intention to share the property beneficially.

It should be noted that Lord Bridge prefaced his remarks on the necessity of a direct contribution with the comment "as I understand the authorities". In fact, earlier authorities suggested that an indirect contribution *could* be sufficient to raise the inference of a common intention where it could be referred to the purchase price, *e.g.* where the legal owner could not otherwise have paid the mortgage (see *e.g. Gissing v Gissing* [1971] A.C. 886, HL, and *Burns v Burns* [1984] F.L.R. 216, CA). This idea was taken up in *Le Foe v Le Foe* [2001] 2 F.L.R. 97, Fam Div. The judge, Nicholas Mostyn Q.C., held that Mrs Le Foe had an interest as a result of her indirect contributions: "the family economy depended for its function on W's earnings. It was an arbitrary allocation of responsibility that H paid the mortgage, service charge and outgoings, while W paid for day-to-day domestic expenditure" (at 973). This more realistic approach to family expenditure is to be preferred both as a matter of authority and as a matter of policy.

Even if indirect financial contributions are taken into account, it seems highly unlikely that the courts will be willing to go further and infer a common intention from non-financial contributions.

> In *Lloyds Bank v Rosset* [1991] A.C. 107, HL, the wife had carried out and supervised renovation works on a property intended as the family home. She had some skill "over and above that acquired by most housewives. She was a skilled painter and decorator who enjoyed wallpapering and decorating . . . " She co-ordinated building work, planned and designed a large breakfast room and small kitchen and papered two bedrooms. Although the judge at first instance thought this was sufficient to justify his drawing the inference that she should have a beneficial interest in the property under a constructive trust, her claim was decisively rejected by the House of Lords. The work which she had done "could not [asserted Lord Bridge] possibly justify" the drawing of such an inference. Indeed Lord Bridge said: "it was common ground that Mrs Rosset was extremely anxious that the new matrimonial home should be ready for occupation before Christmas . . . in those circumstances it would seem "the most natural thing in the world for any wife, in the absence of her husband abroad, to spend all the time she could spare and to employ any skills she might have, such as the ability to decorate a room, in doing all she could to accelerate progress of the work quite irrespective of any expectation she might have of enjoying a beneficial interest in the property."

Lest it be thought that only women's work is vulnerable to being belittled by judges, the case of *Thomas v Fuller-Brown* [1988] 1 F.L.R. 237, CA, should be noted:

> In this case an unemployed builder did extensive work on his partner's property—building a two-storey extension and installing a new staircase, amongst other tasks—but the judge held that he was no more than "a licensee doing the odd job here and there . . . a kept man provided by [the plaintiff] with board and lodging" (at 246). He acquired no interest in the property.

It should be borne in mind that even a direct contribution does not *guarantee* a share in the property. The issue is rather whether the contribution constitutes evidence of the parties' intentions at the time of the purchase: *Re Gorman* [1990] 2 F.L.R. 184 at 291, *per* Vinelott J. There may be circumstances in which a direct contribution may be more appropriately viewed as rent—for example where a number of friends are sharing a property—rather than as a contribution to the purchase price (see *e.g. Savage v*

Dunningham [1974] 1 Ch 181. More dramatically, in *Lightfoot v Lightfoot-Brown* [2005] EWCA Civ 201 the ex-husband's payment of £65,000 earned him no share in the former matrimonial home:

> In this case the parties had divorced and Mr Lightfoot had transferred his share in the property to his former wife. However, he remained living there in the hope of a reconciliation (ultimately dashed when his ex-wife learned of his affair with the nanny). The judge held that paying the mortgage instalments—amounting to £24,000—was explicable on the basis that they were "partly a substitute for the maintenance payments due under the consent order and partly as an acknowledgment that Mr Lightfoot was continuing to live in a house that was no longer his." The further payment of £41,000 was more difficult to explain, but the judge suggested that it was probably paid because Mr Lightfoot expected to remarry his ex-wife and regain his share of the property. In the absence of any evidence that she had promised this, and in the light of the fact that she did not even know of the payment, no constructive trust arose. The Court of Appeal dismissed Mr Lightfoot's appeal on the basis that the judge had considered both types of common intention constructive trust and had decided that no common intention could be inferred from the evidence.

It seems likely that the ex-wife's ignorance of the payment of £41,000 was the clinching factor: it is one thing to infer a common intention when the parties have failed to discuss the contributions each has made, it is quite another to infer such an intention when one party is not even aware that such a contribution has been made.

(2) *The requirement of detrimental reliance*

5–014 As pointed out above, in addition to showing the necessary intention, the court must examine the subsequent course of dealing between the parties to ascertain whether the claimant has relied on the common intention to his or her detriment. Detriment, according to Baron J. in *G v G (Matrimonial Property: Rights of Extended Family)* [2005] EWHC 1560 (Admin), must "hurt". As Lord Bridge emphasised in *Lloyds Bank v Rosset,* the detriment must be of some real weight and significance. In that case, the wife's work in redecorating the house was insufficient on the basis that the monetary value of the wife's contribution to the purchase of a comparatively expensive house "must have been so trifling as to be almost *de minimis."* Detrimental reliance need not be related to the acquisition of the property, but it must consist of something that the person claiming an interest would not have done but for the expectation of an interest in the property.

It is for this reason that the making of financial contributions is in practice so important. Such contributions may constitute evidence from which the parties' common intention can be inferred, and they will also usually establish that the claimant has acted to his or her detriment in reliance on that common intention.

Making indirect financial contributions—such as paying bills or other household expenses—is also sufficient to establish detrimental reliance on an express agreement or understanding, but the relevance of non-financial contributions is rather less certain. Unpaid work in a partner's business was held to constitute detrimental reliance in *H v M (Property: Beneficial Interest)* [1992] 2 F.L.R. 229, Ch D. It is interesting to note that the court referred to the female partner's contribution as mother, helper and unpaid assistant—the implication being that she did work that would normally be remunerated, in addition to domestic work that would not normally be remunerated. Similarly, in *Cox v Jones* [2004] EWHC 1486 (Ch) Mann J. held that Miss Cox's assistance in refurbishing the property was of value because "she was doing something that either Mr Jones would have had to have done himself (but which he had insufficient time to do) or it would have had to have been done by a professional (who would have charged for it)" (para.73). There is an assumption that work that would not normally be remunerated is performed solely out of love and affection and not in the expectation of an interest in the property (although one might argue that that Mann J.'s words in *Cox v Jones* would apply equally to everyday domestic tasks such as cooking and cleaning). The courts have not tended to regard everyday domestic work as sufficient to establish detrimental reliance. The wife's decorating work in *Lloyds Bank v Rosset* [1991] A.C. 107, HL, was considered to be nothing out of the ordinary. By contrast, in *Eves v Eves* [1975] 1 W.L.R. 1338, CA, a claim by an ex-cohabitant succeeded because her work was perceived as being something out of the ordinary. As Brightman J. stated, "I find it difficult to suppose that she would have been wielding the 14lb sledgehammer, breaking up the large area of concrete . . . except in pursuance of some express or implied agreement." In this case the claimant's work was clearly perceived as being more than "ordinary" domestic work.

It has been argued that the rules discriminate against women, in that the legal title to the property is more likely to be vested in the male partner, and because the female partner's income is more likely to be used to pay household bills than the mortgage. These criticisms no longer have the force they once did, since there has been a substantial increase in the number of mortgages taken out by women alone and, at least among cohabiting couples, men are now more likely to move into a house owned by a woman than *vice versa*. Nor are women's earnings generally regarded as a second income to be used for "extras": the cost of houses now often requires two incomes to obtain and service the mortgage, and if a couple are buying a house together it is likely that both names will be on the legal title. However, it remains true that women who adopt the "traditional" role of home-maker will find it difficult to obtain an interest in the property unless they are expressly—and formally—promised a share. Moreover, the law can be subjected to the more general criticism that it does not recognise the realities of family life.

(3) *Quantifying beneficial interests*

Further problems arise when the issue of quantifying the beneficial interests of the **5–015** parties falls to be decided. If the parties have specified the shares that each is to enjoy during their discussions about beneficial ownership, the task of the court is relatively straightforward, although in *Clough v Killey* (1996) 72 P. & C.R. D22, CA, the court suggested that it could depart from the terms of an informal agreement if there was a good reason to do so—for example, where the detriment suffered by the claimant was disproportionate to the interest promised. But what if no shares were ever specified? Or if the parties' common intention has in fact been inferred from their contributions? And if the only evidence before the court is that one party made a contribution to a property registered in the name of another, how is it to decide whether a resulting trust or constructive trust is appropriate?

Before *Lloyds Bank v Rosset* the answer was that a constructive trust would only be found if there was some positive evidence of express discussions between the parties, and a resulting trust would be appropriate if there had been a direct financial contribution to the purchase price. In *Rosset*, however, Lord Bridge stated that a direct financial contribution could give rise to an inferred common intention and hence a constructive trust. It was thought for some time that this type of constructive trust would operate in the same way as the resulting trust, with the shares of the parties being quantified in line with their contributions. In *Midland Bank v Cooke* [1995] 2 F.L.R. 915, CA a different approach was taken:

> In this case title to the matrimonial home had been taken in the husband's sole name. The trial judge held the wife to be entitled to an interest by way of resulting trust by reason of her financial contribution—her half share of a joint wedding present from her in-laws—to the purchase price. This contribution amounted to 6.47 per cent of the purchase price, which was therefore the extent of her interest in the property. But the Court of Appeal allowed her appeal. Once it had been established that both parties were entitled to *some* beneficial interest, the court was entitled to draw inferences as to the parties' probable common understanding about the ownership of the property, and in doing so the court would undertake a survey of the whole course of dealing between the parties relevant to their ownership and occupation of the property and their sharing of its burdens and advantages. This scrutiny would not be confined to the limited range of acts of direct contribution of the sort needed to found a beneficial interest in the first place. On this basis, the wife was entitled to one half of the sale proceeds.

Subsequent cases have endorsed the view that the parties' shares are not to be quantified strictly according to their financial contributions, although the precise approach adopted has differed. In *Oxley v Hiscock* [2004] EWCA Civ 546, for example, Chadwick L.J. stated that:

> "It must now be accepted (at least in this court and below) the answer is that each is entitled to that share which the court considers fair having regard to the whole course of dealing between them in relation to the property." (para.69)

He was clear, however, that this was distinct from the approach adopted in *Cooke*, which required the court to make inferences about the intentions of the parties:

> "It seems to me artificial—and an unnecessary fiction—to attribute to the parties a common intention that the extent of their respective beneficial interests in the property should be fixed as from the time of the acquisition, in circumstances in which all the evidence points to the conclusion that, at the time of the acquisition, they had given no thought to the matter." (para.71)

Slightly less artificial, he suggested, was the reasoning in *Gissing v Gissing* [1971] A.C. 886, HL, that the common intention of the parties was that their shares would be determined at a later date on the basis of what was then fair in the light of the whole course of dealing between the parties. His preference, however, was to

> "accept that there is no difference in outcome, in cases of this nature, whether the true analysis lies in constructive trust or proprietary estoppel." (para.71)

It is hard to quibble with the aspiration that the court should award the claimant a "fair" share, but individual perceptions of fairness may differ widely (contrast for example the courts' rather different interpretation of what is "fair" in the context of divorce settlements in Ch.8). In *Oxley v Hiscock* Chadwick L.J. went on to suggest that equal shares would not be fair, as such a result would "give insufficient weight to the fact that [Mr Hiscock's] direct contribution to the purchase price (£60,700) was substantially greater than that of Mrs Oxley (£36,300)" (para.74). Adding to this the pooling of their resources during the relationship, which justified the inference that they had made equal contributions to the balance of the purchase price (£30,000), he held that the appropriate shares were 60 per cent to Mr Hiscock and 40 per cent to Mrs Oxley. The more mathematically inclined reader will quickly appreciate that Mr Hiscock's financial contribution actually amounted to 59.6 per cent of the purchase price. Similarly, in *Stack v Dowden* [2005] EWCA Civ 857 the Court of Appeal again held that it was not fair for the shares of the parties to be equal in view of the female partner's greater contribution—although in this case the 65 per cent share awarded was rather lower than would have been justified by a strict arithmetical division. This should not, however, be seen as an indication of judicial discrimination: Miss Dowden had claimed no more than 65 per cent. And in *Supperstone v Hurst* [2005] EWHC 1309 the fact that the wife who had contributed the majority of the purchase price was awarded only a 50 per cent share was due to the fact that this is what she had claimed in discussions with her husband's creditors: fairness to the creditors, rather than to the couple, influenced the decision.

These decisions would appear to be a move away from the broad-brush approach established in *Midland Bank v Cooke*—in which the evidence that the parties had been married for twenty years and brought up children together was held to be relevant in inferring their likely intentions—to a stricter contribution-based approach. Certainly the judges in *Oxley v Hiscock* and *Stack v Dowden* gave no indication as to what other factors were deemed relevant in deciding what was "fair". Despite the analogy Chadwick L.J. drew with estoppel, it seems as if the true analogy is the resulting trust: the quantification methods of the resulting trust have crept in under the rhetoric of "fairness". It remains to be seen whether the House of Lords—soon to hear the appeal in *Stack v Dowden* [2005] EWCA Civ 857—will endorse this approach.

One final point should be made. When the court in *Oxley v Hiscock* referred to the need for the division to be "fair", it is important to bear in mind that the court's ability even to consider what division would be fair only arises once the necessary elements of a constructive trust have been established. A comparison of the results in *Burns v Burns* [1984] F.L.R. 216, CA and *Midland Bank v Cooke* illustrates just how arbitrary the rules are. Why should a woman who—as in *Burns v Burns*—had given up 19 years of her life to the care of a man and their two children emerge with nothing, while another (in identical circumstances save that her partner's parents had made them a gift which was used as part of the deposit on a house) becomes entitled to half? If the whole course of dealing between the parties is relevant in determining what shares the parties are to have in the property, why is it not relevant in imputing an intention to share the property in the first place?

Proprietary estoppel

Does the doctrine of proprietary estoppel offer a fairer solution? The basic idea is that **5–016** a person will be prevented from relying upon his or her legal rights—or "estopped"—if this would be unconscionable in the circumstances. Rights may arise by way of estoppel where a promise of an interest in property has been made, the promisee relies on it to his or her detriment, and it would be unconscionable to allow the promisor to go back on the promise. This has obvious parallels with the constructive trust: indeed, in *Lloyds Bank v Rosset* [1991] A.C. 107, HL, Lord Bridge suggested that an agreement followed by detrimental reliance could give rise to either a constructive trust or to an estoppel. However, the scope of estoppel is wider than that of the constructive trust, and this section will focus on the differences between the two.

(1) *Establishing estoppel*

5–017 First, there is less emphasis on the common intention of the parties. An agreement may be sufficient to establish an estoppel, but it is not necessary. An estoppel may be founded on a mistake: for example, where the claimant has made some mistake as to his or her legal rights that the legal owner has encouraged or not corrected. In this case there is no common intention, but there is still a tacit representation by the legal owner. However, as the case of *Lissimore v Downing* [2003] 2 F.L.R. 308 shows, promises that lack specificity will not be sufficient:

> Mr Downing, a founder member of the rock band "Judas Priest", had purchased a large country estate. For eight years he lived there with Miss Lissimore, a pharmacist's assistant earning a modest wage. After the relationship came to an end she claimed an interest in the property. Mr Downing had apparently told her that she was to be "Lady of the Manor" and "did not need to worry her pretty little head about money". If these sound like textbook examples of statements unlikely to attract legal consequences this is unsurprising, given that Mr Downing had consulted his solicitor as to how to avoid a claim by a cohabitant. In this he succeeded. The judge held that it was not the case that "any representations, however vague and unspecific, as to the representor's future intentions, can be used to subject his property generally... to a form of constructive trust or equitable obligation arising under a proprietary estoppel." (para.17)

Once the claimant has established a representation or some encouragement by the owner, the onus shifts to the other party to prove that the claimant did not rely upon it:

> In *Campbell v Griffin* [2001] EWCA Civ 990, Mr Campbell had been promised "a home for life" by the elderly couple with whom he lodged. As they became increasingly frail he cared for them, out of "friendship and a sense of responsibility" as he admitted to the court. The court held that it did not matter if the claimant had mixed motives as long as he was influenced by the promise, and that on the facts he had relied on the assurance to his detriment.

As the above case shows, domestic contributions may be taken into account in determining whether the claimant has relied to his or her detriment on the owner's representation. In addition, the benefit to the owner will be taken into account:

> In *Gillett v Holt* [2000] 2 F.L.R. 266, CA, Mr Gillett had worked for Mr Holt since he was a schoolboy and the latter had promised to leave him the bulk of his estate in his will. The court found that Mr Gillett had acted to his detriment in

reliance on this assurance, subordinating his wishes to those of Mr Holt, depriving himself of the opportunity to better himself in other ways and spending money on the farmhouse where he lived. Robert Walker L.J. stressed that "detriment" was "not a narrow or technical concept. The detriment need not consist of the expenditure of money or other quantifiable financial detriment, so long as it is something beneficial. The requirement must be approached as part of a broad inquiry as to whether repudiation of an assurance is or is not unconscionable in all the circumstances." (at 232).

In that case Robert Walker L.J. also emphasised that the elements of representation, reliance and detriment are all intertwined and that "the fundamental principle that equity is concerned to prevent unconscionable conduct permeates all the elements of the doctrine. In the end the court must look at the matter in the round." Despite such suggestions of flexibility and justice, proprietary estoppel is subject to many of the same limitations as the common intention constructive trust. Thus in *Lissimore v Downing*, even if Mr Downing's representations had been sufficiently precise, her claim would have failed as the court held that she had suffered no detriment:

> In this case Miss Lissimore had first reduced her working hours and then given up her job as a pharmacist's assistant, with Mr Downing's encouragement. The judge held that this did not constitute a detriment, since she did so without reluctance and "there was no sense in which she was giving up a career." (para.36)

(2) *The remedy*

The major difference between the constructive trust and proprietary estoppel relates to **5–018** the remedies that can be awarded by the court. A constructive trust is, by its very nature, an interest in the property. Estoppel, on the other hand, gives rise to an equity that can be satisfied in whatever way seems appropriate—"the minimum equity to do justice"—which may be anything from the transfer of the entire legal and beneficial estate to absolutely nothing. For example:

> In *Pascoe v Turner* [1979] 1 W.L.R. 431, CA, the defendant and his former housekeeper had lived as husband and wife for many years. He then formed another relationship, and told the defendant that the house and its contents were hers. In reliance on that statement the plaintiff made substantial improvements to the house and bought furnishings for it, using for these purposes a large proportion of her small capital. While the defendant's statement was ineffective to transfer the property to her, as the appropriate formalities had not been observed, the fact that she had relied upon it, and he had encouraged her actions, gave rise to an equitable estoppel. In the circumstances—in particular his ruthlessness in later trying to evict her from the property—this estoppel could only be satisfied by transferring the legal estate in the property to her.

By contrast:

> In *Sledmore v Dalby* (1996) 72 P. & C.R. 196, CA, Mr Sledmore promised his daughter and son-in-law that he would give them the house in which they were living, legal title to which was vested in him and his wife. In reliance on this, Mr

Dalby made some improvements to the property. After the deaths of Mr Sled-more and Mrs Dalby, Mrs Sledmore sought possession of the property. The Court of Appeal held that the equity raised by the original promise and Mr Dalby's work on the property had been satisfied by his occupation of the property, rent-free, for the past 18 years. Since Mrs Sledmore's need for accommodation was greater, she was entitled to possession of the property.

It has been established that the equity raised by an estoppel is itself a proprietary interest (s.116 of the Land Registration Act 2002) but the remedy awarded by the court need not be. It is this remedial flexibility that has proved particularly useful to the court in balancing the interests of the parties. In recent cases the courts have stressed that the remedy awarded should be proportionate to the expectation and the detriment suffered:

> In *Jennings v Rice* [2002] EWCA Civ 159, CA, Mr Jennings had worked for Mrs Royle since 1970. From the 1980s she had ceased to pay him but promised him that it would all be his "one day". He had continued to work for her until her death, even sleeping on a sofa in the living room after a burglary to provide her with some security. Her will made no provision for him, but left the property to, *inter alia*, Mr Rice. The estate was valued at £1.285m, with the house and contents being valued at £420,000. It was held that this was "out of all proportion" to what he might have charged for his services. He was awarded £200,000, which reflected the cost of full-time nursing care. Aldous L.J. noted: "if the conscience of the court is involved, it would be odd that the amount of the award should be set rigidly at the sum expected by the claimant."

Given the increase in house prices noted at the start of this chapter, a "proportionate" interest might never amount to the entire property.

Choosing between estoppel and trusts

5–019   Proprietary estoppel and the common intention constructive trust are both concerned to provide relief against unconscionable conduct, and share many other character-istics. It has accordingly been suggested that further developments in the law might be possible through applying the principles of proprietary estoppel (see *e.g.* Sir N. Browne-Wilkinson in *Grant v Edwards and Edwards* [1986] Ch. 638 at 656, CA), or even that the application of the two doctrines produces the same outcome anyway (see *e.g.* Chadwick L.J. in *Stack v Dowden*), although there is no consensus to this effect (contrast *e.g. Hyett v Stanley* [2003] EWCA Civ 942).

Given that a constructive trust and an estoppel may arise on similar evidence, but lead to different results, how are the two to be distinguished? It is perhaps significant that the cases cited in this section largely involve lodgers, relatives and ex-employees, whereas the constructive trust cases are more likely to involve a couple, whether married or unmarried. Although property law purports to be blind to the status of the parties, the evidence would suggest that the greater flexibility of estoppel is preferred—on grounds of policy—where the dispute does not involve spouses or cohabitants.

Similarly, it is difficult to see any distinction between the circumstances that may give rise to a constructive trust and those that give rise to a resulting trust: both may arise out of a direct financial contribution by the claimant even where there were no discussions about the ownership of the property. The distinction between the two may cease to be of any significance if the courts continue to quantify shares under a constructive trust according to the financial contributions of the parties.

Improvements to the property

Ownership of family property—as opposed to its reallocation at the end of a formal **5–020** relationship—is for the most part unregulated by statute. One exception is the rule that improvements to the family home by a spouse, civil partner, fiancé(e), or a person who has agreed to enter into a civil partnership will confer a share (or enlarged share) in that property. (Had the male cohabitant in *Thomas v Fuller-Brown* [1988] 1 F.L.R. 237, see para.5–013 above, been able to substantiate his claim that he was engaged to the woman whose home he had improved, the outcome of the case would have been very different.) The statutory provisions relevant to these different categories are scattered through various pieces of legislation: for spouses the relevant provision is s.37 of the Matrimonial Proceedings and Property Act 1970, and for civil partners it is s.65 of the Civil Partnership Act. The applicability of the rule to engaged couples is a matter of inference: the Law Reform (Miscellaneous Provisions) Act 1970 applies the legal rules governing the rights of husbands and wives in relation to property to the determination of beneficial interests in property acquired during the currency of an engagement. Since few special rules apply to spouses, this provision is of limited scope. The Act does not give the parties to an engagement any right to seek financial provision or property adjustment orders under the Matrimonial Causes Act 1973 or otherwise, since those powers are only exercisable on divorce and similar proceedings: *Mossop v Mossop* [1988] 2 F.L.R. 173, CA. But it is clear that the statutory principle embodied in s.37 of the Matrimonial Proceedings and Property Act 1970 could, in appropriate circumstances, apply so as to create a beneficial interest in favour of an engaged person who has made contributions to the improvement of the property. By contrast, s.74 of the Civil Partnership Act states explicitly that s.65 is to apply where a "civil partnership agreement"—the equivalent of an engagement—is terminated.

Whatever the status of the applicant, the rule is the same. Provided that the contribution is substantial, and in money or money's worth, the contributor is, in the absence of contrary agreement, to be treated as acquiring a share (or an enlarged share) in the property. In the absence of agreement, it is for the court to quantify the shares according to what it considers to be just. The provision is clearly of narrow application and has rarely been invoked, since upon divorce or dissolution the court has other powers to take account of the contributions made by spouses and civil partners. If the property rights of the parties fall to be determined in the context of a dispute with a third party, as in the recent case of *Hosking v Michaelides* [2004] All E.R. (D) 147, the provision may be invoked:

> The judge accepted evidence that Mrs Michaelides had contributed £20,000 to the cost of a swimming pool at the property. It was accepted that this was a substantial sum, and that the swimming pool should be considered as an "improvement" despite the question as to whether it had actually increased the value of the property. However, given the absence of evidence that it *had* increased

the value of the property, the judge held that Mrs Michaelides was not entitled to a beneficial interest under s.37.

Eager home-improvers should take note.

D: CONSEQUENCES OF OWNERSHIP

5–021 Once the claimant has established an interest in the property, the next task is to ask what the effect of this will be. One consequence of ownership is a right to occupy the property, and the significance of this in the context of relationship breakdown is considered in the next chapter. Another consequence is the right to a share of the proceeds when the property is sold, such shares being governed by the parties' beneficial interests in the property. But what if the parties cannot agree whether the property is to be sold or retained for occupation by one of them alone? In such a case either party may apply to the court for the dispute to be resolved. Occupation of the home can be dealt with either under Part IV of the Family Law Act 1996, the Civil Partnership Act 2004 or the Trusts of Land and Appointment of Trustees Act 1996. By contrast, it is only under the latter that the court has the power to order sale at the instance of a beneficial co-owner, and the following discussion will focus on its provisions.

Before 1996, the Law of Property Act 1925 would usually impose a *trust for sale* on land beneficially owned by more than one person. This meant that the primary duty of the trustees—the legal owners of the land—was to sell the property. The trust for sale reflected the concerns of an earlier generation of property-owners, in particular the idea that property was an investment rather than a place to live. The effect of this was mitigated by the fact that the same legislation normally gave the trustees a *power to postpone sale*. The courts also developed the idea of a "collateral purpose": when asked to order that the property should be sold, the purpose for which the home had been acquired would be taken into account. For example:

> In *Re Evers' Trust* [1980] 1 W.L.R. 1327, CA, a cohabiting couple bought a new home together for themselves, their child, and the female partner's two children from a previous relationship. When they split up, the male partner applied for the property to be sold. The court held that sale should be postponed until the youngest child reached the age of 16: the property had been purchased as a family home, and the purpose of providing a home for the children and their carer had not been brought to an end by the departure of the male partner (who had a secure home with his mother and did not need to realise his investment).

The Trusts of Land and Appointment of Trustees Act 1996 replaced the artificial trust for sale by a *trust of land;* and under the Act those beneficially interested will usually have a right to occupy the property (s.12). Anyone who has an interest in property subject to a trust of land—which will include anyone with a beneficial interest in that property—may make an application to the court for an order (s.14) and the court may make orders regulating the occupation of the property or its disposal. In deciding what is to happen to the property, the court is directed to consider a number of matters (s.15). These include—the statutory list is not exhaustive—the intentions of the parties who created the trust, the purposes for which the property is held, the welfare of children who occupy (or might reasonably be expected to occupy) the property as a home, the circumstances and wishes of the adults concerned, and the interests of any secured creditor of any beneficiary. This list was influenced by the factors that the courts took into account in deciding cases under the old law, although the Law Commission clearly intended that the welfare of children would be accorded more importance than under the old law (Law Commission, *Transfer of Land: Trusts of Land*, Law Com No 181 (1989), para.12.9). In the light of this, the approach of the Court of Appeal in *W v W (Joinder of Trusts of Land and Children Act Applications)* [2003] EWCA Civ 924 appears misconceived.

> The case involved a dispute between an unmarried couple with two young daughters. The mother left the family home and her request that the property be sold was granted, a decision that was upheld by the Court of Appeal. The reasoning of the court was unsatisfactory in a number of respects. First, although the welfare interests of the children were acknowledged, the court did not accept that the purpose of the trust was to use the property as a family home. According to Arden L.J., "[t]he purpose established at the outset of the trust which, on the judge's finding, did not include the provision of a home for children, could only change if both parties agreed. There was no evidence from which the judge could find that the mother agreed to the additional purpose." (para.24) To insist on a specific agreement between the parties is unrealistic in view of the dynamics of family life. Secondly, the wishes of the father were given scant consideration, despite the fact that he had an equal interest in the property and that the court is directly required to consider the wishes and circumstances of all of the beneficiaries.

In this case it was envisaged that there would be a separate application under the Children Act 1989 to retain the property as a home for the two girls (on the court's jurisdiction in this respect see paras 7–023 *et seq.*). Because of this possibility, the real impact of the reasoning in this case is likely to be in cases involving creditors (as to which see further below). The restrictive interpretation of what constitutes a 'family home' may erode still further the rights of occupants against creditors.

What if the dispute is between two childless adults? Under the old law, sale would be ordered once the relationship had come to an end: the purpose of providing a home for the couple would not survive the end of the relationship (although it would be possible for one party to retain the home by buying the other's share). The same result is likely to be achieved under s.15 of the 1996 Act, although an explicit agreement between the parties may lead to a different outcome. In *Holman v Howes* [2005] All E.R. (D) 169, for example, the court found that the purchaser had explicitly promised his ex-wife that she could occupy the property for as long as she wished, and refused sale.

E: RIGHTS AGAINST THIRD PARTIES

Property law is a complex subject; and there are many important issues that have to **5–022** be resolved beyond the questions of the parties' rights to beneficial interests in, or occupation of, family property. This section summarises the law governing a number of key issues relevant to the family home. First, in what circumstances will the court order a sale of property at the instigation of a third party? This will determine whether the family is able to remain in occupation of the home. Secondly, to what extent will a third party be bound by a beneficial interest? This may affect how much of the equity in the home can be salvaged from the sale, especially if the debts exceed the value of the property. Thirdly, is there any evidence that one of the parties has been unduly pressurised into creating a charge over the property? These questions, in contrast to those considered in Part D, are relevant to intact families seeking to maintain their home against a third party. The key issue to consider is the balance struck by the law between protecting the family home and respecting the economic interests of creditors and mortgages. Ultimately, as will be seen, the fact that a property is used as a family home carries less weight than the financial interests of third parties over the property.

Ordering sale

5–023   A secured creditor (*e.g.* a mortgagee or a person claiming under a charging order) or trustee in bankruptcy may desire the family home to be sold to discharge the owner's debts, and may apply to the court to request a sale. The rules that apply to applications by a trustee in bankruptcy are different from those applicable to applications by a creditor, and will be considered in turn:

(1) *Bankruptcy cases*

5–024   On bankruptcy, all of a debtor's assets vest in a trustee in bankruptcy, who has a duty to realise them for the benefit of the creditors. Where the bankrupt had a beneficial interest in property—for example, as joint tenant or tenant in common of the family home—the trustee will usually apply to the bankruptcy court for an order for sale. The protection afforded to the family home differs according to the status and rights of those occupying it. If the bankrupt jointly owned the beneficial interest, or was solely entitled to the beneficial interest but was married, in a civil partnership, or had children living in the property, then the court is by statute (ss.335A(2), 336(4) and 337(5) of the Insolvency Act 1986) required in such cases to have regard to (as appropriate) the interests of the bankrupt's creditors, to the conduct of the spouse or former spouse "so far as contributing to the bankruptcy", to the needs and financial resources of the spouse or former spouse, to the needs of any children and to all the circumstances of the case. But after one year from the bankruptcy, the court is required (unless the circumstances of the case are "exceptional") to assume that the interests of the bankrupt's creditors outweigh all other considerations (s.336(5)). In practice, the trustee will usually wait for this year to elapse, and the question will therefore be whether the bankrupt can show that the circumstances of the case are sufficiently exceptional to justify *further* postponement of the sale. It is difficult to persuade the court that this is so:

> In *Re Citro (a Bankrupt)* [1991] 1 F.L.R. 71, CA, the bankrupt based his claim to postponement on the welfare of his children and the hardship for them that would result from eviction. But Nourse L.J. refused to accept that hardship to the children could properly be classed as exceptional in an ordinary bankruptcy case: " . . . it is not uncommon for a wife with young children to be faced with eviction in circumstances where the realisation of her beneficial interest will not produce

enough to buy a comparable home in the same neighbourhood, or indeed elsewhere; and, if she has to move elsewhere, there may be problems over schooling and so forth. Such circumstances, while engendering a natural sympathy in all who hear of them, cannot be described as exceptional. They are the melancholy consequences of debt and improvidence with which every civilised society has been familiar." (at 78)

The courts have been willing to find that the illness of the bankrupt's spouse is an exceptional circumstance, although whether this justifies the refusal of sale or merely a delay depends on the nature of the illness. Thus in *Judd v Brown* [1998] 2 F.L.R. 360 sale was refused where the wife was suffering from ovarian cancer, as a relatively short period would allow matters to be resolved either way (*i.e.* either she would die, in which case the property could be sold, or she would recover, in which case there would presumably no longer be exceptional circumstances and the property could be sold). By contrast, the ongoing problems of the wife in *Hosking v Michaelides* [2004] All E.R. (D) 147 justified only a short postponement of sale. In a suitably compelling case, sale may be postponed indefinitely, as in *Claughton v Charalambas* [1999] 1 F.L.R. 740. In this case the wife suffered from chronic ill-health, the house had been specially adapted to her needs, and the creditors would receive nothing from the sale of the property anyway.

The implementation of the Human Rights Act 1998 has not affected this approach, as the courts have tended to adopt the view that the Insolvency Act already carries out the balancing exercise between the individual and the creditors required by Art.8. However, doubts as to the compatibility of the law were expressed in *Barca v Mears* [2004] EWHC 2170 (Ch), and the judge suggested that rather than requiring a bankrupt to show that the "exceptional circumstances" were of an exceptional *kind*—such as illness—it would be possible to adopt an interpretation that included cases "in which the consequences of the bankruptcy are of the usual kind, but exceptionally severe" (para.40). On the facts of the case this slightly more generous interpretation made no difference.

It should also be noted that even the limited protection outlined above does not apply if the bankrupt is the sole owner of the property, has no children residing in the household, and is neither married nor in a civil partnership.

(2) *Creditors*

Again, a distinction must be drawn between homes in sole ownership and those that **5–025** are jointly owned. In the first situation the court has no discretion to refuse sale, even when the property is occupied by young children, as confirmed by *Pickering v Wells* [2002] 2 F.L.R. 798. In the second situation the creditor may apply for sale under s.14 of the Trusts of Land and Appointment of Trustees Act 1996. At first sight the position of a secured creditor seeking sale under s.14 would appear to be weaker than that of a trustee in bankruptcy, since the interests of such a creditor are merely one of a number of factors to be taken into account under s.15 of the 1996 Act (see para.5–021 above). Despite early indications that a more family-friendly approach might be adopted under the 1996 Act (see *Mortgage Corporation v Shaire* [2001] Ch. 743), the interests of creditors have prevailed in the majority of cases, as the courts have both emphasised the importance of creditors' interests and downplayed the importance of the other interests listed in s.15 (see *e.g. Bank of Ireland v Bell* [2001] 2 F.L.R. 809, *Pritchard Englefield (a firm) v Steinberg* [2004] EWHC 1908 (Ch), and

First National Bank v Achampong [2003] EWCA Civ 487). One of the few cases where sale has been refused is *Edwards v Lloyds Bank* [2004] EWHC 1745 (Ch), although it is hard to escape the suspicion that the factor that justified a delay in this case was not the presence of two children in the home, not the fact that the debt had been incurred by the occupant's ex-husband, who had forged his wife's signature on the documentation, but rather the fact that delay would not be prejudicial to the creditors, since the value of the home more than covered the extent of the debt.

The result is that whether the application is brought by a trustee in bankruptcy or by a creditor makes little difference—save that in the former case the family will usually enjoy at least a year's grace before the property has to be sold.

Are third parties bound by informally created rights?

5–026 This section considers how far a purchaser (a term which in this context has a wide definition and includes a mortgagee), will be bound by an interest that has been created informally. It first sets out the basic rules that apply, and then indicates how their application has been reduced where the property is being purchased with the assistance of a mortgage. It should be noted by way of preliminary that even if the beneficial interest is binding on the mortgagee, the court may still decide to order sale under the Trusts of Land and Appointment of Trustees Act 1996 (see *e.g. Bank of Baroda v Dhillon* [1998] 1 F.L.R. 524, CA). Whether or not the interest of the claimant is binding on the mortgagee thus affects only the amount that the claimant will receive on sale, rather than whether or not the property can be sold.

(1) *The basic rules*

5–027 The rules differ according to whether title to the land is registered or unregistered. In unregistered land, an equitable interest under a trust will bind the purchaser of a legal estate in land only if the purchaser has actual or constructive notice thereof. The question is usually whether the purchaser has made such inspections as ought reasonably to have been made (s.199 of the LPA 1925):

> In *Kingsnorth Finance Co. Ltd v Tizard* [1986] 1 W.L.R. 783, Ch D, the finance company was held to be bound by an interest under a constructive trust belonging to the owner's wife, notwithstanding the fact that a surveyor had inspected the property and seen no evidence of occupation by her or any other female. The court held that although the owner had hidden his wife's belongings, his inconsistent statements to the surveyor should have alerted the company to the need for further inquiries.

Similar but not identical rules operate in registered land. Under Sch.3 para.2 of the Land Registration Act 2002, an equitable interest will bind a purchaser if the person who owns the interest was in "actual occupation" at the time of registration. A purchaser will not, however, be bound by an interest (i) which belongs to a person whose occupation would not have been obvious on a reasonably careful inspection of the land at the time of the disposition and (ii) of which the person to whom the disposition is made does not have actual knowledge at the time. This reflects a shift away from treating occupation as a "plain factual situation" connoting simply physical presence (see the earlier case of *Williams and Glyn's Bank v Boland* [1981] A.C. 487, HL) to the idea of *discoverable* occupation.

(2) *Claims by a mortgagee*

The above rules have been modified by a number of decisions that have particular **5–028**
application to disputes with mortgagees. Because of the risk that someone other than
the legal owner might be able to assert an interest in the property, banks, building
societies and other mortgage lenders take precautions. They normally require spouses,
and other adults who are likely to share the occupation of the property, to execute a
document authorising the owner of the legal estate to enter into the transaction—for
example, mortgaging it to raise money for improvements or other purposes—and
giving that transaction priority to their equitable interest. However, the lender or other
purchaser claiming under the document will be at risk of such a waiver being set aside
on the ground on undue influence (see para.5–029 below).

Even in the absence of any such express waiver, the mortgagee may still claim
priority in the vast majority of cases. First, where a mortgage has been taken out to
fund the purchase of the family home, it will take priority over any beneficial interest,
as established by the House of Lords in *Abbey National Building Society v Cann* [1991]
A.C. 56, HL. The same principle applies if a subsequent mortgage is taken out to pay
off the first. Secondly, even if a second mortgage is taken out for other purposes (*i.e.*
the equity in the property has increased by a sufficient amount to enable the parties to
raise a further sum against the security of the house) the court may infer that the
beneficiary has agreed to this, and that his or her beneficial interest is to be postponed
to the second mortgage (see *e.g. Bristol and West Building Society v Henning* [1985] 1
W.L.R. 778, CA). Under this rule the beneficial owner is only bound to the extent that
he or she consented. Thus if the legal owner misrepresents that the mortgage will be
for £10,000 and borrows £20,000, the beneficial owner is only bound by the first
£10,000 of the mortgage. Thirdly, where the legal title is held by two or more persons,
any sale—including a mortgage of the property—will overreach the beneficial interests
in the property (see *City of London BS v Flegg* [1988] A.C. 54, HL, and *Birmingham
Midshires Mortgage Services v Sabherwal* (1999) 80 P. & C.R. 256, CA). This means
that the equitable owner has only a right to a share of the proceeds of sale rather than
an interest in the property—and therefore no interest capable of binding a third
party.

In brief, a beneficial interest will not have priority over a mortgage if the mortgage
was used to acquire the property, or the owner of the beneficial interest knew of the
mortgage, or the mortgage was executed by two or more legal owners.

Protection against undue influence and misrepresentation

As noted above, the fact that anyone who occupies the family home may be required **5–029**
to sign a form consenting to his or her equitable rights being postponed to the interest
of the mortgagee may raise the issue of undue influence. Another possibility—
especially since joint ownership of the home has become common—is that a partner
is asked to join in a mortgage or other transaction necessary to secure credit for the
family's business. English law has no equivalent of the "homestead" legislation that
exists in some other jurisdictions and restricts the use that can be made of the family
home in providing security for business debts. If the consent of one legal owner has
been procured by the other's undue influence, or by a misrepresentation, should the
former be able to avoid liability? In other words, when should the bank or building

society be bound by the interest of the victim of another's undue influence or misrepresentation?

In *Barclays Bank v O'Brien* [1994] 1 A.C. 180, HL, Lord Browne-Wilkinson identified the competing considerations that the court should take into account. First, wives who are subjected to undue influence can reasonably look to the law for some protection when their husbands have abused the trust and confidence reposed in them.

However, sympathy should not obscure the important public interest in ensuring that the wealth tied up in the matrimonial home does not become economically sterile: if banks were unwilling to accept the matrimonial home as security, the flow of loan capital to business enterprises would be reduced.

This is not the place for a comprehensive account of the many reported cases on this issue. The House of Lords reviewed the law in *Royal Bank of Scotland v Etridge (No.2)* [2001] 3 W.L.R. 1021, HL, which involved eight conjoined appeals. In each case the wife was a joint (or the sole) legal owner of the matrimonial home. In each case the home had been used to secure the husband's, or his company's, debts. The first question was whether undue influence had been established. Their Lordships were keen to sweep away some of the terminology that has complicated this area of the law. It was stressed that the burden of proof lay upon the person claiming to have been wronged. Lord Nicholls suggested that proof that the claimant placed trust and confidence in the other, coupled with a transaction that was not explicable upon ordinary motives would be sufficient to raise a presumption of undue influence. Such a presumption was rebuttable: as Lord Scott pointed out, it would make no sense to presume that undue influence had occurred once the judge had found that there was no actual undue influence. However, certain relationships—such as parent–child, doctor–patient—raised a presumption of undue influence as a matter of law. Even within such relationships, not all transactions would be vulnerable to challenge, only those that could not be explained by ordinary motives. This reasoning is less favourable to wives than earlier cases: there is no presumption of undue influence between husband and wife and the willingness of a wife to sign a guarantee will often be explicable by her desire to safeguard the family business.

Once undue influence has been established, the next question is whether the bank has notice of it. A bank is put on inquiry "in every case where the relationship between the surety and the debtor is non-commercial" (*per* Lord Nicholls at 1048). (The following discussion follows *Etridge* in assuming the surety to be a wife but the same approach should be taken in other non-commercial cases.) The bank must satisfy itself that the practical implications of the transaction have been explained to the wife. For past transactions, confirmation from the solicitor that he has explained the risks to the wife will suffice. For the future, banks will be required to communicate directly with the wife to confirm the name of the solicitor whom she wishes to act for her and to explain that it will require confirmation from the solicitor that she has been advised about the effect of the transaction. The solicitor need not be acting for the wife alone but will not be regarded as the bank's agent. This means that the bank will not be imputed to have notice of the advice that the solicitor gives (or fails to give) to the wife. *Etridge* also set out the "core minimum" of the advice that a solicitor should give a wife. There should be a face-to-face meeting, at which the solicitor explains the nature of the legal documents and their practical consequences and the seriousness of the risks involved. He should stress that the wife has a choice as to whether or not to sign the documents, and check whether she wishes to proceed and whether she is content for him to confirm to the bank that she has been advised by him.

Finally, even if the party influenced succeeds in getting the mortgage set aside, this does not guarantee that the family home will be retained. In *Alliance and Leicester v Slayford* [2000] EGCS 113, CA, it was held that "there is no abuse of process in a mortgagee, who has been met with a successful *O'Brien* type defence taken by the wife of the mortgagor, merely choosing to pursue his remedies against the mortgagor by suing on the personal covenant with a view to bankrupting him, even though this may lead to an application by the trustee in bankruptcy for the sale of the property in which the wife has an equitable interest."

F: OWNERSHIP OF PERSONAL PROPERTY

The rules relating to the ownership of personal property are (happily) less complex. In **5–030** part this is due to the nature and value of such property: since chattels, for example, tend to be less expensive than houses, the acquisition of the property in question is not spread over such a long period, and it is less likely to be used as security for debts. Moreover, the relatively low value of much personal property means that it is not worth litigating about ownership.

The basic rule is that money belongs to the person who earns it, and other forms of property belong to the person who pays for them. No formalities are required to create a trust over personal property (see, *e.g. Paul v Constance* [1977] 1 W.L.R. 527, CA, *Rowe v Prance* [1999] 2 F.L.R. 787, Ch D), but delivery or change of possession is necessary to make a gift (see *e.g. Re Cole* [1964] Ch. 175, CA).

The rules relating to the ownership of the money contained in a bank account show a more realistic appreciation of the way in which couples deal with their property than the rules relating to the family home:

> In *Jones v Maynard* [1951] Ch. 572, Ch D, the bank account was in the sole name of the husband, but both spouses paid money into it, and withdrew money from it. It was held that the money in the account was jointly owned. The judge, Vaisey J., expressed his view that "a husband's earnings or salary, when the spouses have a common purse and pool their resources, are earnings made on behalf of both; and the idea that years afterwards the contents of the pool can be dissected by taking an elaborate account as to how much was paid in by the husband or the wife is quite inconsistent with the original fundamental idea of a joint purpose or common pool. In my view the money which goes into the pool becomes joint property."

The limitations of this should, however, be recognised. As with the rules relating to the family home, a claim will succeed as long as there has been some financial contribution by the claimant, regardless of its amount—but the spouse or partner who has no income and cannot contribute to a joint pool is entitled to nothing. The ownership of property bought with money from the joint fund depends on whether it is intended for joint or individual use: if the former, it will be jointly owned, if the latter, it will be owned by the person who bought it.

The status of the parties has no impact on the ownership of property, save in the following situations, which are all of narrow scope:

(1) Housekeeping allowances

5–031 The Married Women's Property Act 1964 was intended to reverse the common law rule under which the husband was entitled to any savings made by his wife out of a housekeeping allowance. The (unsatisfactorily drafted) Act provides that such savings shall, in the absence of contrary agreement, be treated as belonging to husband and wife in equal shares. It seems that the provisions of the 1964 Act are rarely invoked, no doubt in part because the household arrangements that it was intended to cover are less common now that a high proportion of women work outside the home. The sex-specific nature of the provision also means that it falls foul of Art.5 of Protocol 7 of the European Convention on Human Rights, and the fact that it does not apply to civil partners may also lead to claims of discrimination. The Family Law (Property and Maintenance) Bill 2005 proposed that the rule in the 1964 legislation should apply equally to allowances by a wife to a husband, and between civil partners. As the bill's sponsor, Rob Marris MP, noted, this change is necessary to enable the UK to ratify Art.5 of Protocol 7, which the government committed itself to doing in 1997. However, as noted above, the bill failed to secure a second reading.

(2) Gifts between engaged couples

5–032 The Law Reform (Miscellaneous Provisions) Act 1970 makes special provision for gifts between engaged couples. Any gift made to one's fiancé(e) can be recovered after the engagement is terminated if it was given on the condition (express or implied) that it would be returned if the marriage did not take place (s.3(1)). There is a presumption that an engagement ring is an absolute gift, but this presumption can be rebutted by showing that the gift was conditional (s.3(2)). The difficulties that this may pose are illustrated by the recent case of *Cox v Jones* [2004] EWHC 1486 (Ch):

> In this case it was a matter of dispute between the parties as to whether the engagement ring was a conditional gift or not. Mann J. decided the point in favour of Miss Cox on the basis that it was implausible that, in the context of a romantic holiday, Mr Jones would have told her that the ring was a conditional gift.

Since it is difficult to imagine an engagement ring being given in circumstances that are *not* romantic, an ex-fiancé seeking to recover the ring may have a difficult task.

The same rules—minus any reference to rings—apply to same-sex couples who have agreed to contract a civil partnership (s.74(5) of the CPA).

(3) Presumption of advancement

5–033 The presumption of advancement (see para.5–009 above) applies equally to personal property as to real property.

(4) Improvements to personal property

5–034 Section 37 of the Matrimonial Proceedings and Property Act 1970, along with s.65 of the Civil Partnership Act 2004, described above at para.5–020, applies to personal property as well as to real property, although there are no reported cases where a claim to personal property has been based on this section.

G: CONCLUSION

The law described in this chapter is clearly unsatisfactory in a number of respects. In **5–035** theory, ownership of the family home is governed by rules of property law, which make no concessions to the status of the parties involved. In practice, the courts have drawn distinctions between spouses and cohabitants, between couples who organise their financial affairs at arms' length and those who share everything, and between couples and other family members. Family law considerations have crept into property law, resulting in considerable uncertainty. At the same time, the law demands proof of express conversations or direct financial contributions, requirements that do not necessarily fit the way in which families organise their domestic economy. Domestic contributions will be disregarded in determining whether a claimant can establish an interest, but will be taken into account in determining the extent of any interest. And there is considerable artificiality in the way that the law imputes intentions to parties who are unlikely ever to have heard of a trust, whether resulting or constructive. As Carnwath L.J. noted in *Stack v Dowden* [2005] EWCA Civ 857,

> "To the detached observer, the result may seem like a witch's brew, into which various esoteric ingredients have been stirred over the years, and in which different ideas bubble to the surface at different times. They include implied trust, constructive trust, resulting trust, presumption of advancement, proprietary estoppel, unjust enrichment and so on. These ideas are likely to mean nothing to laymen, and often little more to the lawyers who use them." (para.75)

Other common-law jurisdictions have dealt with the issue by developing more flexible property law doctrines—such as unjust enrichment in Canada, reasonable expectations in New Zealand and joint endeavour in Australia. In addition, many jurisdictions have enacted specific legislation dealing with the property rights of cohabiting couples, and some have extended rights to a wider range of dependants. In 1993, the Law Commission declared that it planned to examine this area of the law with a view to making proposals for reform. Almost a decade later, in *Sharing Homes: A Discussion Paper* (2002) the Commission admitted that it had not been able to devise a reform of property law that would fit "the infinitely variable circumstances affecting those who share homes" (para.1.27). It suggested that reforms might be achieved by way of family law. In 2005 it began work on a new project, this time focusing solely on cohabiting couples, with the intention of finding an appropriate family law solution. The recent reforms over the border in Scotland contained in the Family Law (Scotland) Act 2006 may provide a useful model.

The property rights enjoyed by the parties in the family home are relevant not only in the context of family assets but also in influencing the level of protection they enjoy in other contexts. Property rights are, for example, a significant factor for the courts in regulating occupation of the home in cases of domestic violence, as the next chapter will show.

Chapter 6

PROTECTION FROM VIOLENCE AND HARASSMENT

A: INTRODUCTION

The topic of domestic violence is a controversial one. First, there is the question as to **6–001** what constitutes domestic violence. Different definitions have been put forward over time, but the one formulated by the Inter-Ministerial Group set up to tackle the issue of domestic violence best reflects the broad ambit of domestic violence:

> "any incident of threatening behaviour, violence or abuse (psychological, physical, sexual, financial or emotional) between adults who are or have been intimate partners or family members, regardless of gender or sexuality."

Secondly, the very adjective "domestic" has been criticised. It has been argued that this trivialises the issue, which may lead to it being taken less seriously by the authorities. Edwards, for example, argued that it "serves to neutralise the full horror, viciousness and habituation of the violence, concealing the imprisonment of its sufferers, neutralising the seriousness and the dangerousness of the aggressor, thereby rendering its victims a different and lesser standard of response from the justice system and ultimately a lesser standard of protection" (*Sex and Gender in the Legal Process* (1996), p.180). There has, however, been a shift in attitudes in recent years. In *R v McNaughton* [2003] EWCA Crim 3479 it was stressed that:

> "the seriousness of an incident of violence is not diminished merely because it takes place in a 'domestic environment.' Whenever and wherever it occurs, an offence of violence is an offence of violence."

Indeed, the fact that violence is "domestic" may now seen as an aggravating rather than a mitigating factor (CPS, *Policy for Prosecuting Cases of Domestic Violence* (2005), para.1.2).

A third issue of controversy is whether men tend to be the perpetrators, and women the victims, of domestic violence. The evidence would suggest that women are more likely to be victims of domestic violence than are men, more likely to be the victims of repeated attacks, and more likely to suffer serious injury as a result of such attacks (see S. Walby and J. Allen, *Domestic violence, sexual assault and stalking: Findings from the*

British Crime Survey (Home Office Research Study 276, 2004). On the other hand, the same research confirms that women are sometimes the perpetrators of violence against their partners or ex-partners and it should be recognised that men, as well as women, may be reluctant to report that they have been the victims of violence.

Such findings also have relevance for the debate over the causes of domestic violence. Some see domestic violence as the result of individual pathological deviance, others blame environmental factors, such as the social conditions in which the parties live, while yet others ascribe it to the position of women in society. The debate is of importance, since identifying the causes of domestic violence would enable action to be taken to address them, but none of these theories provides a complete explanation: violence is too common to be attributed to individual deviance, and it is not confined to any one social group, while blaming the inferior position of women does not explain why violence occurs in some relationships but not others.

Given the seriousness with which domestic violence is now regarded, should it be a matter for criminal rather than civil law? Three points should be noted: first, while there is no specific crime of inflicting domestic violence, physical violence, threats and harassment are all punishable under the general criminal law. Significantly, the Domestic Violence, Crimes and Victims Act 2004 made common assault an arrestable offence, which means that the police have the power to arrest without a warrant a person whom they suspect of having committed an assault. There is, however, a wide spectrum of behaviour classifiable as domestic violence that is not defined as criminal, and it is interesting to note that only 17 per cent of the respondents to the British Crime Survey who had experienced domestic violence actually defined the behaviour as criminal. Secondly, the victim may not want the perpetrator to be prosecuted: imprisonment of the aggressor may well lead to unemployment and consequent financial hardship for the victim and any children, and may even exacerbate the problem by provoking further violence. Thirdly, criminal sanctions alone may be insufficient to protect the victim of domestic violence. The principal function of the criminal law is, after all, the punishment of the offender in the interests of society as a whole; and the interests of individual family members are subordinate. In contrast, the main aim of the civil law in this context is to regulate and improve matters for the future—in particular by making orders about the future use of property or the future behaviour of the parties—rather than making judgements upon, or punishing, past behaviour.

It is the role of the civil law that is considered in this chapter, although attention will also be paid to the criminal sanctions used to enforce civil remedies. The issue of domestic violence raises issues that go beyond the scope of this book, for example the provision of healthcare and the re-housing of those who have fled from a violent home. It also raises issues that are examined elsewhere in this book, such as how far evidence of violence should influence the court in deciding whether to make orders relating to residence or contact (para.12–030 below), and when a child may be in danger and should be taken into care (para.13–019 below). There is an increasing awareness of the effect that witnessing domestic violence may have upon a child, and the Adoption and Children Act 2002 redefined "harm" to include "impairment suffered from seeing or hearing the ill-treatment of another." This chapter will focus upon the civil remedies available to a person who can prove that he or she has been a victim of violence. Part IV of the Family Law Act 1996 rationalised the earlier law by establishing a comprehensive and coherent body of statute law and giving the courts with jurisdiction in family matters a single, consistent set of remedies, which are discussed in Part B. Part

C considers other civil remedies available under the court's inherent jurisdiction, and—more significantly—the Protection from Harassment Act 1997, which was not primarily intended to deal with "family" situations, but may have considerable relevance when a relationship has broken down. Both have been amended to some extent by the Domestic Violence, Crimes and Victims Act 2004, in line with the recommendations contained in *Safety and Justice: The Government's Proposals on Domestic Violence* (Home Office, 2003).

B: ORDERS UNDER PT IV OF THE FAMILY LAW ACT 1996

Under Pt IV of the Family Law Act, any court—whether the magistrates' court, the **6–002** county court or the High Court—may make either a non-molestation order, or an occupation order regulating the occupation of a home. This section considers first when such orders may be made and secondly the sanctions available to ensure that the court's orders are obeyed. The law is complex, and this chapter seeks only to give a broad outline. The student is advised to refer to the legislation for the nuances of the scheme.

It should be noted that many of the distinctions drawn by the Family Law Act were not part of the original scheme as recommended by the Law Commission (*Domestic Violence and Occupation of the Family Home* (1992) Law Com. No.207). The Law Commission's proposals were initially put before Parliament in the Family Homes and Domestic Violence Bill 1995, which had passed through most of the necessary stages in both Houses of Parliament when the *Daily Mail* and other newspapers ran a campaign against it, alleging that it would undermine marriage, because it was perceived as conferring new rights on cohabiting couples. The Bill was withdrawn, for somewhat complicated political reasons, and, when it was re-introduced as part of what was to become the Family Law Act 1996, certain distinctions between married and cohabiting couples were made that had not been part of the Law Commission's original scheme. The legislative history goes some way to explaining the complexity of the Act (and demonstrates the difficulties of legislating in areas of sensitive social policy). It should also be noted that both married and cohabiting couples enjoyed rights to protection against domestic violence before the 1996 Act, under the Domestic Violence and Matrimonial Proceedings Act 1976, and that the aim of the 1995 Bill was to rationalise the law.

The 1996 Act has subsequently been amended by the Civil Partnership Act 2004—a measure that was considerably more radical in scope than the 1995 Bill but which did not attract the same virulent opposition in the press.

Non-molestation orders

The Family Law Act 1996 confers on the courts a wide power to make orders **6–003** prohibiting one person from "molesting" another. The discretion of the courts is increased still further by the fact that the Act does not define the term "molestation". The Law Commission stated that molestation includes, but is wider than, violence, and that the term:

> "encompasses any form of serious pestering or harassment and applies to any conduct which could properly be regarded as such a degree of harassment as to call for the intervention of the court."

The following illustrations of conduct that has been held to constitute molestation may be helpful:

> In *Vaughan v Vaughan* [1973] 1 W.L.R. 1159, CA, a husband was held to have molested his wife when he called at her house early in the morning and late at night, called at her place of work, and made "a perfect nuisance of himself to her the whole time".

Again:

> In *Horner v Horner* [1982] Fam. 90, CA, the husband repeatedly telephoned the school at which the wife was a teacher, and made disparaging remarks about her. He also hung scurrilous posters about the wife on the school railings addressed to the parents of the children she taught.

But merely disseminating unfavourable information about a person does not automatically constitute harassment: thus in *C v C (Non-Molestation Order: Jurisdiction)* [1998] 1 F.L.R. 554, Fam Div, the fact that the applicant's former wife had given information about his behaviour during the marriage to the *People* and the *Daily Mail* with the intention of embarrassing and humiliating him was not regarded as molestation. The distinction between this and the earlier cases is that, while the husband might be embarrassed by the revelations, they did not affect his health, safety or well-being.

(1) *Who may apply?*

6–004   Under the Family Law Act it is only possible for an individual to apply for a non-molestation order if the perpetrator is an "associated person." The previous legislation applied only to spouses and cohabitants, but this was thought to be too restrictive. Section 62 of the 1996 Act consequently introduced the broad concept of an "associated person", which included spouses and cohabitants (current or former), engaged or formerly engaged couples, relatives, parents of a child, parties to the same family proceedings and "those who have lived in the same household otherwise than merely by reason of one of them being the other's employee, tenant, lodger or boarder". Further categories have since been added. The Domestic Violence, Crimes and Victims Act 2004 added those who "have or have had an intimate personal relationship with each other which is or was of significant duration." (s.62(3)(ea) of the FLA 1996, as amended). Those seeking enlightenment from the Explanatory Notes as to the meaning of this somewhat opaque phrase will be disappointed: they state, rather unhelpfully, that the relationship need not be sexual but that platonic friends are excluded. So, indeed, are one-night stands, although the film *Fatal Attraction* illustrates all too graphically the emotions they may occasion. (It should be noted that a remedy may be available under the Protection from Harassment Act in such a case, see further paras 6–019 *et seq.*).

The Domestic Violence, Crimes and Victims Act 2004 also included same-sex couples within the category of "cohabitants", but its formulation of those "living together as husband and wife or (if of the same sex) in an equivalent relationship" was swiftly overtaken by the passage of the Civil Partnership Act 2004, which redefined cohabitants as those "living together as husband and wife or as if they were civil partners" (s.62(1)(a) of the FLA, as amended). The Civil Partnership Act also added civil partners, and those who had agreed to enter into a civil partnership, to the list of associated persons.

The scope of the concept of "associated persons" is widened still further by the generous statutory definition of "relative". This includes one's parents, grandparents, children, grandchildren, step-parents and stepchildren, plus siblings, aunts, uncles, nieces, nephews, and, since 2004, first cousins. The latter group may be "of the full blood or of the half blood or by affinity", and affinity can now be created by civil partnership as well as by marriage. In addition, the relatives of one's cohabitant—whether of the same or opposite sex—are also associated persons.

Given this expanded list, the reader may have to spend quite some time working out exactly how many persons they are "associated" with for the purpose of the Family Law Act. The risk that the courts will need to spend time debating whether particular individuals are indeed "associated" for the purposes of the Act is mitigated by the suggestion in *G v F (Non-Molestation Order: Jurisdiction)* [2000] 2 F.L.R. 533 that any doubt should be resolved in favour of the applicant.

The recent changes, by sacrificing certainty of definition to the need for protection in specific cases, raise the question of whether a list of associated persons is really appropriate in this context. Hayes and Williams have argued that it is cumbersome and that it would have been better to recommend that an order should be obtainable by anyone who could prove a proper need for the law's protection: [1992] Fam. Law 497. At present, victims of molestation who do not fall within the class of associated persons must seek other remedies (see below).

(2) When will an order be granted?

In deciding whether to make the order and, if so, in what terms, the court is directed **6–005** to have regard to "all the circumstances including the need to secure the health, safety and well-being of the applicant or any relevant child" (s.42(5)).

The court may make the order in such terms as it thinks fit and tailor it to the needs of the particular case. A standard form of wording is that the respondent is restrained from "assaulting, molesting, annoying or otherwise interfering with the applicant or any child living with the applicant." The general prohibition may be followed by a more precise injunction against the specific types of behaviour complained of. As was noted in a similar context:

> "Harassment can and does take many forms. A determined defendant who . . . is prohibited from committing a particular type of harassment is likely to find a different way of harassing the target of his or her conduct." (*per* Dyson LJ, in *R v Evans* [2005] 1 W.L.R. 1435, a case under the Protection from Harassment Act 1997)

Orders may be made for a limited or unlimited period. The means by which such orders may be enforced by the courts in case of breach are considered further below (para.6–016).

Occupation orders

6–006 An occupation order regulates the occupation of the family home. It may require one party to leave part or all of the home or "a defined area in which the dwelling house is included"—for example a block of flats or the street where the house is situated (s.33). Alternatively, it may require one party to allow the other to remain in the home. Under s.40, additional provisions, including obligations to repair and maintain the home, pay the rent or mortgage or other outgoings, may be included.

An occupation order may be linked with, or be distinct from, a non-molestation order. In cases of domestic violence, an occupation order may be sought to ensure the safety of the victim: obtaining a non-molestation order against a violent partner may offer little real protection if the couple remain under the same roof. But molestation or violence is not a pre-requisite to the obtaining of an occupation order: the procedures of the Family Law Act may also be invoked to regulate the occupation of the property on relationship breakdown—although given the limitations of the scheme it is likely to provide only a stop-gap solution. In the longer term, the court has powers to make orders in relation to the family home on divorce or dissolution (see Ch.8), or, if the parties have not formalised their relationship, under the Trusts of Land and Appointments of Trustees Act 1996 (see para.5–021 above).

(1) *Who may apply?*

6–007 The class of persons who may apply for an occupation order is considerably narrower in scope than the class of persons who may apply for a non-molestation order. Only associated persons may apply for an occupation order, but not all associated persons will be able to do so. First, the order must relate to a dwelling house that was, or was intended to be, the home of the applicant and an associated person (s.33(1)(b)). The logic of this is clear: it would be odd if a relative with whom you had never shared a home, or indeed a person with whom you enjoyed "an intimate personal relationship" could apply to the court to be allowed to occupy your home. Secondly, the legislation draws a further distinction between "entitled" and "non-entitled" applicants. This nomenclature is somewhat confusing, as a non-entitled applicant may still apply for an order. Implicit in this two-fold classification, therefore, is a third, unmentioned category of those associated persons who are neither entitled nor non-entitled applicants and so have no right to apply for an occupation order (see the summary in fig. 1 below).

(a) Applications by entitled persons

6–008 There are two sub-categories of entitled persons. The first is one who has a right under the general law to occupy the property, *i.e.* by virtue of a beneficial estate or interest or contract (s.33(1); see also Ch.5 on such rights). The second is a person who has "home rights" in the property. At common law, a married woman had a right to be provided with a roof over her head as part of her husband's common law duty to maintain her. The right to occupy the matrimonial home was placed on a statutory footing by the Matrimonial Homes Act 1967 and is no longer sex-specific—nor, since the Civil Partnership Act 2004, is it restricted to married couples. The current position is that a spouse or civil partner who does not have a right under the general law to occupy the property will automatically have "home rights". This means that a current spouse or civil partner will always be an entitled applicant. It should be noted that "home rights" do not confer any beneficial interest in the property, simply the right to occupy it. The effect that this right of occupation has as against a third party is considered below at para.6–014.

The underlying policy of these two categories of entitled applicants seems to be that the court's powers should be more extensive in the case of a person who can point to some recognised legal, equitable, or statutory right than in the case of a person who has merely had the use of a family home.

(b) Applications by non-entitled persons

A person who is not an entitled applicant can only apply for an occupation order if he **6–009** or she is the former spouse or civil partner, cohabitant, or former cohabitant of the person who owns the property. As explained below, non-entitled persons are treated less favourably than entitled persons.

Why does the law draw this distinction? The Law Commission noted that the grant of an occupation order "can severely restrict the enjoyment of property rights, and its potential consequences to a respondent are therefore more serious than those of a non-molestation order which generally only prohibits conduct which is already illegal or at least anti-social."

The combined result of these provisions is that an associated person who has not had a sexual relationship with the owner of the property and does not have an interest in the property will not be entitled to apply for an occupation order. Thus, for example, an elderly woman living with her son would not be able to apply for an occupation order against him unless she had an interest in the property.

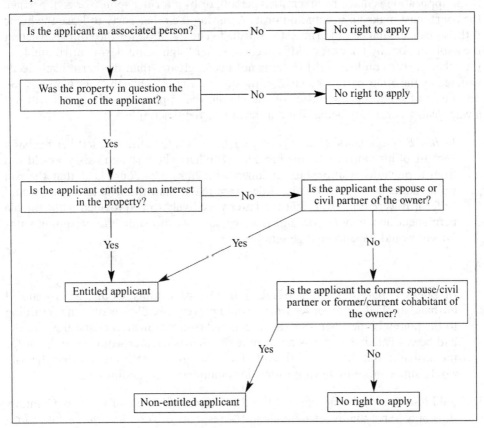

Fig 1

(2) *For how long may an occupation order last?*

6–010 The potential duration of an occupation order depends on the status of the applicant. The period for which an occupation order may be made in favour of an entitled person is at the court's discretion. By contrast, an order in favour of a non-entitled person can only last six months. A further distinction is then drawn between cohabitants (whether current or former) on the one hand and ex-spouses/ex-civil partners on the other: in the case of the latter, the order may be extended for successive six-month periods, but an order in favour of a non-entitled cohabitant or former cohabitant can be extended only once. In this way, the Act seeks to give preference to claims founded on formal relationships or on property rights.

(3) *Exercise of the discretion to make orders*

6–011 In determining whether or not an occupation order should be made, the court's discretion is more structured than when considering the desirability of a non-molestation order. Indeed, in certain circumstances the legislation directs that an occupation order must be made. This section looks first at the "balance of harm test", which, if satisfied, determines the outcome of the case, and then the factors to be applied if no question of harm arises, which are set out in table 1 below.

(a) The balance of harm test

6–012 If the application is made by an entitled person, or by a former spouse or civil partner, the court must make an occupation order requiring the other party to leave the home if the so-called balance of harm test is satisfied. The question for the court is whether the applicant or any relevant child is likely to suffer "significant harm" attributable to the other party's conduct if the order is not made, greater than the harm likely to be suffered by the other party, or a child, if the order is made. While the Law Commission saw this as facilitating the ouster of the abuser, the application of the test will not always lead to an order being made in favour of the "victim":

> In *B. v B (Occupation Order)* [1999] 1 F.L.R. 715, CA, the wife left her husband because of his violence, taking her baby with her. The husband's six-year-old son from a previous relationship remained with him. The court held that the son would suffer more harm if the order were made than the wife and baby would suffer if it were not, given that the latter were likely to be provided with suitable permanent accommodation and that the son, who was already becoming withdrawn, would have to change schools.

Again:

> In *Banks v Banks* [1999] 1 F.L.R. 726, Oxford County Court, a 73-year-old husband applied for an order which would prevent his 79-year-old wife returning to the family home when she was discharged from the mental hospital where she had been treated. There was no dispute that her behaviour would be difficult for the husband, but the court refused to make an order on the ground that the wife would suffer more by having to live in unfamiliar surroundings.

It should also be noted that, contrary to the recommendations of the Law Commission, it is only harm that is attributable to the respondent's conduct that is taken into account. The effect of this seems to be to preserve the decision of the House of Lords in *Richards v Richards* [1984] 1 A.C. 174, HL:

The wife left the matrimonial home with the children, but was unable to find suitable accommodation for them; and she then applied for an order excluding the husband from the matrimonial home so that she could return there with the children. The wife said that she could not bear to be in the same household as the husband; but the judge found that she had no reasonable ground for refusing to live under the same roof as her husband, and expressed the view that it would be "thoroughly unjust" to turn him out of the house. Nevertheless, the judge granted an ouster order because of the importance that he considered case law required him to give to the interests of the children. The House of Lords held that he had been wrong to make the order.

Applying the balance of harm test to these facts it would appear that the harm caused to the wife and child by their poor living conditions was not "attributable to" Mr Richards' conduct.

By contrast, where the applicant is a non-entitled cohabitant, the court is directed merely to take the harm to the parties into account: the balance of harm does not determine the outcome of the case.

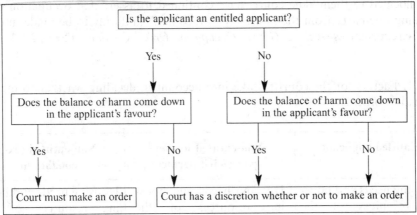

Fig 2

(b) The factors to be taken into account in exercising the discretion

Where there is no question of either party suffering significant harm, the court has a **6–013** discretion whether or not to make an order.

> In *Chalmers v Johns* [1999] 1 F.L.R. 392, CA, the mother and father had had a long-standing tempestuous relationship. Eventually the mother left the flat (of which they were joint tenants) with the seven-year-old child and moved into temporary council accommodation at some distance from the child's school. An order was made against the father. The Court of Appeal held that the judge had been wrong to make the "draconian" ouster order against the father at an interim hearing. Neither the mother nor the child could be said to be likely to suffer significant harm attributable to the father's conduct, and so the court had a broad discretion whether or not to make an order.

The court is enjoined to take all the circumstances of the case into account, but the factors that it is specifically directed to take into account vary according to the status of the parties. In the case of a non-entitled former spouse or civil partner, the court is directed to a longer list of factors than in the case of an entitled applicant, and the list is even longer if the applicant is a non-entitled cohabitant or former cohabitant (see table below).

The lists are largely self-explanatory, but one item merits further consideration, namely the reference to "the nature of the relationship" in the case of any non-entitled cohabitant or former cohabitant. In the original version of the Family Law Act this was amplified by s.41, which required the court, when considering the nature of the relationship, to "have regard to the fact that the parties have not given each other the commitment involved in marriage." This was one of the amendments that was made to placate those who felt that the legislation would undermine marriage. In practice it appeared to have little influence on the court's deliberations, and the Domestic Violence, Crimes and Victims Act 2004 substituted a less dogmatic direction that judges should have regard to "the level of commitment involved" in the particular cohabiting relationship.

Of more significance is the law's traditional deference to property rights. In *Chalmers v Johns* (above) it was decided that it would be harder on the father to eject him from the flat than it would be for the mother and child to continue in the accommodation allocated to them. The courts have continued to assert that occupation orders excluding one party from the house are "draconian" and only to be made in exceptional circumstances (see, *e.g. G v G (Occupation Order: Conduct)* [2000] 2 F.L.R. 36, CA).

Table 1: Factors for the court to take into account in deciding whether to make an occupation order

Entitled applicant	Non-entitled former spouse/civil partner	Non-entitled (ex-) cohabitant
Housing needs and housing resources of the family	Housing needs and housing resources of the family	Housing needs and housing resources of the family
Financial resources	Financial resources	Financial resources
The likely effect of the court's decision on the family's health, safety or well-being	The likely effect of the court's decision on the family's health, safety or well-being	The likely effect of the court's decision on the family's health, safety or well-being
Conduct	Conduct	Conduct
	Length of time since the parties lived together	Nature of the relationship and in particular the level of commitment involved in it
	Length of time since the marriage or civil partnership was dissolved or annulled	Length of time during which they cohabited

Entitled applicant	Non-entitled former spouse/civil partner	Non-entitled (ex-) cohabitant
	Existence of any pending proceedings under MCA, CPA, CA or relating to the ownership of the home	Whether there any children of both or for whom both have parental responsibility
		Length of time since the parties lived together
		Existence of any pending proceedings under CA or relating to the ownership of the home

(4) *The effect of an occupation order on third parties*

In 1965 it was held in *National Provincial Bank v Ainsworth* [1965] A.C. 1175, HL, that **6–014** a wife's common law right to occupy the matrimonial home was a personal right incapable of binding a third party even if the third party had notice of the wife's rights. The Matrimonial Homes Act 1967 was primarily intended to remedy this defect in the law, and it did so by giving spouses in occupation of the matrimonial home rights of occupation and also by providing machinery whereby a spouse could make those rights bind third parties. Part IV of the Family Law Act 1996 re-enacts the substance of the Matrimonial Homes Act, and the Civil Partnership Act 2004 extends the same protection to those who have registered a civil partnership (Sch.9). The home rights of spouses or civil partners can be protected against a third party through registration of either a Class F land charge (in unregistered land), or a notice (in registered land). In contrast, there is no machinery for making cohabitants' occupation orders have this effect.

Emergency protection

In emergencies, both non-molestation and occupation orders may be granted *ex* **6–015** *parte*—*i.e.* at a hearing of which notice has not been given to the other party. The Law Commission noted that there was a danger that malicious or misconceived applications would be granted but thought that this was outweighed by the need for emergency protection in cases of imminent physical violence. The Act accordingly provides that *ex parte* orders may be made where the court considers it "just and convenient to do so" (s.45(1)). In so deciding, it must take a number of factors into account: whether there is a risk of significant harm to applicant or child if the order is not made, whether the applicant will be deterred if an order is not made immediately and whether there is reason to believe that the respondent is aware of the proceedings but is deliberately avoiding service of the proceedings (s.45(2)). It is likely that the *ex parte* order will be of very short duration, lasting only until the earliest date when a hearing on notice can be arranged. Moreover, the court must afford the respondent the opportunity to make representations as soon as is just and convenient (s.45(3)).

It was originally thought that the *ex parte* procedure should only apply to non-molestation orders, which provided more immediate protection against violence. However, in view of the fact that, where the parties live together, an occupation order will often be the only effective means of ensuring that a non-molestation order is heeded, it was thought appropriate that it should also be possible to make such orders speedily. In 2004, the majority of applications for both types of orders were made *ex parte*.

Enforcement of orders

6–016   The Domestic Violence, Crimes and Victims Act 2004 has made significant changes to the ways in which non-molestation and occupation orders can be enforced. First, breach of a non-molestation order (but not an occupation order) is made a criminal offence punishable by up to five years' imprisonment (see the new s.42A of the Family Law Act 1996). Previously, breach of a non-molestation was only punishable as a contempt of court, for which the maximum sentence was two years. Sentences for contempt had to reflect the seriousness of the contempt in the light of this two-year limit (see *e.g. Hale v Tanner* [2000] 2 F.L.R. 879, CA), and the courts accordingly encouraged litigants to bring proceedings under the Protection from Harassment Act 1997 (see paras 6–022 *et seq.* below) for cases warranting a more severe sentence (see *e.g. Robinson v Murray* [2005] EWCA Civ 935 and *Carabott v Huxley* (2005) 102(34) L.S.G. 30). While it remains possible to enforce non-molestation orders by way of proceedings for contempt of court, it is not possible to punish the *same* breach as a contempt of court *and* as an offence under s.42A. It seems likely that the latter course will be preferred, not only because it is possible to impose a longer prison sentence in such a case, but also because a wider range of sentencing options will be available.

Since the breach of a non-molestation order is now a criminal offence, it will be possible for the police to arrest the person in breach without a warrant or a power of arrest. This leads on to the second change made by the 2004 Act. Under the old law, it was common practice—and indeed required in many cases—for a power of arrest to be attached to a non-molestation order, authorising the police to arrest without warrant and bring before the court any person reasonably suspected of being in breach of such an order. (In 2004, for example, 20,890 non-molestation orders were made with a power of arrest attached, and only 2,467 without.) The 2004 Act, by contrast, abolishes this option, although it remains possible for a power of arrest to be attached to an occupation order (see the amended s.47(2)).

Thirdly, the 2004 Act makes it more difficult for a court simply to accept an undertaking from the defendant, since it is no longer able to do so if it appears to the court that the respondent "has used or threatened violence against the applicant or a relevant child" or that "for the protection of the applicant or child it is necessary to make a non-molestation order so that any breach may be punishable under s.42A." (see the new s.46(3A) of the 1996 Act). This means that if it is apparent that the applicant needs the protection of a non-molestation order, it will not be possible simply to accept an undertaking from the perpetrator. The protection offered by an undertaking is also increased by the fact that it is now possible for a warrant of arrest to be issued to enforce an undertaking, since any undertaking is enforceable as if it were an order of the court (s.46(4)).

The remedies available to enforce an occupation order remain unaltered: thus a breach of an occupation order does not constitute a criminal offence, and proceedings for contempt are the only means of punishing a breach of such an order. It also remains possible to attach a power of arrest to an occupation order (s.47). It may seem odd that a breach of an occupation order is treated less severely than breach of a non-molestation order, but, as the government explained in the explanatory notes to the 2004 Act, occupation orders may be granted where there is no history of violence or molestation. If there is such a history, it is likely that any occupation order would be accompanied by a non-molestation order.

C: OTHER CIVIL REMEDIES

Although the concept of "associated persons" within the Family Law Act is generous, **6–017** there are inevitably some people with a legitimate claim to legal protection who do not come within its scope. The fact that a person falls outside the definition of an "associated person" does not necessarily mean that he or she is without legal protection against molestation.

Injunctions under the Supreme Court Act

One option is to seek an injunction against such behaviour. The courts have an **6–018** apparently wide power to grant injunctions "in all cases in which it appears . . . to be just and convenient to do so" (s.37 of the Supreme Court Act 1981). But in fact this provision is nothing like as wide in scope as would appear at first sight. In particular, the court can only grant an injunction in support of some recognised legal or equitable right, so the victim is obliged to show that the conduct complained of constitutes a specific tort or some other legal wrong. As the legal tort of nuisance does not encompass all behaviour that might be regarded as constituting a nuisance in the popular sense of the word, this is a significant limitation. For example, in *Hunter v Canary Wharf Ltd* [1997] 2 F.L.R 342, the House of Lords held that the tort of nuisance was only available to defend property rights, which means that a mere licensee—whether a cohabitant, relative, or adult child—cannot claim in nuisance in respect of harassment experienced at home. More fundamentally, there has been a debate as to whether harassment constitutes a tort at all. Although this was eventually resolved in the affirmative (see *e.g. Burris v Azadani* [1996] 1 F.L.R. 226), doubts about the existence and scope of legal remedies in this context were one factor leading to the passage of the Protection from Harassment Act 1997, which will now be considered.

The Protection from Harassment Act 1997

The 1997 Act was not primarily intended to deal with family relationships, but rather **6–019** to provide a remedy against the attentions of "stalkers". Research suggests, however, that the typical stalker is not a stranger to the victim: the British Crime Survey found that in the majority of cases the offender was known to the victim, and in 20 per cent of cases was a current or ex-partner. While the Act may be used in a variety of contexts, this section will focus on its applicability to cases involving domestic violence.

The key features of the Act are as follows:

(1) The prohibited conduct: "harassment"

6–020 Section 1 of the Protection from Harassment Act 1997 provides that a person must not pursue a course of conduct which amounts to harassment of another, and which he knows or ought to know amounts to harassment of the other.

The Act contains no precise definition of harassment, although s.7(1)(a) does provide that harassing a person includes "alarming a person or causing a person distress". In *Hipgrave v Jones* [2005] 2 F.L.R. 174 Tugendhat J. spelt out the spectrum of conduct that could fall within the Act:

> "Harassment can cover a very wide range of conduct. It may involve actions alone, or words alone (s.7(4)), or both. The actions may be so grave as to amount to criminal offences against public order, or they may be little more than boorishness and insensitive behaviour, so long as it is sufficient to cause distress. The words may be, at one extreme, incitements to, or threats of, violence that cause alarm, or at the other extreme, unwelcome text messages sent, for example, to a woman wrongly perceived to be a girlfriend." (para.20)

Thus "harassment" may cover less obviously threatening behaviour—such as sending letters, gifts or flowers—that is repeated on numerous occasions. The British Crime Survey found that some of those surveyed had received unwanted letters on more than 50 occasions. Whether or not such conduct amounts to harassment will of course depend upon the reaction of the recipient: in *King v DPP* 2001 W.L. 989471 the initial actions of the defendant—sending a letter and giving the woman a begonia—did not alarm her and did not therefore amount to harassment (although his subsequent actions, videotaping her and removing her underwear from her rubbish, definitely did, and the protection of the Act was successfully invoked).

The expression "course of conduct" requires that harassment should have occurred on at least two occasions. As was pointed out in *Lau v DPP* [2000] 1 F.L.R. 799, QBD, the fewer the occasions, and the longer the gaps between them, the less likely it was that a court would find that there had been a course of conduct.

> *R. v Hills* [2001] 1 F.C.R. 569, held that two incidents—the first in April and the second in October—were not sufficiently linked to constitute a course of conduct, especially as the parties had continued to live and sleep together.

This cautious approach was approved in *Pratt v DPP* [2001] EWHC Admin 483, although in this case the offender was convicted despite the continued cohabitation of the parties. Research has shown that it is not unknown for harassment to occur in ongoing relationships, although it is more often triggered by the ending of the relationship.

> In *Woolford v DPP* 2000 W.L. 664496, the ex-husband had left a card that read "Congratulations on your new home, love Daddy" on the very same night that his ex-wife had moved—secretly, or so she had thought—to her new home. This, combined with telephone messages, one of which informed the ex-wife that he was in the former matrimonial home, was held to amount to harassment and he was convicted. The Court of Appeal upheld the conviction, but noted that the offence was at the very bottom of the scale.

The other point to note about *Woolford* is that the events complained of took place over a very short period—less than 24 hours. A "course of conduct" need not therefore be a lengthy vendetta: indeed, in *Kelly v DPP* [2002] EWHC 1428 (Admin) three telephone calls within the space of five minutes was held to constitute a course of conduct.

Questions have also arisen concerning the Act's requirement (in s.1(2)) that the person whose conduct is in question should know that the conduct in question amounts to harassment. The Act provides that a person "ought to know" his conduct amounts to harassment if a "reasonable person in possession of the same information would think the course of conduct amounted to harassment of the other" But what if the person suffers from a mental illness?

In *R. v Colohan* [2001] EWCA Crim 1251, a man who suffered from schizophrenia wrote a number of abusive letters to his MP. The court held that the purpose of the 1997 Act was protective and that the conduct from which it sought to provide protection was "particularly likely to be conduct pursued by those of obsessive or otherwise unusual psychological make-up and very frequently by those suffering from an identifiable mental illness" (at 761). The Act must therefore require the jury to apply the objective test of what a reasonable person would think, unmodified by the individual characteristics of the offender.

(2) *Defences*

Whatever the precise meaning of the word "harassment" in the 1997 Act, it seems **6–021** clear that by itself the prohibition might make many common forms of activity which cause annoyance—investigative journalism, debt collecting and the work of enquiry agents, for example—illegal. Section 1(3) therefore provides that the statutory prohibition of harassment does not apply if the person concerned can show that his or her conduct was "pursued for the purpose of preventing or detecting crime", or under any statute or rule of law or to "comply with any condition or requirement imposed by any person" under any statute, or "that in the particular circumstances the pursuit of the course of conduct was reasonable". It is for the defendant to show that the course of conduct is within one of these exempting provisions.

By way of additional defence, s.12 empowers a Secretary of State to issue a certificate that actions done on behalf of the Crown relate to national security, the economic well-being of the United Kingdom or the prevention or detection of serious crime. Such a certificate prevents the Act applying to the conduct specified in the certificate.

The defendant might also argue that the actions claimed by the applicant to constitute harassment are in fact an exercise of free speech and so protected by Art.10 of the European Convention. Such an argument is unlikely to succeed if the "speech" in question has been accompanied by unreasonable and oppressive conduct (see *e.g.* *Thomas v Hughes* [2001] EWCA Civ 1233, *Howlett v Holding* [2006] EWHC 41 (QB)).

(3) *Remedies*

The Act provides an unusual combination of criminal sanctions and civil remedies, in **6–022** that the same conduct may constitute both a civil wrong and a criminal offence. This approach can be explained by the underlying policy of the Act. The Conservative government responsible for the 1997 Act wanted the police to be able to arrest a person reasonably suspected of harassment, and it is for that reason that the Act makes pursuing a course of conduct prohibited by s.1 an arrestable offence (s.24(2)(n) of the Police and Criminal Evidence Act 1984, inserted by s.2(3) of the Protection from Harassment Act 1997). The Government wanted the police to be able to investigate complaints of harassment and take proceedings against culprits; and whereas the police have the right and duty to do so in the case of criminal offences they have no such powers in respect of torts and other civil wrongs. Finally, the Government wanted the victim of harassment to have effective protection against any repetition of the conduct in question; and to that end the Act empowers the criminal courts to make restraining orders and the civil courts to grant injunctions.

(a) Criminal sanctions

6–023 Section 2 provides that a person who pursues a course of conduct in breach of the Act's provisions is guilty of a criminal offence punishable by up to six months' imprisonment. Section 4 also provides that a person whose course of conduct causes another to fear, on at least two occasions, that violence will be used against him is guilty (subject to defences similar to but not identical with those set out above) of a more serious criminal offence punishable by up to five years' imprisonment. Moreover, the court may impose a so-called "restraining order" on a person convicted under these provisions (s.5), or indeed on a person acquitted of such an offence if this is deemed necessary to protect another from harassment (see s.5A, inserted by the Domestic Violence, Crimes and Victims Act 2004). A restraining order prohibits the defendant from further conduct (described in the order) amounting to harassment or putting a person in fear of violence. Breach of such an order is itself a criminal offence punishable by up to five years' imprisonment; as such, it is an arrestable offence, and the police will be able to arrest without warrant a defendant reasonably suspected of being in breach of the restraining order or prohibitory injunction (s.24(6) of the Police and Criminal Evidence Act 1984).

(b) Civil remedies

6–024 The Act in effect creates a new tort of harassment: a person who is or may be the victim of harassment prohibited by s.1 can bring an action in the High Court or the county court. The fact that the remedy arises where a harassment is "apprehended" means that the victim need not wait for a second incident to occur before obtaining an injunction. This is useful in the light of the evidence that harassment may escalate. There is another reason why a civil remedy may be available even if criminal sanctions are not: as was confirmed in *Hipgrave v Jones* [2004] EWHC 2901 (QB), the civil standard of proof applies to proceedings under s.3.

The court may award damages (including damages for any anxiety or financial loss caused by the harassment (s.3(2)) and it may grant an injunction for the purpose of restraining the defendant from pursuing any conduct which amounts to harassment (s.3(3)). The grant of an injunction is not an automatic response to a finding that harassment has occurred: as Tugendhat J. stressed in *Hipgrave v Jones*, "an injunction should be no more extensive than is necessary and proportionate." If the plaintiff considers that the defendant has done anything prohibited by the injunction, the plaintiff may apply for a warrant of arrest; and s.3(6) provides that it is an offence, punishable by up to five years' imprisonment, to do anything prohibited by the injunction "without reasonable excuse".

D: CONCLUSION

For a long time it was a valid criticism that English law governing domestic violence **6–025** was based on a hotchpotch of enactments of limited scope passed into law to meet specific situations (*Richards v Richards* [1984] 1 A.C. 174 at 206, HL). The Family Law Act 1996 seemed at last to provide a coherent (if not always easily comprehensible) codification of the law; and it is in this respect that the 1997 Act seems to have turned the clock back. It is true, as explained above, that the technique that the 1997 Act adopts is defensible in principle and skilful in application, but it can hardly be said that it makes any contribution to a rational and integrated code. The Protection from Harassment Act has been more widely used than was initially anticipated, which may indicate either that it fulfils a previously unmet need, or that it is too widely defined.

In addition, concern has been expressed about the way in which the legal system as a whole deals with the issue of domestic violence. In *Lomas v Parle* [2003] EWCA Civ 1804, for example, Thorpe L.J. noted that "the present interface between the criminal and family courts . . . is expensive, wasteful of resources and time consuming" (para.52). The government favours the development of an "Integrated Domestic Violence Court" that could hear the criminal and civil aspects of the same case (see *e.g. Domestic Violence: A National Report* (March 2005), para.56).

These initiatives should be contrasted with the concerted efforts being made in other areas to divert family disputes away from the courts (see *e.g.* paras 8–002 and 12–033). In fact, the reverse trend can be noted in the context of domestic violence: it has been stressed that cautions are to be used sparingly, and, as noted above, the circumstances in which a court may accept an undertaking have been reduced.

One further point that may strike the reader is the importance of property rights in this context—such rights may determine the rights of the parties under the Family Law Act or the availability of a remedy under the inherent jurisdiction of the court. Given that control of the family finances is seen as an aspect of domestic violence (see above, para.6–001) and that this may affect the victim's ability to acquire property (see Ch.5), this may pose a problem in some cases. This issue also has relevance for the issue of family maintenance, which is considered in the next chapter.

Chapter 7

FAMILY MAINTENANCE

A: INTRODUCTION

The topics dealt with in this chapter may at first sight seem to be unrelated, but in fact **7–001** they all deal with the fundamental question as to whether one should be maintained by one's family, through one's own employment, or by the state. As we shall see, the answers given to this question tend to vary according to the context in which the question is posed.

In English law, a husband has a common law obligation to support his wife and children, although in practice this has now been supplanted by the various statutory (and non gender-specific) procedures for enforcing maintenance obligations through the courts. Identical statutory obligations to maintain now apply between civil partners. Parenthood also creates obligations: both parents of a child have an obligation to support the child, whether the child was born within marriage or as the result of a one-night stand. By contrast, there is no common law obligation of support between cohabiting partners, and there is no statutory procedure whereby one cohabitant can obtain maintenance from the other.

What is the relationship between such private obligations and the provision that the state makes for needy members of society? It is consistent with the emphasis on the responsibility of parents to support their children that a parent in receipt of income support must apply for child support (see Part C, below). Such consistency is, however, lacking in the "cohabitation rule". This refers to the practice whereby the state will take the resources of an applicant's cohabitant into account when assessing the applicant's eligibility for means-tested benefits, on the assumption that support is being provided, even though the cohabitant is under no obligation to share those resources. The justification for this is that it would be unfair if couples could gain financial advantages by not marrying, since the resources of spouses are also aggregated when assessing eligibility for means-tested benefits. This leads on to a further point, the way in which the state promotes particular family forms through financial incentives. This is far from straightforward, since the fact that the state provides support for needy members of society means that considerable resources are expended on supporting families that might not be regarded as ideal. However, while changes to the tax and benefit system reflect the key shift in family law from marriage to parenthood, it remains the case that those who have formalised their relationship receive significant advantages in the context of pensions.

The text first discusses the role of the state in providing maintenance for the family, including the means used to promote the alternative favoured by the current government, namely the employment of adult family members (Part B). It then turns to the issue of support from one's family. Given the absence of any obligation of support between wider kin, or even adult children and elderly relatives, this falls into two categories, support for children and support for a spouse or civil partner, which are considered in Parts C and D respectively. One point to note is that such support obligations are only enforced where the relationship between the adults has broken down. The state assumes that if two adults are living together, then it is up to them to decide how resources will be shared between them and any dependent children. The assumption that resources will be shared equitably is not borne out by research, as some of the material discussed in the previous chapter illustrates.

B: FAMILY MAINTENANCE—THE ROLE OF THE STATE

7–002 Two issues fall to be considered in this section: first, the role that the state plays in supporting intact families, and, secondly, the extent of its responsibilities where the family unit has broken down. The state has long played a role in supporting families: since the Elizabethan Poor Law the state has assumed some obligation to provide for those who would otherwise starve, and in the nineteenth and twentieth centuries public policy gradually became much more broadly concerned with the welfare of children and families. The commitment of the state to provide for the welfare of its citizens reached a peak in the years following World War II. Statute embodied the principle that benefits were, as Finer J. put it in *Reiterbund v Reiterbund* [1974] 1 W.L.R. 788 at 797, "the subject of rights and entitlement and ... no shame attached to the receipt of them". Today most families derive substantial support—in such diverse areas as public health, medical treatment, housing, and education—from the state. By contrast, the state's responsibilities where the family unit has broken down are somewhat more controversial. Changes in family life over the past few decades—in particular the increase in divorce and the rise in births outside marriage—meant that an increasingly large proportion of the social security budget was devoted to the support of lone parents. This became particularly controversial in the 1980s as the proportion of lone parents in receipt of maintenance from a former partner actually fell. Right-wing political philosophies—seeking to diminish the role of the state and to reinforce the obligations of individuals and families to be self-supporting—became influential, and changes were made to improve both the employment prospects of parents and the system whereby maintenance obligations were enforced, including the radical Child Support Act 1991 (see para.7–009 below).

The influence of those philosophies has been enduring, and survived the election of the Labour Government in 1997. The Blair Government committed itself to modernisation of a welfare system which it thought did not sufficiently help people to fulfil their potential; and the Government specifically adopted the principle that the welfare system should support families and children as well as tackling child poverty and social exclusion. But the "new welfare state" was to be based on the philosophy of "work for those who can, security for those who cannot". The Government also committed itself to raising the proportion of parents meeting their family financial obligations after separation (see further Part C).

The amounts payable by the state, and indeed the types of benefits that are available, change fairly frequently. Of more enduring importance are the following questions. How should support be calculated? Should benefits be calculated on an individual or a family basis? And should the tax and benefit system be used to promote an ideal family form or be targeted to those in need regardless?

(1) *Promoting certain family forms or supporting families in need?*

There are still a number of respects in which the tax system promotes formal relation- **7–003** ships. Admittedly, the married couples' tax allowance is now severely restricted in scope, since it applies only if one of the spouses was born prior to April 6, 1935. (It has, however, been extended to civil partners, and there may be a few septuagenarian civil partners who will benefit from this.) Of more importance is the fact that individuals are not liable to pay inheritance tax on assets inherited from a spouse or civil partner (see para.9–021 below), and spouses and civil partners can transfer assets between themselves without being liable to pay Capital Gains Tax. In addition, a person may rely on the National Insurance contributions made by his or her spouse or civil partner in claiming a state pension.

Broadly, however, the system of tax and benefits focuses on providing support for families in need, particularly those with children.

(2) *Universal, contributory or means-tested?*

Should the state provide set benefits for everyone, regardless of their means? Or should **7–004** individuals have to "earn" their entitlement to benefits by making National Insurance contributions? Alternatively, should provision depend on the income and assets of an individual? The current tax and benefit system contains examples of all three methods of allocating support, but those allowances or payments of most relevance to families tend to fall into either the first or third categories. Child benefit, for example, is a non means-tested benefit payable to any person who is responsible for a child, whatever his or her means or family status. In 2006–7, the amount payable was £17.45 for the first child (and £11.70 for each subsequent child) per week. The concept of a "child" has an extended meaning in this context: the benefit is in certain situations—basically if the young person is in full-time education or is undertaking approved training—payable until he or she reaches the age of 20 (see reg.3 of the Child Benefit (General) Regulations 2006, SI 2006/223).

Also universal in its application is the scheme introduced by the Child Trust Funds Act 2004. Since April 2005, a voucher worth £250 (plus an extra £250 for those living in low-income households) has been available on behalf of any child born since September 2002 to form the building block for a tax-free savings account in the child's name. Up to £1,200 can be added to the account each year—by parents, friends and family—until the child reaches the age of 18, at which point he or she can access the money.

Such sums clearly fall far short of the cost of bringing up a child. More substantial support is provided by means of tax credits, which have largely replaced the allowances for children that were previously provided as part of the benefit system. Working Families' Tax Credit was originally introduced in 1999 "to make work pay for low and middle-income families" (S. McKay, *Working Families' Tax Credit in 2001* (DWP, 2003). The aim was to ensure that families were not worse off in work than they would have been upon benefits, by reducing the amount of tax payable. Since the Tax Credits Act 2002, two separate tax credits have been available: Working Tax Credit, for families in employment, and Child Tax Credit, which may be paid whether or not the adult members of the family are employed. Both are means-tested, and so the amount each family receives depends upon their circumstances. Both are paid directly to the primary carer, rather than to the main breadwinner, the assumption being that money so paid is more likely to be spent on the children. Assistance with the costs of child care is also provided, as part of the government's general policy of promoting employment. Up to 80 per cent of the costs of childcare is payable as part of Working Tax Credit, with a weekly maximum of £175 for one child and £300 for two.

(3) *Whose means are relevant?*

7–005   If a particular benefit is means-tested, then the question arises as to whose means are relevant for the purpose of assessing an individual's eligibility. In the context of Income Support, for example, claims are made in respect of a family unit and only one member of the family is entitled to make a claim. The capital and income of couples living in the same household—whether married, in a civil partnership or cohabiting—are aggregated for the purpose of determining the parties' entitlement. This does not apply to spouses and civil partners who have separated, even if the relationship has not been formally terminated: in this case each is eligible to claim as an individual.

Until recently the "cohabitation rule"—that a couple who were cohabiting should not be in a better position than a married couple in terms of entitlement to benefits—applied only to heterosexual cohabitants, but the Civil Partnership Act 2004 introduced parity of treatment in this respect (to the disadvantage, it should be noted, of same-sex couples in receipt of benefits, who previously would have been able to claim as individuals). The rule has always been controversial, partly because there was no compensatory entitlement to the benefits that married couples were accorded, and partly because of the extremely wide definition of "living together as husband and wife" that the system employed. The first objection has lost some of its force now that state support is targeted at families with children rather than married couples, but the second remains. Whereas the decision whether a couple are or are not "married" involves no investigation of their personal relationship, or any value judgement about which of the normal incidents of marriage (such as the use of a common name or the existence of sexual relations) is essential to the concept, the decision whether or not a couple are "living together as husband and wife" does involve precisely such judgements. Six factors are often cited as relevant for these purposes: membership of the same household; stability; financial support; a sexual relationship; children; and public acknowledgement. It is not necessary for all of these factors to be established for a couple to be deemed to be living together as husband and wife. In particular, the level of commitment necessary for such a finding is likely to be much less than that required by rules that confer rights on cohabitants (see, for example, the requirement that couples must have been cohabiting in the same household for two years in order to bring a claim under the Inheritance (Provision for Family and Dependants) Act 1975, see para.9–009, below). Nor is there any requirement that cohabitants should support one another, which means that a cohabitant may be left with a choice between the relationship and a guaranteed source of income.

It is clear from the Civil Partnership Act 2004 that the same approach is to apply to cohabiting same-sex couples. The general approach is that:

> "two people of the same sex are to be regarded as living together as if they were civil partners if, but only if, they would be regarded as living together as husband

and wife were they instead two people of the opposite sex." (see *e.g.* Sch.24 para.5)

(4) *Families apart?*

The fact that the assets of married and cohabiting couples are aggregated for the **7–006** purposes of the means test indicates a policy that individuals should look to their partners, rather than to the state, for support. The "liable relative" procedure takes this idea a step further and allows the amount paid by way of means-tested benefits to be recovered from a partner in certain circumstances. The legislation has always contained provisions whereby the authorities could recover payments of income support (and now jobseekers' allowance) from "liable relatives". The relevant provisions are contained in Pt V of the Social Security Administration Act 1992, which provides that a man is liable, for the purposes of income support, to maintain his wife and his children, and a woman to maintain her husband and her children. Although spouses cease to be "liable" for this purpose once their marriage is ended by divorce, they remain liable during any period of separation preceding the divorce. Liability for one's children, by contrast, continues even though the parents have divorced, and is enforced through the Child Support Agency (see further para.7–013 below).

Further questions of policy are raised by the increasing tendency for separated couples to share the care of their children (see further para.12–027 below). If the children are living with each parent for an equal amount of time, to whom should the relevant benefits and tax credits be paid?

> In *Hockenjos v Secretary of State for Social Security* (No 2) [2004] EWCA Civ 1749, a separated couple shared the care of their two children between them. Child Benefit was paid to the mother. For this reason, the father (the founder of one of the pressure groups for fathers' rights, "Fathercare") was not eligible to receive a supplement to income-based jobseekers' allowance that was payable to those with responsibility for a child, since "responsibility" was tested by receipt of Child Benefit. The Court of Appeal held that the rule could not be justified as it contravened Council Directive No 79/7/EEC on the equal treatment of men and women in matters of social security. As Ward L.J. noted, "[t]o be forced to treat only one as responsible where there is a shared residence order in force and in operation is grotesque. It is degrading to fathers who actually—and lovingly— tend to their children" (para.174). The father was accordingly awarded the full allowance for any week in which he shared responsibility for his children.

While the precise allowance at stake in that case is no longer available, the same point applies to payments of tax credits. Similar problems arise in relation to Child Benefit itself: at present, if Child Benefit is payable for one child, then the payment cannot be split between separated parents; if, however, it is payable for two children, then the payments may be apportioned between the parents at the discretion of the Inland Revenue (see s.144(3) and Sch.10 para.5 of the Social Security Contributions and Benefits Act 1992, and *R (Ford) v Inland Revenue* [2005] EWHC 1109 (QBD)).

(5) *The promotion of employment*

Current government policy is to promote employment rather than dependence on the **7–007** state. This is a particular issue in relation to lone parents, who are less likely than partnered parents to be in paid employment (see para.1–014). The twin themes of government support and individual responsibility were apparent in the recent Green Paper issued by the Department for Work and Pensions, *A New Deal for Welfare: Empowering people to work* (2006, Cm 6730). For example:

> "The Government is helping to make provision available to enable lone parents to work, but in return we believe that lone parents have a responsibility to make serious efforts to return to work, especially once their youngest child reaches 11." (p.52)

The measures outlined in that paper largely concerned the incentives to be used to persuade lone parents into employment (*e.g.* work-focused interviews and premiums to ensure that lone parents were better off in employment). There is, however, another dimension to the relationship between employment and family responsibilities, namely the extent to which it is possible to combine work and family life. The government has stated that its role:

> "is to support families and ensure that they have meaningful choices about how they live their lives." (*Choice for parents, the best start for children: a ten-year strategy for childcare* (2004), para.2.3.)

Such support takes a variety of forms: the ability of new parents to take leave, the right to request flexible working hours, and the availability of child-care. The Work and Families Bill 2005, currently before Parliament, builds on the proposals set out by the Department of Trade and Industry in *Work and Families, Choice and Flexibility* (2005). In brief, the bill will extend the current entitlement to leave enjoyed by new mothers and fathers (including those who have adopted a child), as well as widening the scope of the right to request flexible working hours initially introduced by the Employment Act 2002. At present a parent (natural, adoptive or foster) or guardian, or the partner of any of these persons, may request flexible working hours in relation to a child under the age of six. The provisions in the new bill would allow a similar request to be made by a person who is caring for another adult. It should of course be noted that this is only a right to request flexible working hours: there is no obligation on the employer to grant such a request. Finally, a separate bill, the Childcare Bill 2005, deals with the responsibilities of local authorities to provide child care facilities.

Such provisions have the power to transform the relationship between work and family life. Whether they achieve this remains to be seen.

C: ENFORCING ADULTS' OBLIGATIONS TO SUPPORT CHILDREN

7–008   The history of the law's attempts to ensure that parents support their children—particularly in the case of parents who were not married to each other—is long and complex. For many years it was the role of the court in divorce or affiliation proceedings to decide whether maintenance should be paid and, if so, at what level. In the 1980s there was concern that the number of lone parents in receipt of maintenance was actually falling, and in 1990 the then Conservative Government published a White Paper, *Children Come First*, which gave the following diagnosis of the problem:

"The present system of maintenance is unnecessarily fragmented, uncertain in its results, slow and ineffective. It is based largely on discretion ... The cumulative effect is uncertainty and inconsistent decisions about how much maintenance should be paid. In a great many instances, the maintenance award is not paid or the payments fall into arrears and then take weeks to re-establish ... "

The proposed solution was to transfer the task of assessing and enforcing maintenance to a new administrative body, and the Child Support Act 1991 was enacted to achieve this. The court does retain a residual role to award maintenance as well as capital provision, as will be explained below. However, since the case-load of the Child Support Agency—currently around 1.4 million—far outnumbers the few thousand orders made by the courts, it is appropriate to consider the newer scheme first.

The Child Support Act 1991

The 1991 Act was enacted—with all-party support—in an attempt to give effect to the **7–009** philosophy that all parents had a moral duty to maintain their children until they were old enough to look after themselves; and that although events might change the relationship between the parents they could not change the parents' responsibilities towards their children. It reflected a determination to create an efficient system whereby parents would be required to support their children at a realistic level, and was justified not only by pragmatic considerations of reducing unnecessary public expenditure, but also by the ideological determination to challenge what had become the common assumption—that the state (or taxpayers) should assume financial responsibility for the family when a marriage or other relationship broke down. The essence of the scheme involved a fundamental change in technique: the legal system, dealing on a case-by-case discretionary basis with the assessment of child main-tenance, was supplanted by an administrative system assessing maintenance according to mathematical formulae. But the legislation proved deeply controversial. The con-fident claims for the improvements that would be effected by the introduction of skilled management techniques were not vindicated. The complexity of the formulae led to mistakes and delays in assessing liability. The newly created Child Support Agency could not cope with its case load, and the House of Commons Social Security Committee was only one of many official bodies which assessed the Agency's admin-istrative performance as "dire". As the Consultation Paper issued by the newly elected Labour Government in 1998 noted:

(the) "system of child support we inherited is a mess. It is failing our children, 1.8 million of whom receive no maintenance from their fathers. It is failing parents— the mothers on Income Support who see every penny of maintenance go straight to the Exchequer—and the fathers who lose contact with their children. It is failing the taxpayer who is picking up the bill for the non-resident parents who don't support their children." (*Children First: a New Approach to Child Support*)

The Child Support, Pensions and Social Security Act 2000 accordingly amended the way in which maintenance was calculated under the Child Support Act 1991. Due to delays in setting up the infrastructure, in particular the new computer systems, the new provisions were not brought into effect until March 3, 2003, and applied only to those whose liability for child support began after that date. The old rules continued to apply to earlier cases. It was initially intended that the new scheme should be extended to earlier cases but, three years on, two-thirds of the caseload of the Child Support Agency consists of cases assessed according to the old scheme. For this reason, and because it is difficult to evaluate the reforms without some knowledge of the system that preceded them, the text gives a brief account of the original scheme as well as the changes made by the 2000 Act before examining the latest proposals for reform.

(1) *The basis of liability*

7–010 The Child Support Act is based on the premise that it is the responsibility of parents, rather than the State, to support their children. But who counts as a parent for these purposes, and in what circumstances will the responsibility of support be imposed?

(a) Liability only on natural parents

7–011 The Act—in contrast to the principle developed in matrimonial law and accepted in the Children Act 1989—does not impose any financial obligation on a step-parent or other person who has treated the child as a child of the family. The Act is based on the principle that children should look to their natural parents for support. The only modification to this is that adoptive parents and persons treated as parents under the Human Fertilisation and Embryology Act (see Ch.10) are subject to the same obligations as biological parents.

(b) Liability only arises if parent and child are not living in the same household

7–012 The Child Support Act is thus concerned with the situation in which a family relationship has broken down (or where there was no co-residence between the parties in the first place). A child is only a "qualifying child" for the purposes of the Act if either or both parents are "non-resident parents"—a term introduced by the 2000 Act to replace the more pejorative "absent parent"—and the child is residing with a "person with care". The Act follows the traditional pattern of English law of refusing to define the level of support appropriate to a child living under the same roof with the parents. Different rules also apply if the child is in the care of the local authority.

(2) *Meeting the responsibility for maintaining a child*

7–013 For the purposes of the Child Support legislation, a non-resident parent is to be taken to have met his or her responsibility to a qualifying child by making periodical payments assessed in accordance with the formula laid down in the Act. Parents are in principle free to make their own agreements about child support and to abstain from using the services of the Agency, but they cannot by private agreement exclude the right subsequently to apply for a maintenance assessment.

If the person with care of a qualifying child is in receipt of income-related benefits, different considerations apply. In this case, the legislation *requires* the person with care to authorise the taking of action to recover child support maintenance from the non-resident parent (s.6 of the 1991 Act). Failure to do so may result in the giving of a "reduced benefit direction"—*i.e.* the amount of the relevant benefit will be reduced in accordance with the provisions of the Act. This will not be done if there are reasonable grounds for believing that there is a risk to the parent with care, or of any child living with him or her "suffering harm or undue distress" as a result of a direction. Of course, if the mother does not know the identity of the father, or claims not to, there will often be little in practice that the Agency can do.

(3) *Quantifying child support maintenance: the formulae*

Under the original provisions of the Child Support Act, calculations of maintenance **7–014** were closely tied to income support levels, both in assessing how much was needed for maintenance and how much the so-called "absent parent" should have left to live on. The formulae were extremely complex and made no allowance for the living costs of any new spouse or partner of the absent parent, nor for the living costs of the any step-children living with the absent parent, since it was thought that children should look to their birth parents for support. In addition, the CSA's calculations were rendered far more difficult by the possibility of departure directions (see below, para.7–015), with the result that over 100 pieces of information could be required to make the assessment.

In 1998 it was suggested that a move to the Australian system, involving "the deduction of a specified percentage of income according to the number of children involved" would be preferable (Davis et al., *Child Support in Action* (Hart Publishing, London, 1998)). This idea was taken up in *Children First*, and enacted in the 2000 Act.

Under the new scheme, the income of the parent with care is ignored and "non-resident parents" simply pay a percentage of their net income—15 per cent if there is one qualifying child, 20 per cent if there are two and 25 per cent if there are three or more. The figure of 15 per cent was chosen because it was "roughly half the average that an intact two-parent family spends on a child" (*A new contract for welfare: Children's rights and Parents' responsibilities*, Ch.2). There is an upper limit of £2,000 per week on the income to which a maintenance assessment applies, which means that the maximum assessment is £26,000 per annum (for three or more children).

There are, inevitably, qualifications to this simple scheme, relating to the income of the non-resident parent, the extent to which the non-resident parent has contact with the child(ren), and the number of children living with the non-resident parent.

First, those earning under £100 weekly only have to pay £5 weekly, regardless of the number of qualifying children (the flat rate). The percentage levy is reduced for those with net incomes between £100 and £200 weekly (the reduced rate): see Child Support (Maintenance Calculations and Special Cases) Regulations 2000, SI 2001/155, r.3 for the way this is worked out. Nothing is payable if the non-resident parent has income of less than £5 per week or is a child (*i.e.* under the age of 16), a person aged 16 or 17 who is receiving Income Support or Jobseekers' Allowance (or whose partner is receiving those benefits), a person receiving an allowance in respect of work-based training for young people, a student or a prisoner. Certain persons in hospital and nursing homes are also exempt.

Secondly, since the Government wished to encourage continued contact and shared care, the amount payable is reduced according to the number of nights that the child spends with the non-resident parent. When a child spends at least 52 nights a year (one night a week) with the non-resident parent, the latter's liability is reduced by one seventh of the weekly rate (and by two sevenths for between 104 and 155 nights, etc.). An example of how this would work where there are two qualifying children who spend different amounts of time with the non-resident parent is provided by *Child Support: A guide to how child maintenance is worked out* (CSL102):

"John and Sandra share the care of their two children. Their son, Jack, spends Friday night to Sunday afternoon (104 nights a year) with John and the balance of the week with Sandra. Their daughter, Zoe, spends one night a week at John's home (52 nights a year). John's child maintenance of £40 (net income of £200 a week) is reduced by 3/14 (2/7 plus 1/7 divided by 2). He has to pay £31.43 a week" (p.18).

Thirdly, the legislation addresses the problem that the old system did not take into account support for step-children living in the same household. The Government expressed the view that the system should not force fathers "to choose between supporting their first and second families". The formula is thus to be adjusted in its application to a non-resident parent who has children or step-children living in the household. The adjustment involves ignoring 15, 20 or 25 per cent of the non-resident parent's income, depending on the number of children in the current household. Thus:

"Graham and Theresa are divorced with one child who lives with Theresa. Graham lives with his new partner, Paula, and their two children. Graham's net weekly income is £280. Because he has two children living in his current family, his net weekly income is reduced by 20 per cent (£56) before his child maintenance is worked out. Child maintenance is 15 per cent (because he has to pay for one child) of £224 (£280–£56) which is £34. Graham's child maintenance is £34 a week." (*Child Support: A guide to how child maintenance is worked out* (CSL102), p.10)

The Government suggested that its scheme involved "a slight preference to children in the first family." It is difficult to see how this is the case, given that higher amounts are allowed for children living with the non-resident parent. In the above example, the notional amount used to support the two children living with Graham is £56 (20 per cent of £280); if he had had two children with Theresa he would have been liable to pay only £44.80 for their support (20 per cent of £224).

The legislation also makes provision for the parent who has children living in several different households. In this situation the amount payable will be divided between the children. For example:

"Mike is the non-resident parent of Ruth's daughter, Tracey. He is also the non-resident parent of Jill's sons, Kevin and Tony. Mike is required to pay child maintenance for three children in total so his maintenance will be 25 per cent of his net weekly income of £360. This is £90. This amount is divided between Ruth and Jill in proportion to the number of qualifying children each of them has—1/3 to Ruth and 2/3 to Jill. Mike pays child maintenance of £30 a week to Ruth and £60 a week to Jill." (*Child Support: A guide to how child maintenance is worked out* (CSL102), p.20)

(4) *Departing from the formulae*

7–015 In addition to the above, the amount of maintenance payable may be varied in certain specified circumstances. Even the original provisions made some allowance for "special cases", although this was limited to the introduction of another formula. The Child Support Act 1995 went further and incorporated an element of discretion into the scheme, providing that a "departure direction" could be made on certain grounds if it was "just and equitable" to do so. The new system retains a discretionary element and allows either parent to apply for a "variation" (see the Child Support (Variations) Regulations 2000, SI 2001/1 56).

The grounds on which a variation can be made are similar, although not identical, to those that justified a departure direction under the 1995 Act. The first two permit downward variations. The first group relates to "Special Expenses", which include costs incurred in maintaining contact with a child, debts incurred for the benefit of the family before the breakdown, and the costs of making payments in relation to a mortgage over the previous family home (unless the non-resident parent still has an interest in it). The second group relates to "Property or Capital Transfers"—and is concerned with the common arrangement under which the husband transferred property or capital to the wife on the understanding that he would not have to make any maintenance payments. Variations are only permitted on this ground if the transfer took place before the Child Support Act came into force on April 5, 1993, which means that this ground is of diminishing relevance. The third ground allows the maintenance payable to be varied upwards where the non-resident parent has assets exceeding £65,000, or seems to enjoy a lifestyle inconsistent with the amount of income declared to the Agency, or has unreasonably reduced his or her income (*e.g.* by investing in assets which do not produce income or by diverting income to others).

In all of the cases specified, the Secretary of State must be of the opinion that it would be just and equitable to agree to a variation, having regard to the welfare of any child likely to be affected. In addition, certain general principles are stated to be relevant: first, that parents should be responsible for maintaining their children whenever they can afford to do so, and secondly, where a parent has more than one child, his obligation to maintain any one of them should be no less of an obligation than his obligation to maintain any other of them.

(5) *Relevance of the child's welfare*

In exercising discretionary powers under the Child Support Acts, regard is to be had **7–016** to the welfare of any child likely to be affected by the decision. This duty extends beyond the "qualifying children" in respect of whom a maintenance assessment may be made. It seems that (for example) a child support officer should "have regard" to the effect of relevant decisions on the non-resident parent's other children or step-children, or even, perhaps, on a parent who is a "child". But the requirement to "have regard" is weak, and in any event there is no straightforward redress for those who consider that it has not been fully observed.

(6) *The role of the courts in relation to child support*

The corollary of the introduction of a formula to assess maintenance payments was **7–017** that responsibility for doing so should be shifted from the courts, whose awards were thought to be both unpredictable and low in amount, to the Child Support Agency. The general principle laid down in the Act is, therefore, that when a child support officer has jurisdiction to make an assessment, the courts may not exercise any power to make or vary any maintenance order in respect of the child.

A child support officer will always have jurisdiction to make an assessment where the parent with care is in receipt of benefits. However, prior to the 2000 amendments, the jurisdiction of the CSA was excluded in non-benefit cases if there was either a written agreement that had been made before 1993, or a consent order (as to which see also para.8–006, below). The court also had the power to vary such an order. This led to the practice (as described in *V v V* [2001] 2 F.L.R. 799, Fam Div) of the courts making an order by consent for nominal periodical payments at the start of the proceedings, and varying it to the level it thought fit at the end of the proceedings. Under the new provisions, a court order made after April 5, 2002 will only have the effect of excluding the jurisdiction of the CSA for one year. After that time, either party may apply to the CSA. Unless either party does so apply, the court retains the power to vary or revoke the order.

The court also has jurisdiction in other cases where the child support officer does not, and the residual role of the court is considered further below (paras 7–020 *et seq.*).

(7) *Collection and enforcement of child support maintenance*

7–018 The Conservative Government believed that the Child Support Act would create an "efficient and effective service" to the public, ensuring that maintenance was paid regularly and on time, so that the "habit of payment" was quickly established and was not compromised by early arrears. The legislation accordingly conferred extensive enforcement powers on the Child Support Agency—for example, power to make a "deduction from earnings order" whereby an employer would be required to pay part of a person's wage or salary entitlement directly to the Agency. Where such an order would not be appropriate—for example because the person concerned was not in employment, or such an order had already proved ineffective—application could be made to the magistrates' court for a liability order, which gave the Agency power to seek even harsher measures (including, ultimately, the right to apply to the court to commit a defaulter to prison). These powers constituted a complete code for the enforcement of orders.

But, notwithstanding this wide range of legal powers, the expectations of the Conservative Government were not fulfilled. The changes made by the 2000 Act involved both "carrots" and "sticks" to tempt or oppress non-resident parents into paying. The carrots included the "more customer-focused service", which it was hoped would increase "compliance and support among non-resident parents", together with the lower payments required in some cases under the new formula. The sticks included more drastic penalties for non-compliance, extending to a power to disqualify a non-resident parent from driving. It was also hoped that the simpler formula would enable the CSA to spend less time on calculating what maintenance is payable and more on ensuring that it is paid.

Once again, these hopes have not been realised. Little use has been made of the new penalties for enforcement (in 2005–06 there were, for example, a mere five driving licence disqualification sentences). The *Child Support Agency Operational Improvement Plan 2006–2009*, published in 2006, noted that around 30 per cent of non-resident parents from whom the Agency requested payment had failed to pay and that as of April 2005 unpaid maintenance amounted to £3.3 billion.

Parents with care, who have no power to enforce maintenance orders themselves, are understandably aggrieved by this situation, and one such parent, Mrs Kehoe, brought a challenge under the Human Rights Act 1998, claiming that her inability to enforce maintenance payments constituted a breach of Art.6 of the European Convention. The House of Lords, by a majority, dismissed her claim. Lord Bingham noted the theoretical advantages of the Child Support Agency:

"[i]t might well be thought that a single professional agency, with the resources of the state behind it and an array of powers at its command, would be more consistent in assessing and more effective in enforcing payment than individual parents acting in a random and uncoordinated way." (*R (Kehoe) v Secretary of State for Work and Pensions* [2005] UKHL 48, at para.6)

The verdict of Mrs Kehoe perhaps reflects the operation of the Agency more accurately:

"[m]y only remedy is to constantly pressurise the CSA which takes no real responsibility for ensuring maintenance is paid and for whom I am just a nuisance."

One way of limiting the effect of these problems on those who should be receiving maintenance would be for the state to guarantee that a minimum sum would be paid to the parent with care even if the non-resident parent paid irregularly or not at all. This is a safety-net that other countries have adopted, and in 2005 the Select Committee on Work and Pensions noted that "[i]n the light of the poor performance of the CSA in enforcing child support there might be a case for guaranteeing child support" (Second Report, *The Performance of the Child Support Agency*, HC 44-I, para.145). The government, however, refused to consider even the Select Committee's tentative suggestion of further research, arguing that parents on benefit would lose their incentive to comply with the Agency (*The Child Support Agency: Government Response to the Committee's 2nd Report of Session 2004-05*, HC 477).

(8) *Conclusions on the child support scheme*

The fact that 30 per cent of non-resident parents are not paying any maintenance does **7–019** at least mean that 70 per cent are paying *some* maintenance—but as the Agency's *Annual Report* for 2004–05 noted, only 70 per cent of those paying actually paid the full amount.

At a theoretical level, the amendments introduced by the 2000 Act reflect a different view of the obligations owed by a non-resident parent to his or her child. Support is pegged to the level of the non-resident parent's actual income, rather than to the amounts payable by way of Income Support, reflecting the idea that children should be entitled to the same level of support that they would have enjoyed had the relationship between the parents continued (or, in some cases, existed). The sums paid under the old and new schemes do differ slightly: as of March 2006 the mean liability was £18 under the old scheme and £24 under the new (CSA, *Summary of Statistics* (DWP, 2006), table 15). A more significant difference lay in the relative proportions of nil assessments: 57 per cent under the old scheme, compared to a mere 13 per cent under the new. It should also be noted that under the new scheme the first £10 of maintenance paid is to be disregarded in calculating the parent with care's entitlement to means-tested benefits. This might suggest that even if non-resident parents are not paying more, their children are in fact receiving more. However, as of March 2006 only 42,000 parents with care were benefiting from the maintenance disregard—a relatively small proportion of the Agency's caseload.

At the time of writing, the future of the Child Support Agency is unclear. On February 9, 2006—the same day that its "Operational Improvement Plan" was announced—the Secretary of State for Work and Pensions stated that the current system of child support in the UK needed to be "completely redesigned and could never in its current state be made fit for purpose" To this end Sir David Henshaw was asked to develop proposals, his terms of reference being:

> "(1) How best to ensure that parents take financial responsibility for their children when they live apart; (2) The best arrangements for delivering this outcome cost effectively; (3) The options for moving to new structures and policies recognizing the need to protect the level of service offered to the current 1.5 million parents with care."

The reader will note the continuing emphasis on child support as the responsibility of the child's parents rather than of the state, as well as the desire for cost-effectiveness, which would seem to signal that there is no intention to return to the court-based system of assessing maintenance. While proponents of an integrated court-based scheme point to the advantages in having all issues relating to finance and contact dealt with by the same body, it should be noted that in these other areas there is a determined effect to deflect families from litigating as far as possible (see further para.8–002 and 12–033 below). It is therefore likely that some variation of the current system will be proposed—and perhaps equally likely that the familiar cycle of optimism and disillusionment will be repeated.

Assessment by the courts of the obligation to support children

7–020 If the Child Support Agency is dealing with a case, the court has no power to make, vary or revive any order relating to financial support. This principle was intended to confine the courts' involvement in relation to child/parent finances to exceptional cases, and it has largely been effective in doing so. But there are a number of cases in which the private law remains significant. A court may still order capital provision for a child, as long as such provision is not effectively capitalized maintenance (see *Phillips v Pearce* [1996] 2 F.L.R. 230, Johnson J.). There is also a residual role to order maintenance in situations to which the Child Support Act does not apply, or where the legislature has accepted that extra provision may be appropriate. Examples of the former include the case in which maintenance is sought from a step-parent or for a child aged 17 or 18 who is not in full-time education. It is even possible for a court to order maintenance in favour of a child over the age of 18 who is in full-time education or training (see *e.g. B v B (Adult Student: Liability to Support)* [1998] 1 F.L.R. 373, CA). Extra provision may be appropriate if the non-resident parent earns more than £2000 per week—the maximum figure to which the Child Support Act formula applies—or if the child is disabled.

The powers of the court to make financial orders in favour of children are to be found in a variety of different statutes of varying scope. For example, the court has power in divorce, dissolution or nullity proceedings to make financial and property adjustment orders in favour of "children of the family"; and the court is directed to give first consideration to the welfare of children of the family in exercising its extensive powers to make financial orders (see para.8–014, below). There are also powers to make financial orders for children of the family in other proceedings between spouses and civil partners while the relationship is subsisting (see Part D below). This current section will concentrate on the court's powers to order provision under the Children Act 1989, which differ from those already outlined in that the focus is on the provision to be made for the child, rather than between the parties to a formal relationship. The 1989 Act reformed and assimilated other provisions whereby parents—including step-parents—could be ordered to make provision for children of the family (see s.15 and Sch.1). This section sets out who may be ordered to make provision, who may apply for provision, the orders that may be made and the principles that the court will apply in exercising its discretion.

The reader will observe in the following account that the cases tend to involve claims against rich fathers who were not married to the mothers of their children, reflecting the residual scope of the court's role, the fact that such women have no other means of securing capital provision from their erstwhile partners, and, as Thorpe L.J. pointed out in *Re P (Child: Financial Provision)* [2003] EWCA Civ 837, the fact that the affluent are less likely to be deterred by the costs of litigation.

(1) *Who may be ordered to make provision?*

Under Sch.1 of the Children Act 1989, only parents may be ordered to make provision **7–021** for their children. In this context, however, "parent" has an extended meaning. It includes biological parents (whether married to one another or not) and adoptive parents. It also includes "any party to a marriage (whether or not subsisting) in relation to whom the child . . . is a child of the family." Section 105 of the Children Act 1989 provides that the expression "child of the family" in relation to the parties to a marriage means:

(1) a child of both of those parties; and

(2) any other child, not being a child who is placed with those parties as foster-parents by a local authority or voluntary organisation, who has been treated by both of those parties as a child of their family.

An identical definition applies to civil partners (see Sch.6 para.48 of the CPA 2004). The inclusion of children "treated" as a child of the family by both parties to a marriage or civil partnership makes the existence of a biological relationship (or even a formal legal relationship, such as adoption) between the child and the adult irrelevant to the question of whether the court has jurisdiction to make orders. But although the definition is very wide it is not all-embracing. In particular, it only applies where adults in question have formalised their relationship: a parent's cohabitant (if not themselves a biological parent) cannot be ordered to make provision for the parent's child, regardless of how long the parties have shared a home. Nor, indeed, is it automatic that a step-parent will be regarded as having treated the child as a child of the family. The courts have held, for example, that it is impossible to treat an unborn child as a child of the family (see *A v A (Family: Unborn Child)* [1974] Fam. 6, CA). If a man marries a woman who is pregnant by someone else, the baby will be a child of their family if the husband treats it as such after birth, even if the wife has deceived him into thinking that he is the father. However, if the relationship breaks down before the birth, the child will be outside the definition whatever the husband may have said about his intentions to treat the baby as his own.

The question of whether the couple has indeed "treated" the child as a child of their family is one of fact, to be judged objectively:

In *Re A (Child of the Family)* [1998] 1 F.L.R. 347, CA, a child was born to a 17-year-old. The girl's parents helped her look after their grandchild and eventually cared for her on a full-time basis. The court held that the grandchild was a child of the grandparents' marriage. It was right to be cautious in deciding that grandparents were treating the child as a child of their family and it would be wrong to hold that the relationship had been established where the grandparents had done no more than society would expect in looking after a grandchild in response to some family crisis. In this case, however, the child called the grandparents "Mum" and "Dad", and the grandparents not only provided primary care for the child but took decisions about medical treatment and education. On the facts, therefore, the grandparents' commitment went beyond the ordinary natural affection and close ties inherent in the relationship, and justified the finding that they had assumed responsibility for the child and treated her as the child of their marriage.

(2) *Who may apply for an order?*

7–022   The list of those who may apply for an order is a long one, consisting of parents (as defined above), guardians, special guardians, any person in whose favour a residence order is in force with respect to a child, and even an adult child. In this last case, however, the powers of the court to order provision have been restricted in a number of ways. First, no order may be made if the parents are living together in the same household (so that it is still impossible for a child to compel parents who are living together to provide support). Secondly, the court's powers on such an application are limited to making periodical payment or lump sum orders, rather than an order for the transfer or settlement of property. Thirdly, in this context the powers are only available to be used against a legal parent. The draftsman has carefully excluded the possibility of applications being made by a step-child against his step-parent or against others who have cared for the child during minority (see Sch.1, para.16(2)).

In addition, there are certain circumstances in which the court may make financial orders even though no application for such an order has been made. The Children Act 1989 provides that the court may make a financial order whenever it makes, varies, or discharges a residence order—and a residence order may be made (whether or not applied for) in any family proceedings if the court considers that the order should be made.

(3) *The orders which may be made*

7–023   There is now a wide range of orders available to the court. The court may order a "parent" to make periodical payments (secured or unsecured—see para.8–009, below, for the difference between the two), to pay a lump sum, and to transfer (or settle) property for the child's benefit. In an appropriate case, these powers may be exercised to deal with the family home. A local authority tenancy might (for example) be transferred to the mother for the children's benefit; or a home belonging to the parents or either of them might be settled on trusts permitting the children to reside there with one of the parents during the children's minority. The flexibility of these powers is well illustrated by the decision in *J v C (Child: Financial Provision)* [1999] 1 F.L.R. 152, Hale J.:

The father won £1.4 million in the National Lottery. The child was living with her mother and half-sisters in a house rented from a Housing Association. The court ordered that the father provide £70,000 to buy a house. This would be settled on trust for the child to live there with her mother and half-sisters. The capital would revert to the father when his daughter reached age 21 (or six months after she finished full-time education, if later). The trustees would have power to deal with the situation in which the mother married or cohabited, and disputes about the exercise of that power would be resolved by the court. The father was also ordered to pay £12,000 to furnish the house, together with £9,000 to buy the mother a second-hand Ford Mondeo car.

The relationship between different types of orders was explored in *Phillips v Peace* [2004] EWHC 3180 (Fam):

> As the result of earlier litigation, the father had been ordered by the court to settle property for the benefit of his child. On a subsequent application by the mother, the court noted that it could not order the father to settle or transfer further property, since "[o]rders for the benefit of a child for the transfer and settlement of property are to be regarded as different methods of dealing with the same, one-off, need for property adjustment in an appropriate case." (*per* Singer J., para.20). While it would be possible under the terms of the legislation to order a second lump sum, such provision could not be used to circumvent the prohibition on a second property adjustment order.

(4) *Principles to be applied in exercising the discretion to make orders*

The Children Act 1989 lays down guidelines for the exercise of the court's powers **7–024** which are similar but not identical to those governing the comparable powers of the court on divorce or dissolution. The court's attention is directed to "the manner in which the child was being, or was expected to be, educated or trained", and it is to "have regard to all the circumstances", including matters such as the income, earning capacity, property and other financial resources which the applicant, the parents and the person in whose favour the order would be made has or is likely to have; those persons' financial needs, obligations and responsibilities; the financial needs, income, earning capacity (if any), property and other financial resources of the child, and any physical or mental disability (see Sch.1, para.4(1) of the Children Act 1989). One factor not explicitly mentioned in this list is the parents' standard of living (contrast para.8–029). Despite this omission, it was held in *F v G (Child: Financial Provision)* [2004] EWHC 1848 (Fam) that it is permissible to take the parent's standard of living into account. Similarly, while the 1989 Act does not stipulate that the child's welfare is to be either the "first" or the "paramount" consideration in this context, it was emphasized in *Re P (Child: Financial Provision)* [2003] EWCA Civ 837 that welfare must be "a constant influence on the discretionary outcome" (*per* Thorpe L.J. at para.44).

Although the 1989 Act focuses on the needs of the child, it is clear that provision for the child—for example in the form of a house—will also benefit the child's carer. More directly, the child's needs may include an allowance for the parent caring for the child. In deciding on the appropriate level of financial provision the courts have consistently held in recent years that a child is entitled to be brought up in circumstances that bear some sort of relationship to the non-resident parent's own standard of living and resources (see *e.g. J v C (Child: Financial Provision)* [1999] 1 F.L.R. 152; *Re P (Child: Financial Provision)* [2003] EWCA Civ 837; *F v G (Child: Financial Provision)* [2004]

EWHC 1848 (Fam)). Whether the non-resident parent is ordered to settle property (which will revert back to the settlor when the child reaches adulthood) or transfer it outright will depend on the nature of the relationship between the adult parties. The former option was preferred in *A v A (A Minor: Financial Provision)* [1994] 1 F.L.R. 657, but in *Francis v Manning* [1997] EWCA 1231 the Court of Appeal distinguished *A v A* by confining it to its particular facts and ordered the transfer of the former family home:

> "Where a very rich man fathers a child on his mistress, she cannot by application under CA 1989 obtain an order which would have the effect of conferring capital on the child for use and enjoyment in later life. A completely different approach is necessarily adopted where a family unit is created without marriage and where on the disintegration of the family the court has the opportunity to preserve the family home for the benefit of a child and for the parent who happens to assume the responsibility for primary care."

This effectively draws the dividing line between co-residential relationships and sexual relationships that do not involve cohabitation—although it should be noted that in that case consideration for the transfer was provided in the form of the father's release from the joint debts and deferred payment.

Finally it should be noted that the legislation contains additional provisions (similar to provisions in the divorce legislation) to be applied in cases in which the "parent" against whom the order is sought is a step-parent or other person who is not the child's mother or father. In such cases, the court must have regard to whether the person concerned had assumed responsibility for the maintenance of the child, and, if so, the extent to which and the basis on which he assumed that responsibility and the length of the period during which he met that responsibility; whether he did so knowing that the child was not his child; and the liability of any other person to maintain the child (Sch.1, para.4(2)).

D: COURT ORDERS FOR MAINTENANCE

7–025 Three different procedures are available whereby one spouse may, during the legal continuance of the marriage, seek a court order for maintenance from the other, and each is replicated for the benefit of civil partners in the Civil Partnership Act 2004. Maintenance for a child of the family may also be ordered, as long as the court has jurisdiction (see para.7–020, above).

(1) *Application in the High Court or County Court*

7–026 Section 27 of the Matrimonial Causes Act provides that either party to a marriage may apply to the High Court or to a divorce county court for an order on the ground that the other party has failed to provide reasonable maintenance for the applicant, or has failed to provide or to make a proper contribution towards reasonable maintenance for any child of the family (as defined above, see para.7–021). Civil partners may make an application under the almost identically-worded Pt 9 of Sch.5 of the 2004 Act. In deciding whether there has been such a failure, and if so what order to make, the court is to "have regard to all the circumstances of the case", including the matters to which the court is specifically required to take into account when exercising its powers on divorce or dissolution.

If the applicant establishes that there has been such a failure, the court can make orders for periodical payments (secured or unsecured) and a lump sum, but it lacks the power to make the pension sharing orders or property adjustment orders that are available upon divorce, dissolution or nullity. In practice there have been very few applications to the superior courts for maintenance provision during the marriage, and it is unlikely that this option will prove any more popular among civil partners.

(2) *Application in the Magistrates' Court*

Since 1878, magistrates' courts have had power to make financial orders in domestic **7–027** cases, and their powers are now codified in the Domestic Proceedings and Magistrates' Courts Act 1978—a reforming Act intended to bring the family jurisdiction of the magistrates' courts into line with the reformed law administered in the divorce court under the Matrimonial Causes Act 1973. These powers may now be exercised in favour of civil partners under Sch.6 of the 2004 Act. The ground upon which an order can be made is that the other party has failed to provide reasonable maintenance for the applicant or a child of the family, or that he or she has deserted the applicant or been guilty of behaviour such that the applicant cannot reasonably be expected to live with the other spouse. In such circumstances the court may order periodical payments and/ or a lump sum (not exceeding £1,000). There is also power (now rarely exercised) to make orders by consent and to make orders reflecting payments previously made voluntarily, but this last provision is virtually a dead letter.

(3) *Separation orders made by High Court or County Court*

Under the Matrimonial Causes Act 1973, a petition for judicial separation can be **7–028** presented to the court by either party to the marriage on the ground that one of the "facts" from which the court could infer irretrievable breakdown—adultery, behaviour, desertion, or living apart for the requisite period—has been established (s.17(1)). The court does not need to be satisfied that the marriage has irretrievably broken down. A judicial separation decree (1) makes it no longer "obligatory for the petitioner to cohabit with the respondent" (s.18(1)); and (2) deprives the parties of their mutual rights of intestate succession (s.18(2)). But in practice it is the fact that the court has power, on or after the making of a decree of judicial separation, to make financial provision and property adjustment orders that accounts for the significant number of judicial separation petitions. People who need to make proper arrangements for living apart, but object to divorce or have no wish to remarry, will often seek judicial separation. It remains to be seen whether any civil partners will wish to take advantage of the equivalent separation orders available under s.56 of the 2004 Act: if they do, the same powers will be exercisable by the court.

E: CONCLUSION

It is clear from the above discussion that the rules relating to family maintenance are **7–029** not entirely consistent. The parallel jurisdictions of the CSA and the courts may be problematic in certain cases: as Wilson J. noted in *V v V* [2001] 2 F.L.R. 799, "the level of child maintenance bears upon the content of the other orders for capital and/or income provision which it is for the court to make; and ... [it is] absurd that its resolution of that one issue has to be foregone." (at 803). Another problem is that the justification for awarding support is not consistent: the Child Support Act bases liability on biological parenthood, while under the Matrimonial Causes Act, Children Act and Domestic Proceedings and Magistrates Courts Act, orders may be made against (at least some types of) social parents.

The extent to which support is provided by an ex-spouse after divorce, and the account that is taken of employment prospects and the availability of state benefits are considered further in the next chapter, which examines the way that assets are dealt with upon divorce.

Chapter 8

DEALING WITH ASSETS UPON RELATIONSHIP BREAKDOWN

A: INTRODUCTION

The way in which the law deals with the parties' assets upon relationship breakdown **8–001** is important not merely because of its financial implications for the parties but also for what it tells us about the way the particular relationship under consideration is perceived. Allowing the parties to make their own arrangements would suggest that they were viewed as independent and equally able to argue for their own rights. Requiring them to share the property equally would, by contrast, indicate that relationship was viewed as a partnership, with each party having an equal entitlement to the assets. Laws couched in terms of obligations of "protection" and "support" would imply a different type of relationship, one that involves ongoing responsibilities to the other, weaker, partner beyond the end of the relationship.

In the context of cohabiting relationships, it is the *absence* of a special set of rules to reallocate property at the end of the relationship that is most striking. The question of whether a cohabiting couple may enter into a contract to regulate how their assets should be divided on relationship breakdown is discussed further below, and the possibility of a tenancy in the name of one cohabitant being transferred to the other is considered in the conclusion. In other cases the division of assets will be governed by property law (see Ch.5).

This chapter is therefore largely concerned with the division of assets when a formal relationship is terminated. The same rules are applicable upon the dissolution of a civil partnership as upon divorce: s.72 of the Civil Partnership Act 2004 declares explicitly that Sch.5 "makes provision for financial relief in connection with civil partnerships that corresponds to provision made for financial relief in connection with marriages by Pt 2 of the Matrimonial Causes Act 1973." And the same rules also apply upon proceedings for annulment or legal separation. The court has extensive discretionary powers to deal with the assets of the parties (in sharp contrast to the lack of discretion during the subsistence of the marriage or civil partnership). The Matrimonial Causes Act 1973 (and Sch.5 of the Civil Partnership Act 2004) lists a number of relevant factors rather than any guiding principle and directs the court to take "all the circumstances of the case" into account in exercising its discretion. Such a broad discretion poses its own problems. As Lord Nicholls observed in *Miller v Miller; McFarlane v McFarlane* [2006] UKHL 24:

> "Of itself this direction leads nowhere. Implicitly the courts must exercise their powers so as to achieve an outcome which is fair between the parties. But an important aspect of fairness is that like cases should be treated alike. So, perforce, if there is to be an acceptable degree of consistency of decision from one case to the next, the courts must themselves articulate, if only in the broadest fashion, what are the applicable if unspoken principles guiding the court's approach." (para.6)

Lord Nicholls had himself embarked upon the task of laying down some general principles in the earlier case of *White v White* [2000] 2 F.L.R. 981, HL. The first, uncontroversial, principle was that the role of the court was to achieve a fair outcome, taking all the circumstances into account. More novel was the suggestion that "in seeking to achieve a fair outcome, there [was] no place for discrimination between husband and wife and their respective roles", while, to ensure that no such discrimination occurred:

> "a judge would always be well advised to check his tentative view against the yardstick of equality of division. As a general guide, equality should be departed from only if, and to the extent that, there is good reason for doing so. The need to consider and articulate reasons for departing from equality would help the parties and the court to focus on the need to ensure the absence of discrimination." (*per* Lord Nicholls at 989)

These dicta have given rise to considerable debate, and although many of the issues have now been clarified by the decision in *Miller; McFarlane*, new questions are posed by that case. The two main judgments—delivered by Lord Nicholls and Baroness Hale of Richmond—emphasised three key themes: needs, compensation, and sharing. Behind this apparent consensus lay subtle differences of emphasis. Lord Nichols spoke of needs in general terms, while Baroness Hale, focusing on the reasons that might justify redistribution of property, noted that the most common rationale for redistribution was that "*the relationship has generated needs* which it is right that the other party should meet." (para.138, emphasis in original). This raises questions as to how needs *not* arising from the relationship—but, for example, from one party's disability—should be addressed. Similarly, the discussion of "sharing" revealed differences of opinion as to what should be shared (see further para.8–022 below). But both were agreed on the importance of compensation—which would be aimed "at redressing any significant prospective economic disparity between the parties arising from the way they conducted their marriage" (*per* Lord Nicholls, para.13, see also Baroness Hale, para.140). The reader will find the themes outlined above recurring throughout the chapter, since the decision of the House of Lords in this case—like *White v White* before it—has implications across the whole topic.

The wealth of case-law on the division of assets on divorce—in contrast to the paucity of cases on obtaining a divorce—might give the impression that the financial consequences of divorce are usually resolved by the courts in adversarial litigation. This is far from being the case, and Part B considers the extent to which the parties can make their own arrangements, along with the procedural innovations designed to make disputes that do come to court less adversarial. It also looks at the possibility that cohabiting couples may regulate their affairs by means of a contract. However, the majority of the chapter is devoted to the way in which the courts have resolved disputes between spouses, since the principles developed by the courts may influence the way in which the parties decide to divide their assets (and is likely to influence the way in which the courts deal with the assets of civil partners). Part C accordingly summarises the orders that the court can make, Part D outlines the factors that the court is directed to take into account, and Part E looks briefly at the circumstances in which an order of the court may be varied or set aside. The structure of the chapter thus follows the possible stages through which a couple may pass in dealing with the issue of how to divide their assets on relationship breakdown.

The chapter concludes with a brief assessment of the current law, and a comparison with the limited rights that are currently available to cohabitants upon relationship breakdown.

B: Private Ordering and its Limits

The first point to be made is that there is no requirement that the court should **8–002** scrutinise the financial arrangements made by the parties upon the legal termination of their relationship. A comparison of the numbers of orders made by the courts with the number of divorces granted reveals that in a considerable number of cases couples must be making their own arrangements, even if orders made by consent are taken into account. For obvious reasons, there are no official statistics on the number of cohabiting relationships that break down each year, but such breakdowns are vastly under-represented in the few cases involving trusts law that come before the courts. Thus private ordering is possible if both of the parties agree not to involve the court.

But what if one of the parties subsequently wishes to resile from an agreement? How far will a contract made before the relationship is formalised, or an agreement entered into at its end, be binding upon the parties if one of them later wishes to escape from the bargain? Slightly different considerations apply according to the stage at which the agreement is made, but two broad policy considerations can be discerned. It has for the past three decades been policy to encourage the parties to resolve matters for themselves rather than resorting to costly adversarial litigation that may engender further bitterness and hostility. Mediation is particularly encouraged by the courts: the successful mediated outcome in *Al-Khatib v Masry* [2004] EWCA Civ 1353 led Thorpe L.J. to express his "conviction that there is no case, however conflicted, which is not potentially open to successful mediation, even if mediation has not been attempted or has failed during the trial process" (para.17). But this emphasis on the desirability of resolving matters by private agreement has not wholly supplanted a much older and at first sight inconsistent philosophy. In this traditional view, the community as a whole has an interest in the financial arrangements made by a couple on divorce. The right to maintenance is a matter of public concern which cannot be bartered away by private contract (see *Hyman v Hyman* [1929] A.C. 601, HL) and accordingly a spouse's rights are not to be bargained away by private agreement. It is for this reason that statute provides that any provision in a maintenance agreement restricting the parties' right to apply to the court is void (s.34(1) of the MCA 1973). It is likely that the same considerations of public policy will apply to contracts between civil partners. By contrast, somewhat different principles apply to cohabitation contracts, and the enforceability of such contracts has long been a matter for debate.

Even if the issue does reach the court, it is not necessarily resolved in an adversarial fashion. Ambitious procedural reforms took effect from June 5, 2000 (Family Proceedings (Amendment No.2) Rules 1999) and the court will attempt to lead the parties to an agreement at a financial dispute resolution meeting.

The different types of agreements will be considered in the order in which they may occur:

Cohabitation contracts

8–003   There are certain legal requirements that must be observed in order to create a valid contract, and these do not differ whether the contract is one between commercial entities or domestic partners. The parties must intend to create a legally enforceable arrangement, there must be an offer and an acceptance, the terms of the agreement must be sufficiently precise and, unless the agreement is contained in a deed or a document under seal, there must be consideration. In addition, depending on the nature of the property, certain formalities must be observed: thus, for example, if the contract involves the sale or disposition of an interest in land it must be made in writing (s.2 of the Law of Property (Miscellaneous Provisions) Act 1989, and see para.5–006 above).

In a domestic context, there is obviously the risk that the necessary legal requirements will be overlooked, or that the court will fail to be convinced that the parties did indeed have the necessary intention to create legal relations (although the more formal the contract, the more likely it is that this requirement will be satisfied). There is also the further requirement that the terms of the agreement should not be illegal or contrary to public policy. It has been thought in the past that this might pose an obstacle to the enforceability of a cohabitation contract, on the basis that it could be seen as contrary to public policy to afford legal recognition to a non-marital relationship. In recent years, it has been thought unlikely that a court would strike down a cohabitation contract on this basis, given the rise of cohabitation and the recognition afforded to cohabitants elsewhere in the law. As yet, however, there is no modern authority upholding a contract between cohabitants, although it was suggested in *Sutton v Mishcon de Reya* [2003] EWHC 3166 (Ch) that such a contract would be upheld. The contract in that particular case, by contrast, was deemed to be a contract *for* cohabitation—involving as it did a wealthy Swedish businessman who agreed to enter into a master–slave relationship with an air steward—and the claim for the contract to be enforced was struck out.

Prenuptial agreements

8–004   In addition to the policy that the state has an interest in the financial arrangements made by the spouses on divorce, there is the further objection that prenuptial agreements are contrary to public policy as they envisage the ending of the marriage before it has even begun. It has been noted that this "seems to . . . be of less importance now that divorce is so commonplace" (*M v M (Prenuptial agreement)* [2002] 1 F.L.R. 654, Fam Div, *per* Connell J.), and the current position is that a prenuptial agreement is not binding on the court but may be taken into account as part of the circumstances of the case. The issue is how much weight should be accorded to it. Earlier cases signaled a degree of hostility to such agreement: in *F v F* [1995] 2 F.L.R. 45, CA, for example, it was held that pre-nuptial contracts were of limited significance, with Thorpe L.J. indicating his reluctance to have "standards that are intended to be of universal application throughout our society" controlled and limited by private contracts. More recently, in *K v K (Ancillary Relief: Prenuptial Agreement)* [2003] 1 F.L.R. 120, Fam Div, the pre-nuptial agreement played a more important role:

> The couple had been dating for two months when W found that she was pregnant. She did not want to be a single mother and stated that if H did not marry her she would have an abortion. He was opposed to abortion but did not want to rush into marriage and thought that they should have a long engagement to see if they were suited. Family pressure was brought to bear on him and he agreed to the marriage. The parties entered into a pre-nuptial agreement to limit any claim W might have on H's capital. Each had independent legal advice, which was to the effect that such an agreement would not be binding, especially if children were involved. The marriage broke down after a year and the judge held that "an injustice would be done to the husband if I ignored the agreement insofar as capital for the wife is concerned." However, the agreement made no mention of maintenance for the wife, and periodical payments of £15,000 were ordered to reflect the fact that she would be caring for the child. A further sum of £1.2m was ordered to provide a home for the child during his minority, which would revert to the husband when the child finished full-time education.

Despite the weight attached to the prenuptial agreement in that case, it is by no means the case that every pre-nuptial agreement will be accorded equivalent significance. The case of *J v V (Disclosure: Offshore Corporations)* [2003] EWHC 3110 (Fam) suggested a number of circumstances that might render it inappropriate to take such an agreement into account:

> "This contract was signed on the very eve of the marriage, without full legal advice, without proper disclosure and it made no allowance for the arrival of children. It must . . . fall at the very first fence, quite apart from the fact that the terms were obviously unfair, preventing the wife from claiming against the husband's assets." (*per* Coleridge J. at para.40)

Separation agreements

By contrast, the parties are encouraged to reach their own agreements upon divorce: **8–005** in *X v X (Y and Z intervening)* [2002] 1 F.L.R. 508, Fam Div, it was noted that there was no public policy objection to such an agreement—"indeed, quite the contrary." An agreement not embodied in a court order may be liable to variation as a "maintenance agreement" under the provisions of s.35 of the Matrimonial Causes Act 1973; and in any event cannot effectively exclude the court's jurisdiction to make orders in the exercise of its divorce jurisdiction. But although the court may have jurisdiction to depart from the agreed terms in the exercise of its discretion, it will be reluctant to do so. The courts lean in favour of upholding agreements; and it has been said that the court must start from the position that a solemn and freely negotiated bargain, by which a party with competent legal advice defines his own requirements, ought to be adhered to unless some clear and compelling reason is shown to the contrary.

The leading case is still *Edgar v Edgar* [1980] 1 W.L.R. 1410, CA:

> The wife of a multi-millionaire entered into an agreement whereby she accepted from her husband property then worth some £100,000, and agreed not to seek any further capital or property provision from him whether by way of ancillary relief in divorce proceedings or otherwise. Three years later she petitioned for divorce, claimed a substantial capital sum, and at first instance was awarded a lump sum of £2 million. But the Court of Appeal held that the wife had shown insufficient grounds to justify going behind the original agreement and she was restricted to the amount she had received under the agreement. It was immaterial that there may have been a disparity of bargaining power between the husband and the wife, since on the facts he had not exploited the disparity in a way unfair to the wife, who had had the benefit of proper professional advice and had deliberately chosen to ignore it.

The approach articulated in *Edgar* has stood the test of time (see *e.g. A v B (Financial Relief: Agreements)* [2005] EWHC 314 (Fam)). It is clear, however, that the circumstances in which the order was made are of considerable importance. In *G v G (Financial Provision: Separation Agreement)* [2000] 2 F.L.R. 18, Fam Div, it was suggested that the most relevant questions were: "(a) How did the agreement come to be made? (b) Did the parties themselves attach importance to it? Have the parties themselves acted on it?" It is unlikely that an agreement that was exploitative would be upheld by the courts.

Consent orders

8–006   The parties may present their agreement to the court and ask it to make a consent order (s.33A of the MCA 1973). This allows the court to scrutinise the terms of the agreement. The court has a statutory duty to consider "all the circumstances" (including those particularised in s.25 of the Matrimonial Causes Act 1973, discussed above); but it is not obliged to become a "forensic ferret" (*Harris v Manahan* [1997] 1 F.L.R. 205). On the contrary, its scrutiny is restricted to a "broad appraisal of the parties' financial circumstances as disclosed to it in the statutory form, without descent into the valley of detail" (*Pounds v Pounds* [1994] 1 F.L.R. 775 at 780, CA, *per* Waite L.J.) In particular, the court is entitled to assume that parties represented by solicitors know what they want, and the court will rely on the lawyers' help in determining whether there are any features which would render the implementation of a concluded agreement unfair (*Hall & Co v Simons* [1999] 1 F.L.R. 536, CA).

If the circumstances of the parties subsequently change, it is possible for them to seek a variation of a consent order in the same way as any other order made by the court. The formal justification for this is that such an order derives its legal effect from the decision of the court rather than from the agreement of the parties that led up to it: *De Lasala v De Lasala* [1980] A.C. 546. Thus, it is more difficult to challenge an agreement that has been enshrined in an order of the court. As Thorpe L.J. put it in *Rose v Rose* [2002] EWCA Civ 208: "from such an order a party cannot resile and he may only seek release by action or application that asserts a vitiating element, such as misrepresentation, mistake, material non-disclosure or a subsequent fundamental and unforeseen change of circumstances."

Unfortunately, a number of cases have demonstrated that on occasion the scrutiny supposedly given by the courts in order to ensure that the settlement is fair and equitable does not always achieve that objective:

> In *Harris v Manahan* [1997] 1 F.L.R. 205, CA, a district judge made a consent order, the effect of which was that a 51-year-old wife (with no earnings and no prospects of any) was not to be entitled to any periodical payments, but was to have her claims for support settled for all time by being given a share of the sale proceeds of the family home. Unfortunately, the house did not sell for the price the parties had anticipated, and eventually the mortgagees took possession. The wife (who was left with no capital assets and no income other than Income Support) applied to the court to set aside the consent order on the ground that it had been vitiated by the inadequate legal advice her solicitors had given. The court held that her application had been rightly dismissed: there had to be finality in litigation, and to that end the wife might (as Ward L.J. put it) have to be the victim sacrificed on the "high altar of policy".

Financial dispute resolution appointments

Under the procedure introduced in 2000, the parties are encouraged to reach a **8–007** settlement at a Financial Dispute Resolution appointment. The nature of FDR and the status of an agreement approved by the judge was considered in *Rose v Rose* [2002] EWCA Civ 208:

> The judge gave an indication as to what order he thought would be appropriate. The parties subsequently came to an agreement and the judge indicated that he was happy with it. However, no order was actually drafted at the court and the husband subsequently decided that he was unhappy with the agreement. The Court of Appeal noted that there were three possible outcomes of FDR: directions for adjournment, or directions for a trial, or else an order, and effectively held that since it was not either of the first two, it must be an order. It was noted that "[t]he whole purpose and effect of the FDR would be lost or compromised were parties free to analyse and re-evaluate a crucial decision of the previous day or the previous week and to decide on further reflection that they made the wrong choice." (*per* Thorpe L.J. at 991)

It was noted that while FDR could take many different forms, district judges were better qualified to offer "early neutral evaluation" of the likely outcome than to act as mediators, a role for which they had had no training. Further, "[t]he FDR is an invaluable tool for dispelling unreal expectations but in the finely balanced case it is no substitute for trial" (*per* Thorpe L.J. at 988).

C: ORDERS THE COURT CAN MAKE

Before 1970, the court's powers were largely confined to ordering cash payments, and **8–008** the allocation of property was determined by principles of trusts law. A change in approach was prompted by two factors: first, the recognition that trusts law was not an appropriate tool for doing justice between the parties, and, secondly, the perceived need to ensure adequate provision for wives unwillingly divorced under the Divorce Reform Act 1969 by economically dominant husbands. The Matrimonial Proceedings and Property Act (consolidated in the Matrimonial Causes Act 1973) greatly extended the court's powers, and the parties' strict legal entitlements to particular assets are now of only limited relevance.

> In *White v White* [2000] 2 F.L.R. 981, HL, the House of Lords was called upon to consider the significance of the fact that the parties had carried on a dairy farming business in partnership during their marriage. It dismissed the argument that there should be a strict valuation of the parties' shares according to property law. According to Lord Nicholls, "[t]he need for this type of investigation was swept away in 1970 when the new legislation gave the courts its panoply of wide discretionary powers."

The orders available to the court under the 1973 Act are divided into financial provision and property adjustment orders—the former being primarily concerned with income, the latter with capital. (Although, rather oddly, an order to pay a lump sum—perhaps of many millions of pounds—is classified as a financial provision order). The Act has been amended—first by the Pensions Act 1995 and then by the Welfare Reform and Pensions Act 1999—to recognise the increasing importance of pension funds. The same orders are now available in relation to civil partnerships under Sch.5 of the 2004 Act.

(1) *Financial provision orders*

8–009 The court can make an order for *periodical payments* of income (which may be made weekly, monthly, or annually). Such an order may be either "unsecured" or "secured": if the latter, the payer is required to set aside a fund of capital (usually stocks and shares) to which recourse can be had to make good any default in making the stipulated payments. A secured periodical payments order can therefore be effectively enforced even if the debtor dies, disappears, disposes of other property, or ceases to earn. However, secured orders are now rare, since if capital is available it is likely to be dealt with by ordering appropriate transfers between the parties.

Periodical payments orders (secured or unsecured) may also be made for a specified term, and the factors that the court will take into account in deciding whether any term is appropriate are considered below (see para.8–037 *et seq.*).

All periodical payments orders come to an end if the payee remarries or forms a new civil partnership. But a periodical payments order does not automatically terminate if the payee simply cohabits. In that case, the payer must apply to the court, which has power to reduce or extinguish the order. The court is likely to exercise this power if the new partner can provide financially for the couple (see *Atkinson v Atkinson* [1988] Fam. 93, CA). This approach has not been affected by the rise in cohabitation: as Thorpe L.J. noted in *Fleming v Fleming* [2003] EWCA Civ:

> "the conclusion that cohabitation is not to be equated with marriage remains as sound today as it was then." (para.9)

It is clear that this approach is influenced by the consideration that cohabitation does not give either party rights against the other's assets.

The fact that the court has the power to make a periodical payments order tells us little about the amount that should be ordered, or indeed the underlying purpose of such an order. In the past such an order was primarily a means for providing support for the weaker partner after the termination of the relationship. However, a wider role is envisaged by the decision of the House of Lords in *Miller v Miller; McFarlane v McFarlane* [2006] UKHL 24. Lord Nicholls suggested that periodical payments could be ordered for the purpose of compensation as well as maintenance:

> "If one party's earning capacity has been advantaged at the expense of the other party during the marriage it would be extraordinary if, where necessary, the court could not order the advantaged party to pay compensation to the other out of his enhanced earnings when he receives them. It would be most unfair if absence of capital assets were regarded as cancelling his obligation to pay compensation in respect of a continuing economic advantage he has obtained from the marriage." (para.32, and see also Baroness Hale at para.154)

An alternative to periodical payments is an order that one party pay a *lump sum* to the other. The court may order payment by instalments; and payment of the instalments may be secured. The advantages of a lump sum payable in instalments rather than periodical payments were set out in *R v R (Lump sum payments)* [2003] EWHC 3197 (Fam):

> "The beauty of including this obligation in a lump sum order rather than somehow in an order for periodical payments is that it will endure beyond the wife's remarriage . . . and will bind the husband's estate in the unlikely event of his death within the 20-year period." (para.49)

In that case the court ordered an initial instalment of £30,000, to be followed by 240 further payments equivalent to the wife's repayments under her mortgage, to enable her to rehouse herself without the need to take capital from the family farm.

(2) *Property adjustment orders*

There are three main types of property adjustment order. The court may order that **8–010** property be transferred between the parties, or settled, or that a settlement be varied. In each case the transfer, settlement or variation may be made for the benefit of the other party or a child of the family

An order requiring the settlement of property may be particularly useful in dealing with the former home of the parties, to ensure that it is available for occupation as a home for dependent children, whilst preserving both parties' financial interest in it. The order might state that the home is to be transferred to the primary carer for the duration of the child(ren)'s minority (a so-called *Mesher* order (*Mesher v Mesher* [1980] 1 All E.R. 126n, CA). A variation of this allows the wife to retain the house until she dies or remarries or becomes dependent on another man: (see *Martin v Martin* [1978] Fam. 12, CA; *Clutton v Clutton* [1991] 1 F.L.R. 242, CA). It would of course be possible for a similar order to be made—with suitable amendments—in favour of a husband or civil partner. The problems posed by such orders were recognised in *B v B (Mesher Order)* [2003] EWHC 3106 (Fam), where such an order was refused because the wife would have difficulty in building up capital assets of her own and would suffer a financial burden if the property had to be sold greater than the benefit that would accrue to the husband.

The possibility of a nuptial settlement being varied obviously depends on there being such an arrangement to vary. It is comparatively rare for such settlements to be made today. In the past this power has been used to deal with assets which might otherwise not have been subject to the court's adjustive powers, but the fact that the court now enjoys wide powers means that less use is now made of this option. Despite this, the same power now exists in relation to civil partnerships (see Sch.5 para.7(1)(c) of the CPA).

(3) *Pension sharing orders*

8–011   In one sense, a pension scheme (under which contributions are invested by trustees who pay out benefits on retirement or death) is simply a savings medium; but if the terms of the scheme meet with Inland Revenue approval, it is a savings medium with very valuable tax benefits. In particular, the contributions made by the employer are not treated as the income of the employee, the employee does not pay income tax on any contributions to the scheme made out of earnings, and the trustees can invest the fund with virtual immunity from taxation. A price has to be paid for these benefits, however. In particular, in order to make the scheme comply with Revenue requirements there will be severe restrictions on access to (and transfer of) the accumulating funds. For long, these restrictions led to the value of the funds being largely ignored on divorce, but the introduction of "portability" of pension rights—so that an employee could take the pension with him on changing jobs—served to highlight the injustice often caused. It affected women more than men, because the major responsibility for family care and home-making remained with women and the consequent limitation on their earning power often prevented them from building up pension entitlements comparable with those of men. Once the Social Security Act 1985 allowed a person changing jobs to transfer the "Cash Equivalent Transfer Value" to a new pension scheme it was difficult to see why this should not happen on divorce. The amount of wealth tied up in pension schemes was after all huge—equivalent to some 70 per cent of the wealth tied up in housing—and more than 11 million people belonged to such schemes. A powerful campaign for justice for the divorced wife built up.

It was, of course, always possible to take pension rights into account by what came to be called "offsetting". For example, the wife would take the family home whilst the husband would keep the pension. More direct methods of reallocation have now been introduced. First, the 1995 Pensions Act introduced "earmarking" (now termed "attachment"), which allows the court to order that part of the pension should be paid to the divorced spouse as and when it falls due. The 1999 Welfare Reform and Pensions Act goes much further: it allows the court to make a pension sharing order under which part (or all) of the cash equivalent transfer value is used to provide pension scheme rights for the divorced spouse. Neither Act is retrospective: attachment is only available in respect of petitions for divorce presented after July 1, 1996, and pension-sharing orders can only be made if the petition was presented after December 1, 2000. Furthermore, it should be noted that, as with all the powers listed in this section, the court has no obligation to make any particular type of order.

It will be interesting to see what use of these provisions is made as between civil partners, and how any such orders are influenced by the division of labour between the parties.

(4) *Power to order sale*

Finally it should be noted that the court now has (s.24A of the MCA and Sch.5 **8–012** para.10 of the CPA) an express power, on making an order for financial relief (other than an order for unsecured periodical payments) to order a sale of any property. In effect, the power is ancillary to the making of the other orders already considered. This power can be exercised even if a third party also has a beneficial interest in the property (although any such person must be given an opportunity to make representations to the court).

D: THE EXERCISE OF THE COURT'S DISCRETION

English law is remarkable not only for the extent of the powers which it gives to the **8–013** court over the income and assets of divorcing spouses but also for the fact that the discretion is (as the Government's Consultation Paper, *Supporting Families* put it in 1998) "almost unfettered". Unlike in many civil jurisdictions, there is no rule or norm of sharing the property equally upon divorce. The objectives of the law have varied over the past 30 years. In 1970, concern about the impact of divorce on women (and particularly the "innocent" wife divorced against her will) had led Parliament to adopt what was known as the "minimal loss" principle. The courts were directed that they should in principle seek to keep the parties, so far as it was practicable and, having regard to their conduct, just to do so, in the financial position in which they would have been if the marriage had not broken down. This principle implied that marriage was a life-long partnership: financial obligations survived the ending of the relationship. The problem with this objective was that the assets that had sustained a particular standard of living for one household were usually insufficient to sustain that level for two households. It was also at odds with the idea that the parties should be able to move on and form—or regularise—new unions. As Lord Scarman noted in *Minton v Minton* [1979] A.C. 593, HL, "[a]n object of the modern law is to encourage each to put the past behind them and to begin a new life which is not over-shadowed by the relationship which has broken down." The legislation was subsequently amended by the Matrimonial and Family Proceedings Act 1984. This removed the "minimal loss" principle, provided that the welfare of the children was to be the "first" consideration for the courts, and required the court to have regard to the desirability of imposing a clean break. Thus the scheme of the legislation—the 1973 Act, as amended, in relation to spouses, and the 2004 Act in relation to civil partners—is, in outline, as follows:

(a) it is the duty of the court in deciding whether to exercise its powers, and, if so, in what manner, to have regard to all the circumstances of the case, first consideration being given to the welfare while a minor of any child of the family who has not attained the age of 18;

(b) the court is directed "in particular" to have regard to certain specified matters;

(c) the court is required to go through a complex decision-making process designed to facilitate, in appropriate cases, the making of a "clean break" between the parties.

The decisions of the House of Lords in *White v White* and *Miller; McFarlane* do nothing to change the structure of this approach, but it is important to bear in mind that the breadth of the discretion afforded to the courts may conceal significant policy shifts in practice. The following discussion will highlight the impact that *White* has had, and that *Miller; McFarlane* is likely to have, on this area of law.

First consideration to the welfare of children

8–014   The Act requires the court, in deciding whether and how to exercise its financial powers, to "have regard to all the circumstances of the case, first consideration being given to the welfare while a minor of any child of the family who has not attained the age of eighteen" (s.25(1) of the MCA; see also the similarly worded Sch.5. para.20 of the CPA). This provision arises in the context of the exercise of the court's powers to make orders in relation to the parties, and is not solely related to the making of orders relating to the children. Thus:

> In *C v C (Financial Relief: Short Marriage)* [1997] 2 F.L.R. 26, CA, the Court of Appeal upheld substantial awards to a wife notwithstanding the fact that the marriage had lasted for only nine and a half months. The statutory obligation to give first consideration to the welfare of the parties' four-year-old invalid child was a material factor in this decision.

A major concern is the need to "stretch" the available assets to cover the family's changed needs for housing. The direction to give first consideration to the children's welfare often justifies giving the home outright to the parent with whom the children are to live. This has not been affected by the decisions in *White* or *Miller; McFarlane*: indeed, in the latter case Baroness Hale emphasised that:

> "The invariable practice in English law is to try to maintain a stable home for the children after their parents' divorce . . . Giving priority to the children's welfare should also involve ensuring that their primary carer is properly provided for, because it is well known that the security and stability of children depends in large part upon the security and stability of their primary carers." (para.128)

Thus:

> In *B v B (Financial Provision: Welfare of Child and Conduct)* [2002] 1 F.L.R. 555, Fam Div, the entire equity in the former matrimonial home was transferred to the wife. The sum was only enough to rehouse her and her son, and, bearing in mind the husband's conduct (child abduction and emptying the building society of £37,000, which he had sent to his mother in Sicily), it was thought to be inappropriate for him to retain any interest in the property.

The court may even take the view that the requirement to give first consideration to the welfare of the children requires a mother with care of the children to receive periodical payments for her own support at least until the children no longer need her full-time care, although this will depend on the resources available.

> In *K v K (Ancillary Relief: Prenuptial Agreement)* [2003] 1 F.L.R. 120, Fam Div, the court ordered a large lump sum for housing, and periodical payments for both

wife and child. The high level of the award was justified by the father's wealth, but the suggestion by the judge that "[a] child is entitled to be brought up by a mother in circumstances which bear some sort of relationship to a father's current resources and standard of living" (at 133) is of more general relevance.

However, there are a number of significant limitations on the scope of the direction to give first consideration to the children's welfare.

(1) *First, but not paramount*

In deciding issues relating to the upbringing of children, the court regards the welfare **8–015** of the child as the "paramount" consideration even if that means that the just claims of the child's parents or other affected have to be overridden (see further Ch.14). In considering financial matters, in contrast, the court need not go so far, and is required merely to give "first" consideration to the welfare of the child in question. This means that it must simply consider all the circumstances, always bearing the children's welfare in mind, and then try to make a just financial settlement between the adult parties. The distinction between "first" and "paramount" was stressed in *Suter v Suter* [1987] 2 F.L.R. 232, CA, and in *Akintola v Akintola* [2002] EWCA Civ 1989, the court had to consider whether the judge had attached too much weight to the child's welfare in ordering that the wife should retain the matrimonial home, an argument that is unlikely to surface in the context of decisions relating to the upbringing of children. On the facts supplied, however, it was decided that the judge had not elevated the duty to give first consideration to the child's welfare "to something unacceptably high."

(2) *Applies only to children of the family*

The expression "child of the family" is widely defined in the legislation (see para. **8–016** 7–021, above) and extends to any child who has been treated by both of the parties as a child of their family. In particular, it will extend to step-children who have lived in the spouses' home. But the definition does not encompass all the children who may, actually or prospectively, be affected by the orders made in the matrimonial proceedings in question: for example, a child born to the husband and his cohabitant after the breakdown of the husband's marriage is likely to fall outside the definition. The legislation thus seems now to embody the principle that the court is to put the interests of the children of a first marriage or civil partnership before the interests of other children affected.

(3) *Applies only during minority of children*

The court is only required to give first consideration to the welfare "while a minor" of **8–017** any child of the family who has not attained the age of 18. This has two particular consequences. First, the court is not obliged to give such consideration to the welfare of any child of the family who has at the date of the hearing already attained the age of 18, even if the child is undergoing advanced education or training or is disabled, for example. Secondly, this provision does not require the court to take account of the fact that children in practice often stay in their homes until a later age. This does not of course mean the court will ignore such interests, but simply that they do not have any special priority:

> In *Richardson v Richardson (No.2)* [1994] 2 F.L.R. 1051, Fam Div, the question was in effect whether the wife should be forced to realise capital tied up in a home

"large enough and suitable enough for girls who [had] attended private school, had bright academic prospects", and were not likely to be truly independent for another five years. The court held that, although the children were no longer minors, they were still dependent on the wife whose ability to earn was restricted by the demands her children made on her time, and who could not sell the family house until they attained independence through education. Accordingly, the term of the wife's periodical payments order was extended for five years to enable the wife to fulfil the responsibilities to her daughters.

The duty to consider "all the circumstances"

8–018 Section 25 of the Matrimonial Causes Act lists eight specific factors to which the court is directed to have regard (see also Sch.5 para.21 of the CPA). There is a vast body of case law, and the following discussion seeks only to highlight points of particular significance. One principle that can be stated at the outset is that no one factor prevails over any of the others, although it is possible to discern shifts in the importance attached to different factors by the courts at different times. Moreover, the list is not exhaustive. The court must have regard to "all the circumstances of the case". It follows that the court must not simply confine its attention to the matters specified; it must also (as Scarman L.J. put it in *Trippas v Trippas* [1973] 1 W.L.R. 134 at 144, CA) investigate all other circumstances "past, present, and, in so far as one can make a reliable estimate, future" which are relevant to a decision of any particular case. The fact that the court has to look to the future, rather than simply deciding on the division of present assets on the basis of past contributions, was emphasised by Baroness Hale in *Miller; McFarlane*: "the checklist in s.25(2) is not simply concerned with totting up the present assets and dividing them in whatever way seems fair at that time" (at para.129).

The specified factors are as follows:

(1) *The income, earning capacity, property and other financial resources which each of the parties to the marriage has or is likely to have in the foreseeable future, including in the case of earning capacity any increase in that capacity which it would in the opinion of the court be reasonable to expect a party to the marriage to take steps to acquire* (s.25(2)(a) of the MCA 1973)

8–019 The fact that this provision refers to the property of each of the parties is a further reminder of the fact that a marriage or civil partnership, by itself, has no impact on property rights. During the relationship the assets may have been vested in one of the parties, which puts the onus on the other to apply for provision. Although it was asserted that, upon divorce, the court did not have "too nice a regard" to the legal or equitable rights of the parties (*per* Lord Denning in *Hanlon v The Law Society* [1981] A.C. 124, HL), who owned what was significant when applicants were limited to a claim for their needs, and respondents were allowed to keep the surplus. *White v White* cast doubt on this approach, but it is clear from *Miller; McFarlane* that "there is still some scope for one party to acquire and retain separate property which is not automatically to be shared equally between them" (*per* Baroness Hale at para.153, endorsed by Lord Mance at para.170). Whatever the approach to be taken, the first step must be to gain an idea of the value of the parties' assets.

(a) Ascertaining the value of the assets

The parties have an obligation to supply relevant information about their finances, and **8–020** a failure to do so may result in the court inferring the availability of undisclosed resources (see *e.g. Minwalla v Minwalla and DM Investments SA, Midfield Management SA and CI Law Trustees Ltd* [2004] EWHC 2823 (Fam)). The powers of the court to set aside an order in cases of material non-disclosure are considered below (see para.8–043).

While openness is encouraged, it has been suggested that lengthy financial inquiries may not be appropriate:

> "even in the longer marriage cases where a 50/50 split is the aspiration, many applicants would, I feel sure, be prepared to compromise over precision providing sensible admissions at a high figure were made, in order to avoid acrimonious, lengthy and very expensive proceedings." (*per* Coleridge J., *J v V (Disclosure: Offshore Corporations)*[2003] EWHC 3110 (Fam), para.129)

(b) What assets are relevant?

The short answer to this is any and all. Assets acquired before or during the relation- **8–021** ship, and even after its legal termination, may be taken into account by the courts, as may expectations of future assets (for example through inheritance: see *e.g. Re G (Financial Provision: Liberty to Restore Application for Lump Sum)* [2004] EWHC 88 (Fam)). The task of ascertaining the assets of the parties is further complicated by the fact that, as Coleridge J. pointed out in *J v V (Disclosure: Offshore Corporations)*[2003] EWHC 3110 (Fam):

> "[t]he concept of a financial resource is a very broad one. It covers far more than merely property that is in the direct legal ownership of possession of one or other of the parties. Any arrangement that provides financial benefit to a party falls to be considered, evaluated and ultimately included as an asset. Mere voluntary and unenforceable arrangements can sometimes fall into this net especially if they arise out of a family arrangement or moral obligation of one kind or another." (para.43)

The principle established by *Thomas v Thomas* [1995] 2 F.L.R. 668, CA, was that the court would not act in direct invasion of the rights of a third party, or put a third party under pressure to act in a certain way, but could take into account the potential availability of wealth from sources owned or administered by others. This was applied in *M v M (Maintenance Pending Suit)* [2002] EWHC 317:

> The parties had enjoyed an extremely high standard of living during the marriage, due to the generosity of the husband's father. Upon divorce the husband claimed that his father was no longer prepared to finance the same standard of living. The court took the view that the father was not as stringent as the husband was claiming, given that the husband had recently been on a luxurious cruise at the father's expense, and based its award on the assumption that the father would continue to fund the husband.

Another matter that has given rise to problems is the extent to which a new partner's earnings and earning capacity should be taken into account. It is clear that the court has no power to order that a third party, such as the husband's second wife or cohabitant, should provide for the applicant or the children of the first family; and it must not make an order which can only be satisfied by dipping into a third party's resources. However, the fact that the third party has means available may be relevant—so that in *Suter v Suter and Jones* [1987] 2 F.L.R. 232, CA, for example, the man with whom the wife was sharing her life was expected to contribute to her living expenses. In such a case it would be preferable to describe the man's contribution as relevant to the wife's needs rather than as a specific resource.

(c) The source of the assets

8–022   The fact that such assets may be taken into account by the court does not mean that the source of the assets is not relevant. Two different approaches should be distinguished. First, if assets acquired during the marriage are insufficient to meet the needs of both parties, then the court may well take other assets into account. By contrast, if the assets of the parties are more than sufficient to meet their needs, the source of the assets may be taken into account in justifying a departure from equal division. Thus in *M v M (Financial Relief: Substantial Earning Capacity)* [2004] EWHC 688 (Fam) the court held that the wife was not entitled to half-share in assets accrued since separation, since "the post-separation accrual does not arise from the trading of capital which existed at separation, rather it has accrued from the husband's own hard work post-separation, albeit that part of his bonus is referable to a scheme that was 'invented' during the marriage." (*per* Baron J. at para.62). Similarly, in *P v P (Inherited Property)* [2004] EWHC 1364 (Fam), [2005] 1 F.L.R. 576, the wife was awarded only 25 per cent of the assets, since the bulk of them had been inherited:

> "Fairness may require quite a different approach if the inheritance is a pecuniary legacy that accrues during the marriage than if the inheritance is a landed estate that has been within one spouse's family for generations and has been brought into the marriage with an expectation that it will be retained in specie for future generations." (*per* Munby J. at para.37)

In *Miller; McFarlane* their Lordships were agreed that the source of assets was a relevant factor, although one that might diminish in significance over the course of the marriage. However, a difference of opinion emerged in relation to the treatment of business assets. Lord Nicholls was unwilling to draw a distinction between one spouse's business assets and other assets that were more obviously family assets: for him, the dividing line was between assets acquired during the marriage (other than those acquired by gift or inheritance) and those acquired before the marriage. The former should be shared equally, while the division of the latter would depend on the duration of the marriage. By contrast, Baroness Hale suggested that a distinction should be drawn between "family assets" and other assets. The former were to be narrowly defined as:

> "those things which are acquired by one or other or both of the parties, with the intention that there should be continuing provision for them and their children during their joint lives, and used for the benefit of the family as a whole." (at para.149, quoting Lord Denning in *Wachtel v Wachtel* [1973] Fam. 72, at 90)

This would include the family home, furniture, family savings, insurance policies and holiday homes, as well as family businesses or joint ventures in which both parties worked. Such assets were the fruits of the marital partnership, and as such there would be a strong case for such assets to be shared equally. By contrast:

> "If the assets are not "family assets", or not generated by the joint efforts of the parties, then the duration of the marriage may justify a departure from the yardstick of equality of division." (para.152)

This means that the spouse who has accrued substantial assets through his or her business could certainly expect to retain more than half of those assets, although the precise proportions would depend on the duration of the marriage.

When applied to the appeal in *Miller v Miller*, these different approaches did not lead to any difference in outcome. Both justified the relatively high award in favour of Mrs Miller by reference to the huge increase in Mr Miller's wealth during the marriage and the high standard of living enjoyed by the parties; both justified a departure from equality, Lord Nicholls on account of the work carried out by Mr Miller prior to the marriage, Baroness Hale because the key assets were "assets generated solely by the husband during a short marriage" (para.158). That their respective approaches *could* lead to different outcomes is clear.

The approach suggested by Baroness Hale—which was explicitly endorsed by Lord Mance and implicitly by Lord Hoffmann—takes a more individualistic approach to the marriage partnership than that of Lord Nicholls. The business assets of one of the spouses are seen as the product of that spouse's efforts, and the fact that one spouse has provided domestic support is not seen as a contribution to the accumulation of the business assets (although it would be viewed as a contribution to the *family*, see further para.8–032 below). The spouse who has given up a lucrative career in order to support the other may be entitled to compensation—itself an individualistic notion—but it may be more difficult to apply compensatory principles to a spouse who did not develop a career before marriage. Equally, the fact that one spouse's career has been more successful than the other's does not, according to this approach, necessarily require any disparity to be addressed:

> "If . . . questions of need and compensation had been addressed, one might ask why a court should impose at the end of their marriage a sharing of all assets acquired during matrimony which the parties had never envisaged during matrimony." (*per* Lord Mance at para.170)

It is important, however, to keep the implications of *Miller; McFarlane* in perspective. The decision does not require the court to exclude those resources that do not fall within Baroness Hale's concept of family assets from consideration, and it will not affect the outcome in the majority of cases where the parties do not have the luxury of surplus assets.

(d) The nature of the assets

The nature of the assets must also be taken into account in deciding what division is **8–023** appropriate. In *Wells v Wells* [2002] EWCA 476, the original order left the wife with considerably greater security than the husband. In allowing the appeal, it was emphasised that there should be a "fair division of both the copper-bottomed assets and the illiquid and risk-laden assets" (*per* Thorpe L.J. at 102). The liquidity of the assets was also an issue in *N v N (Financial Provision: Sale of Company)* [2001] 2 F.L.R. 69, Fam Div:

> In this case, the wife was awarded £1m, out of total assets of £2.6m. The judge held that the court had to consider not only the nature of the assets but also the steps necessary to achieve their liquidation. The husband was accordingly given several years in which to sell his shareholding in a company to raise the necessary sum. It was noted that before the decision in *White*, the court would have "strained to prevent a disruption of the husband's business and professional activities except to the minimum extent necessary to meet the wife's needs." However, "those old taboos against selling the goose that lays the golden egg have largely been laid to rest . . . Nowadays the goose may well have to go to market for sale, but if it is necessary to sell her it is essential that her condition be such that her egg-laying abilities are damaged as little as possible."

The way in which such assets are divided is likely to be affected by *Miller; McFarlane*, but the principle that risks should be shared equally is not.

(e) Income

8–024   In many cases the parties will not have extensive capital assets, and the challenge will be how to make the income that previously supported one household stretch to supporting two. The situation in *McFarlane v McFarlane* [2006] UKHL 24 was rather different. The parties had been married for 16 years, and it was common ground that there were insufficient assets to achieve a clean break. As Baroness Hale pointed out:

> "The main family asset is the husband's very substantial earning power, generated over a lengthy marriage in which the couple deliberately chose that the wife should devote herself to home and family and the husband to work and career." (para.154)

Whether the husband's earning power fell within her own definition of a family asset—and if so, why there should be a distinction between earning power and the product of one's success in business—might be questioned. The key issue for the court was the level at which periodical payments should be set, and for how long. The House of Lords held that such payments should not merely reflect Mrs McFarlane's needs, but also compensation for the sacrifice of her own career (and, according to Baroness Hale, the sharing of the fruits of the partnership). Her entitlement to such compensation was such that it would be inappropriate to place any time limit on the order (see further below para.8–037).

(f) Earning capacity

8–025   The question of earning capacity is frequently a source of dispute. The court is concerned with what each party could reasonably earn; and the legislation—evidently influenced by the belief that the parties should put the failed relationship behind them and if need be retrain to fit themselves for employment—now specifically refers to "any increase in earning capacity which it would be reasonable to expect" either party to take steps to acquire. This involves two separate issues. The first is a question of fact: has the spouse in fact any earning potential? The second is one of judgement:

what would it be "reasonable" to expect? On this latter point, one recurring theme is the middle-aged wife who has not worked during the marriage. It will often not be considered to be reasonable to expect her to retrain after a long absence from the labour market.

> In *Barrett v Barrett* [1988] 2 F.L.R. 516, CA, the wife was 44, her years of caring for the children had severely limited her career opportunities and she had been unable to find full-time employment. Periodical payments were ordered for an indefinite period, as it could not be predicted when the wife would be able to support herself.

By contrast, a more robust approach is taken where the wife is younger or the absence from paid work shorter:

> In *T v T (Financial Relief: Pensions)* [1998] 1 F.L.R. 1072, Fam Div, the wife was 47 but the marriage had been childless and she had worked in a bank for the first half of the marriage. Although she had not worked for nine years and had been told that she was unemployable, the court held that she should make real attempts to find work "even if the location is not ideal, the work is not what she would prefer, and she would prefer not to have to do it." (at 1080)

Similarly, in *Q v Q (Ancillary Relief: Periodical Payments)* [2005] EWHC 402 (Fam), it was held that the earning capacity of the wife—a former hairdresser with no qualifications—would be nil for the next four years but once her youngest child had reached the age of nine, she "ought then to start building up an earning potential" (at para.23). The courts' perception of the period of time that the primary carer should be able to devote to child-care responsibilities is inevitably influenced by the resources available (contrast *K v K (Ancillary Relief: Prenuptial Agreement)* [2003] 1 F.L.R. 120, Fam Div, above para.8–004).

In the wake of *Miller; McFarlane* it will also be relevant to investigate whether the weaker spouse gave up a career to support the other, in which case an element of compensation may be appropriate.

(g) The availability of state benefits

The breakdown of a marriage means that many families—deprived of their main **8–026** wage-earner—become dependent on state benefits; and the courts have to consider how far the availability of such benefits affects its discretion. In cases where there are children, the Child Support Agency will now seek to compel the "non-resident parent" to support them in accordance with the formula laid down by the Child Support Act, and this will usually make the question of a court order under the divorce legislation irrelevant. The two principles that the courts had been accustomed to apply before that Act came into force may still be relevant in exceptional cases in which periodical payments are sought for a wife. The first principle is that a husband was not to be allowed to throw onto the state the cost of supporting his dependants (saying, for example, "there is no point in my paying anything because it will simply reduce my wife's income support"). The second principle is that the husband would be allowed to keep for himself and his new family at least a subsistence level of income, taking into account expenses on travel to work, housing and so on.

(2) *The financial needs, obligations and responsibilities which each of the parties to the marriage has or is likely to have in the foreseeable future (s.25(2)(b) of the MCA 1973)*

It is obviously vital that the division of the assets should be such as to secure the basic needs of the parties and their children. Although the parent who is caring for the children will be deemed to have the greater need for housing (see *B v B*, above, para.8–014), the importance of housing both parties, where possible, has been emphasised by the courts (see, *e.g. Cordle v Cordle* [2001] EWCA Civ 1791). If the family's assets are unequal to the task of supporting both parties then the availability of state benefits may be taken into account, as noted above. But how far are the needs of the parties relevant in higher income cases?

(a) Reasonable requirements

8–027   Before the decision in *White*, the courts tended to focus on the "reasonable requirements" of the spouse claiming provision. What was "reasonable" was gauged by reference to the lifestyle and assets of the parties. However, while the "reasonable requirements" of the rich may seem like luxuries to others—for example, in *Conran v Conran* [1997] 2 F.L.R. 615, Fam Div, the wife's reasonable requirements included houses in Belgravia, Dorset and France—such an approach tended to leave the spouse claiming provision with a relatively small proportion of the assets. By contrast, in *White*, Lord Nicholls stressed that there was nothing in s.25 of the Act to indicate that "reasonable requirements" should limit the amount awarded to the spouse:

> "If a husband and wife by their joint efforts over many years, his directly in the business and hers indirectly at home, have built up a valuable business from scratch, why should the claimant wife be confined to the court's assessment of her reasonable requirements, and the husband left with a much larger share? Or, to put the question differently, in such a case, where the assets exceed the financial needs of both parties, why should the surplus belong solely to the husband?"

Yet even before the House of Lords adopted a narrower approach to such joint efforts in *Miller; McFarlane* the concept of reasonable requirements had begun to resurface. The justifications for focusing on the reasonable requirements of the wife have varied from case to case. In *S v B (Ancillary relief: Costs)* [2004] EWHC 2089 (Fam) the shortness of the marriage was the decisive factor:

> "whatever the extent of ·the husband's wealth, the extreme shortness of the marriage placed a low ceiling, referable only to need, upon this wife's recovery." (para.46)

In *P v P (Inherited Property)* [2004] EWHC 1364 (Fam) equal division was deemed inappropriate given that the bulk of the assets had been inherited (see para.8–022 above), while in *J v V (Disclosure: Offshore Corporations)* [2003] EWHC 3110 (Fam) the key factor was that the considerable assets had been built up before the marriage. Coleridge J. opined that:

> "once the court departs from equality, fractions tend to become arbitrary and carry almost no logical significance. It is far safer and better, I find, in cases of this

kind, properly to recognise the wife's contribution by looking carefully at her financial needs." (para.114)

Similar factors influenced the court in *Minwalla v Minwalla and DM Investments SA, Midfield Management SA and CI Law Trustees Ltd* [2004] EWHC 2823 (Fam), along with the consideration that the total assets were unknown. There are clearly a number of cases in which the reasonable requirements of the weaker spouse remain not merely relevant but decisive.

(b) Obligations and responsibilities

The impact of child care responsibilies has already been discussed in the context of **8–028** earning capacity, and is also relevant in the context of the contributions that the carer has made in the past and will make in the future. It should be noted that the child in relation to whom such obligations arise need not be a child of the marriage. Thus in *Fisher v Fisher* [1989] 1 F.L.R. 423, CA:

> The wife had a child by a third party some years after the divorce. The husband argued that by allowing the pregnancy to occur she had voluntarily made herself incapable of self-support, but the Court of Appeal accepted that it was impossible to ignore the wife's responsibility to her child.

This raises a further question: how far should the new obligations of one of the parties justify a departure from equal division? This appears to be a point on which there is no consensus as yet. In *S v S (Financial Provision: Departing from Equality)* [2001] 2 F.L.R. 246, Fam Div, it was held that equality would discriminate against the husband because he had responsibilities to his new family, whereas the wife had no children dependent on her. By contrast, in *H-J v H-J* [2002] 1 F.L.R. 415, Fam Div, it was stressed that the wife should not be asked to take less simply because the husband had chosen to take on new responsibilities. Either could be argued to be consistent with the approach set out in *White*, and the point remains unresolved.

(3) The standard of living enjoyed by the family before the breakdown of the marriage (s.25(2)(c) of the MCA 1973)

There is no automatic entitlement for either or both parties to keep the same standard **8–029** of living as had been enjoyed during the relationship. The parties' standard of living will be relevant in determining the "reasonable requirements" of the applicant, while the higher awards that followed the decision of the House of Lords in *White* meant that in big money cases each would have sufficient to maintain a high standard of living anyway. In *Miller; McFarlane*, the high standard of living enjoyed by the Millers during their relatively brief marriage was a relevant factor in justifying generous provision, but did not require an award that would enable Mrs Miller to maintain that standard for the rest of her life. Lord Nicholls specifically rejected the suggestion made in the lower courts that Mrs Miller had had a legitimate expectation that she would be living on a higher economic plane as a result of her marriage, since this would effectively reintroduce the discredited "minimal loss" principle. Similarly, Baroness Hale saw the relatively generous provision as a means of ensuring "a gentle transition from that standard to the standard that she could expect as a self-sufficient woman" (para.158).

If the resources of the parties have diminished since the marriage, it may not be reasonable for the same standard of living to be maintained:

In *Wells v Wells* [2002] EWCA Civ 478, it was noted that the family fortunes had been dependent upon the husband's business, and that had the marriage survived the parties would have shared adversity just as they had shared prosperity during the marriage. Any assessment of the wife's income needs thus had to reflect the bad times as well as the good times.

The converse is also true: in *Preston v Preston* [1981] 3 W.L.R. 619, CA, the family had enjoyed a modest standard of living during the marriage, while the husband was building up his business, but the lump sum reflected the success of the business and the luxurious standard of living that she would have enjoyed had the marriage continued.

If the marriage was particularly short, it may be assumed that the spouse did not have time to become accustomed to a particular standard of living. An extreme example of this is *Attar v Attar (No.2)* [1985] F.L.R. 653, where the parties had lived together for only seven weeks, part of which was their honeymoon.

(4) *The age of each party to the marriage and the duration of the marriage* (s.25(2)(d) of the MCA 1973)

8–030   The age of the parties will be relevant to the court's assessment of their needs and resources. If a spouse is young and healthy he or she will be able to work and the need for support will be much less, while an elderly and infirm spouse's needs will be much greater. Of course, the presence of children may mean that even a younger spouse will not be able to work for a time.

Of more relevance—especially in the wake of *White* and *Miller; McFarlane*—is the duration of the relationship. There is a preliminary question as to how duration is to be assessed. Earlier cases excluded periods of pre-marital cohabitation from consideration. More recently, the courts have recognized the artificiality of this approach. Thus in *CO v CO (Ancillary Relief: Pre-Marriage Cohabitation)* [2004] EWHC 287 (Fam), Coleridge J. noted that:

> "Committed, settled relationships which often endure for years in the context of cohabitation (often but not always with children) outside marriage must, I think, be regarded as every bit as valid as those where the parties have made the same degree of commitment but recorded it publicly . . . by marriage." (para.44)

While s.25(2)(d) refers specifically to the duration of the *marriage*, it is possible for pre-marital cohabitation to be taken into account as part of the court's duty to consider "all the circumstances of the case." By contrast, the mere fact that the parties have been dating is accorded less significance: in *M v M (Short Marriage: Clean Break)* [2005] EWHC 528 (Fam) it was decided that although the parties had had a close and "apparently exclusive" relationship for four years preceding their marriage, there was "no mutual commitment to make their lives together" until they became engaged, and this period was consequently disregarded in determining the duration of the marriage (as it was by the House of Lords in hearing the appeal: *Miller; McFarlane*).

How does the duration of the marriage affect the division of the assets? Previously, the courts' focus on the reasonable requirements of a spouse might lead to an elderly spouse receiving less after a lengthy marriage than a younger spouse after a short marriage, with awards being based on the sum needed to produce a set sum for the rest of the recipient's life (sometimes worked out using the so-called *Duxbury* calculation, after the decision in *Duxbury v Duxbury* [1987] 1 F.L.R. 7, CA). However, the potential injustice of an award that reflected an elderly spouse's expected longevity rather than the length of the marriage was recognised in *A v A (Elderly Applicant: Lump Sum)* [1999] 2 F.L.R. 969, Fam Div:

> In this case the husband was aged 79. His wife had capital assets in excess of a million pounds and a spendable income of more than £100,000 a year. It was held that to deal with his claim on the basis of a computation related to the husband's statistical expectation of life would be unfair to him. What would happen if he was one of those who lived longer—perhaps substantially longer—than the average? The husband had the right to recognition in money terms of his significant contributions over a long marriage and this justified a larger award than would be made under a *Duxbury* calculation.

Post-*White*, it would appear that equal division is more likely to be deemed appropriate if the relationship has been a lengthy one (see *e.g. Lambert v Lambert*). But again, it should be borne in mind that the duration of the relationship is just one of the factors to be taken into account. Equal division of the assets acquired during the two-and-a-half year marriage was thought appropriate in *Foster v Foster* [2003] EWCA Civ 565, in which the spouses had been involved in a joint venture, but inappropriate at the end of a 19-year marriage in *P v P (Inherited Property)* [2004] EWHC 1364 (Fam) on the basis that the bulk of assets were inherited. The decision of the House of Lords in *Miller; McFarlane* placed considerable emphasis on the duration of the marriage in relation to non-family assets (see para.8–022 above), but in this it simply confirmed trends already apparent.

Even if the marriage is of relatively short duration, this does not mean that only a low award will be made to the weaker spouse, particularly if there are children. Thus in *Re G (Financial Provision: Liberty to Restore Application for Lump Sum)* [2004] EWHC 88 (Fam), which involved a four-year marriage during which two daughters had been born, it was noted that:

> "Their daughters' impact on the situation changes entirely my perspective of what is fair. It has changed the past, it changes the present, and it should transform the future." (*per* Singer J., para.43)

(5) *Any physical or mental disability of either of the parties to the marriage* (s.25(2)(e) of the MCA 1973)

While the disability of a spouse may invite considerable sympathy, it was emphasised **8–031** in *Wagstaff v Wagstaff* [1992] 1 All E.R. 275, CA, that it was only one of the factors to be taken into account. Any disability will of course influence other factors, such as the earning capacity and needs of the party in question (although note the conflicting views expressed in *Miller; McFarlane* as to whether the court was only concerned with needs arising from the marriage itself, above para.8–001).

(6) *The contributions which each of the parties has made or is likely to make in the foreseeable future to the welfare of the family, including any contribution made by looking after the home or caring for the family* (s.25(2)(f) of the MCA 1973)

The extent to which "contributions" should be taken into account has long been a **8–032** matter of importance and difficulty, and the past few years in particular have seen extensive debates over this issue. The starting point was the widespread feeling in the 1960s that the law governing property regimes did not give adequate recognition to the contributions made, particularly by housewives, towards the acquisition of so-called "family assets". Section 25(2)(f) allowed the courts to take such contributions into account, although in practice the extent to which credit could be given for past contributions obviously depended on the resources available, and there remained an assumption that "domestic" contributions were less valuable than building up the assets. *White v White* signalled a new approach, emphasising that there was to be no discrimination between husband and wife:

> "If, in their respective spheres, each contributed equally to the family, then in principle it matters not which of them earned the money and built up the assets. There should be no bias in favour of the money-earner and against the home-maker and the child-carer." (*per* Lord Nicholls at 989)

As noted above, *White* did not state that equal shares were to be awarded, rather that any departure from equal division should be justified. This led to a number of cases in which it was argued in favour of the money-earner that (invariably) he had made an exceptional contribution to the family assets, which should be reflected in the overall award.

> In *Cowan v Cowan* [2001] EWCA Civ 679, Thorpe L.J. noted that fairness "permits and sometimes requires the recognition of the product of the genius with which only one of the spouses may be endowed". The husband's innovative ideas, hard work and entrepreneurial flair were recognised by his being allowed to retain 62 per cent of the family assets.

Such arguments in turn led to some disquiet about the inquiry that the court was being required to undertake. As was pointed out in *H v H (Financial Provision: Special Contribution)* [2002] 2 F.L.R. 1021, Fam Div, the issue of who made what contribution calls for "a detailed retrospective at the end of a broken marriage just at a time when parties should be looking forward not back." There were concerns that too great an emphasis was being placed on contributions, to the exclusion of other relevant factors (see *e.g.* Coleridge J. in *G v G (Financial Provision: Equal Division)* [2002] EWHC 1339). And there was the additional problem that in cases of exceptional wealth, the contribution of the spouse who had built up the assets could almost always be described as "special".

These issues were recognised in *Lambert v Lambert* [2002] EWCA Civ 1685:

> The parties married in 1974 and parted 23 years later, by which time their joint assets totalled over £20m. The husband argued that their wealth came from his business, which he had started before the marriage. At first instance, the judge held that the husband's contribution could be regarded as exceptional, and awarded the wife 37 per cent of the assets. The Court of Appeal allowed her appeal and awarded her 50 per cent. Thorpe L.J. noted that "[i]f all that is regarded is the extent of the breadwinner's success then discrimination is almost bound to follow since there is no equal opportunity for her to demonstrate the scale of her comparable success ... The more driven the breadwinner the less available will he be physically and emotionally both as a husband and a father."

Thorpe L.J. envisaged that it would still be possible to argue that one spouse had made a special contribution, if "only in exceptional circumstances" (at 158). Following this, in *Norris v Norris* [2002] EWHC 2996 the wife claimed—unsuccessfully—that she deserved more than 50 per cent because she had been more than a homemaker. The court held that this was the case in many marriages, and that her contribution could not be described as special.

The decision in *Lambert* does not mean that equal division will invariably be appropriate. First, the court may still find that one party has made a "special" contribution, if only in "exceptional" circumstances, a possibility endorsed by the House of Lords in *Miller; McFarlane* (see Lord Nicholls at para.68 and Baroness Hale at para.146). Such exceptional circumstances were held to exist in *Sorrell v Sorrell* [2005] EWHC 1717:

> In this case the husband's business had been spectacularly successful, and he had generated the family fortune of over £100m by his talents. The court noted that he was "regarded within his field and the wider business community as one of the most exceptional and talented businessmen" (para.112). Bennett J., awarding the wife 40 per cent of the assets, noted that his decision was not based solely on the size of the family fortune but on the factor that "there is within the husband "exceptional and individual" qualities as the generator of the fortune." (para.116)

Whether the court would have found that the husband's contribution was exceptional if the fortune he had amassed had been less sizeable is a moot point.

It is also possible that even if the court holds that the contributions of the parties are equal, a departure from equality may be justified by other factors—for example the duration of the marriage, the needs of the parties, or the fact that a large proportion of the assets have derived from third parties (see *e.g. G v G (Matrimonial Property: Rights of Extended Family)* [2005] EWHC 1560 (Admin) and *P v P (Inherited Property)* [2004] EWHC 1364 (Fam)). As Thorpe L.J. pointed out in *Lambert*, "[a] finding of equality of contribution may be followed by an order for unequal division because of the influence of one or more of the other statutory criteria as well as the over-arching search for fairness" (at para.26).

Finally, it should be noted that *Miller; McFarlane* signals a rather different approach. Baroness Hale pointed out that s.25(2)(f) is concerned with contributions to the welfare of the family, rather than to the wealth of the parties, and suggested that:

> "Only if there is such a disparity in their respective contributions to the welfare of the family that it would be inequitable to disregard it should this be taken into account in determining their shares." (para.146)

This must be read together with her comments on the appropriate approach to business assets accrued during the marriage (see para.8–022 above). Domestic contributions are not seen as playing a role in the generation of such assets. As a consequence, the focus is likely to shift to the source of the assets and the duration of the marriage.

(7) The conduct of each of the parties if that conduct is such that it would in the opinion of the court be inequitable to disregard it (s.25(2)(g) of the MCA 1973)

8–033 The extent to which the conduct of the parties should be relevant in determining the financial outcome of divorce has long been controversial. Fault played a significant role in the deliberations of the court when the grounds for divorce were themselves based on the commission of a matrimonial offence, but, after the breakdown principle was introduced in 1969, questions arose as to whether it was still appropriate to take conduct into account. The legislation directed the court to take account of the conduct of the parties in determining how far the "minimal loss principle" (see above para. 8–013) should apply. However, the Court of Appeal limited the scope of this in *Wachtel v Wachtel* [1973] Fam. 72, CA, by holding that conduct would only be considered where is was "obvious and gross", which implied something more than responsibility for the breakdown of the marriage. This was based on the belief that the policy of the divorce law was to minimise the bitterness, distress and humiliation of divorce, so that in most cases it would be wrong to allow considerations of what was formerly regarded as guilt or blame to affect the financial orders made on divorce. But it was accepted that there would be a "residue of cases, where the conduct of one of the parties had been such that it would be "inequitable" to disregard it."

This approach was reflected in the drafting of s.25(2)(g), which was inserted by the Matrimonial and Family Proceedings Act 1984 when the "minimal loss principle" was removed. The following cases illustrate what conduct is regarded as "obvious and gross":

> In *Evans v Evans* [1989] 1 F.L.R. 351, CA, a wife obtained a divorce from her husband, after a short marriage, in 1951. Over the next 35 years, the husband meticulously complied with court orders for maintenance. In 1985, the wife was convicted of inciting others to murder the husband under a contract-killing arrangement and she was sentenced to four years' imprisonment. The husband ceased to make the maintenance payments, and the Court of Appeal held that the wife's conduct had been such as to make it right to discharge the order.

Again:

> In *Clark v Clark* [1999] 2 F.L.R. 498, CA, the 40-year-old wife met an 80-year-old millionaire at a Christmas party and (as the judge found) married him for his money. The marriage lasted for six years and was never consummated. The wife was ashamed of being married to such an old person and wanted to live wholly apart from him (at one stage requiring him to live in a caravan) whilst still exploiting his wealth. The Court of Appeal said that it would be hard to conceive graver marital misconduct, and that the wife's conduct was "as baleful as any to be found in the family law reports". But (whilst reducing the award of more than half a million pounds made by the judge) the court did not dissent from the belief that it would be excessively harsh to leave her with nothing.

In a number of cases the courts have also taken the financial misconduct of the parties into account, on the basis that such conduct reduces the assets available for distribution (see, *e.g. Le Foe v Le Foe and Woolwich plc* [2001] 2 F.L.R. 970, Fam Div, in which the husband "embarked on a low, deceitful and ruthless subterfuge to strip the majority of the equity out of the family home", *per* Nicholas Mostyn Q.C.).

Despite the well-established understanding that less serious misconduct would be disregarded in deciding what each spouse should be awarded, it was suggested in *M v M (Short Marriage: Clean Break)* [2005] EWHC 528 (Fam) that the shortness of the marriage should not count against a wife who had not been responsible for bringing it to an end. It was not suggested that this would be taken into account under s.25(2)(g) but rather as part of the overall circumstances of the case. This approach, endorsed by the Court of Appeal (see *Miller v Miller* [2005] EWCA Civ 984) caused some consternation, since it seemed to suggest that responsibility for the breakdown of the marriage would be a relevant factor in determining financial provision. On appeal, however, the House of Lords categorically stated that such an approach was erroneous:

> "Parliament has drawn the line. It is not for the courts to re-draw the line elsewhere under the guise of having regard to all the circumstances of the case . . . In most cases fairness does not require consideration of the parties' conduct . . . Where, exceptionally, the position is otherwise, so that it would be unequitable to disregard one party's conduct, the statute permits that conduct to be taken into account." (*per* Lord Nicholls, *Miller; McFarlane* para.65)

(8) *The value to each of the parties to the marriage of any benefit which by reason of the dissolution or annulment of the marriage, that party will lose the chance of acquiring* (s.25(2)(h) of the MCA 1973)

The fact that divorce ends the legal status of marriage means that any rights flowing **8–034** from that status—for example, rights to succeed on a spouse's intestacy—also come to an end. In recent years the loss of rights under occupational and other pension schemes has been the focus of considerable attention, and the courts have acquired new powers to deal with such assets (see above, para.8–011).

An attachment order requires the pension fund manager or trustee to divert payments from the pensioner to the other spouse (so that the court could, for example, order that half the pensioner's retirement pension be paid over to the ex-spouse) but such an order can only become effective when the benefits become payable—*i.e.* on retirement—and the payments will inevitably cease as and when the pensioner ceases to be entitled (for example, on his death). It appears that little use has been made of the "attachment" provisions. The limitations of the concept of attachment are well illustrated by *T v T (Financial Relief: Pensions)* [1998] 1 F.L.R. 1072, Fam Div.):

> The husband and wife were aged 46 and 47 respectively, and it was decided that it would be impossible to predict what maintenance the wife might need when the husband reached 60 in 2011. Even if an order were made, it would not offer the wife any certainty, as it might be subject to variation at a later date. Moreover, under the terms of the pension scheme, the husband could delay taking his pension until 2026. It was decided that the court would be in a much better position to determine the issue once the husband had retired.

Given that the average age at divorce is 40.9 years for men and 38.7 years for women, this is likely to be a common problem.

By contrast, the pension-sharing provisions introduced by the Welfare Reform and Pensions Act 1999 do not require the applicant to remain dependent upon the choices and life-span of the respondent. Instead, pension rights can be transferred to the applicant at the time of the divorce, although few such orders have been reported.

Even though the court now has these enhanced powers, many cases may still be dealt with by the traditional and simple technique of "offsetting", *i.e.* the court allocates an enlarged share of other assets to one party in compensation for the loss of pension expectations.

Seeking a "clean break"

8–035 In *Minton v Minton* [1979] A.C. 593 at 608, Lord Scarman stated that the "clean break" principle informed the modern legislation, and that:

> "the law now encourages spouses to avoid bitterness after family breakdown and to settle their money and property problems. An object of the modern law is to encourage each to put the past behind them and to begin a new life which is not overshadowed by the relationship which has broken down."

The desirability of a clean break was a key theme in the 1984 reforms (see para.8–013 above), and the Matrimonial Causes Act now contains a number of provisions concerned with the attainment of the "clean break" objective (again, these provisions are replicated in Sch.5 of the Civil Partnership Act 2004). The reader should, however, bear in mind that these provisions relate to what is merely one aspect of the court's discretion, and above all that it is not the court's function to strive for a clean break regardless of all other considerations (see *Clutton v Clutton* [1991] 1 F.L.R. 242 at 245, CA). The following discussion of the statutory provisions should be read in the light of these comments:

(1) *The duty to consider the termination of financial obligations* (s.25A(1))

8–036 If the court decides to exercise its financial powers in favour of a party to the marriage, it must consider "whether it would be appropriate so to exercise those powers that the financial obligations of each party towards the other will be terminated as soon after the grant of the decree as the court considers just and reasonable." This duty arises whenever the court decides to exercise its property adjustment or financial provision powers in favour of a party to the marriage. (It has no application to orders for children.) Both its scope and its limitations were explained by Baroness Hale in *Miller; McFarlane*:

> "Section 25A is a powerful encouragement towards securing the court's objective by way of lump sum and capital adjustment . . . rather than by continuing periodical payments. This is good practical sense. Periodical payments are a continuing source of stress for both parties. They are also insecure. With the best will in the world, the paying party may fall on hard times and be unable to keep them up. Nor is the best will in the world always evident between formerly married people. It is also the logical consequence of the retreat from the principle of the life-long obligation. Independent finances and self-sufficiency are the aims. Nevertheless, s.25A does not tell us what the outcome of the exercise required by s.25 should be. It is mainly directed at how that outcome should be put into effect." (para.133)

Even if a once-and-for-all settlement is desirable, it may not be possible on the facts of the case. There may be insufficient assets available to achieve a fair result, and the court may thus decide to order periodical payments, either to meet the needs of the recipient or to provide compensation (as in *Miller; McFarlane*). Thus in *V v V (Financial Relief)* [2005] 2 F.L.R. 697 the periodical payments ordered after a 31-year marriage amounted to 40 per cent of available income, the judge noting that this was not a big money case but one involving "a solid, secure income which is capable of providing decently for both sides" (*per* Coleridge J., para.37).

It remains to be seen how the decision in *Miller; McFarlane* will affect cases such as *Parlour v Parlour*—heard alongside *McFarlane* in the Court of Appeal (*McFarlane v McFarlane; Parlour v Parlour* [2004] EWCA Civ 872). Mrs Parlour's situation was very different to that of Mrs McFarlane: her marriage was shorter, the job that she had given up less lucrative; and her husband's income as a professional footballer significantly higher but at the same time less likely to continue into the future than Mr McFarlane's. In cases of this kind there may still be an argument for the "planned progression to a clean break" envisaged by the Court of Appeal, the reason for the periodical payments being to ensure the fair division of assets rather than to address future needs or compensation.

If there is insufficient income to make a periodical payments order at an appropriate level, the court may still choose to make a nominal order—*i.e.* an order for the payment of a nominal sum, such as a penny a year—that can be varied upwards if and when the circumstances of the payer improve (see *e.g. SRJ v DWJ (Financial Provision)* [1999] 2 F.L.R. 176, CA). Such orders may also be made to give one party a "last backstop", *i.e.* some protection against unforeseen changes of circumstances such as ill-health or unemployment. On one view, therefore, making a nominal order is inconsistent with the notion of a clean break; but the courts have refused to hold that such orders are undesirable in principle (see *Hepburn v Hepburn* [1989] 1 F.L.R. 373 at 376, CA, *per* Butler-Sloss L.J.; and *Whiting v Whiting* [1988] 2 F.L.R. 189, CA).

(2) The duty to consider specifying a term for any periodical payments order (s.25A(2))

If the court does decide to make a periodical payments order in favour of a party to **8–037** the marriage, s.25A(2) then imposes on it a mandatory duty "in particular" to "consider whether it would be appropriate to require those payments to be made or secured only for such term as would in the opinion of the court be sufficient to enable the party in whose favour the order is made to adjust without undue hardship to the termination of his or her financial dependence on the other party." It follows that in each case in which the court decides to make a periodical payments order, it must then consider whether the order should be for a specified term. In making that decision, the court is required to consider whether such a period would be sufficient for the applicant to adjust "without undue hardship" to the changed circumstances. Can and should the applicant find a way of adjusting his or her life so as to attain financial independence from the other spouse? Is it possible to predict the time by which such an adjustment will have occurred; for example, because child-care responsibilities are likely to have ceased?

These are matters about which the court must be satisfied by evidence; it must not rely on wishful thinking: see *Flavell v Flavell* [1997] 1 F.L.R. 353, CA; *G v G (Periodical Payments: Jurisdiction)* [1997] 1 F.L.R. 368, CA, para.8–041, below. It should also be noted that this provision is directed to ending *dependency*, and does not apply with the same force where periodical payments are necessary to produce a fair result according to the principles enunciated in *White v White*, or to provide compensation, as in *Miller, McFarlane* (*per* Lord Nicholls at para.39). In *McFarlane v McFarlane*, it was thought inappropriate to impose a five-year term on the periodical payments order, particularly in the light of the high threshold that had to be surmounted by an applicant seeking to extend the term (as to which see *Fleming v Fleming* [2003] EWCA 1841, and para.8–041 below).

(3) *Power to direct that no application be made to extend the specified term (s.28(1A))*

8–038   Unless the court has directed that no application for an extension of the term can be entertained, the court will have jurisdiction to vary a specified term order by extending the term specified at any time during the currency of the order. It has been said (in *Whiting v Whiting* [1988] 2 F.L.R. 189, CA) that to make such a direction is "draconian" and inappropriate in cases in which there is real uncertainty about the future—particularly when young children are involved. On the other hand, unless such a direction is made the paying spouse is left at risk of an extension being ordered at a later date, although such extensions are not lightly granted (see para.8–041 below). In *D v D (Financial Provision: Periodical Payments)* [2004] EWHC 445 (Fam) the court decided not to exercise its power to bar a future application to extend the ten-year term, since the order was intended to achieve equality between the parties, which might be undermined by future events.

(4) *The power to dismiss a claim for periodical payments (s.25A(3))*

8–039   If complete finality is to be achieved, the court must exercise the power specifically conferred upon it by statute to dismiss all claims for periodical payments and to direct that the applicant be debarred from making any further application for a periodical payments order. The court will also direct that no application under the provisions of the Inheritance (Provision for Family and Dependants) Act 1975 (see Ch.9) will be permitted by the spouse for provision out of the other's estate.

E: RECONSIDERING FINANCIAL ARRANGEMENTS

8–040   The broad heading of this section covers a number of different issues. First, in what circumstances may an order be varied by the court? Secondly, what principles apply when the court is hearing an appeal from a lower court? Thirdly, what is the position if one of the parties later discovers that the other did not make full disclosure at the time of the hearing, or if the circumstances of the parties change radically?

(1) *Variation of orders*

8–041   The court has the power to vary an existing order for periodical payments (s.31 of the MCA 1973). This can include varying the period for which the payments are to be made, as well as the amount that is payable: thus in *Flavell v Flavell* [1997] 1 F.L.R. 353 the original two-year period was varied to an indefinite period as there was no prospect of the wife being able to support herself. Equally, the court can order that the payments are to be terminated. In *Miller, McFarlane* it was thought appropriate that husband should bear the burden of applying for the order to be terminated should circumstances change, rather than requiring the wife to justify the extension of the order.

Although the court has no power to vary a lump sum or property order, under s.31(7A) of the Act it is now possible to order that periodical payments be "capitalised", *i.e.* replaced by a lump sum. These new powers were used in *Harris v Harris* [2001] 1 F.C.R. 68, CA:

> The parties had agreed that the wife should receive a lump sum and £10,800 periodical payments per year for herself. The husband subsequently suffered a serious illness and had to take early retirement. The judge ordered that the wife's periodical payments be capitalised, the sum being calculated on a "joint lives" basis—*i.e.* the periodical payments that the wife would have received while both she and her husband were still alive. He awarded her £120,000, based on estimates as to the life expectancy of the husband. Upon appeal, the Court of Appeal confirmed first, that the new provisions had retrospective effect, and, secondly, that as the original order for periodical payments had been made on the basis that there would be no provision in the event of the husband's death, the judge had been correct to capitalise the payments on a joint lives basis.

In exercising its powers the court is to have regard to all the circumstances of the case: there is no need to show that the original order was flawed in any way. However, it was noted in *Fleming v Fleming* [2003] EWCA Civ that the court's obligations to consider whether it would be appropriate to terminate financial obligations/achieve a clean break "are much enhanced . . . where there has been a previous term ordered" (para.13). As noted in *Miller; McFarlane*, this means that any person applying for the term to be extended must surmount a high threshold.

(2) *Appeals*

If one of the parties wishes to appeal against a decision, the appeal must be lodged **8–042** within 14 days. The leave of the appellate court may be necessary. The courts have frequently stressed the need for finality in litigation and pointed to the way in which family resources may be wasted upon litigation. One extreme example of this was *Piglowska v Piglowski* [1999] 1 W.L.R. 1360, HL, in which the total value of the assets was £127,400 and the legal costs incurred in deciding upon their division exceeded £128,000. The House of Lords took the opportunity to lay down some general principles by which the hearing of appeals should be governed:

> Lord Hoffmann quoted from *Bellenden (formerly Satterthwaite) v Bellenden* [1948] 1 All E.R. 343, CA, to the effect that "[i]t is only where the decision exceeds the generous ambit within which reasonable disagreement is possible, and is, in fact, plainly wrong, that an appellate body is entitled to interfere" (*per* Asquith L.J., at 345). He went on to stress that an appellate court must bear in mind the advantage that the first instance judge had in seeing the parties and the other witnesses. It should not engage in a "narrow textual analysis" of the judgment, but take into account that judgements could always be better expressed and assume that the judge directed himself correctly unless the contrary could be shown. It should also recognise that value judgements—for example regarding the weight to be accorded to each spouse's wishes—could vary, and that appellate courts should accordingly "permit a degree of pluralism in these matters."

The Access to Justice Act 1999 included a provision that no further appeal could be made to the Court of Appeal unless it raised an important point of principle or practice, or there was some other compelling reason for the Court of Appeal to hear it (see s.55 of the Act).

(3) *Appeals out of time on the basis of a flaw in the trial process*

8–043   What if a spouse does not initially wish to appeal against the order, but subsequently discovers that the outcome was less fair than was it originally appeared? The sanction for failure to disclose any matter relevant to the exercise of the court's discretion is that the order is liable to be set aside:

> In *Jenkins v Livesey (formerly Jenkins)* [1985] A.C. 424, HL, a wife did not disclose the fact that she intended to remarry. That fact would materially have affected the terms of the divorce settlement under which the husband was relieved from paying periodical maintenance but gave up his entire interest in the family home. Since any periodical payments would have come to an end on the wife's remarriage, it is most unlikely that he would have agreed to these terms had he known the facts. The order was set aside.

Again:

> In *T v T (Consent Order: Procedure to Set Aside)* [1996] 2 F.L.R. 640, Fam Div, the husband led his wife to believe that there was no free market in the shares of his corporate hospitality company. A consent order was made on that basis. He did not reveal that negotiations for a takeover by a public limited company were taking place; and shortly after the making of the order he received £1.6 million for his holding. The consent order was set aside for non-disclosure.

Not every failure to disclose information will justify the order being set aside. The non-disclosure must be material, but need not be fraudulent, although, as Thorpe L.J. pointed out in *Shaw v Shaw* [2002] EWCA Civ 1298, it is hard to envisage a case where a material non-disclosure would be unintentional. It is necessary to show that the court would have made a "substantially different" order had full disclosure been made: see *P v P (Consent Order: Appeal Out of Time)* [2002] 1 F.L.R. 743, Fam Div.

(4) *Appeals out of time on the basis of changes in circumstances*

8–044   What is to happen if there is a change of circumstances after the making of an order whether by consent or otherwise—which was unforeseen by either party? For example:

> In *Barder v Caluori* [1988] A.C. 20, HL, the court by consent made a "clean break" order under which H was to transfer the matrimonial home to W within 28 days. Four weeks later, W killed her children and committed suicide. All her property would go under her will to her mother. The House of Lords held that the husband should be given leave to appeal out of time; and, on the appeal, that the order should be set aside.

When should leave to appeal out of time in this way be given? The House of Lords held that where there had been an unforeseen change of circumstances, leave should be given if four conditions were satisfied:

(1) the basis or fundamental assumption underlying the order had been undermined by a change of circumstances;

(2) such change had occurred within a relatively short time (usually no more than one year) from the making of the original order;

(3) the application for leave had been made reasonably promptly; and

(4) the granting of leave would not prejudice unfairly third parties who had acquired interests for value in the property affected.

The courts have not been prepared to set aside orders merely because assets have appreciated dramatically in value (see *Cornick v Cornick* [1994] 2 F.L.R. 530, Fam Div, where the husband's shares rose in value by nearly 600 per cent in 18 months) provided that the valuation before the court at the time of the order was correct (contrast *Thompson v Thompson* [1991] 2 F.L.R. 530, CA, where a small business was sold for more than twice the valuation put before the court two weeks earlier, and the court set aside the consent order). Similarly, the redundancy of one of the parties does not justify the fresh hearing (see, *e.g. Maskell v Maskell* [2001] EWCA Civ 858). But they have been prepared to set aside orders where the parties' needs have changed dramatically (as in *Barder* itself, and in *Williams v Lindley* [2005] EWCA Civ 103, where the wife became engaged to a wealthy older man one month after receiving a lump sum of £125,000 to re-house herself and the children).

If the court does give leave to appeal out of time against the order, it will on the appeal substitute whatever order would have been appropriate on the basis of all the facts as they are known to be at the date of the appeal hearing. Thus:

> In *Smith v Smith (Smith intervening)* [1991] 2 F.L.R. 432, CA, the wife had committed suicide five months after the initial order of the court. The court held that it was wrong simply to say that at the date of the appeal the wife had no housing needs, so that no order should be made in her favour. Rather, the court should ask what order it would have made had it known that the wife had only five months to live.

A change in the law may constitute a supervening event, but in *S v S (Ancillary Relief: Consent Order)* [2002] EWHC 223, it was held that a consent order made six weeks before the decision in *White* could not be re-opened: the effect of *White* was radical but not unforeseen.

F: CONCLUSION

The law in this area has undergone radical change in the past few years. The **8–045** implications of *White v White* are still being worked out, and the decision of the House of Lords in *Miller, McFarlane* provides further scope for debate. It is almost inevitable that the principles enunciated in the latter will before long be tested. On the facts of *Miller v Miller* it may not have mattered whether the departure from equality was justified by the earning capacity that the husband brought to the marriage or the fact that the bulk of his wealth lay in business assets, a point that Baroness Hale failed to resolve, but it is easy to imagine a case where this will be crucial.

This chapter has focused on the rules that govern the division of property on divorce, rather than upon relationship breakdown more generally, as there are few rules that apply specifically to cohabiting couples in this context. Support may be provided for a child of the relationship under the Child Support Act 1991, and the court may even order the transfer of property under s.15 of the Children Act 1989 (see Ch.7), but such obligations are based on parenthood rather than upon past cohabitation.

One provision that does deal with the position of a cohabitant upon relationship breakdown is tucked away in Sch.7 of the Family Law Act 1996 (and is one of the provisions of that Act to have come into force). It is only applicable to cohabitants who are living in rented accommodation, but given that 40 per cent of cohabiting couples rent, and that those who do so are less likely to marry and more likely to split up, it is of no small importance. (Its relative obscurity may explain why it escaped the ire of the Act's opponents. An alternative explanation might be that the reallocation of tenancies is seen as less problematic than suspending the rights of a home-owner). Schedule 7 of the Act allows the court to transfer a tenancy to the spouse or cohabitant (as defined in s.62 of the Act) of the tenant. This is of particular significance in the context of public sector tenancies, which confer a security of tenure and the right to buy the property. The transferee may be ordered to pay compensation for the tenant's loss of the right to buy.

In sharp contrast to the lack of rights for cohabiting couples on relationship breakdown, and the wide discretion available to the courts when dividing the assets of spouses or civil partners, is the way in which assets are dealt with upon the death of one of the parties, which forms the subject-matter of the next chapter.

Chapter 9

RIGHTS ON DEATH

A: INTRODUCTION

Despite the rise in relationship breakdown, it still remains true that more marriages **9–001** are ended by death than by divorce. Cohabiting relationships are more likely to break down before the death of either partner, but the law looks more sympathetically upon a bereaved cohabitant than upon one whose relationship has come to an end during the joint lives of the parties, and rights have been conferred on both heterosexual and same-sex cohabitants in this context. Furthermore, following the Civil Partnership Act 2004 civil partners will be treated in the same way as spouses on the death of a partner. The division of assets upon death is therefore an important topic for the family lawyer.

The first point to note is that any adult of sound mind may make a will disposing of his or her property. As long as the appropriate formalities laid down in the Wills Act 1837 have been observed, the will determines the distribution of the estate. The freedom to make a will in whatever terms one chooses is a firm principle within English law, and it is only in limited circumstances that the terms of a will may be challenged. Making a will allows an individual to give effect to his or her views about family life and family obligations, to reward (or punish) family members.

But not every adult makes a will, and those under the age of 18 have no power to do so. The law thus provides a default regime in cases of intestacy. These rules are based on certain assumptions about the way in which the intestate would wish his or her estate to be divided, although it is open to question whether some of these assumptions remain valid at the start of the twenty-first century.

This chapter briefly outlines the intestacy rules (Part B) and then considers the ways in which family members and dependants may challenge the provision that has been made for them (Part C). Finally, the special treatment of the family home—whether rented or owner-occupied—is examined (Part D).

B: DIVISION OF THE ESTATE UPON INTESTACY

The intestacy rules are set out in s.46 of the Administration of Estates Act 1925. The **9–002** rules are complex, since they are required to cover a wide variety of situations: was the intestate survived by a spouse, civil partner, children, grandchildren, parents, grand-parents, siblings, nieces, nephews, uncles, aunts, cousins or any combination of such persons? Any of the persons in this list may be entitled to a share, but their entitlement (and the extent of their share) will depend on who else has survived the deceased.

(1) *The intestate who is survived by a spouse or civil partner*

9–003   It is convenient to start, as s.46 of the Act does, with the intestate who is survived by a spouse or civil partner. The rules have always privileged the surviving spouse, reflecting the equally strong preference demonstrated in wills: according to the Inland Revenue, on average three-quarters of the estate is left to the surviving spouse. Whether the testamentary preferences of civil partners will follow the same pattern remains to be seen.

The *proportion* that a spouse or civil partner receives on intestacy depends on which other relatives survived the deceased. Three situations need to be distinguished.

First, if the deceased left issue (which for these purposes means children and grandchildren, whether born within a formalised relationship or not) the surviving spouse or civil partner is entitled to all of the personal chattels, the first £125,000 of the estate (the "statutory legacy") and a life interest in one-half of the balance (if any). The other half of the balance is held on trust for the issue, to be divided equally between the children of the deceased (with the share of a child who pre-deceased the intestate passing to his or her children). Upon the death of the spouse or civil partner, the half share which was enjoyed under a life interest will also pass to the issue in equal shares.

> Example: Fred dies intestate, leaving a wife, and two children. His estate consists of the family home (worth £300,000), its contents (£20,000), a car (£5,000) and various bank accounts (worth £175,000). His wife will inherit the £25,000-worth of chattels (the contents of the house, and the car), plus £125,000, plus a life interest in half the balance (in this case half of £350,000, *i.e.* £175,000). The two children share the remaining £175,000 equally. When the wife dies any money remaining from her £175,000 will pass automatically to the children: as she has only a life interest she cannot dispose of it by will.

Secondly, if the intestate leaves a spouse plus one or more parents, siblings or nieces and nephews, but no issue, the spouse receives the personal chattels, the first £200,000 of the estate and an *absolute* interest in half of the balance. The remainder passes to the surviving parent(s), or, if there is no surviving parent, to the siblings of the intestate, with the share of a sibling who pre-deceased the intestate passing to his or her children.

Thirdly, if there are no other close relatives then the surviving spouse takes the whole estate.

The level of the statutory legacy reflects a number of (conflicting) principles. As the recent consultation paper issued by the Department of Constitutional Affairs explained:

> "First, it is clear that at all times overwhelming priority has been accorded to the surviving spouse. Secondly, prominence has been given to securing the marital home for the use of the surviving spouse. Thirdly, the expectations of the children

and other relatives have been acknowledged." (DCA, *Administration of Estates—Review of the Statutory Legacy* (2005), para.82)

It further added that the proposed new levels—£350,000 instead of £125,000 and £650,000 instead of £200,000—would also take account of future increases in value. The steep rise in the level of the statutory legacy reflects the rise in house prices since it was last set: given the importance attached to securing the family home for the surviving spouse it is logical that the statutory legacy should reflect this rise.

Might it not be simpler to provide that the surviving spouse inherits the entire estate under the intestacy rules? This option was recommended by the Law Commission in 1988 but concern was expressed about the position of children from a previous relationship.

Example: Teresa has two children from a previous relationship. She marries Simon, leaves her entire estate to him by will, and then dies. When Simon subsequently dies intestate, Teresa's children have no automatic rights to inherit.

Given that there are 400,000 married step-families with dependent children—and a still larger number where the children are no longer dependent—the problem is a very real one. It is questionable, however, whether it is an issue that should be addressed through the level of the statutory legacy. Where the amount of the estate is less than the statutory legacy, the children of the intestate will not receive anything. It is not obvious that the needs of children whose parents left relatively small estates are less compelling. A preferable approach would be to provide that the surviving spouse takes a percentage share of the estate. This would also reduce the need to update the level of the statutory legacy at regular intervals.

The upper level of the statutory legacy reflects the fact that parents and siblings would not have the same expectation of inheriting and are far less likely to be dependent on the deceased. The DCA noted that "the predominant guiding factor in setting the upper level seems to have been to try to ensure that the surviving spouse should be made absolutely secure before other relatives should benefit" (para.14). With the level at £650,000, the surviving spouse will inherit the entire estate in an estimated 96 per cent of cases.

Finally, given that English law recognises polygamous marriages lawfully contracted overseas, it may at some point be necessary for the courts to consider how the intestacy rules operate where the deceased left multiple spouses. As yet, this point has not arisen.

(2) *The intestate who dies single*

If a single person dies intestate, the estate will be distributed according to whether he **9–004** or she has been survived by (in order of priority) issue, parents, siblings (of the whole blood and half blood respectively), grandparents, or uncles and aunts (again, with those of the full blood being preferred to those of the half blood). The policy of the intestacy rules is to prefer close kin and to pass wealth to the generation below rather than the generation above (so, for example, the parents of the deceased only stand to inherit if their child left no issue). The issue of relatives who have predeceased the intestate may take their share of the estate: thus the scope of the rules is extended to nieces and nephews, as well as to cousins. If the intestate is not survived by any of these relatives the estate will pass to the Crown as *bona vacantia*.

In sharp contrast to the favourable treatment of formalised relationships, a bereaved cohabitant has no rights of intestate succession in the partner's estate. Unmarried partners would thus be well advised to make wills to secure provision for each other. The Law Commission reviewed this area of the law in 1988 and canvassed whether the intestacy rules should be reformed to allow a cohabitant to receive a set share of his or her deceased partner's estate. Although the Public Attitude Survey indicated strong support for such reform, the Law Commission decided against recommending such a reform on the basis that it would sacrifice the simplicity and clarity of the existing scheme. Instead, the Commission recommended that cohabitants should have enhanced rights to apply for discretionary provision, a recommendation which was enacted in the Law Reform (Succession) Act 1995 (see further Part C below).

There are other ways in which the rules do not reflect the complexity of modern life. While half-brothers and -sisters are included, no other relations by marriage receive any mention. Those who wish to make provision for step-children or others not listed in the intestacy provisions must do so by will.

C: THE INHERITANCE (PROVISION FOR FAMILY AND DEPENDANTS) ACT 1975

9–005 As noted above, under English law anyone of full age and mental capacity can make a will disposing of all his property. But although freedom of testation is still the basic principle of English succession law, the Inheritance (Provision for Family and Dependants) Act 1975 permits certain specified persons to apply to the court for reasonable financial provision to be made out of the deceased's estate. An application can be made whether or not the deceased left a will, and whether or not any will made provision for the applicant. There are three elements to any claim: first, is the person entitled to apply; secondly, was the provision made for the applicant unreasonable; and thirdly, if so, what level of provision should be ordered by the court? These three elements will be considered in turn.

(1) *Who can apply?*

9–006 The main "gate-keeping" provision of the Inheritance Act is that only certain categories of people can apply—spouses and civil partners, whether current or former, children, children of the family, cohabitants and any person "who immediately before the death of the deceased was being maintained . . . by the deceased".

(a) (Former) spouses and civil partners

9–007 Spouses and civil partners may apply as of right, regardless of whether they were actually living with the deceased at the time of death. Former spouses and civil partners will only be able to bring a claim if they have not since formalised another relationship.

(b) Children and children of the family

9–008 A claim may be brought by a child of the deceased or a person who was treated as a child of the family "in relation to a marriage" or, now, in relation to a civil partnership. If, by contrast, the deceased had been cohabiting with a person who had a child from a previous relationship, the child would not be a "child of the family" for these purposes. The child might, however, be able to claim as a "dependant".

(c) *Claims by cohabitants*

Before 1995 a cohabitant could only make a claim if he or she qualified as a **9–009** dependant. The Law Reform (Succession) Act 1995 amended the 1975 Act by allowing a claim by a cohabitant who had been living with the deceased in the same household immediately before the date of the death, and for at least two years before that date, as the husband or wife of the deceased (s.1(3)(1A) of the 1975 Act). This definition excluded same-sex cohabitants, but the Act has now been amended again—this time as a result of the Civil Partnership Act 2004—to include those 'living as the civil partner of the deceased' (s.1(1B)(b)).

The different criteria that need to be satisfied in order for a cohabitant to bring a claim have been considered in a series of recent cases.

(i) Was the claimant living as the husband or wife of the deceased?: In most cases a **9–010** cohabitant will find no difficulty in satisfying this requirement, but the facts of *Re Watson (deceased)* [1999] 1 F.L.R. 878, Ch D were relatively unusual:

> In this case, the parties' relationship stretched back over 30 years, although their responsibilities to their parents "seemed to get in the way of marriage" and it was not until 1985 that the applicant (then aged 54) moved into the deceased's house. She assumed responsibility for the housekeeping, washing, shopping, cooking and gardening but did not have sexual relations. The judge held that the appropriate question for the court was whether, in the opinion of a reasonable person with normal perceptions, it could be said that the two people in question were living together as husband and wife. This did not mean that it would be sufficient for the relationship to have been one that a husband and wife *might* have had (because that would bring almost all relationships between men and women living in the same household within the statute), but at the same time the court would not ignore the "multifarious nature of marital relationships". The judge opined that it was not unusual for a happily married husband and wife in their mid-fifties not merely to have separate bedrooms but to abstain from sexual relations. The parties had shared living space and meals and the woman had performed the tasks stereotypically associated with a housewife. The judge was therefore satisfied that they had been living together as man and wife.

(ii) Were the parties living in the same household?: It is not necessary for the parties to **9–011** be living under the same roof to be deemed to be living in the same household. As was pointed out in *Gully v Dix* [2004] EWCA Civ 139:

> "they will be in the same household if they are tied by their relationship. The tie of that relationship may be made manifest by various elements, not simply their living under the same roof, but the public and private acknowledgement of their mutual society, and the mutual protection and support that binds them together . . . " (*per* Ward L.J.)

Yet it may be difficult to show that two individuals who maintain separate establishments are actually sharing a household:

In *Churchill v Roach* [2002] EWHC 3230, Arnold—long separated from his wife—began to live with Muriel, but was (mistakenly) concerned that she would thereby become his "common law wife" and asked her to leave. For the next five years they spent weekends and holidays together. In 1998 he sold his house and bought the cottage adjoining hers. The two properties were turned into one (although still held under separate titles). The judge held that before 1998 "there were two separate establishments with two separate domestic economies. There was, of course, a degree of sharing when the two met at weekends and some of those weekends were long. But that does not mean that they lived in one household." After 1998, they were living together in one household—but Arnold's death in early 2000 occurred before the two-year requirement could be satisfied.

A similar problem faced the claimant in *Kotke v Safarini* [2005] EWCA Civ 221, a decision under the Fatal Accidents Act 1976, which employs a similar definition of "cohabitant."

9–012 **(iii) Were the parties living in the same household immediately before the date of the death?:** This requirement posed a potential problem in *Gully v Dix* [2004] EWCA Civ 139:

> The parties had lived together since 1974. In 1999 the male fell over the bannisters and sustained head injuries which meant that he was unable to work, or indeed to look after himself. As the judge noted, he was "incontinent when drunk, which was often." This led to temporary separations of up to a week at a time. After he threatened to kill himself in August 2001 the female partner left. He spoke to her daughter—promising to stop drinking—but the messages were never passed on, and he was found dead in his bed in October 2001. The estate was worth £170,000 and under the intestacy rules would pass to a brother that he had not seen in 30 years. The court held that on the facts they were still living together. She had only taken a small suitcase of clothes and so was clearly not intending to leave permanently; the doctor had advised her to stay away for her own safety; and neither party regarded the relationship as at an end. He wanted her back, and, the judge opined that she would have gone back if asked: "The very fact that her daughter concealed the telephone calls from her is an indication that, to those who knew her, it was obvious that she would have returned to live with the deceased the moment he asked her to do so."

Thus it appears from these three cases that the courts are more willing to find that an existing cohabiting relationship has continued, although the parties are physically separated, than that a developing relationship has become a cohabiting one.

(d) Those maintained by the deceased

9–013 The Inheritance (Provision for Family and Dependants) Act 1975 included amongst the statutory class of "dependants", a person who "immediately before the death of the deceased was being maintained, either wholly or partly, by the deceased". Until express provision was made for a surviving cohabitant in 1995, this provision was often invoked by a surviving cohabitant, and remains relevant for relationships that do not meet the threshold criteria under the 1995 Act, as well as for friends, relatives or other dependants. For example:

In *Rees v Newbery and the Institute of Cancer Research* [1998] 1 F.L.R. 1041, Ch
D, the deceased, a man of substantial means, was a close friend of the applicant.
He had allowed him to live in a flat which he owned at a rent much below market
levels, and had instructed his solicitors to draft a will whereby the applicant would
be entitled to continue in occupation of the flat on similar terms. The judge held
that the provision of the flat had been a provision of maintenance for the
applicant, who succeeded in a claim for reasonable provision out of the deceased's
estate.

Again:

In *Re B, deceased* [2000] 1 All E.R. 665 CA, the deceased was born severely brain
damaged, and damages of a quarter of a million pounds were awarded to her.
Part of this sum was spent in buying a house where the applicant (the child's
mother) could care for her, having given up her job to do so. The child's father left
a short time after her birth. The child survived to age 14; and the mother did not
wish the father to take the half share in the child's property to which he was
entitled under the rules of intestate distribution. She accordingly applied for
reasonable provision (over and above her entitlement on intestacy) to be made for
her out of her daughter's estate; and the question arose as to whether she had
"been maintained" by her daughter for the purposes of the 1975 Act. The Court
of Appeal held that it had been wrong to strike out her claim: the child's damages
had been used to meet her mother's needs so that she in turn could care for her
daughter.

These debates on what constitutes maintenance are not merely exercises in semantics.
Both Parliament and the courts have been concerned that the 1975 Act should not
become the vehicle for the court to rewrite a will merely because it considers the will
to have been unjust. The function of the court is restricted to dealing with situations
of dependency.

Re B illustrates a number of points of contention. First, is a person "dependent" if
he or she contributes to the relationship? It may be easier for a person who has
received support or accommodation in return for care or housekeeping services to
establish dependency than for one who had been making an equal or greater financial
contribution (see, *e.g. Bishop v Plumley* [1991] 1 W.L.R. 582, CA). In *Churchill v Roach*
[2002] EWHC 3230, above para.9–011, it was decided that the female partner was
partly dependent on the deceased—in that the net flow of benefits was from him to
her—so she qualified under this category.

Secondly, s.3(4) of the Act requires the court, in deciding whether reasonable
provision has been made, to have regard to the extent to which the deceased assumed
responsibility for the applicant. Is it therefore necessary to establish that the deceased
"assumed responsibility" for the applicant in order for the applicant to apply for
provision? This would have posed problems for the applicant in *Re B* as her daughter
was of limited mental capacity. The court was willing to infer that responsibility had
been assumed from the fact that the deceased made a substantial contribution to the
applicant's needs.

It may seem odd that the legislation does not grant a claim to a person who was
caring for another, or who had made a substantial contribution to the other's welfare.
This is because the legislation, in contrast to the intestacy rules, is largely about needs

rather than rights. It should also be remembered that a person who has made a contribution to the *property* of the deceased might be able to claim an interest by way of a trust, as detailed in Ch.5. But there will inevitably be cases that fall between these two sets of rules, and this may need to be addressed in the future, to recognise the role of informal carers looking after an increasingly elderly population.

(2) Applicant has to establish lack of reasonable financial provision

9–014 The second hurdle is that the applicant must establish that the "disposition of the deceased's estate effected by his will or the law relating to intestacy" is "not such as to make reasonable financial provision" for him or her. The underlying principle is that it is not the function of the court to undertake a redistribution of the deceased's estate to achieve a *fair* distribution. Instead, the provision must be shown to be unreasonable: the test, set out in *Re Coventry* [1980] Ch. 461, requires a judge to ask "whether, in all the circumstances, looked at objectively, it was unreasonable that the deceased's will did not make greater provision for the claimant's maintenance." Thus:

> In *Barass v Harding* [2001] 1 F.L.R. 138, CA, the former wife of the deceased was described as being in "parlous financial circumstances". However, given the fact that the parties had divorced in 1964 and had had no continuing relationship—apart from a "semi-business arrangement" whereby she occupied a flat he owned for a peppercorn rent—his failure to make provision for her was not unreasonable.

It may be difficult for an adult child—at least one who is capable of earning his or her own living—to show that a parent had not made reasonable financial provision. In some cases such an applicant will already have received significant sums during the parent's lifetime (see *e.g. Robinson v Fernsby* [2003] EWCA Civ 1820). Even if the child has received nothing from the parent, this does not mean that the court should rewrite the latter's will to make provision for the former:

> In *Re Jennings (dec'd)* [1994] Ch. D. 286, a 50-year-old had been brought up from the age of four by his mother and step-father. There was no contact between biological father and son after the parents' divorce, and the only thing the father did for his son was to send him ten shillings in a birthday card on his second birthday. The father left the residue of his estate (which amounted to some £300,000) to charities. The son had been successful in business and was in reasonably comfortable financial circumstances. The Court of Appeal dismissed his claim on the basis that the failure to make financial provision for the son was not unreasonable.

The few cases in which a claim by an adult child have succeeded have tended to involve express promises—either to the child or another—that property will be given to the child (see *e.g. Espinosa v Bourke* [1999] 1 F.L.R 747).

(3) The court's extensive powers

9–015 If the court considers that the will or intestacy does not make reasonable financial provision for the dependant, it may make any of a range of orders, for example for periodical payments of income or for the payment of a lump sum. The level of provision that the court can order depends on the status of the applicant, as follows:

(a) The surviving spouse or civil partner

Provision for a surviving spouse or civil partner is to be such as would be reasonable **9–016** for such a person to receive, regardless of whether that provision is required for his or her maintenance. The court is specifically directed to consider the provision that the applicant might reasonably have expected to receive if the relationship had been terminated by divorce or dissolution rather than by death (s.3(2) of the I(PFD)A). In *P v G, P and P (Family Provision: Relevance of Divorce Provision)* [2004] EWHC 2944 (Fam) Black J. held that:

> "what the statute contemplates in a case such as this is not that the entire fictional ancillary relief case should be played out within the Inheritance Act claim but that the court should simply reach sufficient of a conclusion about how it would have been resolved to take that factor into account in considering what would be reasonable financial provision under the 1975 Act." (para.236)

Having concluded that the likely outcome on divorce would have been an equal division of the assets, the judge emphasised that this was only one factor to be taken into account under the 1975 Act and awarded the widow £2m, which increased her share to more than 50 per cent of the estate. The discrepancy can be justified by the obvious difference between divorce and death.

> "I am struck by the force of the repeated observations in the decided authorities about the difference between divorce where there are two surviving spouses for whom to make provision and death where there is only one. It seems to be probable that this difference will not infrequently be reflected in greater provision being made under the 1975 Act than would have been made on divorce, and that this may legitimately be so even where the estate is a relatively large one, as it is here." (para.242)

Similarly, the duration of the marriage is a less significant factor if it ends in death rather than divorce. As Wall L.J. noted in *Fielden v Cunliffe* [2005] EWCA Civ 1508:

> "a widow is entitled to say that she entered into it on the basis that it would be of infinite duration . . . The fact that the marriage has been prematurely termi-nated by death after a short period may therefore render the length of the marriage a less critical factor than it would have been in the case of a divorce." (para.30)

Even so, as he went on to suggest:

> "there is . . . a clear difference between a widow who had been married for many years and who had made an equal contribution to the family of the deceased, and a woman in Mrs Cunliffe's position, who had been married only a little over a year, and who had . . . made no contribution to the family business and only a very small contribution to the family wealth." (para.34)

A departure from equality—this time downwards—was therefore justified.

(b) Other applicants

9–017 The court can only order such provision as is required for the applicant's "maintenance." The interpretation of this is relatively generous: it may, for example, include the housing needs of the applicant, as in *Churchill v Roach* [2004] [2002] EWHC 3230 (see para.9–011 above).

(4) *Evaluating the Act*

9–018 There is little empirical evidence about the working of the 1975 Act; and it may be that payments are made out of court to those falling within the specified categories to avoid the potential cost of an action. In recent cases, the courts have emphasised the sometimes ruinous costs of litigating over relatively small estates and have encouraged alternative methods of dispute resolution.

D: THE FAMILY HOME

9–019 Special consideration should be given to the rules relating to the family home, whether rented or owner-occupied.

(1) *The statutory transmission of tenancies*

9–020 Spouses, civil partners, cohabitants (whether of the same or opposite sex) and members of the tenant's family have the right to succeed to a tenancy on the tenant's death. The courts have a discretion as to the allocation of the tenancy if there is more than one person entitled to succeed to it and they do not agree on the outcome. The law on this topic is complex, and the details may be found in the Housing Acts 1985 and 1988 and Sch.8 of the Civil Partnership Act 2004.

(2) *Determining ownership and occupation of the family home*

9–021 As noted in Ch.5, it will be important to ascertain the beneficial ownership of the family home when the legal owner dies. If another person has a beneficial interest in the property, the value of the deceased's estate will be reduced accordingly. This is obviously important for the potential beneficiaries, but is also significant in terms of liability for inheritance tax. At present the vast majority of estates are below the threshold for inheritance tax (currently set at £285,000 for the year 2006–07 and due to rise to £300,000 in 2007–08 and £312,000 in 2008–09), but this will be affected by rising house prices. Inheritance tax is not payable on any part of the estate that passes to the surviving spouse or (by virtue of the Tax and Civil Partnership Regulations 2005, SI 2005/3229) civil partner, but these exemptions do not extend to cohabitants.

Where the owner died intestate, the surviving spouse may request that the family home be appropriated towards his or her share of the estate. Otherwise, occupation of the family home will depend on the terms of the will, and on whether the spouse (or indeed any other person) has a proprietary interest in the home. Home rights do not survive the death of the surviving spouse or civil partner.

Mention should also be made of the special rules that apply where the property is held under a joint tenancy:

(a) Joint tenancy: the right of survivorship

In many cases the title deeds or register will provide that the parties own the property **9–022** as beneficial joint tenants. This means that they do not own individual shares in the property, but are both entitled to the entire property (as distinct from a tenancy in common, under which the parties have individual shares in the property). Where a couple—or indeed other home-sharers—are joint tenants, the doctrine of survivorship will apply. This means that the surviving joint tenant is entitled to the entire estate. If the parties were joint tenants in equity, the survivor is entitled to the entire beneficial interest, whereas if they were joint tenants at law but not in equity, the survivor will hold on trust for the estate of the deceased.

(b) Severance of the joint tenancy

The right of survivorship represents what many couples living happily together would **9–023** wish. But when a relationship breaks down, one or both partners may want to ensure that their interest in the family home will pass to someone else—perhaps to a new partner, or to children from a previous relationship. It is not possible to achieve this simply by making a will, since making a will does not displace the right of survivorship. It is first necessary to sever the joint tenancy: this turns the *beneficial* joint tenancy into a tenancy in common in equal shares. (It should however be noted that the *legal* joint tenancy cannot be severed.) The parties can then make wills disposing of their interests as they wish (see, *e.g. Chandler v Clark* [2002] EWCA Civ 1249).

There are a number of ways in which severance can be achieved, but much the simplest is for the one joint tenant to give written notice to the other under the provisions of s.36 of the Law of Property Act 1925. Solicitors who are consulted in a situation of this kind may be liable in professional negligence if they fail to give advice about severance. If the client decides that severance is appropriate, the written notice should be given immediately, without waiting to inspect title deeds: see *Carr-Glyn v Frearsons (A Firm)* [1999] 1 F.L.R. 8, CA.

Advice on severance needs to be cautious, however, since it will not be advantageous if the other joint tenant dies first:

> In *Kinch v Bullard* [1999] 1 F.L.R. 66, Ch D, the wife decided to sever the joint tenancy of the matrimonial home, and signed a notice. But her husband suffered a heart attack, and the wife (realising that severance would not be in her interests if he died before her) destroyed the letter when it was delivered in the post. But the court held that the tenancy had been severed. The notice was effective as soon as it had been delivered (see s.196(3) of the Law of Property Act 1925); the severance was immediately effective and could not be reversed.

E: CONCLUSION

The rules described in this chapter reveal differing views of the family. The intestacy **9–024** rules are based on status and blood relationships, while the family provision legislation takes a more functional approach, extending rights to those who were supported by the deceased regardless of whether there was any legally recognised family tie. However, in other ways the concept of the family evidenced by the former is wider than that shown by the latter: even cousins may have a claim under the intestacy rules, if closer relatives are lacking, while claims for provision are limited to the close family circle unless the deceased was actually maintaining the claimant. The privileged position of the spouse or civil partner—under both sets of rules—is also worthy of note. By contrast, in other areas of family law the focus has shifted from formal relationships to parenthood, and it is the parent-child relationship that forms the subject-matter of Part III.

PART THREE

CHILDREN, THE FAMILY AND THE LAW

INTRODUCTION

The family as a private unit

A new-born child is physically incapable of caring for itself, and mentally incapable of **III–001** reaching reasoned decisions about its own future. Others must therefore assume the burden of care and of decision-taking for the baby. The growing child may increasingly demand a say in the decisions that have to be taken about such matters as education and leisure activities. The fact that society casts on the family the function of socialising children increases the possibility of conflict, for the child may not want to do what the parents or other carers would wish. Against this background, no one should be surprised that studies of child development and family dynamics often reveal a hotbed of conflict. Yet most of these conflicts are resolved without any reference to the law, much less to the courts. As Ch.1 emphasised, the family is traditionally seen as a private unit—a realm that the state cannot and should not seek to enter *(Prince v Massachusetts* (1944) 321 U.S. 158 at 166, *per* Rutledge J.: and see *per* Lord Donaldson M.R., *Re M and N (Wards) (Publication of Information)* [1990] 1 F.L.R. 149 at 164). The traditional view is that it is for parents to discipline their children and to make choices on their behalf. The Human Rights Act, after all, guarantees the protection of the right to family life. Yet there remain cases which cannot properly be resolved by private ordering, not least where parents cannot agree between themselves; while the traditional view has also come into conflict with beliefs, strongly articulated in recent years, which assert children's rights to autonomy and, in particular, to have a say in decisions which affect their future. Increasingly, therefore, the law does have to provide answers to questions about who is to be entitled to take decisions about a child's upbringing, and to provide procedures whereby those issues may be litigated.

Family and the State

A further potential source of conflict arises if the parents or other carers are unable or **III–002** unwilling to adopt the values and child-rearing practices deemed appropriate by the state—whether because the parents have a different scale of values (a matter of particular significance in a multi-cultural society) or because the parents are (through illness, poverty or other factors) unable to achieve the levels of parenting skill judged acceptable by contemporary standards. Since the end of the Second World War in 1945 the State has assumed increasing responsibilities to provide a wide range of services to benefit children and families, and to care for children whose own families are unable or unwilling to provide "good enough" parenting. In many cases, of course, the relationship between the state (acting through local authorities) and the family is an entirely consensual one, with no element—or at least no apparent element—of compulsion. But it has for long been recognised that the State sometimes needs to intervene against the wishes of a child's family in order to provide protection for a child against abuse or neglect. The circumstances that justify such intervention have, in recent years, become a matter of acute controversy. Will local authority "care" truly protect a child from abuse? There is a sad history of official inquiries revealing that children in care may even be at increased risk of abuse; whilst there is a growing body of evidence linking local authority care with subsequent under-achievement. In any event, to remove a child from home and parents (perhaps eventually to be transferred to a new family by the process of legal adoption, which destroys all legal links between the child and the birth parents, to other parents) must constitute a dramatic interference with the birth parents' rights to family life.

The legal structure for determining issues about children's upbringing: the Children Act 1989

III–003 The legal procedures governing the upbringing of children and defining the circumstances in which the state may take compulsory measures of child care were revolutionised by the Children Act 1989, which was accurately described by Lord Chancellor Mackay as "the most comprehensive and far reaching reform of child law which has come before Parliament in living memory". The Act sought to provide a comprehensive, clear, and consistent code for the whole of child law, and undoubtedly effected considerable simplification and rationalisation. But it is not a complete code for children—child support, assisted reproduction and adoption being perhaps the most obvious examples of areas not governed by the 1989 Act—and subsequent amendments have encumbered its original form.

The law relating to children is almost inevitably complex; but the reader should not allow the mass of detail to conceal the fact that there are major issues of principle involved:

(1) *The courts as coercive agencies of the state*

III–004 In particular it is necessary to remember that the courts, in this as in other respects, exercise the coercive judicial power of the state, and ultimately court orders are enforceable by sanctions, including imprisonment. As the judge noted in *FM (A Child by AM his Litigation Friend) v Singer and others* [2004] EWHC 793:

> "The court's view as to what is in the best interests of a child will invariably not accord with the wishes of one of the parents but it is the court's view, when embodied in an order of the court, which must prevail." (para.5)

But this raises certain problems. It is one thing to imprison a person for an attack on a former partner in breach of a court order (see Ch.6). It is quite another to imprison the victim of that attack, who, fearing for the safety of the child, ignores the terms of a court order for contact with the perpetrator. The enforcement of contact orders has become a particular problem for the courts in recent years, and the means deployed are considered further below (para.12–031). The key point for present purposes is that once an order has been made it is capable of being (and in appropriate circumstances will be) enforced by the physical power of the state (although *FM (A Child by AM his Litigation Friend) v Singer and others* illustrates the practical problems of such enforcement).

(2) *The question of standing: who can bring cases to the court?*

Although this sounds a very technical issue, it is in fact one of great importance—and **III–005** difficulty. Should a neighbour who thinks that parents have an unsatisfactory life-style be allowed to ask the court to make an order about how the parents should bring up their child? Should a pressure group be able to apply for an order overriding parental agreement to some form of medical procedure—perhaps the termination of a daughter's pregnancy? Should a grandparent be able to seek an order that the child be sent to a particular school? Should a local authority be able to apply for an order that a child be removed to a children's home because the authority considers that the parents' attitude to the child's upbringing is unsatisfactory? And what about the child himself? Can a rebellious teenager apply to the court for an order overruling the parents' refusal to allow him to live with or even go on a foreign holiday with a friend? In deciding these matters, it must be remembered that the process of litigation can itself be profoundly destructive: as an experienced judge of the Family Division put it, "nothing can raise the temperature of a family dispute more than an ill-considered, unfounded application for a residence order" (even if the parties refrain from the "intemperate and bilious" language used in the case then before the court: *Re R. (Residence: Contact: Restricting Applications)* [1998] 1 F.L.R. 749 at 759, *per* Wilson J.). There are accordingly restrictions on who can bring cases to court (see paras 12–004 *et seq.*, and Ch.13).

(3) *On what principles should the court act?*

It is tempting—and easy—to say that the child's welfare should always be the para- **III–006** mount concern. But views as to what is best for a child have changed over the years:

> In *Re Thain* [1926] Ch. D. 676, a judge refused to attach weight to the suggestion that a child would be harmed if she were removed from the couple who had cared for her for five years since infancy. The judge said that "at her tender age, one knows from experience how mercifully transient are the effects of partings and other sorrows, and how soon the novelty of fresh surroundings and new associations effaces the recollection of former days and kind friends".

This view would not be accepted by twenty-first century child psychiatrists, who give great importance to the attachments which a child forms in early infancy.

Views also differ between contemporaries. For example, there are still people who believe that the biblical text "He that spareth the rod hateth his son" justifies inflicting severe corporal punishment on children. On the other hand, there are those who believe that parents should be prohibited from administering any form of corporal punishment on a child (see further para.11–003 on whether parents are able to inflict such punishments).

Judges do not rely solely on their own perceptions as to what would best promote the welfare of a child, and will usually be assisted by expert evidence in reaching their decisions (including medical evidence and the evidence of experts in child development), although they are not bound to follow the recommendations of experts. Of course, disciplines such as medicine and psychology are no more set in stone than the law is, but judges can do no more than accept the best advice currently available, while bearing in mind that such advice may in years to come seem as wrong-headed as the view that attaching leeches to a sick body is likely to improve the patient's health.

(4) *Relationship between standing and governing principles*

III–007   Perhaps it must be accepted that opinions change over the years and differ between individuals, but it may be that once an issue is before it the court must simply do its best on the available evidence. But this makes it clear that there is a relationship between the two issues of, on the one hand, determining the circumstances in which people are to be allowed to bring cases about the child's future to the court, and on the other hand the issue of what test is to be applied in the cases which do come before the court. Thus, if it is the state which wants to interfere, the court cannot act merely on the basis of its perception of the child's welfare, for this would be to permit children to be removed from their families simply on the basis that a court considered that the state could do better for the child than his or her family (as the then Lord Chancellor, Lord Mackay put it in 1989: see p.139 N.L.J. 508). On the other hand, if the parents themselves disagree about the child's upbringing then it is difficult to think of plausible reasons for denying them the right to bring the matter to the court—indeed, attempts to do so would probably be inconsistent with the right under Art.6 of the Convention to a fair trial of civil rights and obligations, and it is equally difficult to think of any more satisfactory principle than to require the court to take whatever course the evidence suggests will be best for the child. But does it follow that we should allow the neighbour or pressure group the same unqualified right which a parent has to put parental decisions into question by a court—with all the attendant tension and uncertainty—even if the court would be guided solely by its perception of the child's interests in deciding the matter? As we shall see, the legislation answers this question by allowing certain people an unfettered right to bring issues to the court, allowing others to do so if the applicant can obtain the leave of the court, whilst altogether prohibiting others from making applications.

The scope of the Children Act 1989

III–008   The orders that the court can make under the Children Act 1989 can conveniently be divided into four main groups. First of all, there are the so-called "s.8 orders" as defined in s.8 of the Act which include residence and contact orders, as well as orders dealing with specific aspects of a child's upbringing. Such orders are conveniently described as "private law" orders because they are the orders usually made in proceedings brought by private individuals on or after the breakdown of their relationship. It is, however, important to note that these orders can be made in any family proceedings, so that the court has power to make a residence order in favour of a relative, for example, in a case in which a local authority has applied for a care order and it equally has power to make a contact order in proceedings brought by an applicant for an adoption order.

The second main group of orders are often called "public law" orders because they can only be made on the application of local authorities or other specially qualified agencies. Public law orders include care and supervision orders, which involve a degree of state intrusion into the family and therefore require certain conditions to be satisfied.

The third group of orders is the orders for financial relief with respect to children which can be made in proceedings started under s.15 and Sch.1 of the Children Act 1989. These orders have been dealt with in Ch.7.

The fourth and last group of orders can loosely be described as "ancillary orders". They include orders requiring a welfare report (s.7), orders directing a local authority to investigate a case with a view to bringing care proceedings (s.37), and orders requiring the assessment of a child who is subject to an interim care or supervision order (s.38). Such orders—the aim of which is often to amass the necessary information before the court makes a final decision—are dealt with at the most appropriate places in the text.

Organisation of the text

Chapter 10 deals with the basic questions concerning parentage, including the issues **III–009** that arise where the child has been born following assisted reproduction. Chapter 11 goes on to examine the distinct legal concept of parental responsibility—which determines who is entitled to take decisions about a child's upbringing. If there is disagreement between those who have parental responsibility for a child, then it may be necessary to invoke the assistance of the court, and Ch.12 considers the circumstances in which an application can be made to the court and the range of orders that the court can make. If those caring for the child neglect their responsibilities, or harm the child, it may be necessary for the State to intervene to protect the child, and Ch.13 considers the circumstances in which this is legally possible. Throughout all these areas of law the welfare of the child must be considered, and the factors that the court must take into account in evaluating the welfare of any individual child are discussed in Ch.14. The final chapter examines the law relating to adoption, now reformed by the Adoption and Children Act 2002. It may seem odd to consider adoption—which is, after all, a way of creating family ties—at the end of the book, but in fact the order chosen reflects the stages through which a child may pass. Even if a child is given up for adoption at birth, the law will still designate the birth mother as the legal mother until the process of adoption is completed, and the question as to who has parental responsibility will also be relevant. More frequent is the situation where a child has already suffered many of the problems to which the law struggles to find solutions and is adopted from care.

Chapter 10

LEGAL PARENTAGE

A: INTRODUCTION: WHAT IS A PARENT?

Words describing family relationships—for example "aunt" or "brother"—are often **10–001** used in different senses by different people; and, in particular, words connoting a relationship are often used to indicate a social reality, rather than a biological fact. For example, someone brought up from birth by foster-parents may well refer to them as "mother" and "father"; and it is not unusual for a young child to look on the mother's partner as his or her "dad" whether or not the man concerned is biologically the child's parent. For many years, the law rarely had to concern itself with these ambiguities and differences of linguistic usage. Leaving on one side legal adoption (which only became possible in this country in 1926: see Ch.15, below), the law did not take account of social or psychological parentage. For the common law, parentage concerned genetics (*Re B (Parentage)* [1996] 2 F.L.R. 15, Fam Div, at 21, *per* Bracewell J.) and genetic factors alone determined the identity of a person's parents.

While this remains the position at common law, in recent years the courts have had to grapple with the impact of scientific developments. As Hedley J. pointed out in *W and B v H (Child Abduction: Surrogacy)* [2002] 1 F.L.R. 1008, Fam Div, "our scientific capabilities are racing ahead of our ethical grasp of the issues involved." (at 1009). Blood testing and DNA sampling have made it easier to determine the paternity of a child, but the courts still have to address the question as to when such tests should be ordered and how samples should be taken. What, for example, should be the position of the law where there is a danger that proof that the mother's husband is not the father of her children will lead to the breakdown of the family unit? Developments in assisted reproduction pose even more difficult questions. Should legal parentage be ascribed to the persons who have provided the genetic material for the child, the woman who has carried the child to term, or the persons who intend to bring up the child? Also, what should be the position if someone's genetic material is used by mistake? In 2002, mixed-race twins were born to a white woman as the result of a mix-up at an IVF clinic that attracted much media attention and illustrated how human error might add an extra layer of complication. The court had the task of construing statutory provisions that had not been drafted with this eventuality in mind: *Leeds Teaching Hospital NHS Trust v A* [2003] EWHC 259, and see below para.10–010). This case also demonstrates how there may be a disjunction between legal parenthood and social parenthood.

This chapter looks first at how parentage may be established (Part B), and then considers the particular rules that are applicable to assisted reproduction and surrogacy arrangements (Parts C and D respectively). It concludes by considering whether a child has a right to know the truth about his or her genetic parentage (Part E).

B: ESTABLISHING PARENTAGE

10–002 At common law, the man and woman who provide the genetic material (the sperm and egg, or "gametes") that results in conception and birth are the child's parents. The rule is simple: in the past, however, it posed certain difficulties in that there were no sophisticated or reliable methods available to identify the child's genetic parents. Motherhood was said to be a biological fact that could be proved demonstrably by parturition—*i.e.* in most cases someone would have seen the mother give birth (see *The Ampthill Peerage* [1977] A.C. 457 at 577). But paternity remained for long almost impossible to prove, leading one judge to comment cynically that paternity was a matter of opinion rather than a matter of fact. Yet it was important to be able to decide the question, if only in order to try to make the father financially responsible for the child's upkeep. The law therefore took refuge in presumptions:

The common law presumptions

10–003 The law presumed that the husband of a married woman was the father of any child born to her during the marriage. This presumption could only be rebutted if there were evidence establishing beyond reasonable doubt that the husband could not have been the father—for example because he had been out of the country throughout the time when the child could have been conceived. A husband who could have had intercourse with his wife at the likely time of conception would be held to be the father of her child even if there were evidence that the wife had also had intercourse with "one, two or 20 men" (*per* Sir F. Jeune, P., *Gordon v Gordon* [1903] P. 141 at 142). It should be borne in mind that at this period a finding of illegitimacy would have had severe consequences. As Thorpe L.J. pointed out in *Re H and A (Children)* [2002] EWCA Civ 383, "in the nineteenth century, when science had nothing to offer and illegitimacy was a social stigma as well as a depriver of rights, the presumption was a necessary tool" (at 30).

It was also presumed that the man named on the birth certificate was the child's father, but the value of this was limited by the fact that restrictions were for long placed on the entry of any name other than that of the husband. Finally, the fact that a person had been found to be the father of a child in proceedings under the Children Act 1989 (and certain other statutes) was held to create a rebuttable presumption that he was indeed the child's father (Civil Evidence Act 1968, as amended by Sch.16, para.2 of the Courts and Legal Services Act 1990).

Are the presumptions still relevant?

10–004 The law still presumes paternity in the above situations, at least for the purpose of extracting child support (s.26 of the Child Support Act 1991, as amended by the Child Support, Pensions and Social Security Act 2000). However, the importance of the presumptions has been reduced in two ways. First, it is no longer necessary to provide evidence to rebut the presumption of legitimacy beyond all reasonable doubt. It is sufficient if the paternity of the child is "more probable than not" (s.26 of the Family Law Reform Act 1969). Secondly, developments in blood testing and DNA sampling have made parenthood something that can be established positively as a matter of virtual certainty provided that the necessary tissue samples are available (as Waite L.J. put it in *Re A (A Minor) (Paternity: Refusal of Blood Test)* [1994] 2 F.L.R. 463 at 469).

It has been known for well over 50 years that comparison of the characteristics of the child's blood with the blood characteristics of the child's mother and of a particular man could provide conclusive evidence that the man could *not* be the father of the child. Evidence of this kind might therefore indirectly establish that a particular man *was* the child's father, by a process of elimination. More recently, the development of DNA profiling has greatly increased the accuracy with which parentage may be established. The presumption of legitimacy thus has little to offer: as Thorpe L.J. commented in *Re H and A (Children)* [2002] EWCA Civ 383, CA, "it seems to me that the paternity of any child is to be established by science and not by legal presumption or inference" (at 30). This of course assumes that the issue of paternity actually falls to be resolved by the court. There is no requirement that the paternity of the child be tested before the details of the man assumed to be the father are entered on the birth certificate, and research indicates that in a surprisingly large number of cases the birth certificate is misleading.

The availability of samples

The application of scientific methods of testing assumes the availability of the neces- **10–005** sary samples. Two issues arise: how should the courts deal with a refusal by an adult to give a sample, and when may a sample be taken from a child?

To give the court power to compel people to submit to the taking of samples would have been a serious interference with personal liberty, and the Family Law Reform Act 1969 accordingly introduced a compromise. The court may give a direction for the use of tests (s.20); but failure to comply with such a direction is not a contempt of court punishable by fine or imprisonment (as would usually be the case for a failure to comply with a court order). Indeed, the Act specifically provides that in general a sample shall not be taken without the consent of the person concerned (s.21(1)). However, the court is empowered to draw such inferences from a refusal as it thinks fit, and *In Re A (A Minor) (Paternity: Refusal of Blood Test)* [1994] 2 F.L.R. 463 at 473, the Court of Appeal held that if a claim were made against someone who could possibly be the father, and that person chose to exercise his right not to submit to be tested, the inference that he was the father would be "virtually inescapable" unless he could give very clear and cogent medical or perhaps other reasons for the refusal. In that case:

> A prosperous businessman refused to undergo a test because the mother had been working as a prostitute and there were known to be two other men who might on the facts equally be the father. He said it would be unreasonable and unjust to put him alone at risk of having paternity conclusively established against him. But Waite L.J. said (at 473) that any man who is unsure of his own paternity and

harboured the least doubt as to whether the child he is alleged to have fathered may be that of another man now has it within his power to set all doubt at rest by submitting to a test. The accuracy of scientific testing now made it impossible for any man in such circumstances to be forced against his will to accept paternity of a child whom he does not believe to be his.

This approach applies even if the effect of making a finding of paternity will be to rebut the presumption (see above) that a married woman's husband is the father of her child: see *F v Child Support Agency* [1999] 2 F.L.R. 244, Fam Div. The recent case of *Secretary of State for Work and Pensions v Jones* [2003] EWHC 2163 (Fam) demonstrates that it also outweighs the presumption that the man registered on the birth certificate is the child's father:

> In this case the mother was living with Mr Jones at the time of conception but returned to her husband before the birth of her child, K. Her husband was registered as the father, having agreed to treat K as his own. Some time later the mother sought a maintenance assessment under the Child Support Act 1991, naming Mr Jones as the father. Mr Jones ticked the "Yes" box on the enquiry form in answer to the question of whether he was the father but added a question mark and wrote "maybe". He then failed to comply with the court's direction that he take a DNA test and did not attend the hearing. The magistrates decided that he was not the father, but on appeal Butler-Sloss P. held that they had erred in law. There were two possible routes to the conclusion that Mr Jones was K's father: the first was the mother's evidence combined with Mr Jones' answer on the enquiry form and his refusal to undergo testing; the second was his refusal to undergo testing, which even by itself would raise a virtually inescapable inference that he was the father.

In order to carry out DNA tests it will obviously also be necessary to take samples from the child. It is specifically provided that samples may be taken from a consenting person of 16 or over, and from a child under that age "if the person who has the care and control of him consents" (s.21(2) and (3)). If the person with care and control of the child does not consent, the court may order that samples be taken if it considers that this would be in the best interests of the child. This may give rise to difficult questions, for example where proving that one man was not the father might lead to the break-up of the family. It seems that today there is a general assumption that it is best for the truth to be established, and in many cases the court will make a direction for testing, even if, as in *Re H and A (Children)* [2002] EWCA Civ 383, the court is faced with a stark choice between establishing the truth and maintaining the stability of the parties' marriage:

> In this case, the wife had been having sex with both her husband and another man around the time of conception of the twins. The wife had told the other man that he was the father and had shown the children to him. After they quarrelled, he applied for parental responsibility and contact. The husband stated that if tests established that the other man was the father, he would leave his wife and the children. At first instance the judge refused to order tests. However, the appeal was allowed. The establishment of scientific fact was to be preferred over uncertainty with its attendant risks of gossip and rumour. Moreover, the court thought

that it was simplistic to assume the continued stability of the marriage in view of the wife's deception.

Similarly, in *Blunkett v Quinn* [2004] EWCA Civ 2816 (Fam) it was held to be in the best interests of the child to have his parentage determined at the earliest opportunity, despite the (married) mother's request for the proceedings to be adjourned because of her subsequent pregnancy.

Safeguards

The legislation contains safeguards intended to protect the integrity of the sampling **10–006** and testing system. Tests ordered by the courts can only be carried out by an accredited body (s.20(1A) of the Family Law Reform Act 1969, inserted by the Child Support, Pensions and Social Security Act 2000). But the fact that these safeguards are not observed does not prevent scientific evidence being admitted if it is credible:

> In *Re Moynihan* [2000] 1 F.L.R. 113, HL, the issue was entitlement to succeed to a peerage. One of the possible claimants had been born after the mother had received assisted reproduction treatment at a clinic in Los Angeles. The husband attended a Harley Street clinic some years later and samples were taken. The Committee of Privileges—notwithstanding the fact that the samples were not taken in pursuance of a blood test direction and that the prescribed procedures had not been followed—admitted evidence, based on the testing of those samples, that the husband could not be the father of the child concerned.

C: HUMAN ASSISTED REPRODUCTION

The practice of artificial insemination—"manual introduction of sperm into the **10–007** cervix" as Bracewell J. put it in *Re B (Parentage)* [1996] 2 F.L.R. 15 at 21, has long been known as a possible means of human conception, and does not necessarily involve any complex technology or medical skill. Artificial Insemination by a Donor ("AID") began to be used on a wide scale after the end of the Second World War; and, by the 1980s, every year some thousands of children were being conceived in this way.

In such cases, the man who provides the sperm is unquestionably the genetic father of any resulting child; but the question of whether the law should insist on regarding him as the child's legal father (often in preference to the mother's husband, who might well have suggested artificial insemination as the best way of coping with his infertility) began increasingly to be asked. But it was the development of scientific techniques involving the creation of live human embryos outside the human body (*in vitro* fertilisation or "IVF"—fertilisation in a glass or test tube) which prompted the Government to set up the Committee into Human Fertilisation and Embryology (1984, Cmnd 9314, Chairman Dame Mary Warnock); and the Warnock Committee explained the basic IVF procedure as follows:

> "A ripe human egg is extracted from the ovary, shortly before it would have been released naturally. Next, the egg is mixed with the semen of the husband or

partner, so that fertilisation can occur. The fertilised egg, once it has started to divide, is then transferred back to the mother's uterus." (para.5.2)

This envisages the couple in question providing the genetic materials, and in most IVF cases the genetic materials of the intending parents are used. IVF may, however, also involve an egg and/or semen donated by third parties. Use of a donated egg is less common than the use of donated sperm, and use of both together even less so. Questions of prevalence apart, the result is that there need no longer be any genetic link between the child eventually delivered and the woman who bears the child. In such a case, to which of the following should parentage be attributed? The possible options are:

(i) The genetic parents, *i.e.* the persons who have donated the egg and/or sperm (notwithstanding the fact that they had never had any contact with the child or its mother and that in the great majority of cases they would be wholly ignorant of the fact that a child had even been born).

(ii) The carrying parent, *i.e.* the woman who has borne the child to delivery (notwithstanding the fact that she may have provided none of the genetic material from which the child's inherited characteristics will be derived).

(iii) The social parents, *i.e.* those who arranged for the child to be conceived and born and who intend to care for the child in exactly the same way as would the parent of a child conceived and born in the traditional way.

The widespread use of such procedures—it has been estimated that there were 12,000 conceptions as a result of donated sperm or eggs before 1990—made it imperative to legislate. The Human Fertilisation and Embryology Act 1990 established the Human Fertilisation and Embryology Authority, and endowed it with extensive powers to control, by licensing and otherwise, the provision of treatment. The Authority issues directions under the Act and Codes of Practice to govern procedures. The issue of access to treatment services lies outside the scope of this work: for present purposes the important provisions of the Act are those that lay down rules regarding the legal parentage of children. The position can be summarised as follows.

(1) *Maternity*

10–008   As under the common law, the woman who bears a child will, at the child's birth, always be regarded as the legal mother (s.27(1)).

(2) *Paternity*

10–009   The common-law rule that the father of a child is the person who provides the sperm that leads to conception is displaced by statute in certain situations, as follows:

(a) where AID/IVF is provided to a married woman

10–010   The husband of a woman who is artificially inseminated (or who has been implanted with an embryo not created from the husband's sperm) is treated as the father of the child, unless it is proved that he did not consent to the treatment (s.28(2)). The meaning of consent was considered in *Leeds Teaching Hospital NHS Trust v A* [2003] EWHC 259:

Two couples—one black, one white—had been receiving treatment at the same IVF clinic. By mistake, Mrs A's eggs were mixed with Mr B's sperm. The mistake became apparent when Mrs A gave birth to mixed-race twins. The court held that s.28(2) did not apply as Mr A had only consented to *his* sperm being mixed with his wife's eggs, and not to the event that had actually occurred, namely his wife being inseminated by a third party. It was further held that s.28(2) did not apply "to any child who, by virtue of the rules of common law, is treated as the legitimate child of the parties to a marriage" and that the common law presumption was displaced by the DNA tests that had established that Mr B was the biological father of the twins, although the point was not fully reasoned. Thus Mr B was the legal, as well as the biological, father of the twins.

Once parentage is determined under the provisions of the 1990 Act, it is conclusive for all purposes:

In *Re CH (Contact: Parentage)* [1996] 1 F.L.R. 569, a married couple tried unsuccessfully to have a child. They received fertility treatment; and were eventually advised that AID would be the most appropriate procedure. The husband gave his written consent to such treatment, and the child was born. The marriage broke down, and the mother established a new relationship. She sought to deny the husband contact, arguing that he was not the child's biological father, and that, just as the law did not recognise any presumption that a step-parent should have contact (see *Re H (A Minor) (Contact)* [1994] 2 F.L.R. 776, CA) so it should deny any presumption of contact to her former husband. Judge Callman refused to accept this: Parliament had legislated to place the husband in the same position as the biological father, and to sever that tie would be contrary to the wishes of Parliament.

It should be noted that this is one context where a civil partner is treated differently to a spouse. The lesbian civil partner of the mother will not be the legal parent of the child. Whether she *should* be treated as the child's legal parent is currently under debate (see the consultation paper issued by the Department of Health: *Review of the Human Fertilisation and Embryology Act: A Public Consultation* (2005), para.8.22).

(b) where a course of treatment is provided to "a man and a woman together"

The Act also contains a provision that goes some way to equate the position of a **10–011** heterosexual couple living together in a stable relationship outside marriage with that of a married couple; again, there is no equivalent in the Civil Partnership Act 2004. Where sperm has been used "in the course of treatment services" provided for a man and a woman "together" under the licensing procedure established by the 1990 Act then the man is treated as the child's father (s.28(3)). It is clear that this is different to s.28(2): as Butler-Sloss P. noted in *Leeds Teaching Hospital NHS Trust v A* [2003] EWHC 259, for the purposes of s.28(2) it is the husband's *lack* of consent that is relevant, while the partner making a claim under s.28(3) has to show some positive involvement. This too is under consideration as part of the Department of Health's review, although the consultation paper notes that "it is difficult to see how unmarried couples could be treated in the same way as married couples in s.28 given the lack of legal definition of an unmarried couple." (*Review of the Human Fertilisation and Embryology Act: A Public Consultation* (2005), para.8.15). Similarly, in relation to the recognition of same-sex couples who have not formed a partnership, the question arises as to "how would any automatic recognition of parenthood be achieved given the lack of legal ties between the couple?" (para.8.24)

There has been some difference of judicial opinion as to the interpretation to be put on the expression "treatment services" in this context. It seems unnecessary for the man himself to receive any specific treatment, but it is certainly not sufficient for the man merely to be living with a woman patient (*Re Q (Parental Order)* [1996] 1 F.L.R. 369 at 372, Fam Div), and it is not possible to say that a man in a coma is "receiving treatment together with" his partner (*R. v Human Fertilisation and Embryology Authority, Ex p. Blood* [1997] 2 F.L.R. 742, CA). In *Re R (IVF: Paternity of Child)* [2005] UKHL 33 Lord Hope suggested that the underlying assumption of the section was that the process "is in reality a joint enterprise—that the treatment is being sought by the woman and the man together because they both wish to receive the benefit of the treatment to bring a child into being jointly as their child." (at para.11).

> In this case the parties had cohabited, and tried for a child through IVF, using sperm provided by an anonymous donor. The first cycle of treatment was unsuccessful and the relationship came to an end. The mother did not inform the hospital of this and went through a second, successful, cycle of treatment. At first instance it was held that the former cohabitant was the legal father of the child: the original consent form signed by the parties had envisaged two cycles of treatment, and from the clinic's point of view treatment was still being provided to the parties together. However, the Court of Appeal came to a different conclusion, and the decision—together with the reasoning of Hale L.J.—was endorsed by the House of Lords. It was held that the time at which legal paternity is created is the time when the embryo that subsequently results in the birth of the child is placed in the mother. If treatment is not being provided to both parties at this point, then s.28(3) does not apply. Since by this stage the parties were no longer a couple, the ex-cohabitant was not the legal father of the resulting child, who was accordingly legally fatherless.

Furthermore, Butler-Sloss P. held in *Leeds Teaching Hospital NHS Trust v A* [2003] EWHC 259, that "[a] fundamental error resulting in the use of the sperm of another in place of the use of sperm of the man taking part in the treatment must vitiate the whole concept of "treatment together" for the purposes of the 1990 Act" (para.37).

(c) where a man donates sperm for the purposes of "treatment services"

10–012 In each of the two cases discussed above, the Act treats the woman's partner as the child's father (irrespective of the fact that he has not himself provided the genetic material from which conception resulted). It is provided in those cases that "no other person is to be treated as the father of the child". The application of this rule will usually mean that a sperm donor is not to be treated as the child's legal father. However, the Act (in an attempt to protect donors participating in recognised infertility treatment from the legal responsibility which they would otherwise in theory bear as father of a child at common law: see *Re B (Parentage)* [1996] 2 F.L.R. 15, Fam Div) goes further. It is provided that a man who donates sperm for the purposes of "treatment services" provided under the HFEA 1990—in effect, at an officially licensed centre which is bound to follow certain prescribed procedures in relation to the giving of donors' consents and otherwise (Sch.3)—is not to be treated as the child's father (s.28(6)(a)).

This rule did not affect the outcome in *Leeds Teaching Hospital NHS Trust v A*, as Mr B had not consented to his sperm being used for treating others, and the common law rule applied, with the result that he was the legal as well as the genetic father. In addition, if AID is achieved otherwise than at an officially licensed centre, the common law rules continue to apply (see *e.g. B v A, C and D (Acting By Her Guardian)* [2006] EWHC 2 (Fam), para.11–017 below).

(3) *Use of sperm after donor's death*

The new technologies make it possible that a child will not only be born but actually **10–013** *conceived* after the death of the donor. If the deceased donor was the husband or partner of the child's mother, does the law recognise him as the child's father? Until recently the answer to this question was no, but the *Blood* case led to this being challenged:

> In *R. v Human Fertilisation and Embryology Authority, Ex p. Blood* [1997] 2 F.L.R. 742, CA, sperm was removed from the husband whilst he was in a coma. In those circumstances, the Human Fertilisation and Embryology Authority initially refused to release the sperm; but eventually the deceased's widow was allowed to export the sperm to Belgium, where she was treated with it, conceived, and bore a son. As the law then stood, the deceased Mr Blood could not as a matter of law be treated as the child's father. Mrs Blood then challenged this provision on the basis that it was incompatible with the European Convention. She withdrew her case after the Health Secretary conceded this point.

The Human Fertilisation and Embryology (Deceased Fathers) Act 2003 was subsequently passed. This amends the 1990 Act to allow the deceased husband or partner of a woman to be registered as the father of her child, if he had consented in writing to the treatment continuing after his death *and* to being named as the father on the birth certificate (s.28(5A)–(5I)). It applies whether or not the sperm of the deceased husband or father was used to create the embryo, thus projecting the effect of s.28(2) and (3) beyond the grave.

A number of points should be noted about this change. First, the number of cases where it will be relevant will depend on the willingness of clinics to allow the gametes of a deceased person to be used. Secondly, the legislation is permissive only: it is not compulsory for the deceased donor to be registered as the father, and it is up to the mother to elect in writing if she wishes him to be registered. The mother is not given absolute freedom of choice, though: the new provision does not apply if another person is to be treated as the father by virtue of s.28(2) or (3), which means that existing relationships are prioritized over past ones. Finally, registration is purely symbolic, and the deceased father is not treated as a father for any other purposes (to do so would cause havoc with the administration of the deceased's estate).

(4) *"Fatherless" children?*

The rules created by the Human Fertilisation and Embryology Act 1990 have to deal **10–014** with almost impossibly complex circumstances, and they can no doubt be justified on the basis of a pragmatic assessment of what is expedient in the majority of cases. Unhappily, their effect may be to create the possibility that a child will be legally fatherless. Clinics are directed to consider a child's need for a father in deciding whether to provide treatment, but the courts have not allowed this consideration to dictate the construction of the statutory provisions (see *Re R (a child),* above).

The question as to whether a child born as the result of AID has a right to know the identity of his or her genetic parents is considered further below (see para.10–024).

D: Surrogate Parenting

10–015 The word "surrogate" simply means "substitute". Surrogate parenting is not a modern invention—it can be found in the Bible (see Genesis ch. 30 verses 1–10). Nor does it require the use of any sophisticated scientific techniques.

> In *Re an adoption application AA 212/86 (Adoption: Payment)* [1987] 2 F.L.R. 291, the intending father and surrogate mother had (in the judge's words) "physical congress with the sole purpose of procreating a child".

On the other hand, surrogacy may also be linked to IVF treatment. The terminology is lucidly explained in the review of current arrangements and regulation of the practice (1998, Cm. 4068) chaired by Professor Margaret Brazier:

> "Surrogacy is the practice whereby one woman (the surrogate mother) becomes pregnant, carries and gives birth to a child for another person(s) (the commissioning couple) as the result of an agreement prior to conception that the child should be handed over to that person after birth. The woman who carries and gives birth to the child is the surrogate mother, or 'surrogate'. She may be the genetic mother ('partial' surrogacy—*i.e.* using her own egg) or she may have an embryo—which may be provided by the commissioning couple—implanted in her womb using in-vitro fertilisation (IVF) techniques ('host' or 'full' surrogacy)." The commissioning couple "are the people who wish to bring up the child . . . They may both be the genetic parents, or one of them may be, or neither of them may be genetically related to the child".

Thus, either the commissioning mother or the surrogate mother or indeed a third woman may provide the egg, while the genetic father may be the husband or partner of the commissioning mother, an anonymous donor, or even the husband or partner of the surrogate mother.

Surrogacy and parentage

10–016 The applicable rules depend on whether the procedure is carried out at a clinic regulated by the Human Fertilisation and Embryology Authority or independently: if the former, then the rules laid down in the 1990 Act will apply as set out above; if the latter, then the common law applies. In either case, the result is that the surrogate mother is the legal mother of the child, but under the 1990 Act the legal father may be her husband or partner, assuming he consents or is involved in the process as required by s.28(2) and (3) respectively, while under the common law the genetic father—who might not be the commissioning father—will be the legal father. Since such a result is at odds with the purpose of the surrogacy arrangement, the Act makes provision for parentage to be transferred to the commissioning parents by means of a parental order. If the criteria for a parental order cannot be satisfied, it may still be possible for the commissioning parents to adopt the child.

(1) *Parental orders*

The 1990 Act allows a "parental order" to be made in respect of a child carried by the   **10–017** surrogate as the result of AID or of an embryo being implanted in her (but not, it will be noted, where the child is the result of sexual intercourse between the commissioning father and the surrogate mother). The main features of the law are as follows.

(a) Application by commissioning parents

A parental order can only be made on the application (made within six months of the   **10–018** birth of a child whose home is with them) of an adult married couple, and it can only be made if the gametes of the husband or the wife or both were used to bring about the creation of an embryo (s.30(1)(a) and (b)). It is fundamental that the child should have a genetic link with either the husband or wife or both (*Re Q (Parental Order)* [1996] 1 F.L.R. 369 Fam Div, at 370, *per* Johnson J.). There is no equivalent provision in the Civil Partnership Act 2004, so civil partners who enter into a surrogacy arrangement cannot use this procedure (although this too is currently under review: see *Review of the Human Fertilisation and Embryology Act: A Public Consultation* (2005), para.8.22).

(b) Surrogate and legal father to consent

The court must be satisfied that the surrogate and the legal father of the child "have   **10–019** freely, and with full understanding of what is involved, agreed unconditionally to the making of the order" (s.30(5)); and a consent given by the surrogate within six weeks of the child's birth is ineffective (s.30(6)). For these purposes, the question of identifying the child's father is to be resolved by reference to the rules set out above. Thus:

> In *Re Q (Parental Order)* [1996] 1 F.L.R. 369, Fam Div, sperm had been provided by a donor at a treatment centre, and accordingly the donor was not to be treated as the child's father. The surrogate mother was a single woman, and accordingly the provisions deeming a husband to be the father of a child born as a result of AID did not apply. The commissioning husband—although he had had many meetings with the surrogate—was never "treated" with the surrogate. Accordingly the child was legally fatherless, and the only consent required was that of the surrogate.

This provision is clearly modelled on the adoption law, but adoption law makes provision for dispensing with the agreement of a person who cannot be found or is incapable of giving agreement, or if the welfare of the child requires such consent to be dispensed with (see para.15–035 below). In contrast, the 1990 Act only allows the court to dispense with parental agreement on the first of these grounds (s.30(6)).

(c) No financial inducements

10–020 The court must be satisfied that no money or other benefit (other than for expenses reasonably incurred) has been given or received by the commissioning parents for or in consideration of either the making of the order, the giving of the consent which is required to the making of an order, the handing over of the child to the commissioning parents, or the making of any arrangements with a view to the making of the order, unless such payments have been authorised by the court. Authorisation may, however, be retrospective:

> In *Re C: Application by Mr and Mrs X under s.30 of the Human Fertilisation and Embryology Act 1990* [2002] 1 F.L.R. 909, Wall J., the commissioning couple had been advised that £10,000 was the usual sum payable for "expenses reasonably incurred." However, the surrogate refused to accept less than £12,000 and the couple, assuming that this was for loss of earnings, agreed to pay this sum. It subsequently transpired that the surrogate mother had not been in paid employment and was on income support. The justices refused a parental order on the basis that they could not be sure that the sum related to reasonable expenses. However, Wall J. authorised the sum retrospectively on the basis that it was not disproportionate to the amount that was usually allowed and the couple had acted in good faith in making the payment. In addition, the child was much cherished and it was clearly in her interests for the order to be made.

(d) The effect of a parental order

10–021 A parental order provides for a child to be treated in law as the child of the commissioning parents (s.30(1)). Regulations made under the Act extend the application of certain provisions of adoption law (now the Adoption and Children Act 2002) to parental orders.

The Registrar General is required to enter the fact that a parental order has been made in the Parental Orders Register, which (like the births register) is open to public inspection. As with adoption, provision has been made for those concerned to trace the records of the original birth entry; and the child may thus identify the surrogate mother.

(2) *Adoption*

10–022 It will be obvious from the above discussion that not all commissioning couples will be able to satisfy the strict legislative criteria for a parental order. This does not mean that they will be unable to become the legal parents of the child: the possibility of adopting the child may be open to them. The effect of an adoption order is that the child is treated in law as the child of the adopters, and not of any other person; and such an order—considered in detail in Ch.15, below—effectively overrides the rules set out above (ss.27(2) and 28(5)(c) of the HFEA 1990 and s.67 of the Adoption and Children Act 2002).

One complication is that legally only a local authority or authorised adoption agency may place a child for adoption: independent placements are unlawful. Two points should be noted, however: first, no offence is committed if the child is placed with a relative (as defined in s.97 of the Adoption and Children Act), so a placement with a commissioning father who is also the genetic father would not be an offence; secondly, the court may decide to ratify an initially illegal placement if this is deemed to be in the best interests of the child (see further para.15–018 below).

Are surrogacy agreements enforceable?

The above discussion assumes that all the parties are willing to abide by the original **10–023** agreement. But what if the parties change their minds? Publicity given to the practice of surrogacy in the mid-1980s (and particularly to the establishment of commercial agencies introducing commissioning parents to a surrogate) led to the enactment of the Surrogacy Arrangements Act 1985. This Act makes it a criminal offence for any person to initiate or take part in negotiations with a view to the making of a surrogacy arrangement, to offer or agree to negotiate the making of a surrogacy arrangement, or compile any information with a view to its use in making, or negotiate the making of, surrogacy arrangements; but these prohibitions apply if (and only if) the actions in question were done on a commercial basis. The Act defines "commercial basis" by reference to the making of "payments"; but it is specifically provided that this word does not include payment to or for the benefit of a surrogate mother or prospective surrogate mother (s.2(3)). The intention was therefore to make the agency criminally liable, whilst leaving the surrogate mother herself free to accept payments whether or not they were confined to expenses.

There is, however, an important distinction between the surrogate's right to *accept* payments and her ability to *enforce* payments. Section 36 of the Human Fertilisation and Embryology Act provides that no surrogacy arrangement is enforceable by or against any of the persons making it. Hence, for example, the surrogate mother could not sue for any money agreed to be paid to her, whilst any provisions dealing with the future care of the child would be unenforceable. All this may suggest that the law takes a deeply ambivalent attitude towards surrogacy; but surrogacy is apparently used in appropriate cases—for example, where the commissioning mother has no womb—by treatment centres licensed under the Human Fertilisation and Embryology Act (see, e.g. *Re Q (Parental Order)* [1996] 1 F.L.R. 369). The questions as to whether the law should continue to prohibit "commercial" surrogate agency practice and whether surrogacy contracts should remain unenforceable was deliberately excluded from the terms of reference of the 1998 Brazier Review (1998, Cm. 4068); and the Review noted the lack of clear and consistent policies. The Review therefore confined itself to recommending legislation more effectively banning payments other than genuine and vouched expenses, dealing with the registration of agencies, and the creating of a code of practice having the force of law.

The scale on which surrogacy is carried on is unclear, but the Brazier Review considered that numbers were rising and likely to continue to do so. The practice is likely to remain controversial; although informed medical opinion seems to have moved towards acceptance of surrogacy as an "acceptable option of last resort". But the risks are not to be understated, as emerges from the facts of *Re Q (Parental Order)*:

> The surrogate felt "emotionally torn in half by the separation from the baby" and said that she had not really been prepared for feeling exactly the same about the baby as she had felt about her own children. Stung by the hospital's refusal to allow her to see the child after birth she decided to take steps to bring the child up herself. In the event, she changed her mind and decided to honour her agreement with the commissioning parents. Had she not done so it would have been impossible for the parental order to be made.

E: THE CHILD'S RIGHT TO KNOW ABOUT HIS OR HER ORIGINS

10–024 The law governing assisted reproduction and surrogacy now accepts that the child's legal parents may not be the child's genetic parents; yet genetic parentage may be seen as a matter of great relevance by the child and others. Should the law give a child a right to know the truth about his or her genetic parentage? The question is a difficult one, about which conventional views have changed over the years. There has been a move to greater openness within the context of adoption, and Parliament in 1975 accepted that an adopted child should have the right of access to the register that might reveal the identity of the child's birth parents (see para.15–006 below). Provisions of the Children Act 1989 are intended in appropriate cases to promote contact between the child and his birth relatives, and these provisions now extend to surrogate births where a parental order has been obtained. Similarly, *Re H and A* (above) shows the importance attached to ascertaining the truth, in contrast to earlier authorities that placed a higher value on maintaining the family unit.

By contrast, until recently those born as the result of assisted reproduction were entitled to very limited information under the Human Fertilisation and Embryology Act. The legislation stipulated that the register kept by the Human Fertilisation and Embryology Authority relating to the provision of treatment services and those born as a result of such services could not include information that might identify the donor. Even the provision of non-identifying information—such as the race, height and hair colour of the donor—was dependent on the donor making such information available to be passed on. And even this limited information could not be accessed until the child attained the age of 18, although those aged over 16 could make inquiries about any relationship to an intended spouse.

This was challenged by the offspring of sperm donors, and in *Rose and EM (a child represented by her mother as litigation friend) v Secretary of State for Health and HFEA* [2002] EWHC 1593 (Admin) the court endorsed the importance of being able to find out about one's genetic inheritance. In 2001, the Department of Health began a public consultation exercise on the issue. An overwhelming majority of respondents felt that non-identifying information should be provided but barely half thought that the donor should be identified. Despite this lukewarm support, the rules were changed, and identifying information will be available to children born as a result of sperm, eggs or embryos donated after April 1, 2005—but, as before, only when they reach the age of eighteen (Human Fertilisation and Embryology Authority (Disclosure of Donor Information) Regulations 2004 SI 2004/1511), which means that such information will not become available until 2024 at the earliest. Those aged 16 or 17 can, however, check whether they are related to an intended spouse or civil partner.

Past donors have been reassured that any changes will not be retrospective. However, the Government has also proposed that a voluntary contact register be set up to enable children born as the result of AID to contact those donors who wish to make contact with their genetic offspring. Such a register would be the only means that existing children would have of ascertaining their genetic parentage.

Such measures do of course presuppose that the child is aware that he or she was born as the result of AID. It seems that in practice those bringing up AID children rarely disclose the circumstances surrounding the conception, so that in many cases the children will not even know that their genetic parentage is different from their social parentage. Such children will not be in a position to seek any information that may be recorded. In this sense a child's "right" to know about his or her origins depends as much upon the attitudes of the parents as upon the facilities provided by the law.

F: CONCLUSION

It is clear that the attribution of legal parentage is affected by the relationship status **10–025** of the parents: the Human Fertilisation and Embryology Act treats the co-parents of women undergoing treatment differently according to whether they are spouses or civil partners, or heterosexual or same-sex cohabitants. The attribution of legal parentage to the husband of the woman undergoing treatment is of course sometimes a fiction in that he is not always the child's biological father: would it be any more of a fiction to attribute legal parentage to a lesbian civil partner in the same situation? The fact that same-sex couples can now adopt jointly (see para.15–016 below) means that the system of registration must now cope with parents of the same sex in this context: it would not be impossible to devise an appropriate form. Similarly, only married couples may apply for a parental order: civil partners and cohabitants must seek to adopt the child instead.

Thus legal parentage does not always correspond with social parenthood. The fact that a certain person is deemed by the law to be the legal parent of a child tells us nothing about the factual relationship between the parties. Being the legal parent of a child carries with it certain rights and obligations (for example, the right to inherit from the child in question according to the rules set out in Ch.9, and the probably more onerous obligation to provide financial support for the child as detailed in Ch.7). However, the key concept in determining what rights and duties a parent has in relation to the child is not parentage, but parental responsibility, which is the subject of the next chapter.

Chapter 11

PARENTAL RESPONSIBILITY AND CHILDREN'S RIGHTS

A: INTRODUCTION

The fact that a person is the legal parent of a child carries with it certain legal **11–001** consequences but does not, of itself, mean that person is entitled to exercise "all the rights and duties of a parent." The ability of a parent to make certain decisions will depend on whether he or she has "parental responsibility". But not all parents have parental responsibility, and not all those who have parental responsibility are legal parents. For example, as explained below, if the father is not married to the mother of the child, he will not acquire parental responsibility automatically. Also, if a child has been taken into care, the local authority acquires parental responsibility to enable it to make day-to-day decisions involving the child. Parts B and C accordingly examine what parental responsibility entails, and who may exercise it.

Even having parental responsibility does not guarantee the right to make decisions about the upbringing of a child. First, another person may have day-to-day control of the child. While a child can only have two legal parents (and sometimes only one), there is no such limit on the number of persons who may have parental responsibility for a child. The way in which the court resolves disputes between parents (and others) is considered in Chs 12 and 14. This leads on to the second point. Although the general policy of the Children Act 1989 is that parents have responsibility for making decisions about their children, when a court is asked to determine any question involving the upbringing of a child, the welfare of the child is its paramount consideration. Thus if the parties involve the court in their dispute, it is the child's best interests rather than their own wishes that will prevail. Moreover, the wishes of *both* parents may be overridden, for example where there is a dispute with foster parents or the local authorities. It is however important to emphasise that the welfare of the child is not by itself sufficient to justify state intervention, reflecting another aspect of parental responsibility, namely the privilege of bringing up one's children without state interference. As Baroness Hale put it in *R (Williamson) v Secretary of State for Education and Employment* [2005] UKHL 15:

> "Children have the right to be properly cared for and brought up so that they can fulfil their potential and play their part in society. Their parents have both the primary responsibility and the primary right to do this. The state steps in to

regulate the exercise of that responsibility in the interests of children and society as a whole. But "the child is not the child of the state" and it is important in a free society that parents should be allowed a large measure of autonomy in the way in which they discharge their parental responsibilities. A free society is premised on the fact that people are different from one another. A free society respects individual differences." (para.72)

The welfare principle, and the extent to which the welfare of the child is aligned with the wishes of the parents, is considered in detail in Ch.14.

Thirdly, the extent to which the parent can make decisions for the child may also depend on the understanding and wishes of the child in question. The rights, as well as the welfare, of children are becoming an increasingly important consideration, and it has been recognised that the duration of parental responsibility may in practice cease some time before the child attains the status of an adult at the age of 18. Part D briefly outlines the concept of children's rights, a theme that affects all of the topics discussed in this section of the book to a greater or lesser extent.

B: THE CONCEPT AND CONTENT OF PARENTAL RESPONSIBILITY

Responsibilities rather than rights

11–002   The common law described the relationship between parent and child in terms of rights, and early legislation followed this approach. But long before the Children Act 1989 it was accepted that the interests of parents might better be described as "responsibilities" or "duties". The Children Act 1989 therefore adopted the term "parental responsibility". It was thought that use of the word "responsibility" would illuminate and reinforce the view (eloquently put forward by Lord Chancellor Mackay: (1989) 139 New L.J. 505) that "the reason and sole justification for parental status" is "the duty to raise the child to become a properly developed adult both physically and morally".

The new terminology was thus intended to emphasise that the law has moved away from "rights" and towards "responsibilities" as the main attribute of parenthood (*Re S (Parental Responsibility)* [1995] 2 F.L.R. 648 at 657, CA, *per* Ward L.J.). Parental responsibility may itself involve rights: it is defined by the 1989 Act as meaning "all the rights, duties, powers, responsibilities and authority which by law a parent of a child has in relation to the child and his property." Rights and responsibilities are not irreconcilable: as Herring has pointed out, rights may be child-centred (given to parents to carry out their responsibilities to their child) or parent-centred (reflecting the parents' interests in the way their child is brought up). Many will contain elements of both: the right to decide on the child's education could be seen as facilitating the parent's responsibility to ensure that the child received an education as well as the parent's own interest in the form that that education takes.

The content of parental responsibility

11–003   The Act does nothing directly to define or alter the scope and extent of parental responsibility, but it is generally agreed that the following rights and responsibilities are included within its scope:

(1) the right to decide where the child should live and the responsibility to provide a home for the child;

(2) the right to choose the name by which the child will be known;

(3) the right to decide on the child's education and religion;

(4) the right to discipline the child;   .

(5) the right to consent to medical treatment;

(6) the right to withhold consent from a proposed marriage or civil partnership;

(7) the right to veto the issue of a passport and to decide whether to take the child out of the UK;

(8) the right to administer the child's property, to enter into certain contracts on his behalf, and to act for the child in legal proceedings;

The reader will have noticed the absence of any obligation to support one's child in the above list. This is not an incident of parental responsibility, but of legal parenthood—a father who does not have parental responsibility for his child will still be liable to pay child support—a distinction that is not uncontroversial. Another omission from the list is the issue of contact: whether a parent has a right to contact with his or her child is a contentious issue, and suggestions that the right to contact is the right of the *child* ignore the fact that a parent has no *duty* to keep in contact with a child. Moreover, the issue of parental contact is distinct from that of parental responsibility: a father may have contact without parental responsibility and *vice versa*. The issue of contact is considered in more detail in Ch.12.

In addition to debates over the appropriate content of the list, the scope of certain of the listed rights has attracted controversy. Perhaps the most hotly contested is the right of a parent to inflict corporal punishment in disciplining a child. The scope of this right has been restricted in recent years. Corporal punishment is no longer allowed in any schools in England and Wales, and in *R (Williamson) v. Secretary of State for Education and Employment* [2005] UKHL 15 the House of Lords dismissed a claim that the prohibition on corporal punishment infringed the rights of parents to bring their children up, and have them educated, in a Christian tradition that sanctioned the use of physical discipline, holding that that the interference with parental rights was necessary and proportionate. Further:

> In *A v UK (Human Rights: Punishment of Child)* [1998] 2 F.L.R. 959, ECHR a man charged with assaulting his nine-year-old step-son and occasioning him actual bodily harm successfully invoked the defence (embodied in statute: s.1(7) of the Children and Young Persons Act 1933) that a parent was entitled to administer moderate and reasonable physical chastisement. The European Court of Human Rights held that the step-father's treatment of the child amounted to a violation of Art.3 of the Convention ("inhuman or degrading treatment or punishment"), and that English law had not provided adequate protection for the child.

After consultation the Government indicated that it had no plans to change the law. Reform ultimately came about as the result of a backbench amendment to the

Children Bill in 2004. The solution now adopted in the Children Act 2004 attempts to draw a distinction between acceptable and unacceptable levels of punishment. The defence of "reasonable chastisement", which was applicable to a broad range of offences, has been replaced by one of "reasonable punishment", which cannot, for example, be used to justify an assault or battery of a child that caused actual bodily harm, wounding or grievous bodily harm (s.58). "Reasonable punishment" does, however, remain a defence to the less serious charge of assault. That conduct that would otherwise constitute an assault should be deemed to constitute reasonable punishment has been seen as unacceptable by many commentators. The Parliamentary Joint Committee on Human Rights thought that such an approach would not meet the UK's human rights obligations, and the four UK Children's Commissioners have called for a complete ban on smacking. It is clear that such a ban would have considerable public support: a MORI poll commissioned by the Children Are Unbeatable Alliance found that 71 per cent of those questioned would support a change in the law to give children the same protection from being hit as adults enjoy. It is also interesting to note that while the legislature has endorsed the right of parents to administer corporal punishment, the courts in *J v C* [2005] EWHC 1016 regarded a woman's propensity for administering corporal punishment as a factor militating against the making of an adoption order in her favour.

Finally, although couched in terms of rights, this list includes powers that are to be exercised in the interests of the child as well as those that reflect a parent's own wishes. For example, in *Re A (Minors) (Conjoined Twins: Medical Treatment)* [2001] 1 F.L.R. 1, CA, Ward L.J. noted that parental rights and powers—in this case the right to consent to medical treatment—"exist for the performance of their duties and responsibilities to the child and must be exercised in the best interests of the child". This leads on to the next question: what if parental wishes are not consistent with the best interests of the child?

Overruling parental wishes

11–004   It is clear that parental wishes are accorded significant weight by the courts but are not determinative. As Ward L.J. put it in *Re A*:

> "Since the parents have the right in the exercise of their parental responsibility to make the decision, it should not be a surprise that their wishes should command very great respect. Parental right is, however, subordinate to welfare . . . "

In that case the court held that it could exercise its inherent jurisdiction to override the parents' refusal to consent to an operation that would result in the death of the weaker twin. Holman J. made the same point more forcefully in *An NHS Trust v MB (A Child By CAFCASS as Guardian Ad Litem)* [2006] EWHC 507 (Fam), arguing that the wishes of the parents were:

> "wholly irrelevant to consideration of the objective best interests of the child save to the extent in any given case that they may illuminate the quality and value to the child of the child/parent relationship." (para.16)

While in this case the order made happened to coincide with the parents' wishes, the decision was made according to the best interests of the child in question. It is—and for many years has been—the law that when a court determines any question with respect to the upbringing of a child, or the administration of a child's property or the application of any income arising from it, the child's welfare is to be the court's paramount consideration (see now s.1(1) of the Children Act 1989). Hence, if legal proceedings are brought relating to the child's upbringing, questions of entitlement to parental rights become largely irrelevant. The child's welfare will override the wishes of natural parents, and even overrides considerations of doing justice to the parents.

Yet this does not render parental responsibility redundant. First, the ability of the court to override parental wishes depends on the issue actually coming before the court. As the Law Commission pointed out in its *Report on Illegitimacy*, at para.4.19:

> "... under our law, unless and until a court order is obtained, a person with parental rights is legally empowered to take action in respect of a child in exercise of those rights. It is true that if appropriate procedures are initiated he or she may be restrained from exercising those rights if it is not in the child's interests that he or she should do so; but unless and until such action is taken the person with parental authority would be legally entitled to act. It is self-evident that the court cannot intervene until its powers have been invoked, and in many cases this intervention might well come too late to be effective ...."

It thus remains the case that a person who has parental responsibility in respect of a child is entitled to exercise it as he or she chooses, unless restricted by general statutory provisions or a specific court order. In the context of medical treatment, for example, while the courts attach considerable importance to the views of medical practitioners, doctors are not entitled simply to override parental wishes:

> In *Glass v UK* [2004] 1 F.L.R. 1019 it was held that the hospital's decision to impose treatment in the face of the objections from the mother of the patient violated Art.8. The doctors should have sought authorisation from the court.

The court orders that may cut down parental freedom of action are considered in Chs 12 and 13, while the way in which the courts decide what course of action will be in the child's best interests is considered in more detail in Ch.14.

General constraints on parental responsibility

11–005 The general law may restrict parental responsibility in a number of ways. First, statute may prescribe a specific age at which a minor becomes entitled to exercise certain rights, and parental discretion cannot override such stipulations. Secondly, parents may be under obligations to ensure that their children behave in a certain way. For example, parents have the right to decide *how* their children should be educated, but not *whether* their children should be educated, as they are under a statutory duty to ensure that their children receive suitable education (s.7 of the Education Act 1996) and may be subject to criminal penalties if they fail to fulfil this duty (s.444 of the 1996 Act; see further s.116 of the Education Act 2005).

Responsibility as accountability

11–006 The obligation to ensure that one's child is educated appropriately is illustrative of a different conception of parental responsibility, namely accountability. The idea of accountability can also be seen in the criminal law's attitude to young offenders. As the Home Office stated in 1990:

> "When young people offend, the law has a part to play in reminding parents of their responsibilities." (*Crime, Justice and Protecting the Public*, Cmd 965)

In addition to being liable for fines imposed on their children, parents may now find themselves subject to a "parenting order", which mandates parental attendance at counselling or guidance sessions. Such orders were introduced by the Crime and Disorder Act 1998 and their scope extended by the Anti-Social Behaviour Act 2003. The latter also introduced the concept of a parenting contract, which has similar aims but purports to be voluntary on the part of the parent. For present purposes, the significance of these innovations lies in the emphasis on guidance and counseling, and the clear implication that parenting skills can be taught—a far cry from the Victorian idea of the *paterfamilias* with almost absolute and unchallengeable power.

Parental rights and the Human Rights Act 1998

11–007 The implementation of the Human Rights Act 1998 has reinvigorated the debate over parental rights, and this important topic is dealt with at para.14–017 below.

C: Who is Entitled to Exercise Parental Responsibility?

11–008 The rules about who has parental responsibility are set out in the Children Act 1989, as amended by the Adoption and Children Act 2002. In order to understand the current law, a brief historical explanation is necessary.

The relevance of marriage

11–009 Legal systems have traditionally drawn a sharp distinction between "legitimate" children (who are regarded as full members of their legal family) on the one hand, and "illegitimate" children (who to a greater or lesser extent are not given full legal recognition) on the other hand. The general rule was that a child should only be regarded as legitimate if the parents were lawfully married at the time of the child's birth or conception. This principle was carried to an extreme by the common law of England, which classified the illegitimate child as *filius nullius* ("the child of no-one") and thus for legal purposes a stranger not only to his father but also to his mother and to all other blood relatives. In consequence of this doctrine, the illegitimate child (or "bastard") had, at common law, no legal right to succeed to property, to receive maintenance, or to any of the other benefits derived from the legal relationship of parent and child.

These rules increasingly seemed harsh and unjust and over the course of the twentieth-century reforms were gradually enacted. For example, legislation provided that a child could be legitimated by the subsequent marriage of the parents. Eventually the Family Law Reform Act 1987 accepted the general principle that the marital status of the child's parents was not a ground for discriminating against the child. The Act asserted the general principle that references in legislation "to any relationship between two persons shall, unless the contrary intention appears, be construed without regard to whether or not the father and mother of either of them, or the father and mother of any person through whom the relationship is deduced, have or had been married to each other at any time." Hence, in relation to statutes enacted after April 4, 1988, the word "parent" includes a father who was not married to the mother of his child, thereby reversing the common law rule.

However, the principle of the 1987 Act does not to apply to earlier legislation unless express provision is made for that purpose. As a result, a few minor distinctions remain. Succession to the throne of the United Kingdom is governed by the Act of Settlement 1701, the language of which restricts the right of succession to the legitimate, while succession to hereditary peerages is governed by the terms of the relevant letters patent, which limited the succession to heirs "lawfully begotten" (see Law Com. No.118, para.8.26). Both remain unaffected by the 1987 Act, and although the latter rule was challenged in *Re Moynihan* [2000] 1 F.L.R. 113, HL, as being inconsistent with the guarantees of the European Convention, it was upheld by the House of Lords. More generally the right to take property under wills taking effect and settlements made before the implementation of the 1987 Act, is unaffected by the 1987 Act (for a recent example see *Upton v National Westminster Bank* [2004] EWHC 1962). And of somewhat wider application are the rules relating to citizenship (s.9 of the Nationality, Immigration and Asylum Act 2002, was intended to amend s.50 of the British Nationality Act 1981 to enable a child to acquire British citizenship through either his mother or his father, regardless of their marital status, but the regulations necessary to effect such a change have not yet been made) and immigration law, which continue to attach importance to status.

While it is still technically correct to refer to children as either legitimate or illegitimate, there has been a shift away from attaching such labels. In *Re R. (Surname: Using Both Parents')* [2001] EWCA Civ 1344, Hale L.J. expressed her regret that a case had been reported using the term "illegitimate" in its title. For this reason this book eschews the terminology of legitimacy wherever possible. Unfortunately, there is no convenient replacement: references to an unmarried father may not be appropriate if, for example the father is married to someone other than the mother of his child. It is hoped that the reader will forgive the circumlocutions used in trying to steer a path between the unacceptable and the inaccurate.

Deserving and undeserving fathers

While the law no longer stigmatises children born outside marriage, there remains a **11–010** somewhat negative view of their fathers. Even though a genetic father is to be considered a *parent* whether or not he is married to the mother of his child, he will not necessarily have parental responsibility. In 1987 the Law Commission's consultation revealed that influential groups thought that automatically to equate the legal position of the father with that of the mother would give rise to considerable social evils. The relationship between the parents might have been transitory; indeed, the conception of the child might have been the result of rape. In less dramatic (and more typical) cases, there was concern that mothers might be tempted to conceal the father's identity in order to prevent him being able to exercise the authority which would be conferred on him by law. There were also fears that the father's legal right might be exercised in a disruptive way, particularly when the mother had married a third party and established a secure family for herself and the child.

For these reasons, the Family Law Reform Act 1987 (and subsequently the Children Act 1989) preserved the principle that the father who is not married to the mother does not automatically acquire parental responsibility. It was provided, however, that it would be possible to acquire such responsibility by virtue of an order or an agreement (see paras 11–018 and 11–017, below).

While the parents are living together or co-operating, the practical consequences of this denial of parental responsibility are not great, although it may cause inconvenience, for example if a father is unable to consent to medical treatment for his child. The fundamental objection to the present rule is that of principle: an important distinction between children based solely on their parents' marital status remains embodied in the law, while fathers are essentially divided into "deserving" and "undeserving".

While distinguishing between fathers on the basis of their marital status does not contravene the ECHR (see, *e.g. B v UK* [2000] 1 F.L.R. 1), there have been moves to minimise such distinctions. The courts have recognised that a father may have a right to respect for his family life even if he was unaware of the child's existence (*Re H; Re G (Adoption: Consultation of Unmarried Fathers)* [2001] 1 F.L.R. 646, Fam Div). In 1998 the Lord Chancellor's Department issued a Consultation Paper on whether it should be made easier for the father to acquire parental responsibility for extra-marital children. It noted that over three-quarters of births outside marriage were registered with the details of both parents and that almost three-quarters of those who had registered the birth jointly were living together at the same address. There was also evidence of a wide-spread assumption that registering the birth conferred parental responsibility. Legislation has now made this assumption a reality, although it is not retrospective (see further para.11–016 below). Fathers who participate in the registration of their child's birth are now elevated to the ranks of the deserving: but the distinction between deserving and undeserving remains. It should also be noted that fathers who are not married to the mother cannot acquire parental responsibility without the co-operation of the mother (see paras 11–016 and 11–017 below), or the approval of the court (see para.11–018 below).

Automatic parental responsibility

11–011 The current law can now be described. The following persons have parental responsibility automatically, and—unless the child is subsequently adopted—will not lose parental responsibility:

(1) *Both parents, if they are married to one another*

11–012 Section 2(1) of the Children Act 1989, provides that where a child's mother and father were "married to each other at the time of his birth" they each have parental responsibility for a child. This apparently simple phrase has a wider meaning. It applies to a child who was legitimated (by the subsequent marriage of his parents) or was entitled to be treated as legitimate (because although his parents' marriage was void, at least one of them reasonably believed it to be valid at either the time of conception or the time of the marriage, whichever was later).

(2) *The mother, even if she was not married to the father*

Section 2(2) provides that the mother of a child will have parental responsibility even **11–013** if she was not married to the father. It should also be noted that acquiring parental responsibility is not conditional upon attaining adulthood: a teenager who gives birth will still have parental responsibility for her child automatically.

Ways of acquiring parental responsibility

In addition, the following are capable of acquiring parental responsibility in certain **11–014** defined circumstances. Parental responsibility acquired by these means can also be lost:

(1) *The father who is not married to the mother*

If the father is not married to the mother, he does not automatically have parental **11–015** responsibility. As noted above, the Children Act 1989 provided two procedures whereby he could obtain parental responsibility and the Adoption and Children Act 2002 added a third. The father will acquire parental responsibility if he:

(a) Has registered the birth jointly with the mother

Under s.4 of the Children Act 1989 (as amended by s.111 of the Adoption and **11–016** Children Act 2002), a father who has registered the birth jointly with the mother will acquire parental responsibility. The requirement that registration be a joint action reflects the fact that a father who is not married to the mother is not entitled to register the birth without the co-operation of the mother. While the physical presence of both parties is not required, individually the mother cannot register the father's name, and the father cannot register the birth at all without a statutory declaration by the absent party acknowledging the father's paternity, or, alternatively, a parental responsibility agreement or order.

Research suggests that most couples will register the birth jointly: Kiernan and Smith's study of children born in 2001–2 found that where the child was born to cohabiting parents, all but three per cent were jointly registered (K Kiernan and K. Smith, "Unmarried Parenthood: New Insights from the Millennium Cohort Study" (2003) 114 *Population Trends* 23). Of the 15 per cent of mothers who were not in a co-residential relationship at the time of the birth, high rates of joint registration were observed among those who were closely involved with, or alternatively separated or divorced from the father (81 per cent in each case). Only among those who were not in a relationship at the time of birth did joint registrations fall to 27 per cent. This suggests that in the vast majority of cases where there is a relationship between the parents, the father will acquire parental responsibility. Indeed, joint registration has become the most common means of acquiring parental responsibility (otherwise than by marriage) since it came into force on December 1, 2003. In 2004 83 per cent of births outside marriage were registered jointly, and 224,352 fathers acquired parental responsibility as a result. Whether this is likely to have any impact on the way these men approach fatherhood remains to be seen.

(b) Has made a parental responsibility agreement

11–017 Section 4(1)(b) of the Children Act 1989 provides that parents who are not married to one another may by agreement provide for the father to have parental responsibility for the child. In order to provide some protection for mothers in "coercive" relationships, the Act provides that the agreement must be in a prescribed form. Applicants must take the form to a court where a J.P. or court official will witness the signatures (see the Parental Responsibility Agreement (Amendment) Regulations 1994, SI 1994/3157). Thereafter it must be filed in the Principal Registry of the Family Division. Some 3,000 agreements are registered each year. It is likely that this figure will fall in the wake of the implementation of the Adoption and Children Act, since registration of the birth offers a far simpler route to parental responsibility. The option of making an agreement will still be useful if for some reason the birth was not jointly registered, or in respect of past births.

It has been held that a parental responsibility agreement can be made even where a care order (which allows the local authority to exercise parental responsibility and control its exercise by others) is in force (*Re X (Parental Responsibility Agreement: Children in Care)* [2000] 1 F.L.R. 517, Fam Div). This leads to the somewhat odd conclusion that making a parental responsibility agreement is not itself an exercise of parental responsibility.

(c) Has been granted a parental responsibility order

11–018 The father may apply to the court for an order that he "shall have parental responsibility for the child" (s.4(1)(a)). In deciding whether to make an order, the courts have applied the principle that the child's welfare is the paramount consideration. The matters to which the court will usually attach importance are whether the father has shown commitment and attachment to the child and his reasons for seeking the order (*Re H (Minors) (Local Authority: Parental Rights) (No.3)* [1991] 2 All E.R. 185, CA). However, it was stressed in *Re M (Contact: Parental Responsibility)* [2001] 2 F.L.R. 342, Fam Div, that these were not the only relevant factors: "parental responsibility is not a reward for the father, but an order which should only be made in the best interests of [the child]" (at 365–6).

The courts have drawn a distinction between the status that parental responsibility confers and the day-to-day exercise of the rights comprised in parental responsibility:

> In *Re M (Contact: Family Assistance: McKenzie Friend)* [1999] 1 F.L.R. 75, CA, the father had displayed considerable commitment to the children, and they to him; and he was paying £400 monthly for their support. The mother had a genuine fear of the father and opposed the application. But the Court of Appeal held that it was "startlingly obvious" that the order should have been made. The "fundamental aspect of the parental responsibility order . . . is that it is a matter of status" (*per* Ward L.J.). It was "essential for the well-being of the children, especially where they are denied face to face contact, to begin to know that their father was concerned enough to make an application to be recognised as their father, and that his status as their father has the stamp of the court's approval". The court noted that other procedures were available under the Children Act if the father abused his rights.

An avowedly "creative" solution to restrain any potential misuse of parental responsibility by the father was adopted in *B v A, C and D (Acting By Her Guardian)* [2006] EWHC 2 (Fam):

> In this case a lesbian couple, Ms A and Ms C, had advertised for a man who would be interested in fathering a child. Mr B responded and a child (D) was conceived following sexual intercourse between Mr B and Ms A. After D's birth in 2000 it became clear that Mr B wanted greater involvement than the couple thought appropriate. A contact order was made in his favour in 2001, but the issue of parental responsibility was deferred. The dilemma facing Black J.—balancing the possible disruption to D's family from Mr B against the consistent message from the case-law that fear of misuse should not preclude the making of a parental responsibility order—was eased by Mr B's offered undertakings not to interfere in specified areas of D's upbringing. The order was made upon the condition that he would not visit or contact D's school, or contact any health professional involved in D's care, without the prior written consent of either Ms A or Ms C.

Although generalisations on matters of fact are always dangerous in the context of a highly discretionary jurisdiction, it seems that only rarely will a parental responsibility order be denied to a father who genuinely wishes to secure recognition of his legal relationship with the child. If, however, the father has made the application for a parental responsibility order for "demonstrably improper and wrong motives" the court retains a discretion to refuse the order. Thus:

> In *Re P (Parental Responsibility)* [1998] 2 F.L.R. 96, CA, the father (who had begun a sexual relationship with the mother when he was in his 60s and she was 15 or 16) had established a good relationship with the child. But the father had been found to have indecent photographs in his possession and to be deeply confused over sexual boundaries. Moreover, he made it clear that he would use a parental responsibility order to monitor the child's health and schooling, and to vet potential child minders. The Court of Appeal held that it had been right to refuse the order: he intended to use the order for improper or inappropriate means and to interfere with and possibly undermine the mother's care of the child.

Similarly:

> In *Re M (Contact: Parental Responsibility)* [2001] 2 F.L.R. 342, Fam Div, there was a history of conflict between the parents. The father and his family were described by the court as "uncontrolled and threatening", and, while the father was genuinely concerned about his daughter, there was a risk that he might misuse his parental responsibility. In addition, the child was disabled to the extent that she would be unaware of her father's concern for her (in contrast to *Re M (Contact: Family Assistance: McKenzie Friend)* [1999] 1 F.L.R. 75, CA, above). The court therefore refused to make an order.

In addition, the court will not grant parental responsibility to a parent who is mentally incapable of exercising it:

In *M v M (Parental Responsibility)* [1999] 2 F.L.R. 737, Fam Div, the father had been severely injured in a road accident. His IQ was 54, he had a reading age of eight years and a mathematical reasoning age of six years. His short-term memory had been severely affected and he had difficulty in identifying the current date or even the year. The judge refused to make a parental responsibility order. Far from being able to exercise parental responsibility—for example, to weigh up the merits of rival schools or the potential benefits and risks of medical treatment—the father was in need of something akin to parental responsibility to be exercised by others over himself.

These cases do indicate that the courts take some account of the way in which parental responsibility will be exercised, rather than regarding it as a pure question of status. The court may also decide that a parent is no longer entitled to exercise parental responsibility and terminate an existing parental responsibility order. In general, however, an order will be made if the father can satisfy the conditions set out in *Re H*: in 2004 over 10,000 parental responsibility orders were made, with a further 952 being withdrawn and only 214 refused.

(2) *A step-parent*

11–019 Until the Adoption and Children Act 2002, the only ways in which a step-parent could acquire parental responsibility was by obtaining a residence order or adopting the child. There was concern that such step-parent adoptions distorted family relationships by extinguishing the relationship with the original parent (see further para. 15–008, below). A simpler solution was thus adopted. Section 4A of the Children Act 1989 (inserted by s.112 of the 2002 Act), now provides that a step-parent can acquire parental responsibility by agreement with the other parents (or at least those who have parental responsibility) or by order of the court. This provision, which came into force on December 30, 2005, goes some way to recognising the diversity of modern family life. Civil partners can now acquire parental responsibility in relation to their partner's children in the same way. It should be noted, however, that a parent's cohabitant—whether of the same or opposite sex—cannot take advantage of this procedure.

(3) *Adoptive parents*

11–020 The adoptive parents of an adopted child have parental responsibility; and the making of an adoption order operates to extinguish the parental responsibility vested in any other person immediately before the making of the order. In addition, those who are in the course of adopting a child may acquire parental responsibility: s.25 of the Adoption and Children Act 2002 provides that parental responsibility is conferred upon prospective adopters where a child is placed with them either with parental consent or as a result of a placement order (see para.15–023). The freedom of action of the prospective adopters is curtailed somewhat by the fact that the adoption agency also acquires parental responsibility as a result of the placement order and is entitled to determine how the other parties involved exercise their parental responsibility.

(4) *Commissioning parents in whose favour a parental order has been made*

11–021 The making of a parental order under s.30 of the Human Fertilisation and Embryology Act 1990 also operates to deprive the surrogate and her husband or partner of parental responsibility and to vest parental responsibility in the commissioning parents.

(5) *Special guardians*

The Adoption and Children Act 2002 also introduced the concept of "special guar- **11–022** dianship", which is essentially a halfway house between the often temporary nature of fostering and the permanence of adoption (see para.15–013, below, for further information). It provides that special guardians will have parental responsibility for a child for the duration of the special guardianship order, and will be entitled to exercise it "to the exclusion of any other person with parental responsibility" (see s.14C(1) of the Children Act 1989, inserted by s.115 of the 2002 Act).

(6) *The child's guardians*

The Children Act provides procedures whereby parents, guardians and special guardi- **11–023** ans may appoint other individuals to be the child's guardian by will or written instrument. The provisions are rather complex. Section 5(6) provides that a guardian should have parental responsibility when his or her appointment takes effect; and broadly speaking, an appointment only takes effect on the death of the last person to have parental responsibility for a child (see s.5(7)). For example:

> H appoints a guardian for his child. He dies, but W survives. The person appointed by H will only be able to exercise parental responsibility on W's death (see s.5(8)).

However, the position would be different if there were a residence order in H's favour alone: the appointment of the guardian would then be effective immediately on H's death (see s.5(7)(b)), although parental responsibility would be shared with W. The policy underlying these provisions is that one spouse should not ordinarily be able to dictate from beyond the grave how the other should care for the child during the survivor's lifetime; but that if one person has responsibility for the child under a residence order, then it is reasonable that he or she should be able to control the arrangements immediately following the death. An appointment by a special guardian will also take place upon that person's death, even if a parent with parental responsibility is still alive, reflecting the balance of responsibilities between special guardians and parents.

The court also has the power to appoint a guardian if the person responsible for the child has died (for the precise provisions see s.5).

(7) *A person in whose favour a residence order has been made*

The Children Act adopts the general principle that the person who is actually looking **11–024** after a child should have the necessary powers and legal authority to do so. In pursuance of this policy, where the court makes a residence order (*i.e.* an order settling the arrangements about the person with whom the child is to live: see para.12–018, below) in favour of a person who is not a parent or guardian of the child, that person will thereby have parental responsibility for the child for so long as the order remains in force (s.12(2)). It is of course possible that a residence order will be made in favour of a father who does not have parental responsibility: in such a case the court will also make an order under s.4 conferring parental responsibility (s.12(1)). The difference is that in the latter case the father's parental responsibility will not come to an end if the residence order terminates.

In a few unusual cases the court has made a residence order specifically to deal with parental responsibility:

Re G (Residence: Same-Sex Partner) [2005] EWCA Civ 462 concerned a lesbian couple who had been together for eight years. Two children had been born to one of them by anonymous donor insemination. The other sought a joint residence order, which was opposed by the mother, who wished to move to Cornwall with her new partner. At first instance the order was refused but the Court of Appeal granted it as a means of recognizing the co-parent's role, since this was the only means by which parental responsibility could be conferred upon her (for the sequel see *CG v CW and G (Children)* [2006] EWCA Civ 372, para.14–015).

It should also be noted that s.12(3) provides that the parental authority flowing from the making of a residence order is limited in two specific respects: first, it does not include the right to withhold consent to the making of adoption orders; and secondly, it does not confer any right to appoint a guardian for the child.

(8) *The local authority*

11–025 The local authority will acquire parental responsibility in a number of situations: if an emergency protection order or care order has been made in its favour (see s.44(4)(c) and s.33(3)(a) respectively) or if a placement order has been made in the course of adoption proceedings (see s.25 of the Adoption and Children Act 2002). These orders are considered in detail elsewhere (see Chs 13 and 15). For present purposes it is sufficient to note that the scope of the parental responsibility flowing from the making of a care order is limited in so far as it does not extend to giving agreement to adoption or to the appointment of a guardian, nor does it give the local authority the right to cause the child to be brought up in a different religious persuasion from that in which he would have been brought up had the order not been made (s.33(6)). On the other hand, a local authority may decide that adoption is in the child's best interests, and it may be difficult for the parents to withstand this decision (see Ch.15).

(9) *Anyone in whose favour an emergency protection order has been made*

11–026 Anyone is entitled to apply for an emergency protection order, and once such an order is made the applicant acquires parental responsibility (s.44(4)(c), and see further para.13–011). Given the limited duration of such orders—which, even if extended, last for a maximum of 15 days—the applicant's opportunity to exercise parental responsibility is necessarily limited, and the statute warns that such a person should only take "such action in meeting his parental responsibility for the child as if reasonably required to safeguard or promote the welfare of the child (having regard in particular to the duration of the order" (s.44(5)(b)). In practice, it is extremely rare for anyone other than a local authority to apply for an emergency protection order.

Ways of losing parental responsibility

11–027 It is a fundamental principle of the Children Act that parental responsibility is not easily lost: in particular, a person with parental responsibility does not lose it solely because another person also acquires parental responsibility (s.2(6)). But a person who has acquired parental responsibility by any of the means described above may lose it: the child may be adopted by a new family; a residence order may be revoked; a care order may terminate; and, where parental responsibility has been conferred by agreement, order, or joint registration, it may be terminated by court order if the circumstances justify it (s.4(2A)). Thus:

In *Re P (Terminating Parental Responsibility)* [1995] 1 F.L.R. 1048, Fam Div, the nine-week-old child had multiple fractures (including a fractured skull) and other serious injuries as a result of which she would be permanently disabled both mentally and physically. The parents originally denied that they had had anything to do with the violent injuries inflicted on the child, and made a parental responsibility agreement apparently believing that this would give some advantages in the care proceedings that were pending. Investigations subsequently established the father's guilt, and he was sentenced to four and a half years' imprisonment. The court held that the continuation of a parental responsibility agreement would have "considerable potential ramifications for future adversity" to the child; it would be "deeply undermining" to the mother; it would unsettle the foster parents who were caring for the child; and it would be a message to others that the father had not by his conduct forfeited responsibility.

The case of *B v A, C and D (Acting By Her Guardian)* [2006] EWHC 2 (Fam) further suggests that where parental responsibility is granted upon certain conditions, breach of those conditions might lead to the court being invited "to reconsider the whole question of parental responsibility" (para.91).

What all of the above examples have in common is that parental responsibility is terminated by an order of the court. It is not possible to terminate parental responsibility merely by agreement between the parties—another example of the fact that it is more difficult to lose parental responsibility than to gain it.

Shared parental responsibility

It will be clear from the above discussion that there may be a number of persons with parental responsibility for a child, possibly in different households. For example, if a court makes a residence order in favour of the two grandparents of a child born to married parents, they will both have parental responsibility, but the child's parents do not thereby lose parental responsibility. As a result, there are four people with parental responsibility for the child; and s.2(7) specifically provides that where more than one person has parental responsibility for a child, each of those persons may act alone and without the other in "meeting that responsibility". In effect, parental responsibility is enjoyed jointly and severally. **11–028**

This principle is often convenient in practical terms: it will be sufficient to find one person with parental responsibility in order to give agreement to emergency surgery, for example. But the convenience is purchased at the cost of creating potential difficulties where those who share parental responsibility are not on good terms. Section 2(8) provides a partial remedy for this problem: parental responsibility does not entitle a person to act inconsistently with any order made with respect to the child under the Act. If the court makes a residence order in favour of one of the parents on divorce, the other—although still possessing parental responsibility—would not be entitled to do anything incompatible with the residence order (such as removing the child from home).

Notwithstanding the apparently clear rule that joint parental responsibility is exercisable by either parent alone, a number of cases have suggested that there are certain exercises of parental responsibility that should not be unilateral. According to

Butler-Sloss P. in *Re J (Specific Issue Orders: Child's Religious Upbringing and Circumcision)* [2000] 1 F.L.R. 571:

> "There is, in my view, a small group of important decisions made on behalf of a child which, in the absence of agreement of those with parental responsibility, ought not to be carried out or arranged by one parent carer although she has parental responsibility under s.2(7) of the Children Act 1989. Such a decision ought not to be made without the specific approval of the court. Sterilisation is one example. The change of a child's surname is another." (at 577)

The courts have also suggested that one parent should consult the other about the child's education (*Re G (Parental Responsibility: Education)* [1994] 2 F.L.R. 964, CA).

Such decisions certainly establish that where there is a dispute about such matters between two persons who have parental responsibility, the matter should be referred to the court; and it seems that a third party who knowingly accepts the instructions of one person in such a situation may not be able to rely on the defence of acting with consent. But the decisions have not escaped criticism. In any event the difficulty is primarily a practical one. The reality seems often to be that each person with parental responsibility will have the power effectively to authorise actions that others would strongly oppose; and the only effective safeguard in such circumstances is to obtain orders from the court defining the areas of responsibility (see further Ch.12).

The most dramatic example of a potential clash between people with parental responsibility arises in cases in which the court makes a care order. In many cases, the parents will be opposed to the making of the order, and it is not easy to see why a local authority should wish to obtain a care order unless it envisages a real prospect of having to exercise or to threaten to exercise compulsion against the parents. But the Act adheres to the philosophy that the fact that a local authority has acquired parental responsibility should not deprive the parents of their responsibility; and it seeks to deal with—the often very real—potential conflict by providing that the local authority should have power "to determine the extent to which a parent or guardian of the child may meet his parental responsibility for the child" (s.33(3)(b)). In effect, therefore, this provision gives the local authority power to restrict the parents' exercise of parental authority; but it is also provided that the authority may only exercise that power if satisfied that it is "necessary" to do so in order to safeguard or promote the child's welfare (s.33(4), and see further *Re G (Care: Challenge to Local Authority's Decision)* [2003] EWHC 551 (Fam) and para.13–012 regarding the obligations on local authorities to involve parents in the decision-making process).

Responsibility not transferable

11–029 Section 2(9) prohibits surrender or transfer of parental responsibility. Children are not a marketable commodity; and this provision—reflecting the common law—prevents parents from allowing children to be privately adopted or even "sold". The prohibition on surrendering parental responsibility underlines the policy adopted by the 1989 Act that the sanction of a court order is required before a person can be rid of parental responsibility. In one respect this represents a significant change in policy: it abolished the procedure by which a local authority could in certain circumstances—often with the consent of the parents—acquire parental authority by administrative action.

How does the fact that parental responsibility is not transferable affect such routine situations as a child being left in the care of a nanny or au pair whilst the parents are away on a business trip or foreign holiday, or a child being sent to boarding school or on an adventure training course? Section 2(9) expressly permits a person with parental responsibility to arrange for "some or all of it to be met" by one or more persons acting on behalf of the person with parental responsibility. It also expressly provides that the "person with whom any such arrangement is made may himself be a person who already has parental responsibility for the child". It seems that this provision is intended to encourage parents to make their own arrangements for what they consider to be best if their relationship breaks down, but no such agreement can exclude the power of the court to impose a different solution. The Act also provides that the making of such an arrangement does not affect any liability—perhaps prosecution for child neglect—arising from a failure to meet the responsibility (see s.2(11)).

Action by a person without parental responsibility

It is not necessary for a person to have parental responsibility to be entitled to take **11–030** action in a child's interests (perhaps, but not necessarily, in an emergency). Section 3(5) provides that a person who "has care" of a child without having parental responsibility may do "what is reasonable in all the circumstances of the case for the purpose of safeguarding or promoting the child's welfare". This provision makes it clear that someone caring for a child in the parent's absence may, for example, arrange emergency medical treatment; and it has been suggested that a foster-parent might rely on this provision to justify a refusal to hand over the child to the parents in the middle of the night (see White, Carr and Lowe, *The Children Act in Practice* (2nd edn, Butterworths, 1995, para.3.71)). It is quite clear that some provision to legitimise short-term and emergency measures is necessary to protect the position of people such as schoolteachers, doctors and paramedics. But the scope of the present provision is not clear, and it seems that relatives or others caring for an orphaned child would be best advised to apply to the court for a court order that will confer parental responsibility on them:

> In *B v B (A Minor)(Residence Order)* [1992] 2 F.L.R. 327, CA, a grandmother was caring for her daughter's child. She found that the local education authority was reluctant to accept that she had the power to give consent to the child going on school trips and insisted on having the mother's written consent.

Authority without obligation?

Conversely, in some cases the Children Act confers authority but does not provide any **11–031** machinery whereby the person with such authority can be made to discharge any duty of support. For example, although a guardian has "parental responsibility" for a child, the Act provides no machinery whereby a guardian can, as such, be required to provide financial support for the child. Again, a person who has parental responsibility as a consequence of having a residence order made in his favour does not thereby come under any obligation to provide financial support for the child (see para.7–021 above).

D: "PARENTAL RESPONSIBILITY" AND CHILDREN'S RIGHTS

11–032 Can it really be true that a parent can legally prohibit a 16- or 17-year-old from leaving home or even from staying with friends or going on a holiday? And what is to happen if parent and child disagree about medical treatment—for example, about whether a 15-year-old girl should have a prescription for the contraceptive pill?

The common law was quite clear. It recognised that a wise parent would not seek to enforce his views against the wishes of a mature child; and the law would refuse to lend its aid to a parent who sought to impose his will on a child who had attained the "age of discretion". But as a matter of law the parent retained his authority until the child reached the age of majority (which was 21 until the Family Law Reform Act 1969 reduced it to 18). The fact that a particular child's intellectual or emotional development was advanced was irrelevant in deciding whether or not parental authority continued (see the judgment of Parker L.J. in *Gillick v West Norfolk and Wisbech Area HA* [1985] F.L.R. 736, CA).

The *Gillick* decision

11–033 This traditional understanding of the common law position of a parent was over-turned by the decision of the House of Lords in *Gillick v West Norfolk and Wisbech Area HA* [1986] A.C. 112, HL:

> Mrs Victoria Gillick, the mother of four daughters under the age of 16, sought an assurance from the authority that her daughters would not be given contraceptive treatment without her prior knowledge and evidence of her consent. The authority refused to give such an assurance. Mrs Gillick therefore asked the court to declare that DHSS advice to the effect that young people could in some circumstances be given contraceptive advice and treatment without their parent's knowledge and consent was unlawful and wrong, and that it adversely affected Mrs Gillick's right as the children's parent. The House of Lords, by a 3–2 majority, held that her application should have been dismissed.

Twenty years later the ability of those under the age of 16 to seek confidential medical advice on contraception and abortion was again challenged in court, but Silber J., noting the advances in children's rights since *Gillick*, held that "it would be ironic and indeed not acceptable now to retreat from the approach adopted in *Gillick* and to impose additional new duties on medical professionals to disclose information to parents of their younger patients.": *R (ota Axon) v Secretary of State for Health* [2006] EWHC 372 (Admin), para.80.

The *Gillick* rationale—mature children entitled to take their own decisions?

11–034 The basis of the *Gillick* decision seemed to be that, in the absence of an express statutory rule (for example, the rule requiring parental consent to the marriage of a minor child), all parental authority "yields to the child's right to make his own decisions when he reaches a sufficient understanding and intelligence to be capable of making up his own mind on the matter requiring decision" (*per* Lord Scarman at 186).

The question of whether a child had sufficient understanding and intelligence must be an issue of fact in each case, depending on the complexity of the issues involved, and the child's emotional and intellectual maturity. Some decisions (including the decision of whether to seek contraceptive advice) require a very high level of maturity and understanding; but less complex issues would require a correspondingly less highly developed intellectual and moral understanding. The fact that the level of understanding required varies according to the seriousness of the issue involved was one factor that persuaded Silber J. in *Axon* that the same basic principles were applicable to access to abortions as to advice on contraception.

Limitations on *Gillick* doctrine

The scope of the decision in *Gillick* is restricted by the fact that it is not applicable if **11–035** a statute prescribes a specific age of legal capacity. It also depends on the willingness of the courts to find that a particular child has sufficient understanding to make the decision, and on the opportunity for children to challenge parental decisions. Controversially, there appear to be some decisions that even a competent child cannot make, for example the right to refuse medical treatment. These three issues will be considered in turn:

(1) *Statutory restrictions*

The *Gillick* approach permits the courts to apply a broad and realistic test, which **11–036** seems much more sensible than the strictly chronological tests applicable where capacity is fixed by statute, especially when those statutory age limits are scattered across a range of statutes and do not seem to reflect any coherent concept of child development. Why, for example, is it possible to buy a crossbow at the age of 17 (according to the Crossbows Act 1987) but to be barred from buying fireworks until the age of 18 (under the Fireworks (Safety) Regulations 1997)? But the courts are still bound by such statutes. Hence it is still the law that at one minute to midnight on the eve of a young person's eighteenth birthday he or she cannot make a will because s.7 of the Wills Act 1837 so provides, and it is still the law that such a person cannot (generally speaking: see the Minors Contracts Act 1987) make an enforceable contract. But come midnight he or she can do both these things.

The fact that the *Gillick* principle does not affect the many important areas in which the child's legal capacity is governed by statute is a serious limitation on the scope of the doctrine, but there cannot be any doubt that this limitation exists. It is equally, of course, a limitation on parental responsibility, since a child cannot make a will or contract even with parental consent.

(2) *The opportunity to challenge parental responsibility*

Gillick and *Axon* both concerned the ability of a child to obtain access to treatment by **11–037** a third party. What is the position if the disagreement between the child and parent relates to the child's upbringing? It was suggested by Lord Fraser in *Gillick* that wise parents relax their control and allow increasing independence, while Lord Scarman seemed to suggest that a parent loses the right to make decisions once the child is competent to decide for him- or herself. In everyday family life it is likely that children enjoy increasing autonomy, and negotiate with their parents on the boundaries of what is permissible. But in cases of fundamental and irreconcilable disagreement, is there any means by which a child can seek a court order to enforce his or her own choices? As the next chapter will show, it is possible for a child to seek leave to apply for an order under s.8 of the Children Act 1989, which is capable of dealing with almost any aspect of a child's upbringing. The court must he satisfied as to the child's competence, but even if this is decided in the child's favour the court may still decide that the issue is not one that it should resolve:

> In *Re C (A Minor)(Leave to Seek Section 8 Order)* [1994] 1 F.L.R. 26 a 15-year-old girl sought leave to seek a s.8 order to enable her to go on holiday with her friend's family. The judge refused to grant leave, partly because he felt that the issue was a trivial one, and not the sort of issue that Parliament had envisaged would be brought to the courts by children, and partly because he thought that it would be wrong to give the girl the impression that she had won some kind of victory over her parents.

While the judge's desire to discourage litigation of this kind is understandable, it might be questioned whether the girl's request was any more "trivial" than some of the issues that warring parents bring before the courts (see *e.g. Re N (A Child)* [2006] EWCA Civ 357, which concerned a proposed two-week holiday in Slovakia). *Re C* illustrates that it may be difficult in practice for even a child adjudged competent by the court to obtain the court's support for a course of action contrary to parental wishes.

(3) *The inability to refuse treatment*

11–038 If a child has the right to consent to medical treatment it might be thought that he or she must equally have the right to refuse such treatment. But this appears not to be true. In a series of cases the courts have held that, whilst such a refusal is a very important consideration in the clinical judgement of the doctors taking the decision as to whether to proceed or not, a person under the age of 18 has no power to override a consent to treatment given by someone who has parental responsibility or by the court exercising its inherent *parens patriae* jurisdiction over children. Thus:

> In *Re W (a minor) (medical treatment: court's jurisdiction)* [1993] Fam. 64, CA, the judge took the view that a 16-year-old girl suffering from anorexia had sufficient understanding to make informed decisions about her treatment; but he overruled her refusal to accept treatment in a specialist unit. The Court of Appeal upheld the judge's decision, although Lord Donaldson was doubtful as to whether the girl did have sufficient understanding, noting that "it is a feature of anorexia nervosa that it is capable of destroying the ability to make an informed choice". The court seemed to accept dicta in the earlier case of *Re R. (A Minor) (Wardship: Medical Treatment)* [1992] Fam. 11, CA, to the effect that although the parents of a *Gillick* competent child had no right to determine whether or not treatment should be given, yet they still retained the right to give a valid consent (thus overruling their child's own decision). It has subsequently been held that in such circumstances, reasonable force may be used to carry out the treatment (*Re C (Detention: Medical Treatment)* [1997] 2 F.L.R. 180, FD).

Similarly:

> In *Re M (Medical Treatment: Consent)* [1999] 2 F.L.R. 1097, Fam Div, a healthy, active 15-and-a-half-year-old girl suffered heart failure without any prior warning,

and doctors concluded that she would die unless she had a heart transplant within a week or so. The patient's view was "I don't want to die, but I would rather die than have the transplant and have someone else's heart" and she did not want to be on medication for the rest of her life. The judge accepted that the views of this intelligent young person carried considerable weight, but considered that seeking to achieve what was best required him to give authority for the transplant to be carried out.

This means that as long as consent is provided by someone—be it the child, the parents, or the court—the treatment can legally go ahead. (Whether a doctor would decide that it was in the best interests of the child to impose treatment is another matter.) In contrast, a mentally competent adult patient "has an absolute right to refuse to consent to medical treatment for any reason, rational or irrational or for no reason at all, even where that decision will lead to his or her own death" (see *Tameside and Glossop Acute Services Trust v CH* [1996] 1 F.L.R. 762 at 769, Fam Div, *per* Wall J., and *Re B (adult: refusal of treatment)* [2002] EWHC 429).

The difficulty with the cases is that they deny a person under 18 the right to make a decision simply by reason of his or her age; and the notion that a *Gillick*-competent person should be compelled against his or her will to undergo treatment which he or she conscientiously wishes to reject seems repugnant to some commentators. It may also be thought that the policy adopted in the decided cases is inconsistent with the policy apparently underlying the Children Act 1989—for example, s.44(7) provides that the child "may, if he or she is of sufficient understanding to make an informed decision, refuse to submit" to an examination or other assessment directed to be made by the court in certain circumstances (see para.13–011, below). Despite the increasing importance that is attached to the wishes and autonomy of children in other contexts (see *e.g. Re Roddy (A Child: Identification: Restriction on Publication)* [2003] EWHC 2927 and *Mabon v Mabon* [2005] EWCA Civ 634), the courts remain reluctant to allow children to make decisions that will result in their death (see *e.g. Re P (Medical Treatment: Best Interests)* [2003] EWHC 2327).

The reader must decide whether it is right that youth should be a sufficient basis for exercising compulsion on a person who fully understands the issue, whereas old age is not. They might ponder the words of Munby J. in *Re Roddy (A Child)(Identification: Restriction on Publication)* [2003] EWHC 2927:

> "Are we, in other words, to take children's rights seriously and as our children see them? Or are we to treat children as little more than the largely passive objects of more or less paternal or judicial decision-making?" (para.46)

Making the capacity to decide depend on age certainly gives rise to apparent anomalies, as evidenced by the sad facts of *Re E (A Minor) (Wardship: Medical Treatment)* [1993] 1 F.L.R. 386, Fam Div:

> A 15-year-old boy and his parents were Jehovah's Witnesses, and refused to agree to the blood transfusion treatment which doctors considered appropriate to treat his leukaemia. Ward J. held that when viewed objectively the boy's welfare led to only one conclusion, *i.e.* that he should receive treatment; and this was carried out. It is understood that when the boy reached majority he refused further transfusions and died.

E: CONCLUSION

11–039 The use of the expression "parental responsibility" is intended to convey a message; but the message is in fact rather misleading. First, certain rights and responsibilities are conferred independently of whether a particular person has parental responsibility. For example, a father or step-parent may not have parental responsibility but the former will, and the latter may, have the obligation to support the child in question (see further Ch.7). Secondly, a person's ability to exercise parental responsibility may be limited by the circumstances of the case if the child is in fact living with another adult. In addition, the exercise of parental responsibility may be constrained by an order of the court. Such constraint may be general, as where a care order is made in favour of the local authority (see para.11–028 above and Ch.13 below), or specific, where some particular aspect of parental responsibility is restricted by court order. The next chapter will consider the potential for such restrictions.

Chapter 12

The Courts' Powers to Make Orders Dealing with Children's Upbringing: The Private Law

A: Introduction

As discussed in the previous chapter, a person with parental responsibility is entitled **12–001** to exercise it without—at least in the usual course of events—consulting other persons with parental responsibility. The scope for disagreement between parents whose relationship has broken down is obvious, and some idea of the scale of the problem may be conveyed by the fact that in 2004 alone the parents of 149,275 children divorced (to say nothing of the uncounted number of cohabitants with children who separated). No doubt most parents will be able to decide with whom the children should live and to resolve any disputes arising out of the tensions of post-separation parenting—if not without difficulty, then at least without litigating. But there will inevitably be a number of cases in which parents or other carers simply cannot agree, and seek an order from the court to resolve their dispute. Under the Children Act 1989 there are three key questions that must be posed.

First, does the court have jurisdiction to make an order? The somewhat complex rules on this point are discussed in Part B below. Secondly, what orders are available to the court in private proceedings—*i.e.* proceedings in which the dispute is between two private individuals rather than the family and the state? Part C explains the orders that can be made under s.8 of the Act—in brief, residence orders, contact orders, specific issue orders and prohibited steps orders—and discusses a number of key issues that have arisen in recent years. The text then examines certain ancillary powers, for example the court's power to order welfare reports or make family assistance orders (Part D).

The final question is: should the court exercise its discretion to make an order (and, if so, in what terms)? The Act provides that the welfare of the child should be the paramount consideration for the court and sets out a checklist of the factors that are to be taken into account. Some idea of the way in which the courts approach their task may be gleaned from the discussion in Part C. A more detailed description of the welfare principle is contained in Ch.14: this separate treatment is justified by the fact that the welfare principle applies to the public proceedings involving state intervention discussed in Ch.13 as well as to disputes between individuals.

The structural elegance of the scheme based on these three questions is in sharp contrast with the messiness of family life that results in parents litigating over arrangements for their children. Despite attempts to encourage parents to mediate and make their own arrangements, the number of applications to the court continues to climb.

Finally, despite the elegance of the Children Act, it is not a complete code for children, and two further topics fall to be considered. The first relates to the court's inherent jurisdiction to make orders, and its relationship with the Children Act, and is considered in Part E. Secondly, one drastic outcome of relationship breakdown may be the abduction of a child by one of its parents. This issue is considered in Part F. The approach taken by the courts in such cases differs significantly from that taken in domestic cases—it is, according to Singer J. in *Re C (Abduction: Interim Directions: Accommodation by Local Authority)* [2003] EWHC 3065 (Fam), governed by "a self-contained code, specific and specifically tailored to the *sui generis* nature of such applications in our domestic law" (at para.39)—and the strict rules applied provide an interesting comparison to the focus on welfare in the 1989 Act.

B: DOES THE COURT HAVE JURISDICTION?

12–002 The 1989 Act does not assume that orders relating to children will automatically be made when parents divorce: it is the clear message of s.1(5) that an order should not be made unless this would be better for the child than not making an order (see further para.14–008). But the Act also recognises that the need to resolve issues relating to children may arise in the context of various parental disputes that do not involve the children directly, and the court has jurisdiction to make an order in certain family proceedings, as set out below, even if no-one has applied for an order. In addition to this "spin-off" jurisdiction, it is possible for an application to made for any s.8 order directly, although such "freestanding" applications are governed by somewhat complex rules relating to the standing of the applicant.

The "spin-off" jurisdiction

12–003 The 1989 Act is based on the principle that the existence of family litigation is a sufficient justification for the court to exercise its powers over any children involved. If a question arises in any family proceedings with respect to the welfare of the child the court may make an order under s.8 if it considers it right to do so. "Family proceedings" are defined in s.8(3) as either proceedings under specified statutes (Pts I, II and IV of the Children Act itself, the Matrimonial Causes Act 1973, the Adoption and Children Act 2002, the Domestic Proceedings and Magistrates' Courts Act 1978, Pt III of the Matrimonial and Family Proceedings Act 1984; the Family Law Act 1996 and ss.11 and 12 of the Crime and Disorder Act 1998), or any proceedings under the inherent jurisdiction of the court in relation to children (see further Part E). Some of these statutes impose a specific duty upon the court to consider the arrangements proposed by the parties for their children's upbringing (see *e.g.* s.41 of the Matrimonial Causes Act 1973 in the context of divorce). Under some of the other statutes the relationship with the 1989 Act is less obvious, but the list gives the courts the flexibility so often needed in dealing with matters relating to children. Thus, for example, if a man seeks to exclude the woman with whom he is living from the family home under the Family Law Act 1996, the court can make orders relating to the children if it deems this necessary.

"Free-standing" applications

This brings us to the second main category of "family proceedings", the so-called **12–004** "free-standing" applications, which allow applications to be made specifically for s.8 orders. The rules are intended to provide what the Law Commission (Law Com. No.173, para.4.41) described as a filter protecting the child and the family against unwarranted interference whilst at the same time ensuring that the child's interests are properly protected.

The scheme of the Act is effectively to create four categories of applicant: first, those who are entitled to apply for any of the s.8 orders, subject to certain limitations; secondly, those who are entitled to apply for only certain types of orders; thirdly, those who may seek leave to apply for an order; and finally, those who are subject to further restrictions.

(1) *Persons entitled to apply for any s.8 order*

The class of persons automatically entitled to apply for an order has grown in recent **12–005** years. Section 10(4)(a) of the 1989 Act now provides that any parent or guardian (including a special guardian), and any person in whose favour a residence order is in force, is entitled to apply for any s.8 order. In addition, a step-parent or civil partner who has parental responsibility will also be able to apply (and as to how such persons may acquire parental responsibility see para.11–019 above).

This provision, in effect, defines those who are deemed to have a legitimate interest in seeking the court's intervention, irrespective of the particular circumstances of the case. For example, one spouse should be able to apply for a residence order even if he or she does not want to bring divorce proceedings. Again, while a father who was not married to the mother does not automatically have parental responsibility for the child (see Ch.11), it was thought reasonable to give him the right to apply to the court for an order relating to the child's upbringing. This right is automatic and does not depend on the existence of "family life" between father and child: thus in *Leeds Teaching Hospital NHS Trust v A* [2003] EWHC 259, it was noted that Mr B, the legal and biological father of the children concerned, would be able to apply for a s.8 order even though he had no factual relationship, and hence no family life, with the children.

The reason why the Act includes anyone in whose favour a residence order has been made in the class of those entitled to apply for orders is less self-evident, but in fact follows logically from the scheme of the Act. As we have seen, a person who has a residence order thereby has parental responsibility. Accordingly, such a person may need to seek a specific issue order, or a prohibited steps order, to enable that responsibility to be properly met.

Equally logically, certain restrictions on applying for a s.8 order are imposed in the context of adoption proceedings. Under the Adoption and Children Act 2002, if the child has been placed for adoption, the leave of the court is required for an application for a residence order, and no application for contact may be made under the 1989 Act (although such application may be made under the 2002 Act). Further restrictions are imposed where there is a placement order or special guardianship order (see Ch.15 for an explanation of these terms).

In addition, further restrictions may be imposed by the court, as making applications can be detrimental to the child (as well as being what Butler-Sloss L.J. described as "a waste of public money and a waste of the court's time" (*Re H (Child Orders: Restricting Applications)* [1991] F.C.R. 896 at 899, CA). The legislature was conscious that vexatious or harassing applications might be made even by a parent; and s.91(14) therefore gives the court power, on disposing of any application, to make an order that any named person be debarred from making any application for an order under the Act without leave of the court. For example:

> In *Re N (Section 91(14) Order)* [1996] 1 F.L.R. 356, CA, there had been a multiplicity of proceedings about a child. There was no dispute that the father should have contact with the child, but the father continued to make applications about matters such as medication, karate lessons, walking to school and the like. The Court of Appeal held that the judge, having made a contact order, had been right to order that the father make no further applications without leave of the court, since she had rightly been concerned that there had been too much in the way of litigation and that the child needed to know exactly where he stood.

But the power to impose such a restriction is not limited to cases in which the applicant has made repeated and unreasonable applications. Provided the welfare of the child so requires, the court may impose a leave requirement in cases where there has been no such history.

> In *Re P (Section 91(14) Guidelines) (Residence and Religious Heritage)* [1999] 2 F.L.R. 573, CA, there had been highly charged litigation about the future of the child of Orthodox Jewish parents who fervently believed that the child's placement with Roman Catholic foster-parents was unacceptable. The litigation had been corrosive of the adults' relationships, the strain had taken its toll on the foster parents, and future litigation over the child's residence would be damaging to the child. The court imposed a leave requirement.

Re P also confirmed that since an order under s.91(14) is not an *absolute* bar on seeking the court's assistance, it is not inconsistent with Art.6 of the European Convention on Human Rights, which guarantees the right to a fair trial. Nevertheless, it has been emphasised that the power to make s.91(14) orders is to be exercised with great care and sparingly (see *e.g. Re C (Prohibition on Further Applications)* [2002] 1 F.L.R. 1136, CA, and *Re B (Section 91(14) Order: Duration)* [2003] EWCA Civ 1966).

(2) Persons entitled to apply for residence and/or contact orders

12–006 Two groups fall within this category: those who are entitled to apply for either a residence order or a contact order, and those who are only entitled to apply for a residence order. Both, however, require the leave of the court to apply for other s.8 orders (and of course restrictions may be placed on their ability to apply for residence or contact orders under s.91(14)). The justification for this category is that some people may have or have had a sufficiently close link with the child to justify their being entitled to apply for contact, or to justify their seeking to have care of the child in their home, without it being appropriate for them to have the right to make applications which would interfere with the specific decision-taking powers of those who have "parental responsibility" for the child. The detailed provisions are contained in s.10(5): briefly, those who are entitled to apply for a residence or contact order are as follows:

(a) *Anyone to whom the child has ever been a "child of the family"*, for example **12–007** anyone who has at any time been the child's step-parent. For this purpose the applicant must either have been married or in a civil partnership: a party to an unformalised relationship cannot qualify under this head).

(b) *Anyone with whom the child has lived for three out of the past five years.* The **12–008** period need not necessarily be continuous, but must not have ended more than three months before the application (s.10(10)). Again, the principle seems to be that such a person has established a case to have a claim for contact or even residence considered on the evidence by a court, even though he or she should not be entitled as of right to get the court to decide on other specific aspects of parental responsibility (such as where the child should go to school or whether the child should undergo medical treatment).

(c) *Anyone who has the consent of* either: **12–009**

    (i) (if a residence order is in place) all those who have a residence order (the principle presumably being that, if those people see no reason why the court should not hear a contact or residence application, others— perhaps at a greater distance in terms of factual relationship with the child—should not be allowed to stand in the way); or

    (ii) (where the child is in care under a care order) anyone who has the consent of the local authority (the principle being presumably that in such a case the local authority is effectively "in the driving seat" and will have to act in accordance with the guidelines governing the exercise of its statutory discretions (see s.22(5)); or

    (iii) in other cases, the consent of everyone with parental responsibility for the child (see s.10(5)).

In addition, there is a further group of persons who are only entitled to apply for a residence order, namely local authority foster parents with whom the child has been living for at least one year immediately prior to the application (s.10(5A)). This brings the law into line with adoption law, as such persons can also apply for an adoption order after the child has been living with them for a year (see para.15–032 below).

(3) *Persons who require leave to apply*

The Act adopts what is sometimes described as the "open door" policy; and it **12–010** provides that the court may make a s.8 order if an application for the order has been made by a person who has obtained the leave of the court to make the application (s.10(1)(a)(ii)). The Rules (see r.4.3 of the Family Proceedings Rules 1991) stipulate that an applicant must make the request for leave in writing setting out the reasons for the request and providing a draft of the application in respect of which leave is sought. In effect, therefore, anyone (unless debarred under the rules summarised at paras 12–013 *et seq.*, below) may bring an issue to the court's notice. The decision whether to allow the application to proceed is dependent on the exercise of a judicial discretion. There are two separate sets of principles to be applied in determining applications for leave to apply for an order: the first relates to anyone other than the child in question, and the second to the child:

(a) Applications by persons other than the child concerned:

12–011 Section 10(9) provides that in deciding whether to grant leave or not the court is to have "particular regard" to—

(a) the nature of the proposed application for the s.8 order;

(b) the applicant's connection with the child;

(c) any risk there might be of that proposed application disrupting the child's life to such an extent that he would be harmed by it; and

(d) where the child is being looked after by a local authority—

    (i) the authority's plans for the child's future; and
    (ii) the wishes and feelings of the child's parents.

The Court of Appeal has held that these specific guidelines mean that the court is *not* bound to apply the general principle that the child's welfare is the paramount consideration (see *e.g. Re A (minors) (residence orders: leave to apply)* [1992] Fam 182, CA). The court must therefore direct itself by reference to the statutory guidelines. Earlier cases required an applicant to show "a good arguable case", but in *Re J (Leave to issue application for residence order)* [2002] EWCA Civ 1346, the Court of Appeal expressed its disapproval of this practice:

> This case involved an application by the child's grandmother. At first instance it was refused, but on appeal the Court of Appeal held that the requirement that applicants show "a good arguable case" was no longer appropriate. First, the statutory checklist (which contained no such condition) should be given proper weight. Secondly, "trial judges should recognise the greater appreciation that has developed of the value of what grandparents have to offer" (*per* Thorpe L.J. at 118). Finally, protection of the applicant's rights under Art.6 of the ECHR (and potentially under Art.8) required, as a minimum, that applications should not be dismissed without full enquiry. The application for leave was allowed.

The reasoning reflects both the greater importance attached to members of the extended family, and the increased importance of procedural and substantive rights. It has subsequently been held that the court is still entitled to consider the likelihood of the order being granted, since this is germane to the nature of the order being sought, and is merely prohibited from disposing of the application on the basis that is had no reasonable prospects of success: *Re R (Adoption: Contact)* [2005] EWCA Civ 1128.

Of course, the great majority of cases in which applications for leave are made do not present great difficulties; and in particular, only rarely will grandparents or other close relatives be denied leave to seek contact. However, the fact that leave to make an application has been given does not mean that there is any presumption that the application itself will be successful.

(b) Applications by the child concerned

Section 10(8) of the Children Act provides that where the application is made by the **12–012** child concerned the court must be satisfied that he or she has sufficient understanding to make the proposed application, but is not required to apply the further guidelines governing applications by others discussed above. The question of whether the child has "sufficient understanding" is determined by reference to the gravity and complexity of the issues involved as already explained at para.11–034 above in the context of the *Gillick* decision; but there are particular—and potentially damaging—aspects of the legal process that the child should understand:

> In *Re C (Residence: Child's Application for Leave)* [1995] 1 F.L.R. 927, Stuart-White J., there had been much litigation between parents about the upbringing of a 14-year-old girl. Eventually, the girl (who had been living with her father) sought leave to apply for a residence order in favour of her mother. The judge pointed out that "once a child is a party to proceedings between warring parents, that leads the child to be in a position in which the child is likely to be present hearing the evidence of those parents, hearing the parent cross-examined, hearing perhaps of many matters which at the tender age of the child, it would be better for her not to hear"; and the child herself might be subjected to cross-examination.

For this reason, the level of understanding required is high: as Sir Thomas Bingham M.R. put it in *Re S (A Minor) (Independent Representation)* [1993] Fam. 263 at 276:

> "Where any sound judgment on the issues calls for insight and imagination which only maturity and experience can bring, ... the court ... will be slow to conclude that the child's understanding is sufficient."

It may be, however, that these decisions need to be reconsidered in the light to the increasing importance attached to children's rights (see e.g. *Mabon v Mabon* [2005] EWCA Civ 634). Even if the court concludes that the child is competent, there is a discretion whether or not to grant leave (see e.g. *Re C (A Minor) (Leave to seek s.8 order)* [1994] 1 F.L.R. 26, Johnson J.). The courts will take into account the likelihood of the child's application for the substantive order being successful, although this criterion is not mentioned in the statute and it remains to be seen whether this is affected by the decision in *Re J (Leave to issue application for residence order)* [2002] EWCA Civ 1346 (above, para.12–011).

The extent to which children are involved in the process by other means is considered further below (para.14–010).

(4) *Restrictions on applying for residence and other orders*

Finally, there are two specific restrictions on applying for s.8 orders, both of which **12–013** relate to the role of local authorities.

(a) Local authorities not to be allowed to circumvent care order procedure by seeking residence order:

One of the cardinal principles adopted by the Children Act is that local authorities **12–014** (and other state agencies) should not be entitled to interfere in family life without good cause. The principle is that the state is only to be allowed to intervene in the upbringing of a child if the child is at risk because of a failure in the family. To allow a local authority to apply for residence orders on the basis simply that the child's welfare would be best served in this way would be to undermine that policy. Accordingly the Act provides that no local authority may apply for a residence or contact order, and the court is prohibited from making such orders in favour of a local authority (s.9(2)). There are other provisions in the legislation designed to promote the same policy objective, but they are best considered in the context of the court's jurisdiction to make care orders (see Ch.13, below).

(b) Restrictions on applications by local authority foster parents:

12–015   At the same time, the Children Act is intended to assist local authorities in providing support for families in need, and this support may often involve a child being "looked after" by a foster-parent found by the local authority. Once a court has decided that it would be in the child's best interests to make a care order in his or her favour, the local authority should be able to determine how to discharge its responsibilities to the child.

Whether or not the child is subject to a care order, the Act places further restrictions on applications by local authority foster-parents. The Act provides that a person who has been the child's local authority foster parent within the last six months may not even seek leave to apply for a residence or other s.8 order unless that person is a relative of the child, or has the permission of the local authority, or the child has been living with him or her for at least one year (see s.9(3), as amended by the Adoption and Children Act 2002).

The general policy seems fairly clear. First, parents who allow their child to be cared for on a short term basis by a local authority foster parent should have the confidence that the foster parent will not be allowed to go to court with the claim that a residence order in the foster parent's favour would better promote the child's welfare than allowing the child to return to his parents. Secondly, the local authority should be able to plan for the future of the children in their care without the fear that those plans will be upset by litigation started by a comparatively short-term foster parent.

However, once "family proceedings" are before the court, the court (as we have seen at para.12–003, above) has power to make orders if it considers that it should do so, "even though no ... application has been made" (s.10(3)). In a controversial decision, the Court of Appeal held (by a majority) that this power may be exercised to make an order in favour of foster-parents who were debarred under s.9(3) from seeking leave to apply for such an order:

> In *Gloucestershire CC v P* [1999] 2 F.L.R. 61, CA, the local authority had placed the child with foster parents, but then decided that the child's interests would be best served by his being adopted by others. The child's grandparents sought a residence order. The foster-parents wanted a residence order, but were debarred by s.9(3) from seeking leave to make the application. The Court of Appeal held that in a situation where the child's welfare was paramount it would be wrong to fetter the wide discretion that the Act conferred to make an order. However, the grant of a residence order to foster-parents in this way would be most exceptional and would only be made on cogent grounds where the child's needs clearly so required.

C: PRIVATE LAW ORDERS UNDER THE CHILDREN ACT 1989

This section deals with the s.8 "menu" of orders, which, as already stated, are usually **12–016** made in private law proceedings, but which may be made in any family proceedings. It first sets out the four types of orders, followed by the conditions and directions that may be attached to such orders, and finally discusses key issues in the making and enforcement of the various orders. The factors taken into account by the courts in deciding what, if any, order should be made are considered in Ch.14.

The "menu" of orders

(1) *Contact orders*

A contact order is defined by s.8(1) as: "an order requiring the person with whom a **12–017** child lives, or is to live, to allow the child to visit or stay with the person named in the order, or for that person and the child otherwise to have contact with each other." Such an order enables the court to give effect to the general assumption that it is desirable for a child to preserve links with both parents; and contact orders may be used in other cases involving relatives and people who wish to preserve a link with the child. Contact orders may if necessary be very specific and detailed—sometimes, for example, providing that contact should be supervised, or take place at a particular location (perhaps a contact centre of the kind now found in many towns). Contact may also be direct (*i.e* face-to-face) or indirect (*e.g.* by letter). The number of applications for contact has shown a dramatic increase since the early years of the Children Act, and in 2004 the courts made 70,169 orders for contact (*Judicial Statistics 2004*).

(2) *Residence orders*

In accordance with the "plain words" approach adopted by the Children Act, the **12–018** legislation no longer refers to ambiguous and obscure concepts such as "custody." A residence order is simply "an order settling the arrangements to be made as to the person with whom a child is to live," and 31,878 residence orders were made in 2004 (*Judicial Statistics 2004*).

Although the general policy of the Children Act is to use plain language, so that orders mean what they say but mean no more than they say, the making of a residence order has important ancillary consequences. First, the making of a residence order automatically prohibits change of the child's surname without the written consent of all those who have parental responsibility or the approval of the court (s.13(1)(a)). Secondly, the person in whose favour a residence order has been made can remove the child from the jurisdiction for up to one month—for example for a holiday. Any longer periods of absence require the consent of all persons with parental responsibility or the leave of the court. Thirdly, the making of a residence order automatically terminates any care order, so that an application for a residence order may be a technique for seeking to remove a child from local authority care. Finally—and perhaps most importantly—the making of a residence order confers "parental responsibility" on the person in whose favour it is made if that person does not already have it (s.12(2)). Thus in *Re M (Sperm Donor Father)* [2003] Fam. 94, a shared residence order was made in favour of a lesbian couple to enable both to have parental responsibility for the child, and in *Re G (Residence: Same-Sex Partner)* [2005] EWCA Civ 462 the court went a step further in making a shared residence order in favour of a lesbian mother and her *ex*-partner for the same reason.

The making of a residence order does not, however, deprive any other person of his or her parental responsibility. Thus, the making of a residence order in favour of the child's father does not deprive the mother of her right to take decisions about education or any other matter (although of course she must not act inconsistently with the terms of any court order, and thus could not remove the child from the father's home).

(3) *Prohibited steps orders*

12–019 A prohibited steps order is defined as "an order that no step which could be taken by a parent in meeting his parental responsibility for a child, and which is of a kind specified in the order, shall be taken by any person without consent of the court." Such orders may, for example, prohibit the removal of a child from his home, direct that a child should not be brought into contact with a named person or taken to a particular place, or forbid the carrying out of medical treatment on the child. They may thus be extremely useful in situations of family breakdown, and 9,556 such orders were made in 2004 (*Judicial Statistics 2004*).

A prohibited steps order can be made against anyone whether or not that person has parental responsibility and whether or not he is a party to the proceedings. For example:

> In *Re H (Prohibited Steps Order)* [1995] 1 F.L.R. 638, CA, a man with whom the mother had been living sexually abused her daughter. The Court of Appeal held that it had power to make a prohibited steps order against the man forbidding him from seeking contact with any of the children, notwithstanding the fact that he was not a party to the proceedings and had not been heard. If, having been served with the order, he wished to contest it he would be enabled to do so.

The main limitation is that the action prohibited must be of a kind which could be "taken by a parent in meeting his parental responsibility" (as defined by s.3; see para.11–003, above). If not, the court will not have jurisdiction to make the order, as in *Croydon LBC v A* [1992] Fam. 169, Hollings J. In this case an order prohibiting the mother from having contact with the violent father, who had been convicted of assaulting the child, was not within the scope of the section, since one adult having contact with another for their own purposes was not a "step which could be taken by a parent in meeting his parental responsibility for a child". By contrast in *Re Z (A Minor) (Freedom of Publication)* [1996] 1 F.L.R. 191, CA, the mother's decision whether or not to consent to her daughter's appearing in a television programme was an exercise of her parental responsibility and so could be restrained by a prohibited steps order.

(4) *Specific issue orders*

12–020 A specific issue order is an "order giving directions for the purpose of determining a specific question which has arisen, or which may arise, in connection with any aspect of parental responsibility for a child," and enables the court to make rulings about particular matters, such as the religion or education of the child, the name by which he or she should be known and applications to take the child abroad. In this respect, a specific issue order (of which 3,893 were made in 2004) serves a different purpose from a residence order or a parental responsibility order, which confer general powers to take decisions about the child's upbringing. A specific issue order differs from a prohibited steps order in that it may mandate positive action, as well as prohibiting certain actions.

As with the prohibited steps order, the only restriction on the kind of application that the court can deal with under this heading is that the order must deal with some aspect of parental responsibility (for an unusual example see *Re F (Specific Issue: Child Interview)* [1995] 1 F.L.R. 819). Recent examples include an order for the immunization of two children at the request of their non-resident fathers in *Re C (Welfare of Child: Immunisation)* [2003] EWHC 1376 (Fam); approved on appeal [2003] EWCA Civ 1148, and a refusal to order circumcision at the request of a Muslim mother against the opposition of the Jain father, on the basis that the boy had been brought up in both faiths and should decide for himself which, if any, he wanted to follow (*Re S (Specific Issue Order: Religion: Circumcision)* [2004] EWHC 1282 (Fam)).

Conditions and directions

The courts have the power to give directions about how a s.8 order is to be carried into **12–021** effect, and to impose conditions upon the parties (see s.11(7)). Residence orders may thus contain directions about how the child is to be prepared for a change of home, or conditions that the residential parent must remain in a particular place (and hand over all passports and travel documents), or that the child is not to be allowed to come into contact with a named third party. Contact orders may (and very often do) contain detailed provisions about the arrangements to be made. But the power is not limitless; and in particular the courts have been concerned that judges should not use the power to impose conditions in an attempt to control the lives of the adults concerned:

> In *Re D (Residence: Imposition of Conditions)* [1996] 2 F.L.R. 281, the mother's boyfriend was a man with a record of violence. The court made a residence order in her favour, but attached a condition that she should not bring the children into contact with him or allow him to live at any address at which she was living with the children. The Court of Appeal held that this was wrong: the court should not try to overrule the mother's right to live her life as she chose. Of course, if she did choose to live with him, the court might decide that the children's welfare would be better served by their living with their grandmother or with their father.

The power to attach directions to orders must be confined within the primary purpose of the s.8 order:

> In the remarkable case of *D v D (county court: jurisdiction)* [1993] 2 F.L.R. 802, CA, the judge hearing a mother's application for a residence order was strongly critical of action taken by the police and social services in investigating complaints made by the father about the child's treatment, and made a "direction" that they should take no further action without prior leave of the court. It was held that the power to make "such incidental, supplemental or consequential provision as the court thinks fit" could not extend to prohibiting public authorities from discharging their statutory and common law powers.

The principle of subsidiarity is of course of general relevance: the power to impose conditions should not be used effectively to negate the terms of the main order:

> In *Birmingham CC v H* [1992] 2 F.L.R. 323, Fam Div, the local authority applied for an interim care order (see para.13–014 above) in respect of a baby. The baby's 15-year-old mother was desperately anxious to fulfil her role as a mother and it was argued on her behalf that the court should instead make a residence order in her favour subject to conditions to secure the baby's protection (requiring the mother to reside at a particular institution, comply with all reasonable instructions from the staff, and even to hand over the child to the care of the staff if so required). Ward J. held that this course was inappropriate, since it would be inconsistent with a residence order "to say that a condition of it should be that, effectively, some other person assume the parental responsibility which goes with the exercise of that order and to do so at the instance of that other without any judgment of the court" (p.325). An interim care order was therefore made.

Restrictions on the court's power to make orders

12–022   The Children Act 1989 contains a number of provisions restricting the power that the court would otherwise have to make orders:

(1) *Age*

12–023   The Act provides that no court shall make a s.8 order with respect to a child who has attained the age of 16 unless the circumstances of the case are exceptional and that (with the same proviso) no court is to make an order which is to have effect after the child is 16 years old (see s.9(7) and (6) respectively). The one exception is that a residence order made in favour of a person who is neither the parent nor the guardian of the child concerned may continue until the child attains the age of 18 (s.12(5), as inserted by the Adoption and Children Act 2002), which ensures the continuation of the parental responsibility that accompanies such an order.

(2) *Specific issue orders and prohibited steps orders may not be used to achieve the same result as a residence or contact order*

12–024   Under s.9(5), the court is prohibited from making a specific issue order or prohibited steps order "with a view to achieving a result which could be achieved by making a residence or contact order". The reason for such a prohibition is obvious where local authorities are concerned: as noted above, a local authority may not apply for a residence or contact order, and it should not be able to evade the more demanding requirements of public law simply by framing its application as a specific issue order or prohibited steps order.

> In *Nottingham CC v P* [1993] 2 F.L.R. 134, CA, a father had persistently abused his eldest daughter by having sexual intercourse with her and committing buggery upon her. The judge found that the other children were also seriously at risk, as the mother was weak and unable to protect them. The local authority however "persistently and obstinately refused" to seek a care order (presumably for financial reasons) but did apply for a prohibited steps order excluding the father from the home and prohibiting him from having any contact with the children. It

was held that this was prohibited by s.9(5). Regulating who was to live in the household with the child was something that could be achieved by a residence order, and, likewise, regulating contact was something that could be achieved by a contact order, even if it was an order for no contact. The Court of Appeal dismissed the local authority's appeal. The children remained at risk.

The prohibition in s.9(5) extends to all applicants, even those who are entitled to seek a residence or contact order, perhaps because of concerns that an order might place a child in a person's care without conferring parental responsibility.

Key controversies

Post-separation parenting may give rise to a number of difficulties, and in recent years the issues of residence and contact, in particular, have attracted considerable attention. Some of the key controversies are as follows: **12–025**

(1) *In whose favour are residence orders made?*

While the majority of children remain with their mothers after parental divorce or separation, there is no presumption that a residence order should be made in favour of the mother. The current pattern reflects the fact that the mother is likely to be the primary carer of the child, and the courts have shown themselves willing to make residence orders in favour of fathers who have taken on this role: **12–026**

> In *Re H (Agreed Joint Residence: Mediation)* [2004] EWHC 2064 (Fam) the child had remained with his father after his parents separated. The judge found that the child's "primary attachment is to his father. He was there in the difficult days of the initial separation, he was solid and dependable .... I do not consider that the special bond that was created at that time has ever been broken despite the fact that the mother has increased her role." (*per* Baron J. at para.60). A residence order was accordingly made in the father's favour.

Nor indeed is there any presumption in favour of the child's biological parent:

> In *Re H (A child) (residence)* [2001] EWCA Civ 742, a mother sought to challenge the residence order that had been made in favour of her mother three years earlier. Thorpe L.J. noted that there was no reference to any presumption in favour of the natural parent in s.1 of the Children Act and "judicial overlay on that section must obviously be treated with caution" (at 285). Furthermore, the concept of the "natural parent" was not fixed: it could refer to the psychological parent rather than to the birth parent. The challenge thus failed and the residence order in favour of the grandmother remained in force.

Similarly, in *CG v CW and G (Children)* [2006] EWCA Civ 372, residence was transferred to the biological mother's former lesbian partner (see further para. 14–015). Of course, the absence of any presumption that residence should be awarded to birth parents in general, or the mother in particular, does not mean that the courts' interpretation of the welfare principle will not favour such a practice. This is further considered in Ch.14.

(2) Should a shared residence order be made?

12–027   The Children Act provides that where a residence order is made in favour of two or more persons who do not themselves live together, the order may specify the periods during which the child is to live in the different households concerned (s.11(4)); and it thus clearly envisages that there may be occasions on which the court will wish to make what is sometimes called a "shared residence order" (perhaps providing for the child to spend a week with one parent and then a week with the other, but probably more commonly providing that the child spend weekdays with one parent and weekends with the other). The question of whether it is appropriate to make such an order is governed by the principle that the child's welfare is the paramount consideration (see Ch.14, below). There has been a significant shift in the courts' willingness to make shared residence orders (*per* Thorpe L.J. in *Re R (Residence: Shared Care: Children's Views)* [2005] EWCA Civ 542 at para.11). Earlier cases suggested that a shared residence order would only be appropriate in exceptional circumstances, or if there was a positive benefit to the child in making such an order, but in *D v D (Shared Residence Order)* [2001] 1 F.L.R. 495, CA, the court pointed out that the Children Act contained no such restrictions. In that case, the children lived with their father for 140 days each year and with their mother the rest of the time, and the shared residence order reflected the reality of the situation. Subsequent cases have adopted a generous interpretation of what constitutes the "underlying reality" of the situation. For example, in *A v A (Shared Residence)* [2004] EWHC 142 (Fam), a shared residence order was made "not only to reflect the reality that the children are dividing their lives equally between their parents, but also to reflect the fact that the parents are equal in the eyes of the law, and have equal duties and responsibilities towards their children." The decision in *Re A (Temporary Removal from the Jurisdiction)* [2004] EWCA Civ 1587 reflected the increasing importance attached to the second factor. In this case the mother planned to move to South Africa for two years with her daughter, but the Court of Appeal felt that a shared residence order was still appropriate as "a formal recognition of an underlying reality, namely that both parents have parental responsibility which they will continue to exercise." The "underlying reality" being recognised in these cases is the reality of the parents' continuing responsibilities rather than the children's lives: in such circumstances the only difference between a shared residence order and a combination of orders granting residence to one parent and staying contact to another is symbolic. This is not to deny its importance: the number of applications for shared residence orders does suggest that parents value their contribution to their children's upbringing being designated as "shared residence" rather than "contact". Despite the new emphasis on continuing parental obligations, it remains unlikely that a shared residence order would be made where the child spent no time with one parent: the order thus must bear at least some relation to the reality of the child's life (see *e.g. Re A (children) (shared residence)* [2001] EWCA Civ 1795).

   Subject to that limitation, the recent case-law shows that a shared residence order may be made even where children do not spend equal amounts of time in each household, even where the parents' homes are geographically distant (see *e.g. Re F (children) (shared residence order)* [2003] All E.R. (D) 258), and even where the parents remain in conflict (*e.g. A v A (Shared Residence)* [2004] EWHC 142 (Fam)). As Thorpe L.J. noted in *Re C (A Child)* [2006] EWCA Civ 235:

> "the whole tenor of recent authority has been to liberate trial judges to elect for a regime of shared residence, if the circumstances and the reality of the case support that conclusion and if that conclusion is consistent with the paramount welfare consideration. The whole tenor of authority is against the identification of restricted circumstances in which shared residence orders may be made." (para.19)

The implications of this shift for other areas of the law—*e.g.* in relation to entitlement to housing and benefits—should be noted (see *e.g. R (Bibi) v Camden London Borough Council* [2004] EWHC 2527 (Admin) and *Hockenjos v Secretary of State for Social Security (No.2)* [2004] EWCA Civ 1749).

(3) *Should the residential parent be prevented from moving?*

Under s.13 the consent of every person with parental responsibility, or the leave of the **12–028** court, is required if the residential parent wishes to take the child out of the jurisdiction for more than one month. (The rules are even stricter if there is no residence order in force: in such cases the leave of the court or the consent of every person with parental responsibility is required for *any* move). A person who removes the child from England and Wales—Scotland and Northern Ireland being, for these purposes, different jurisdictions—without these conditions being satisfied commits an offence under s.1 of the Child Abduction Act 1984 (see paras 12–047 *et seq.* below). The residential parent may seek a specific issue order to authorise the move (equally, it is open to the parent opposed to the move to seek a prohibited steps order to prevent it). Given that the decision of the residential parent to move to a different country may obviously have a profound impact on the ability of the other parent to maintain contact with the child, especially if a contact order is not enforceable in the jurisdiction where the child is living, how do the courts approach the question as to whether the carer should be allowed to remove the child from the jurisdiction?

The interests of the child in question are the paramount consideration for the court. However, the tendency of the courts has been to focus upon the position of the primary carer. In the past it was suggested that there was a presumption that the wishes of the primary carer should receive the endorsement of the court (see, *e.g. Poel v Poel* [1970] 1 W.L.R. 1469, CA). More recently, in *Payne v Payne* [2001] EWCA Civ 166, Thorpe L.J. regretted the use of the term "presumption"—in line with the general shift away from presumptions in family law—although he went on to add that the impact on the primary carer would usually be the crucial factor. There are two reasons for this: first, the rights of the primary carer, and, secondly, the impact that refusing to allow the move may have upon the carer and the home environment, which will in turn affect the welfare of the child involved. An illustration of the first point is provided by *Re G-A (a child) (removal from the jurisdiction: human rights)* [2001] 1 F.C.R. 43, CA:

> In this case the mother, the primary carer, wanted to move to New York to take up a job that she had been offered there. The court allowed the move, noting that the father's right to family life had to be balanced against the mother's right to private life, which included the freedom to work where she chose.

The court's perception of the potential impact of a refusal on the carer (and children) is apparent in *Re B (children) (removal from the jurisdiction)* [2001] 1 F.C.R. 108, CA.

> In this case the mother wished to move to Denmark with her children. At first instance this was refused, but the Court of Appeal authorised the move, noting that the judge had paid insufficient attention to the impact of the refusal on the mother. Would she be able to provide the children with a loving and carefree atmosphere in the home if she was prevented from executing her reasonably formulated plan?

Similarly, in *Re B (Removal from the Jurisdiction); Re S (Removal from the Jurisdiction)* [2003] EWCA Civ 1149, Thorpe L.J. explained how refusing a move dictated by the career plans of the residential parent's new partner might have an impact on the welfare of the children involved:

> "The mother's attachment and commitment to a man whose employment requires him to live in another jurisdiction may be a decisive factor in the determination of a relocation application. That does not entail putting the needs and interests of an adult before the welfare of the children. Rather the welfare of the children cannot be achieved unless the new family has the ordinary opportunity to pursue its goals and to make its choices without unreasonable restriction."

Despite this emphasis on the position of the primary carer, it is certainly not the case that *any* proposed move will be endorsed by the court. The Court of Appeal has set out various factors to consider in deciding whether a move should be permitted (see *Payne v Payne* [2001] EWCA Civ 166 and *Re B (Removal from the Jurisdiction); Re S (Removal from the Jurisdiction)* [2003] EWCA Civ 1149).

First, was the resident parent's application realistic and genuine? If not, refusal of permission to relocate would be inevitable, as in *R v R (Leave to remove)* [2004] EWHC 2572 (Fam), where the court felt that the mother's plans to move to Paris were a yet further manifestation of her tendency to run away from situations and idealise new solutions. Secondly, was the other parent's opposition based on genuine concern for the child or driven by ulterior motives? What would be the detriment to him, and to his relationship with the child, if the move were allowed, and how far would such detriment be offset by the extension of the child's maternal family (on the assumption that the mother is taking the child back to her country of origin)? Thirdly, what impact would a refusal have on the residential parent, and, if she was caring for her child within a new family, upon that family and her new partner? The answers to these appraisals "must then be brought into an overriding review of the child's welfare as the paramount consideration, directed by the statutory checklist insofar as appropriate." (*per* Thorpe L.J., *Payne v Payne*, para.40).

The applicability of these principles to various types of relocation cases has been considered in a number of recent cases. The Court of Appeal has confirmed that the principles outlined in *Payne* are equally relevant where the residential parent plans to relocate to her country of origin or to move abroad for work purposes. If, by contrast, the planned move is of short duration, a different approach may be required—"the more temporary the removal, the less regard should be paid to the principle stated in *Payne*" (*per* Thorpe L.J. in *Re A (Temporary Removal from Jurisdiction)* [2004] EWCA

Civ 1587, para.13). A different approach again—this time giving more weight to the views of the other parent—is appropriate if residence is shared between the parents, as in *Re Y (Leave to Remove from Jurisdiction)* [2004] 2 F.L.R. 330. Finally, if both parents are seeking to relocate, the principles set out in *Payne* have no application: the court is simply faced with a straightforward choice between the two alternatives: *Re B (Children)* [2005] EWCA Civ 643.

What of moves within the jurisdiction? There are no statutory restrictions on such moves, and in *Re E (Minors) (Residence Orders)* [1997] 2 F.L.R. 638, CA, it was held that conditions restricting where the residential parent was to live should only be included in "exceptional circumstances". An example of what is considered to be "exceptional" is provided by *Re S (a child)* [2002] EWCA Civ 1795:

> In this case the child suffered from Down's Syndrome and would be unable to understand the loss of contact with her father and family. Her need for stability and reassurance was held to outweigh the impact on the mother's mental health (which would itself have an impact on her daughter) and the fact that her living conditions would be improved by the move.

While the courts continue to state that conditions should only be imposed in exceptional circumstances, recent cases do suggest an increasing willingness to impose conditions where the move would effectively exclude one parent from the child's life. Thus:

> In *B v B (Residence: Condition Limiting Geographic Area)* [2004] 2 F.L.R. 979 the mother wished to move to Newcastle but the judge opined that her plans lacked clarity and purpose and that the move was intended to frustrate the father's contact with his child. A condition requiring the mother to reside within the area of the M25 was thus imposed.

One theme running through all the topics considered in this section is the importance of both parents in the child's life. The issue of contact with a non-residential parent has become a significant social, legal, and political issue in recent years and raises a number of controversial questions.

(4) *Is there a* right *to contact?*

In recent years the courts have tended to eschew the language of rights in this context. **12–029** If anyone has a right to contact, it is the child rather than the parent, but in practice contact may be ordered against the wishes of children if this is deemed to be in their best interests, whereas there is nothing that the law can do to compel contact if the non-residential parent does not wish it. Furthermore, in deciding whether contact should be ordered the determining factor is not what the child wants, but what is in the child's best interests.

By contrast, the jurisprudence of the European Court of Human Rights offers stronger support for a right to contact. The court has emphasised the importance of contact for both parent and child, stating in *Kosmopolou v Greece* [2004] 1 F.L.R. 800 that "the mutual enjoyment by parent and child of each other's company constitutes a fundamental element of family life" (para.26). The state has obligations to protect this aspect of family life even in intra-family disputes, the key question being whether the authorities "have taken all necessary steps to facilitate contact as can reasonably be demanded in the special circumstances of each case" (see *Hokkanen v Finland* (1995) 19 EHRR 139, *Sylvester v Austria* [2003] 2 F.L.R. 210). Lack of co-operation between the parents does not exempt the authorities from taking action but rather imposes "an obligation to take measures that would reconcile the conflicting interests of the parties, keeping in mind the paramount interests of the child" (*Zawadka v Poland* [2005] 2 F.L.R. 897, para.67). As that last case makes clear, however, the rights of the parties may have to yield to the welfare of the child: thus in *Süss v Germany* [2006] 1 F.L.R. 522 the court held that there was no violation of Art.8 as the national courts' decisions to suspend access "can be taken to have been made in the child's best interest." (at para.91). Even so, "although measures against children obliging them to reunite with one or other parent are not desirable in this sensitive area, such action must not be ruled out in the event of non-compliance or unlawful behaviour by the parent with whom the children live" (*Ignaccolo-Zenide v Romania* (2001) 31 EHRR 7, para.107). Thus it is clear that even the European Convention affords no absolute right to contact, although it requires careful scrutiny of any decision to suspend contact.

(5) *Is there a presumption in favour of contact?*

12–030 While there is a widespread assumption among the judiciary that it is generally in the interests of a child to maintain contact with both parents, the courts have stated that there is no presumption that the court should make an order that a child spend equal—or indeed any—time with each parent. In *Re S (Contact: Promoting Relationship With Absent Parent)* [2004] EWCA Civ 18, for example, Butler-Sloss P. firmly rejected suggestions that there should be a presumption of equality of time spent by a child with each parent:

> "This approach to contact would not be in the best interests of many children whose welfare is the issue before the court. The court is not and should not be tied to a certain number of days which would be automatically ordered to be spent by the absent parent with the child. Children of all ages and circumstances may be the subject of contact orders and one blanket type of order may inhibit the court arriving at the decision which reflects the best interests of each individual child." (para.26)

Similarly, in *Re L; Re V; Re M; Re H (Contact: Domestic Violence)* [2000] 2 F.L.R. 334, CA, Thorpe L.J. stated that there was no presumption that contact would be ordered at all. Moreover, the assumption that contact will be in the best interests of the child might be weaker if there were no existing relationship between the child and the parent. He suggested that distinctions should be drawn between cases in which contact is sought to maintain an existing relationship, to revive a dormant one, or to create a non-existent one, and that "the judicial assumption that to order contact would be to promote welfare should surely wane across the spectrum" (at 364).

It should, however, be noted that there is certainly a *perception* that there is a presumption in favour of contact (see para.12–031 below), and in practice the courts will order contact unless there are good reasons not to do so.

(6) *Is there a presumption against contact in cases of domestic violence?*

12–031 The strength of the assumption that contact is beneficial is demonstrated by the fact that there is no presumption *against* contact even in cases of domestic violence. In recent years there has been increased awareness both of the link between domestic violence and child abuse and of the effect that witnessing domestic violence may have upon children. In 2002, for example, the Adoption and Children Act amended the 1989 Act to make it clear that if seeing or hearing the ill-treatment of another leads to the impairment of the child's health or development, this falls within the definition of "harm" for the purposes of the Act. Similarly, Butler-Sloss P noted in the conjoined appeals of *Re L; Re V; Re M; Re H (Contact: Domestic Violence)* [2000] 2 F.L.R. 334, CA, that violence to a partner is itself a failure in parenting, in that the perpetrator has failed to protect the child's carer or the emotional well-being of the child. In that case, the Court of Appeal relied extensively on the expert psychiatric evidence provided to the court by Sturge and Glaser (see [2000] Fam. Law 615) but rejected their central recommendation that there should be an assumption against contact in cases of domestic violence. Instead, it stressed that all the circumstances of the case should be taken into account in assessing what the welfare of the child required. Factors to be weighed in the balance would be the seriousness of the violence, the risks that contact might entail and the ability of the offending parent to recognise his past conduct and make genuine attempts to change. Repentance by the perpetrator, however genuine, gives no guarantee that contact will be ordered:

> In *Re V*, one of the above appeals, the son had witnessed a knife attack on his mother by his father. While the father had undergone counselling and claimed to be a changed person, the son was opposed to any contact with him, refusing to read his letters and showing signs of distress when the hearing was taking place. The court held that contact could not be seen as a reward for the parent's good behaviour, and that in this case it had to be refused as it was not in the best interests of the son.

The Court of Appeal in *Re L* also instigated a change in practice in cases where domestic violence was alleged, requiring courts to investigate allegations of domestic violence. Indeed, even if the allegations are abandoned the judge may need to continue with the investigation to ensure that the welfare of the children involved is adequately protected (see *e.g. Re F (Restrictions on Applications)* [2005] EWCA Civ 499). Guidance on the appropriate approach to be adopted by the courts was published by the Children Act Sub-Committee in 2002 (*Guidelines for Good Practice on Parental Contact in Cases where there is Domestic Violence*), and new application forms have been introduced with the aim of identifying domestic violence. Despite such activity it is clear that not all judges have been alert to the changes in policy and practice. In *Re H (A Child)* [2005] EWCA Civ 1404, for example, Wall L.J. noted tartly that the case had been "a paradigm of how a difficult and sensitive contact dispute should not be handled" (para.111), and stressed the importance of using the CASC Guidelines.

If there are concerns about the safety of contact, various options are available. Supervised contact may address the fears of the residential parent, although research has shown that few contact centres actually supervise contact. (Aris *et al., Safety and child contact: an analysis of the role of child contact centres in the context of domestic violence and child welfare concerns (L.C.D.,* 2002)). Where direct contact is not desirable or feasible, an order can be made for indirect contact, for example by letter or greetings card, as was the case in all four appeals in *Re L*. Such arrangements may impose a positive obligation on the residential parent to pass on the other parent's communications (see *e.g. Re O (Contact: Imposition of Conditions)* [1995] 2 F.L.R.

124, CA). Even such indirect contact may be refused if it would affect the well-being of the child. In *Re C (Contact: No order for Contact)* [2000] 2 F.L.R. 723, FD, the son had said that he would kill himself due to his unhappiness over contact and had torn up letters from his father. The court refused contact. In addition, the impact that even indirect conduct may have on the child's carer will also be relevant to the welfare of the child (see *e.g. Re M and B (children) (contact: domestic violence)* [2001] 1 F.C.R. 116, CA, although contrast *Re L (Contact: Genuine Fear)* [2002] 1 F.L.R. 621, Fam Div, where the court thought that indirect contact could be managed by the mother).

It should also be noted that a very different picture of the family justice system is presented by the recent report by HM Inspectorate of Court Administration, *Domestic Violence, Safety and Family Proceedings* (2005), which noted that:

> "The perception of the presumption of contact in domestic violence cases is experienced by women as dangerous to themselves and their children." (p.19)

In addition, the pressure on parents to make their own arrangements without the intervention of the court may mean that victims of domestic violence are not adequately protected in such cases.

(7) *How can contact be enforced?*

12–032   As the domestic violence cases show, the residential parent will often have good reason for opposing contact with the other parent. Yet this will not always be true, and in recent years the courts have had to grapple with a number of cases in which the resident parent has refused to allow contact to take place.

One way in which a parent may frustrate contact is by making allegations against the other parent, in the hope that the delay needed to investigate those allegations will confer an advantage in subsequent proceedings. It is clear that a strict attitude is taken by the courts to false allegations against the other parent: in *Re T (Order for Costs)* [2005] EWCA Civ 311, a costs order was made against a mother who had made groundless allegations against the father.

The problem posed by the obduracy of the residential parent may be compounded by the refusal of the child to see the other parent. In such a case the court will consider whether the child's refusal is genuine or the result of the influence of the residential parent (see *e.g. Re T (Contact: Alienation: Permission to Appeal)* [2002] EWCA Civ 1736). The term "parental alienation syndrome" (PAS), coined by an American psychiatrist, has begun to infiltrate the law reports, although such a syndrome is not recognised in either of the international classifications of mental illness. As Butler-Sloss P. pointed out in *Re L; Re V; Re M; Re H (Contact: Domestic Violence)* [2000] 2 F.L.R. 334, CA, while some mothers are responsible for alienating their children, this "is a long way from a recognised syndrome requiring mental health professionals to play an expert role" (at 351). The courts have preferred the term "implacable hostility" (see *e.g. Re O (Contact: Withdrawal of Application* [2003] EWHC 3031 (Fam)).

This is not to deny that the views of the children in question may have been influenced by one parent (see *e.g. In re M (Children)(Contact: Long-term Best Interests* [2005] EWCA Civ 1090). But it is also important to recognise that a child may have independent reasons for refusing contact, as the domestic violence cases discussed above indicate (and see also *Re C (Prohibition on Further Applications)* [2002] 1 F.L.R. 1136, CA).

The problem is not that the court lacks powers to enforce its orders, but rather that its existing powers may be inappropriate in the circumstances of the particular case. For example, failure to comply with a contact order is punishable by imprisonment as a contempt of court, but the courts have been understandably reluctant to impose custodial sentences on the child's primary carer. Only if there has been a persistent failure to comply will a prison sentence be appropiate (see *e.g. Re S (Contact Dispute: Committal)* [2004] EWCA Civ 1790). And, as Butler-Sloss P. noted in *Re S (Contact: Promoting Relationship With Absent Parent)* [2004] EWCA Civ 18, such drastic enforcement measures bring their own problems for the future relationships of the parties:

> "It will hardly endear the father to the child who is already reluctant to see him to be told that the father is responsible for the mother going to prison." (para.28)

Similar problems are posed by the imposition of a fine:

> "Most mothers do not have enough money to pay a significant fine and this sanction is seldom used, particularly since she is the primary carer of the child": *Re S (Contact: Promoting Relationship With Absent Parent)* [2004] EWCA Civ 18, *per* Butler-Sloss P., at para.28.

In considering whether the residential parent should be imprisoned or fined, the interests of the child at the heart of the dispute are not the court's paramount consideration. By contrast, if other options—such as transferring residence to the other parent—are considered, the focus must be the best interests of the child and not the punishment of the recalcitrant parent. If both parents are equally capable of caring for the child, then the court may well decide that it is in the child's best interests to reside with the parent most likely to facilitate contact. In extreme cases it may even be found that the children are suffering harm as a result of their parent's opposition to contact: in *V v V (Contact: Implacable Hostility)* EWHC 1215 (Fam) it was held that the disruption that would be caused by the move was outweighed by the emotional harm that the children would suffer if they remained with their mother. But Bracewell J recognised that transferring residence to the other parent might not be an option:

> "the other parent may not have the facilities or capacity to care for the child full-time, and may not even know the child." (para.10)

Ultimately, the court may have to abandon attempts to ensure that contact actually takes place, not because of the lack of means to enforce the order but because it would not be in the best interests of the child to have contact with a parent from whom he or she is estranged or who has, through lapse of time, effectively become a stranger. As Butler-Sloss P. noted in *Re S (Contact: Promoting Relationship With Absent Parent)* [2004] EWCA Civ 18:

> "One aspect of proportionality which has to be weighed in the balance is the extent to which a court should go to force contact on an unwilling child and on the apprehensive primary carer. At this point the factor of proportionality becomes all-important since there is a limit beyond which the court should not strive to promote contact and the court has the overriding obligation to put the

welfare of the child at the forefront and above the rights of either parent."
(para.28)

It is clear that the courts do not lightly abandon attempts to enforce contact. As
Bracewell J. noted in *V v V (Contact: Implacable Hostility)* EWHC 1215 (Fam), giving
up "is the worst option of all and sometimes the only one available. This is the option
which gives rise to the public blaming the judges for refusing to deal with recalcitrant
parents. This option results in a perception fostered by the press that family courts are
failing in private law cases and that family courts are anti-father" (para.10).

(8) *Reforming the system*

12–033 In addition to the problems of hostile parents and reluctant children, the fact that
there are a number of problems with the current system is amply illustrated by *Re D
(Intractable Contact Dispute: Publicity)* [2004] EWHC 727 (Fam), a dispute that
involved 43 hearings conducted by 16 different judges over a period of almost five
years, at the end of which the "wholly deserving father left [the] court in tears" having
abandoned his case. There have been numerous calls for reform from the courts (see
in particular *V v V (Contact: Implacable Hostility)* [2004] EWHC 1215 (Fam) and *Re
D (Intractable Contact Dispute: Publicity)* [2004] EWHC 727 (Fam)), and various
options have been canvassed by the Government (see *e.g. Making Contact Work*
(2002), *Parental Separation: Children's Needs and Parents' Responsibilities* (2004) and
Parental Separation: Children's Needs and Parents' Responsibilities: Next Steps (2005)).
At the time of writing, Parliament was debating the Children and Adoption Bill 2005,
the relevant provisions of which can be broadly classified into three categories: those
aimed at re-education, those improving the support that will be offered by outside
agencies, and those promising more effective enforcement. Under the new system the
court will be able to require either parent "to take part in an activity that promotes
contact with the child concerned" (cl.1) by means of either a "contact activity
condition" attached to a contact order, or a "contact activity direction", which may be
made independently of an order. "Contact activities" are to take the form of classes,
counselling, or similar forms of guidance, and may, for example, aim to persuade
recalcitrant parents of the benefits of contact or to address violent behaviour. The role
of outside agencies is to be enhanced: officers from CAFCASS (the Children and
Family Court Advisory and Support Service) may be asked to monitor the parties'
compliance with the order and associated conditions or directions, and will be under
a duty to carry out a risk assessment if they suspect that a child is at risk of harm.
Changes are also proposed to the family assistance order (see further para.12–036
below). Finally, a new mode of enforcing contact by means of "an unpaid work
requirement" is to be introduced. The Bill is likely to become law later this year.
   The law, of course, has its limits. There is an increasing emphasis on parents making
their own arrangements (via Parenting Plans, mediation, and in-court conciliation),
although HM Inspectorate of Court Administration warned against the dangers of
such a policy in cases of domestic violence in its report *Domestic Violence, Safety and
Family Proceedings* (2005). What is really required, as the Government noted in the
Foreword to *Parental Separation: Children's Needs and Parents' Responsibilities: Next
Steps* (2005), is a change in parental attitudes:

"In time, it needs to become socially unacceptable for one parent to impede a
child's relationship with its other parent wherever it is safe and in the child's best

interests. Equally, it should be unacceptable that non-resident fathers absent themselves from their child's development and upbringing following separation."

But the reader should not be left with the impression that intractable contact disputes are common. In the vast majority of cases the parties agree on arrangements for contact without resorting to litigation. Of the minority—approximately 10 per cent—who do take the issue to court, only a very few become embroiled in long-running court battles (see L. Trinder *et al.*, *A Profile of Applicants and Respondents in Contact Cases in Essex* (2006)).

(9) How far can s.8 orders be used to control adult behaviour?

The above discussion has identified a number of occasions on which the court has held **12–034** that it is inappropriate to attempt to control adult behaviour through the use of s.8 orders (see *e.g. Croydon LBC v A* [1992] Fam. 169 and *Re D (Residence: Imposition of Conditions)* [1996] 2 F.L.R. 281). One particular issue that has arisen is whether it is possible to use such an order to require an abusive or violent parent to leave the family home. The courts have consistently held that this should be achieved under the appropriate statutory regime—*i.e.* the Family Law Act 1996—rather than by means of a s.8 order (*Re D (Prohibited Steps Order)* [1996] 2 F.L.R. 273; *Pearson v Franklin (Parental Home: Ouster)* [1994] 1 F.L.R. 246). This of course depends on the other adult being willing to take steps to exclude the violent partner (the order in *Re H (Prohibited Steps Order)* [1995] 1 F.L.R. 638, para.12–019 above, was only possible because the man had already been excluded from the family home). In some cases the problem may be not that the adult parties have separated but that they have not. In such cases, if the child is at risk it may be appropriate for the local authority to commence care proceedings (see Ch.13).

D: ANCILLARY ORDERS

There are a number of ancillary orders relating to children that the court may make **12–035** in family proceedings, either to assist it in making its decision, or to assist the family.

(1) The Family Assistance Order

Courts are not equipped to act directly as welfare agencies. But there is no reason why **12–036** they should not ensure that help from such agencies is available to those who appear before them. One such form of assistance is a "family assistance order" under s.16 of the 1989 Act, which requires that a CAFCASS officer or an officer of the local authority be made available to "advise, assist and (where appropriate) befriend" the child, the child's parent or guardian, or any other person with whom the child is living or in whose favour a contact order has been made. The objective is to enable short-term independent help to be provided to the family (*Re C (Family Assistance Order)* [1996] 1 F.L.R. 424 at 425, Johnson J.). However, a number of factors—some legal, some financial—have resulted in only limited use being made of such orders. First, the order can only be made if the circumstances are "exceptional", and orders can only be made for a period of up to six months (although they can be renewed). Secondly, assistance cannot be imposed upon the parties against their wishes: all the persons named in the order (except the child) must consent to its being made. Thirdly, while the consent of the local authority (upon whom the burden of providing the assistance will fall) is not required for the order to be made (see *e.g. Re E (family assistance order)* [1999] 3 F.L.R. 700, FD), the court cannot actually require it to carry out the order. This is illustrated by *Re C (Family Assistance Order)* [1996] 1 F.L.R. 424, Johnson J., where the local authority simply declined to carry out the order because of budgetary constraints. The judge held that in the circumstances there was nothing appropriate or sensible that he could do; and—as appears in a number of places in this book—it is clear that the Children Act deliberately allocates many decisions involving the expenditure of money to the local authority, whose decision is only open to challenge, if at all, in proceedings for judicial review.

The legal limitations on the making of a family assistance order are addressed by the Children and Adoption Bill 2005, which will remove the requirement that the circumstances be "exceptional", and will allow such orders to be made for a maximum of twelve months. It is also envisaged that the family assistance order will have a specific role to play in the context of contact, with a CAFCASS officer being directed to give "advice and assistance as regards establishing, improving and maintaining contact" and to report back to the court. The other problems identified above—the need for the parties' consent and the local authority's co-operation—remain.

(2) *Ordering a Welfare Report*

12–037   Civil litigation in England is usually conducted on the basis of the so-called adversarial system, in which the court listens to such evidence as the parties choose to put before it. By contrast, in Children Act cases the courts make frequent reference to their quasi-inquisitorial role. One example of this is their power to commission welfare reports from independent persons. Section 7(1) provides that a court considering any question with respect to a child under the Act may request that a report be made to the court "on such matters relating to the welfare of that child as are required to be dealt with in the report". Extensive use is made of this power: CAFCASS, which took over the task of providing reports in 2000, responded to 30,813 requests for reports in 2004–5 (CAFCASS, *Annual Report and Accounts 2004–5*).

The primary function of a reporter is to assist the court by providing the court with the factual information on which it can make a decision (*Scott v Scott* [1986] 2 F.L.R. 320). He or she has power to inspect the court file; and will usually interview all the parties, visit the parent's home, see the children and others involved, observe the children with their parents in their homes, and talk to doctors and teachers if that would be appropriate in the circumstances. This means that preparing a welfare report is a time-consuming occupation, which may conflict with the principle that delay is likely to prejudice the welfare of the child. The court must therefore decide, applying the criterion of what would best promote the child's welfare, whether the benefits of having a report outweigh the disadvantage of delay (see *Re H (Minors) (Welfare Report)* [1990] 2 F.L.R. 172, CA). If a report is provided, the court is not bound to follow the recommendations of the reporter, but it must give reasons for departing from such recommendations.

It should be noted that the number of welfare reports produced has remained fairly static despite the increase in litigation in recent years, and as noted above, the Government has suggested that the efforts of CAFCASS should be directed away from the writing of reports to in-court conciliation and monitoring compliance with contact orders. CAFCASS itself has taken a similar view (see *Every Day Matters: New*

Directions for CAFCASS (2005), para.34.2). The implications of this for the court's awareness of the wishes and feelings of the child are considered further below (see para.14–010).

(3) *Power to direct local authority investigation*

If matters arising in private law proceedings suggest that a care or supervision order **12–038** might be appropriate, the court may direct the local authority to undertake an investigation of the child's circumstances and to consider whether they should apply for a care or supervision order (or take other action with respect to the child). This course has been deemed appropriate in certain intractable contact disputes, on the basis that the resident parent is causing the children "emotional harm" (see *e.g. Re M (Intractable Contact Dispute: Interim Care Order)* [2003] EWHC 1024 (Fam)).

What if the local authority, having made their investigation, decides not to seek an order? Section 37(3) provides that the authority must inform the court of their reasons (and also state what other steps they propose to take in relation to assisting the child, etc.); but their decision is—perhaps subject to the possibility of judicial review—final:

> In *Nottingham CC v P* [1993] 2 F.L.R. 134, CA, both the trial judge and the Court of Appeal considered that a care order would be appropriate; but the local authority refused to make an application. As the President of the Family Division put it: "if a local authority doggedly resists taking the steps which are appropriate to the case of children at risk of suffering significant harm it appears that the court is powerless".

E: FAMILY PROCEEDINGS UNDER THE INHERENT JURISDICTION

Section 8(3) of the Children Act 1989 provides that "family proceedings" include any **12–039** proceedings under the "inherent jurisdiction of the High Court in relation to children".

(1) *Wardship and the inherent jurisdiction*

The origins of the court's "inherent jurisdiction" over children lies in the doctrine that **12–040** it was the Crown's prerogative as *parens patriae* (father of the nation) to have the care of those who could not look after themselves: the crown has a duty to protect its subjects and "particularly children who are the generations of the future" (*per* Lord Donaldson of Lymington M.R., *Re C (A Minor) (Wardship: Medical Treatment) (No.2)* [1990] Fam. 39 at 46). This jurisdiction was delegated to the Court of Chancery, and for many years was normally invoked by making the child a "ward of court". Once a child had been made a ward—which occurred as soon as an application was made—no important step in the life of the ward could be taken without leave of the court. Typically, therefore, the ward could not marry, be subjected to surgery or enter into long-term business associations without the court's approval.

In recent years it has come to be appreciated that wardship was the *result* of an exercise of the inherent jurisdiction and not the *ground* for the exercise of that jurisdiction. The court may therefore be asked to exercise its inherent jurisdiction to take decisions that are necessary for the protection and well-being of the child (for example, by authorising medical treatment) even if the child has not been made a ward of court. Such decisions are "one-offs": thus, for example, the fact that the court exercises its inherent jurisdiction to order medical treatment for a child does not mean that the permission of the court is required for other important steps in the child's life, unlike the position where the child is made a ward of court. As Wall L.J. noted in *Wyatt v Portsmouth NHS* [2005] EWCA Civ 1181:

> "In the overwhelming majority of cases in which the inherent jurisdiction of the court over children . . . is invoked, the "best interests" decision by the court determines the issue once and for all." (para.112)

Even in cases where this is not true—as in the long line of cases concerning the appropriate medical treatment of Charlotte Wyatt (see *Portsmouth NHS Trust v Wyatt* [2004] EWHC 2247 (Fam); *Wyatt v Portsmouth NHS Trust (No.3)* [2005] EWHC 693 (Fam))—the appropriate solution may be to deal with further issues as they arise under the inherent jurisdiction rather than by making the child a ward of court. Wall L.J. went on to eschew any on-going role for the court in medical cases:

> "it is, in our view, not the function of the court to oversee the treatment plan for a gravely ill child . . . . The court's function is to make a particular decision on a particular issue." (para.117)

A further important distinction between wardship and the inherent jurisdiction is that the former is only exercisable in relation to a child, while the latter may be invoked to protect vulnerable *adults*—for example those at risk of forced marriages (see *e.g. Re SK (Proposed Plaintiff)(An Adult by way of her Litigation Friend)* [2004] EWHC 3202 (Fam)) or those who are incapable of consenting to marriage (see *e.g. M v B, A and S (By the Official Solicitor)* [2005] EWHC 1681). This section will focus solely on the court's powers in relation to children, but the wider role of the inherent jurisdiction in relation to adults (see in particular *Re SA* [2005] EWHC 2942) should not be forgotten.

(2) *A residual role*

12–041 Wardship became an increasingly popular way of dealing with disputes over children during the second half of the twentieth century, in particular after jurisdiction was transferred to the Family Division in 1970: in 1991 there were nearly 5,000 applications to make children wards of court. The attractions of wardship were its flexibility—no grounds needed to be satisfied and the court had a wide range of powers at its disposal—and its immediacy. However, the popularity of wardship placed a burden on scarce judicial resources, and the Children Act 1989 imposed significant restrictions on the use of the inherent jurisdiction by local authorities. As a result, a local authority may no longer use the inherent jurisdiction to require a child to be placed in care (s.100(2)): this is now a matter that requires the specific statutory criteria set out in s.31 of the Act to be satisfied (see further Ch.13). In closely defined circumstances a local authority may still invoke the inherent jurisdiction for other purposes, but it must first obtain the leave of the court, and the court may only grant such leave if it is satisfied that the result which the authority wishes to achieve could not be achieved through the making of an order under the statutory code, *and* that there is reasonable cause to believe that if the court's inherent jurisdiction is not exercised the child is likely to suffer significant harm.

No specific restrictions were placed on applications by private individuals, but the courts have discouraged what they regard as unnecessary recourse to their inherent jurisdiction:

In *Re T (a minor) (child: representation)* [1994] Fam. 49, CA, Waite L.J. said that the "courts' undoubted discretion to allow wardship to go forward in a suitable case is subject to their clear duty, in loyalty to the scheme and purpose of the Children Act legislation, to permit recourse to wardship only when it becomes apparent to the judge in any particular case that the question which the court is determining . . . cannot be resolved under the statutory procedures in Pt II of the Act [which deals with 'private law' procedures] in a way that secures the best interests of the child; or where the minor's person is in a state of jeopardy from which he can only be protected by giving him the status of a ward of court, or where the court's functions need to be secured from the effects potentially injurious to the child, of external influences (intrusive publicity for example) and it is decided that conferring on the child the status of a ward will prove a more efficient deterrent" than the use of proceedings for contempt of court.

It appears that this judicial discouragement has been effective, and in the wake of the 1989 Act the number of applications dwindled to a few hundred each year. Statistics on the resort to the inherent jurisdiction are no longer available but it has been suggested that the numbers are "negligible" (*Hansard* (HC) vol.385 col.837W, May 16, 2002). Despite these constraints, the inherent jurisdiction does still have an important role to play in a number of contexts, and may be invoked for the following reasons:

(a) Immediacy

It is still the law (see s.41(2) of the Supreme Court Act 1981 as amended by Sch.13, **12–042** para.45(2) of the CA 1989) that a child becomes a ward on the issue of a summons making the application (unless he or she is already subject to a care order); and that thereafter no important step may be taken in the ward's life without leave of the court. It is not easy to achieve this result so speedily and effectively in any of the statutory procedures established by the Children Act 1989. If there is a danger that potentially irreversible damage might be done to a child's welfare (perhaps by taking a child out of the country, or by withdrawing medical treatment), the wardship jurisdiction may be favoured over other options. Thus:

In *Re M (Medical Treatment: Consent)* [1999] 2 F.L.R. 1097, FD, Johnson J. was telephoned at his home on a Friday evening and told that application was to be made to carry out a heart transplant on a teenager who refused to consent. The judge organised representation by solicitor and counsel, the patient was interviewed, representations made, and on Saturday morning the judge made his order.

(b) Flexible procedures

Re M (above) also illustrates the flexibility of wardship. Once the wardship court is **12–043** seised of the case it can continue to do whatever is appropriate as and when action is desirable, without it being necessary to make a fresh application for a particular specific issue or prohibited steps order. It can almost be said that the court becomes the child's legal parent:

In *Re K (Adoption and Wardship)* [1997] 2 F.L.R. 221, a child, found under a pile of corpses in Bosnia, was taken to an orphanage in Bosnia and eventually brought to this country by middle-class professionals who cared for her devotedly and made her one of their family, speaking only English and baptised a Christian. They applied to adopt her, but gave a misleading factual account of the circumstances. In a number of other respects the adoption proceedings were deeply flawed, not least because they failed to reveal that the child had relatives in Bosnia who were anxious and able to care for her. An adoption order was made; but when the true facts emerged it was set aside by the Court of Appeal. The child was made a ward of court. The President of the Family Division accepted expert evidence that to return the child to her family (now resident in Switzerland) would involve a high risk of injury and serious disturbance; and he concluded that her welfare required that she remain for the present time and for the foreseeable future in the care of the applicants under the authority of the court. It was however to be clearly understood that she was not the applicant's daughter, and active and effective steps were to be taken to make her acquainted with her relatives and to get to know her true family background and of her cultural and religious heritage as a Bosnian Muslim. To that end the applicants were required to supply three-monthly reports; and the case was to be relisted for review before the President.

Applications under the inherent jurisdiction are also used to deal with complex medical decisions (see *e.g. Practice Note—Official Solicitor: Sterilisation* [1996] 2 F.L.R. 111, and *Re A (Minors)(Conjoined Twins: Medical Treatment)* [2001] 1 F.L.R. 1).

(c) Extensive powers

12–044   No precise limit has ever been placed on the wardship jurisdiction; and it has been said that the wardship judge has theoretically limitless power to protect the ward from any interference with his or her welfare, direct or indirect (*Re K (Wards: Leave to Call as Witnesses)* [1988] 1 F.L.R. 435 at 442). As such proceedings are "family proceedings" for the purpose of the Children Act, the court has the power to make s.8 orders, but it can also grant injunctions. For this reason, the inherent jurisdiction has often been invoked in cases in which media publicity would damage the child's welfare. In recent years, however, the courts have been increasingly sensitive to the potential conflict between the best interests of the individual child and the public interest in freedom of expression protected by Art.10 of the European Convention, and in *Re S (Identification: Restrictions on Publication)* [2004] UKHL 47 Lord Steyn roundly declared that a new approach was appropriate:

"The House unanimously takes the view that since the Human Rights Act 1998 came into force in October 2000, the earlier case-law about the existence and scope of inherent jurisdiction need not be considered in this case or in similar cases. The foundation of the jurisdiction to restrain publicity in a case such as the present is now derived from convention rights under the European Convention." (para.23, and for the new approach to be adopted see para.1–024 above).

On the facts of that case, the public interest in the full reporting of the criminal trial of a mother accused of murder outweighed the distress that such reporting would cause to her child (and in a similar vein see *A Local Authority v PD and GC (By Her Guardian)* [2005] EWHC 1832 (Fam)). It was emphasised in the later case of *A Local Authority v W, L, W, T and R (By The Children's Guardian)* [2005] EWHC 1564 (Fam) that *Re S* had not been based on any preference in favour of the rights set out in Art.10, and that:

> "The exercise to be performed is one of parallel analysis in which the starting point is presumptive parity." (*per* Sir Mark Potter P, para.53)

The different result achieved in that case—prohibiting publicity about the identity of a mother who had pleaded guilty to a charge that she had knowingly infected the father of her child with HIV—was justified by the fact that the children might themselves be suspected of being infected with the HIV virus and their future placement might be prejudiced. It is clear that there remains some scope for invoking the inherent jurisdiction of the court to restrain publicity, particularly if the publicity relates directly to a child.

(d) Filling gaps in the statutory scheme

The theoretically unlimited power of the court to protect children has led on occasion **12–045** to the use of the inherent jurisdiction to deal with what are regarded as "lacunae" in the statutory provisions (see *e.g. Re C (Adoption: Freeing Order)* [1999] 1 F.L.R. 348, Wall J.). This course is not unproblematic. There would seem to be force in the argument (unsuccessfully advanced in *Re C*) that use of the inherent jurisdiction to compensate for the perceived shortcomings of a legislative code is equivalent to rewriting an Act of Parliament. The line between a perceived lacuna in the statutory scheme and a result that contravenes the statutory code enacted by Parliament may be a fine one: contrast, for example, the willingness of the court to invoke the inherent jurisdiction to achieve a result expressly prohibited by the legislation and relevant regulations in *Re W and X (Wardship: Relatives Rejected as Foster Carers)* [2003] EWHC 2206 (Fam) with the more cautious approach adopted in *W v J (Child: Variation of Financial Provision)* [2003] EWHC 2657 (Fam).

(3) *Limitations on the availability of inherent jurisdiction*

This leads on to an important limitation on the availability of the inherent jurisdiction. **12–046** It is a well-settled principle of administrative law that the inherent jurisdiction of the courts is not to be allowed to interfere with action properly taken under a comprehensive legislative code: *A v Liverpool CC* (1981) 2 F.L.R. 222, HL. This imposes restrictions on the use of the inherent jurisdiction not only where the issue in question is specifically dealt with by the Children Act 1989, but also where other statutory powers are exercisable. For example, the fact that a child is subject to immigration control does not prevent the court from making that child a ward of court, but, as Munby J. noted in *R (Anton) v Secretary of State for the Home Department; Re Anton* [2004] EWHC 2730/2731 (Admin/Fam), a judge of the Family Division "cannot in the exercise of his family jurisdiction grant an injunction to restrain the Secretary of State removing from the jurisdiction a child who is subject to immigration control—even if the child is a ward of court" (para.33). In such a case any remedies lie in administrative law.

On further limitation of note is that there is no jurisdiction in respect of an unborn child. In *Re F (in utero) (Wardship)* [1988] 2 F.L.R. 307, CA, a pregnant woman who had a history of severe mental disturbance disappeared shortly before the expected date of her child's birth. An application was made to ward the unborn child; and it was intended to ask the court to make orders to help trace the mother and to ensure that she lived in a suitable place until the birth. The Court of Appeal held that, for three reasons, the wardship jurisdiction was not available. First, a foetus has no right of action, and is incapable of being a party to an action. Secondly, the only practical consequence of warding the foetus would be to control the mother, and, in such a sensitive field, which affected the liberty of the subject, it was for Parliament (rather than the courts) to take any necessary action. Finally, conflicts of interest could arise between the foetus and the mother—for example, if a mother wanted her pregnancy to be terminated; and the wardship jurisdiction was not appropriate for the resolution of such conflicts since wardship was concerned to promote only one of those interests, the welfare of the child. Once again, the court was forced to bow to the difficulties of constraining adult actions in the interests of children.

F: INTERNATIONAL CHILD ABDUCTION

12–047 The abduction of a child by his or her parent can be seen as an extreme reaction to some of the problems discussed earlier in this chapter. The mode of dealing with the issue is very different from that adopted either under the Children Act 1989 or under the inherent jurisdiction. Child abduction is largely governed by an international convention—the 1983 Hague Convention on the Civil Aspects of International Child Abduction—the aim of which is to return abducted children to the country where they are habitually resident as speedily as possible. The welfare of the *individual* child is given little consideration: the Convention is premised on the assumptions that child abduction is harmful to children and should be discouraged, and that when it has occurred, it is in the best interests of children for questions about their future to be determined by the courts in the country where they are habitually resident. This difference in approach was noted in *Re W (Abduction: Domestic Violence)* [2004] EWCA Civ 1366:

> "The experience and the instinct of the trial judge is always to protect the child and to pursue the welfare of the child. That instinct and experience is sometimes challenged by his international obligation to apply strict boundaries in the determination of an application for summary return." (*per* Thorpe L.J., para.23)

While child abduction is governed by a separate code from the other issues considered in this chapter, there is inevitably some overlap. For example, if a child is at risk of abduction it may be advisable to seek a prohibited steps order explicitly prohibiting such a move, or to make the child a ward of court. Moreover, it is important to recognise the common problems at the root of the legal disputes: parents who are not allowed to remove the child from the jurisdiction by legal means may resort to abduction. It was initially expected that the Convention would be invoked to deal with cases where the child was kidnapped by the non-resident parent. However, research has shown that most "abductions" are by the mother of the child in question: one survey found that 70 per cent of abductions are by mothers (see N. Lowe and A. Perry, *International Child Abduction—The English Experience* (Nuffield, 1997)). In many of these cases the mother was returning to her home country after her relationship with the father had broken down. The incidence of domestic violence explains why many choose to resort to self-help rather than to invoke the assistance of the court. It is open to question whether it is in the best interests of children to be automatically returned in such situations.

There has been an explosion of case-law on this topic in recent years, and this section merely highlights the salient principles. This section will deal first with the rules that apply when the other country is also a signatory to the Hague Convention, then with the rules that apply when dealing with an abduction from a country that has not signed the Convention. (The discussion will focus on abductions from outside the UK: abductions from Scotland and Northern Ireland are governed by the Family Law Act 1986, which provides that orders relating to matters such as residence and contact—for a full list see s.1—made in any part of the UK can be enforced in any other part as if made there)

Since the whole point of multi-lateral Conventions is that each signatory adopts the same rules, it is reasonable to expect that a similar approach would be adopted in other signatory countries. It should however be noted that while the basic principles to be applied do not vary, individual countries may interpret them in different ways. What follows thus relates only to the approach taken when the English courts are considering whether a child should be returned to another country.

The 1983 Hague Convention on the Civil Aspects of International Child Abduction

As noted above, the basic principle of the Convention—which was implemented by the **12–048** Child Abduction and Custody Act 1985—is that the abducted child should be returned to the country of his or her habitual residence as soon as possible. Article 12 of the Convention provides that "the authority shall order the return of the child forthwith" if less than a year has elapsed since the abduction. The speed with which the English authorities return children to their country of habitual residence is in sharp contrast with the delays that are endemic in other parts of the family law system: the survey by Lowe and Perry found that returns were completed within an average of six-and-a-half weeks. During this period various measures will usually be put in place to prevent the onward abduction of the child (see *e.g. Re C (Abduction: Interim Directions: Accommodation by Local Authority)* [2003] EWHC 3065 (Fam)).

(1) When is the removal of a child wrongful?

The removal or retention of a child will be wrongful if "it is in breach of rights of **12–049** custody attributed to a person, an institution or any other body, either jointly or alone, under the law of the State in which the child was habitually resident immediately before the removal or retention" (see Art.3(a) of the Convention).

The terms used in this provision require some explanation. The scope of the Convention clearly depends on the meaning that is attached to "rights of custody". As Thorpe L.J. explained in *Hunter v Murrow (Abduction: Rights of Custody)* [2005] EWCA Civ 976, the concept is specific to the context:

> "in determining whether or not the father exercised rights of custody immediately prior to X's removal this court applies not English law but the English perception of the autonomous law of the Hague Convention." (para.29)

Thus a parent with parental responsibility has "rights of custody" for these purposes, even if the child is not living with that parent. In addition, the English courts have held that a father who does not have parental responsibility may still have "rights of custody" in certain circumstances, for example if he has become the child's primary carer:

> In *Re F (Abduction: Unmarried father: Sole Carer)* [2002] EWHC 2896, the parents were separated and the father cared for his three children, plus a fourth whose paternity was more doubtful. The mother then abducted the fourth child and took him to Australia to live with her and her new husband. Charles J. made an order that the removal of the child was wrongful, and Butler-Sloss P. refused to set aside this order, holding that the father had "inchoate rights of custody"—*i.e.* he had no formal rights but there was a reasonable prospect that his application for such rights would succeed. Even if the father was not related by blood to the child, as the child's primary carer for the past three years he would stand a good chance of obtaining a residence order. He thus possessed rights of custody within the meaning of the Hague Convention

However, the scope of this is not unlimited. Merely sharing the task of caring for a child with the mother does not confer rights of custody on the father (see *e.g. Re C (Child Abduction) (Unmarried Father: Rights of Custody)* [2002] EWHC 2219), even where the mother is not actually present (see *e.g. Re J (Abduction: Acquiring Custody Rights By Caring For Child)* [2005] 2 F.L.R. 791).

The removal of a child will also be wrongful if the *court* is deemed to have rights of custody, which will be the case if an application relating to the child has been made to prevent the removal of the child by one parent pending the court's determination of the other parent's rights (*Re H (Abduction: Rights of Custody)* [2000] 1 F.L.R. 374, HL). Again, this is subject to limitations:

> In *Re C (Child Abduction) (Unmarried Father: Rights of Custody)* [2002] EWHC 2219, Munby J. held that the mere issue of proceedings was insufficient (unless it took the form of an application for the child to be made a ward of court). A court would only be invested with rights of custody if the matter had actually come before a judge, even if this had only been for the purpose of giving directions.

By contrast, in an attempt to reduce the need for legal proceedings, it was held in *Re H (Child Abduction)(Unmarried Father: Rights of Custody)* [2003] EWHC 492 (Fam) that rights of custody could be established by letters exchanged between the parents' solicitors confirming that the mother had no plans to take the child out of the jurisdiction, since:

> "the very fact that the mother, through her solicitors, gave that confirmation and did not merely assert that it was none of his concern or business, shows a recognition by her and her solicitors at that time that this father, in all the history and circumstances of the case, already had some right, or at the least an inchoate right, to determine the child's place of residence." (*per* Holman J. at p.158)

While the desire to avoid litigation is laudable, the case does stretch the concept of "rights of custody" beyond its natural meaning. It should also be borne in mind that the more extensive the definition of "rights of custody", the more difficult it will be for a mother to flee with her child from a violent partner.

The second concept that needs further explanation is that of "habitual residence". This is largely a question of fact, based on physical presence in the country and intention to remain there (see *e.g. Al Habtoor v Fotheringham* [2001] EWCA Civ 186). As Thorpe L.J. noted in that case, it is possible to lose habitual residence in a single day when leaving a country to live elsewhere, but only obtain it in the second country "after a period that demonstrates that the residence has become habitual and is likely to continue to be habitual" (at 963).

(2) *Are there any circumstances in which the child will not be returned?*

The Convention does allow that there are certain situations in which a child need not **12–050** be returned to the country of habitual residence, which are as follows:

(a) Consent, acquiescence or non-exercise of rights of custody

The removal or retention of a child will not be wrongful if a person who has rights of **12–051** custody was "not actually exercising custody rights at the time of removal or retention or had consented to or subsequently acquiesced in the removal or retention." (Art.13(a)). It was confirmed in *Re P (Abduction: Consent)* [2004] EWCA Civ 971 that "consent does not fall to be considered for the purpose of establishing the wrongfulness of the removal or a breach of rights of custody pursuant to Art.3 but only for the purpose of invoking an exercise of the court's discretion pursuant to Art.13" (para.22). It may seem odd that the consent of the other parent is not relevant to the wrongfulness of the removal, but as the judge went on to explain:

> "If a child is removed in *prima facie* breach of a right of custody, then it makes better sense to require the removing parent to justify the removal and establish that the removal was with consent rather than require the claimant, asserting the wrongfulness of the removal, to prove that he or she did not consent." (para.33)

The same considerations presumably apply to the question of whether a parent is actually exercising rights of custody.

(b) Danger to the child

Article 13(b) of the Convention provides that a state is not bound to order the return **12–052** of a child if it is established that "there is a grave risk that his or her return would expose the child to physical or psychological harm or otherwise place the child in an intolerable situation." What counts as harm for these purposes? The courts have emphasised that a high threshold must be satisfied; how high is illustrated by the fact that in *Re S (a child)* [2002] EWCA Civ 908, the court ordered the return of a child who had been brought to the UK by her mother because of the escalating violence in Israel. Even violence or abuse within the family may not be sufficient to persuade the courts that the return of the child would place the child in an intolerable position, since the courts take into account the degree of protection that the country of habitual residence may be able to offer. Thus:

> In *Re H (children) (abduction)* [2003] EWCA Civ 355, the court ordered that the children be returned to Belgium despite the evidence of the father's violence, as

they would not be returning to live with him, and it should not be assumed that the Belgian authorities would be unwilling or unable to take action.

An order for the return of the child may effectively compel the return of the abductor if he or she is the child's primary carer. In *S v B (Abduction: Human Rights)* [2005] EWHC 733 (Fam), the mother argued that the effect on her psychological health if the order for return were to be made would render her incapable of providing adequate care for her child. The court noted that while it was appropriate to take such evidence into account, the evidence did not suggest that there was a grave risk of danger to the psychological health of the child. Sir Mark Potter P did however note that the fact that the intolerable situation was brought about by the parent's own actions did not mean that it could not be taken into account:

> "The principle that it would be wrong to allow the abducting parent to rely upon adverse conditions brought about by a situation which she has herself created by her own conduct is born of the proposition that it would drive a coach and horses through the 1985 Act if that were not accepted as the broad and instinctive approach to a defence raised under Art.13(b) of the Convention. However, it is not a principle articulated in the Convention or the Act and should not be applied to the effective exclusion of the very defence itself." (para.49)

Despite this concession, it remains the case that this defence is very difficult to establish. The contrast with the approach of the domestic courts where a parent is seeking leave to relocate (see para.12–028) is a stark one.

(c) The wishes of the child

12–053 If the child objects to being returned and "has attained an age and degree of maturity at which it is appropriate to take account of its views", the court may refuse to order the return of the child (see Art.13 of the Convention). The court found that the defence was established in *Re J (Abduction: Child's Objections to Return)* [2004] EWCA Civ 428, it being noted that the child in that case:

> "is of an age and degree of maturity at which it is appropriate to take account of his views. His views are clear and coherent. They are rationally based. They are not unduly influenced by the views of his mother." (para.89)

As such judicial pronouncements suggest, there is more to this defence than a simple expression of wishes by the child. Moreover, the court is not obliged to respect the wishes of the child even if satisfied of the child's maturity. As Thorpe L.J. noted in *Zaffino v Zaffino (Abduction: Children's Views)* [2005] EWCA Civ 1012:

> "in the exercise of the discretion arising under Art.13 . . . the court must balance the nature and strength of the child's objections against both the Convention considerations (obviously including comity and respect for the judicial processes in the requesting State) and general welfare considerations." (para.19)

In this case a 13-year-old girl was returned to Canada with her younger siblings, despite her objections. It is interesting to note that in this case the decision that the younger siblings should be returned influenced the decision that the same option was appropriate for the older children, in contrast to earlier cases in which the opposite occurred (see *e.g. Re T (Abduction: Child's Objection to Return)* [2000] 2 F.L.R. 192).

(d) The passage of time

If proceedings were commenced more than a year after the child was abducted, the **12–054** general rule that the child should be returned still applies, "unless it is demonstrated that the child is now settled in its new environment" (see Art.12 of the Convention). Even once it has been shown that the child is settled in its new environment, the court retains a discretion to return the child: *Cannon v Cannon* [2004] EWCA Civ 1330. In that case, Thorpe L.J. stressed that it would be more difficult to establish that the child was settled where the delay in proceedings was attributable to the fact that the child had been concealed from the applicant:

> "[i]n cases of concealment and subterfuge the burden of demonstrating the necessary elements of emotional and psychological settlement is much increased." (para.61)

Despite this high threshold, the return of the child was refused when the case was reheard, although the judge did stress that this was an exceptional case: *Re C (Abduction: Settlement)(No.2)* [2005] 1 F.L.R. 938.

Non-Convention countries

The above rules do not apply where the child has been abducted from a non- **12–055** Convention country: as Baroness Hale stated in *Re J (Child Returned Abroad: Convention Rights)* [2005] UKHL 40:

> "[t]here is no warrant, either in statute or in authority, for the principles of the Hague Convention to be extended to countries which are not parties to it." (para.22).

Instead, the court will decide what it is in the best interests of the child. It may be decided that it is in fact in the best interests of the child to be returned to the home country, taking into account the child's degree of connection with each country, the length of time he has spent in each country, the effect of the decision on the primary carer and the legal system of the other country. There is, however, no presumption that return will be in the child's best interests, as Baroness Hale went on to emphasise:

> "The most one can say, in my view, is that the judge may find it convenient to start from the proposition that it is likely to be better for a child to return to his home country for any disputes about his future to be decided there. A case against his doing so has to be made." (para.32)

G: Conclusion

While there is a proliferation of case-law on s.8 orders and child abduction, it should **12–056** be remembered that only a minority of separating parents resort to the law, and fewer still resort to the drastic measure of abduction. This is in line with the ethos of the Children Act 1989 that parents should have responsibility for determining issues relating to their children's upbringing and that the courts should only make an order where it is necessary.

Yet the absence of litigation should not be equated with the absence of conflict. If parents agree between themselves, the solution adopted might not be what is best for the child but might rather reflect the power balance between the parents. Similarly, conciliation may result in an agreed solution, but little real co-operation. One recent study of different types of conciliation services noted that:

"Perhaps the most pressing concern, however, is how little impact the conciliation session and the adoption of new contact arrangements had on parental relationship quality, shared decision-making and contact problems. It is these issues, rather than the mere quantity of contact, that are most likely to impact on children's adjustment." (L. Trinder *et al.*, *Making contact happen or making contact work: The process and outcomes of in-court conciliation* (DCA, 2006), p.86).

It remains to be seen whether the solutions proposed in the Children and Adoption Bill 2005 manage to address these wider issues.

The focus now shifts from parents disputing between themselves to disputes between the child's carers and the state. The next chapter accordingly considers the circumstances in which the state may intervene more directly in the child's life.

Chapter 13

COURT ORDERS DEALING WITH CHILDREN'S UPBRINGING: THE STATE'S ROLE

A: INTRODUCTION—STATE INTERVENTION: THE HISTORICAL BACKGROUND

The relationship between the State and the family has been considered at various **13–001** stages in this book. The State's role in the upbringing of children can, for example, be seen in its definition of parenthood, and in the concepts of welfare applied by the courts in determining disputes between family members. In such cases the State's influence is indirect, but in some situations the State has a more direct role to play—for example in providing support for the family or taking over responsibility for family members, sometimes even against the wishes of the family. This chapter focuses on this direct role, and the fundamental issues that it raises about the basis of State intervention and the importance attached to the interests of different members of the family.

Support for the family takes a number of different forms. It can be seen in the financial support that is provided through the benefits and tax systems (see, *e.g.* Ch.7), in the provision of housing, and in the health and education services. The Children Act 1989 contains provisions dealing with family centres and day care services such as nurseries, play-groups, child-minding, out-of-school clubs and holiday schemes. The government has emphasised the importance of "high quality universal services" (DfES, *Every Child Matters* (2004), para.3.5), and has identified a number of ways in which the well-being of children is to be promoted.

Important though such issues are, this chapter will focus on a rather different kind of support. For years the community's duties to needy children were largely a matter for the Poor Law, but in the twentieth century it gradually came to be appreciated that more far-reaching measures were required. In 1948, as part of the creation of the modern welfare state after the Second World War, the Children Act 1948 imposed a general duty on local authorities to provide care for children deprived of a normal home life. The focus of the 1948 Act was on supporting children within their families. Yet supporting individual members of the family may necessitate their removal from their family. In what circumstances should the State be able to intervene against the wishes of the adult family members? Provisions allowing community intervention were in existence even before the 1948 Act, but there have been many shifts of opinion as to the balance to be struck between protecting the child on the one hand, and preserving the right of parents to bring up children as they wish without interference from social workers or other agents of the state on the other hand. The difficulty of finding the right balance is exacerbated by the fact that both intervention and non-intervention may lead to disaster. On the one hand, in Cleveland in 1987 a large number of children were removed from their homes by the local authority because of suspicions of sexual abuse. The method used to diagnose such abuse was controversial and was later discredited. The crisis created pressure for reform, and the subsequent inquiry, chaired by Mrs Justice Butler-Sloss (*Report of the Enquiry into Child Abuse in Cleveland 1987*, 1988, Cm 412), was one of the influences on the public law provisions of the Children Act 1989. On the other hand, there is a long list of children who have died at the hands of their relatives where the local authority failed to take adequate (or sometimes any) protective measures. The report into the murder of Victoria Climbié (by her great-aunt and the latter's boyfriend) detailed the inaction of social workers, police and doctors:

> "Victoria was known to no less than [three] housing authorities, four social services departments, two child protection teams of the Metropolitan Police Service, a specialist centre managed by the NSPCC, and she was admitted to two different hospitals because of suspected deliberate harm ... The extent of the failure to protect Victoria was lamentable. Tragically, it required no more than basic good practice being put into operation." (*The Victoria Climbié inquiry: Report of an Inquiry by Lord Laming* (2003), para.1.16)

As this extract suggests, the powers to protect Victoria existed, but were not put into implementation. Subsequent measures have focused on promoting co-operation between different agencies. Under the Children Act 2004, for example, each local authority must establish a Local Safeguarding Children Board, which, as the latest government guidance, *Working Together to Safeguard Children* (2006), explains, is "the key statutory mechanism for agreeing how the relevant organisation in each local area will co-operate to safeguard and promote the welfare of children in that locality, and for ensuring the effectiveness of what they do" (para.3.1).

There are clear parallels between the issue of child protection, and that of domestic violence, which was discussed in Chapter 6. In some cases there will be a direct link, with violence being directed against both an adult partner and the children. Even if the child is not a direct victim of the violence, witnessing domestic violence may itself be harmful. Both domestic violence and child protection raise questions about the appropriate level of state intervention. In particular, both raise questions as to the relationship between the criminal law and protective measures. Discussion of the offences that may be committed by the more extreme forms of bad parenting is outside the scope of this chapter, which is concerned solely with civil proceedings designed to protect the child, but three points should be noted for present purposes. First, the commission of a criminal offence is not a necessary precondition for state intervention: protection is afforded in a far wider range of circumstances. Secondly, where a parent's actions are the subject matter of a prosecution, it should be borne in mind that the criminal law requires a charge to be proved beyond reasonable doubt, rather than simply on the balance of probabilities. Being acquitted of a criminal charge does not necessarily mean that the accused did not commit the actions in question or that he or she will not be found to have done so in civil proceedings. Thirdly, it should be borne in mind that children may be "villains" as well as "victims"—the necessity for state intervention may arise because a child is beyond the control of his or her parents.

Once the state has intervened to protect a child, what should happen next? There have been shifts in policy regarding the measures that should be taken once a child has been removed from the family unit. Should the authorities work towards the rehabilitation of the child with the family or find a substitute family? The current policy of promoting adoption is discussed in more detail in Ch.15, along with the other means of providing long-term substitute care.

A further issue to be considered is the way that responsibility is shared between different State agencies. Should the local authority be able to decide for itself when a child should be taken into care, or must the sanction of the court be given? How far can the courts control the way in which local authorities exercise their powers, and in what circumstances can local authorities be called to account for their actions? The approach of the Children Act 1989 is that the court must decide whether a care order is appropriate, but a local authority should have responsibility for a child once a care order had been made.

The Children Act 1989

The reader will have seen in the earlier chapters of this book how the Children Act **13–002** 1989 rationalised and codified the private law relating to children. The Act has also had a revolutionary impact on the public law. Previously, the legislation governing the relationship between the child, the family and the state was complex, confused and sometimes inconsistent, and could be circumvented by making the child a ward of court. The Children Act provided a more consistent approach, preventing the courts from exercising their inherent jurisdiction to require a child to be placed in the care of the local authority (see para.12–041, above), and providing for greater integration between public and private law proceedings. The Act codified and reformed the law governing the powers and duties of local authorities in relation to the provision of support for children and families. It also made sweeping changes in the law governing the circumstances in which a local authority might intervene compulsorily in the upbringing of a child, and in the legal position of children looked after by local authorities. As in private law proceedings, the non-intervention principle emphasises that an order should only be made where this would be better than making no order at all. The Act envisaged a partnership—between the State and the parents, between the local authorities and the courts, and between the different agencies responsible for child protection. With regard to the partnership between the State and parents, even where the welfare of the child cannot be secured by voluntary agreement with the parents, the Act emphasises that parents should be included in the decision-making process. How this operates in practice is considered below.

The Children Act 1989 is a remarkable legislative achievement, and it is impossible for the lawyer not to admire the technical skill of its construction. But the Act left a number of important issues—particularly about the circumstances in which compulsory state intervention is justified—to be resolved by judicial decision; and there is no shortage of case law (including decisions of the House of Lords) on the interpretation of some of the Act's provisions. Secondly, it is important not to exaggerate the contribution that the law can make to child care. The very process of state intervention may harm the families involved. And a number of inquiries—notably the Utting Report into the safeguards protecting children living away from home (*People Like Us*, 1997) and the Waterhouse Report into sexual abuse in Welsh Children's Homes (*Lost in Care*, 2000)—have demonstrated only too vividly the failings of the public care service. As the Secretary of State for Health put it in giving the Government's response to *People Like Us*, the Report "painted a woeful tale of failure. Many children who had been "taken into care" to protect and help them had not been protected and helped. Instead some had suffered abuse at the hands of those who were meant to help them. Many more had been let down, never given the attention they needed, shifted from place to place, school to school and then turned out when they reached 16 . . . ".

The approach of this chapter

13–003 This chapter looks briefly at the general duties of a local authority to provide services for children in need (Part B), and then examines in more detail the circumstances in which the state may intervene to protect children (Part C). Part D goes on to consider the situation of those children looked after by local authorities (where do they live, what duties does the local authority owe to them, and what remedies are there if the care plan is not implemented?). The rather different issue of the "problem child" is discussed in Part E, which focuses on the way in which provisions to protect children intersect with laws designed to deal with children who have committed offences or are otherwise problematic. Finally, Part F examines the remedies available where a local authority has failed.

B: LOCAL AUTHORITIES' POWERS AND DUTIES TO PROVIDE SERVICES FOR CHILDREN

13–004 The Children Act 1989 drew together local authority functions in respect of children, and created a significant range of new duties. Part III of the Act imposes a general duty to safeguard and promote the welfare of children in the authority's area who are "in need". The main provisions of Part III are as follows:

(1) *Services for children "in need"*

13–005 Every local authority has a general duty to provide a range and level of services appropriate to the needs of children in their area so as to safeguard and promote the welfare of such children; and, so far as is consistent with that duty, to promote their upbringing by their families (s.17(1)).

The definition of "in need" is clearly important. The Act adopts a wide definition—a child is in need if he is disabled, or if his "health and development" is likely to be affected unless the local authority provides services (s.17(10)). What this means in practice is determined by the individual local authority. Research has shown that many local authorities adopt a narrow definition—often conflating "in need" with "at risk"—out of concern that they would not have the resources to cope with the demand if services were offered to a broader range of children in need (*The Children Act Now* (2001)). Yet even if a child is assessed as being in need, the local authority has no enforceable duty to provide a child with the services needed, as confirmed by a 3–2 majority of the House of Lords in *R (G) v Barnet London Borough Council; R (W) v Lambeth London Borough Council; R (A) v Lambeth London Borough Council* [2003] UKHL 57. As Lord Hope of Craighead noted, "[a] child in need within the meaning of s.17(10) is eligible for the provision of those services, but he has no absolute right to them" (para.85). Section 17 thus only imposes what is sometimes termed a "target" duty rather than one that is mandatory.

The requirement that local authorities should promote children's upbringing by their families (s.17(1)(b)) reflects the belief that this is generally in the best interests of children. Local authorities have statutory duties to make appropriate provision for services (ranging from advice, through home help, to travel and holiday facilities or assistance) to be available for children in need while they are living with their families (Sch.2, para.8). Support may be provided by a variety of means, including payments and vouchers (ss.17(6), 17A and 17B). In addition, s.17(6)—as amended by the Adoption and Children Act 2002—specifically provides that the local authority may provide accommodation for a child in need, and, indeed, for the child's family "if it is provided with a view to safeguarding or promoting the child's welfare" (s.17(3). Once again, however, a distinction must be drawn between what the local authority is empowered to do and what it is obliged to do. The conjoined appeals in *R (G) v Barnet London Borough Council; R (W) v Lambeth London Borough Council; R (A) v Lambeth London Borough Council* [2003] UKHL 57 all involved issues relating to accommodation. The House of Lords held—again, by a 3–2 majority—that the local authority was not under a duty to provide accommodation for the family of a child in need. It stressed that the provision of housing was a matter for the local housing authority, and was governed by its own statutory code. Thus, in the words of Lord Scott of Foscoe:

> "the local authority is entitled . . . to adopt a general policy under which it is made clear that it will make accommodation available to the children of the family in order to prevent the children becoming homeless, but will not permit the parents to use the children as stepping stones by means of which to obtain a greater priority to be rehoused than that to which they would otherwise be entitled." (para.141)

The adoption of such a policy may be encouraged by the pragmatic calculation that, faced with the prospect of their children being provided with accommodation away from the family, parents will make extra efforts to find accommodation for the family as a whole.

Despite the difficulties in enforcing a local authority's general duties under s.17, it should be borne in mind that the section plays an important preventive role in the field of child protection. It has been noted that the expectation of Parliament in passing the Children Act 1989 "was that local authorities would . . . take reasonable steps to reduce the need to bring proceedings for care or supervision orders" (*per* Hale J., in *Oxfordshire CC v L (Care or Supervision Order)* [1998] 1 F.L.R. 70 at 74). A local authority seeking a care order should be asked whether the child's welfare could not better be promoted by support furnished under the Act than by invoking its powers of compulsory intervention (see specifically Sch.2, para.7). Since taking children into care is an expensive option, there may be financial advantages to providing services to children in their families. It is clear that a high proportion of children defined as being "in need" are so defined because of family problems: information from a sample week in February 2005 found that 37 per cent of the children on the database were in need because of abuse or neglect, with a further 13 per cent suffering from family dysfunction (DfES, *Children in Need* (2006), table 5).

(2) *Accommodation*

13–006 In addition to their powers to provide accommodation under s.17, local authorities have a *duty* to provide accommodation for children in need in specified circumstances under s.20. The duty arises in relation to children who require accommodation as a result of their being abandoned, or there being no person who has parental responsibility, or as a result of the person who has been caring for the child being prevented from providing the child with suitable accommodation or care (s.20(1)). In addition, there is a duty to provide accommodation for children in need who have attained the age of 16 "and whose welfare the authority consider is likely to be seriously prejudiced if they do not provide him with accommodation" (s.20(3)). It is clear that in each of these cases the duty is to provide accommodation for the child, not for the child's family.

Even if the child's family is able to provide accommodation, the local authority has a *discretionary power* to provide accommodation for the child if to do so would safeguard or promote the child's welfare (s.20(4)). This does not mean that a local authority can simply remove a child against the wishes of its parents on the ground that this course will promote the child's welfare: the provision of accommodation under s.20 depends on the co-operation of the parents or other persons with parental responsibility. The local authority may not provide accommodation against the wishes of a person with parental responsibility, as long as the latter is willing and able to provide the child with, or arrange, accommodation. Moreover, persons with parental responsibility retain the right to remove a child from accommodation, without prior notice. This power of parental veto does not apply if the child is 16 or over (so a child of this age can refuse to return to the parental home); nor if a special guardian, or any person in whose favour a residence order has been made, agrees to the child being accommodated.

The respective powers of parents and local authorities were considered in *R v Tameside MBC Ex. p J* [2000] 1 F.L.R. 942, QBD:

> The parents had agreed to the local authority providing accommodation for their disabled daughter, as they could no longer cope with her. After three years the local authority suggested that she be transferred to foster parents. The parents opposed this, and sought judicial review of the decision. It was held that the local authority did not have the power to place the child with foster parents against her parents' wishes. Although it had "mundane day-to-day powers of management . . . a move of the kind envisaged in this case goes much further and trespasses into the kind of decision-making that is ultimately exercised by those with parental responsibility" (*per* Scott Baker J. at 948). At the same time, the parents were not entitled to dictate where the authority *should* accommodate their daughter. The local authority was entitled to present the parents with a choice between looking after her themselves or agreeing to the local authority's plans, and retained the ultimate sanction of applying for a care order.

Such factors should be borne in mind in evaluating the balance of power between parents and local authorities. While the provision of accommodation under s.20 is termed "voluntary" accommodation, research has demonstrated that in fact parents often believe that they must accept the provision of accommodation for their child if an application for a care order is to be avoided. Hunt and McLeod have described how some parents in this situation feel a pervasive sense of powerlessness and agree to "voluntary" care in the hope that this would "get Social Services off our backs" and avert the loss of their children (*Statutory Intervention in Child Protection*, 1998). Nevertheless, the distinction in law between the provision of services to those who are willing to accept them and subjecting families to compulsory state intervention is of enormous conceptual importance.

C: PROTECTIVE MEASURES

The Conservative Government responsible for the Children Act 1989 took a deliberate **13–007** decision to reject the notion that state intervention could be justified simply on the basis that the child's welfare so required. In its view, there was a crucial distinction between the criteria upon which the court could resolve disputes between members of a family (where a broad discretion guided by the principle of the child's best interests would be appropriate and defensible) and cases in which state intervention could be justified. As the then Lord Chancellor, Lord Mackay of Clashfern, explained:

> "The integrity and independence of the family is the basic building block of a free and democratic society and the need to defend it should be clearly perceivable in the law . . . to provide otherwise would make it lawful for children to be removed from their families simply on the basis that a court considered that the state could do better for the child than his family. The threat to the poor and to minority groups, whose views of what is good for a child may not coincide closely with that of the majority, is all too apparent . . . " (1989) 139 N.L.J. 505 at 507 (and see also the citations from Lord Mackay's parliamentary speeches in the opinion of Lord Nicholls, *Lancashire CC v A* [2000] 2 A.C. 147, HL).

Thus, under the 1989 Act, state intervention is only permitted if there is evidence that the child is being harmed, or is likely to suffer harm, within the family. This is emphasised in *Working Together to Safeguard Children* (2006):

> "Only in exceptional cases should there be compulsory intervention in family life: for example where this is necessary to safeguard a child from significant harm. Such intervention should—provided this is consistent with the safety and welfare of the child– support families in making their own plans for the welfare and protection of their children." (para.1.5)

This section first sets out the range of available protective orders. It then discusses each in the context of the process as a whole, beginning with the powers available in case of an emergency, then going on to look at the way in which the local authority will obtain information about the child, and the nature of care proceedings. It goes on to examine the conditions—usually termed the "threshold criteria"—that have to be satisfied before the court has power to make a care or supervision order, and considers how the court decides whether or not to make an order.

The range of protective orders

13–008 Four different protective orders are available under the Children Act 1989: the child assessment order, the emergency protection order, the supervision order and the care order. In addition, the last two may be made on an interim basis. The justification for this proliferation of orders is that each performs a distinct function—as signalled by the names of each order. However streamlined the procedure for dealing with applications for care orders, it is self-evident that there will be cases in which emergency action needs to be taken before the requisite full judicial hearing. A child cannot, for example, be left with parents who are starving him or her, and care must be given to a child whose parent has been arrested and detained in respect of a criminal offence. Moreover, there may be cases in which the parents refuse to allow the child to be examined, even though there is cause for concern about the child's welfare. Thus the child assessment order enables an assessment of the child to be carried out to ascertain whether further action needs to be taken, while the emergency protection order mandates swift and short-term protection. Interim care and supervision orders may be made for a period of up to eight weeks (and extended as necessary). A supervision order is a less intrusive order than a care order, since it simply places the child under the supervision of a designated local authority (s.31(1)) whose duty it is to "advise assist and befriend" the child. The child will continue to live at home unless the supervisor directs otherwise, while under a care order the child is taken into the care of the local authority.

Behind that brief outline lies a series of complex rules as to the circumstances in which the court may make each order. First, there has to be an application for an order. The integrated approach of the Children Act is reflected in the fact that if there are *private* family proceedings before the court, the local authority may intervene to seek a care or supervision order. Alternatively, the court can direct the local authority to make an investigation of the child's circumstances and to consider whether to apply for a care or supervision order, or to take other action (s.37). The general philosophy of the Act, however, is that the decision is one for the local authority. If the authority concludes that it does not wish to seek a care or supervision order, the court cannot require the authority to seek such an order, and it has no power to make such an order of its own motion, however clear it may be that the necessary conditions are satisfied and that the making of an order is required to protect the child:

> In *Nottingham County Council v P* [1994] Fam. 18, CA, a man had persistently sexually abused his daughter; and the judge considered that her two younger sisters were at serious risk of abuse. All the individuals concerned were prepared to accept a supervision order, but the local authority refused to make the necessary application. The President of the Family Division expressed "deep concern" at the court's inability to direct the local authority to take the steps necessary to protect the children; but pointed out that "if a local authority doggedly resists taking the steps which are appropriate to the case of children at risk of suffering significant harm . . . the court is powerless . . . "

Moreover, in contrast to the position under the private law, the ability of an individual to instigate protective measures is severely constrained. While any person can apply for an emergency protection order—reflecting the fact that there may be circumstances in which action needs to be taken speedily—applications for the other three orders may only be made by a local authority or an "authorized person"—and at present the only authorised person is the NSPCC.

There are certain other general constraints on the court's powers. The court cannot make any of the above orders if the child has reached the age of 17 (or is aged 16 and has married). In addition, certain criteria—discussed in detail below—have to be satisfied in order for the court to have the power to make any of the above orders. Finally, while an order can only be made if the relevant criteria are satisfied, the fact that the court *can* make an order does not necessarily mean that it *should*. The court must go on to consider whether the making of an order would promote the child's welfare and would be better for the child than making no order at all (s.1(3) and (5)).

Emergency powers

Two different sets of powers are available in cases of emergencies. In addition to the emergency protection order noted above, it is possible for the police to take action to protect children.

13–009

(1) *Police protection*

Section 46(1) of the Children Act provides that a constable may remove (or prevent the removal of) a child if he has "reasonable cause to believe that the child would otherwise be likely to suffer significant harm": Significantly, no court order is necessary, so whether or not this condition is satisfied is a matter for the individual officer. In *Langley v Liverpool City Council* [2005] EWCA Civ 1173 it was held that this discretion is subject to certain constraints if an emergency protection order has already been made in relation to the child. In such a situation, although it is possible for a police officer to exercise his powers under s.46, he should not do so if he knows that an emergency protection order is in force, unless there are compelling reasons to do so. As Dyson L.J. noted:

13–010

> "the statutory scheme clearly accords primacy to s.44. Removal under s.44 is sanctioned by the court and it involves a more elaborate, sophisticated and complete process than removal under s.46." (para.38)

Working Together to Safeguard Children (2006) endorses the primacy of the emergency protection order, advising that police powers "should only be used in exceptional circumstances where there is insufficient time to seek an Emergency Protection Order or for reasons relating to the immediate safety of the child" (para.5.51).

Research has shown that "police protection is an unplanned response to a child protection crisis that is notified to the police or discovered by officers undertaking ordinary policing duties" and that it is used in relation to over 6,000 children each year (see J. Masson, "Police protection—protecting whom?" [2002] JSWFL 157). The child cannot be kept in police protection for more than 72 hours, but the police may themselves apply for an emergency protection order.

(2) *The emergency protection order*

Protection is maximised by the fact that anyone can apply for an emergency protection order, although the conditions for such orders vary according to the status of the applicant. Local authorities and other authorised persons must be able to show that

13–011

there is reasonable cause to believe that the child is suffering or likely to suffer significant harm, that their enquiries in respect of the child are being frustrated because access to the child has been refused and the authority "has reasonable cause to believe that access to the child is required as a matter of urgency" (s.44(1)(b) and (c)). In other cases—for example where the applicant is a concerned neighbour—it must be shown that there is reasonable cause to believe that the child is likely to suffer significant harm if the child is not moved (or if the child does not remain where he or she is).

While it is possible for an application to be made without notice, it was stressed in *X Council v B (Emergency Protection Order)* [2004] EWHC 2015 (Fam) that this should not be done as a matter of course:

> "An *ex parte* application will normally be appropriate only if the case is genuinely one of emergency or other great urgency—and even then it should normally be possible to give some kind of albeit informal notice to the parents—or if there are compelling reasons to believe that the child's welfare will be compromised if the parents are alerted to what is going on." (*per* Munby J. at para.57)

The judge also emphasised how important it was:

> "that both the local authority and the justices in the [family proceedings court] approach every application for an EPO with an anxious awareness of the extreme gravity of the relief being sought and a scrupulous regard for the European Convention rights of both the child and the parents." (para.41)

An emergency protection order requires any person who is in a position to do so to produce the child, and authorises the applicant to remove the child, or to prevent the child's removal from a hospital or other place in which the child was being accommodated (s.44(4)(c)). While the order is in force, the applicant has parental responsibility for the child, but the Act imposes severe limits on the exercise of that responsibility and the applicant may only take action reasonably required to safeguard or promote the welfare of the child (s.44(5)). Moreover, the court may give directions about who is to be allowed contact with the child, and about medical examination or other assessment procedures (s.44(6)). A child of sufficient understanding may refuse to undergo such procedures.

Sometimes an order is sought because of suspicions that the child is being abused by a parent or step-parent. In such cases, the best form of protection would be to exclude the person in question from the family home until the issue could be fully explored. The courts found difficulty in making orders under the Children Act which would have this effect, and the Act was accordingly amended by Sch.6 of the Family Law Act 1996 (inserting new ss.38A, 38B, 44A and 44B into the 1989 Act). The court has the power to include an "exclusion requirement" in an emergency protection (or interim care) order if it has reasonable cause to believe that excluding a particular person will remove the risk of harm to the child. The person concerned may be required to leave the house and not to re-enter it during the duration of the order, and may be excluded from a defined area in which the house is situated. A power of arrest (see para.6–016, above) may be attached to such orders. Obviously such an order cannot be made unless there is another adult in the household capable of caring for the child (s.44A(2)(b)(i)), and that person must consent to the exclusion of the other before an order can be made. Alternatively, the court may accept undertakings instead of imposing an exclusion requirement (s.44B).

An emergency protection order is not to continue beyond eight days (although the court may order one extension of no more than seven days under s.45(5)). While application may be made to discharge the order after 72 hours, there is no appeal against a decision to grant or refuse an emergency protection order (s.45(10)). The lack of an appeal mechanism has been the subject of some criticism, and in *X Council v B (Emergency Protection Order)* [2004] EWHC 2015 (Fam) Munby J. suggested that judicial review might be available "to correct error or injustice." (para.40). Moreover, the fact that the order *can* be made for eight days does not mean that an order always should be made for this period: Munby J. went on to emphasize that the order should be made for the shortest possible period and a local authority is under a duty "to keep the case under review day by day so as to ensure that parent and child are separated for no longer than is necessary to secure the child's safety" (para.49). The shortness of the periods involved reflects the fact that the order is intended to deal only with emergencies: longer-term protection should be secured by other means, which will now be considered.

Should an application for a care or supervision order be made?

The decision of whether or not to seek compulsory intervention can be a difficult one; **13–012** and the Department of Health's original *Guidance* (1991) stated that "applications for a care or supervision order should be part of a carefully planned process" (vol.1, para.3.2). This is because (as Lord Clyde put it in *Lancashire CC v B* [2000] 2 A.C. 147, HL), "very considerable harm may be done by an intervention, however well intentioned . . . [t]he making of an application is a step not lightly to be embarked upon. The stress which care proceedings may well impose on the parents may even itself be damaging to the child". Although there may be cases where starting care proceedings is a "matter of obvious necessity", many care proceedings "may be something not to be embarked upon without careful deliberation and a professional objectivity".

Some idea of the scale of the task faced by local authorities may be obtained from the fact that there were 552,000 referrals to social services departments in the year ending March 31, 2005. Of these, 290,300 led to an initial assessment being carried out in order to gauge what the needs of the child might be and whether any further action was required. In deciding whether intervention might be necessary, the key question for the local authority is whether the child is suffering, or likely to suffer, significant harm. If the local authority has reasonable cause to *suspect* that this is the case, it has a duty to make inquiries under s.47 of the 1989 Act, and an estimated 68,500 children were the subject of s.47 inquiries in the year up to March 2005.

The Children Act 2004 places increased emphasis on the wishes of the child in such cases, stating that the local authority "shall, so far is reasonably practicable and consistent with the child's welfare—(a) ascertain the child's wishes and feelings regarding the action to be taken with respect to him; and (b) give due consideration (having regard to his age and understanding) to such wishes and feelings of the child as they have been able to ascertain" (s.47(5A) of the 1989 Act, as inserted by the Children Act 2004). Similarly, *Working Together to Safeguard Children* (2006) advises that s.47 inquiries "should always involve separate interviews with the child who is the subject of concern and—in the great majority of cases—interviews with parents and/or

caregivers, and observation of the interactions between parent and child(ren)"
(para.5.62).

If the parents refuse to co-operate, then the local authority may seek an emergency
protection order (see para.13–011 above) or child assessment order to enable it to
carry out its inquiries. The child assessment order was intended to provide for cases in
which there is reasonable concern about the child but insufficient grounds to obtain an
emergency protection order or care order (see *An Introduction to the Children Act 1989*
(HMSO), para.6.41). Before making such an order under s.43 of the 1989 Act, the
court must still be satisfied that there is reasonable cause to suspect that the child is
suffering or is likely to suffer significant harm and that an assessment of the child's
health or development is necessary to enable the applicant to determine whether or
not the child is in fact suffering or likely to suffer significant harm. A child assessment
order permits the making of an assessment; but the child may only be kept away from
home in specified circumstances, and may (if of sufficient understanding) refuse to
submit to any assessment. It seems doubtful whether the child assessment order has
been effective in meeting the objectives of those who campaigned for its introduction:
there are very few applications and no reported case law. However, as Munby J. noted
in *X Council v B (Emergency Protection Order)* [2004] EWHC 2015 (Fam), where the
objective is to assess the child, the child assessment order may provide an equally
effective (and less intrusive) approach than the emergency protection order.

Where the local authority's inquiries indicate that its suspicions were well-founded,
the next step is to convene a child protection conference. In 2005, over half of the s.47
inquiries—37,400—led to child protection conferences. Such conferences bring
together key professionals, family members, and—where appropriate—the child, the
aim being:

> "to bring together and analyse in an inter-agency setting the information which
> has been obtained about the child's developmental needs, and the parents' or
> carers' capacity to respond to those needs to ensure the child's safety and promote
> the child's health and development within the context of their wider family and
> environment; to consider the evidence presented to the conference, make judg-
> ments about the likelihood of a child suffering significant harm in future and
> decide whether the child is at continuing risk of significant harm; and to decide
> what future action is required to safeguard and promote the welfare of the child,
> how that action will be taken forward, and with what intended outcomes."
> (*Working Together to Safeguard Children* (2006), para.5.80)

This illustrates the emphasis on partnership, both between different agencies and
between the authorities and the parents. The professionals involved may include social
services staff, members of the police force, medical practitioners, community health
workers, teachers, and representatives from voluntary agencies such as the NSPCC.
The guidance emphasises that children should be given the opportunity to attend
(depending on their age and understanding), and that family members should be
involved in the process, and only excluded in exceptional circumstances.

Over 80 per cent of such conferences led to a child being registered on the child
protection register in 2004–5. The most common reason for a child to be so registered
was neglect, accounting for 43 per cent of registrations in 2004–5. Physical abuse
accounted for 15 per cent of registrations in that period, sexual abuse for 9 per cent,
and emotional abuse for 19 per cent.

Once a child is registered, the conference should also draw up a child protection plan, setting out what needs to be done, and appoint the lead statutory body and a key worker to take responsibility for putting the plan into effect. Regular reviews must be held as long as the child remains on the register—which will be until it is considered that the child no longer needs the safeguard of a child protection plan, or until the child is no longer the responsibility of the local authority.

It will be clear from the above discussion that there are a number of ways in which the local authority can act to protect a child short of applying for a care or supervision order. It must be satisfied that the child's needs can only be properly met by compulsory measures before making such an application. The willingness of local authorities to use alternative measures can be demonstrated by the fact that there were only 8,493 applications for care orders, and 3,102 applications for supervision orders, in 2004—a small figure when compared to the number of referrals and s.47 inquiries.

The nature of care proceedings

Once the local authority has decided that it is appropriate to apply for a care or **13–013** supervision order, it will need to put together evidence to convince the court that the threshold criteria are met and that an order should be made. This section considers a number of issues relevant to the gathering of information, and the court's approach to the evidence before it.

(1) *Interim orders*

Notwithstanding many improvements in court structures and procedures introduced **13–014** in the wake of the Children Act, there may well be circumstances—for example, where there is a need to obtain and consider expert medical evidence—in which an application for a care or supervision order cannot be dealt with at once. In many of these cases, the child might be at risk in the period pending final determination of the application for a care order; and s.38 accordingly permits a court that is adjourning proceedings for a care or supervision order, or directing an investigation under s.37, to make an interim care order (or an interim supervision order) if it is satisfied that there are reasonable grounds for believing that the threshold criteria set out in s.31(2)—set out below at para.13–019—are met.

The threshold for making an interim order is thus lower than for the making of a final care order, and, in finding that "reasonable grounds for believing" exist, the court is not prejudging the question of whether the threshold criterion for the making of a full care or supervision order will be satisfied. Interim orders may be made for up to eight weeks, but may be extended for further periods of up to four weeks (such time limits reflecting the original expectation of those who drew up the 1989 Act that care cases would last no longer than 12 weeks, as noted by Baroness Hale of Richmond in *Re G (Interim Care Order: Residential Assessment)* [2005] UKHL 68). On each application the court has to be satisfied that the evidence justifies the making of an order but is inevitably circumscribed in the inquiries that it can make (see, *e.g. Re B (Interim Care Orders: Renewal)* [2001] 2 F.L.R. 1217, Fam Div).

The effect of an interim care order is, so long as it is in force, broadly comparable to that of a final order; and in particular the local authority is required to receive and keep the child in its care, is given parental responsibility, and has the power to determine the extent to which parents and others having parental responsibility are allowed to meet such responsibilities (s.31(11)).

One distinct feature of an interim care or supervision order is the court's power to give directions regarding the examination or assessment of the child under s.38(6) (including a direction that there should be no examination or assessment). This power is clearly related to the need to obtain information before making a final care order. The precise scope of s.38(6) has been a matter of dispute in a number of recent cases, one key issue being whether it encompasses "treatment" as well as "assessment". This point has recently been resolved by the House of Lords in *Re G (Interim Care Order: Residential Assessment)* [2005] UKHL 68:

> In this case care proceedings had been initiated in relation to the mother's third child (her second child having died from non-accidental injuries and her first having as a consequence of this been placed with its father). The court ordered a residential assessment of the family—the child and her parents—at a specialist hospital for 6–8 weeks. This was followed by a second order for a further 6 weeks at the hospital, on the basis that the issues had not been sufficiently addressed. The hospital then recommended that the family should remain there for a further 4 months, to enable the mother to undergo psychotherapy. The local authority refused to fund this further period of treatment, and Johnston J. held that s.38(6) did not give him the power to order such treatment. The appeal was allowed by the Court of Appeal, but on appeal the House of Lords restored the decision of Johnston J. Baroness Hale of Richmond, delivering the main judgment, emphasised that the purpose of s.38(6) was to obtain information, not to provide services for the family.

This does not mean, however, that it is only the child that may be the subject of an assessment. The House of Lords in *Re G* accepted its earlier decision that the interaction between the child and parent could properly be the subject of an assessment:

> In *Re C (Interim Care Order: Residential Assessment)* [1997] 1 F.L.R. 1, HL, teenage parents were suspected of physically abusing their baby causing him perhaps permanent brain damage. The local authority obtained an emergency protection order; and the baby was living with foster parents. A lengthy investigation by social workers concluded that there might be a possibility of the baby being rehabilitated with the parents, but this could only be determined on the basis of a residential assessment of the parents and their baby directed to the parents' ability to cope with the baby over long periods of time and in stressful situations. Such an assessment would be costly and might pose risks to the child, and the local authority accordingly refused to agree to, or pay for, the residential assessment proposed. The House of Lords held that the power to direct an assessment was not limited to assessments of the child, but extended to an assessment of the capabilities of a parent properly to care for the child at home.

However, as Baroness Hale pointed out in *Re G*, it would not be a proper use of the court's powers to seek to bring about a change in the parent's behaviour. As she concluded:

"In short, what is directed under section 38(6) must clearly be an examination or assessment of the child, including where appropriate her relationship with her parents, the risk that her parents may present to her, and the ways in which those risks may be avoided or managed, all with a view to enabling the court to make the decisions which it has to make under the Act with the minimum of delay. Any services which are provided for the child and his family must be ancillary to that end. They must not be an end in themselves." (para.69)

This interpretation of s.38(6) was influenced by two factors: first, the relationship between s.38(6) and (7), and, secondly, the need to avoid delay. Under s.38(7) the court may prohibit an examination or assessment which the local authority would otherwise be able to commission under the parental responsibility vested in it by an interim care order. This, as Baroness Hale pointed out, was a response to the concerns raised by the Cleveland report (see para.13–001 above), which had recommended that children should not be subjected to repeated medical examinations. The purpose of the provisions in s.38(6) and (7) was therefore not merely to obtain information but also "to enable the court to control the information-gathering activities of others" (per Baroness Hale at para.64). Secondly, the fact that interim care orders were intended to be temporary measures only indicated that lengthy assessments of the kind recommended by the hospital would be inappropriate.

The outcome for the family in Re G raises the question of whether the courts should have the power to order that treatment services be provided for families. In Re G the family actually remained at the hospital, despite the legal wrangles, and treatment was successful, with the result that when the family was discharged the local authority did not need to seek a care order. The cost of providing services of this kind is likely to be significantly less than the cost of looking after children under a care order. Whether local authorities will be influenced by the successful outcome of the treatment in Re G or the House of Lords' decision that there is no duty to provide such services remains to be seen.

One final point on the scope of s.38(6) relates to the wishes of the child. The section expressly provides that the child, if of sufficient understanding to make an informed decision, may decline to undergo an assessment directed to be made under this provision. It has been held that the High Court may, in the exercise of its inherent jurisdiction, override such a refusal (South Glamorgan CC v W and B [1993] 1 F.L.R. 574, Fam Div). This decision is controversial, and may well be vulnerable to attack under the Human Rights Act.

The fact that an interim care or supervision order will last for only a limited period before it needs to be renewed does give the court the power to review the case when it returns to court. However, such orders should not be made solely for this purpose. It was stressed in Re S (FC) (see below, para.13–036) that an interim order should only be made to safeguard the interests of a child until the court was in a position to decide whether a care order should be made, and should not be used to exercise a supervisory role over local authorities. As Lord Nicholls acknowledged, it would not always be possible to remove all uncertainties about the future of the child before making an order. A distinction had to be drawn between those matters that could be resolved by a limited period of "planned and purposeful delay", in which case an interim order would be appropriate, and those that would have to be worked out at a later date by the local authority.

(2) *The importance of ascertaining the truth*

13–015   There may be cases in which parents are prepared to accept that the threshold criteria are satisfied, but strongly dispute some of the matters alleged against them. Should the court insist on all the allegations being tried or should it simply accept that it has jurisdiction to make the order, and go on to the next, "welfare", stage?

> For example, in *Re M (Threshold Criteria: Parental Concessions)* [1999] 2 F.L.R. 728, CA, three children alleged that their adoptive father had sexually abused them. He was prosecuted and acquitted. The adoptive parents did not resist the making of a care order and admitted that they had caused the children significant harm—for example, by using inappropriate punishments. But they did strongly deny the allegations of sexual abuse, and argued that the court should not investigate those allegations since the parents were not resisting the making of the care order. The Court of Appeal held that, whilst it was as important in family as in other civil cases that there should be no unnecessary litigation in the courts, and that in some cases a concession which provided the basis for finding the threshold criteria proved would be adequate to meet the justice of the case and the best interests of the children, this was not such a case. Questions of whether the adoptive parents would be allowed any contact with the children would have to be resolved, whilst the care plan for the children would have to deal with such issues as whether they required therapy, and this depended on what had actually happened.

Whilst there will be some cases in which the court can properly accept a compromise solution, the general principle is that a parent's consent to the making of a care order is not sufficient for the purpose of satisfying the threshold conditions, and that no agreement between the parties can relieve the court of its duty to satisfy itself by evidence that the conditions have been met (see also *Re D (child: threshold criteria)* [2001] 1 F.L.R. 274, CA). It is also the case that the court can embark on a hearing of the factual evidence even if all the parties have asked for the proceedings to be withdrawn: see *A County Council V DP, RS, BS (By the Children's Guardian)* [2005] EWHC 1593 (Fam).

(3) *Listening to the child*

13–016   The need for the child's interests to be properly represented was dramatically illustrated in the case of Maria Colwell in the 1970s:

> Maria's mother applied, under the legislation then in force, for her to be returned to her care. Although the local authority was aware that the mother's partner was a source of considerable risk to Maria, it also believed that the policy of the local magistrates' court was to favour return of children in care to their parents unless there was clear evidence that this would be contrary to the child's interests. The local authority concluded that it would probably not be able to satisfy the court, and therefore it decided not to oppose the revocation of the care order. Maria was returned home and was killed by her step-father.

Such cases demonstrate the need for a non-adversarial procedure, in that the court must be able to ensure it has all the information needed to make a decision on the child's future. But they also demonstrate the need for the child's case to be put forward by someone who is wholly committed to the child and does not simply put forward what seems a reasonable compromise taking account of all the various competing factors.

The Children Act 1989 provides that in care and certain other proceedings (for a full list see s.41(6)) the court must appoint a children's guardian to represent the child "unless satisfied that it is not necessary to do so in order to safeguard" the child's interests (s.41(1)). Since April 2001, children's guardians—formerly known as guardians *ad litem*—have been provided by CAFCASS. The role of the children's guardian, who is qualified in social work, is to advise both the child and the court. The report to the court must indicate the wishes and feelings of the child wherever possible, but the guardian's role is not simply to put forward the child's point of view but to set out the suitability of the various available options. The children's guardian is not legally qualified, and one of his or her duties will be to appoint a solicitor for the child (unless one has been already appointed). It should be noted that the solicitor may represent both the guardian and the child, but if their instructions conflict the case should be conducted in accordance with the child's instructions, provided that the solicitor considers the child is capable of understanding the matter: see s.41(5)).

(4) *Evidence*

The rules on the admissibility of evidence reflect the nature of care proceedings. As **13–017** Butler-Sloss P. noted in *Re T (Abuse: Standard of Proof)* [2004] EWCA Civ 558:

> "The strict rules of evidence applicable in a criminal trial, which is adversarial in nature, are to be contrasted with the partly inquisitorial approach of the court dealing with children cases in which the rules of evidence are considerably relaxed." (para.28)

Many cases involve an assessment of whether or not a child has been or is likely to have been physically or psychologically damaged; and in such cases the court will almost invariably have available to it evidence from paediatricians, child psychiatrists or child psychologists. The opinion of such persons on any relevant matter about which they are qualified to give expert evidence is—contrary to the general rule that witnesses must only speak to the facts—admissible (s.3 of the Civil Evidence Act 1972).

In a number of recent cases it has been clear that a child has suffered harm, but less clear whether that harm can be attributed to natural causes, the "rough and tumble of family life," or non-accidental injury. Medical evidence tends to be given greater weight than the evidence of the parties—see, *e.g. Re B (Non-accidental Injury: Compelling Medical Evidence)* [2002] EWCA Civ 902—but there are, inevitably, matters upon which medical opinion is divided. A recent spate of cases in which the criminal convictions of mothers accused of killing their children have been quashed has led judges to sound a note of caution about relying on expert evidence. Thus in *W v Oldham Metropolitan Borough Council* [2005] EWCA Civ 1247 Wall L.J. emphasised the importance of considering the evidence as a whole—

> "in a child case involving complex and serious injuries, the expert evidence has to be carefully analysed, fitted into a factual matrix and measured against assessments of witness credibility." (para.44)

—while adding reassuringly that "family judges rarely decide cases on the evidence of a single expert" (at para.42). In that case it was suggested that it would be appropriate for the court to grant permission to instruct a second expert if the question to be addressed "goes to an issue of critical importance for the judge's decision in the case" (at para.39). In addition. the courts have been quick to stress that they are aware of the limitations of expert evidence:

> "the judgment in *Cannings* has, amongst other things, reminded the family court that even the most distinguished expert can be wrong, of the possible dangers of an over-dogmatic expert approach, and of the likelihood in the future of change and revision of medical views having regard to research . . . " (*per* Charles J. in *A County Council v K, D, and L* [2005] EWHC 144 (Fam), para.51)

Ultimately, the decision is one for the judge, not for the expert, which has implications for the way in which the evidence is presented (see *e.g.* the suggestions of Charles J. in *A County Council v K, D, and L* [2005] EWHC 144 (Fam)).

(5) The burden of proof

13–018   Like other courts, the courts administering the care jurisdiction can only act on the basis of proof, and the onus of proving the case rests on the applicant. Having heard the admissible evidence, the court must be satisfied on the balance of probabilities—*i.e.* it must be "more likely than not"—that the events in question occurred. In *Re H and R (Child Sexual Abuse: Standard of Proof)* [1996] 1 F.L.R. 80, HL, Lord Nicholls suggested that:

> "the more serious the allegation the less likely it is that the event occurred and, hence, the stronger should be the evidence before the court concludes that the allegation is established on the balance of probability." (p.586)

This suggestion has given rise to much debate. It would appear that Lord Nicholls was not setting a higher test for more serious allegations, merely pointing out that a factor to be taken into account in deciding whether the allegation was true is that it is inherently less probable that serious abuse has occurred. The Court of Appeal has recently confirmed this approach in *Re T (Abuse: Standard of Proof)* [2004] EWCA Civ 558 and *Re U (Serious Injury: Standard of Proof); Re B* [2004] EWCA Civ 567, firmly rejecting the suggestion in *Re ET (Serious Injuries: Standard of Proof)* [2003] 2 F.L.R. 1205 that in cases of serious allegations the difference between the civil and criminal standards of proof was largely illusory. Thus it is entirely possible that different conclusions will be reached in civil and criminal proceedings:

> In *A Local Authority v S, W and T (By his Guardian)* [2004] EWHC 1270 (Fam): it was held that although the stepfather had been acquitted of murder and manslaughter, some form of non-accidental shaking injury was the overwhelmingly probable cause of injury.

With these points in mind, the threshold criteria that must be satisfied before an order can be made will now be considered.

The threshold criteria

The court only has jurisdiction to make a care or supervision order if it is satisfied that **13–019** the conditions set out in s.31(2) are satisfied. Only if the threshold criteria are satisfied will the court go onto the next stage and consider whether it should in fact make a care or supervision order. Under s.31, the court must be satisfied:

(a) that the child concerned is suffering, or is likely to suffer, significant harm; and

(b) that the harm, or likelihood of harm, is attributable to—

(i) the care given to the child, or likely to be given to him if the order were not made, not being what it would be reasonable to expect a parent to give to him; or

(ii) the child's being beyond parental control.

"Harm" is defined in s.31(9) as meaning "ill-treatment or the impairment of health or development, *including, for example, impairment suffered from seeing or hearing the ill-treatment of another.*" The phrase in italics was added by the Adoption and Children Act 2002 and reflects the growing concern as to the effect that witnessing domestic violence may have upon children. "Development" means "physical, intellectual, emotional, social or behavioural development; "health" means "physical or mental health"; and "ill-treatment" includes sexual abuse and forms of treatment which are not physical.

Notwithstanding Lord Chancellor Mackay's statement that the Children Act 1989 was so clearly drafted that ordinary people would be able to understand it without needing to consult lawyers or other experts, there has been a mass of reported case law on the construction of these provisions.

(1) *What harm is "significant"?*

In many cases—for example where a child has been severely injured or neglected—the **13–020** answer will be clear, but in other cases the decision may be more difficult:

> In *Re A (children) (interim care order)* [2001] 3 F.C.R. 402, Fam Div, the children alleged that their father had assaulted them. The mother did not want the children to give evidence against him, on the basis that they needed a continuing relationship with him and they would be stigmatised by the Muslim community if he was imprisoned as a result of their evidence. It was held that the mother's actions had caused significant harm to the children because of the conflict of loyalties to which they were exposed.

More unusually:

> In *Haringey London Borough Council v C, E and Another Intervening* [2004] EWHC 2580 the child in question was the product of an alleged "miracle birth". The court concluded that child had in fact been removed from unknown parents and that if his "future care is founded upon a lie he will likely suffer profound harm." (*per* Ryder J., para.89)

The recently published *Working Together to Safeguard Children* (2006) emphasises that:

> "There are no absolute criteria on which to rely when judging what constitutes significant harm. Consideration of the severity of ill-treatment may include the degree and the extent of physical harm, the duration and frequency of abuse and neglect, the extent of premeditation, and the presence or degree of threat, coercion, sadism, and bizarre or unusual elements." (para.1.25)

The Act provides that "where the question of whether harm suffered by a child is significant turns on the child's health or development, his health or development shall be compared with that which could reasonably be expected of a similar child" (s.31(10)); and this would seem to be an invitation for the local authority to lead expert evidence comparing the child's development with that which would be expected on the basis of statistical data about such matters as weight, size, and so on. It seems clear that the reference to a "similar" child is intended to compare like children with like children—a blind child with a blind child, a Down's Syndrome child with a Down's Syndrome child, for example. But although there will be many cases in which the "significance" of the harm cannot really be questioned, there will be others in which the answer is less clear. *Working Together to Safeguard Children* also warns of the need to be "sensitive to differing family patterns and lifestyles and to child rearing patterns that vary across different racial, ethnic and cultural groups", while emphasising that "child abuse cannot be condoned for religious or cultural reasons" (para.10.9).

In practice, any court left in doubt about whether the harm suffered might truly be described as "significant" would be unlikely to be satisfied about the benefits of making an order (see further para.13–029).

(2) Is the child suffering harm?

13–021   Under the Law Commission's draft legislation it was sufficient for the local authority to show that the child *had* suffered significant harm, but the Conservative Government was concerned about the possibility of children being removed from their parents by over-zealous social workers on the basis of some long-past failure, and the Act consequently provided that it must be shown that the child *is* suffering harm (or alternatively is likely to suffer such harm).

That wording soon gave rise to difficulty. For example, it would surely be absurd to deny the court the power to make orders in cases in which the child had been removed from an appalling situation of violence and risk under the Act's emergency provisions, merely because at the time of the substantive hearing the child was being well cared for in hospital or by foster-parents. The difficulties came to a head in *Re M (A Minor) (Care Order: Threshold Conditions)* [1994] 2 AC 424, HL:

> A husband brutally murdered his wife in the presence of their four-month-old son and their three other children by attacking her with a meat cleaver. The local authority applied for a care order with a view to the child being placed for adoption outside the family. But at the time of the hearing before the judge, the child was living happily with his mother's cousin and his half-siblings. The Court of Appeal held that the child had to be shown to be suffering such harm *at the date of the hearing*, but the House of Lords allowed the appeal and ruled that, if interim local authority arrangements had been continuously in place from the

date at which protective measures were first taken down to the time of the hearing, the court could properly look back to the earlier date.

It must be admitted that this interpretation does not solve all possible difficulties—when, for example, do "arrangements for the protection of the child" begin?—but it seems to provide a reasonable pragmatic solution in the great majority of cases.

(3) *Is the child likely to suffer harm?*

It was the Conservative Government's clearly articulated policy that compulsory measures should be available in cases in which a child was seriously at risk, notwithstanding the fact that no harm had actually yet been suffered. Consistently with the decision in *Re M*, the date at which the question of "likelihood" has to be resolved is the date on which protective measures were initiated: *Southwark LBC v B* [1998] 2 F.L.R. 1095, Fam Div. But how is the court to interpret the word "likely"? **13–022**

> In *Re H and R (Child Sexual Abuse: Standard of Proof)* (above) the House of Lords by a 3–2 majority ruled that the question was whether, on the basis of the facts as admitted or found, there was a "real possibility"—a possibility that could not sensibly be ignored having regard to the feared harm in the particular case—that the child would suffer significant harm.

Thus it is not necessary to establish that it is more likely than not that the child will suffer harm.

The fact that another child in the family has suffered harm may indicate that there is a real possibility of harm, but this will depend on the circumstances. The Court of Appeal stressed in *Re K (Children)* [2005] EWCA Civ 1226 that if life-threatening injuries have been caused to one child by one of the parents (about which both have lied) then there have to be unusual circumstances (or at least full and reasoned explanation) if the court is not to find that the threshold criteria are satisfied in relation to their other child. In an appropriate case the court may be satisfied that the parent's relationship with the other child is so different that the latter is not at risk (see *e.g. Re T (children) (interim care order)* [2001] EWCA Civ 1345).

More difficult is the situation where it has been alleged that another child in the family has suffered harm but these allegations have not been proved, as was the case in *Re H and R (Child Sexual Abuse: Standard of Proof)* [1996] 1 F.L.R. 80, HL:

> A 15-year-old girl alleged that her step-father had sexually abused her over a period of seven years, and that on four occasions he had raped her. The father was prosecuted for rape but acquitted. When the local authority subsequently sought a care order in relation to the girl's younger sisters—the girl herself having been accommodated elsewhere—the judge noted that he was "more than a little suspicious" that the step-father had done what was alleged but held that it was not proved on the balance of probabilities. In such a case the court had no power to make a care order. The allegation that the step-father had sexually abused a child had not been proved, and there were no other facts upon which a finding of significant harm could be based.

As a result, if the court is not satisfied on the balance of probabilities that an alleged incident of harm has taken place, no account can be taken of that alleged incident in evaluating whether the child is *likely* to suffer significant harm. Once again, there is tension between the objectives of protecting children from abuse and protecting adults from unwarranted state intervention. It is important to remember that a finding that sexual abuse has not been proved "does not equate with a finding that . . . abuse did not occur, any more than a finding of not guilty equates with a finding of innocence" (*per* Rose L.J., *Re G and R (Child Sexual Abuse: Standard of Proof)* [1995] 2 F.L.R. 867 at 881). The risk that the family justice system will fail adequately to protect the vulnerable is all too obvious. But the difficulty should not be exaggerated: it is in practice rare for the factual substratum on the basis of which the court is invited to make a finding of significant harm to be limited to a single matter; and (as Lord Nicholls of Birkenhead put it in *Re H and R (Child Sexual Abuse: Standard of Proof)* (above):

> " . . . there will be cases where, although the alleged maltreatment itself is not proved, the evidence does establish a combination of profoundly worrying features affecting the care of the child within the family. In such cases, it would be open to a court to find . . . on the basis of such facts as are proved that the threshold criterion is satisfied."

For example:

> In *Re G and R (Child Sexual Abuse: Standard of Proof)* [1995] 2 F.L.R. 867, CA, the children had severe behavioural problems. The judge held that allegations of sexual abuse against the father had not been made out; but the Court of Appeal held that the evidence—which included much evidence of poor parenting and of the children being severely disturbed—"overwhelmingly established" that a two-year-old was likely to suffer significant harm if she were returned to the care of her parents.

The problems that face the court where it is proved that the child has suffered harm, but not who caused it, are considered below (para.13–024).

(4) *Is the harm attributable to lack of parental care or the child being beyond parental control?*

13–023   A child might be suffering, or at risk of suffering, significant harm by reason of illness, accident or other misfortune; and it would obviously be absurd to give the court power to remove the child from caring parents in such cases. The Children Act 1989 therefore stipulates that the harm must be "attributable" either to lack of parental care or to the child being beyond parental control.

(a) Lack of reasonable parental care

13–024   The Act provides that the harm or likelihood of harm which has been established must be shown to be "attributable to . . . the care given to the child, or likely to be given to him if the order were not made, not being what it would be reasonable to expect a parent to give to him" (s.31(2)(b)(i)).

The interpretation of this provision has given rise to some difficulties. However, it is clear from the fact that the Act refers to the care given by "a" (rather than "the") parent that judgments about the standard of care to be expected are to be answered by reference to what a hypothetical reasonable parent would provide for the child in question (*Lancashire CC v A* [2000] 2 A.C. 147, HL, *per* Lord Nicholls). The fact that a parent is unable to provide such a level of care does not necessarily indicate that the parents are at fault, as there may be reasons beyond their control. In addition, lack of parental care may be demonstrated where the parent has failed to protect the child from harm.

Problems may arise where the child has sustained injuries but it is unclear whether those injuries were inflicted deliberately or the recent of an accident. In such a case medical evidence will often be of critical importance, but the explanation provided by the parents will also be relevant. Unconvincing or inconsistent explanations may lead the court to conclude that the injuries were non-accidental. In addition, other aspects of the parents' behaviour may satisfy the threshold criteria:

> In *CL v East Riding Yorkshire Council* [2006] EWCA Civ 49 it was not possible to establish whether the child's injuries were accidental or not. Despite this, it was noted that the judge was entitled to find that the threshold criteria were satisfied on the basis of the parents' failure to call an ambulance, since this suggested that the child "was likely to suffer significant harm due to the parents' failure to ensure that he received immediate treatment" (*per* Wall L.J., para.55). The fact that they had lied about the child's injuries could also fall within the scope of s.31(2).

A rather different problem arises where it is clear that the injuries were non-accidental but not who caused them. Today the task of caring for children—particularly for children who do not live in stable two-parent families—is often shared between parents who are living apart, grandparents and other relatives, and official and unofficial child-minders. What is to happen if a child suffers non-accidental injury but it cannot be shown that one of the child's parents was responsible for inflicting it?

> In *Lancashire CC v A* [2000] 2 A.C. 147, HL, a seven-month-old baby was looked after by a paid child minder during the day while the child's parents were at work. The baby was found to have suffered at least two episodes of violent shaking which resulted in subdural haemorrhages, retinal haemorrhages and cerebral atrophy. It was impossible to decide whether this harm—undoubtedly significant—had been caused by the child's mother or father or by the child minder. The House of Lords rejected an argument that the threshold criterion could only be satisfied if it were shown that the harm was attributable to the care or absence of care given to the child by the parent against whom the order was sought. In a case in which the care of the child was shared, and the court was unable to identify which of the carers was responsible for the deficient care, it would be sufficient for the court to be satisfied that the deficit was attributable to any of the primary carers.

The factor which outweighed all others in reaching this decision on the interpretation of the threshold criteria was (as Lord Nicholls put it) "the prospect that an unidentified and unidentifiable carer might otherwise be free to inflict further injury on a child he or she had already severely damaged". This was considered to outweigh the fact that the threshold criteria may now be satisfied in a case in which there is no more than a possibility that the parents were responsible for the child's injuries.

The House of Lords in *Lancashire CC v A* also pointed out that the fact the threshold criteria were satisfied did not inevitably mean a care order would be made.

In the words of Lord Clyde, satisfying the threshold criteria "merely opens the way to the possibility that an order may be made". For these reasons, the House considered that the decision was not inconsistent with the Convention right embodied in Art.8 of the European Convention on Human Rights: the interference with the parents' family was justified as being necessary for the protection of the child's rights.

The test to be applied by the court in such cases was formulated by Butler-Sloss P. in *North Yorkshire County Council v SA* [2003] EWCA Civ 839 as:

> "Is there is a likelihood or real possibility that A or B or C was the perpetrator or a perpetrator of the inflicted injuries?" (at para.26)

The "real possibility" test employed in this context should be contrasted with the higher standard of the balance of probabilities required to establish that harm has actually occurred. The distinction can be justified by the fact that in those cases where the perpetrator cannot be identified it is at least certain that the child has been harmed, and the obvious need for protection should not be affected by the difficulty of deciding who was responsible for inflicting the injuries.

It should also be noted that recent changes to the criminal law make it easier to convict parents who have killed their child. Previously, if it was unclear which of the parents was responsible for killing the child, neither could be convicted. Section 5 of the Domestic Violence, Crimes and Victims Act 2004 introduced the new offence of "causing or allowing the death of a child or vulnerable adult". As a result, it is sufficient to show that a person who lived in the same household as the victim either caused the death or was aware of the risk of harm and failed to take such steps as could reasonably be expected to protect the victim.

(b) Child beyond parental control

13–025   The question of whether a child is or is not beyond parental control is one of objective fact; and it is immaterial that the parents are in no way culpable:

> In *M v Birmingham CC* [1994] 2 F.L.R. 141, Fam Div, a 13-year-old girl had developed a wayward, uncontrollable and disturbed pattern of behaviour, sometimes involving violence and the making of unfounded allegations against those with whom she came into contact. She absconded from the unit in which attempts were made to treat her; and she took drug overdoses. The judge held that she had presented and continued to present a serious problem to anyone who had the duty of caring for her. The fact that her mother was a caring person who had tried to get appropriate help to deal with the child's problems did not affect the fact that the harm she was likely to suffer was attributable to her being beyond parental (or indeed any other) control. The threshold criterion was thus satisfied.

Should the court make an order?

13–026   The court cannot make a care or supervision order unless the threshold criteria are satisfied, but (as noted above) it does not follow from the fact that the threshold criteria have been satisfied that the court *must* make a care or supervision (or indeed any) order. If it decides not to do so it may either make a s.8 order (whether or not there is an application for such an order), or no order at all. While this gives the court considerable flexibility, there are a number of constraints on the court's powers. First, it should be noted that it is not possible for the court to make s.8 orders alongside a care order, although it is possible to make such orders as an alternative to a care order. Furthermore, if the court decides to make a residence order in public law proceedings, it must also make an interim supervision order unless satisfied that the welfare of the child will be sufficiently safeguarded without such an order being made (s.38(3)). After all, it should not be forgotten that the court will only be making an order in this context if it has already determined that the threshold criteria have been satisfied.

In deciding how to exercise its discretion, the court must apply the principle that the child's welfare is paramount and take into account the factors listed in s.1(3). In addition, it must ask whether making the care or supervision order (or indeed any other order) would "be better for the child than making no order at all" (s.1(5)). The enactment of the Human Rights Act has added a new dimension to the exercise of the court's discretion: any interference in family life must not only be in accordance with the law and necessary, but also proportionate. As Thorpe L.J. noted in *Re B (Care: Interference with Family Life)* [2003] EWCA Civ 786:

> "where the application is for a care order empowering the local authority to remove a child or children from the family, the judge in modern times may not make such an order without considering the . . . Art.8 rights of the adult members of the family and of the children of the family. Accordingly, he must not sanction such an interference with family life unless he is satisfied that that is both necessary and proportionate and that no other less radical form of order would achieve the essential end of promoting the welfare of the children." (para.34)

With these points in mind, a number of specific issues should be considered. What should the approach of the court be at the welfare stage where there are lingering suspicions as to whether a child has suffered harm, or doubts as to the perpetrator of any harm? And how does the court exercise its discretion whether or not to make an order?

(1) *The problem of lingering suspicions*

In approaching the exercise of its discretion, the court must act on the basis of proven **13–027** fact rather than mere suspicion or mere doubts. If the evidence before the court is not sufficient to establish on the balance of probabilities that a particular incident occurred, the court is not entitled to take it into account at the "welfare" stage (see *e.g. Re M and R (Child Abuse: Evidence)* [1996] 2 F.L.R. 195, CA). As Lord Nicholls noted in *Re O and N (children) (non-accidental injury)* [2003] UKHL 18:

> "On the one hand there is the family protection purpose of the threshold criteria. On the other hand there is the general principle that at the welfare stage the court has regard to all the circumstances. On balance I consider that to have regard at the welfare stage to allegations of harm rejected at the threshold stage would have the effect of depriving the child and the family of the protection intended to be afforded by the threshold criteria." (para.38)

(2) *The problem of the unidentified perpetrator*

As noted above, the court may find that the threshold criteria are satisfied even where **13–028** it is unclear which of the parents was responsible for inflicting harm on the child. But the identity of the perpetrator is also relevant at the "welfare" stage: if, for example, the parents have separated, it will be crucial to the local authority when formulating its care plans to know whether the child would be at risk from both, or just one of, the parents. However, if it is impossible to ascertain which of the parents was responsible for the child's injuries, the court has to proceed on the basis that either parent is potentially the perpetrator of the injuries in deciding whether a care order should be made, and the local authority must make the same assumption in formulating its care plan (see *Re O and N (children) (non-accidental injury)* [2003] UKHL 18). However, Lord Nicholls did add that the court could take into account any views expressed by the judge at the preliminary hearing as to the likelihood of either parent being responsible for the injuries.

(3) *What order is appropriate?*

13–029   Under s.1(3)(g) the court must have regard to the range of powers available to it, and therefore will need to consider whether any other order (such as a residence order in favour of a relative) is more likely to promote the child's welfare. In evaluating what benefits the making of a care order will give the child, the court will take into account the local authority's plans for the child. Under s.31A (as inserted by the Adoption and Children Act 2002), the local authority is required to prepare a care plan, and s.31(3A) directs that no care order may be made unless the court has considered a s.31A care plan. The importance of the plan is increased by the wide range of options open to the local authority once a care order has been made: it may decide that the child should remain living with its parents, or should live with foster-carers on a temporary basis, or even that it is in the best interests of the child to be adopted. The flexibility conferred by the Children Act is in most cases a considerable benefit, but does mean that the court must carefully analyse the precise effect that the orders sought will have on all those affected.

One factor to be considered is whether the local authority requires parental responsibility. If so, a care order is likely to be more appropriate than a supervision order, since the latter does not confer parental responsibility on the local authority. Whether or not the local authority requires parental responsibility will thus be an important factor in deciding which order is appropriate:

> In *Re O (Supervision Order)* [2001] 1 F.L.R. 923, CA, Hale L.J. reviewed the advantages of a care order. It was held that, in view of the level of the risk to the child, the local authority did not need the power to remove the child without a court order. Nor did it need parental responsibility or the power to control the exercise of the parents' parental responsibility, since the care plan gave no indication that such control was necessary. A supervision order was proportionate to the risk and could (and should) be made to work: the local authority should deliver the necessary services and the parents should co-operate.

The court will also be influenced by the fact that a care order is a greater intrusion into family life than a supervision order. A supervision order places the child under the supervision of a designated local authority (s.31(1)) whose duty it is to "advise, assist and befriend" the child. The child will continue to live at home unless the supervisor directs otherwise. While Sch.3 sets out detailed directions that can be given to children or their parents by the supervisor, it should be noted that there are no sanctions for breach (other than the risk that the local authority will seek a care order from the court). A supervision order is intended to be a short-term measure and will normally come to an end after one year (Sch.3, para.6(1)). The supervisor may apply to extend the order, but it cannot be extended beyond three years from the date when it was made. However, as Hale L.J. pointed out in *Re O (Supervision Order)* [2001] 1 F.L.R. 923, CA, there would be no difficulty in obtaining a further order if the child was still at risk of harm after the three years had elapsed.

By contrast, a care order lasts until the child is 18 unless it is brought to an end earlier (see para.13–038 below on the circumstances in which a care order will be terminated). Despite the drastic nature of a care order, if such an order is the only way of achieving the desired outcome, it should be made. It should be noted that while the European Court of Human Rights has emphasised that care orders should be temporary measures and that the ultimate aim should be the reunification of the family, it has also accepted that the child's interests should prevail and would justify the severance of ties with the rest of the family where this is necessary (see *K and T v Finland* [2001] 2 F.L.R. 707, ECHR; *P, C and S v UK* [2002] 3 F.C.R. 1, ECHR; *KA v Finland* [2003] 1 F.L.R. 696, ECHR).

D: CHILDREN LOOKED AFTER BY A LOCAL AUTHORITY

If the court has made a care order, the local authority is required by the Children Act **13–030** 1989 to receive the child into their care (s.33(1)), and to provide accommodation for the child (s.23(1)). Such a child is described as a "looked after" child, as is a child who is accommodated under a voluntary arrangement under s.20 (see para.13–006 above). As at March 31, 2005, 18,800 children were being "looked after" under voluntary arrangements, and a further 39,400 under care orders. It will be obvious that this figure far exceeds the number of care orders made annually, or even the number who began to be looked after in that year (a total of 24,500), since it includes children who began to be looked after in previous years.

The local authority must take a number of factors into account in deciding how to fulfil its duties to the children it is looking after. In addition to the general duty under s.17(1)(b) to promote the welfare of children in need and "so far as is consistent with that duty, to promote their upbringing by their families", the Act imposes on local authorities a specific statutory duty to safeguard and promote the welfare of the children that they are looking after (s.22(3)). The local authority must also "so far as is reasonably practicable" ascertain the wishes and feeling of (a) any child they are looking after (or proposing to look after); (b) his parents; (c) any other person who has parental responsibility for him; and (d) any other person whose wishes and feelings the authority considers to be relevant. In making any decision with respect to such a child, the local authority is obliged to give due consideration to the wishes and feelings of such persons as well as to the wishes and feelings of the child ("having regard to his age and understanding"), and to the child's "religious persuasion, racial origin and cultural and linguistic background" (s.22(5)).

This section considers a number of issues, some of general relevance to all looked-after children, others pertaining to the position of the child who is subject to a care order. First, how are "looked-after" children actually looked after? Secondly, if a child is subject to a care order, how is the local authority's implementation of its care plan regulated? Thirdly, what provision is made for children subject to care orders to have contact with their birth families?

Accommodation

13–031 There are various ways in which a local authority may provide accommodation for the children it is looking after: the child may remain in the family home, or live with foster-parents or in a care home. A new permanent family may be secured by adoption. This section considers the different options and how they are regulated. After all, as Munby J. noted in *F v Lambeth LBC* [2002] 1 F.L.R. 217, Fam Div, "if the State is to justify removing children from their parents it can only be on the basis that the State is going to provide a better quality of care than that from which the child in care has been rescued" (at 234). It should also be noted that the child may move between the different options outlined below, or between different placements: of the children who ceased to be looked after in the year ending March 31, 2005, almost 30 per cent had five or more placements during their care history.

(1) *Parents*

13–032 In an appropriate case—and subject always to the provisions of the Placement of Children with Parents, etc. Regulations 1991, which are designed to ensure that a child is not returned to a situation of danger—the care plan for the child may entail the child remaining in the parental home. As of March 31, 2005, 10 per cent of looked after children were living with at least one of their parents.

(2) *Foster care*

13–033 By far the most popular option is to place a child with a local authority foster parent: in 2005, 68 per cent of children were looked after in such placements. Any persons with whom a child is placed by the local authority are termed local authority foster parents, even if they are friends or relatives of the child. The only exceptions to this are parents, or persons who have parental responsibility for the child or in whose favour a residence order was in force before the care order was made (s.23(4)). A growing proportion of "looked after" children are placed with relatives or friends: as of March 2005, approximately 7,500 "looked after" children were living with relatives or friends.

It is obviously important that foster parents should be able to provide a good standard of care for the children entrusted to them, and there are consequently detailed regulations dealing with the approval of foster parents and the decision-taking procedures leading to a placement of a child (see the Fostering Services Regulations 2002, SI 2002/57). Relatives and friends are now subjected to the same degree of scrutiny, which posed a problem in *Re W and X (Wardship: Relatives Rejected as Foster Carers)* [2003] EWHC 2206 (Fam):

> In this case the grandparents had been rejected as potential foster parents. As a result, it was not possible for the court to make a care order and allow children to remain with their grandparents. The local authority did not want to move the children from the grandparents, and a clinical psychologist gave evidence that a further move would be extremely detrimental to the children. As Hedley J. noted, "the ideal solution was simply not available for these children" (para.10). He accordingly invoked the inherent jurisdiction of the court (see para.12–045 above), and made a supervision order combined with orders under s.8.

Prior to the introduction of the 2002 Regulations, relatives and friends acting as carers were subject to less scrutiny. They were also paid less, but this practice was successfully challenged:

> In *R. ota L v Manchester CC* [2002] 1 F.L.R. 43, QBD, foster carers challenged Manchester City Council's policy of paying a lower rate to any carers who were related to, or friends of, the foster-child(ren). Munby J. held that the policy was irrational and unlawful, and, in addition, that it breached both Art.8 and Art.14, since it discriminated against the parties on the basis of their family status.

The result of these changes is that relatives and friends should now be treated in the same way as other foster-parents.

(3) *Children's homes*

Children may also be accommodated in children's homes or residential schools, but **13–034** over the years there has been a sharp decline in the number of such placements, and in 2005, only 13 per cent of "looked after" children were accommodated in this way. Inquiries—notably the Utting Report into the safeguards protecting children living away from home (*People Like Us*, 1997)—have revealed serious shortcomings in the provision of these services for children, which are now regulated by the Children's Homes Regulations 2001.

(4) *Adoption*

Increasing numbers of children are adopted from care—3,800 in 2004–5—although **13–035** the absolute numbers remain small. The Government has stated that it wishes to increase this figure and to reduce the time that elapses before looked-after children are placed for adoption. These issues are considered in more depth in Ch.15.

Implementing the care plan

As noted above, the local authority must produce a care plan, and the court must **13–036** consider that plan before making a care order. Once the care order has been made, however, the court has no further supervisory role, and is restricted by statute from exercising its inherent jurisdiction. Nor can it reserve for itself a supervisory role by making a care order subject to conditions: as Butler-Sloss L.J. has put it, when a care order is made "the local authority is thereafter in the driving seat . . ." and the court cannot impose conditions upon nor seek undertakings from a local authority to whom the court has entrusted the child by virtue of a care order (*Re C (Interim Care Order: Assessment)* [1996] 2 F.L.R. 708 at 711, CA).

The lack of any power to supervise the implementation of a care plan caused considerable disquiet, and attempts were made to secure a greater role for the courts (*Re W and B; Re W (Care Plan)* [2001] EWCA Civ 757). However, the Court of Appeal's innovations were rejected by the House of Lords in *Re S (FC) (Minors) (Care Order: Implementation of Care Plan); Re W (Minors) (Care Order: Adequacy of Care Plan)* [2002] UKHL 10, and Lord Nicholls emphasized that the matter should be dealt with by Parliament. Parliament responded in the Adoption and Children Act 2002, and a local authority is now required to appoint a person to review each case (s.118, inserting s.26(2A) into the 1989 Act, and see the Review of Children's Cases (Amendment) Regulations 2004, SI 2004/1419). The local authority is itself required by regulations to keep each case under regular review, and reviews must take place within the first four weeks of the child beginning to be looked after. A second review must take place within three months of the first, and after that reviews are to be carried out at intervals of not more than six months. The responsibility of the new Independent Reviewing Officers created by the 2002 Act is to chair these regular reviews and monitor the local authority's compliance with the care plan. As a last resort, an Independent Reviewing Officer may refer a case to CAFCASS to take legal action if the failure to implement the care plan risks breaching the child's human rights.

It should of course be borne in mind that the fact that a care plan is not fully implemented might not be due to the failings of the local authority. A care plan that was appropriate at the time that the care order was made may cease to be feasible—for example if the plan was to return the child to the birth parents but new problems subsequently emerge. As the previous section emphasised, being looked after by the local authority is rarely a static situation.

Contact with parents

13–037   Cases in which children in care continue to live in the parental home are infrequent; and one of the most important issues to be decided in planning the child's future is the extent to which the parents are to be allowed to have contact with their child. There is now a greater emphasis on such contact: as Thorpe L.J. noted in *Re W (Section 34(2) Orders)* [2000] 1 F.L.R. 502, CA, one of the objectives of the Children Act 1989 was to impose a clearer and higher duty on local authorities to promote contact between children in care and their parents. In addition, the European Court of Human Rights has consistently stressed that any restrictions on contact should be scrutinized carefully, and, in *P, C and S v UK* [2002] 3 F.C.R. 1, ECHR, found a breach of Art.8 on the basis that depriving the parents of contact was not necessary to safeguard the child.

The local authority's plans for contact between parents and child will be relevant to the decision whether or not a care order should be made (see s.34(11)). If the court disagrees with the local authority's proposals it might decline to make a care order *(Re T (A Minor) (Care Order: Conditions)* [1994] 2 F.L.R. 223, CA)).

The Act requires a local authority to allow a child in care "reasonable contact" with the parents and a number of other persons specified in s.34(1). Section 34(3) provides that such persons, together anyone who obtains leave, may apply to the court for an order setting out what contact will be allowed between the child and the applicant, and s.34(2) gives a similar right to the child and the local authority to make applications. The authority may only *deny* contact on its own initiative if satisfied that it is "necessary" to do so to safeguard or promote the child's welfare, and if the refusal is decided on as a matter of urgency and does not last for more than seven days (s.34(6)). If contact is to be prevented in the longer term, the authority must obtain an order from the court to this effect. Thus the local authority may not refuse contact "unless they have first persuaded a judge that such a refusal is necessary" (*Re W (Section 34(2) Orders)* [2000] 1 F.L.R. 502, CA, *per* Thorpe L.J. at 507). Overall, the legislative balance is tilted in favour of contact, since the court has no power to prohibit a local authority from allowing contact but may prevent it from refusing contact *(Re W (Section 34(2) Orders)* [2000] 1 F.L.R. 502, CA).

In deciding whether to allow or refuse contact, the court will have regard to the welfare principle. The court recognise the importance of contact (as Simon Brown L.J. put it in *Re E (A Minor) (Care Order: Contact)* [1994] 1 F.L.R. 146 at 154–155):

> "first, in giving the child the security of knowing that his parents love him and are interested in his welfare; secondly, by avoiding any damaging sense of loss to the child in seeing himself abandoned by his parents; thirdly, by enabling the child to commit himself to the substitute family with the seal of approval of the natural parents; and, fourthly, by giving the child the necessary sense of family and personal identity. Contact, if maintained, is capable of reinforcing and increasing the chances of success of a permanent placement, whether on a long-term fostering basis or by adoption."

One further factor is that contact may be a step towards rehabilitation with the parents.

> In *Kirklees Metropolitan District Council v S (Contact to Newborn Babies)* [2006] 1 FLR 333, Bodey J. upheld an order for daily contact on the basis that it was an interim order and "was only intended to run for a number of weeks before being reviewed, with a view either to rehabilitation, or else to a likely reduction in quantum." (at para.36) She did, however emphasise that order for daily contact supervised by the local authority was "exceptionally unusual." (para.31)

The possibility of rehabilitation is an increasingly important consideration given that the European Court of Human Rights has stressed that care should ideally be only a temporary measure, and that any restrictions on contact with a child in care will be subjected to strict scrutiny by the court (see, *e.g. K and T v Finland* [2001] 2 F.L.R. 707, ECHR). There will of course be some cases, as Hale J. recognised in *Berkshire CC v B* [1997] 1 F.L.R. 171 at 176, Fam Div, in which the child clearly needs a new family for life and contact with the birth family would bring little or no benefit. In general, however, contact is only to be terminated where rehabilitation is not an option and post-adoption contact would not be beneficial (*Re H (Termination of Contact)* [2005] EWCA Civ 318).

It should however be borne in mind that the lack of an order refusing contact does not necessarily mean that contact will take place. The various pressures—on birth parents, new carers and local authorities—that can lead to the dimunution or cessation of contact in practice were fully described in J. Masson, C. Harrison and A. Pavlovic, *Lost and Found: Making and remaking working partnerships with parents of children in the care system* (1999). Recent research confirms that a high proportion of children lose contact with their parents: of the sample of children who had been identified as suffering or likely to suffer significant harm, one-third had lost contact with their birth mother by the time of the follow-up study, and over half were not in contact with their birth father (M. Brandon *et al.*, *Living with significant harm: a follow up study* (Centre for Research on the Child and the Family, 2005), p.47).

Ending the care order

A care order will last until the child reaches the age of 18 unless it is brought to an end **13–038** earlier. The child, the local authority, and any person with parental authority may apply to the court for the discharge of a care order (s.39(1)), and applications for discharge must be decided by reference to the child's welfare. There are a number of provisions designed to inhibit repeated fruitless applications: after an unsuccessful application has been made for the discharge of a care or supervision order, no further application can be made within the following six months, unless the leave of the court is required (s.91(15), and note too the court's powers under s.91(14), discussed at para.12–005).

A care order will also be brought to an end if the court makes a residence order or special guardianship order, and application for such orders constitute an alternative method of questioning its continued existence. Finally, the making of a placement order under the Adoption and Children Act 2002 will terminate a care order (s.21 of the 2002 Act), as will the making of the adoption order itself.

Leaving care

13–039   Most children who are looked after by the local authority return to their parents within a year. For those who cannot return to their parents, the local authority will need to decide what arrangements will be most suitable in the long term. Some children will be adopted and so leave the care system (on the process by which a child may be adopted, and the extent to which adoption is to be preferred to long-term fostering, see Ch.15). Others will remain subject to a care order until the age of 18. In the latter case the duties of the local authority will continue beyond the young person attaining adult status. The local authority should appoint a personal adviser and prepare a "pathway plan" in preparation for the young person's departure from care (see s.23D and 23E respectively), as well as keeping in touch with the young person and providing assistance (as set out in s.23C). The local authority owes similar duties to children aged 16 or 17 who have been looked after for at least 13 weeks since attaining the age of 14 (see s.23A and 23B).

E: THE PROBLEM CHILD

13–040   So far this chapter has been primarily concerned with the compulsory measures that may be directed against adult family members for the protection of vulnerable children. But what if it is the *child* who is the problem? The treatment of delinquent children is a topic in itself: this section simply addresses a number of points at which the system of child protection and the issue of delinquency intersect.

(1) *Secure accommodation orders*

13–041   Local authorities are not allowed to place any children that they look after in secure accommodation for more than 72 hours without an order from the court (s.25). Such an order can only be made if the child has a history of absconding and is likely to abscond from other accommodation and suffer significant harm, or if the child is likely to injure himself or others if kept in any other form of accommodation. While the child's welfare is a relevant consideration when deciding whether to make such an order, it is not the paramount consideration. Moreover, it was stressed by Charles J. in *S v Knowsley Borough Council* [2004] EWHC 491 (Fam) that the welfare of the child should be assessed on the basis:

"that the local authority is the decision-maker and thus on the basis whether a placement of the child in secure accommodation is within the permissible range of option s open to a local authority exercising its duties and functions to promote and safeguard the welfare of the child who is being looked after by it." (para.45)

This reflects the fact that once a care order has been made, a local authority has parental responsibility and the ability to take decisions about the child's welfare, subject only to limited scrutiny by the courts. In 2004 945 such orders were made.

The existence of secure accommodation orders underlines the fact that children may need protecting from themselves in certain circumstances. The fact that secure accommodation orders have been challenged in a number of cases indicates that the children concerned may not appreciate this: as Brooke L.J. has commented "[e]ven if the availability of such orders is a manifestation of the wish of a benevolent state to protect its children from harm, they will not be seen in this light by young people of C's age and maturity" (Re C (Secure Accommodation Order: Representation) [2001] 2 F.L.R. 169 at 183). The court stressed the importance of affording the procedural rights in Art.6(3) to children faced with such an order. In Re K (Secure Accommodation Order: Right to Liberty) [2001] 1 F.L.R. 526, CA, the Court of Appeal dismissed a claim that such an order amounted to a deprivation of liberty within Art.5 of the ECHR, on the basis that Art.5(1) of the Convention permitted restrictions on liberty for the purpose of educational supervision, which was being provided to the child in this case. Thorpe L.J. went further and argued that the deprivation of liberty could be seen as the exercise of parental responsibility for the child's welfare, but the majority of the Court of Appeal did not agree, partly because such orders went beyond normal parental control, and partly because they could be used even where the local authority had not acquired parental responsibility for the child.

(2) *Duties owed to children detained in Young Offender Institutions*

In *R. ota the Howard League for Penal Reform v Secretary of State for the Home* **13–042**
Department [2002] EWHC 2497 (Admin) the court was asked to consider whether local authorities owed any duties to children detained in Young Offender Institutions. As the judge noted, the evidence "painted a deeply disturbing picture of the YOI population":

"Over half of the children in YOIs have been in care. Significant percentages report having suffered or experienced abuse of a violent, sexual or emotional nature. A very large percentage have run away from home at some time or another. Very significant percentages were not living with either parent prior to coming into custody and were either homeless or living in insecure accommodation. Over half were not attending school, either because they had been permanently excluded or because of long-term non-attendance ... " (para.11)

Evidence of the bullying, drug use, self-harming and suicide attempts that occurred within YOIs was also given. The judge held that the duties that a local authority would normally owe to children under either s.17 or s.47 "do not cease to be owed merely because the child is currently detained in a YOI" but that such duties would have to take effect "subject to the necessary requirements of imprisonment." The judge further held that under human rights law the Prison Service was under obligations to have regard to the "welfare principle" and to take effective steps to protect children in YOIs from ill-treatment. Subsequently, it was agreed that the Youth Justice Board would devote £1m in order to fund extra social worker places at YOIs, to ensure that the duties of local authorities were carried out. In addition, it is one of the functions of the new Local Safeguarding Children Boards to consider what arrangements should be put in place to safeguard children in custody.

(3) *The delinquent child and the care system*

13–043 The extent to which the criminal law should be influenced by considerations of the child's welfare—or the care system influenced by the child's criminality—is a difficult and controversial issue. In 1969, the Children and Young Persons Act allowed the court to make care orders on the basis that the child had committed an offence and was in need of care and control; but little use was made of this provision, and other methods of dealing with young offenders—notably police cautioning and, in appropriate cases, prosecution—were in practice preferred. In 1989, the Children Act made it clear that delinquency and child protection were to be governed by somewhat different considerations, and the relevant provisions of the Children and Young Persons Act 1969 were repealed. However, in the 1990s there was increasing concern about some aspects of youth behaviour, which were reflected in the Crime and Disorder Act 1998. Section 11 of the 1998 Act allows a magistrates' court to make a "child safety order" if a child under 10 years of age has, for example, committed an act which would be an offence were he not under the age of criminal responsibility or has acted in a manner causing harassment, alarm or distress to others or has infringed the provisions of a curfew notice made by a local authority under powers conferred by s.14 of the Act. Such an order places a child under the supervision of a social worker or member of a youth offending team and will impose requirements to ensure that the child receives appropriate care, is subject to proper control, and is prevented from repeating the behaviour which has triggered the proceedings. The Act initially provided that a care order could be made if the child safety order was breached, even if the threshold criteria were not satisfied, but this was controversial, and the possibility was removed by the Children Act 2004 (s.60). It remains possible for the court to make a "parenting order" under the 1998 Act, requiring the parent or guardian to attend counselling and guidance sessions (see further para.11–006 above).

F: REMEDIES AVAILABLE WHERE THE LOCAL AUTHORITY HAS FAILED

13–044 The decision of a local authority may be challenged through the normal appeal process, but a number of other options may also be available. As the cases described below indicate, the claim may relate to the failure of the local authority to take a child into care, the interference with family life caused by doing so, or the harm caused to the child while in local authority care.

(1) *Complaints procedures*

13–045 Section 26 of the Children Act 1989 requires local authorities to establish procedures for considering representations (including complaints) made to them by a wide range of people likely to be affected by decisions about the exercise of local authority powers and the discharge of their duties. At least one person who is independent of the authority must participate. The Department of Health and the Social Services Inspectorate have given guidance on the conduct of reviews, and the local authority is required by law to have "due regard" to the findings of the panel. It appears that such procedures are often cheaper, quicker and more satisfactory than judicial review (see, e.g. *R. v Hampshire CC, Ex p. H* [1999] 2 F.L.R. 359 at 366, CA). However, the decision as to whether panel recommendations should be followed remains one for the local authority and—as in *Re T (Accommodation by Local Authority)* [1995] 1 F.L.R. 159, Johnson J., where the review panel, after a "searching and vigorous enquiry" had upheld the complaint—the local authority may refuse to accept the recommendations. In that event, a complaint may in some circumstances be taken to the Ombudsman (Local Commissioner for Administration).

As part of the Government's policy of involving children in the decision-making process to a greater extent, the Adoption and Children Act 2002 amended the 1989 to provide that children making complaints under s.26 should have "assistance by way of representation" (s.26A, and see the Advocacy Services and Representations Procedure (Children) (Amendment) Regulations 2004, SI 2004/719).

(2) *Judicial review*

The lawfulness of a local authority's decision (as distinct from the merits of the **13–046** decision) may be challenged by way of judicial review. However, the fact that many of the duties imposed upon local authorities are only "target" duties will restrict the extent to which an authority's decision not to provide services can be challenged by way of judicial review: see *R. ota A v Lambeth LBC* [2002] 1 F.L.R. 353, CA. The court may find that the decision of the local authority was irrational and unreasonable, but even so it can only direct the local authority to reconsider the issue, and cannot require it to provide the services in question (*Re T (Judicial Review: Local Authority Decisions Concerning Child in Need)* [2003] EWHC 2515 (Admin)).

Furthermore, the courts have emphasised judicial review should not be used as a substitute for challenging decisions through the usual processes:

> In *R. ota X v Gloucestershire CC* [2003] EWHC 850 (Admin), a couple sought permission to apply for judicial review in order to prevent the local authority from applying for orders in relation to their unborn child. The judge held that judicial review was a remedy of last resort, and that the proceedings should be defended as and when they were commenced.

(3) *Action in negligence*

In the past actions in negligence against local authorities exercising the discretion **13–047** conferred on them by child care legislation were firmly discouraged. Claims were struck out as disclosing no reasonable cause of action, a practice endorsed at the highest level (see *e.g. X (minors) v Bedfordshire CC* [1995] 2 A.C. 633, HL). However, the European Court of Human Rights expressed its disapproval of this practice in *Osman v UK* [1999] 1 F.L.R. 193, ECHR, and in *Barrett v Enfield LBC* [1999] 2 F.L.R. 426, HL, the House of Lords held that it was wrong to strike out a claim for damages in respect of a failure to provide a proper standard of care to a child looked after by a local authority. Successful claims were subsequently made by adults who, as children, had suffered abuse while resident in children's home (see *e.g. C v Flintshire County Council* [2001] 2 F.L.R. 33, *KR v Bryn Alyn Community (Holdings) Ltd* [2003] 1 F.L.R. 1203).

Yet even though there is no longer any blanket immunity from actions in negligence for local authority exercising their statutory duties under the child protection legislation, the court may still be of the opinion that no duty of care is owed in a particular situation. For example, it has been held that there is no common law duty of care to parents not to make negligent allegations of child abuse. A majority of the House of Lords held in *D v East Berkshire Community Health NHS Trust; MAK v Dewsbury Healthcare NHS Trust; RK v Oldham NHS Trust* [2005] UKHL 23 that to impose such a duty would result in a conflict of interests for the professionals involved. As Lord Rodger pointed out:

> "Acting on, or persisting in, a suspicion of abuse might well be reasonable when only the child's interests were engaged, but unreasonable if the interests of the parents had also to be taken into account. Of its very nature, therefore, this kind of duty of care to the parents would cut across the duty of care to the children. (para.110)

No such policy reasons precluded a duty being owed to the child in this situation (see the decision of the Court of Appeal on this point: [2003] EWCA Civ 1151). Similarly, in *A v Essex County Council* [2003] EWCA Civ 1848, it was held that it was:

> "not fair, just and reasonable to impose upon the professionals involved in compiling reports for adoption agencies a duty of care towards the prospective adopters. We would certainly not rule out a duty of care towards the child, but that does not arise in this case." (*per* Hale L.J., para.56)

—although on the facts of that case the adoption agency were negligent in failing to pass on the information that it had decided the parents should have (and see further para.15–022 below).

As the above account indicates, the courts are more willing to accept a duty of care to the child than to the parents. There remains a question as to whether a local authority could be held to be negligent for failing to take action to protect a child. Even if the courts were to decide that the decision not to institute care proceedings— which necessarily involves the weighing of competing public interests—could be made the subject of an action in negligence, it might be difficult to establish the necessary elements of an action in negligence—for example that the relationship between the children and the social workers was sufficiently close to justify the imposition of a duty of care. The individuals affected may, however, be able to establish that the inaction of the authorities has breached their human rights.

(4) Human rights

13–048   In the absence of a remedy in the domestic courts, cases have been taken to the European Court of Human Rights. The UK has been found to be in breach of Art.3 for failing to protect children from inhuman and degrading treatment, and in breach of Art.13 for failing to provide a domestic remedy for such complaints (see, *e.g. Z v UK* [2001] 2 F.L.R. 612, ECHR; *E v UK* [2002] 3 F.C.R. 700, ECHR; and *DP and JC v UK* [2003] 1 F.L.R. 50, ECHR). In *Z v UK* (which involved a claim by the children in the *Bedfordshire* case) and *E v UK* the local authority had been aware that the children were suffering abuse but failed to protect them. The court noted the "pattern of lack of investigation, communication or co-operation", which had dogged the case. However, there are limits on what is expected of local authorities.

In *DP and JC v UK* (above), it was held that there was no breach of Art.3 where the local authority was not aware that the children were being sexually abused by their stepfather. While the local authority had had frequent contact with the family, the latter's problems were explicable on the basis of the problems that were already known to the local authority and there was no reason to suspect a deeper problem.

The UK has also been found to be in breach of its human rights obligations where local authorities *have* intervened.

In *P, C and S v UK* [2002] 3 F.C.R. 1, ECHR, the mother, an American citizen, was suspected of suffering from Munchausen Syndrome by Proxy and her elder son was in care in the US. She met the father, who was researching this condition, and they subsequently married. When the mother became pregnant, the local authority decided to undertake a risk assessment under s.47. As the parents did not co-operate with this, the authority decided that an emergency protection order should be taken out as soon as the child was born. The ECHR held that it was within the proper role of the authority to seek such an order, but that the way in which it was implemented breached Art.8. The child's safety could be ensured while she was in the hospital, especially while the mother was confined to bed, and there was no need to remove her immediately. It also held that there was a breach of Art.6, as in the circumstances of the case the mother needed representation in order for the proceedings to be fair, even if such representation would not have affected the outcome of the case (and see also, *Venema v The Netherlands* [2003] 1 F.L.R. 551, ECHR).

Of course, since the enactment of the Human Rights Act 1998, it is no longer necessary to take the case to the European Court in order to obtain redress for a breach of human rights (see para.1–015 above). The courts have emphasised that any complaints that an individual's human rights have been breached by the local authority's actions "should be dealt with within the context of the care proceedings and by the court which is dealing with the care proceedings.": *Re L (Care Proceedings: Human Rights Claims)* [2003] EWHC 665 (Fam), *per* Munby J., para.25, endorsed by the Court of Appeal in *Re V (Care Proceedings: Human Rights Claims)* [2004] EWCA Civ 54. Free-standing applications under the Human Rights Act are therefore discouraged while care proceedings are taking place, although they may be appropiate once the care proceedings have come to an end.

While the courts are increasingly alert to the human rights of the various parties, it has been affirmed by the House of Lords that the overall scheme of the Children Act 1989 complies with the Human Rights Act. As Wall L.J. noted in *Re V (Care Proceedings: Human Rights Claims)* [2004] EWCA Civ 54:

"The short message from *Re S; Re W* is that whatever its imperfections, the 1989 Act is HRA 1998 compliant." (para.115)

G: CONCLUSION

Having begun the chapter with a discussion of some of the crises to affect the issue of **13–049** child protection in recent years, and, in the last section, examined the remedies available against a local authority that has failed in some way, it is perhaps appropriate to redress the balance by pointing out that the cases with happy endings are unlikely to come to the attention of the media or the courts. It has been noted that:

> "Out of sight, skilled and diligent professionals arrange vital protection for vulnerable children and provide or organise effective support for their parents and wider families." (P. Dale, R. Green and R. Fellows, *Child Protection Assessments Following Serious Injuries to Infants: Fine Judgments* (John Wiley & Sons Ltd, 2005), p.12)

There is, however, a lack of information on the effects of state intervention. While the DfES provides comprehensive statistics on "looked-after" children, follow-up studies tend to be small-scale. The evidence from one such study is not exactly reassuring. Of an initial cohort of 105 children identified as suffering significant harm between 1993 and 1994, information was available on 77 in 2001–2, and it was found that 57 per cent of them had suffered further neglect or abuse (M. Brandon *et al.*, *Living with significant harm: a follow up study* (Centre for Research on the Child and the Family, 2005), p.49).

Most children who are looked after by the local authority return to their parents within a year. For those who cannot return to their parents, the local authority will need to decide what sort of placement will be most suitable in the long term. Chapter 15 considers the process by which a child may be adopted, and the extent to which adoption is to be preferred to long-term fostering. Before this, however, it is necessary to consider the welfare principle in more detail, since it plays an important role in both private and public law proceedings relating to children, and this forms the subject-matter of the next chapter.

Chapter 14

Should the Court make an Order? The Welfare Principle

A: Introduction

The family justice system seeks to promote the welfare of children, and, on one view, **14–001** any exposition of that system should begin by setting out the courts' approach to ascertaining and promoting the welfare of those with whom it is concerned. Why then does this book relegate the main systematic treatment of this topic—it has of course been mentioned in passing in many earlier parts of the text—almost to the end? The answer lies in the structure of the legislation, and in the approach to it that the lawyer must take. Although the child's welfare is the paramount consideration for the court when it is considering whether to make orders in both public and private law proceedings, this is not the same as a rule that any order that promotes the child's welfare can be made. In public law cases, the question of welfare does not even arise unless and until the court has decided that it has jurisdiction to make an order—usually because it has been established that the child has suffered or is at risk of suffering "significant harm". Even in private law proceedings there are constraints on the court's powers, as not every person can invoke the court's jurisdiction. The reader should have an understanding of the types of orders that can be made before proceeding to the issue as to how the court exercises its discretion.

Part B considers the circumstances in which the welfare principle will apply, and the factors that the court is directed to take into account in assessing the best interests of the child are set out in Part C. One key debate in recent years has been whether the welfare principle is compatible with the European Convention on Human Rights, and this is considered in Part D.

B: The Fundamental Principle: Child's Welfare Paramount

Section 1 of the Children Act 1989 reasserts the principle established in the context of **14–002** wardship and first placed on a statutory footing in 1925, namely that when a court determines any question with respect to the upbringing of a child, or the administration of a child's property or income, the child's welfare shall be the court's paramount consideration. This means that the principle only applies where such questions are directly in issue in a matter properly before the court. Three important qualifications on the applicability of the welfare principle flow from the wording of the Act.

(1) *Issue must relate to child's upbringing, or the administration of his property or income*

14–003   Questions of where the child should live or be educated clearly do relate to the child's upbringing, and so the court's decisions on such matters—for example under s.8 of the Children Act—will be decided by reference to the welfare principle. But in *Re A and W (Residence Order: Leave to Apply)* [1992] Fam. 182, CA, the court held that the decision of whether to grant or refuse an application for leave to apply for a s.8 order was not such a question. It was only after the court had granted leave, and heard the application, that the question of upbringing arose. It seems therefore that the child's welfare will not be the paramount consideration in many of the procedural issues that have to be resolved in the conduct of litigation.

Again, although the child's welfare is the paramount consideration in deciding questions about the *administration* of the child's property, it is not the paramount consideration in deciding whether or not to make an order requiring a parent to maintain the child (although the Court of Appeal has held that it is still a very important factor: see *Re P (Child: Financial Provision)* [2003] EWCA Civ 837 at para.7–024 above).

The welfare principle does however govern a decision about whether the child's money should, for example, be invested in buying a house where he could live, or whether it would be better to invest the money and use the income to pay rent and so on.

The question of precisely what questions do relate to the child's upbringing can be a difficult one. In *Kelly v BBC* [2000] 3 F.C.R. 509, Fam Div, it was suggested that upbringing "applies only to those processes of which the child is the object, and not to those in which the child is the subject" (*per* Munby J. at 539), although this distinction may be difficult to apply in practice and would seem to pay insufficient attention to the active role of the child.

(2) *The question of upbringing must be the central issue for decision*

14–004   There are many disputes between family members that may have a profound effect on children and the way in which they are brought up—perhaps the most obvious example being the grant of a divorce to the parents of a child. But the welfare of the child is not the governing factor for the court in this situation, nor in any other case where the question of upbringing arises only incidentally.

(3) *The matter must be within the court's jurisdiction*

14–005   To say that the court can only make orders if the matter is properly before it and within its jurisdiction may seem a statement of the obvious; but there are reasons why in the present context this general principle needs to be kept in mind. First—as already pointed out—there is no jurisdiction to make care or supervision orders unless specific criteria are satisfied (see Ch.13, above). Secondly, the general principle may be displaced by statute in specific circumstances. One example is the Child Abduction and Custody Act 1985 (see para.12–047 above), which is premised on the assumption that it is generally appropriate for children to be speedily returned to the country from which they have been wrongfully removed and under which the welfare of individual children is excluded from the court's consideration. Another is the Child Support Act 1991 (see Ch.7).

With these points in mind, the key elements of the welfare principle can now be considered.

C: THE WELFARE PRINCIPLE

The Children Act 1989 states three key elements to the application of the welfare **14–006** principle by the courts. These are laid down in the 1989 Act, but apply to all cases in which a court determines any question relating to the matters set out in para.14–003 above. First, the court is directed to have regard "to the general principle that any delay in determining the question is likely to prejudice the welfare of the child" (s.1(2)). Secondly, in considering whether to make any particular order, the court "shall not make the order or any of the orders unless it considers that doing so would be better for the child than making no order at all" (s.1(5)). Thirdly, the court is to have "particular regard" to a checklist of factors set out in s.1(3) in certain situations. These three components will be considered in turn:

No delay

As the Official Guide to the Children Act puts it, the Act recognises that "the child's **14–007** sense of time may be more acute than an adult's and that delay in determining the proceedings may in itself be harmful to the child" (para.3.23), and that delay in court proceedings may put stress on all those involved which may rub off generally in damage to the child. However, it is important to note that the legislation merely states that delay is "likely" to be prejudicial. It certainly does not seek to prescribe that a case should never be adjourned, or to prevent the court from a deliberate decision that delay might be beneficial: see *C v Solihull MBC* [1994] 2 F.L.R. 290 at 304, *per* Ward J. The Act is aimed at minimising mere "drift", and the welfare of the child may well be served by purposive delay. It may, for example, be inappropriate to make an order where matters are still in a state of flux (see, *e.g. Re C (a child)* [2001] 3 F.C.R. 381, CA). More time may be needed to prepare reports or to explore the possibility of a negotiated solution. Similarly, in the case of *Re K (Non-accidental injuries: Perpetrator: New evidence)* [2004] EWCA Civ 1181, it was held that the delay that would be occasioned by the admission of new evidence was outweighed by considerations of justice, the public interest in identifying the perpetrator, and the possibility of the children being reunited with their mother if she was excluded as a perpetrator.

Is the order necessary?

When the Law Commission was examining the law in the 1980s, it expressed concern **14–008** over what it believed to be the common tendency to assume that some order about children should always be made in divorce and other matrimonial proceedings, effectively as "part of the package" provided by the legal system (*Report on Guardianship and Custody* (Law Com. No.172, 1988), para.3.2). The Commission thought that there was a risk that orders allocating "custody" and "access" (according to the terms then used) might polarise the parents' roles and perhaps alienate the child.

Section 1(5) was an attempt to meet this concern. In effect, the court needs to justify a decision to make an order: it must ask itself what, precisely, would be the effect of making an order, and whether this would or would not be positively in the child's interests. An order should only be made if the court reaches a decision that an order would be better for the child than making no order.

There will obviously be many cases in which the court will find no difficulty in satisfying itself that to make an order would be better for the child than not to do so. If there has been a dispute that the court has had to resolve, the case for making an order would seem to be almost unanswerable. In fact, in *Re P (Parental Dispute: Judicial Determination)* [2002] EWCA Civ 1627, an order that the mother should be able to determine where the children were to go to school was held to amount to a failure to adjudicate. Thorpe L.J. noted that "in the end, the parents have a right to a judicial determination" (at 289) and stated that it was not open to a judge to give more or less absolute decision-making powers to one of the parents.

Moreover, the Court of Appeal has recently held that even if the parents are now in agreement an order may still be appropriate:

> In *Re G (Children)* [2005] EWCA Civ 1237 the unmarried parents had agreed after much discussion that the father should have parental responsibility and that a residence order should be made in favour of the mother. The judge refused to make the residence order on the basis that it was not the role of the court simply to rubber-stamp agreements between the parties. The Court of Appeal allowed the appeal and held that the order should be made. Ward L.J. noted that s.1(5) "does not, in my judgment, create a presumption one way or another. All it demands is that before the court makes any order it must ask the question: will it be better for the child to make the order than making no order at all?" (para.10)

It is interesting to note that the reasons given for making the residence order in this case appear to focus more on the benefits to the parents in making the order, and only tangentially on the benefits to the children involved. Ward L.J. suggested that the order would give the mother security and peace of mind, which would be "an integral and important factor in producing stability in the lives of the children in care of the parent" (para.11). Rather more tenuously, he suggested that the order was advantageous to the children involved because it was better for matters to be resolved by agreement between the parents rather than by the court—an argument that could equally have been used to refuse making an order in this case. The critical factor—and the one least related to the welfare of the children—was that the court should be cautious about going behind "agreements carefully negotiated in difficult questions of this kind" (para.13). The court should, he suggested, instead respect the view of the parents that an order would be beneficial to the management of their children's lives.

Even when there is no dispute, an order may be desirable to clarify the position for third parties. For example:

> In *B v B (A Minor) (Residence Order)* [1992] 2 F.L.R. 327, CA, a teenage mother's child was being cared for by its grandmother. The court made a residence order in the grandmother's favour in part to confer parental responsibility on her—there had been problems with the local education authority, for

example, who questioned whether the grandmother could authorise school trips and so on—and in part to make it plain that the birth mother was not to take the child away from her grandmother's care.

The welfare checklist

The welfare checklist consists of a list of factors to which the court should have regard **14–009** in determining issues relating to the child's welfare. The hope was that such a list would help achieve greater consistency and clarity in the application of the law. It may of course be questioned whether it leads to greater objectivity: many of the factors listed are relatively open-ended and capable of more than one interpretation on the facts of any particular case. Furthermore, the list may itself give rise to debate: some commentators may feel that it gives too little weight to the interests of other family members, others that the reference to the child's cultural and religious background is in fact intended to support parental wishes in these areas. The reader should consider the assumptions underpinning the inclusion of particular factors on the checklist.

It should be noted that the court is only *obliged* "to have regard in particular" to the matters specified in the checklist in two cases: first, where an application is opposed; and, secondly, where the application relates to a care or supervision order (s.1(4)). However, as the checklist is merely an aid to ascertaining the child's welfare, it is unlikely that the outcome of the case will turn on whether reference to the check-list is mandatory or not. For example:

> In *Dawson v Wearmouth* [1997] 2 F.L.R. 629, CA, (the facts of which are described below at para.14–013), the issue was whether a change to the child's surname should be allowed. There were two possible procedures. One was for the father to seek a specific issue order under s.8. Given that the application was opposed, the court would be required to refer to the check-list. The other was to seek an order under s.13 (which prohibits the change of a child's surname in cases in which a residence order is in force), in which case reference to the check-list would not be mandatory. The Court of Appeal held that the distinction was more apparent than real: in either case, the judge would "invariably have regard to the considerations identified in [the checklist] in his search for welfare as the paramount consideration even if under no specific duty so to do" (at 635). Although the case subsequently went to the House of Lords, there was no appeal on this aspect of the matter.

A second preliminary question to consider is the use to be made of the checklist. It has been said that it provides a "useful and important discipline in ensuring that all relevant factors are carefully considered and balanced" (*B v B (Residence Order: Reasons for Decision)* [1997] 2 F.L.R. 602 at 607–608, CA, *per* Holman J.), and it will be a useful aide-memoire in almost all cases. But is the judge required to go laboriously through the specified matters item by item? In *H v H (Residence Order: Leave to Remove)* [1995] F.L.R. 529 it was held that this was not required:

> "Perhaps one should remember, that when one calls it a checklist, that it is not like the list of checks which an airline pilot has to make with his co-pilot, aloud one to the other before he takes off. The statute does not say that the judge has

to read out the seven items in s.1(3) and pronounce his conclusion on each. Sometimes judges will do that, maybe more often than not; but it is not mandatory." (*per* Staughton L.J. at 532; and see also *B v B (Residence Order: Reasons for Decision)* [1997] 2 F.L.R. 602, CA).

Finally, it should also be noted that, while some of the factors in the checklist overlap (*e.g.* the characteristics and needs of the child, and the abilities of each parent to meet those needs), others may conflict on the facts of the case (*e.g.* the wishes of the child and his or her perceived needs). Moreover, since the court's assessment of the welfare of the child will depend on *all* the circumstances of the case, care should be taken in applying the authorities cited.

With these points in mind, the specific factors listed in the checklist should be considered:

(1) *The ascertainable wishes and feelings of the child concerned (considered in the light of his age and understanding)*

14–010   The relevance of a child's own wishes has been re-enforced by the *Gillick* decision (see paras 11–033 *et seq.*), and by Art.12 of the United Nations Convention on the Rights of the Child, which proclaims the right "of the child who is capable of forming his or her own views to express those views freely in all matters affecting the child, the views of the child being given due weight in accordance with the age and maturity of the child." It has been said that the right of a child to be heard is a cornerstone of the Children Act (see *Re H (A Minor) (Care Proceedings: Child's Wishes)* [1993] 1 F.L.R. 440 at 450, *per* Thorpe J.). In practice, a number of difficult issues are raised. For example, how old does a child have to be before its views are accorded significant weight? How is the requirement of "understanding" interpreted? What if the child's wishes conflict with the court's perception of the child's welfare? And how are the wishes of the child to be ascertained in the first place?

A study of the lower courts carried out by Smart *et al* (*Residence and Contact Disputes in Court: Vol.1* (DCA, 2003), ch.7) found that the courts did listen to children who were deemed old enough to make informed decisions. The weight that is given to the wishes of children of different ages is neatly illustrated by the decision in *Re S (Contact: Children's Views)* [2002] EWHC 540:

> In this case the father sought contact with his three children, V, JO and JA, aged 16, 14 and 12 respectively. It was held that there was no point in making an order in respect of V, who was opposed to contact. JO was prepared to have limited contact with his father, but only on his own terms, and the court simply ordered that he make himself available for contact by mutual agreement. The judge noted that the father had not grasped the fact that his children were young adults and that hectoring them, and not listening to them, was likely to be counter-productive. He also doubted the quality of contact that was only achieved by a court order against the wishes of the children. The youngest child had maintained contact with his father, and the order allowed him some choice—"commensurate with his age"—about what form contact should take.

As the judge in that case appreciated, young adults may vote with their feet and refuse to comply with the orders that the court has made—although in *R (CD) v Isle of Anglesey County Council* [2004] EWHC 1635 (Admin) it was stressed that the inability of a disabled child to literally vote with her feet would not detract from the weight to be attached to her wishes. In that case Wilson J. held that a care plan was unlawful on the basis that it (*inter alia*) failed to give due consideration to the wishes of the child:

"Notwithstanding my 11 years of service in the Family Division, I cannot recollect a case in which, otherwise than in relation to secure accommodation, it has been considered seriously arguable that a 15-year-old child should be required to reside at an establishment to an extent substantially contrary to his or her wishes and feelings.... Of course a 15 year old who does not suffer substantial disabilities... can, as is the frequent experience of the Division, vote with his or her feet. C can do no such thing; but it would, for obvious reasons, be wrong to pay any less respect to her wishes and feelings in consequence." (para.61)

In addition the views of far younger children may be taken into account, especially where domestic violence has occurred:

In *Re G (a child) (domestic violence: direct contact)* [2001] 2 F.C.R. 134, Fam Div, the child's father had been responsible for the death of her mother. He sought contact with her while he was in prison serving a sentence for manslaughter but the court refused. Butler-Sloss P. noted that the reluctance of a three-year-old child to attend contact would not normally carry much weight, but in this case, as the child was traumatised by the events that had occurred and suffered from nightmares, the case against direct—*i.e.* face-to-face—contact was overwhelming.

While this was an extreme situation, a number of recent cases indicate that the court is reluctant to order contact against the wishes of a child where domestic violence has occurred: see *Re L, Re V, Re M, Re H (Contact: Domestic Violence)* [2000] 2 F.L.R. 334 (discussed at para.12–030, above); *Re M and B (children) (contact: domestic violence)* [2001] 1 F.C.R. 116 (younger child was eight years old and "had a perfectly clear perception of whether or not she wanted to receive communication from her father"); and *Re U (a child)* [2003] EWCA Civ 27. Lest it be thought that the wishes of the child and mother always coincide in such cases, it should be noted that in *I v N* [2003] EWHC 327 the court ordered contact against the wishes of the mother, at least in part because of the child's express wish that contact should continue.

The court will also take into consideration how the children in question reached their decisions: are their expressed wishes genuine or the result of pressure from one or both of their parents? This has been a particular consideration in a number of recent contact cases. The case of *In re M (Children)(Contact: Long-term Best Interests* [2005] EWCA Civ 1090 illustrates how the court's perception of the child's understanding may affect the outcome of the case. In this case the children were teenagers— one was almost 16 and the other 13—and the judge noted that at this age their views would normally carry great weight, but:

"Their understanding in this case is corrupted by the malignancy of the views with which they have been force-fed over many years of their life, until so blinded by them that they cannot see the truth either of their mother's good qualities or of the good it will do them to have some contact with her." (para.26)

By contrast:

> In *Re M, T, P, K and B (Care: Change of Name)* [2000] 2 F.L.R. 645, Fam Div, the children had been the victims of abuse and were taken into care. The local authority applied to change the surname of each of the children, at their own request. It was noted that the evidence was "all one way insofar as the wishes of the children are concerned", as they were afraid that their father, or members of his extended family, would track them down. The judge also held that the children's wishes were the result of long deliberation, had not been planted by others, and were not transient or equivocal. The application to change their names was granted.

Despite the importance that is attached to the wishes expressed by children, the courts have emphasised that decisions in these cases are for the court, and not for the child. One weighty consideration is the danger of putting the burden of making a choice on the child:

> In *Adams v Adams* [1984] 5 F.L.R. 768, CA, for example, Dunn L.J. remarked that the pressures on children were "quite sufficient when the marriage has broken down and one of the parents has left home without putting on the additional burden of being made to feel that they have to decide their own future."

Another factor to bear in mind is that it is the child's welfare, and not the child's wishes, that is the paramount consideration for the court (see further para.11–038 above). The court may be of the opinion that to accede to the wishes of the child would not be in the child's best interests.

There is a further question regarding the information about the child's wishes that is available to the court. There is no requirement that the judge should see, let alone hear, the child. The way in which the wishes of the child are conveyed to the court differs significantly between public and private proceedings. In the former, the child will usually be separately represented: s.41(1) of the 1989 Act provides that in certain specified proceedings—including applications for care orders—the child shall be separately represented unless the court is "satisfied that it is not necessary to do so in order to safeguard his interests." This means that a CAFCASS officer will normally be appointed as a "children's guardian", and will report to the court on the wishes of the child and matters relating to the welfare of the child. It should be noted, however, that the role of the children's guardian is not simply to act as a mouthpiece for the child's wishes but to advise the court on what is in the child's best interests. The children's guardian will also appoint and instruct a solicitor to present the child's case in court: again, the solicitor acts on the instructions of the children's guardian rather than the instructions of the child—although a child of sufficient understanding may choose to be represented by his or her own solicitor (see para.13–016 above).

In private proceedings the situation is rather different. The court may, but is not required to, call for a welfare report under s.7 (see above para.12–034). At present CAFCASS supplies around 30,000 welfare reports each year, but the government's proposal that CAFCASS officers—termed in this context child and family reporters—

should devote less of their time to writing reports raises questions about how the wishes of children are to be conveyed to the court.

At present the circumstances in which a child may be separately represented in private proceedings are somewhat limited. Under r.9(5) of the Family Proceedings Rules 1991 the court may appoint a person to be the guardian ad litem of the child, but the scope of this rule has been cut down by two recent developments: first, the indication that separate representation should be used only in cases of "significant difficulty" (see *President's Direction: Representation of Children in Family Proceedings Pursuant to Family Proceedings Rules 1991, Rule 9.5* [2004] 1 F.L.R. 1188); and, secondly, the fact that judges below the level of circuit judge may no longer appoint a guardian (*The Appointment of Guardians in Accordance with Rule 9.5 and the President's Practice Direction*).

One promise of reform has not yet been made good. Section 122 of the Adoption and Children Act 2002 added proceedings under s.8 of the 1989 Act to the list of specified proceedings in s.41(6), which would entail the appointment of a children's guardian and a solicitor, as in public law proceedings. While this provision has come into force, as yet the necessary amendments to the Family Proceedings Rules required to give effect to it have not been made. Subsequent research commissioned by the government "does not indicate that separate representation would be right for all children in all cases." (Baroness Ashton, Hansard (HL), January 11, 2006, vol.677 col.WS12). It remains to be seen what rules will be devised to secure the representation of children in s.8 cases.

The above discussion has focused on the representation of children in court proceedings, but as already described (see paras 1–004 and 12–033) current policy is to divert disputing parents away from the court wherever possible. Whether children will have a greater voice in these alternative modes of dispute resolution is open to doubt.

(2) *The child's physical, emotional and educational needs*

The need to provide for a child's physical care is self-evident: the court would not, for **14–011** example, make a residence order in favour of a parent who was homeless and had no prospect of obtaining housing. It is true that it has been said that in most cases "disadvantages of a material sort must be of little weight" (*Stephenson v Stephenson* [1985] F.L.R. 1140 at 1148) but a basic minimum of physical provision is required.

There was a time when the courts tended to apply presumptions in assessing a child's needs—for example that young children, and girls approaching puberty, should be with their mother, while boys over a certain age should be with their father. Although the more modern approach is not to make any such presumption (and see para.12–026 above), it seems that there is still a likelihood that the courts will think it natural that young children should be with their mothers. As the House of Lords pointed out in the Scottish case of *Brixey v Lynas* [1996] 2 F.L.R. 499 at 505:

> " . . . the advantage to a very young child of being with its mother is a consideration which must be taken into account in deciding where lie its best interests . . . It is neither a presumption nor a principle but rather recognition of a widely held belief based on practical experience and the workings of nature . . . where a very young child has been with its mother since birth and there is no criticism of her ability to care for the child only the strongest competing advantages are likely to prevail."

But where this is not the case, the courts may grant a residence order in favour of a father:

> In *Re D (a child) (residence: ability to parent)* [2001] 2 F.C.R. 751, CA, the father obtained a residence order when his daughter was only one year old, due to concerns over the mother's drinking habits. The order was confirmed at a final hearing and upheld on appeal. There were concerns about the mother's medical condition, and while she was available as a full-time carer, the importance of this was much diminished where the attachment between mother and child had been interrupted, and the father had been caring for the child for longer than the mother.

In considering questions of education, the court will often be primarily concerned with the dangers of uprooting a child from a school where satisfactory progress is being made. But there may be cases in which there is a clash of values to be resolved:

> In *May v May* [1986] 1 F.L.R. 325, CA, the question was whether two boys, aged six and eight, should live with their father or their mother. There was no conflict about the competence of either parent, but there was a conflict of values between them. The father attached importance to academic achievement, punctuality, tidiness, and giving assistance in the household. The mother and her cohabitant had, in contrast, a much more free and easy approach to life and to such issues as the amount of time that the children should spend working, watching television, and so on. The Court of Appeal refused to upset the trial judge's decision that the children should live with the father.

It is not easy to see what kind of "expertise" could provide any useful guidance in cases such as that, involving no more (and no less) than a choice between different values.

(3) *The likely effect on the child of any change in his circumstances*

14–012 This is one of the matters on which the views of child development specialists have been persuasive. The courts today generally start from the proposition that stability is all important for children's welfare, and accordingly they will be reluctant to interfere with the *status quo* unless there is clear justification for doing so. For example:

> In *Re B (Residence Order: Status Quo)* [1998] 1 F.L.R. 368, CA, a residence order was made in favour of the father of a four-year-old child. The father had given up his work to care for the child full time. Two years later the mother (who had remarried) applied for and was granted a residence order. Although the welfare officer had reported that there was no overwhelming reason for moving the child, the judge took the view that short-term distress caused by the change would be relatively insignificant compared to the benefits the child would gain from the improvements in the contact arrangements that he thought would follow the change. The Court of Appeal held that this decision was plainly wrong, and that the overwhelming importance for securing the child's future was preservation of the *status quo*.

This would seem to indicate that the arrangements that the parties make before the court order are likely to have an impact on the court's final decision (which may lead to skirmishes about residence before the final hearing: see, *e.g. S v N* [2003] All E.R.) (D) 260). However, *Re A (children) (shared residence)* [2001] EWCA Civ 1795 demonstrates that the initial arrangements are not necessarily determinative:

> In this case, the mother left the family home in 2001 but retained contact with her children. A residence order subsequently provided that the two younger children were to live with her. The father argued that the judge had changed their residence without giving reasons, but the Court of Appeal held that the previous arrangements had merely been temporary and that it was not a true *"status quo"* case.

The case illustrates how even apparently objective concepts such as the *status quo* may be open to interpretation. The status quo may, in fact, involve a variety of different elements. For example, in *Re B (Children)* [2005] EWCA Civ 643 the mother had been the child's primary carer, but the court held that this was only one aspect of the status quo, given she was planning to relocate to a country with a new partner who had had little opportunity to get to know the children and where the children would be unable to speak the language (see further para.12–028 above).

In addition, the importance of stability may be outweighed by other considerations.

> In *Re M (Child's Upbringing)* [1996] 2 F.L.R. 441, CA, the court decided that a Zulu child, who had been cared for in England by a white woman, should be returned to his parents (the woman's former servants) in South Africa. In this case, considerations of the child's cultural background outweighed the importance of maintaining the *status quo* (although the arrangement ordered did not work out and the child returned to England within a relatively short period).

A perhaps more common example involves the transfer of residence to one parent where the other has been opposing contact to the detriment of the child. Thus, in *V v V (Contact: Implacable Hostility)* [2004] EWHC 1215 (Fam), the court held that the disruption that would be caused by the move (against children's wishes, it should be noted) was outweighed by the emotional harm being caused by the mother's attitude. As Bracewell J. noted:

> "the mother's continued care of the children is incompatible with the children enjoying and benefiting from a normal relationship with their father." (para.43, and see further para.12–031 above)

(4) *The child's age, sex, background and any characteristics of his which the court considers relevant*

As noted above, while there is no presumption that young children should be in the care of their mother, or that a child should live with a parent of the same sex, the children's age and sex obviously affect their needs, as the House of Lords' decision in *Brixey v Lynas* [1996] 2 F.L.R. 506, HL, has again emphasised (see above, para.14–011). **14–013**

The statutory reference to "background" may involve the court in a consideration of the child's cultural and religious background (as in *Re M (Child's Upbringing)* [1996] 2 F.L.R. 441, CA, above). If the child's background involves competing cultures, the court will try to preserve both aspects of the child's background. Thus in *Re S (Change of Names: Cultural Factors)* [2001] 2 F.L.R. 1005, Fam Div:

> A Muslim girl eloped to Gretna Green with a Sikh man. They had a child together, but the marriage was not a success and, after the divorce, the mother wanted to change her son's Sikh names on the basis that the Muslim community would not otherwise accept him. The court held that the child should be known by Muslim names in order to ease his integration into the community. However, his Sikh names would not be formally changed, as this would eliminate his half-Sikh identity. A similar compromise was suggested in relation to religious issues: the court ordered that the child should be brought up as a Muslim but encouraged to respect the Sikh faith as well.

There may, however, be situations in which the child's religious background is accorded less weight:

> In *Re P (Section 91(14) Guidelines) (Residence and Religious Heritage)* [1999] 2 F.L.R. 573, CA, the Orthodox Jewish parents of a Down's Syndrome baby were unable to care for her, and she was fostered with non-practising Catholic foster parents after strenuous efforts to find an Orthodox family to care for her had yielded no result. When the child was eight the parents applied for the child to be returned to them. They claimed that a child had a presumptive right to be brought up by her own parents in her own religion, and that although a move would cause short-term trauma, the long-term benefits of culture and heritage would shift the balance decisively in favour of the parents. The Court of Appeal rejected this claim. The undoubted importance to an Orthodox Jew of religion (providing a way of life permeating all activities) was a factor to be put in the balance but could not be overwhelming (not least because of the child's limited capacity to understand and appreciate religious matters). Moreover, the child would not appreciate the reasons why she was being moved from the family in which she had lived for seven years; and for this reason what Butler-Sloss L.J. described as the "some-times over-emphasised *status quo* argument" had "real validity in this case".

The court has even held that a child may be required to change his religion:

> In *Re R (A Minor) (Residence: Religion)* [1993] 2 F.L.R. 163, CA, a boy of nine had been living wholly within what the judge described as the "stifling" religious conditions of the Exclusive Brethren. In accordance with the beliefs of the Brethren the boy believed he should neither live with nor even see his father because the father had (in the Brethren's view) done wrong; and the boy believed that if he lived with his father (his only surviving parent) he would no longer be able to have anything to do with the Brethren whose beliefs he shared "with extraordinary depth of feeling for a boy of his age". The Court held that to be bound by the child's religious beliefs would amount to an abandonment of its

duty to decide what the child's welfare, viewed objectively, required. A residence order in favour of the father was made accordingly.

In the light of the decision of the European Court in *Palau-Martinez v France* [2004] 2 F.L.R. 810, however, it would be necessary for the court to consider "direct, concrete evidence" about the impact of the religion in question on the child's upbringing (para.42), rather than assuming it to be harmful.

It might seem odd to describe the child's surname as a "characteristic", but in practice the courts have attached considerable importance to the name by which a child is known, seeing it as integral to the child's sense of identity.

> *Re D, L and LA (Care: Change of Forename)* [2003] 1 F.L.R. 339, Fam Div., involved informal name changes instituted by one child's foster parents and by the others' prospective adopters. Butler-Sloss P. noted that no foster parent should unilaterally change a child's name. "To change that is to change the child's identity. The right of a child and both parents to respect for that part of family life still exists, even though the child has gone into a foster placement." (at 346)

The use of surnames in particular gives rise to deeply felt disputes (*Dawson v Wearmouth* [1999] 1 F.L.R. 1167 at 1178, HL, *per* Lord Hobhouse). In that case:

> A woman registered the name of her child in the name of her husband (Wearmouth), even though she was separated from him, and even though another man (Dawson) was the father of the child, as both she and her two children from the marriage had continued to use the name of Wearmouth. When the father discovered this, he applied for an order that the child be known by the name of Dawson and that the mother be prohibited from allowing him to be known by the name of Wearmouth or any other surname. The trial judge made such an order on the basis that it would give the child a reminder of his father's place in his life. The Court of Appeal allowed the mother's appeal, attaching importance to the fact that the child's surname was registered as Wearmouth and that there were no countervailing considerations suggesting that the mother had been wrong to choose that name. The House of Lords dismissed the father's appeal on the basis that the Court of Appeal had correctly evaluated the factors relevant to the child's welfare.

It is perhaps more common for a father to seek to prevent a change of name after the end of the relationship.

> In *Re R (Surname: Using Both Parents')* [2001] 2 F.L.R. 1358, CA, the mother, who was planning to move to Spain with her mother and the mother's partner, began to use the latter's name for herself and her son. The father opposed the change. The Court of Appeal noted that the new surname had a relatively insecure foundation—the mother did not use it for all purposes and might change it if she remarried—and had been adopted without any consultation with the father. The long-term benefit of maintaining an outward link with the father was weighed against the short-term issues of convenience and avoiding confusion. It was decided that the balance came down in favour of refusing to allow the change,

although Thorpe L.J. pointed out that the Spanish practice of combining surnames could provide a solution in this case.

(5) *Any harm which the child has suffered or is at risk of suffering*

14–014   "Harm" is defined by ss.105(1) and 31(9) of the 1989 Act as "ill-treatment or the
impairment of health or development", and accordingly has a broad meaning (see
further para.13–019).

As the discussion of contact orders (para.12–031, above) indicated, in recent years
the courts have become increasingly sensitive to the effect that domestic violence may
have on the child, either because he or she has witnessed it directly or because of the
impact on the parent who was the victim of the violence. The reluctance of the child
to retain contact with a violent parent will be an important factor (see
para.14–010).

The ability of a parent to protect a child from harm at the hands of a third party
may also be relevant in deciding what orders should be made.

> In *Re E (children) (residence order)* [2001] EWCA Civ 567, there were a number
> of concerns about the mother, including the fact that she had had a number of
> unsatisfactory relationships, including one with a violent partner. It was con-
> cluded that the children were at some risk from violence, and a residence order
> was made in favour of the father.

Similarly, in the public law case of *Re O-S (Children: Care Order)* [2001] EWCA Civ
2039, the fact that the mother's relationship with her children's violent father was still
continuing was influential in the decision to make a care order and to approve the local
authority's plan for adoption (contrast the reluctance to make orders under s.8 that
directly constrain adult behaviour, para.12–034 above)).

Another issue that has attracted considerable attention in recent years is the risk of
sexual abuse. In such cases, the court will have to weigh up the evidence as to whether
such behaviour has occurred or not, and then determine the risk of harm on the basis
of the facts which have been proved (see *In Re M and R (minors) (child abuse:
evidence)* [1996] 2 F.L.R. 195, CA).

The fact that there is a proven risk of sexual abuse is in any event only one element
in the decision-making process. It has been said that in seeking to protect children
from sexual abuse, society may cause other, and possibly greater, harm to the children
it seeks to protect (*per* Balcombe L.J., *Re H (Minors) (Wardship: Sexual Abuse)*
[1991] 2 F.L.R. 416). Hence, the court must exercise its discretion, weighing in the
balance all the relevant factors in order to assess the relative weight of advantages and
risks to the child of the possible courses of action. For example:

> In *Re B (A Minor) (Child Abuse: Custody)* [1990] 2 F.L.R. 317, Ward J. found
> that it was "overwhelmingly likely" that a four-year-old boy had seen sexual
> behaviour between his parents which he ought not to have seen, that he had seen
> indecent videos and that there was a serious lack of awareness on the part of the
> child's parents as to "quite where boundaries are to be drawn". However, the
> abuse was not of the most serious kind, and the risk of further abuse did not
> outweigh the advantage of preserving links with a "warm playful father" who had
> a good relationship with his son.

(6) *How capable is each of his parents, and any other person in relation to whom the court considers the question to be relevant, of meeting the child's needs?*

This aspect of child welfare raises similar issues to those discussed under the second **14–015** heading, since the court's assessment of the ability of a parent to meet a child's needs will inevitably depend on its perception of what those needs are. Each parent will need to show that he or she is capable of caring for the child, either personally or with assistance:

> In *Re D (A Child)* [2005] EWCA Civ 743, the court was of the opinion that the father had failed to demonstrate this, noting that "[t]he whole balance tips significantly in favour of the mother's proposal once the father revealed that he would be heavily dependent on the unexplored availability of the extended family." (para.10)

The problem in this case was not the fact that the father would be reliant on his family, but rather that his family's ability to provide support had not been demonstrated.

Given the importance that is attached to retaining links with both parents, the willingness of each parent to promote contact may be an issue:

> In *Re J (children) (residence: expert evidence)* [2001] 2 F.C.R. 44, CA, the expert evidence cast doubt on the father's ability to meet "the children's emotional need for a constructive and healthy relationship with their mother." The report of the court welfare officer noted that the father appeared to hold the mother in contempt and had not denied that he was sexist. There was concern that the eldest child was adopting similar attitudes. A residence order was initially made in favour of the father, but the Court of Appeal allowed the appeal on the basis that the judge had not given sufficient weight to the expert evidence and remitted the case for a rehearing.

Similarly, the attempt of one parent to exclude the other from the children's lives may backfire:

> *CG v CW and G (Children)* [2006] EWCA Civ 372 involved a dispute between two women. Two children had been conceived by one of them during their eight-year relationship by anonymous donor insemination, and had been brought up by them jointly. After the relationship came to an end, the biological mother sought to exclude her former partner from the children's lives. A shared residence order was made to confer parental responsibility on the former partner (see para. 11–024). Despite a court order preventing the biological mother from relocating from the Midlands to Cornwall, she and her new civil partner moved there with the children. The judge granted residence to the former partner, and this was upheld by the Court of Appeal. The crucial issue in the case was the risk that the biological mother would continue to marginalise her former partner and flout court orders, and this outweighed the potential disadvantage of changing the children's residence.

In that case the Court of Appeal also emphasised how attitudes to same-sex parents have changed. While in that case the court was faced with a choice between two women who were both living with their lesbian partners, it is highly unlikely that any court would today decide that a parent living in a same-sex relationship was by that reason alone any less capable of meeting the child's needs than a parent living in a heterosexual relationship (and note the earlier cases in which it was accepted that the care offered by a same-sex couple might on the facts be preferable to the other alternatives: *C v C (A Minor) (Custody: Appeal)* [1991] 1 F.L.R. 223; *B v B (Minors) (Custody, Care and Control)* [1991] 1 F.L.R. 402).

One further issue to be considered under this heading is whether there is any presumption that the biological parents are to be preferred to members of the extended family or unrelated carers. In the seminal case of *J v C* [1970] AC 668, HL, foster parents were preferred to the child's biological parents:

> The question was whether a 10-year-old boy should be returned to his "unimpeachable" natural parents in Spain, or whether he should continue to live with the English foster parents who had looked after him for most of his life. It was held that to return a child who had been brought up as an English boy with English ways to a strange environment, and to parents who would have difficulty in coping with his problems of readjustment, would be inconsistent with his welfare.

While *J v C* preceded the Children Act, it should be noted that the checklist in s.1(3) is largely based on the factors that earlier courts tended to take into account in making decisions about children's welfare. The case of *Re M (Child's Upbringing)* [1996] 2 F.L.R. 441, CA (para.14–012) might suggest that *J v C* would be decided differently today, although it should be noted that *J v C* was not cited in *Re M* (and the result in the latter case should also give pause for thought). The important point for present purposes is that the House of Lords in *J v C* held that the welfare test applied even when the dispute was between unimpeachable parents and someone who had no biological links with the child at all. More recently, in *Re H (a child: residence)* [2002] 3 F.C.R. 277 at 285, CA, Thorpe L.J. noted that there was no presumption in favour of the natural parent in s.1 of the 1989 Act and "judicial overlay on that section must obviously be treated with caution" (see further, at para.12–016). He returned to this issue in *CG v CW and G (Children)* [2006] EWCA Civ 372, noting that any preference for the natural parent only applied in disputes between a parent and non-parent and doubting its relevance in cases where the disputing parties had both acted as parents, even if one of them was not the child's biological parent:

> "in the eyes of the child the natural parent may be a non-biological parent who, by virtue of long settled care, has become the child's psychological parent. That consideration is obviously pertinent to any resolution of the competing claims of same sex parents. As in the present case the family may be created by mutual agreement and with much careful planning. Both partners seek the experience of child-bearing and child-rearing in one capacity or another. Where, as here, the care of the newborn, and then the developing baby, is broadly shared the children will not distinguish between one woman and the other on the grounds of biological relationship. Depending on circumstances the psychological attachment may be to each more or less equally or more to the biological parent or more to the non-biological parent." (para.44)

If the applicant is not the child's parent even in this extended sense, there remains an assumption that it will usually be in the best interests of the child to remain with its natural parents. Even this will, however, have to give way to the particular needs of the child. In *Re C (a child) (residence order)* [2003] EWCA Civ 407, Thorpe L.J. held that there would have to be "good, substantial and sufficient reasons" for preferring a relative to the child's biological parent, but that such reasons need not "be so exceptional as to merit the label compelling" (at para.13). Much will therefore depend upon the facts of the individual case. For example:

> In *Re N (Residence: Appointment of Solicitor: Placement with Extended Family)* [2001] 1 F.L.R. 1028, CA, a residence order was initially made in favour of the child's uncle and aunt, with whom he had lived for several years. However, the Court of Appeal felt that the trial judge had given insufficient weight to the factors indicating that "a child ought to be brought up within his birth family", namely the child's sense of identity, avoiding confusion of family roles, and cultural factors. (It should also be noted that the social workers and psychologists involved in the case disagreed as to what would be in the child's best interests, which illustrates the scope for disagreement between different professions, and the difficulty in establishing any objective concept of welfare). The case was remitted to the High Court for a rehearing.

In that case, the child had been placed with his relatives following the death of his mother in a car crash rather than because of any parental failings. This should be contrasted with *Re M (Residence)* [2002] EWCA Civ 1052:

> In this case, a widow with four children married a convicted murderer, and they had a son together. After her death (from natural causes), the local authority took all five children into temporary care and then placed them with their maternal uncle. The court held that there were no grounds for making a care order and ordered that, while the eldest four children should remain with their uncle, the youngest child should return to his father. The Court of Appeal allowed the uncle's appeal and made a residence order in his favour, on the basis that the judge should not have rejected the expert evidence relating to the father's personality defects and the slim chances of his being able to parent his son satisfactorily.

Re M was of course an exceptional case. On balance, the case-law suggests a continuing preference for parental care, although couched in more moderate terms than in the past (see *e.g. Re KD (a minor) (ward: termination of access)* [1988] 1 All E.R. 577). In the vast majority of cases, of course, children will remain with at least one of their biological parents: a child cannot be taken away from the parental home simply on the basis that another couple would be able to provide a better upbringing. In private law disputes, the courts are unlikely to prefer untried alternatives with relatives as long as one of the parents is willing and able to provide the child with a home, and members of the extended family will usually be required to obtain leave before applying for a s.8 order.

(7) *The range of powers available to the court under the Children Act in the proceedings in question*

This provision requires the court to consider what it can achieve by exercising its **14–016** powers under the legislation. In particular, the court may want to consider imposing conditions on the making of a residence order, or the desirability of making contact orders with other relatives—particularly bearing in mind the fact that the Act expressly permits the court to make an order if it considers that it should do so "even though no . . . application has been made" for the order (s.10(1)(b)). Similarly, in the context of public law cases, the court will consider whether a care order or supervision order is the most appropriate route, and whether any of the s.8 orders might provide a viable alternative (see further para.13-029).

D: THE WELFARE PRINCIPLE AND HUMAN RIGHTS

14-017 One fertile source of debate in recent years has been the issue of whether the welfare principle in s.1 of the 1989 Act is compatible with Art.8. Does the principle that the welfare of the child is *paramount* give sufficient weight to the rights of parents (and other adult family members)? Alternatively, how far is the welfare of a child to be taken into account in balancing claims under Art.8 of the Convention?

The English courts have consistently asserted that the welfare principle is consistent with the terms of the Convention (see *e.g. Re KD (a minor) (ward: termination of access)* [1988] 1 All E.R. 577, endorsed in *Re B* [2002] 1 F.L.R. 196). There are two strands to this argument. First, it is argued that the current application of the welfare principle already takes the Art.8 rights of the parties involved into account. Thus, for example, it was suggested in *Re H (Contact Order) (No.2)* [2002] 1 F.L.R. 22, CA, that:

> "a proper application of the checklist in s.1(3) is equivalent to the balancing exercise required in the application of Art.8, which is then a useful cross-check to ensure that the order proposed is in accordance with the law, necessary for the protection of the rights and freedoms of others, and proportionate."

Given that the checklist in s.1(3) makes no mention of the rights of *any* of the parties involved, this reasoning does not appear convincing. Contrast, for example, the following statement from Sir Thomas Bingham M.R. in *Re O (Contact: Imposition of Conditions)*:

> "it cannot be emphasised too strongly that the court is concerned with the interests of the mother and the father only in so far as they bear upon the welfare of the child."

The second argument is that the rights of the adults involved are in any case subject to the welfare of the child. It is true that Art.8(2) recognises that an interference with the rights of individuals under Art.8(1) may be justified by reference to the "protection of health or morals, or for the protection of the rights and freedoms of others." It is also true that the jurisprudence of the European Court has endorsed the importance of the best interests of the child:

> In *Hoppe v Germany* [2003] 1 F.C.R., ECHR, the father claimed that the limits on his contact with his daughter breached his human rights under Art.8 of the Convention. The court held that a fair balance had to be struck between the interests of the child and those of the parent, and, when striking such a balance,

particular importance had to be attached to the best interests of the child, which, depending on their nature and seriousness, might override those of the parent. In this case the father's insistence on his rights and disregard for his daughter's psychological health justified the limitations imposed by the court.

But it is important to note that the welfare of the child does not *automatically* justify an interference with the parents' rights under Art.8(1): it *may* do so depending on the circumstances. While the European Court has on occasion suggested that the interests of the child are "paramount" (see *e.g. Yousef v The Netherlands* [2003] 1 F.L.R. 210, ECHR, and *Zawadka v. Poland* [2005] 2 F.L.R. 897, ECHR), it has not been consistent in this usage. The better view is therefore that Art.8 requires the courts to balance the respective rights of the parties—including those of the child—rather than simply ask what course is in the child's best interests. Many academic commentators, therefore, remain unconvinced that the welfare principle is truly compatible with Art.8, and various alternatives have been proposed (see *e.g.* J. Herring, "The Human Rights Act and the welfare principle in family law—conflicting or complementary?" (1999) C.F.L.Q. 223; J. Eekelaar, "Beyond The Welfare Principle" (2002) CFLQ 237; A. Bainham, *Children: The Modern Law* (3rd edn, 2005), p.40; S. Choudhry and H. Fenwick, "Taking the Rights of Parents and Children Seriously: Confronting the Welfare Principle under the Human Rights Act" (2005) 25 O.J.L.S. 453).

One context in which the competing rights of different family members has to be considered is that of adoption, which forms the subject matter of the next chapter.

Chapter 15

ADOPTION

A: INTRODUCTION

There are numerous historical examples, both literary and actual, of children being brought up by persons other than their biological parents, but it was not until 1926 that adoption was placed on a legal footing. The 1926 Adoption Act was limited in scope, amounting to little more than a process whereby, with minimal safeguards, the courts registered and ratified a private contract whereby the adopters acquired some but by no means all of the legal attributes of parentage. Since that date, there have been significant changes: first, in the use that is made of adoption, secondly, in the extent to which the process is regulated, and, thirdly, in the way that adoption is perceived.

The key changes in the use of adoption relate to the number of adoptions, the age at which children are adopted, the reasons for adoption, and the identity of the adoptive parents. In the 1950s and 1960s adoption was seen primarily as a method whereby a healthy, white (and usually illegitimate) baby was placed with a childless couple who would bring him or her up as their own child. The number of adoption orders increased steadily to a peak of 25,000 in 1968. Half of the children adopted in that year were babies less than a year old and 97 per cent of those babies were illegitimate. In many cases the adopters were one of the child's birth parents and a step-parent (see further below para.15–008). In other cases the process was shrouded in secrecy: adoption agencies were active in meeting the need to ensure that pregnant women gave birth in secrecy, and adoptive parents would often conceal the child's origins from the outside world and indeed from the child. (See, for example, Mike Leigh's film *Secrets and Lies*, which involves a meeting between a woman and the adult daughter that she gave up as a baby—indeed, without even seeing her, since she was unaware that her daughter was of mixed race.) By contrast, in 2004, only 4,539 adoption orders were made, and in the year ending March 31, 2005 a mere 5 per cent of the children adopted from care (for whom more detailed statistics are available) were less than a year old.

One reason for this is that greater regulation has slowed the process down, making it more difficult to complete the adoption in under a year (see further Part D). The fall in the number of adoption orders, and in the number of babies adopted, is also clearly linked to the availability of abortion and contraception on the one hand, and the greater acceptance of child-bearing outside marriage (whether within a two- or one-parent family) on the other. It is still the case that the majority of adopted children—around three-quarters in 2004—were born outside marriage, but the numbers adopted are now a much smaller proportion of the total number born outside marriage (42 per cent in 2004). The main reason for adoption is no longer the marital status of the mother, but the failings of the parents as carers: in the year ending March 31, 2005, the majority of children—3,800—were adopted from care (compared with 8.7 per cent in 1968). The second main reason for adoption today is also linked to changes in family formation, as it is used to confer the status of a parent on the new partner of a parent (see further para.15–008 below). These changes have implications for many of the issues discussed in this chapter.

The second set of changes relate to the increased regulation of the process whereby the suitability of couples to adopt is assessed. In part, this can be seen as another example of the modern emphasis on accountability, but it also flows from the changes described in the previous paragraph. Assessing the suitability of a person to adopt a child who has been emotionally scarred by earlier events is clearly a more difficult task than deciding whether a baby should be placed with a particular person.

The third set of changes relate to changing views about the role of adoption. Should adoption be a means of effectively "transplanting" a child to a new family, so that the adoptive parents become, for all legal purposes, the child's parents? Should links with the birth family be maintained? Do children have a right to information about their birth parents, and do the birth parents have any rights to information about their children? The concept of "transplanting" a child carries rather different connotations where that child is adopted from abroad, and the special considerations that apply to such adoptions are briefly considered at the end of the chapter.

Finally, it should be noted that adoption law has now been extensively reformed, a process that has taken more than a decade. As part of the last Conservative Government's programme of family law reform, the Department of Health carried out an impressively thorough *Review of Adoption Law and Practice* and in 1993 the Government issued a White Paper (*Adoption: The Future*), which set out decisions on a number of matters. Further consultation on some particularly difficult areas followed; and in 1996 the Government published another White Paper (*Adoption—A Service for Children*), which incorporated a 104-clause draft Adoption Bill. In the event, no legislation was introduced, possibly because of the difficulties that the government had experienced in enacting the Family Law Act 1996, possibly because of lack of parliamentary time before the government fell in 1997. Some reform was achieved in 1999, but the Adoption (Intercountry Aspects) Act 1999 was the result of a private member's bill and dealt only with a small part of adoption law. In 2000 a Cabinet Committee was set up to examine reform. New proposals for reform were put forward (*Prime Minister's Review: Adoption*, Performance and Innovation Unit, 2000), which were shortly followed by a White Paper (*Adoption: a new approach—A White Paper* (2000)). The Adoption and Children Act 2002, which makes radical changes to the law of adoption, is based on the recommendations put forward in the 2000 White Paper, although certain changes were made in the course of the parliamentary debates. Further delay occurred before implementation, and it was not until December 30, 2005 that the Act came into force. As yet, therefore, there are no reported decisions on its provisions, but some assistance can still be gleaned from cases decided under the old law, with due attention being paid to the changes in the legislative scheme. In addition, the—already lengthy—Act has been supplemented by detailed Regulations, and by statutory guidance.

This chapter looks first at the concept of adoption, and how the legal concept fits with the reality of modern adoption (Part B). Part C then sets out the legal position as to who can adopt, and the role of adoption agencies in assessing and preparing potential adopters is discussed in Part D. Part E considers the rights of the birth parents in the adoption process. The final decision as to whether or not an adoption order should be made is for the court, and the basis upon which such decisions are made are described in Part F. The chapter concludes with a brief discussion of inter-country adoption.

B: The Concept of Adoption

This section discusses the legal concept of adoption under the current law and its consequences for the parties. It then goes on to examine how the reality of the modern adoption process fits with the "legal transplant" theory, and finally considers what alternatives to adoption exist.

15–002

(1) Adoption as a "legal transplant"

English law adopted the model of the "legal transplant": the adoptive parents did not merely have care of the child but became, for all legal intents and purposes, the child's parents. An adoption order transfers a child from one family to another; and, once made, the order is irrevocable:

15–003

> In *Re B (Adoption: Jurisdiction to Set Aside)* [1995] Fam. 239, CA, a child was born in a nursing home in 1959 to a Kuwaiti Arab father and a Roman Catholic mother. The matron arranged for him to be adopted by an Orthodox Jewish couple, who believed that the child was Jewish. When they discovered that he was not they arranged for him to be received into the Jewish faith and continued to bring him up in the Jewish tradition. When he grew up, the boy decided to emigrate to Israel but (apparently because of his appearance) was suspected of being a spy and was declared *persona non grata*. He made inquiries into his origins and traced his birth father in Kuwait; but he could not find work in Kuwait or in any other Arab state. He felt that he did not belong to either the Jewish or Arab communities. He applied to the court to set aside the adoption order. The President of the Family Division (whose decision was upheld by the Court of Appeal) refused to do so: to allow a mistake such as had occurred in this case to invalidate an adoption order would undermine the whole basis on which legal adoption in the country was founded. This was that the child became the child of the adopters for all legal purposes and save in certain prescribed and restricted circumstances an order once made was irrevocable. (For an extreme case in which an adoption order was revoked see *Re K (Adoption and Wardship)* [1997] 2 F.L.R. 221, para.12–043 above.)

The conceptual differences between adoption and other methods of providing long-term substitute care for children have been summarised as follows (see *J v C* [1970] A.C. 668 at 930, HL, *per* Lord Upjohn):

(1) An adoption order is permanent and irrevocable; other orders dealing with the child's upbringing can in theory be varied.

(2) Adoption affects legal status—and thus such matters as the child's succession rights and citizenship. Other court orders dealing with upbringing do not have such consequences.

(3) Adoption severs the legal family ties between the child and the birth parents and their relatives. Once an adoption order has been made, the parents no longer have standing even to apply for contact (see *Re R (A Minor) (Adoption: Access)* [1991] 2 F.L.R. 78, CA) although, like anyone else, they could seek leave to apply to the court for contact with the child (see para.15–043 below).

(2) *The legal consequences of adoption*

15–004 Adoption not only vests parental responsibility for a child in the adopters but also extinguishes the parental responsibility—and indeed the parental status—of the birth parents (s.46 of the Adoption and Children Act 2002). Section 67 of the 2002 Act provides that the effect of an adoption order is that the child is thenceforth treated as if he or she had been born as the child of the adopters or adopter. In theory, therefore, the rights of parent and child should be exactly the same as if this were in fact the case, and this is indeed the general position. For example, the adopted child is treated for succession purposes as a member of his adoptive family and not of his birth family; and a child adopted by a British citizen becomes a British citizen if he or she was not one already (see s.1(5) of the British Nationality Act 1981).

But there are certain statutory modifications of the general principle. For example, the prohibited degrees of marriage between the adopted child and the birth family are unaffected. Moreover, although the child is brought within the prohibited degrees in relation to his or her adoptive parents, the legislation does not create any prohibitions on marriage with other members of the adoptive family (so that, surprisingly, an adopted child may legally marry his adoptive sister, or even his adoptive grandmother; see para.3-010 above).

A further legal fiction is that an adopted child will always be legitimate—regardless of the marital status of the adopter or adopters (s.67(2)). Given the reduced significance of the concept of legitimacy—and the fact that, in a further departure from strict logic, adoption does not affect succession to peerages—the effect of this is largely symbolic.

(3) *The legal transplant model and the reality of modern adoption*

15–005 Maintaining a fiction that an adopted child is in fact as well as law the child of the adoptive parents depends on the child being unable to remember, and having no subsequent contact with, the birth parents. How does the legal fiction fit with the reality of modern adoption? Three situations should be considered. First, what if the child wishes to trace his or her birth parents (or the birth parents wish to trace the child)? How far should the law facilitate this? Secondly, what if the child was adopted at an older age and knows the identity of his or her birth parents? How prevalent is this, and how do the courts approach the issue as to whether links with the birth family should be retained? Thirdly, the tendency for children to be adopted by their relatives, or by a parent and step-parent, has already been noted: again how prevalent is this, and what is the law's policy on such adoptions? Finally, how far should adoptive parents receive support from the state over and above that provided for birth parents?

(a) Tracing one's family

The legal transplant model reached its apogee in the Adoption Act 1949, which **15–006** introduced a procedure under which the court could make an adoption order without the mother knowing the adopters' identity. The law came to accept the desirability of complete secrecy and it was assumed that there would be no contact at all. It was thought that such contact would be undesirable not only in the child's interest, but in the interests of the adopting parents (who might find themselves harassed by the birth parents), and of the birth mother, who might have agreed to place her child for adoption only on the basis that she could conceal from everyone—including perhaps her husband—the fact that she had ever borne a child. Despite this, it was regarded as good practice for a child to be brought up knowing that he had been adopted and about the circumstances leading up to the adoption. Adoptive parents were thus given written background information about the child and the birth family in an attempt to help them bring up the child in the knowledge of the adoption from an early age. To this extent the legal transplant model was modified.

It subsequently came to be recognised that many adopted people wished to go further and to trace their genetic origins, and that, sometimes, the birth parents wished to know what had become of their child. The culture of secrecy began to be questioned. The Children Act 1975 began the process of removing some of this secrecy from the statutory adoption process, introducing measures whereby adopted children might, as adults, be able to trace their birth parents, and the Children Act 1989 went further, establishing the framework for an adoption contact register for relatives to indicate their desire to be traced. The 2002 Act similarly requires the Registrar-General to maintain both the Adopted Children Register (s.77) and the Adoption Contact Register (s.81). Neither is open to public inspection or search, although the index to the former is open to the public (s.78).

The current position is that on attaining the age of 18, an adopted child may apply either to the Registrar-General (if the adoption took place before December 30, 2005, see s.79(6) and Sch. 2 of the 2002 Act) or to the adoption agency (if the adoption took place after that date) for access to the original birth records, which will reveal his or her original name and parentage, in so far as this was recorded. (In some cases the information available may be sparse, especially if the child was abandoned at birth: see K. Adie, *Nobody's Child* (Hodder and Stoughton, 2005)). The risk that a 16- or 17-year-old might inadvertently marry a person to whom he or she is related is addressed by the provision for a person who is intending to marry to obtain information from the Registrar-General on this point (s.79(7)). Birth relatives of the adopted person can have their details recorded in the Adoption Contact Register, and the information will be passed on if the adopted person has given notice indicating a wish to contact his or her relatives (s.80). A study carried out after the Adoption and Contact Register had been in existence for almost a decade found that the details of 18,276 adopted persons and 8,007 relatives had been recorded, leading to only 490 matches (J. Haskey and E. Errington, 'Adoptees and relatives who wish to contact one another: the Adoption Contact Register' (2001) 104 *Population Trends* 18). It should also be noted that since December 30, 2005 it has been possible for relatives to indicate that they do *not* wish to be contacted (Adopted Children and Adoption Contact Registers Regulations 2005, SI 2005/924, r.7(1)(b)). Similarly, the adopted person may indicate a desire only to be contacted by specific relatives (r.6(1)). Intermediary services that help with tracing are regulated by the Adoption Information and Inter-mediary Services (Pre-Commencement Adoptions) Regulations 2005 SI 2005/890 (the position in relation to post-commencement adoptions is considered further below).

At present, therefore, the law is asymmetrical, giving greater rights to the adopted child than to the birth parents. It should, however, be borne in mind that the adopted person may not know that he or she was adopted. While in 2005 only 210 adoption orders were made in relation to children under the age of one, ten times that number of adoptees were under the age of one at the time that they started to be looked after (the adoption process can be a lengthy one). While openness is encouraged, it is obviously possible that some of those who were adopted at a very young age will never learn of this fact. In addition, an adopted person has no absolute right of access to his or her birth certificate. Under the 2002 Act, an adoption agency may apply to the High Court for an order that will prevent the adopted person obtaining a certified copy of the record of his birth. The High Court may only make such an order if the circumstances are exceptional (s.60(3)), which strikes a balance between the interest of the adopted person in obtaining information about his or her identity and the need to protect the birth family in cases such as the following:

> In *R. v Registrar General, Ex p. Smith* [1991] 1 F.L.R. 255, CA, a patient in Broadmoor Hospital brutally and sadistically murdered a fellow prisoner (appar-ently under the delusion that the victim was his adoptive mother). Disturbed and unstable, he continued to express hatred for his adoptive parents. He exercised his statutory right to seek the information that would enable him to trace his birth certificate, and thereby to be in a position to trace his birth parents. There were real fears that he would seek to harm the birth parents, whom he blamed for his problems, and the Court of Appeal accepted that, in the circumstances, it had been right to deny him the statutory right of access to his birth certificate.

In most cases, however, it will be possible for an adopted person to find out the identity of his or her birth mother (and father if he is named on the birth certificate), and to use this information as a basis for tracing the birth family. But what about other information held by the adoption agency that arranged the adoption? Prior to the Adoption and Children Act 2002 there was little guidance on when it would be appropriate for an adoption agency to disclose information to an adopted person: the issue was left to the discretion of the individual agency (see reg.15(2) of the Adoption Agencies Regulations 1983 (SI 1983/1964)), and practice consequently varied. The 2002 Act established a new framework to clarify what information must be kept, and whether the agency had a duty or a discretion to disclose such information. This new scheme applies only to adoptions that took place after December 30, 2005, and the details are set out in the Disclosure of Adoption (Post-Commencement Adoptions) Regulations 2005 SI 2005/888. Briefly, the adoption agency is always required to keep the case record set up in respect of the adopted person. It is also required to keep a range of information—including any information that was supplied by the birth family to be passed on to the adopted person, any information supplied by the adoptive parents relating to matters arising after the making of the adoption order, and information about entries on either register—unless it decides that it would be preju-dicial to the adopted person's welfare, or not reasonably practicable, to keep such information (reg.4). Whether such information can be disclosed depends on whether it falls into the category of "protected" information. Such information, as defined in s.57 of the 2002 Act, is essentially information that identifies any persons involved in the adoption process. The adopted person has no right to receive such information (s.58(4)), but the adoption agency has the power to disclose the information if it considers it appropriate to do so (s.61(4)). Before doing so it must "take all reasonable steps to obtain the views of any person the information is about as to the disclosure of the information about him." (s.61(3)). Additional considerations apply if the protected information is about a person who is a child at the time that the application is made (s.62). The new statutory scheme, combined with the detailed regulations, thus clarifies what information can be disclosed, and when.

Finally, it should be noted that the modern practice is to provide adopted children with a life-story book, containing information about their birth family, which might obviate the need for the adopted person to rely on the provisions discussed above. The National Adoption Standards, published by the Department of Health in 2001, state that:

> "Birth parents and families will be supported to provide information that the adopted child needs. This will include information about the adopted child's birth and early life, the birth family's views about adoption and contact and up-to-date information about themselves and their situation." (D.6)

It is clear that both the current law and practice of adoption has moved a long way from the earlier system of secret adoptions.

(b) Contact with the birth parents

The second situation is rather different. If an adoption order is made in respect of an **15–007** older child, should that child continue to have contact with the birth family? The trend towards post-adoption contact began in the 1980s, and there is evidence that it is now actively promoted:

> "Post-adoption contact has developed from a marginal activity arranged by a few individuals to a key element of professional activity in adoption. . . . Adoption agencies have developed many of their practices so as to create a climate which supports the maintenance or establishment of contact because of their experience of its benefits for children adopters and parents . . . Prospective adopters are often required to meet birth parents as part of their preparation for adoption; the suitability of those opposed to contact is questioned." (J. Masson, "Thinking about contact   a social or a legal problem?" [2000] C.F.L.Q. 15, p.29)

Yet the existence of such contact arrangements should not obscure the fact that, after adoption, the birth parents are no longer the child's legal parents and it is the adoptive parents who have the right—as any other parent would have—to exercise parental authority by restraining (or permitting) contact between the child and others. In some cases, the birth parents (and others, such as the child's grandparents) have evidently been concerned that the adopters might prevent contact, and have asked the court to make legally binding provision for continuing contact. In the past the courts have tended to be reluctant to do so, on the basis that the decision on whether to permit contact is a matter for the adopters to decide in the exercise of their parental responsibility. It remains to be seen whether the 2002 Act—under which the court is now specifically required to consider whether there should be contact arrangements when making a placement order or adoption order—will make any difference. The relevant provisions will be considered in Part F when examining the role of the court in the adoption process: the important point for present purposes is that the greater importance attached to open adoption makes it more likely that the adopted child will have contact with his or her birth family. In such cases the factual tie subsists even though the legal ties have been cut.

(c) Relative adoptions

15–008 A third type of adoption that brings the fiction at the root of the legal transplant theory into sharp focus is adoption by relatives. The prevalence of such adoptions has fluctuated over the decades, as has official policy regarding such adoptions. In the 1960s and 1970s adoption became widely used by relatives; in particular, a very large proportion of all adoptions (nearly 70 per cent in 1975) were in favour of a parent (usually a mother) and step-parent. The popularity of such adoptions was founded to a substantial extent on the wish of mothers who had re-married to integrate their children into their new families for all legal purposes. Adoption by a biological parent may seem unnecessary, but adoption by the step-parent alone would have had the effect of terminating the mother's parental status, as the law then stood.

The factual situation in such cases was far removed from that on which the traditional notion of adoption had been based; and in 1972 the Houghton Committee expressed concern about the dangers of adoptions by relatives. In particular, the Committee was concerned that adoption might be used to conceal the truth about the child's parentage (so that, for example, the child adopted by her grandparents might be led to think that her mother was her sister). Another important concern was that adoption by one birth parent and a step-parent might be used to sever the child's relationship—in law and in fact—with the other birth parent. These concerns were influential and the Children Act 1975 introduced specific provisions designed to discourage adoptions by step-parents and relatives, unless there were special circum-stances making adoption desirable in the interest of the child's welfare. But these provisions were found to be unsatisfactory and not easy to apply in practice, and were repealed by the Children Act 1989. Throughout the 1990s, step-parent adoptions accounted for around half of all adoptions, although the numbers have fallen again in the past couple of years and in 2004 only 23 per cent of adoptions were by step-parents. It should also be noted that under the old law adoption by one of the birth parents and his or her *unmarried* partner, was not possible, as joint adoption orders could only be made in favour of married couples (see further para.15–016 below). It was possible, however, for a residence order to be granted as a means of regularising the position between a child and adult—and conferring parental responsibility—without severing the child's relationship with his or her birth parents.

The 2002 Act both eased adoption by the partners (both married and unmarried) of parents and—at least potentially—rendered it unnecessary in the case of step-parents. First, it is now unnecessary for the parent and new partner to apply to adopt jointly, as the Act makes provision for the partner of a parent to adopt the child alone, without affecting the status of *that* parent, although the status of the *other* birth parent is extinguished (s.51(2) and s.67(3)(a)). Secondly, it is now no longer necessary for step-parents to go through the process of adoption in order to acquire parental responsibil-ity, as they will be able to do so by means of a parental responsibility order or agreement (s.4A of the Children Act 1989 as inserted by s.112 of the ACA 2002). This option, it should be noted, is only open to the spouse or civil partner of a parent and not to a partner who has not formalised the relationship with the parent (see further para.11–019 above). In addition, it remains possible for a residence order to be used to confer parental responsibility (see further para.11–024).

It should of course be noted that acquiring parental responsibility is not the same as acquiring the legal status of a parent. Parental responsibility is revocable, and the acquisition of parental responsibility by a step-parent does not extinguish the parental responsibility of either birth parent. It remains to be seen whether the new provision in s.4A has an impact on the number of applications for adoption by step-parents, or whether couples value the symbolic and legal effect of an adoption order in defining them as a family.

(d) Support for adoptive parents

Should adoptive parents receive support from the state? The legal transplant theory **15–009** would suggest that they should not: since the child is treated as the child of the adopters, rather than as a child that they are bringing up for the benefit of others, there appears no justification for providing adoptive parents with any greater support than other parents. Yet once again, this conflicts with the nature of modern adoption. Older children, particularly those adopted from care, may have special needs: the case of *A and B v Essex CC*, below, para.15–022, offers an extreme example of the problems that adoptive parents may face, and the White Paper noted that 67 per cent of looked-after children had mental health problems. These problems have been recognised for some time: the Adoption Act 1976 established a framework for post-adoption support, but provision of such services was patchy. The White Paper emphasised the importance of support for adopters, both before and after adoption, but the 2002 Act only imposes a duty to assess an applicant's need for services, not a duty to *provide* them (s.4). Financially-stretched local authorities are unlikely to devote considerable resources to meeting what is only a "target duty" (see also para.13–005, above).

(4) *Alternatives to adoption*

The above discussion has illustrated that although there may be a legal fiction that the **15–010** adopted child is actually the child of the adoptive parents, there is no longer a *social* fiction to this effect in the majority of cases. In some cases it may not be appropriate to terminate the legal relationship between the birth parents and the child, even if the child is no longer living with the birth parents. In such situations a number of alternatives to adoption are available, namely foster-care, a residence order and the new concept of "special guardianship" All three provide some recognition of the role of the child's carer short of full parental status.

(a) Foster care

As noted in Ch.13, a high proportion of "looked-after" children—68 per cent in **15–011** 2004–5—are placed with foster parents. In such cases the birth parents retain parental responsibility, and, if there is a care order in force, the local authority will also have parental responsibility. By contrast, the foster parents do not have parental responsibility. In many cases fostering may be a short-term option—of the 54,200 placements with foster-parents in 2004–5, 11,800 lasted for less than eight days. The average duration was rather longer, at 281 days, and fostering may be a step towards adoption as well as an alternative to it. The present government perceives it to be desirable for fostering to offer greater security and permanence, and recent developments facilitate adoption by foster parents (see further below para.15–031).

However, not all foster parents will want to adopt, as *Re F (Adoption: Welfare of Child: Financial Considerations)* [2003] EWHC 3448 (Fam) demonstrates:

> In this case three young boys had been placed with foster parents in a placement organised by an external foster agency. This placement was costing the local authority £131,000 *per annum*, of which the foster parents received £53,500. If the foster parents became local authority foster parents they would receive a maximum of £30,000 *per annum*, and if they adopted the boys they would lose even this, and they were not prepared to give up the money. The local authority wanted to move the children to (as yet unidentified) potential adopters, via a bridging placement. The move was not supported by the guardian, the child psychologist, an independent social worker or their current social worker. Black J. held that in the circumstances, the mother's refusal to consent was not unreasonable and that it was not in the best interests of the children to be moved.

In this case the theoretical security that adoption would confer did not outweigh the actual benefits of the current arrangements:

> "I do not accept that it is in the interests of these particular children to abandon the known and loving family they are living in and step into the unknown in pursuit of the benefit of adoption with as yet unidentified adopters." (*per* Black J. at para.99)

Private fostering arrangements should be distinguished from the arrangements made for looked-after children. Under the Children Act 1989, a child is defined as being privately fostered if he or she is under 16 and is provided with a home for more than 28 days by someone who is not the child's parent or relative and does not have parental responsibility for the child (s.66(1)). As *Working Together to Safeguard Children* (2006) explains, such children:

> "are a diverse, and sometimes vulnerable, group. Groups of privately fostered children include children sent from abroad to stay with another family, usually to include their educational opportunities; asylum-seeking and refugee children; teenagers who, having broken with their parents, are staying in short-term arrangements with friends or other non-relatives; and language students living with host families." (para.11.12).

The fact that such arrangements are made privately does not mean that they are not subject to scrutiny. The local authority must be notified of the arrangement (and changes made to the 1989 Act by the Children Act 2004 require local authorities to promote awareness of the notification requirements: see Sch.8 para.7A of the 1989 Act). It is then under a duty to ascertain that the welfare of the child is being satisfactorily safeguarded (s.67(1)). This entails visiting the foster placement at regular intervals (see the Children (Private Arrangements for Fostering) Regulations 2005, SI 2005/1533). In addition, new *National Minimum Standards for Private Fostering* now apply to such arrangements (DfES, 2005).

While private foster parents are subject to legal regulation, they have no special status in the eyes of the law and do not have parental responsibility.

(b) Residence orders

Foster parents (and other carers) may also apply for residence orders, which do confer **15–012** parental responsibility (see Ch.12 for the constraints on applying for such orders, and for the powers which such orders confer). Such an order does not extinguish the birth parents' parental responsibility, nor does it allow the parties in whose favour a residence order has been made to consent to adoption. However, it does limit the extent to which the birth parents can exercise parental responsibility (and specific issue or prohibited steps orders may be used to impose further restrictions).

A residence order may be more suitable than an adoption order if the circumstances of the case render it inappropriate to terminate the legal relationship with the birth family:

> *Re B (Adoption Order)* [2001] EWCA Civ 347, a young boy enjoyed excellent relationships with both his foster-mother and his natural father. The parties agreed that there should be a residence order in favour of the former, and a contact order in favour of the latter. However, the foster-mother, encouraged by the local authority, then applied for, and obtained, an adoption order. The Court of Appeal allowed the father's appeal. Hale L.J. noted that there was more than one way of securing legal permanence for children and held that a residence order was appropriate in this case. This, unlike the adoption order, would recognise that the child had two families. An adoption order would remove the boy's legal relationship with his father and would only be viable if combined with a contact order "designed to maintain a level of continuing contact between J and his whole paternal family which calls into question the appropriateness of the wholesale transfer in legal terms which adoption brings about." (at para.24)

As noted in this case, a residence order, unlike adoption, does not create the legal relationship of parent and child. In addition, it will come to an end when the child reaches adulthood. This was a factor that influenced the court's decision to make an adoption order in *Re A (Placement of Child in Contravention of Adoption Act 1976, s.11)* [2005] 2 F.L.R. 727. According to the judge:

> "A residence order would be time-limited. It would not reflect the reality of the closeness established from birth between this child and the applicants. In the particular circumstances of the case it would in a sense demean the relationship between child and carers if there were only a residence order." (at para.6)

In this case contact with the birth family was thought to be an additional factor *supporting* the making of an adoption order, since the child would not be at risk of losing her birth family. The case can be distinguished from *Re B* on the basis that in *Re A* the parents actually supported the making of an adoption order.

(c) Special guardianship

A third alternative to adoption is created by the Adoption and Children Act 2002. As **15–013** the government explained in the White Paper that preceded the reforms, adoption will not always be appropriate:

> "Some older children do not wish to be legally separated from their birth families. Adoption may not be best for some children being cared for on a permanent basis

by members of their wider birth family. Some minority ethnic communities have religious and cultural differences with adoption as it is set out in law. Unaccompanied asylum-seeking children may also need secure, permanent homes, but have strong attachments to their families abroad." (*Adoption—a new approach* (2000), para.5.8)

The 2002 Act accordingly created the concept of a "special guardian". The persons who are entitled to apply for a special guardianship order are similar to those entitled to apply for a s.8 order (s.14A(5) of the Children Act 1989, as inserted by the 2002 Act, and see further paras 12–005 *et seq.* above), but not identical, as it is categorically stated that a special guardian "must not be a parent of the child in question" (s.14A(2)(b)). A person who is not listed can still apply with the leave of the court (s.14(4)), and the court has the power to appoint a special guardian in any family proceedings even if no such application has been made (s.14(6)(b)).

The application to become a special guardian is, however, different from an application for a s.8 order in that the local authority must be notified at least three months in advance of any application being made (s.14(7)), and must prepare a report for the court on the applicant's suitability to become a special guardian (s.14(8)). Similarly, the court must have such a report before it can make an order appointing a special guardian in other family proceedings.

If a special guardianship order is made—a decision which is governed by the welfare principle—the special guardian acquires parental responsibility for the child (s.14C(1)(a)). While this does not extinguish the parental responsibility of the birth parents, the legislation confers greater power on the special guardian by providing that he or she can exercise parental responsibility to the exclusion of any other person (s.14C(1)(b)). Like the other alternatives reviewed in this section, a special guardianship order does not have the same degree of permanence as an adoption order, and may be varied or discharged by the court (s.14D).

It should be noted that the ideas underlying special guardianship are not entirely original. Under the Children Act 1975, non-parents could apply for "custodianship" of a child, but this option was little used. Two factors may make special guardianship more popular: first, the changes in the use of adoption may mean that there is more demand for it; and, secondly, s.14F makes provision for support (including financial assistance) to be provided to special guardians (for the details see the Special Guardianship Regulations 2005, SI 2005/1109).

C: ELIGIBILITY TO ADOPT AND TO BE ADOPTED: THE LAW

15–014 The basic rules about who may adopt and be adopted under English law are laid down by statute.

(1) *The person to be adopted*

15–015 English law makes it clear that (in contrast to civil law systems in which adoption is used to establish inheritance rights) adoption is concerned with providing for a child "the social and psychological benefits of truly belonging to a family": *Re R. (Adoption)* [1967] 1 W.L.R. 34 at 41, Buckley J. The 2002 Act provides that the person to be adopted must be under 19 years of age and must never have been married (s.47(8) and (9)). If the child has attained the age of 18 the court will only make an order if the proceedings were commenced before the child's eighteenth birthday (s.49(4) and (5)). In some cases the court has refused to make an adoption order in respect of a child nearly 18 years old if the purpose of the adoption was in reality to confer citizenship rights (*Re B (Adoption Order: Nationality)* [1999] 1 F.L.R. 907, HL). But this does not mean that there is anything to stop the adoption of a "child" who is nearly 18 years old if, in all the circumstances, that will be for his benefit and the other relevant conditions are satisfied:

> In *Re D (A Minor) (Adoption Order: Validity)* [1991] 2 F.L.R. 66, CA, an order was made in respect of a child just six days before his 18th birthday. The child, who was severely handicapped and had a comprehension age of four, had been in the care of foster parents throughout this childhood, but latterly his mother had conducted a campaign of harassment against them and had had to be restrained by injunction. The foster parents applied for an adoption order, apparently because the injunction would terminate when the child reached majority, and they would then be again exposed to harassment. The Court of Appeal held that it was not necessary to show that the making of an adoption order would benefit the child during the six days before he became an adult; the fact that adoption would confer substantial benefits on him was sufficient.

In this, the case can be seen as anticipating the new emphasis on the life-long impact of adoption, which forms part of the statutory checklist introduced by the 2002 Act (see further below, para.15–039).

(2) Who may adopt?

An adoptive parent must generally be at least 21 years of age, although a parent **15–016** adopting his or her own child need only be 18 years of age (ss.50–51). Under the 1976 Act, an adoption order could only be made in favour of either a married couple or a single person. This meant that unmarried couples were not able to adopt jointly, although since it was possible for an adoption order to be made in favour of one member of a cohabiting couple it is difficult to see what purpose this rule served. In addition, it was possible for the court to make an adoption order in favour of one cohabiting partner and a joint residence order in favour of the two partners in appropriate cases: see *e.g. Re AB (Adoption: Joint Residence)* [1996] 1 F.L.R. 27, FD.

By contrast, the Adoption and Children Act 2002 allowed an adoption order to be made in favour of a either a single person or a couple, whether the latter consists of a married couple or "two people (whether of different sexes or the same sex) living as parties in an enduring family relationship" (see ss.50–51 and the definition of "couple" in s.144(4)(b)). The latter provision attracted considerable controversy when it was debated in Parliament, and attempts in the House of Lords to remove it from the Bill were only narrowly defeated. Its detractors argued that non-marital relationships were less stable than marital ones, while its supporters focused on the advantages that the provision would bring to children in care by widening the pool of potential adopters. The Joint Select Committee on Human Rights held that an amendment restricting the right to adopt to married couples was incompatible with the UK's human rights commitments. Not only would a blanket ban on adoption by unmarried couples amount to unjustifiable discrimination on the ground of marital status—thus violating Art.14 (combined with Art.8) of the European Convention—but the rights of the children would also be affected. The Committee noted that there was not always a simple choice between married and unmarried couples as potential adopters:

> "For example, one might have to choose between the child being adopted by an unmarried couple, being adopted by a single person, or not being adopted at all. Without a view of the range of options in an individual case, it is hard to say which option would best advance the child's long-term best interests. . . . preventing adoption by suitable couples, merely on the ground that they are unmarried, restricts the pool of potential adopters who could give children loving family homes, and does not seem to make the best interests of the child the paramount consideration as required by Article 21 of the CRC." (*Twenty-Fourth Report*, 2001–02, para.6)

Thus Parliament eventually voted to allow unmarried couples to adopt jointly, and the Civil Partnership At 2004 further amended the definition of a couple to include civil partners.

There are restrictions on the making of an adoption order in favour of a sole applicant who is married or in a civil partnership. In this case an adoption order can only be made if the court is satisfied that the other spouse or civil partner cannot be found, or is incapable by reason of ill health of applying, or that the parties have separated and are living apart and that the separation is likely to be permanent (see s.51(3)). Clearly, an adoption order should not be made where one of the parties to the marriage is unwilling. Rather oddly, perhaps, these rules do not prevent an adoption order being made in favour of both spouses, even though they are separated:

> In *Re WM (Adoption: Non-Patrial)* [1997] 1 F.L.R. 132, Johnson J., a married couple had adopted a child in El Salvador and brought him to their home in this country. Since the El Salvador order was not recognised by English law, the couple applied for an adoption order here; but by the time of the hearing they had separated. The judge made an adoption order. To do so was not prohibited; and on the unusual facts there would be real advantage to the child, not least in that the arrangements for his future would have to be reviewed by the court hearing a divorce application. (See also *Re C (Foreign Adoption: Natural Mother's Consent: Service)* [2006] 1 F.L.R. 318)

The legislation also contains restrictions on applications by only one of the parents of the child to be adopted. An adoption order may not be made in this situation unless the other parent is dead or cannot be found, or there is no other legal parent (by virtue of s.28 of the Human Fertilization and Embryology Act 1990, see Ch.10), or other reasons justify the child being adopted by the applicant alone (see s.51(4)). These restrictions were reviewed in *In re B (A minor)(Respondent)* [2001] UKHL 70:

> In this case the relationship between the parties had ended before the mother realised that she was pregnant. When the child was born she was placed with foster parents. The father then expressed an interest in looking after his daughter, and she was placed with him when she was two months old. The father then applied to adopt her. The House of Lords held that the reason for justifying the exclusion of the other natural parent need not be comparable with the death or disappearance of the other spouse and allowed the father's application. (The

question of whether adoption by one parent is in the best interests of a child is considered further below, para.15–039.)

These are the minimum requirements laid down by law about the personal attributes of the parties to an adoption: no adoption order can be made in other cases. But in practice, adoption agencies, in the exercise of their discretion in arranging placements, are likely to apply very much more demanding tests, as the next section will discuss.

D: The Role of the Adoption Agency

One of the most remarkable features of the adoption process in England is the way in **15–017** which it has been transformed into a matter in which most of the effective decisions are taken by social workers. In 1926, and for some years afterwards, the activities of adoption agencies in arranging adoption were viewed with some suspicion. Placements were generally arranged by private individuals, such as doctors or the proprietor of the nursing home where the child was born. By contrast, by the mid-1970s it was the private placement that was regarded with suspicion. The Children Act 1975 prohibited the making of arrangements for adoption by private individuals. At the same time it imposed upon every local authority a duty to establish and maintain a comprehensive adoption service (an obligation that continues under s.3 of the Adoption and Children Act 2002). The term "adoption agency" encompasses both the adoption services maintained by local authorities and registered adoption societies. The latter are usually termed "voluntary agencies" and are subjected to considerable regulation under the Care Standards Act 2000 and the Adoption Agencies Regulations 2005 (SI 2005/389). In practice, however, the responsibility for making arrangements for adoption falls largely upon the services maintained by the local authority.

This section briefly considers the sanctions underpinning the prohibitions on independent placements and then outlines the duties of the adoption agency.

(1) Independent placements prohibited

It is now a criminal offence for anyone other than an adoption agency to make **15–018** arrangements for the adoption of a child or to place a child for adoption (s.93 of the ACA 2002). It is also a criminal offence to make or receive any payment in consideration of the adoption of a child (s.95), although an exception is made for expenses incurred in the adoption process (see further s.96). The 2002 Act further underlines the central role of the adoption agency by placing restrictions on who may prepare an adoption report (see s.94 and the Restriction on the Preparation of Adoption Reports Regulations 2005, SI 2005/1711).

It should be noted, however, that the bar on making independent arrangements does not extend to a private placement with a parent, guardian or relative of the child (the latter defined in s.144(1) as a grandparent, brother, sister, uncle or aunt, whether of the full-blood or half-blood or by marriage), or where the prospective adopter is the partner of the child's parent (s.92(4)).

Moreover, even if a placement is illegal, the courts do not regard that fact as a bar to the making an adoption order if a refusal would prejudice the child's welfare (although it was held in *Re G (A Minor)(Adoption: Illegal Placement)* [1995] 1 F.L.R. 403 that such cases should be dealt with by the High Court). Thus:

In *Re A (Placement of Child in Contravention of Adoption Act 1976, S 11)* [2005] 2 F.L.R. 727, the child had been placed with friends of her parents. The judge noted that the parties had acted in good faith and that it was not appropriate for criminal proceedings to be brought, while warning that "[c]ommunities which may employ procedures which are not compliant with the Adoption Act 1976 need to be made fully aware of the potential criminal penalties." Since by this time the child was five and well-integrated into the family, it was in her best interests to make the order for adoption.

(2) *The duties of the adoption agency*

15–019 Although it remains the case that only the court can make an adoption order (see further below, para.15–032), the court cannot itself carry out any adequate investigation of the issues which arise in deciding whether the making of an adoption order would be for the benefit of the child. As Hedley J. pointed out in the context of an application for a care order, "the decision about matching is a decision for the local authority in the execution of an approved care plan, rather than a decision for the court" (*Re R (Care: Plan for Adoption: Best Interests)* [2006] 1 F.L.R. 483, para.17)

Accordingly, it is necessary for these investigations to be made by skilled experts whose assessment will be available to the court; and adoption agencies—whether those established by local authorities or voluntary agencies—have a vital part to play in these matters.

Section 1(2) of the Adoption and Children Act provides that, in reaching any decision relating to an adoption of a child, the paramount consideration for the adoption agency is the welfare of the child "throughout his life", and s.1(4) sets out a checklist of factors to which the agency is to have regard. These are the same factors that the court is required to take into consideration, and are considered in more detail below (paras 15–037 *et seq.*). This section focuses on the practical responsibilities of the adoption agency in determining whether adoption is appropriate for the child and finding suitable adoptive parents.

(a) Investigation, reports and counselling

15–020 The agency has extensive duties to obtain reports about the child, his birth parents, and the prospective adopters. It must also provide a counselling service for the birth parents, the child, and prospective adopters.

The detailed regulations are set out in the Adoption Agencies Regulations 2005, SI 2005/389, and what follows is intended merely to give a flavour of the duties of the adoption agency. It must, for example, investigate the health history of the birth parents and their family, ascertaining details of serious or hereditary diseases. It must also find out the birth parents' wishes and feelings about adoption.

With regard to the prospective adopters, the agency must make a full investigation into their circumstances (including such matters as their financial position, and their previous experience of caring for children), and it must assess their ability to bring up an adopted child throughout childhood. Police checks must be carried out and references obtained. There must be a medical report, which will discuss, for example, whether the prospective adopter's consumption of alcohol gives cause for concern, as well as whether he or she smokes tobacco or uses habit-forming drugs. It is further prescribed that an adoption agency "shall, in determining the suitability of a couple to adopt a child, have proper regard to the need for stability and permanence in their relationship" (reg.4(2) of the Suitability of Adopters Regulations 2005, SI 2005/1712)—although it is doubtful whether this adds anything to the statutory requirement that the parties should have an "enduring" relationship (see s.144(4)(b) of the 2002 Act).

Reports on the child must also be compiled. The child must be medically examined, and a detailed account produced dealing with such matters as personality and social development, educational attainment and the extent of the relationship with the birth family. In addition, the child's wishes and feelings in relation to adoption, his religious and cultural upbringing and contact with the birth family must also be ascertained.

(b) Reference to the adoption panel

In an attempt to introduce a further check on unsuitable placements, adoption **15–021** agencies are required to establish a panel including social workers, a medical adviser, and at least three independent members. Wherever reasonably practicable the "independent persons" must include at least two persons with practical experience of adoption.

The reports compiled by the adoption agency are passed to the adoption panel, whose role is to consider whether the child should be placed for adoption. The agency's assessment of the prospective adopter's suitability to be an adoptive parent must first have been copied to the prospective adopter, who is given an opportunity to make observations about it—presumably in an attempt to meet criticisms that suitable applicants were being rejected by social workers on trivial grounds.

The panel must consider all the information and reports referred to above, and may seek other relevant information, and it must obtain legal advice about each case. It is then for the panel to consider whether adoption is in the best interests of the child, whether a prospective adopter is suitable to be an adoptive parent, and whether the child should be placed with a particular prospective adopter.

The agency must not take a decision on these matters until it has taken account of the panel's recommendations. If the agency decides that the prospective adopter is unsuitable, the agency must notify him or her, provide reasons, and invite representations. (These will be passed on to the adoption panel, which will once again consider the case and make a recommendation to the agency.) Under s.12 of the 2002 Act, rejected adopters have the right to an independent review of their case (for the details see the Independent Review of Determinations (Adoption) Regulations 2005, SI 2005/3332).

Throughout this complex decision-taking process it is for the panel to recommend, but for the agency to decide, whether adoption is in the best interests of the child, whether a prospective adopter is suitable to be an adoptive parent, and whether the child should be placed with a particular prospective adopter—bearing in mind of course that the ultimate decision lies with the court (see further below paras 15–029 *et seq.*).

One final point on matching the child with potential adopters should be noted. Since the adoption agencies established by local authorities operate within a specific area, there is obviously the possibility that potential parents in another area will not come to their attention. There is now a national database of children waiting to be adopted, and of adults who have been approved as potential adopters. This means that if suitable adopters cannot be found locally, the search for a match can be widened.

(c) Providing information to the prospective adopters

15–022 Since adoption now involves older children, often with difficulties, rather than babies, the process of finding suitable adopters must take into account the characteristics of the child as well as the adopter. The Regulations stipulate that the adoption agency must provide the prospective adopters with a copy of the child's permanence record (which, as defined in reg.17, includes extensive information about the child), as well as providing counselling (reg.31 of the Adoption Agencies Regulations 2005, SI 2005/389). They also stipulate that the prospective adopter must be provided with any other information that the agency considers relevant, which clearly allows the agency to exercise some discretion in deciding what information should be provided. In this context the decision of the Court of Appeal in *A and B v Essex CC* [2003] EWCA Civ 1848 is likely to remain relevant.

> In that case a couple had claimed that the local authority had been negligent in failing to inform them of the behavioural difficulties of a child who had been placed with them for adoption. The Court of Appeal upheld the decision of the judge below that the adoptive parents were entitled to damages for the injury, loss and damage that they had suffered during the placement, but on the basis that the agency had failed to pass on information that it had decided that the adopters should have. The professionals compiling reports for adoption agencies owed no duty of care to prospective adopters.

While the child's permanence record must now include an "assessment of the child's emotional and behavioural development" (reg.17(1)(f)), the point made in that case holds good in relation to information that the agency is not under a specific duty to provide. As Hale L.J. emphasised in that case prospective adopters "are not passive recipients of the agency's services. They are actors in the story. They have a trial period within which to get to know the child and adjust to the enormous upheaval of having a new person in their lives" (para.55). This leads on to the next stage in the process, that of placing the child with the prospective adopters.

(d) Placing the child with the adopters

15–023 Once suitable adopters have in theory been identified, the next stage is to place the child with them. If each parent or guardian has consented to the placement—parent, for these purposes, being limited to parents with parental responsibility—then the placement can proceed without a court order (s.19), unless a care order has subsequently been made. In all other cases the agency must seek a placement order from the court (s.21).

Whether the child has been placed for adoption with the consent of the birth parents or as the result of the making of a placement order, the adoption agency will have parental responsibility for the child (s.25). Certain aspects of parental responsibility are also acquired by the prospective adopters also when the child is placed with them, although the status of the birth parents is not extinguished until an adoption order is made. The legislation also provides that the adoption agency can determine how far the birth parents or prospective adopters may meet their responsibility for the child, thus addressing any problems that might arise as a result of multiple persons having parental responsibility.

It is clear that the responsibilities of the adoption agency do not end with the placing of the child with the prospective adopters. The agency must "ensure that the child and prospective adopter are visited within one week of the placement and thereafter at least once a week until the first review", which takes place within four weeks of the child being placed for adoption (reg.36(4)(a) and (3)(a) of the Adoption Agencies Regulations 2005, SI 2005/389). The agency's responsibilities to keep the placement under review continue until the adoption order is made.

Sections E and F will now consider the role of the birth parents (in giving their consent) and of the court (in making a placement or adoption order) respectively.

E: THE ROLE OF THE BIRTH PARENTS

The discussion so far has focused on the position of the child and the prospective **15–024** adopters. But what of the wishes and feelings of the birth parents? This section briefly considers the law relating to the giving of parental consent, along with the broader issue of parental involvement in the adoption process. It should, however, be borne in mind that the birth parents' refusal of consent is not determinative (see further para.15–034 below).

(1) *Whose consent is relevant?*

In considering the role that the birth parents play in the adoption process, it is first **15–025** necessary to establish *which* parents have the power to consent to the child being placed for adoption, or to the adoption itself. The consent of the legal mother is always required, as is the consent of a guardian or special guardian, but the consent of a parent—invariably a father—who does not have parental responsibility is not required. It should be borne in mind, however, that the likelihood of a father *not* having parental responsibility has been reduced by recent reforms (see para.11–016 above).

(a) Giving consent

A number of points should be noted about the way in which consent is given. A **15–026** mother cannot give her consent to adoption in the first six weeks after the child's birth (s.52(3) of the ACA 2002). The policy underlying this provision is that the mother should have time to get over the physical and emotional effects of giving birth. A mother can, however, consent to the child being placed for adoption even within the first six weeks of the child's life, and in this case she must also consent (in writing) to the adoption of the child (reg.35(4) of the Adoption Agencies Regulations 2005, SI 2005/389).

More generally, the agreement of any parent or guardian must be an informed one. A reporting officer is appointed to witness the signature of the parent and must ensure "so far as reasonably practicable that the parent or guardian is (i) giving consent unconditionally, and (ii) with full understanding of what is involved" (reg.72(1)(a) of the Family Procedure (Adoption) Rules 2005, SI 2005/2795). There is, however, no requirement that the birth parents should know the identity of the prospective adopters (s.52(5)), and indeed a parent or guardian may give an advance consent to adoption when agreeing to the child being placed for adoption (s.20).

(b) Withdrawing consent

Where the parents originally consented to the child being placed for adoption, but **15–027** later change their minds, they are entitled to the return of their child, unless an application is or has been made for either an adoption order or a placement order (s.32). This provides an incentive for prospective adoptive parents to apply for adoption orders as soon as they are legally able to do so. The fact that parents have consented to the child being placed for adoption will also make it difficult for them to oppose any subsequent application for an adoption order (see further para.15–032 below).

By contrast, if the child is subject to a placement order—as is likely to be the situation in the majority of cases—the parents are not entitled to the return of their child.

(2) The role of a parent without parental responsibility

15–028 As noted above, as the result of recent reforms fewer fathers will lack parental responsibility. Even so, there will continue to be fathers without parental responsibility, and so the question arises as to their role in the adoption process. Under the old law it was clear that at least some fathers without parental responsibility should be involved in the adoption process. The key question was whether there was "family life" between the father and the child:

> In *Re H; Re G (Adoption: Consultation of Unmarried Fathers)* [2001] 1 F.L.R. 646, FD, Butler-Sloss P. first enquired whether there could be said to be any "family life" between the fathers and the children. In the first case the parents had cohabited and the father was still in touch with the child that had been born during the relationship, although he was unaware of the existence of the second child. It was held that he did have a family life with the second child, and that to place the child for adoption without notice being given to him would be in breach of this right. It was noted that the mother's desire for confidentiality should not prevail unless there were strong countervailing factors such as rape or domestic violence. (There was also the pragmatic consideration that the father might find out anyway). In the second case, the parties had never cohabited and had lost touch. It was held that no family life existed between the father and his child, and that the local authority need not inform him of the adoption.

While the 2002 Act is largely silent on the role to be played by the father without parental responsibility it is likely that this approach will continue. The Regulations make it clear that a father without parental responsibility is not automatically a party to an application for a placement order or adoption order, but that if provision has been made for him to have contact with the child, he will be joined as a respondent (reg.23 of the Family Procedure (Adoption) Rules 2005. It is further provided that an adoption agency may ask the High Court for directions on the need to give a father without parental responsibility notice of their intention to place a child for adoption (reg.108 of the Family Procedure (Adoption) Rules 2005, SI 2005/2795).

Moreover, even if a father later acquires parental responsibility, his role in the adoption process is limited. The fact that he has acquired parental responsibility does not mean that his consent to the placement or adoption becomes necessary: instead, s.52(10) provides that that he "is to be treated as having at that time given consent . . . in the same terms as those in which the first parent gave consent." Once the child is settled with the prospective adopters, there may be little that the father can do to influence the process.

F: THE ROLE OF THE COURT

The court may be required to make a number of decisions in the process leading to the **15–029** adoption of a child. The child may have been the subject of care proceedings, in which case the court will have had to approve the local authority's care plan indicating that adoption is to be sought. If the child is then to be placed for adoption, a placement order must be sought from the court if the consent of the child's parents is not forthcoming. Finally, no adoption is complete without an adoption order from the court, even if the parents are happy for the adoption to go ahead. Despite the importance of such orders, the court's role is essentially limited to ratifying—or not—the arrangements sought by others: it does not choose the prospective adopters and it cannot make an adoption order of its own motion. This section will first consider the orders that the court can make and then the criteria that govern whether or not such orders should be made.

The powers of the court

There are two key orders in the adoption process: first, the placement order, which **15–030** may be made if the consent of the birth parents to the adoption is not forthcoming, and, secondly, the adoption order that must be made to complete the legal process of adoption.

(1) *Placement orders*

Until 1984 a parent could only consent to a specific adoption and that consent could **15–031** be withdrawn after the child had been placed with the prospective adopters and at any time up to the making of the final order. The Children Act 1975 introduced the procedure of "freeing" a child for adoption, in order that any doubts about parental agreement could be resolved by the court at an early stage, and usually before the child had been placed for adoption. Use of this procedure was not mandatory and a child could, therefore, be placed with prospective adopters without being freed for adoption. By contrast, under the 2002 Act a child may only be placed for adoption if the necessary consents are given or a placement order has been made by the court. This is intended to ensure greater certainty for all concerned, and a review by the court before relationships are created and lost by the decisions of adoption agencies.

   If the relevant consents have been given to the child being placed with prospective adopters there is no need for the court to make an order. In other cases—whether because of the absence of parental consent or, if a child has been abandoned, the absence of known parents—a placement order will be necessary. The court can only make such an order if the child is subject to a care order *or* the court is satisfied that the conditions in s.31(2) of the Children Act (which give the court jurisdiction to make a care order) are satisfied, *or* the child has no parent or guardian (s.21 of the ACA 2002). In addition, the court must be satisfied either that the parents consent or that their consent should be dispensed with, and that the welfare of the child requires the order to be made. The criteria for making a placement order thus reflect the principle that children should not be removed from their parents against their wishes unless the care (or lack thereof) given to the child has passed a certain threshold of bad parenting. While it is envisaged that placement orders will be made in care proceedings, it may be difficult to achieve this within the timescales set out in the Protocol for

Judicial Case Management in Public Law Children Act Cases (see [2003] 2 F.L.R. 719).

In addition, before making a placement order the court must "consider the arrangements which the adoption agency has made, or proposes to be made, for allowing any person contact with the child and ... invite the parties to the proceedings to comment on those arrangements" (s.27(4) of the ACA 2002). It may make an order for contact under s.26, either upon the application of the child, a parent or other person having close links with the child (s.26(3)), or upon its own initiative.

(2) Adoption orders

15–032 Although it is clear that the adoption agency takes most of the effective steps in relation to adoption, it remains a fundamental principle that an adoption order can only be made by a court. A number of restrictions on the making of such an order should be noted.

First, an adoption order may not be made unless the child has been living with the applicants for a certain period of time (s.42). Different time periods apply to different types of adopters. If the child has been placed for adoption, or the applicant is a parent of the child, an application may not be made for adoption unless the child has lived with the potential adopter(s) for ten weeks. If the applicant is a partner of the child's parent, the period is extended to six months. Local authority foster parents must wait twelve months, and in any other cases the child must have lived with the applicants for at least three out of the past five years. These provisions reinforce the restrictions against adoptions by non-relatives that have not been arranged through an agency. Secondly, the court must consider whether making an adoption order would promote the child's welfare (see further para.15–036).

Thirdly, the requirements regarding the requisite consents must have been given, or, if consent has not been given the court must be satisfied that it may dispense with such consent. It should be noted that if advance consent has been given under s.19, such consent cannot be withdrawn after the application for an adoption order has been made (s.52(4)), and a parent or guardian cannot oppose the making of an adoption order without the leave of the court (s.47(5)), which will only be granted if there has been a change of circumstances since consent was originally given (s.47(7)). Similar constraints apply if the child was placed for adoption under a placement order or with the consent of the parents (s.47(4)).

Finally, before making an adoption order, the court must consider whether there should be any arrangements for contact between the child and any person "and for that purpose the court must consider any existing or proposed arrangements and obtain any views of the parties to the proceedings" (s.46(6)).

The issues of dispensing with consent, making an order, and contact will now be considered in more depth.

Dispensing with consent

15–033 Under the 2002 Act parental consent cannot be dispensed with when making a placement order or adoption unless either the parent or guardian cannot be found or is incapable of giving consent, or the welfare of the child requires the consent to be dispensed with (s.52).

(1) *Cannot be found or is incapable of giving agreement*

This provision will normally apply to cases in which the whereabouts of the person **15–034**
whose consent is required are unknown and cannot be discovered, or where he or she
lacks the mental capacity to give consent. An applicant relying on this ground must
show that all reasonable steps have been taken to find the parent or guardian,
including making inquiries of relatives. In addition, the courts have held that a person
"cannot be found" for the purposes of this section if there are no practical means of
communication, even if the physical whereabouts are in fact known:

> In *Re R (Adoption)* [1967] 1 W.L.R. 34, the parents lived in a totalitarian country
> and any attempt to communicate with them would involve embarrassment and
> danger. The court dispensed with their agreement. (See also *Re A (Adoption of a
> Russian Child)* [2000] 1 F.L.R. 539, FD.)

(2) *Welfare of child requires consent to be dispensed with*

This provision appears to mark a significant change in the law. Previously, some form **15–035**
of parental default had to be shown before the court could dispense with parental
consent (see s.16 of the 1976 Act). However, the legal criteria rarely proved an obstacle
to an order being made, as the courts tended to be heavily influenced by the decision
that adoption would be for the child's benefit. For example, parental consent could be
dispensed with where that parent was withholding consent unreasonably: the justification that a reasonable parent would consent to an adoption that was in the child's best
interests meant that a parent resisting adoption would by definition be labelled as
unreasonable. From one perspective the 2002 Act merely makes the existing practice
of the court more transparent. There is, however, a subtle difference between an order
being made because it will promote the child's welfare, and an order being made
because the child's welfare requires parental rights to be overridden: the latter does at
least acknowledge that there is a balance to be struck. A number of commentators
have questioned whether the new test is compatible with the European Convention on
Human Rights.

Should the court make an order?

For years adoption law was out of step with the approach taken in other areas of child **15–036**
law, since the welfare of the child was only the *first* consideration. The Adoption and
Children Act 2002 has now brought adoption law into line with the Children Act 1989
in providing that the welfare of the child is to be the court's *paramount* consideration
(see s.1(2) of the ACA 2002), although the formulation of the 2002 Act is slightly
different in that it is the child's welfare "throughout his life" that is relevant.

The 2002 Act also echoes the 1989 Act in stating that the court must bear in mind
that delay is likely to prejudice the child's welfare (s.1(3)), and must refrain from
making an order "unless it considers that making the order would be better for the
child than not doing so." (s.1(6)). It further sets out a checklist of factors to be taken
into account that is very similar to those set out in s.1 of the Children Act. The
differences that exist reflect the distinct nature of adoption. Thus the court is to have
regard to "the likely effect on the child (throughout his life) of having ceased to be a
member of the original family and become an adopted person" (s.1(4)(c)), and the
child's relationship with relatives and other significant persons (s.1(4)(f)). These considerations apply to the making (or revocation) of both placement and adoption

orders, and to orders under s.26 dealing with contact while the child is subject to a placement order (s.1(7)(a)). In considering all such applications, the court is to have regard to the full range of its powers under the Act, and under the Children Act, and can only make an adoption order if this would be preferable to making any other order (or making no order at all).

(1) *The child's wishes*

15–037 Like the 1976 Act, the 2002 legislation requires the court to have regard to the ascertainable wishes and feelings of the child, "considered in the light of the child's age and understanding" (s.1(4)(a)). In practice, if the child's wishes are ascertained it will require clear evidence to justify the court in not giving effect to them:

> In *Re D (Minors) (Adoption by Step-Parent)* (1981) F.L.R. 102, the question was whether an adoption order should be made in favour of the step-father of girls aged 10 and 12, both of whom were in favour of the adoption order being made. It was held that this was a weighty factor.

The *National Adoption Standards* go further, stipulating that the different stages of the adoption process are to be explained to the child, and:

> "Every child will have his or her wishes and feelings listened to, recorded, and taken into account. Where they are not acted upon, the reasons for not doing so will be explained to the child and properly recorded." (A.4)

It will be noted that this focuses on procedure rather than guaranteeing that the child's wishes will be heeded. There is no formal requirement that the agreement of the child to the making of an adoption order be obtained, in contrast to the position in Scotland (the Adoption (Scotland) Children Act 1978 requires the consent of a child over the age of 12 to an adoption order). Autonomy and welfare may conflict on this point: the arguments as to whether a child should have the burden of deciding between two parents apply with even more force to this situation. Given that the Department of Health found that "[a] major reason for placement breakdown is that the child was not emotionally willing to be placed with a new family but was not enabled to say so", maybe the child's voice should be heard more often (see "Adoption and Permanence for Children who Cannot Live Safely with Birth Parents or Relatives", Quality Protects Research Briefing No.5, 2002).

(2) *The child's particular needs*

15–038 The child's need for a stable home is likely to weigh very heavily with the court in deciding whether adoption, rather than some lesser order, is appropriate, and whether contact with the birth family is likely to jeopardise the stability of the new family.

(3) *The impact of becoming adopted*

15–039 Under s.1(4)(c) the court is required to have regard to "the likely effect on the child (throughout his life) of having ceased to be a member of the original family and become an adopted person. This directs the court to consider both the impact of the legal relationship with the birth family being severed, and the impact of a new legal relationship being created.

In many cases the crucial factor will be whether there is any realistic prospect of the child being re-integrated into its birth family; and this should be fully explored before a decision is taken to sever all legal links between the child and the birth family. This was also a consideration under the 1976 Act:

> In *Re C (A Minor) (Adoption: Parental Agreement: Contact)* [1993] 2 F.L.R. 260, CA, the question was (*per* Hoffmann and Steyn L.JJ. at 270) whether a couple should be permanently deprived of all future contact with their four-year-old daughter. Everyone agreed that they loved her and desperately wanted to keep her. They, for their part, could not understand what they had done to deserve having to lose their child. The judge found on the facts that there were no realistic prospects of such re-integration occurring; and that accordingly adoption would be in the child's interests.

The case of *In re B (A Minor) (Respondent)* [2001] UKHL 70, involved the question whether the legal relationship with *half* of the child's birth family should be severed:

> In this case the mother had given her daughter up for adoption, but subsequently agreed that the father (from whom she had separated while unaware that she was pregnant) could look after her. The father applied to adopt his daughter, to ensure that the mother would not be able to take her away at a later date. The Official Solicitor opposed the father's application to adopt on the basis that ending the child's relationship with her mother could not be said to promote her welfare. At first instance the judge decided that in view of the fact that the mother had rejected the child at birth and consented to the adoption, it would be in the child's best interests to make her placement with her father secure. The Court of Appeal reversed this decision, but the House of Lords restored the decision of the trial judge, on the basis that the Court of Appeal should not have interfered where the judge had not misdirected herself. Lord Nicholls did however comment that the circumstances in which it is in the best interests of the child to make an adoption order in favour of one parent, to the exclusion of the other, are likely to be exceptional.

In addition to the stability that the adoptive family can offer, there may be more tangible advantages, such as the benefits resulting from the change in immigration status:

> In *Re B (Adoption Order: Nationality)* [1999] 1 F.L.R. 907, HL, a 15-year-old Jamaican girl given leave to enter the United Kingdom for six months had her application for an extension rejected. A law centre advised that the only way in which she could gain the right to stay would be for the relatives caring for her here to apply to adopt her. The Home Office intervened to oppose the application, and the Court of Appeal held that no adoption order should have been made because, in assessing the benefits to the child, the court should ignore benefits resulting solely from the child's change in immigration status. The House of Lords unanimously held that this approach was contrary to the express terms of the Act: the court could not simply ignore the considerable benefits that would accrue to the child during the remainder of her childhood.

In the past, the courts have refused to make adoption orders that would merely give the child a favourable immigration status as an adult: *Re B (Adoption Order: Nationality)* [1999] 1 F.L.R. 907, HL. In contrast to the 1976 Act, which referred to the effect of the adoption during childhood, the 2002 Act requires the court to consider the lifelong effect of adoption. Whether this makes the courts more willing to make adoption orders to confer immigration advantages remains to be seen, but it seems unlikely that such orders would be made where this was the only advantage accruing from the adoption.

15–040 (4) *The child's background*

The question of what would be beneficial to a child may involve difficult considerations of racial or ethnic identity, and the courts have attached considerable weight to this factor:

> In *Re B (Adoption: Child's Welfare)* [1995] 2 F.C.R. 749, Wall J., the child had two loving and competent parents who wished to care for her in their home in the Gambia. It would not be in the child's interests for the parents' parental responsibility for her to be extinguished; whilst there was a danger that she would lose the advantages of her cultural heritage and her sense of identity as the child of African parents.

Again:

> In *Re N (A Minor) (Adoption)* [1990] 1 F.L.R. 58, a black child was placed with white foster parents under a private fostering agreement. The child remained in their care for more than three years, and they applied for an adoption order. The judge considered that adoption would not be in the child's interest because the child's father would have a useful and important part to play in her life when she wanted to seek out her cultural roots. The child should remain in the foster parents' care, but remain legally her birth parents' child.

On the other hand, there may also be good reason for not matching the child's background too closely, as the case of *Re C (Adoption: Religious Observance)* [2002] 1 F.L.R. 1119, FD illustrates:

> In this case the local authority's plan was for the child (whose background included Jewish, Irish Roman Catholic and Turkish-Cypriot Muslim elements) to be adopted by a Jewish couple who had a low level of religious observance (and had Roman Catholic and Turkish elements in their wider family). The judge noted the difficulty of finding a home that reflected such a mixed heritage, and suggested that it could be in the interests of a child to have a home where only one strand of her heritage was reflected, provided that the adopters were sufficiently sensitive to help her understand her origins. Moreover, "in circumstances where the need to find a permanent alternative home for C has been precipitated by the poverty, physical but in particular intellectual and emotional, of the home which the parents could offer to her, it is paradoxical to seek to replicate in the adoptive home the religious void in their home." (Both parent had learning difficulties and the father had claimed that the child had a "London religion".) The judge approved the plan for adoption.

(5) *Any harm that the child has suffered*

This has the same meaning as in the Children Act 1989 (see para.14–014, above).   **15–041**

(6) *The child's relationship with relatives*

The factors set out in s.1(4)(f) are likely to be particularly relevant in deciding whether **15–042** some order short of adoption would be more appropriate, and whether contact should be ordered. The court is directed to have regard to the child's relationship with his or her relatives and any other relevant person, and in particular:

   (i) "the likelihood of any such relationship continuing and the value to the child of its doing so;

   (ii) the ability and willingness of any of the child's relatives, or of any such person, to provide the child with a secure environment in which the child can develop, and otherwise to meet the child's needs,

   (iii) the wishes and feelings of any of the child's relatives, or of any such person, regarding the child."

Several points are worthy of note: first, contact is seen in terms of its value to the child rather than to the other parties involved; secondly, the legislation is far from suggesting that there is any positive benefit to being brought up by one's relatives, although it does suggest that relatives should be considered as carers before any plan is made for adoption; thirdly, the wishes of the parents are now just one of the factors to be taken into consideration. It remains to be seen how the courts will interpret these factors under the 2002 Act.

Should an order for contact be made?

As noted above, the court is required to consider the arrangements for contact **15–043** between the child and his or her birth family when making either a placement order or an adoption order. The placing of a child for adoption, or the making of an adoption order, operates to extinguish any existing order for contact under the Children Act 1989 (ss. 26(1) and 46(2)(b)). Those adopting the child may be willing to allow contact between the child and his or her birth family, in line with the emphasis on openness (see para.15–007 above). But if they are not, is the court likely to make legally binding provision for continuing contact?

   A number of points should be made. First, the extent of contact between the child and the birth parents may be a relevant factor in deciding whether or not an adoption order is appropriate in the circumstances (see *e.g. Re B (Adoption Order)* [2001] EWCA Civ 347, para.15–012 above). Secondly, if the adoptive parents have agreed to contact, then the court may take the view that no order for contact is necessary, pursuant to the "no order" principle included in the 2002 Act. Thus:

   In *Re T (Adoption: Contact)* [1995] 2 F.L.R. 251, CA, the adopters had agreed that the mother should continue to see the child once a year, and the judge attached an order to that effect to the adoption order. The Court of Appeal held he had been wrong to do so. The finality of adoption and the importance of letting the adoptive family find its feet ought not to be threatened by an order (all the more so since if they wished to stop the birth mother's visits they would have to incur the expense of an application to the court). The principle that the court should not make orders unless the welfare of the child would be better served by doing so than by making no order was to be applied. The onus should be on the birth mother to seek leave to apply for a contact order if she considered the adopters were behaving unreasonably in denying her contact.

This case also illustrates the weak position of the birth-parent after adoption: no longer a "parent" within the definition in the Children Act, he or she needs to seek leave to make any application for contact (or other s.8 order).

Thirdly, if the adoptive parents do not want contact between the child and his or her birth family, the court is unlikely to make legal provision for such contact. The courts have consistently taken the view that, in the ultimate analysis, the decision on whether to permit contact was a matter for the adopters to decide in the exercise of their parental responsibility (*Re V (A Minor) (Adoption: Consent)* [1987] Fam. 57 at 78, *per* Oliver L.J.). It is not surprising, therefore, to find the courts declining to impose provisions about continued contact with which the adopters did not agree. According to Lord Ackner in *Re C (A Minor) (Adoption Order: Conditions)* [1989] A.C. 1, the effect of this would—

> "be to create a potentially frictional situation which would be hardly likely to safeguard or promote the welfare of the child." (at 17)

This view has continued to prevail, despite the greater emphasis on openness in the modern adoption process:

> In *Re R (Adoption: Contact)* [2005] EWCA Civ 1128 the child's half-sister sought leave to apply for a contact order in the context of adoption proceedings. This was refused, and her appeal was dismissed by the Court of Appeal. Wall L.J. noted that contact orders were unusual in adoption proceedings and "the judge was plainly entitled . . . to take into account that the court would be reluctant to make an order in the face of reasonable opposition from the prospective adopt-ers." (para.50). He emphasised that "the critical and most important factor in the case . . . is that L's placement should be as secure, stable and happy as possible." (para.60)

Given these different factors it is unsurprising that there are few reported cases in which contact has been ordered. A rare example is *Re O (Transracial Adoption: Contact)* [1995] 2 F.L.R. 597, CA:

> In this case Thorpe J. held that the security of a 10-year-old Nigerian girl could only be obtained by an adoption order, but considered that the order should require contact with the mother. In this he was influenced in part by the fact that the child was being brought up in a family, and in a locality, where it was very difficult to buttress her Nigerian heritage.

It is unlikely that the 2002 Act will lead to a change in approach.

It should of course be borne in mind that where children are adopted from care, there may be good reasons for them not to have contact with their birth families (see, *e.g. Re M, T, P, K and B (Care: Change of Name)* [2000] 2 F.L.R. 645, FD, see para.14–010, above; and *Re C (Adoption: Religious Observance)* [2002] 1 F.L.R. 1119). Even so, in *Re G (Adoption: Contact)* [2002] EWCA Civ 761, it was mooted that allowing contact would remove "the sense of the ogre", although in that case the children were in care pending adoption.

G: INTER-COUNTRY ADOPTIONS

As noted in the introduction, increasing numbers of children are being adopted from **15–044** overseas, although the numbers remain relatively small—only about 300 each year. The desire to adopt a child from overseas has been fuelled by two trends: first, the well-publicised plight of orphaned and abandoned babies in countries such as Romania and China, and, secondly, the scarcity of babies available for adoption in this country. There is evidence that couples did not always observe the required procedures (see *e.g. Re K (Adoption and Wardship)* [1997] 2 F.L.R. 221, para.12–043 above), and foreign adoption orders were not always recognised by the English courts. The dangers of unregulated adoptions are amply demonstrated by the facts of *Flintshire CC v K* [2001] 2 F.L.R. 476, FD:

> An English couple, the Ks, paid for a private home study report regarding their suitability to adopt and $12,500 to an American adoption agency, which informed them that twins were available for adoption. The twins had previously been placed with another couple, the As, from whom the birth mother had removed them, ostensibly for a brief "closure" visit. The mother then handed the children over to the Ks, and an adoption order was made (in a state with which none of the parties had any connection). The Ks brought the children back to the UK and gave their story to a newspaper. At this stage the local authority stepped in and applied for a care order. The judge noted that the home study report was useless and dangerous, and that the arrangements for the child were ill conceived, ill thought through and poorly implemented. The evidence of the social workers was that the Ks showed no affection for the twins, whose welfare was subordinated to the Ks' involvement with the media (they had had five different minders while the Ks were giving interviews, including two journalists). The care order was granted, and the twins were returned to the USA, for their fate to be decided upon by the authorities in the state where they were born.

The judge in that case commented that "[a] two-tier system, applying lower standards in respect of adoption of a child from overseas, is wholly unacceptable" (at 487).

A solution was needed to regulate both the suitability of those wishing to adopt and the recognition of adoption orders made overseas. The Adoption (Intercountry Aspects) Act 1999, implementing the Hague Convention on Protection of Children and Co-operation in Respect of Intercountry Adoption, was intended to bring this two-tier system to an end. The majority of the 1999 Act was incorporated—with certain amendments—into the Adoption and Children Act 2002, and the revised procedure for domestic adoptions also has implications for adoptions with an international element. Under the Convention, eligibility to adopt a child from overseas is now assessed by the same process as is used for domestic adoptions. It is the responsibility of the country where the child lives to assess whether the child is available for adoption, and both the sending and the receiving country must agree to the adoption. The order itself may be made in either state.

If the child's state of origin is not a signatory to the Hague Convention, then the process remains the same in assessing the eligibility of the person wishing to adopt, but an order made in the child's country of origin will not be recognised, so an adoption order must be made in this country (see s.83 of the 2002 Act).

The fact that the adoption process in the child's state of origin does not meet internationally prescribed standards does not necessarily mean that the arrangement will not be accorded *some* legal recognition. Thus in *Singh v ECO, New Delhi* [2004] EWCA Civ 1075 it was held that while the Sikh religious adoption ceremony that had taken place in India did not meet international standards, on the facts there was family life between the child and the adopters. Munby J. noted that the case had arisen because

> "this boy and his adoptive parents come from a society and embrace a faith which hold to a view of adoption sufficiently different from our own that our law refuses to afford recognition to what I have no doubt was in their eyes, as in the eyes of their community generally, a ceremony of the most profound emotional, personal, social, cultural, religious and indeed legal significance." (para.57)

H: CONCLUSION

15–045 The Adoption and Children Act 2002 will make a number of important changes to the adoption process, although, as this chapter has demonstrated, some of the changes merely make the courts' current approach explicit. The Government has stated that the adoption process is too lengthy and should be speeded up. While some surveys have found that, on average, over three years elapse between the child starting to be looked after by the local authority and the adoption order, it should be borne in mind that this period will often involve attempts at rehabilitation with the birth parents as well as the search for suitable adopters, the evaluation of the placement, and the process of obtaining an order from the court. Given the importance of each of these stages, a little delay might be preferable to a speedy decision that turns out to be the wrong one. Rather than speeding up each separate stage, some new initiatives try to work towards rehabilitation while setting up an alternative placement should rehabilitation fail. Such initiatives may take the form of "contingency planning" (planning a fall-back position), "twin-track planning" (finding potential adopters) or, most ambitiously, "concurrent planning", which involves the child being placed with the prospective adopters while the possibility of rehabilitation is explored (see E. Monck, J. Reynolds and V. Wigfall, *The Role of Concurrent Planning: Making permanent placements for young children* (BAAF, 2003)).

Adoption is intended to provide the child with a new family "for life", but of course adoptive families may suffer the same vicissitudes as other families. The Department of Health noted that in one survey of adult adoptees, seven per cent of those placed for adoption when under the age of 12 months, and 11 per cent of those placed when over 24 months old, rated their experience of growing up adopted either negatively or very negatively ("Adoption and Permanence for Children who Cannot Live Safely with Birth Parents or Relatives", Quality Protects Research Briefing No.5, 2002). The child in *A v Essex County Council* [2003] EWCA Civ 1848 (above at para.15–022) initially returned to being cared for by the local authority when his new parents were unable to cope with his behaviour. However, by the time the case came before the Court of Appeal, Hale L.J. was able to report that:

"The adoptive placement has not broken down. William is still part of the claimant's family and they remain committed to him. Although he has had to go to residential placements for a while, he is currently back living with them." (para.17)

There are at least some happy endings.

INDEX

Accountability
  parental responsibility, 11–006
Adoption, 15–001—15–006, 15–010, 15–014,
    15–045
  and see Adoption agencies; Adoption
    panels
  adoption orders, 15–032
  adoption support, 15–009
  care plans, 13–035
  children, 15–015
  childrens welfare, 15–035, 15–036—15–042
  counselling, 15–020
  courts, 15–029, 15–030
  criminal conduct, 15–018
  intercountry adoption, 15–044
  investigations, 15–020
  parental consent, 15–025—15–027,
    15–033—15–035
  parental contact, 15–007, 15–043
  parental responsibility, 11–020, 15–023,
    15–028
  parents, 15–016, 15–024
  placement orders, 15–023, 15–031
  prohibited degrees, 3–010
  relatives, 15–008
  reports, 15–020
  surrogacy, 10–022
  void marriages, 3–010
Adoption agencies, 15–017, 15–018, 15–019
  and see Adoption
  counselling, 15–020
  information, 15–022
  investigations, 15–020
  parental responsibility, 15–023
  placement orders, 15–023, 15–031
  reports, 15–020
Adoption orders, 15–032
Adoption panels, 15–021
Adoption support, 15–009
Adultery, 4–009—4–012

Affinity
  annulment, 3–007—3–009
Age
  childrens welfare, 14–013
  void marriages, 3–012
Anglican marriage *see* Marriage
Annulment, 3–001, 3–002, 3–003, 3–048
  affinity, 3–007—3–009
  civil partnerships, 3–001, 3–044—3–047
  consent, 3–025
    duress, 3–027—3–030
    fraud, 3–031
    insanity, 3–026
    mistake 3–031
  consummation, 3–019
    capacity, 3–018, 3–020—021
    refusal, 3–022—3–024
  decrees, 3–036—3–039, 3–040—3–043
  financial provision, 3–043
  legitimacy, 3–042
  void marriages, 2–016, 3–004, 3–040
    age, 3–012
    bigamy, 3–014
    formalities, 2–016, 3–013
    polygamy, 3–016
    prohibited degrees, 3–005—3–011
    same sex partners, 3–015
  voidable marriages, 3–017, 3–040, 3–041
    children, 3–042
    consent, 3–025—3–031
    consummation, 3–018—3–024
    gender reassignment, 3–033
    mental disorder, 3–032
    pregnancy, 3–035
    sexually transmitted diseases, 3–034
Anti molestation orders *see* Non molestation
    orders
Artificial insemination *see* Assisted
    reproduction

Assisted reproduction, 10–007, 10–014
  mothers, 10–008
  paternity, 10–009—10–012
  sperm donors
    death, 10–013

Bankruptcy
  sale of property orders, 5–024
Banns, 2–006
Behavioural problems
  children, 13–040, 13–043
    care orders, 13–043
    child safety orders, 13–043
    parenting orders, 13–043
    secure accommodation orders, 13–041
    young offender institutions, 13–042
Benefits, 7–004, 8–026
  income related benefits, 7–005, 7–006
Bigamy, 3–014

Care orders, 13–012, 13–026—13–029
  behavioural problems, 13–043
  care proceedings, 13–013—13–018
  discharge, 13–038
  interim orders, 13–014
  threshold criteria, 13–019—13–025
Care plans, 13–030, 13–036
  accommodation, 13–031
    adoption, 13–035
    childrens homes, 13–034
    foster care, 13–033
    parents, 13–032
  care leavers, 13–039
  parental contact, 13–037
Care proceedings, 13–013—13–018
Carers
  parental responsibility, 11–030
Change of circumstances
  childrens welfare, 14–012
Child abduction, 12–047—12–056
Child benefit, 7–004
Child safety orders, 13–043
Child support, 7–008—7–017, 7–019
  enforcement, 7–018
  judgments and orders, 7–020—7–024
Child tax credit, 7–004
Child trust funds, 7–004
Children, III–009
  and see Childrens homes; Childrens rights;
    Childrens welfare; Local authorities
    powers and duties
  child benefit, 7–004
  child support, 7–008—7–017, 7–019
    enforcement, 7–018
    judgments and orders, 7–020—7–024
  child tax credit, 7–004
  child trust funds, 7–004

Children—cont.
  contact orders, 12–017, 12–029
    applicants, 12–006—12–009
    domestic violence, 12–031
    enforcement, 12–032
  emergencies, 13–009
    emergency protection orders, 13–011
    police, 13–010
  family assistance orders, 12–036
  international child abduction,
    12–047—12–056
  judgments and orders, III–008, 12–001,
    12–016, 12–025, 12–033, 12–035,
    12–056
    applicants, 12–004—12–005
    conditions, 12–021
    directions, 12–021
    enforcement, 12–032
    inherent jurisdiction, 12–039, 12–049
    jurisdiction, 12–002, 12–003
    parents, 12–034
    relocation, 12–028
    restrictions, 12–022—12–024
  legal systems, III–003—III–007
  local authorities
    investigations, 12–038
  medical treatment, 11–038
  need, 13–004—13–006
  prohibited steps orders, 12–019, 12–024
  residence orders, 12–018, 12–026, 15–012
    applicants, 12–006—12–009
    parental responsibility, 11–024
    restrictions, 12–013—12–015
    shared residence orders, 12–027
  secure accommodation orders, 13–041
  specific issue orders, 12–020, 12–024
  wardship, 12–040—12–045
  welfare reports, 12–037
  young offender institutions
    detention, 13–042
Childrens homes, 13–034
Childrens rights, 10–024, 11–001, 11–031
  Gillick competence, 11–037—11–039
Childrens welfare, 12–001, 14–001, 14–002
  adoption, 15–035, 15–036—15–042
  checklists, 14–009, 14–010, 14–016
    age, 14–013
    change of circumstances, 14–012
    characteristics, 14–013
    ill treatment, 14–014
    need, 14–011
    parents, 14–015
  courts, 14–002, 14–003—14–005, 14–006
    checklists, 14–009—14–016
    delay, 14–007
    necessity, 14–008
  human rights, 14–017
  relationship breakdown, 8–014—8–017

Church of England
    marriage ceremony, 2–010
Civil marriages, 2–007
    marriage ceremony, 2–009
Civil partnerships, I–001, 2–001, 2–020,
        2–021, II–004
    dissolution, 4–001, 4–036, II–007
    nullity, 3–001, 3–044—3–047
Clean break, 8–035—8–039
Cohabitation, 1–008, II–005
    see also Civil partnerships
    cohabitation agreements, 8–003
    relationship breakdown, 8–003, 8–045
Consent orders, 8–006
Constructive trusts, 5–010—5–015, 5–019
Consummation, 3–019
    capacity, 3–018, 3–020—3–021
    refusal, 3–022—3–023
        reasonable excuse, 3–024
Contact orders, 12–017, 12–029
    applicants, 12–006—12–009
    domestic violence, 12–031
    enforcement, 12–032
Contracts
    family property, 5–006
Counselling
    adoption, 15–020
Creditors
    sale of property orders, 5–025

Death, II–007, 9–001, 9–024
    family property, 9–019—9–023
    family provision, 9–005—9–018
    intestacy, 9–002—9–004
    sperm donors, 10–013
Deceased persons see Death
Declarations of trust
    family property, 5–005
Delay
    childrens welfare, 14–007
Demography, 1–006
    birth
        unmarried couples, 1–009
    cohabitation, 1–008
    families, 1–013, 1–014
    marriage, 1–007
    minorities, 1–012
    single persons, 1–011
    stepchildren, 1–010
    stepparents, 1–010
Desertion
    divorce, 4–014
Detention
    young offender institutions, 13–042
Discrimination
    human rights, 1–023
Dissolution
    civil partnerships, 4–001, 4–036, II–007

Divorce, 4–001, 4–002—4–005, 4–023—4–026,
        4–027—4–034, 4–037, II–007
    and see Relationship breakdown
    adultery, 4–009—4–012
    desertion, 4–014
    divorce petitions, 4–007
    facts, 4–008
        adultery, 4–009—4–012
        desertion, 4–014
        respondents, 4–013
        separation, 4–015—4–022
    judicial separation, 4–035
    justification, 4–006
    mediation, 4–032
    religions, 4–035
    respondents
        behaviour, 4–013
        separation, 4–015—4–022
Divorce petitions, 4–007
Domestic violence, 6–001, 6–002, 6–017,
        6–025
    contact orders, 12–030
    harassment, 6–019, 6–020
        civil law, 6–022, 6–024
        criminal law, 6–022, 6–023
        defences, 6–021
    injunctions, 6–018
    non molestation orders, 6–003, 6–005
        applicants, 6–004
        emergencies, 6–015
        enforcement, 6–016
    occupation orders, 6–006, 6–011—6–013
        applicants, 6–007—6–009
        duration, 6–010
        emergencies, 6–015
        enforcement, 6–016
        third parties, 6–014

Education
    childrens welfare, 14–011
Emergency protection orders, 13–011
    parental responsibility, 11–027
Estoppel, 5–016—5–018, 5–019

Families, 1–001, 1–002, II–002, III–001,
        III–002
Family assistance orders, 12–035
Family law, 1–001, 1–003—1–005, 1–026,
        II–001
Family proceedings, 12–038
Family property, II–001, 5–001
    see also Personal property
    death, 9–019—9–023
    ownership, 5–002, 5–003, 5–008, 5–021,
        5–035
        constructive trusts, 5–010—5–015, 5–019
        contracts, 5–006
        declarations of trust, 5–005

Family property—*cont.*
  ownership—*cont.*
    estoppel, 5–016—5–018, 5–019
    exemptions, 5–007
    improvements, 5–020
    resulting trusts, 5–009
    transfer of title, 5–004
    sale of property orders, 5–023—5–025
    third parties, 5–022—5–029
Family provision, 9–005—9–018
Financial dispute resolution appointments, 8–007
Financial provision orders, 8–009
Foster care, 13–033, 15–011
Fraud
  annulment, 3–031
Freedom of expression, 1–024

Gender reassignment, 3–033
Gender recognition certificates, 3–033
Gifts, 5–032
Gillick competence, 11–035—11–039
Guardians
  parental responsibility, 11–022

Harassment, 6–019, 6–020
  civil law
    remedies, 6–022, 6–024
  criminal law, 6–022, 6–023
  defences, 6–021
Human rights, 1–015—1–017, 1–025
  childrens welfare, 14–017
  discrimination, 1–023
  families, 1–022
  freedom of expression, 1–024
  local authorities powers and duties
    children, 13–048
  proceedings, 1–020
  right to life, 1–018
  right to respect for private and family life, 1–002, 1–021
  torture
    prohibition, 1–019

Improvements
  family property, 5–020
  personal property, 5–034
In vitro fertilisation *see* Assisted reproduction
Income related benefits, 7–005, 7–006
Intercountry adoption, 15–044
Interim orders
  care orders, 13–014
  supervision orders, 13–014
International child abduction, 12–047—12–056
Intestacy, 9–002—9–004
Investigations
  adoption agencies, 15–020

Investigations—*cont.*
  local authorities, 12–038

Joint tenancies
  severance, 9–023
  survivorship, 9–022
Judicial reviews
  local authorities powers and duties, 13–046
Judicial separation, 4–035
  and see Separation
  maintenance, 7–028

Local authorities
  and see Local authorities powers and duties
  investigations, 12–037
  parental responsibility, 11–025
Local authorities powers and duties
  care plans, 13–030, 13–036
    accommodation, 13–031—13–035
    care leavers, 13–039
    parental contact, 13–037
  child safety orders, 13–043
  children, 13–001—13–003, 13–007, 13–008, 13–040, 13–044, 13–049
    care orders, 13–012—13–029, 13–038, 13–043
    care proceedings, 13–013—13–018
    complaints, 13–045
    duty of care, 13–047
    emergency protection orders, 13–011
    human rights, 13–048
    interim orders, 13–014
    judicial reviews, 13–046
    need, 13–004—13–006
    parenting orders, 13–043
    secure accommodation orders, 13–041
    supervision orders, 13–012—13–029
    young offender institutions, 13–042

Maintenance, II–007, 7–001—7–003, 7–020—7–024, 7–029
  benefits, 7–004
    income related benefits, 7–005, 7–006
  child benefit, 7–004
  child support, 7–008—7–017, 7–019
    enforcement, 7–018
    judgments and orders, 7–020—7–024
  child tax credit, 7–004
  child trust funds, 7–004
  county courts, 7–026
  High Court, 7–026
  judicial separation, 7–028
  magistrates courts, 7–027
  working tax credit, 7–004
Marriage, 1–007, I–001, 2–001, 2–002, 2–003, 2–021, II–003, II–004
  and see Annulment; Divorce; Relationship breakdown

Marriage—*cont.*
  age, 3–012
  banns, 2–006
  civil marriages, 2–007, 2–009
  formalities, 2–014—2–017, 3–013
  intention
    publication, 2–005—2–007
  law reform, 2–019
  marriage ceremony, 2–008
    Church of England, 2–010
    civil marriages, 2–009
  parental consent, 2–004
  presumptions, 2–018
Matrimonial property *see* Family property
Mediation
  divorce, 4–032
Medical treatment
  children, 11–035
Mental disorder, 3–032
Minorities, 1–012

Non molestation orders, 6–003, 6–005
  applicants, 6–004
  emergencies, 6–015
  enforcement, 6–016
Nullity, 3–001, 3–002, 3–003, 3–048
  affinity, 3–007—3–009
  civil partnerships, 3–001, 3–044—3–047
  consent, 3–025
    duress, 3–027—3–030
    fraud, 3–031
    insanity, 3–026
    mistake, 3–031
  consummation, 3–019
    capacity, 3–018, 3–020—3–021
    refusal, 3–022—3–024
  decrees, 3–036—3–039, 3–040—3–043
  financial provision, 3–043
  legitimacy, 3–042
  void marriages, 2–016, 3–004, 3–040
    age, 3–012
    bigamy, 3–014
    formalities, 2–016, 3–013
    polygamy, 3–016
    prohibited degrees, 3–005—3–011
    same sex partners, 3–015
  voidable marriages, 3–017, 3–040, 3–041
    children, 3–042
    consent, 3–025—3–031
    consummation, 3–018—3–024
    gender reassignment, 3–033
    mental disorder, 3–032
    pregnancy, 3–035
    sexually transmitted diseases, 3–034

Occupation orders, 6–006, 6–011—6–013
  applicants, 6–007—6–009
  duration, 6–010

Occupation orders—*cont.*
  emergencies, 6–015
  enforcement, 6–016
  third parties, 6–014

Parentage, 10–001, 10–002, 10–025
  assisted reproduction, 10–007—10–014
  childrens rights, 10–024
  common law
    presumptions, 10–003—10–004
    samples, 10–005—10–006
  surrogacy, 10–015, 10–016
    adoption, 10–022
    enforcement, 10–023
    parental orders, 10–017—10–021
  testing, 10–005—10–006
Parental consent
  adoption, 15–025—15–027,
    15–033—15–035
  marriage, 2–004
Parental contact, 13–037
  adoption, 15–007, 15–043
Parental orders, 10–017—10–021
Parental responsibility, II–006, 11–001,
    11–002, 11–007, 11–028, 11–030, 11–032,
    11–039
  accountability, 11–006
  adoption, 11–019, 15–023, 15–028
  carers, 11–030
  childrens rights, 11–033
    Gillick competence 11–034—11–038
  emergency protection orders, 11–026
  entitlement, 11–008, 11–011—11–013
    fathers, 11–010
    legitimacy, 11–009
  guardians, 11–023
  local authorities, 11–025
  parental responsibility agreements, 11–017
  residence orders, 11–024
  restrictions, 11–005
  special guardians, 11–022
  stepparents, 11–019
  surrogacy, 11–021
  termination, 11–027
  transfer, 11–029
  unmarried fathers, 11–015—11–018
Parental responsibility agreements, 11–017
Parental wishes, 11–004
Parenting orders, 13–043
Parents
  capability, 14–015
Paternity
  assisted reproduction, 10–009—10–012
Pension sharing orders, 8–011
Periodical payments orders, 8–037, 8–037,
    8–038, 8–039
Personal property
  see also Family property

Personal property—*cont.*
  ownership, 5–030
    gifts, 5–032
    improvements, 5–034
    resulting trusts, 5–033
    savings, 5–031
Placement orders
  adoption, 15–023, 15–031
Polygamy, 3–016
Pre marital agreements, 8–004
Pregnancy, 3–035
Prohibited degrees, 3–005—3–011
Prohibited steps orders, 12–019, 12–024
Property adjustment orders, 8–010

Relationship breakdown, 8–040, 8–045
  and see Dissolution; Divorce; Separation
  assets, 8–001, 8–002
    cohabitation agreements, 8–003
    consent orders, 8–006
    financial dispute resolution
      appointments, 8–007
    financial provision orders, 8–009
    pension sharing orders, 8–011
    pre marital agreements, 8–004
    property adjustment orders, 8–010
    sale of property orders, 8–012
    separation agreements, 8–005
  clean break, 8–035—8–039
  cohabitation, 8–003, 8–045
  discretion, 8–013, 8–018—8–019, 8–022,
    8–027—8–034
    benefits, 8–026
    childrens welfare, 8–014—8–017
    earned income, 8–025
    income, 8–024
    liquidity, 8–023
    relevant property, 8–021
    value, 8–020
  judgments and orders, 8–008
    appeals, 8–042—8–044
    variation, 8–041
  periodical payments orders, 8–036, 8–037,
    8–038, 8–039
Relatives
  adoption, 15–008
  prohibited degrees, 3–006
Relocation, 12–028
Reports
  adoption agencies, 15–020
  welfare reports, 12–037
Residence orders, 12–018, 12–026, 15–012
  applicants, 12–006—12–009
  parental responsibility, 11–023
  restrictions, 12–013—12–015
  shared residence orders, 12–027

Respondents
  behaviour
    divorce, 4–013
Resulting trusts, 5–009, 5–033
Right to life, 1–018
Right to respect for private and family life,
  1–002, 1–021

Sale of property orders, 5–023, 8–012
  bankruptcy, 5–024
  creditors, 5–025
Samples
  parentage, 10–005—10–006
Section 8 orders *see individual orders*
Secure accommodation orders, 13–041
Separation, 4–015—4–022
  judicial separation, 4–035
    maintenance, 7–028
  separation agreements, 8–005
Severance
  joint tenancies, 9–023
Sexually transmitted diseases, 3–034
Shared residence orders, 12–027
Single persons, 1–011
Special guardians, 15–013
  parental responsibility, 11–021
Specific issue orders, 12–020, 12–024
Sperm donors
  and see Assisted reproduction
  death, 10–013
Stepchildren, 1–010
Stepparents, 1–010
  parental responsibility, 11–019
Supervision orders, 13–012, 13–026—13–029
  behavioural problems, 13–043
  discharge, 13–038
  interim orders,13–014
  proceedings, 13–013—13–018
  threshold criteria, 13–019—13–025
Surrogacy, 10–015, 10–016
  adoption, 10–022
  childrens rights, 10–024
  enforcement, 10–023
  parental orders, 10–017—10–021
  parental responsibility, 11–021
Survivorship
  joint tenancies, 9–022

Tax credits, 7–004
Testing
  parentage, 10–005—10–006
Torture
  human rights, 1–019
Transfer of title
  family property, 5–004
Trusts
  constructive trusts, 5–010—5–015, 5–019

Unmarried couples, 1–009
  fathers
    parental responsibility, 11–015—11–018

Venereal disease *see* Sexually transmitted
    diseases
Violence, 6–001, 6–002, 6–017, 6–025
  contact orders, 12–030
  harassment, 6–019, 6–020
    civil law, 6–022, 6–024
    criminal law, 6–022, 6–023
    defences, 6–021
  injunctions, 6–018
  non molestation orders, 6–003, 6–005
    applicants, 6–004
    emergencies, 6–015
    enforcement, 6–016
  occupation orders, 6–006, 6–011—6–013
    applicants, 6–007—6–009
    duration, 6–010
    emergencies, 6–015
    enforcement, 6–016
    third parties, 6–014
Void marriages, 2–016, 3–004, 3–040
  see also Voidable marriages
  adoption, 3–010
  age, 3–012
  bigamy, 3–014
  formalities
    defects, 2–016, 3–013

Void marriages—*cont.*
  polygamy, 3–016
  prohibited degrees, 3–005, 3–011
    adoption, 3–010
    affinity, 3–007—3–009
    relatives, 3–006
  same sex partners, 3–015
Voidable marriages, 3–017, 3–040, 3–041
  see also Void marriages
  children, 3–042
  consent, 3–025
    duress, 3–027—3–030
    insanity, 3–026
    mistake, 3–031
  consummation, 3–019
    capacity, 3–018, 3–020—3–021
    refusal, 3–022—3–024
  gender reassignment, 3–033
  mental disorder, 3–032
  pregnancy, 3–035
  sexually transmitted diseases, 3–034

Wardship, 12–040—12–045
Welfare reports, 12–037
Working tax credit, 7–004

Young offender institutions
  detention, 13–042